WHAT WE WEREN'T TAUGHT ABOUT THE BIBLE AND ITS HISTORY

Copyright © 2007 Roger W. Fearing
All rights reserved.
ISBN: 1-4196-1463-0
ISBN-13: 978-1419614637

Visit www.booksurge.com to order additional copies.

ROGER W. FEARING

WHAT WE WEREN'T TAUGHT ABOUT THE BIBLE AND ITS HISTORY

A CHRISTIAN'S PERSPECTIVE OF A JEWISH BOOK

2007

WHAT WE WEREN'T TAUGHT ABOUT THE BIBLE AND ITS HISTORY

TABLE OF CONTENTS

Acknowledgments	xv
Preface	xvii
Introduction	xix
CHAPTER 1...about Genesis	**1**
What's in a Word?	1
The Beginnings	7
Creation	7
The "Garden of Eden"	14
The Fall of Mankind	15
YAHveh's First Covenant with Mankind	17
The Beginning of the First Family	18
The Sons of YAH and the Sons of Men	19
The End of the First Millennium—One Remaining Servant, Noah	20
The Flood	21
YAHveh's Second Covenant with Mankind	23
Replenishing the Earth	23
YAHveh Builds a Nation for Himself	26
YAHveh's Third Covenant with Mankind	26
The End of the Second Millennium—Isaac's (Yitzhak's) Descendants	31
YAHveh's Fourth Covenant with Mankind	32
YAHveh's Fifth Covenant with Mankind	32
Jacob (Yaacov) Builds a Family	33
Jacob (Yaacov) Wrestles with God's Angel	34
Israel's (YisraEL's) Favorite Son Joseph (Yosef)	37
Conclusion	41
CHAPTER 2...about Exodus	**43**
Moses (Mosheh), the Deliverer and Prophet	44
The Reunion of Two Brothers	46
The Testing Begins	47

The First of Many Feasts that Point to the Messiah (PASSOVER/PESACH)	50
YAHveh's Sixth Covenant with Mankind, the Covenant of Marriage to YisraEL	55
YAHveh Establishes a Replica of Heaven on Earth, a Second Eden	57
YisraEL Committed Adultery	60
The Tabernacle (Mishkahn) is Completed and the Articles Arranged	61
Conclusion	62
CHAPTER 3...about Leviticus, Numbers, and Deuteronomy	**65**
YAHveh Prepares YisraEL to March into the Promised Land	65
Miriam (Meeryahm) Became a Leper	67
The Judgment of Forty Years in the Wilderness	67
Forty Years of Bickering	69
The Last Days of the Forty Year Wandering	70
Balaam, an Unworthy Prophet of YAHveh	71
Balak and Balaam Try a Second Scheme to Destroy YisraEL	72
The Final Census and the Exchange of Leadership	73
Mosheh Reviews the Torah Before YisraEL	74
Service to Another ELuah	76
Graven Images	78
The Test of a True Prophet	80
Expressing Our Love for YAHveh Through His Provisions	81
Honoring YAH by Celebrating the Sabbath	82
Honoring Him Through His Appointed Times (Moedim), the Annual Feasts	83
Establishing Clean and Unclean	88
Establishing YAH's Form of Government, Civil Justice, and Welfare	89
Mosheh's Last Days	93
Conclusion	94
CHAPTER 4...about Joshua, Judges, and Ruth	**95**
Joshua (Yoshua), YisraEL's First Judge	96
YisraEL Continues to Conquer Their Inheritance—But not Completely	99
The Story of Ruth	101
The Last of the Judges	102
Conclusion	104

CHAPTER 5...about I Samuel	105
King Saul (Shaul)	107
The Early Years of David (Dahveed)	110
The Final Days of King Shaul	114
Conclusion	115
CHAPTER 6...about II Samuel, I Chronicles, and The Book of Psalms	117
Dahveed is Made King Over the Tribe of YAHuda	118
Dahveed Becomes King Over All YisraEL	119
YAHveh's Seventh Covenant with Mankind at the End of the Third Millennium	120
Bathsheba (Bathshe`bah)	121
King David's Son, Absalom	122
Dahveed Causes YisraEL to Suffer Because of His Poor Judgment	124
Dahveed Appoints the Leaders to Serve in the House of YAH	125
Solomon (Shalomo) Designated to be the Next King of YisraEL	126
The Book of Psalms	126
Conclusion	129
CHAPTER 7...about I Kings 1-11, II Chronicles 1-9, the Book of Proverbs, Song of Solomon, and Ecclesiastes	131
Solomon (Shalomo), the New King of YisraEL	132
Solomon (Shalomo) Makes Plans to Carry Out the Construction of the House of YAHveh	132
Shalomo's Proverbs	134
Conclusion	135
CHAPTER 8...about I Kings 12—II Kings 8 and	137
II Chronicles 10-21	137
The Beginning of the Reign of King Jeroboam (YAHroboam)	137
The Northern and the Southern Tribes of YisraEL	138
YAHveh Sent His Ne'vee, Elijah (ELeeYAHoo), to Warn YisraEL of Her Sins	140
Elisha (ELeeshaw), Elijah's (ELeeYAHoo's) Protégé	142
Elisha (ELeesha) Takes Over Where ELeeYAHoo Left Off	144
The Miracles of Elisha (ELeeshaw)	146
Conclusion	147

CHAPTER 9...about Obadiah, Joel, II Kings 8-14, and	149
II Chronicles 21-25	149

Obadiah's (OhbedeeYAH's) Prophecy Regarding Edom	149
YAHveh Continues His Attempt to Guide YisraEL	
Through Elisha (ELeeshaw)	150
The Ne'vee Joel (YoEL)	153
Conclusion	155

CHAPTER 10...about Jonah, Hosea, Amos, II	
Kings 14&15, and II Chronicles 25-27	157

Jonah (Yonah)	157
Hosea (Hoshea)	158
Amos (Ahmos)	161
Conclusion	162

CHAPTER 11...about the Ne'vee Micah, the Beginning of the	
Prophecies of Isaiah, II Kings 15-18, and II	
Chronicles 27-31	163

Micah (Meecah)	163
Isaiah (YishshaYAH)	165
Conclusion	169

CHAPTER 12...about Isaiah Continued, Nahum, II	
Kings 18-23, and II Chronicles 31-34	171

The Ne'vee Nahum Declares the Ruin of Assyria and the City of	
Nineveh	183

CHAPTER 13...about the Ne'vim Zephaniah, Jeremiah	
1-24, and II Chronicles 35	187

Zephaniah (TzefenYAH)	187
Jeremiah (YirmehYAH)	188
The Final Days of YAHuda,	194
Conclusion	195

CHAPTER 14...about Lamentations, Habakkuk, Job, Jeremiah 25&26, Daniel 1&2, II Kings 24: 1-7, and II Chronicles 36: 1-7   197

Lamentations	197
Habakkuk (Chabahkook)	198
Job (Yov)	199
Jeremiah (YirmehYAH) 25 & 26	200
Daniel (DahneeEL) 1 & 2	201
Conclusion	204

CHAPTER 15...about Ezekiel 1-33, Jeremiah 27-52, II Kings 24&25, and II Chronicles 36&37   205

Ezekiel (YechezkEL) 1-33	205
YirmehYAH 27-52	214
Conclusion	218

CHAPTER 16...about Ezekiel 34-48 and Daniel 3-9   219

Ezekiel (YechezkEL) 34-48	219
Daniel (DahneeEL) 3-9	222
Conclusion	227

Chapter 17...about the Remaining Twenty-One Psalms, Ezra, Daniel 10-12, Esther, Nehemiah, and the Ne'vim: Haggai, Zechariah, and Malachi   229

The Last Twenty-One Psalms	229
Ezra (Ezrah)	231
DahneeEL 10-12	233
Haggai (Hagahee)	235
Zechariah (TzahkarYAH)	236
Esther (Ester)	240
Malachi (Mahlakhee)	243
Nehemiah (NehchemYAH)	245
Conclusion	248

CHAPTER 18…about the 400 Years Remaining Until the First Coming of the Messiah	249
Conclusion	255
CHAPTER 19…about the Gospels of Matthew, Mark, Luke, John, and Acts 1	257
The Introduction to Yeshua, the Messiah	257
Yeshua Qualifies as the Messiah	258
The Birth of Both Yeshua and His Cousin, John the Baptist (Yochanan the Immerser)	258
The Circumcision and Dedication of Yeshua and His Cousin, Yochanan the Immerser, and Their Early Years	259
The Coming of the Magi	261
Yochanan the Immerser and Yeshua the Messiah Begin Their Ministries	263
Yeshua Must Come Face to Face With His Father's (Abba's) Enemy, the Prince of Darkness	264
Yeshua Chooses His First Disciples (Talmidim) and Goes to His Hometown in Galilee	265
Yeshua Attends His First Passover Celebration after Entering His Ministry	266
Yeshua Returns to Galilee and Calls Two More Disciples (Talmidim)	268
Yeshua Chooses Six More Disciples (Talmidim) and Calls Them All to be Apostles (Shelichim)	270
Yeshua's Ministry Intensifies as He Teaches and Focuses on Kingdom Principles Taught Through Parables	272
Yeshua Instructs His Apostles (Shelichim) on How to Minister Through Miracles to the Multitudes	280
Yeshua's Last Celebration of the Feast of Sukkoth Here on Earth	288
Yeshua Celebrates His Last Chanukah	293
Yeshua's Friend, Lazarus, Dies	297
The Days Leading Up to Yeshua's Crucifixion	300
The Crucifixion	317
The Burial	319
The Mandate and Ascension	322
Acts 1	323
Conclusion	323

CHAPTER 20...about Acts 2—15	325
Conclusion	338
CHAPTER 21...about Galatians, Acts 16—19, I&II Thessalonians, and I&II Corinthians	341
Rav Shaul's Letter to the Kahal at Galatia	341
I & II Thessalonians	341
Acts 16—19	345
I Corinthians	352
II Corinthians	364
Conclusion	369
CHAPTER 22...about Romans, Acts 20—28, Colossians, Philemon, Ephesians, and Philippians	371
Acts 20	371
Romans	372
Acts 21-28	385
Colossians	388
Ephesians	391
Philippians	394
Conclusion	396
CHAPTER 23...about I & II Timothy and Titus	397
I Timothy	397
Titus	400
II Timothy	400
Conclusion	401
CHAPTER 24...about James, Jude, and I&II Peter	403
James (Yaacov)	403
Jude (YAHuda)	406
I Peter (Kefa)	407
II Kefa	410
Conclusion	412

CHAPTER 25...about the Letter to the Hebrews, or
    Messianic YAHudi   413

Conclusion   123

CHAPTER 26...about John's Three Letters to the
    Kahal and the Revelation Given to Him by Yeshua   425

I Yochanan   425
II Yochanan   428
III Yochanan   429
Revelation (Also Known as the "Apocalypse of Yochanan")   429
The First Vision   430
The Second Vision   433
The Third Vision   435
The Fourth Vision   435
The Fifth Vision   441
The Sixth Vision   443
The Seventh Vision   444
Conclusion   446

CHAPTER 27...about the History of the Church and
    Christianity Over the Past 2000 Years, Up to and
    Including the Present   449

Constantine and the First Reform   452
Mohammad   454
The Crusades and the Beginning of the Sixth Millennium   456
    The Renaissance, the Reformation, and the Beginning of the
    Spanish Inquisition   457
The Second Reform   458
The Third Reform   460
The Fourth Reform   461
The Fifth Reform   462
The Sixth and Seventh Reform   462
Conclusion   464

Glossary of Hebrew Words   467

ACKNOWLEDGEMENTS

Without the help and encouragement from my wife and helpmate, Bonnie, who assisted me in editing and proofreading, and my daughter, Michelle, who also helped, this book may never have been written. I also want to thank my son-in-law, Edwin Bannworth, and granddaughter, Stephanie, who encouraged us while we labored for three years in order to complete this manuscript.

PREFACE

First of all, let me describe myself and my book. I am not a literary scholar, which you will conclude for yourself as you read. I avoid theological and technical terminology because I do not want to overwhelm, even if I could, my readers. I stick to what I call "folk dialogue".

This book will prove to be somewhat controversial to its readers. To most Christians, it will challenge almost everything they have been taught about the Bible. To most Jews, it will challenge what they have heard about Christian theology. To most Messianics, it will challenge their thinking regarding what they have come to accept about their Hebraic Roots. My purpose is to challenge everyone into rethinking their spiritual traditions.

The best way to describe what I have done to accomplish this is that I have compiled a bible digest that explains from a Hebrew perspective each book of the Bible in a chronological sequence. So, I recommend to the reader that they use a good Chronological Bible as a study tool to go along with this book. I know that they may be hard to find, but by using one, it could prove to be a great help in order for you to get a better grasp of the context and content of what I am trying to convey. I have found both a King James and an NIV version available in some Christian book stores.

{THANKS AND GOOD READING!}

INTRODUCTION

I'm sure that all of you who have decided to read this book are wondering what I could possibly mean by **"WHAT WE WEREN'T TAUGHT ABOUT THE BIBLE AND ITS HISTORY"**. Has the church deliberately kept something from us? No, not deliberately—the church has meant well. Most pastors do have a heart for the Lord, so it's been completely unintentional on their part. However, the problem is that the Bible has been taught to them and in turn to us from the wrong perspective. It's been taught through a "Western perspective" that was derived from a theology based upon a Greek/Roman culture that was full of paganism, secularism, and ideas that were based upon man's point of view. We *should have been taught* from a *Hebrew* perspective—God's point of view. God gave Adam a language that was passed down from generation to generation, right up to Abraham. Abraham was the first Hebrew, thus his language became known as the Hebrew language. So, unless we have an understanding from a Hebraic perspective, how can we truly come to know the heart of our Father? My desire and purpose for writing this book is to help you better understand His heart and for His words to come to life for you in a new and different way.

The Bible is made up of a collection of sixty-six books and letters. They are arranged in two volumes: thirty-nine in the first, referred to as the "Old Testament", and twenty-seven in the second, referred to as the "New Testament". The first was based upon the Hebrew language and culture, and the second was based upon the Greek language but still with the Jewish/Hebrew culture. But as I said before, it has been taught from a Western perspective. The error lies in trying to approach the Bible from the perspective of our own culture—it just doesn't work. An old Indian proverb says that you can never judge a man unless you have walked in his moccasins.

I hope you will read this book with an open mind and spirit. Sometimes we become so comfortable with what we have been taught that when a different perspective is given, we tend to become defensive. No one really likes change, and no one likes having their own spiritual understanding challenged. I assure you that this book is going to challenge your thinking. It's also going to make you question what you've been taught from this Western perspective. At the same time, it's going to answer a lot of your questions and perhaps create some new ones. So please approach what you are about to study with a discerning spirit—*"Test all things; hold fast what is good"* (**I THES 5:21**). Ask the Holy Spirit to help guide you. I don't believe that you will find anything in this book that goes against God's Word—His *original* Word. Now, together, let's explore what our Lord's heart reveals about Himself and about us, and who we truly are in Him. To begin, we need to understand what biblical truth is.

"What is truth?" This was the question that Pontius Pilate asked after Jesus said, *"For this cause I was born, for this cause I have come into the world, that I should bear witness to the truth. Everyone who is of the truth hears My voice"* (**JOHN 18:37b & 38a**). Jesus, who made the claim that He was the Living God, the Creator of all things, the *"Word"* made flesh, the Promised One of whom all of the prophets had ever spoken of, was also *the Truth*. *"I AM the Way, the Truth and the Life. No one comes to the Father except through me."..."Sanctify them by Your truth. Your word is truth"* (**JOHN 14:6 & 17:17**). The *Truth* is Jesus, and the *Word* is Jesus—they are one and the same. *"And the Word became flesh and dwelt among us, and we beheld His glory, the glory of the Father, full of grace and truth"* (**JOHN 1:14**). And the Bible is the Word—therefore, the Bible is the Truth.

The Bible, which is the most purchased and yet least read book in history, has always been challenged concerning its veracity. Is it a book of historical facts or just allegories? Should it be taken literally or figuratively? Is it a reliable spiritual guide? Is it another book of philosophies, or is it something else altogether? One thing is certain—it is the only book known by mankind that has the uniqueness of being written by forty different individuals over a period of sixteen-hundred years, and yet it has a oneness in harmony of thought as though it had been written by only one author. That one author is the Holy Spirit of God.

The only way to even begin to understand the depths and the mysteries of the Scriptures is through faith and by the Spirit. Paul, the writer of two letters that were written to the believers in the city of Corinth, said, *"But the natural man does not receive the things of the Spirit of God, for they are foolishness to him; nor can he know them, because they are spiritually discerned"* (**I CORINTHIANS 2:14**). In our Western culture, the "natural" man approaches the Bible philosophically—he has to because it is in his nature to reason things out logically. We are taught from a Greek philosophy to be "thinkers" and "intellectuals". This may be good up to a point, but this kind of thinking says that if something doesn't make sense or if it can't be proven, then it is foolishness. Many times, having "faith" is looked upon as being "gullible" or "weak". Most cultures struggle with the idea of having a personal god. Consequently, the natural man, having only the ability to understand things from his own particular perspective, perceives spiritual things as foolishness. If he can't touch it, grasp it, or see it, it doesn't exist. Therefore, he reasons that the Bible is only a book that is full of stories for moral living. Again, Paul stated, *"but we preach Christ crucified, to* *the Jews it is a stumbling block and to the Greeks* (or non-Jews) *it is foolishness"* (**I CORINTHIANS 1:23**).

His truth is not intellectual—it is spiritual. So, in order for us to understand His truth, we must become spiritual. How is this done? Jesus explains this to a religious leader, a Pharisee named Nicodemus, when He said, *"Most assuredly, I say to you, unless one is born again he cannot see* (perceive or understand) *the kingdom of God."*…*"Most assuredly, I say to you, unless one is born of water* (or natural birth) *and the Spirit, he cannot enter the kingdom of God"* (**JOHN 3:3 & 5**). Therefore, if we need to understand truth from a spiritual point of view, then we must be born of the Spirit. This is the cornerstone of the foundation and the building blocks of spiritual knowledge. Jesus Himself said, *"God is Spirit, and those who worship Him must worship in spirit and in truth"* (**JOHN 4:24**).

Again, what is truth? Just like most men and women, I have asked myself that question many times. I've also asked myself who am I, where did I come from, and where am I going in this life? There are some who feel that these questions are just too deep to ask and contemplate, so they live as though there is no tomorrow and that today will last forever—that's irresponsible. We should plan for a multitude of tomorrows but live as though today could be our last. These questions continually plagued me. In my search for answers, I found myself always coming back to the question of God and His Bible.

I came from a simple background, having no formal education, just the school of hard knocks. My parents were not spiritual or even religious. My father was a typical blue-collar-factory worker and was a part-time bartender, just to provide for his family. The only interest that he ever showed toward religion was his Sunday-morning sessions with television evangelists. I found many of them interesting as well, and they became the first to sow seeds of faith into my spiritual future. But the only time that I was able to actually go to church or to Sunday school was when, or if, I was able to catch a ride with one of our neighbors.

I lived in a tough ghetto-like neighborhood with a mixture of poor blacks and whites. I lacked the enthusiasm to excel in school and the necessary talent to do well in sports. All that I was able to learn was self-taught later in life. At the age of seventeen, soon after the Korean conflict but before Vietnam, I enlisted in the military, where I spent nearly three years as an Army paratrooper. It was there that I finally received my high school diploma. I also met and wed a young Kentucky girl, but the marriage began to fail within two years. It was during this time that I seriously began asking myself if this is all there is to life—one daily struggle after another and one disappointment after another? Doesn't life have more meaning than just getting up and going to work day after day, just like my parents? Is this all that I'm here for—to just put one foot in front of the other? For a short period of time, I even tried a lifestyle of partying and alcohol but, fortunately for me, never any drugs. It was also during this time that we had a son, but I failed at being a real father to him because of that lifestyle. At times, the questions "who am I really and why am I here" would come to my mind, and I would make a few futile attempts at making a connection with God, but it was always short-lived. One day, I even prayed the "sinner's prayer", and it took hold for awhile, but like the seed that had been sown among rocks, it had no root, and soon it withered away. Once again, I turned my back on God and His Son, Jesus Christ, but He knew that my prayer at the time was sincere, so He never turned His back on me.

After finishing my tour in the military, I worked a number of different sales jobs and eventually became a driver salesman for a major soft drink company. My first wife decided that our marriage wasn't working and ended it in a divorce a short time later. After that, I met Bonnie, who became my true soul mate and my present bride. She has been faithfully by my side for over forty-five years. Soon after our marriage, we moved to Detroit, Michigan, where I worked for another soft drink company, later at a national insurance company, and then a food-vending company. In 1967, we had the unpleasant experience of living through the Detroit riots. It was at that time that we decided to truly dedicate our lives to God. We made a covenant with Him to walk by faith from that moment on and asked Him to somehow just get us back home to Ohio. We held hands, knelt before Him at our bedside, and prayed. If we weren't sure before, we knew then that we were new creatures in Him and that we were "born-again" into a spirit-centered life.

Our loving Heavenly Father answered our prayer by moving us back to my hometown of Sandusky, Ohio. We had neither a home nor a job waiting for us when we arrived, but by faith, the Father provided both in just a few short weeks. Soon after that, He led me to my final vocation, a driver for a well-known delivery-service company, where I spent the next thirty years until my retirement, seven years ago. During those thirty years, He taught us by His Word and by His Spirit. And even though I stumbled several times, which included an adulterous affair and not being the kind of father that I could or should have been to the two children that we share, God has always been faithful to His covenant with us, despite my shortcomings.

On January 1, 1976, Bonnie and I once again knelt down, but this time in front of our television set, and prayed with Pat Robertson during a "700-Club" program and asked for the gift of the Holy Spirit. *"But you shall receive power when the Holy Spirit has come upon you; and you shall be witnesses to Me in Jerusalem, and in Judea and Samaria, and to the end of the earth"* (**ACTS** 1:8). Jesus' apostles took care of the spreading of His Word in Jerusalem, Judea, and in Samaria, but we knew that it was up to us, those in the Church, to do the "end of the earth" thing. We didn't have an immediate "second experience" (the first experience being "born-again"), but within a matter of months, we both believed and received this second experience with the infilling and overflowing of His Spirit. It was accompanied with the manifested evidence of being able to speak to our Heavenly Father in a new, unknown, and unlearned language that seemed to come from deep within our very being. We had a new hunger to be His witnesses and to share our new life with anyone who would give us an ear. Next, the Father introduced us to a para-church organization known as the "Full Gospel Business Men's Fellowship International", where He put us to work in our community and throughout the state of Ohio, ministering and teaching in the power of His Spirit. We saw healing, deliverance, salvation, and the infilling of the Holy Spirit in the lives of many others. We were right in the middle of His Charismatic revival. We joined a local Lutheran church that also believed in ministering in this manner. We were blessed.

Now, several years later and still with a hunger for Him that is even stronger than before, the Father has continued to guide us faithfully. We are now deeply involved in what we believe to be His seventh and final reformation since the death and resurrection of Jesus—the Messianic Movement. This is a movement that is still in its infancy, but is truly able to answer questions that were never answered by the Church. It is with this perspective in mind that I want to share with you the many kingdom principles that I have found in the Scriptures. I will be discussing many things that you may already know, but from this different perspective, which I believe is the same one that the Father originally revealed to His forty writers—a Hebraic perspective.

Let me warn you again, if you try to understand the Scriptures from an intellectual point of view, they will more than likely seem to be nothing but foolishness. If you truly want to find out who you really are, why you are here, and where it all ends, it would be wise for you to become born-again, if you aren't already, just as we did. In order to do this, you must be *serious* with Him and then He will be *serious* with you. First, you must admit that you have blown it by trying to fit in with this world and by trying to philosophically make sense out of both "life" and "God". We've all tried that in one way or another, and you're only kidding yourself if you think you're the exception. Making sense out of life in that manner is like trying to hold onto jelly. We both know, and more importantly, *He* knows that you've made a mess instead. Next, you need to ask Him to forgive you for trying to be your own self-made person. Again, be honest with yourself and with Him; He truly understands because He became like you so that He could! He also made you and wants *you* to give up trying to do *His* job in your life. He sent His Son, Jesus, to pay the debt that you couldn't pay and the one that He never owed. He did this because He loves you and wants you to know Him intimately, fully, and completely. If you accept that payment in Jesus' name and ask Him to take charge from now on, He will—you can trust Him to do it. He will reveal Himself to you because this is His personal promise to you, *"seek and you shall find"* (**MATT 7:7**). Now, if you've done all of that, you can now get on with finding out **WHAT WE WEREN'T TAUGHT ABOUT THE BIBLE AND ITS HISTORY.**

CHAPTER 1
WHAT WE WEREN'T TAUGHT
...about Genesis

What's in a Word?

The Bible starts with the words "In the beginning", and the first book is called *"Beginnings"*. *Genesis* is a Greek word that means *beginnings*. However, the original *beginnings* weren't written in Greek, but rather in Hebrew. The Hebrew word for *beginnings* is *B'resheet*. The first book is made up of many "beginnings": the Earth, mankind, sin, death, families, and nations—one nation in particular, the Hebrew nation, and from them, Israel. Israel was God's chosen people, and His enemies have been trying to wipe them out since the beginning.

Long before there were any Hebrews, God's archenemy, Satan, tried to establish a nation and a religion for himself through Nimrod. We have come to know them as Babel, or Babylon (Confusion). God thwarted this attempt before it could get off the ground. *"Come let Us go down and confuse their language, that they may not understand one another's speech"* (**GEN** 11:7). Then Satan tried to eliminate God's nation, Israel, by reversing this language incident through the Greek Empire. Whenever the Greeks would conquer a country or nation, they would neutralize its government by changing its religion, *language*, educational system, social structure, and culture into their own—a process called *"Hellenizing"*. That's why in about 300 BC/BCE (Before the Common Era), when the Greek Empire was in power, seventy Hebrew scholars translated the thirty-nine books of the Old Testament, known in Hebrew as the *TaNaKh*, into Greek. The TaNaKh became known as the *Septuagint* in order to commemorate the seventy scholars who translated it.

Some have implied that the Greek Scriptures may not be inspired. I do not take that position because all Scripture is inspired. The Greek rendition, however, is only a *translation* of the message. Greek is no more or no less inspired than a German, Spanish, or an English translation. The *message* is what is inspired, not the language that it's written in. The language of the Hebrews and their culture, however, were chosen by God in order to best intimately express Himself and His heart to those whom He created in His image. So why is anyone trying to mess with what God chose? Because the evil one, a.k.a. Satan (or hasatan, which means "the destroyer and accuser" in Hebrew), doesn't want God's people to truly have a full understanding of who God is, and even more importantly, who **WE** are **IN HIM**!

God's original language, the one He gave to Adam in the beginning, was the same language that He gave to all of the "sons of God". Noah spoke it, Shem spoke it, and Abraham spoke it. When God called Abraham and his descendants Hebrews, the language that they and their ancestors had been speaking would naturally be called the "Hebrew language". The Hebrew language is a very spiritual language with many hidden meanings and mysteries, or some might refer to them as "codes", because it is numerical as well as literal. God is the Master of mathematics and design, and His language reflects that. This is how He intended to communicate all of the secrets of His plan for heaven and Earth to His Creation.

Since I truly believe that this was His original language, I would like to familiarize you with some of its words as we go along. I will attempt to substitute some of the words, names, and titles with their Hebrew equivalents, along with their phonetic spelling and pronunciation. However, I will not get into any codes—I'll leave that up to the scholars.

Most English words are derived from other languages, such as Greek, Latin, Spanish, and German, just to mention a few. Many of these words have definitions that are in direct contrast to the original Hebraic language that God created. They at times change the meaning of what the original Scriptures were actually trying to convey. Sometimes the change in the meaning is slight, and at other times the change can be pretty drastic. For example, when we come across the word "church" in our Bibles, according to Webster's dictionary it is an English translation of the Greek word *kirche*. But when we take a closer look at the word "church/kirche", we find that the Greek writers actually used the word *ecclesia*, which means *congregation*. So why did they change the actual word? It's because church/kirche best suited what *they* were trying to convey. "Kirche" has a variety of meanings, such as a group of Christian worshipers, a meeting place for the purpose of worship, a denomination, etc. When we search the Scriptures, we find that this word "church/kirche" (which was mistranslated) was used only twice in the four eyewitness accounts of Jesus' ministry, the gospels. After that, Paul and others used it several times in their letters to the believers who were scattered throughout the Roman Empire. But since the word *ecclesia* means *congregation*, it better describes what Jesus and the others meant because it has a more precise meaning. It conveys the thought that we are individual members of an assembly, a congregation of people, a community, a family, or even a nation. The correct word, *ecclesia*, has much more of a personal reference than a universal one, like the word church/

kirche has. *Ecclesia* better expresses the importance of being members of a community and more accurately fits the description that Paul used in his letter to the believers in Rome. *"For as we have many members in one body, but all the members do not have the same function...so we being many, are one body in Christ, and individually members of one another"* (**ROM 12:4&5**). Therefore, in the future, in order to sidestep the confusion that this discrepancy creates, I will refer to these members as **Believers, His Body, Congregation,** or **Assembly**. In some cases, I will even use the Hebrew equivalent, **Kahal**.

Let's look at a few other discrepancies, beginning with the description of the first thirty-nine books of the Bible that we refer to as the ***Old Testament***. The word *Old* implies that it is no longer relevant—it's something from the past that no longer applies to the here and now. We have come to think of the ***Old Testament*** as just being an *old* historical storybook, too difficult to read and comprehend at times. It's full of great Sunday school stories, but it just doesn't apply to modern day life. We know this isn't true because Paul writes in his second letter to his friend, Timothy, *"All Scripture is given by inspiration of God, and is profitable for doctrine, for reproof, for correction, for instruction in righteousness, that the man of God may be complete, thoroughly equipped for every good work"* (**II TIM 3:16&17**). Then again, in his letter to the believers in Ephesus, he writes, *"Now, therefore, you are no longer strangers and foreigners, but fellow citizens with the saints and members of the household of God, having been built on the foundation of the apostles and prophets, Jesus Christ Himself being the cornerstone"* (**EPH 2:19&20**). We also find Jesus Himself saying, *"Do you think that I came to destroy the Law and the Prophets? I did not come to destroy but to fulfill"* (**MATT 5:17**). The ***New Testament*** didn't even exist when these three statements were made—it wouldn't for another one hundred and fifty years. The writers of these statements were making reference to the ***Old Testament***. So the ***Old Testament*** wasn't old at all, but very relevant for all time. Its writings and teachings were the only **Words of God** available for doctrine, for reproof, for correction, and for instruction in righteousness. When Jesus referred to them as the ***Law and the Prophets***, He meant ***Law*** (Torah) and ***Prophets*** (Ne'vim). The thirty-nine books that we call the ***Old Testament*** are divided into three sections: the ***Torah***, the ***Ne'vim***, and the ***Kethuvim*** (Writings). These make up the Hebrew Scriptures that are known as the ***TaNaKh***, a word derived from the sound of the first Hebrew letter from each section—"Tet (Ta), Noon (Na), and Khet (Kh) equals TaNaKh." The ***Torah***, which we know as the ***Law of Moses*** or ***The Pentateuch***, is the first five books of the Bible: Genesis—Exodus—Leviticus—Numbers—Deuteronomy. The word, Torah, actually means *instructions*. In the future, I will refer to the "Old Testament" as either the ***Scriptures***, as Jesus did when He said, *"You search the Scriptures, for in them you think you have eternal life;*

and these are they which testify of Me" (**JOHN 5:39**), or I will refer to them as the *TaNaKh*, the Hebrew term.

Next, let's look at the last twenty-seven books (mostly letters) of Scripture that are referred to as the *New Testament*. They began to be compiled about thirty years after Jesus' death and resurrection. Then other writings began to be gathered, along with the gospels, after the destruction of Jerusalem in 70 CE (Common Era). All of these writings became the doctrines of the Roman Catholic Church around 150 CE and were later called the *New Testament*. These twenty-seven books were considered to be truly canon, or *equal* in inspiration, because of their harmony and continuity to the first thirty-nine books of Scripture. However, when it began to be called the *New Testament*, the term *"New"* implied that it was a replacement of the *"Old"*. The word *"Renewed"* would have been a more accurate translation, as would the word *"Covenant"* rather than *"Testament"*. God, through the sacrifice of His Son, actually *renewed* His *Covenant* with His people, Israel. Because of their inability to keep His commandments within that Covenant, He was going to eliminate the curse of it through the blood of His Son. He was then going to renew their hearts with a spiritual heart transplant. *"Behold, the days are coming, says the LORD, when I will make a new (renewed) covenant with the House of Israel and with the House of Judah"..."But this is the covenant that I will make with the House of Israel after those days, says the LORD: I will put My law (Torah/ Instructions) in their minds, and write it on their hearts; and I will be their God, and they shall be My people"* (**JER 31:31 & 33**). Again, in future references, I will either use the term *Scripture* or *Renewed Covenant* in order to stay away from further error.

Even the term *Christian* is a Greek translation of the Hebrew word *Messianic*. The first believers were actually called *The Way* or *Nazarenes* and were considered to be just another sect or offshoot of Judaism. They were not called *Christian* until Paul and Barnabus were at Antioch. *"Then Barnabus departed for Tarsus to seek Saul. And when he had found him, he brought him to Antioch. So it was that for a whole year they assembled with the church* (ecclesia) *and taught a great many people. And the disciples were first called Christians in Antioch"* (**ACTS 11:25&26**). When the word Christian was used at Antioch, it was actually used in a derogatory or mocking manner. There are only two other times that the word *Christian* is ever used in the Scriptures—once more in the book of **Acts** and once in **I Peter**.

Now that we have looked at several of the Greek words that are commonly used in the Scriptures and their Hebrew equivalents, let's look at some that are used to describe God. The proper Hebrew name for *Jesus* is *Yeshua*, which means "the Salvation of God". *Jesus* is the English version of His Greek name, *Iesous*, which unfortunately does not have an exact Greek meaning. It is assumed to mean "the salvation of the Lord", but it seems to be only a substitute for His proper Hebraic name. (Did you know that the letter "J" never existed in the English language before 1610 CE? It was introduced at that time and replaced the use of the letters "I" and "Y" in many of our words.) Yeshua was also known as *the Anointed* or *the Promised One*. The Greek word for *the Anointed One* is *the Christ,* and in Hebrew, it is *HaMashiach,* which means *the Messiah.* His ministry as the *Promised* or *Anointed One* was threefold: salvation to each individual who would accept His redemption by faith—sanctification (to be made holy), which was also received by faith—and most importantly, the restoration of the "House of Israel" (all of God's chosen ones—His people).

You will find the words **LORD** *God* used to refer to the Almighty One, the Creator, throughout the English translations of the Scriptures; you will also see *Lord* **GOD** or just **LORD**. The reason for this is that it has been a popular belief among the Jewish sages and rabbis that if you pronounce the **LORD**'s name, **YAH***veh* or ***Jehovah,*** you would be recklessly taking the chance of misusing it and would be guilty of breaking the third commandment. To avoid this, they would simply refer to Him as ***Adonai,*** meaning **Lord**, or ***HaShem,*** meaning *the Name.* To do anything else would be a sign of not fearing or not showing proper humility before the **LORD**. However, throughout the Scriptures, we are encouraged to call upon His Name and to do all things in His Name. I take this literally. Therefore, instead of **LORD** *God*, I will refer to Him as **YAH***veh* **EL***ohim*. Instead of **Lord GOD**, I will refer to Him as ***Adonai* YAH***veh*. In the Renewed Covenant (New Testament), instead of just *Lord*, I will refer to Him as ***Adonai,*** and instead of *God*, I will occasionally refer to Him as ***Eluah.*** Mind you, I am not saying that it is wrong to refer to Him by these other names—I just personally enjoy and am excited in both knowing and using His original chosen language. It makes my relationship with Him even more real, more intimate, and more personal. After all, He is our Father or ***Abba*** (Daddy), and I want to encourage you to know Him in this way as well.

The Hebrew word **YAH***veh* is actually the pronunciation of the Tetragrammaton. The Tetragrammaton is the four English letters **Y-H-V-H** and comes from the four Hebrew letters Yeh-Heh-Vahv-Heh. They are pronounced with the same vowel sounds that are in the word YAHveh (the Hebrew alphabet contains no actual vowels, only sounds) and means *I AM THAT I AM* or *I will be as I will be.* The shortened version of **YAH***veh* is **YAH**, as in the words *Ha-leh-lu-YAH*, which is interpreted as *Praise be to YAHveh.* The word "praise" in the Hebrew is "YAH-hoo-dah". The word **YAH** can be found in many different Hebrew names, such as Isaiah (Yesha-YAH), Jeremiah (Yirmeh-YAH), and Zechariah (TzahkarYAH or Zekar-YAH). YAHveh is also referred to as EL (God) or in the singular, ELuah (the God).

This too is found in many names, such as Daniel (Dah-neeEL) and Michael (Meekhah-EL).

ELohim means the ***Mighty Ones*** in Hebrew. The word *ELohim* is the plural form of EL or ELuah. The Israelites use this plural form when they make their confession of faith—*"Hear, O Israel* (Sh'ma YisraEL), *the LORD our God* (YAHveh Elohenu), *the LORD is one* (YAHveh Echad)"!* (**DEUT** 6:4). The word *Sh'ma* (Sheh-mah') means to listen with your whole being and not just with your ears—just like loving God with your whole being. *"You shall love YAHveh your ELohim with all your heart, with all your soul, and with all your might"* (**DEUT** 6:5). *ELohenu* means *"our ELohim"*. *Echad* signifies unity, as within a marriage. *"Therefore a man shall leave his father and mother and be joined to his wife, and they shall become one* (echad) *flesh"* (**GEN** 2:24). So, when they make this confession, they are actually saying that He is One (*Echad*), but in a plural sense, *"Mighty Ones"*. This confession is known as "the Sh'ma", and they say it once in the morning and again in the evening, every day before retiring. In addition, it is said just before the evening meal at sundown to begin the seventh (Sabbath) day. It is also said at the beginning of each appointed feast day in the evening (a Hebrew day begins at sundown).

To more fully understand the word "echad", the best example to use is found in the marriage unit. Before marriage, a man is dependent upon and a liability to his parents. Afterwards, he is to become dependable and liable for his wife and will be her source, provider, and strength. She is to be the recipient of his provisions and the provider of the love and tenderness needed to raise a strong family. She is to be the source for the life of all of his offspring and future descendants. They shall then submit themselves as a family unit to one another and to YAH. This is a perfect example of the three-strand rope that cannot be easily broken. *"Though one may be overpowered by another, two can withstand him. And a threefold cord is not quickly broken"* (**ECCL** 4:12). This example also illustrates the idea of the triune ELohim. The Father, because of His ability to be omnipresent (present in all places at the same time), is at the same time the Son. The Father (YAHveh) and His Son (Yeshua) coexist through the power of the third Person of the Godhead, the Holy Spirit (Ruach HaKedosh). ***Ruach*** means the ***Breath of YAHveh***, and ***Kedosh/Kadesh*** means ***Holy***. The Ruach (Spirit) seems to be the feminine Person of YAHveh, which means that He could represent a wife or a mother. The Ruach (Spirit) never takes away the glory from the Father, but instead, glorifies Him. The Ruach (Spirit) represents love, tenderness, and complete submission. Without the Ruach (Spirit), creation would not have taken place. Without Him, the birth of the only begotten Son (Yeshua) could not have taken place. YAHveh ELohim, the first Person of the Godhead, represents the masculine Person of YAHveh, or husband and father. He is the final authority, the strength (power), and the judge of all creation. To

Him goes all of the glory and honor. Finally, Yeshua, His Son and the second Person in the Godhead, is the result of the love within this Echad, becoming the full image of YAHveh and having full authority given to Him.

The Beginnings

Now let's take a look at what the first book (Genesis) of The Law of Moses (Torah/Instructions) says about beginnings. The first book of the Torah starts with *"In the beginning"* (**GEN 1:1**). We also find this in the fourth book of the Renewed Covenant, where John begins his eyewitness account of Yeshua's life with these same three words, *"In the beginning"* (**JOHN 1:1**). Genesis goes on to confirm that YAHveh was the one who created the heavens and the Earth, and John goes on to confirm that YAHveh and Yeshua are one (Echad) and the same. Later, in the same chapter, John writes that Yeshua was responsible for creation and was manifested in the flesh to mankind.

"The beginnings" not only refer to the beginnings of time, space, heaven, and Earth, but also to the beginnings of rebellion and sin as well, along with the beginnings of evil and death. A renewed heaven and Earth follow after the flood, along with the beginning of the three races descending from Noah's sons, Shem, Ham (Hahm), and Japheth (Yafeth). Then there was the beginning of a pagan nation called Babylon. After this, was the beginning of a special nation, the Hebrew nation, followed by the beginning of a chosen nation, Israel. Finally came the beginning of a chosen people—Judah (YAHuda), Joseph (Yosef), and his son, Ephraim (Efraeem).

Creation

The Scriptures challenge us to believe in a Creator by faith—not only in His existence but also in His kindness, goodness, love, and His desire to bless His people. *"But without faith it is impossible to please Him, for he who comes to God must believe that He is, and that He is a rewarder of those who diligently seek Him"* (**HEB 11:6**). The beginning of time and space began at the creation of the heavens and the Earth (**GEN 1:1&2**). Before that, YAHveh dwelt in the third heaven, where he created the heavenly host of angels. This third heaven is also known as *"Paradise"* (**II COR 12:3&4**). In Paradise, there is neither time nor space. There are many who ask how long has God existed. The answer is "forever". All this really means is that He had no beginning because He existed in a realm that we have no way of understanding. We are all beings of time and space, and He is not. YAHveh created time and space in order to express what and who He really is—He is *"Love"*. *"He who does not love does not know God, for God is love"* (**I JOHN 4:8**). The greatest expression of love is through choice, so YAHveh developed a system through which all of His creation would be able to choose Him. Even His heavenly host, His angels, was given this choice. All were given the opportunity to choose between that which was good and that which was evil. All of those who would choose that which was good would forever be within the borders of His protection from the evil one. All of those who would choose evil would be subject to His wrath and outside of His protection from the evil one. Therefore, when He created Paradise, He gave those who dwelt there those same options. To those who chose Him as their everlasting ELohim, He promised eternal blessings—to those who did not, eternal punishment. A rebellion broke out in Paradise that was led by the evil one, and YAH ended it by placing those who made the wrong choice in chains until that great and final Day of Judgment (JUDE: 6).

We read that on the first day of His creation, the *"Word"*, Yeshua, created light out of darkness (GEN 1:1&2). That means that He created something out of nothing, given our understanding of the term nothing. Now I ask you, which takes more faith—to believe that an everlasting, ever-living ELohim did this or, as the evolutionists would like us to believe, that nothing created something out of nothing? Those are our only two choices because out of all of science, these are the only feasible possibilities. Of course, you could believe the theistic-evolutionist who says that a Supreme Being is responsible but that He used evolution to do it. I choose the first—it's a no brainer. Why would He use evolution and then lie to us in His written Word? And then you have the argument concerning the age of all things—ten-thousand years, a hundred-thousand, a million, or a billion? Well, the only way you can really settle that debate is—*who was there to record it?* I only know of One. Now, the godless-scientific mind wants to argue that the carbon-two-fourteen test, along with geological and other scientific data, provides the evidence for a very old Earth and universe. There hasn't really been any reliable data on the age of the universe, just theories based upon the same basic technology that is used to predict the weather, and you know how reliable that is. Geology can only be used as proof if you throw out the idea of a Biblical flood. On the other hand, if you use the creation-science, or intelligent-design, idea of a worldwide catastrophic flood, this would explain all of the geological and fossil records. Many scientists, on both sides of the argument, do agree that the carbon-two-fourteen tests have been proven mostly unreliable. The evidence of a prehistoric man evolving from an ape-man on the most part has been disproved as mistaken data, outright fraud, or blatant hoaxes. Well then, what clues do the Scriptures provide us with? As far as the age of the Earth, we can easily trace back through the Biblical records to determine the time from Adam's (Ahdom's) creation until now, which was about six-thousand years.

Scripture tells us that the Creator of all things is a very meticulous ELohim. *"For God is not the author of confusion but of shalom* (peace)*, as in all the congregations of the saints."..."Let all things be done decently and in order"* (I

COR 14:33 & 40). Because of that, we can calculate His time frame from the following verses: *"For a thousand years in Your sight are like yesterday when it is past, and like a watch in the night."…"But, beloved, do not forget this one thing, that with Adonai one day is as a thousand years, and a thousand years is as one day"* (**PSALMS** 90:4 and **II PET** 3:8). Some have said, "Yeah, I've heard that before, but that doesn't necessarily make it so." Well, consider the content of those Scriptures and see how they apply. Throughout the Scriptures, you will see YAHveh using numerical patterns of seven, forty, twelve, and others, such as two, three, and ten. By using the numerical pattern of seven, considered to be one of His holy (kedosh) numbers for His appointed times (moedim), He created the Earth and the heavens in six days (six-thousand years) and rested on the seventh (one-thousand years). Let's take a closer look at this. This seventh millennium is more than likely the time between creation and the flood when He left the complete stewardship of the Earth to man. During YAHveh's rest, man, because of his fallen state, completely polluted the Earth with sin. This would mean that the first millennium after creation became so out of control that YAH had to bring it to judgment through the flood. After His covenant with Noah, He guided men along for another five-thousand years to our present date—a total of six-thousand years. This would mean that we are just now entering the seven-thousandth year, or millennium, which would be the promised millennium of shalom (peace). Some also claim that the Scriptures say that He created it in six literal twenty-four-hour days. This would be correct if a day always meant a period of twenty-four hours. But the word used here for ***day*** is the Hebrew word "yom". It can either mean a specific period of time, such as a twenty-four-hour day, or an unspecified period of time, such as "in the Day of the LORD." In some places, "the Day of the LORD" means "the day of His coming" or "judgment". In other places, "the Day of the LORD" means "the days of His reign". Taking all of this into consideration, ***a day*** could be twenty-four hours, an unspecified length of time in His creation, or it could mean a thousand years.

If this was the pattern that He chose, which seems reasonable to me, then this would mean that He created light, and all that goes with it, over a period of a thousand years. The date of the beginning of this process of creation could be expressed as 10,000 BCE. As you may or may not know, light is more than just what we are able to see. There are many dimensions to light that we cannot see, and I believe that there are many more yet to be discovered. Light is the foundation of all energy, so the command, *"Let there be light"*, could be interpreted as "Let all of the energy in light be released and become the power that My Ruach (Spirit) will use to complete My Creation". At that very moment, the whole universe could have been filled with light, and over the next thousand years, this light could have been condensed into one point in space. His Ruach (Spirit/Breath) then could have taken this light and energy (His "Shchinah Glory" or "Presence") and shaped all of the minerals that are found on this Earth into a beautiful blue globe of molten rock covered with water. When He saw the completion of His work, He said that it was good, and the evening and the morning were the first day. This was a "first-day" event for Him, but not necessarily a twenty-four hour day, as we have said before. He began with nothing but darkness (the evening), and He finished with light (the morning). This was the method that He chose to use in order to teach mankind His pattern of keeping time. Take note: His day begins at the first sign of evening and ends at the next sign of evening—not from one midnight hour until the next midnight hour and then dividing them with a midday hour. That's man's method of measuring time based upon Greek timekeeping and not His. His is a night watch (approximately six p.m. until six a.m.) and a day watch (six a.m. to six p.m.). This is how He taught the Hebrews to keep time, and this is His Scriptural timekeeping method. The date at the end of this period of Creation would have been 9000 BCE.

As was said earlier, YAH could have used this same pattern of seven to also give us a mirrored image of the future. On the first day *of* Creation, He created light out of darkness. Now keeping His pattern in mind, we can see that His second period of 6000 years *after* Creation is a mirrored image of His first 6000 years *of* Creation. In His first millennium *after* Creation (4000—3000 BCE), because of His resting, YAH did not intervene with or intercept the evil that came upon the Earth as a result of man's sin. Instead, He allowed it to continue until the end of His rest, and then He judged it with the flood. This flood separated the good from the evil, mirroring His first-millennium day *of* Creation (10,000—9000 BCE) when he separated light from darkness. Remember, light and darkness also represents good and evil. That's why He renewed His Creation after the flood, making all things good again.

He began His second thousand-year day *of* Creation (9000—8000 BCE) with this beautiful blue globe that was enveloped in water and beginning to undergo a tremendous change in its composition. This change would have started with an evaporation process that was caused by the heat of the molten rock, creating an atmosphere capable of sustaining life as we know it. This atmosphere is biblically known as the "first heaven". When YAH renewed the heaven and the Earth during the second millennium *after* Creation (3000—2000 BCE) with the waters of the flood, it mirrored this second-millennium day *of* Creation.

When He separated the water above from the water below, it created oceans or seas. The waters beneath the atmosphere, or seas, with its tremendous pressure, would have begun cooling the molten rock and the minerals within it, causing the dry land to appear and leaving only a single place, or sea, remaining.

This single place could be where the Pacific Ridge is found today. This ridge, or rim, is made up of a circular range of mountains and faults that extend from our west coast, known as the San Andreas Fault, and follows north to Alaska. It then turns west and goes across the Aleutian Islands and the Bering Straits. From there, it continues west into Siberia and then south toward Japan to the Philippine Islands. It continues further south to just north of Australia and south of Hawaii. It makes another turn to the east and finally back north again to California. This area is known for its volcanic activity and Earthquakes.

Sometime during the third-millennium day *of* Creation (8000—7000 BCE), He created, within that dry land, the properties of life for all living things. First, there would have appeared from this dry land, or soil, trees for shade, trees that yielded fruit, and grass and herbs that yielded seeds that contained all of the necessary formulas and design for reproducing in the future. While all of this was happening, the waters were receding to underground chambers to be stored up for YAHveh's use at a future date. *"This is the history of the heavens and the earth when they were created, in the day that YAHveh ELohim made the earth and the heavens, before any plant of the field was in the earth and before any herb of the field had grown. For YAHveh ELohim had not caused it to rain on the earth, and there was no man to till the ground; but a mist went up from the earth and watered the whole face of the ground"* (**GEN** 2:4-6). From these underground springs, YAHveh watered the Earth until the great flood. So the Earth probably looked something like it does today, except in reverse, with two thirds or more being dry land and one third or less being water. A thousand years of this growth process of the herbs and the trees being absent of death, because death was not introduced until after the "fall", would have produced tremendous giant plants. This has been confirmed through fossil evidence.

It was during His third millennium *after* Creation (2000—1000 BCE) that He fed His people with spiritual waters and food (the Torah), causing growth and maturity to them and mirroring His feeding of the Earth with its waters from within. He also began to raise His seed up through Abraham (Avraham), Isaac (Yitzhak), Jacob (Yaacov)/Israel (YisraEL), Judah (YAHuda), and Joseph (Yosef). He also raised great men of faith up, such as Moses (Mosheh), David (Dahveed), and all of the Ne'vim.

Then came that wonderful fourth-millennium day *of* Creation (7000—6000 BCE) when YAH would redistribute His energy of light (Shchinah Glory) into galaxies, stars, nebulae, planets, and a companion for the Earth, the moon, and a new source of energy for life, the sun. He also commissioned these to be signs for keeping track of days, months, seasons, and years for all of His future appointed feasts (moedim) and celebrations. He also created the millions and billions of years that light would have to travel in order to illuminate the Earth with its starlight and beauty. At this time, the Earth had only one season—a tropical summer paradise, just as the geological and fossil evidence proves, because it too was preserved for us by the flood. All of this evidence could only mean one thing—that the Earth was originally perfectly vertical on its axis (today it is 23 ½ degrees off vertical) as it traveled in its orbit around its new light source, which it had to be in order for it to be able to maintain such a worldwide paradise. The Scriptures also tell us that in the future, this same Shchinah Glory will once again replace all of the lights of the heavens, becoming our final source of light. *"And there shall be no night there: They need no lamp nor light of the sun, for Adonai Eluah gives them light"* (**REV 22:5**).

In the fourth millennium *after* Creation (1000—0 BCE), YAH brought another new *Light* into the world. This new *Light* came in the form of His chosen kings, from King David (Dah-veed) to King Jesus (Yeshua), beginning the Messianic Era (ME/CE/AD).

In the fifth-millennium day *of* Creation (6000—5000 BCE), He created, from out of the Earth, both fish and birds to inhabit the sea and the air. Their existing for this length of time without the hindrance of death would have resulted in a multitude of species for both, including size and variety.

In the fifth millennium *after* Creation (0—1000 ME/CE/AD), YAH said that those who would wait upon Him would mount up as eagles (**ISA 40:31**). He would cause His Spirit to descend from heaven like a dove and baptize (immerse) them with an overflowing of His Holiness (**JOHN 1:32&33**). He would make those who followed Him fishers of men (**MATT 4:18&19**). During this time, the spread of His Scriptures throughout Europe was unprecedented.

Then, in the sixth and final millennium day *of* Creation (5000—4000 BCE), He created the great beasts of the fields, forests, and jungles, which would have included the dinosaurs, herds of cattle, wild beasts, and crawling insects. Then, just as He did with the creatures of the fifth millennium, He commanded them to only produce their own kind. All came from the dust of the Earth, and all would return to it after the "fall". Again, another thousand years would give ample time for a multitude of species of these creatures to inhabit the whole Earth and for many of them to grow, both in size and in variety. YAHveh then spoke to His Echad (Triune Being) and said, *"Let Us make man (Adam/Ahdom) in Our image, according to Our likeness, let them have dominion over the fish of the sea, over the birds of the air, and over the cattle, over all the earth and over every creeping thing that creeps on the earth. So YAHveh created man in His Own image; in the image of ELohim He created him; male and female He created them"* (**GEN 1:26&27**). He provided man (Adam/Ahdom) with the same food source that He had provided for all of His other creatures—the fruit of the trees and the herbs of the field. They were all to be vegetarians in this phase of His creation. That blows the idea of flesh-eating beasts, including the Tyrannosaurus Rex, the Raptors, etc.

WHAT WE WEREN'T TAUGHT ABOUT THE BIBLE AND ITS HISTORY

The sixth millennium *after* Creation (1000—2000 ME/CE/AD) brings us up to our present date. It has been proven during this period in history that the "beast of the Earth", that is the brutality of the nations and its leaders, has brought us to another time of judgment for our sins. Man, who was supposed to be the Creator's crowning glory, has instead brought mostly shame upon His Name. With his ever-increasing knowledge, he has attempted to make himself his own Lord (Adonai) through science, medicine, academics, psychology, and physiology. In doing so, he has looked to himself and missed the One who has provided all the necessary things that would have made him a good steward of Creation. And instead of giving Him the glory and honor, he has kept it for himself. He has turned away from the gift giver and has worshiped the gifts instead. Now it is time for those *"Who are called by His Name, to humble themselves, and pray and seek His face, and turn from their wicked ways, then He will hear from Heaven, and will forgive their sin, and heal their land"* (**II CHRON 7:14**) and bring His Peace (Shalom) upon the Earth.

When YAHveh ceased from His creating the heavens and the Earth, He established a seventh millennium for His rest. This was His example for all of us to follow, honoring the seventh day of the week—it was also His fourth commandment. This seventh day of rest is a rehearsal for a time in the future when He will establish a millennium of rest and shalom (peace) for mankind, who has been struggling with himself and creation as a result of the "fall". If He commanded us to rest on the seventh day, where did we get the idea that the first day of the week was the day of rest? I know that Yeshua was raised from the dead on the first day of the week after His crucifixion, but I can't find anywhere in Scripture where we were told to change His Sabbath to the first day—we've done that on our own. However, I do find something about changing His words in a few places. *"You shall not add to the word which I command you, nor take anything from it, that you may keep the commandments of YAHveh your ELohim which I command you"* (**DEUT 4:2**). This same kind of command is also found in **DEUT 12:32, JOSH 1:7, PROV 30:6,** and **REV 22:18**. If we check history, a guy by the name of Emperor Constantine made a decree to all Christians throughout the Empire of Rome that changed YAHveh's Sabbath to the first day of the week—Sunday, the day of the sun god, Zeus/Jupiter. Not only that, but he also declared Jupiter's birthday, which was the fourth day after the winter equinox, December 25th, as being Yeshua's birthday. Who gave him the authority to add to or take away from the Scriptures? It certainly wasn't YAHveh.

YAHveh saved His crowning glory for last. On the sixth-day *of* Creation, as His final labor, He created Man. He now personally forms Man with His own hands and breathes into him His own ***Breath*** (Ruach/Spirit), making man a spirit being and the most unique of all His creatures. At the same time, he does possess a soul, as do all of YAH's creatures, and like them, lives in a body of flesh and bone. Man was also unique because within him was dwelling his partner in life. *"So YAH created man in His own image; in the image of YAH He created him; male and female He created them"* (**GEN** 1:27). He later took the female from the flesh and bone of the male. Therefore, they were both created in His image. Then we read: *"This is the book of the genealogy of Adam (Ahdom). In the day that YAH created man, He made him in the likeness of YAH....He created them male and female, and blessed them and called them Mankind (Adam/Ahdom or Ahdomah) in the day they were created....And Adam (Ahdom) lived one hundred and thirty years,* **and begot a son in his own likeness, after his image**, *and named him Seth"* (**GEN** 5:1-3). Notice that it states: **"And begot a son in "his own" likeness, after "his" image"**. This tells us that *we* are not made in the image of YAH. Only Adam (Ahdom) was because, like YAH, he was originally sinless. But all of his descendants after him (meaning us) were made in the likeness and image of Adam (Ahdom) with his sinful nature. And since we are naturally born in Adam's (Ahdom's) image, in order for us to become the sons of YAH, we must therefore be born a second time—but this time, born of His Ruach (Spirit) (**JOHN** 1:11&12). There are some who say that chapter two of Genesis disagrees with the order of creation that is given in chapter one. I don't see it that way. I see chapter one as being the chronology of creation and chapter two as a recap of certain segments that expound on man's role and purpose in creation.

Let's pause for a moment and take a look at another one of YAH's numerical patterns—the pattern of two and three (three two-thousand-year periods). It was approximately two-thousand years between the time that YAHveh had finished Creation and the time that He had brought mankind from Adam (Ahdom) to Avraham, the father of the Hebrew nation. In His second two-thousand-year period, He focused on His "sons of faith" until He had brought forth His only begotten Son, Yeshua. Finally, in His third two-thousand-year period, His Ruach (Holy Spirit) spread the Good News in preparation for the restoration of all things back to their original state before the fall.

What I have just shared with you about the order of creation is just my theory and opinion, but so are those of the evolutionists and creationists—they too are just opinions and theories. So, take them for what they're worth—you can be the judge.

The "Garden of Eden"

Exactly what was this "garden", and what made it so unique? The garden was a terrestrial duplication of Paradise. Paradise is YAH'S perfect heavenly habitation. He wanted to make a duplication of it on the Earth because it was there that He planned to dwell and fellowship with man as a father would with his son. He placed it on a high plateau or on top of a mountain, facing east with only one entrance. We will continue to see this pattern of construction in His tabernacle in the wilderness and in both of the permanent houses that were built for Him. YAHveh seldom does anything without it having an immediate application as well as a future one.

The four rivers that are mentioned in Genesis (Pishon, Gihon, Hiddekel, and Euphrates) existed before the flood and were more than likely washed away by it—new rivers formed, taking their place. Although the geography had changed, their basic locations had not. Today there is only one of these rivers in this region that empty into the Mediterranean Sea—the Nile, formerly the Pishon. Two others, the Tigris (Hiddekel) and the Euphrates, merge into one river and empty into the Persian Gulf. They are located in the territory that we call Iraq. The Gihon River is now just an underground spring that empties into the Kidron River just outside of Jerusalem in Israel.

YAHveh brought all of the animals that He had created to Adam (Ahdom) for him to name. (He would once again bring His creatures to another man, Noah, but this time in order to save them from His judgment.) YAH was demonstrating the exalted position that He desired for man by giving him dominion over His Creation. This also tells us that man must have had a language and vocabulary, along with a vast understanding of all things, in order to undergo such a task as this. Man had been created in perfection and had a body that was created and designed to live eternally. YAH's plan was to meet all of man's needs through His vast provisions. However, unlike the other creatures, man didn't have a companion, so YAH decided to provide him with one who would be taken from man's own flesh, bone, and blood instead of from the dust of the Earth. He made them "one" (echad), just as YAHveh is an Echad Being. Adam (Ahdom) also had the authority to name his new companion, so he called her Eve (Cheva), which means "from man". YAHveh had provided man with a harmonious relationship with all of His creatures, just as He will do during the millennium of shalom (peace). This compatibility continued until the fall of mankind. Remember, there was no death, nor war, nor fear, nor hatred—only complete harmony and peace (shalom).

The Fall of Mankind

After YAH had formed man, He gave him only one commandment to keep. He was not to eat the fruit of a certain tree in the garden (the tree of the knowledge of good and evil). Everything else was free for the taking, especially from the Tree of Life. This was all that was required of him in order to maintain his present position in this Earthly Paradise. But an intruder came into this Paradise who was disguised as a serpent. Now whether this creature could actually speak may or may not have been the case, but it was somehow able to communicate with Eve (Cheva) because some type of dialogue went on between them. This dialogue stirred up new feelings within this helpmate of Adam's (Ahdom's) that she apparently had not experienced before—the forbidden fruit suddenly became overwhelmingly desirable. Wow! What the power of suggestion can do under just the right circumstances and the right timing. She became acutely aware of this fruit's beauty, not to mention its ability to make her wise like God, just as the serpent had suggested. What could possibly have been going through Eve's (Cheva's) mind at that moment?—"Maybe Adam (Ahdom) and I have been bamboozled by YAH! Maybe that was why we were told not to touch. Oops! Did He say *"do not touch"*? Hmm...could it be that He didn't like the idea of competition? Maybe He was concerned about losing control. Yeah...that's it! YAH wants to be the only one to run things, and I'll bet He's jealous about the beauty of this other guy too. Just wait until I tell Adam (Ahdom)!"

They were tested, and they failed the test. Freedom of choice brings with it a big responsibility and possibly a consequence. Before the test, they were aware of only one thing—YAHveh's love and companionship. They were one with Him, and He was one with them. They had no doubt or fear—there was nothing there to be afraid of, not even the intruder. All they needed to do was to tell YAH about this creature and his enticing offer. Things would have been really different if they had. Well, that ain't the way it happened. One bite and *boom*—everything changed. All of a sudden, they became aware of everything that they hadn't noticed before, like..."Hey we're naked!" "What does that mean?" "I don't know, but it doesn't feel right!" "Uh-oh...I wonder if ELohim (God) will notice we're naked. We better make something with our hands in order to cover up our nakedness, and then we better hide! We're going to be found out anyway, so we better just fess up and try to fix this thing!"

We can be sure of one thing—He is always ready to forgive us. But that doesn't take care of the consequences; that's a debt that has to be paid for in someway or another. It's like the natural law of gravity or inertia—you just can't change it. You are subject to it, but if you balance it correctly, you can use it to your advantage. You are always subject to the one you obey. If Adam (Ahdom) and his helpmate, Eve (Cheva), would have by their own free will chosen to continue to subject themselves to YAH through their obedience, He would have continued to be their Master (Adonai). But because they chose to obey the serpent (Satan in disguise) instead, they transferred that servant-hood over to him. The result was that instead of Adam (Ahdom) walking with YAH for eternity and resting with Him for a thousand years, he only saw 930 years on this planet, and then he had to pay the price for his sin—death.

YAH was going to provide a way for man to rectify his mistake, but He was going to do it over a long period of time—*six-thousand years*! But man was going to have to give up a few things as a consequence to his mistake: first would be his close relationship with YAH, as he had known it—second, his eternal physical existence—and third, he would have to work for his keep. YAH was then going to provide a covering for him to ward off Satan's plan of utter destruction. He would do this through a series of unilateral contracts known as *covenants*. This would mean that He would always hold up His end regardless of what man might do. Man's obligation would be to follow YAH's instructions, later to be called His Torah, and to train up his children to do likewise. If man failed to do this, YAH would even provide the atonement. The only acceptable atonement was blood. *"For the life of the flesh is in the blood, and I have given it to you upon the altar to make atonement for your souls; for it is in the blood that makes atonement for the soul"* (**LEV 17:11**).

The only provision that YAH made for man to be able to purchase his life back with was the blood that maintained that life—his own blood. But he would have to give up his own life in order to do that. That's an oxymoron—you can't do both. Someone or something else would have to pay that price for him. YAH's solution for that was to allow man to use the creatures that he had named and had become so close to before his fall from YAH's grace as his substitute—but he was to choose only the creatures that YAH would specify as being acceptable.

All the living things that YAH created on the fifth and sixth day have a heart that pumps an ever-flowing river of blood. If that river stops, life leaves that creature and it ceases to exist. In man, however, it is the Breath of YAH (Ruach/Spirit) that provides him with an "eternal" soul. However, the question becomes—under which master will that soul live? It has been left up to each individual to make that decision for himself.

YAHveh's First Covenant with Mankind

Adam (Ahdom) and Eve (Cheva), out of frustration and shame, tried to cover their nakedness by making fig-leaf aprons. This was not a sufficient covering, so YAHveh Himself shed the first blood of two of His creatures in order to provide the clothing, or covering (atonement), that man needed to cover his sin. It was then that He made His first covenant with them. He told them that through the seed of Eve (Cheva), He was going to provide a *Man* who would finally defeat their accuser and adversary. This Seed would be Holy (Kedosh) and would only come through the woman. Man could have no part in this conception because his blood would contaminate any life that it was responsible for reproducing. His sinfulness and the curse of his sinfulness would pass on to all of his descendents. On the other hand, the woman would be the only human participant that could be used because her blood doesn't enter into the child's system, except to feed it while it is in her womb—ask any doctor. The father determines the sex of the child and initiates the child's production of its own blood. If YAHveh was responsible for the conception, then the child's blood would be sinless and therefore holy (kedosh).

Another consequence that was brought on by their disobedience was that they could no longer be residents in His Garden (YAH's Paradise on Earth). This was for a couple of reasons. First, YAHveh was Holy and, therefore, sin could not remain in His presence. Being in His presence in Paradise was the privilege for only those who were submitted to Him. And second, there was also the problem with the presence of the Tree of Life—if they were to eat of it, there would go the consequences for their disobedience. He, therefore, placed fire at the entrance to His Garden to keep them from the Tree of Life. They were banished from YAH's presence and sent *east* of His garden. East was the direction that was symbolically used to depict "departure from YAH", while west was the direction used for "approaching Him". We will look at this more closely in the next chapter.

The Beginning of the First Family

According to the instructions (Torah) of YAH, the firstborn represents the strength and authority of the family. *"Sanctify to Me all the firstborn, whatever opens the womb among the children of Israel both of man and animal; it is Mine"* (**EXOD 13:2**). If the firstborn dishonors the family, the birthright must be passed on to one deserving the honor—the second born, the third, etc. Adam (Ahdom) and Eve's (Cheva's) firstborn was Cain (Kaeen) and their second was Abel (Ahbel). Cain (Kaeen) became a farmer, working the soil for his livelihood by the sweat of his labors. Abel (Ahbel) was a herdsman, tending and caring for YAH's dumb creatures. Adam (Ahdom) and Eve (Cheva) apparently raised their family to fear YAH, to pray and to worship Him, and to depend upon Him for their livelihood. They also must have taught them to recognize YAH's provisions by giving Him an offering in order to show their gratitude. Cain (Kaeen) offered YAH only the works from his labor, but Abel (Ahbel) remembered that only the shedding of blood would pay the price for his sinful nature and that good intentions just wouldn't cut it, so he offered up the life of one of his yearling lambs. YAH saw the two hearts and accepted Abel's (Ahbel's) offering with gladness because He knew that Abel (Ahbel) understood the lesson. This uncovered Cain's (Kaeen's) heart that was full of jealousy and envy, revealing his true character. This in turn brought about hatred and anger, which is the root cause of murder. *"But I say to you that whoever is angry with his brother without cause shall be in danger of the judgment"* (**MATT 5:22**). This led to Cain (Kaeen) murdering his brother, Abel (Ahbel), and then being driven away from his family as the consequence. Cain (Kaeen) pleaded with YAH about his banishment because he was concerned about future generations of brothers and sisters who might want to take vengeance on him or his descendants because of their brother's death. Because of YAH's grace, He declared that his banishment would be sufficient enough and that if anyone were to take vengeance on Cain (Kaeen) or his descendants, they would suffer a seven-fold punishment. YAH also gave him a distinguishing physical characteristic that could easily be identified by others in order to protect him and his descendants. Nowhere in Scripture does it say what this characteristic was. I believe it could very well have been that Cain's (Kaeen's) descendants were given either a darker or a lighter complexion than the others. This could account for the variety of complexions that distinguish the many different races that are found in the world today. Remember, this was by no means a curse—it was just a distinguishing characteristic. Too many times we tend to judge people by their outward appearance before we get to know them. We judge them through our own personal prejudice against their complexion, their physical attributes, their race, or even their cultural background. YAH hates this, and that is why I believe that He made the punishment for harming Cain (Kaeen) or his descendants so severe. We will cover this point more thoroughly when we discuss Noah and his sons.

After Adam (Ahdom) and Eve (Cheva) lost both of their first two sons to evil, they continued having more sons and daughters. The next son that was listed among their descendants was Seth, who also feared YAH and followed His commandments.

The Sons of YAH and the Sons of Men

The Scriptures contain several long lists of begets. The first list is that of Cain (Kaeen) and his descendents (**GEN 4:16-24**), followed by the list of Seth and his descendants (**GEN 5:6-32**). A problem began to develop when these two lineages began to intermarry. *"Now it came to pass, when men began to multiply on the face of the Earth, and daughters were born to them, that the sons of God saw the daughters of men, that they were beautiful; and they took wives for themselves of all whom they chose"* (**GEN 6:1&2**). Who were these sons of God, and who were the daughters of men? Some say that the sons of God were the offspring of the fallen angels. This is not possible because first of all, the fallen angels were confined to chains until the judgment (**JUDE: 6**). Secondly, angels cannot procreate. *"But those who are counted worthy to attain that age, and the resurrection from the dead, neither marry nor are given in marriage; nor can they die anymore, for they are equal to the angels and are sons of God, being sons of the resurrection"* (**LUKE 20:35&36**). As these Scriptures confirm, sons of God are those who qualify to attain the resurrection. Therefore, the term "sons of God" could only pertain to the descendants of Adam (Ahdom) through the lineage of Seth because they were the ones who followed after righteousness. The term "daughters of men" could only pertain to the descendants of Adam (Ahdom) through the lineage of Cain (Kaeen) because they were those who were the rebellious ones. There is no record in the Scriptures as to how many other sons and daughters Adam (Ahdom) had after Seth—it just says that he had others.

Intermarriage was not a problem back then because of the purity of the human body. The human body was originally designed to last forever, and the consequence of sin had not yet taken its complete toll on it. Then too, YAHveh had not yet put a prohibition on intermarrying—instead, He was using it as His tool to populate the Earth. Man must have developed into a near *super human being* with the capability of spawning a tremendous amount of offspring because he lived seven, eight, or even nine-hundred years. The Scriptures describe man's accomplishments during this time as being in music, crafting tools, and mining. If the sons of Cain (Kaeen) accomplished all of these things, just imagine what the sons of YAH would have developed.

Why did man become so wicked in such a short span of time—one-thousand years? They didn't have the care or guidance of YAH. He saw what man had done with what He had given him and what happened when He allowed evil to coexist with good. He had left them to be on their own during His thousand-year Sabbath rest and what a mess they had made. He couldn't allow any of this to continue—it was time to start over and renew His covenant with those who feared Him and had remained faithful to Him. GEN 6:1-8 explains the events that led up to YAH's decision to judge the earth with a flood.

The End of the First Millennium—One Remaining Servant, Noah

There were ten generations through the linage of Seth, from Adam (Ahdom) to Noah, whose names in Hebrew prophetically revealed the promise of "The Redeemer" to future generations. The first man was Adam (Ahdom), which means ***man/mankind***. The second was Seth, which means ***appointed***. The third was Enosh, which means ***mortal***. The fourth was Kenan, meaning ***sorrow***. The fifth was Mahalalel and means ***blessed one***. The sixth was Jared, which means ***come down***. The seventh was Enoch and means ***teaching***. The eighth was Methuselah, meaning ***his death will send***. The ninth was Lamech, which means ***hidden/invisible king***. And finally, the tenth was Noah and means ***rest/comfort***. Thus we have—*"Mankind (is) appointed mortal sorrow. (The) Blessed One (will) come down, teaching (that) His death will send (the) hidden/invisible King (to bring) rest/comfort."* The DNA (or Seed) that would fulfill the first covenant of YAH was being passed down through the patriarchs of these ten houses (families).

In the course of their lives, we can see one that especially stands out—Enoch. He lived three hundred and sixty-five years and, because of his relationship and fellowship with YAHveh, was translated into His presence. We see this happening one other time in Scripture with the prophet Elijah (ELeeYAHoo). *"Then it happened, as they continued on and talked that suddenly a chariot of fire appeared with horses of fire, and Elijah (ELeeYAHoo) went up by a whirlwind into heaven"* (**II KINGS 2:11**). Enoch's son, Methuselah, lived the longest out of all of YAH's "sons of longevity"—nine hundred and sixty-nine years. Then the grandson of Methuselah, Noah, came on the scene. His three sons would establish the three basic races of the Earth.

It was shortly after YAH's Sabbath rest and His acknowledgment of the total corruption of mankind that Noah was born. He chose Noah, who was a righteous man above all others, to be the one to repopulate the Earth—He was about to destroy it so that He could renew it. He told Noah to follow His instructions because the Earth as he knew it was only going to last for another one-hundred and twenty years.

The Flood

It was soon after the birth of Noah's firstborn, Shem, that YAH informed him about His plan of destruction. He gave Noah instructions on how to build an ark. This was not a ship with a bow and a keel (the word for "ark" is the same word that is used for "box" or "container", and it's the same word that was used for the "basket" that Moses was left in, and the "box" that the ten commandment tablets were placed in). Instead, this was an extremely large box with three floors that would have rooms large enough to hold all of his family plus all of the animals that YAH would send to him. He then explained to Noah the purpose for it—He was going to bring rain from the sky and cause the Earth to erupt, bringing forth a flood of water. This would have taken an enormous amount of faith on Noah's part because he had no concept of what rain was or what YAH meant by a flood.

Soon after he began his construction, his wife bore him two more sons, Ham (Hahm) and Japheth (Yafeth). Noah spent the next one-hundred and twenty years laboring on this faith project, all the while experiencing ridicule from his neighbors. The dimensions of this three-story waterproof box were four-hundred and fifty feet long, seventy-five feet wide, and forty-five feet high, with a vented skylight on top that ran its length. Before the great deluge, YAH told Noah that he would be sending him two of every kind of animal, one of each gender, which He desired to save. Some species would be designated as clean, while all others were considered unclean. The clean would arrive in pairs of seven for the purpose of sacrifice. He also commanded him to select seven pairs of each kind of bird. Noah would have been familiar with animal sacrifices because this had been the practice since the garden—the incident between Cain (Kaeen) and Abel (Ahbel) also verifies this. They could not have been for the purpose of consumption because at that time mankind's dietary laws were limited to the herbs of the field and the fruit of the trees and vines. Finally, the day came when everything that YAH had told Noah began to take place, and he and his family, along with the animals, entered the ark.

A number of scientists on both sides of the aisle (evolution vs. intelligent design) believe the theory that a colossal meteor, asteroid, or comet struck the Earth at some early date in history and caused a cataclysmic event to take place. The evolutionists believe it brought about the extinction of the dinosaur. They may be close, but I think it did a lot more than just that. There is no doubt that some kind of cataclysmic event did take place that brought about the global flood of Genesis. Let's look at something that we already have some knowledge about. Our solar system is inundated with evidence of some type of extraterrestrial bombardment. In our exploration of the solar system, we have discovered that virtually all of the inner planets and their moons, along with our own, are highly pockmarked, which had to have had some type of causation. It is as if the entire solar system had passed through some type of cosmic hailstorm. Whether or not it was a comet or a meteor striking the Earth that caused the fountains of the deep to erupt and the clouds to be gathered and release the torrent of rain, something did change the axis of the Earth. This change introduced the four seasons and all of its climates in an instant. Geological and biological evidence shows that some of the great mammoths were frozen instantly with undigested food in their stomachs. Other evidence of the cataclysmic flooding are the many plants that have been sealed in rock (fossils) showing no signs of decay. Marine life has been found on top of mountains. The evidence goes on and on. All of this evidence may be a case for the evolutionist, but the bottom line is that YAH's hand was on the event.

The Genesis account of the flood tells us that from the time that YAH told Noah to enter the ark until the deluge actually began was seven days. We are then told that the heavens and the fountains of the deep were opened for forty days. Seven and forty are spiritual numbers that YAH uses to tell us something. Seven days for the embarkment of His creatures shows us His holy (kedosh) signature for the completion of His work. The forty days of His wrath shows us His holy (kedosh) testing period. Testing is always related to the number forty. When we stop to consider the amount of rain that it would take to cover any of the mountains on the Earth in Noah's day by ninety to one-hundred feet, it could never be accomplished in only forty days. However, if most of the water that we observe on the Earth today were in underground reservoirs, the possibility of what would have occurred when they broke loose can easily be understood. The pressure from the weight of that much water would have changed the geography of the entire face of the planet. Not only that, but it could have been the force that would account for the petrified forests, fossil records, coal reserves, veins of diamonds, rubies, sapphires, emeralds, and the pools of oil. A worldwide flood answers all of these hypotheses. Genesis then tells us that the receding of the waters continued for a full year before Noah was given the word to disembark from the ark.

YAHveh's Second Covenant with Mankind

It is at this time that YAHveh adds to His covenant with mankind by declaring a cessation on this method of invoking His wrath. He confirms it with the sign of the rainbow—YAHveh always confirms His covenants with signs. Noah had begun to sacrifice some of the clean animals that were brought out from the ark. YAH then introduced some new commandments that man was to obey in this new covenant. This began with the eating of flesh as a new dietary law that mankind was called to observe—at the same time, a prohibition on blood consumption was commanded. There seems to be no distinction between clean and unclean here, other than what was to be sacrificed. This was also an extension of the ordinances for the shedding of blood for sin. This would all be a part of His second covenant with man. It was after this that YAH caused the fear of man to come upon the animals of the Earth. The law regarding the shedding of human blood was also expanded to include the blood that was spilt by animals and even those who were responsible for them—this was the establishment of the capitol-punishment ordinance. Noah, his family, and the families of the rest of creation were once more commanded to multiply and replenish the Earth.

Replenishing the Earth

Noah took up farming and planted a vineyard. After his first harvest, he celebrated and became a little inebriated. Apparently, after going into his tent to sleep it off, his robe became disarrayed in such a way that it exposed his nakedness. His second-born son, Ham (Hahm), went into his father's tent and found him in this embarrassing position. Instead of covering him up out of respect, he ran out to his brothers and made sport of his father. Upon hearing of their father's embarrassing situation, they immediately went into his tent with a blanket, and while walking backwards as an expression of honor to him, they covered his nakedness. When Noah heard of this, he pronounced his displeasure with Ham's (Hahm's) show of disrespect by assigning him, along with his descendants, a position of servant-hood under his brothers.

The replenishing of the Earth by Noah's descendants began in Scripture with Noah's youngest son, Japheth (Yafeth). His descendants migrated to the Caucasian Mountains and populated most of what we now call Europe. They became more readily known as the Gentile/Goyim (Gohyeem) nations. Shem,

Noah's oldest, settled throughout the Middle East and was the direct ancestor of both the Hebrew and the Arab nations, as well as those of the Americas. Ham's (Hahm's) descendants migrated to the continents of Africa and Asia (the Far East). Some of Ham's (Hahm's) descendants became a thorn in the flesh for the Hebrews. These descendants included the Cushites, the Puttim, the Canaanites, and the Philistines.

Also from Ham (Hahm) came a mighty hunter known as Nimrod, who was the founder of a city called Babel. He was the ancestor of the nation known as Babylon (today's Iraq). Babylon would be the place where all pagan religions would have their origin. The idols and the panorama of polytheism within these religions would eventually evolve into the gods (elohim) of the Medes and the Persians. These empires would follow in Babylon's footsteps and would fall later in history. From there came the mixing of both the elohim and the philosophies of the Greek and Roman empires. The combining of all of these false elohim just added to the confusion of mankind's misunderstanding of spirituality. You can now see the far-reaching consequences of Ham's (Hahm's) dishonor toward his father. According to the first book of the Torah, Genesis, Nimrod was the "grandson" of Ham (Hahm).

This would put us on YAHveh's timetable at about 2500 BCE. This was when Nimrod decided to build a temple and dedicate it to himself (temples are for idols and not for YAHveh—YAHveh takes up His residence in a *house*, or in Hebrew, *Beit* or *Beth*). Nimrod's desire was to counterfeit YAH's throne on Earth with a high place that would represent Eden. This was pure rebellion against YAH, just as much so as when Lucifer attempted to cause a coup in heaven in order to usurp YAH's throne. YAH had his own plan for duplicating Eden—the Tabernacle in the wilderness of Canaan, about a thousand years later. Nimrod proclaimed himself to be the "ELuah on Earth". He had many wives, one of whom was Ishtar. Their firstborn was named Tammuz, who was considered to be the "Son of ELuah". After Nimrod died, he was given the name "Molech" and was worshipped as the king of the universe. His wife, Ishtar, was later called "Ashtoreth", the queen of heaven, and their son was called "Zeus".

I'm giving you this background information about the origins of many of the pagan elohim and religions because many false theologies have their roots in them. For instance, Molech was also known as Jupiter the el-sun (mighty one of the sun). The el-sun was a predominate deity among many other false religions and went by many other names, too many to mention here. The great influence that they have had on man over the ages has been illustrated in the form of the sun being depicted as a silhouette or halo behind the subject of many sculptures, paintings, and other artifacts. The Roman Emperor Constantine, a worshipper of the el-sun, Zeus/Jupiter, promoted, through art, the enshrinement of many

WHAT WE WEREN'T TAUGHT ABOUT THE BIBLE AND ITS HISTORY

of those whom he had admired throughout history with the symbol of the sun as a halo behind them. Today we see this artwork and the illustrations of many biblical characters, including Yeshua, with these symbols—even in our churches. And if we research history, we can even find the "mother-with-child" image among many pagan deities. These symbols have stealthily crept into our own religious beliefs.

After Nimrod built his city and tower, YAH had had enough of his rebellion, so He responded by confusing the languages of men, thereby halting the construction of such a tower or pinnacle. The people scattered to the "Four Corners of the Earth", a term that we will better understand later. People have a tendency to gravitate toward those whom they feel the most comfortable with, so when YAH confused the languages at the building of the tower of Babel, those who had similar languages and were alike in appearance grouped together to form different cultures and races. This in turn accomplished YAHveh's plan for mankind to multiply and fill the Earth. The Earth divided a century or two later (**GEN 10:25**), and the continents shifted, races and cultures developed, more high places were built throughout the Earth (archeology testifies to this), and the Earth began to be filled. This would also agree with the theory of most geological scientists—that a continental shift did occur and divided the European and African continents from the Americas. This was probably the direct result of the worldwide flood. In all actuality, we are still experiencing the residual effects of that flood with all of our earthquakes and volcanic activity.

At this point, let me address the complexity of the different races that descended from this one man, Noah. As far as skin color is concerned, there isn't such a thing—only skin tone, or complexion. Every human being on the Earth has the same skin color, just different tones. Within each person is a protein called Melanin that is made up of two genes that determine their skin tone. These two genes vary in their strength, and this regulates the tone level of each individual's skin. Let's look at an example. Let's say that "AA" and "BB" represent both the strongest genes and the darkest tone of these genes. Now let's use "aa" and "bb" to represent the weakest and the lightest tone. A medium tone would then be either "Aa and Bb" or "aA and bB". All tones going from darker to lighter, including medium tones, could have varying combinations such as "AA and Bb", "Aa and BB", "aA and BB", "AA and bB", etc. We can see this in our modern times with the race of people found in the country of India. It is not unusual for one family to produce two very dark children and two very light, with other shades in between. This would mean that each of Noah's three sons could very easily have had different skin shades, or tones, just as the people of India do today.

YAHveh Builds a Nation for Himself

The generations of Shem were Arphaxas, Shelah, Eber, Peleg, Reu, Serug, Nahor, Terah, and then Abram (Avram). The longevity of these generations between Shem and Avram began to diminish rapidly after the flood. It seems that the introduction of seasons and climate changes took a heavy toll on the longevity of all life. As a matter of fact, Shem's death occurred about the same time as Avram's. Some scholars believe that Shem may have been the one who was known as the priest-king of the city of Salem, Melchizedek. We will discuss the importance of this later in Chapter Twenty-Five.

Avram, who was an Armenian, heard the voice of YAHveh directing him to leave the land of his fathers in Ur, which was located somewhere in Mesopotamia, and travel to the land of Canaan. By faith, he followed YAH's instructions and gathered up his family, which included his nephew Lot and his family, along with his possessions, and began his journey. This was an example of putting faith into action, and it was counted by YAHveh as righteousness. *"And he believed in YAHveh, and He accounted it to him for righteousness"* (**GEN 15:6**). *"Thus also faith by itself, if it does not have works, is dead"* (**JAM 2:17**).

Avram acted on his faith and traveled south, crossing over the Euphrates River and leaving the land of Mesopotamia behind. He then crossed over the Jordan (Yarden) River into the land of Canaan, just as YAHveh had instructed him. There were no questions nor debate, just blind obedience. By doing this, he earned the name of "Hebrew" (Erbee/Irvim) for himself and his descendants, which means "to cross over" in the Hebrew tongue. This name or description can apply to anyone who is willing to cross over from carnal living into spiritual living. When we, by our own free will, submit ourselves to His calling and are ready to leave everything that we use to count as valuable behind, and when we become born afresh as a new spiritual being, then we are by definition a Hebrew. This is the true meaning of the word. It has nothing to do with ancestry, culture, heritage, or race—it has everything to do with faith.

YAHveh's Third Covenant with Mankind

YAHveh instituted His third covenant, or promise, with Avram. He told Avram that He was going to bless all of the nations on the Earth through his descendants (**GEN 12:3**). He was going to bring forth His Seed (the Messiah) from Avram's seed in order to accomplish this. He then promised to make all of Avram's descendants (Hebrews) into a mighty nation. A famine struck the land of Canaan, so Avram journeyed south to the land of Egypt. There, Avram got himself into trouble by failing to act in faith—he didn't look to YAHveh for his instructions. Out of fear for his life, he lied about Sarai (Saraee) being his wife; instead, he said that she was his sister (although she was his half-sister).

After being found out by the Pharaoh of Egypt, he was given some provisions, along with a few servants and slaves, and sent out of the land. Some of Avram's family and servants must have stayed behind in Egypt because he was later told that some of his descendants would dwell there for another four-hundred years.

Later, in a similar situation, Avram lied again about Sarai (Saraee) being his wife; this time to a man called Abimelech. Men of faith make mistakes because they are human and are made of sinful flesh, just as we all are. YAHveh will even use our decisions, those that are based upon fear and not faith, to shape our future circumstances in order to fit them into His will.

One day, Avram and his nephew Lot found it necessary to separate their clans due to some internal strife that had developed, and they had to go their separate ways. Avram gave Lot his choice of land, and out of Lot's greed, he chose the best land. This later proved to be a dire mistake when he had to hastily depart with his family in order to save them. Lot had teamed up with some pagan neighbors and soon found himself in the crossfire between some warring kings of the land. Here again, no one had consulted YAHveh. Bad choices are always made when consultation is not first sought from the right source. When Avram heard of his nephew's predicament, he rushed to his rescue. Immediately afterward, the king-priest, Melchizedek, of the city of Salem (Shalom/peace—later to become Jerusalem), brought bread and wine to Avram in order to celebrate his victory and recognized him as being a servant of YAHveh. Avram responded to this recognition by dedicating a tenth of all of his possessions to Melchizedek. This later became the amount of the offering ordained by YAH to be given to a priest. A priest is always the one chosen by YAH to be a servant to Him, and this amount is to be his livelihood for that service. Never before in history, or after, has anyone else ever been both a king and a priest at the same time—YAH has promised this position to His only begotten Son, Yeshua, when He returns to set up His Eternal Kingdom here on Earth.

At this point in time, YAHveh added to His third covenant (He never diminishes them) by promising Avram that his descendants would become as the stars in the heavens—without number. In doing so, He told Avram to bring Him a three-year-old heifer, a three-year-old female goat, a three-year-old ram, a turtledove, and a young pigeon. He instructed Avram to cut them all in two, except for the birds. In Avram's time, a covenant was made between two parties by their both passing between the halves. A curse of division would come upon the house and the descendants of the one who would first break the agreement. However, YAHveh had a different plan in this covenant. He caused Avram to fall into a deep sleep and then appeared to him as both a smoking oven and a burning torch that passed between the halves. Because YAH knew that man would be the first to break the covenant between them, He would represent both parties—by doing this, the covenant would be eternal. The burning torch represented the fire of His Holy Spirit (Ruach HaKedosh), and the smoking oven represented the Spirit's refining. YAHveh then gave Avram a little glimpse into the future by showing him his descendants dwelling in Egypt (Mitsrahyim—a land for testing) for the next four-hundred years, where they would be made into a horde of people.

A period of about twenty-five years passed, and Avram and Sarai (Saraee) still had no offspring, so they decided to give YAHveh a helping hand in bringing forth His promise. Sarai (Saraee) offered her maidservant, Hagar, an Egyptian (Mitsrahyim) slave, to be the recipient of Avram's promised seed. Here again, no one consulted YAHveh. The result was Ishmael, Avram's firstborn. Ishmael's descendants would later join up with Nimrod's descendants and become the future enemies of the Hebrews. Remember, nothing happens by accident in YAHveh's overall plan. The mixing of the seed of the Hebrew nation with an Egyptian (Mitsrahyim) woman would take place once again in history with Avram's great-grandson, Joseph, but this time under YAH's total purpose and blessing. The lesson here is—don't get ahead of YAH, just be patient. Ishmael (YishmaEL) was given a blessing and told that he would grow into a nation of twelve tribes; they would dominate the Middle East region even to this day. Twelve is another kedosh (holy/set aside) number used to signify the completion of YAH's purpose in history. This same principle also applies to the twelve tribes of Israel (YisraEL) and to a year being divided into twelve months.

Up until that time, Avram, which means "exalted father", and his wife, Sarai (Saraee), remained childless. YAHveh now changes Avram's name to Avraham, which means "father of multitudes". He promises them a son in their old age. He also changes Sarai's (Saraee's) name, which means "one with potential" or "exalted woman", to Sarah (Sah-rah), which means "Princess".

Even though YAH's covenant with Avraham was unilateral in order to show its exclusiveness, He would now include a sign that would require an act of faith on Avraham's part. The sign was the shedding of personal blood through the act of circumcision by Avraham and by all of his male descendants. This would separate Avraham and his descendants from the rest of the world. This ordinance was to continue as a sign between YAHveh and his people until its fulfillment in the Messiah. At this same time, YAH promised Avraham that he would finally have his "son of promise" the following year and that his name was to be Isaac (Yitzhak), which means "laughter".

In the meantime, a *lot* (a pun on words) began to happen. Either YAHveh or Yeshua as an Angel, along with two other angelic beings, visited Avraham with some startling news. These angelic beings were manifested as humans.

WHAT WE WEREN'T TAUGHT ABOUT THE BIBLE AND ITS HISTORY

Throughout Scripture, we see YAH manifesting Himself, or His angelic hosts, in a variety of forms. These three visitors brought both good and bad news. First was the good news that confirmed that they were to have their own "Son of Promise" within that year. This birth would be a forerunner of the "Promised One", the "Messiah", in that it was preceded by an announcement from angelic beings. However, these two births would differ in that one would be by a virgin, while the other would occur well after natural childbearing years. The bad news was that a great evil had settled in the twin cities of Sodom and Gomorrah and that YAH was going to have to manifest His wrath upon them. The evil seemed to be at least as great as the evil that came upon the Earth before the great flood. YAH told Avraham about His decision to destroy the cities in order to test Avraham's honor and integrity. Avraham pleaded with YAH to reconsider for the sake of those living there who might be righteous. YAH assured Avraham that He would not show forth his wrath if there were any righteous there. Avraham was thinking about his nephew, Lot, and his family and was interceding for them. Of course, YAH already knew this and had sent His other two angels to rescue Lot and his family. YAHveh never brings his judgment of wrath down upon His own unless He first warns them, provides special protection for them, or delivers them out of it. Lot and his family proved not to be all that righteous by the way they conducted themselves during their deliverance. He only had two daughters who were still virgins. His sons-in-law, the two men who were betrothed to Lot's daughters, ignored the warnings and stayed in the city. Even afterward, Lot's wife seemed to show some regret in leaving the lifestyle that she had become accustomed to, and as a result, she too had to suffer the fate of those who were evil. As if that weren't enough, the two daughters who had left with him, out of fear that somehow this experience was going to leave them childless, devised a plot to get their father drunk and committed incest with him in order to guarantee themselves offspring. These offspring in turn would become the ancestors of the Moabites (Moabi) and the Ammonites (Ammoni), who would also become the enemies of the Hebrew people because of their mixing with the descendants of Ishmael (YishmaEL) and Ham (Hahm).

Within a year, just as YAH had promised Sahrah and Avraham, the miracle "promised son", Isaac (Yitzhak), was born. Isaac (Yitzhak) was raised as a herdsman under the watchful eye of his father. Avraham also gave him YAH's instructions/torah regarding the creation of all things and the miracle of the flood, just as they had been handed down through the patriarchs. He was told about the fate of Sodom and Gomorrah, his miraculous birth, and the promise to the Hebrew people. He obviously learned to love and trust YAHveh as his ELohim. One day, Avraham was visited by YAHveh and put to another test. Was his love for his son, his special son, greater than his trust in his ELohim?

Did he really believe YAH when He told him that through this heir he would be the father of many nations? If he really believed, how would he respond to a request from YAH to sacrifice this son on an altar of faith? If he did, would YAH somehow raise him from the dead in order to honor his promise about the multitude of descendants? Or was all of this just a cruel trick, and YAHveh really wasn't any different than the elohim of the other nations? Avraham does, without question, follow YAH's instructions to the letter. He was told to take his son of promise to a certain mountain, later known as Mt. Moriah (Moreeah), just outside of the city of Salem. Even Isaac (Yitzhak) perceived what was about to take place and, without a struggle, submitted to both his father's actions and his authority, trusting completely in his father's wisdom concerning this matter.

YAHveh would one day do the same thing with His only begotten Son, who would also trust in His Abba's (Father's) wisdom. However, Isaac (Yitzhak), unlike Yeshua, but like the rest of us, deserved to die because of his sins. *"For all have sinned and fall short of the glory of God"* (**ROM 3:23**). YAHveh then shows His love and mercy and, as always, provided a substitute sacrifice—a ram with one of its horns caught in a bush. This is an example of Yeshua as the perfect lamb and as the substitute for our sins. Later we will see YAHveh using the horn of a ram as an instrument to illustrate the sound of His voice for His people, and a bush of fire (like the flaming torch) to speak to another man of faith, Moses. The Angel of YAHveh (His Word/Yeshua before He was made flesh) called for Avraham to stay his hand and to do no harm to the lad. At this time, YAHveh again expanded His covenant with mankind through Avraham by proclaiming—*"Then the Angel of YAHveh called to Avraham a second time out of heaven, and said "By Myself I have sworn, says YAHveh, because you have done this thing, and have not withheld your son, your only son, "in blessing I will bless you, and in multiplying I will multiply your descendants as the stars of the heaven and as sand which is on the seashore; and your descendants shall possess the gate of their enemies. "In your seed all the nations of the earth shall be blessed, because you have obeyed My voice"* (**GEN 22:15-17**).

As Isaac (Yitzhak) grew in stature and knowledge, his abba (father), Avraham, began to contemplate his son's need for a bride. Soon after the death of his beloved Sahrah, he realized that the time seemed good because the grief of this event had affected Isaac (Yitzhak) so severely. Avraham knows that in order to pass "the promise of multiplication" on to his descendants, it would have to be done within his own kinsmen to guarantee its purity (YAHveh lists His restrictions regarding intermarriage relationships later in **LEV 18.**), so he commanded his faithful servant, Eliezer, to venture to his brother Nahor's clan to seek out a wife for Isaac (Yitzhak). Eliezer called upon YAHveh to direct him in His selection so that he might please his master, Avraham. YAH answered by arranging the circumstances that singled out Rebekah, the granddaughter of Avraham's brother, as His choice. After avoiding being manipulated by Avraham's nephew and Rebekah's abba, Bethuel, as well as her brother, Laban, Eliezer was able to bring her back to his master's estate without causing any further delay. It was love at first sight for both Isaac (Yitzhak) and Rebekah, and they were betrothed to one another.

The End of the Second Millennium—Isaac's (Yitzhak's) Descendants

Isaac's (Yitzhak's) wife, Rebekah, discovered that she was also barren like her mother-in-law, Sahrah. Isaac (Yitzhak) patiently waited twenty years without an heir before he petitioned YAH, who heard and answered his prayer. Rebekah not only conceived, but she found herself with twins. She too went to YAHveh in prayer because there was a definite struggle going on inside of her womb. He informed her that there were two leaders of two different nations inside of her and that the one who would exit her womb last would be the one through whom He would pass the seed of the "Promised One". The first would be the strongest, but he would serve the second. At birth, the first to be delivered was covered with red hair—a very unusual distinguishing mark for a Hebrew child. Some say that this was the beginning of redheaded people. He was named Esau because he was stout, strong, and hairy. He was also nicknamed Edom/Red because of his red hair and reddish complexion. Both of the names, Esau and Edom, are derived from the same root word as the word Adam (Ahdom), which describes the Earth's crust and its color. The second to birth was named Jacob, or James (Yaacov/YAHacov), which means "supplanter", "superceder", "replacer", or even "overcomer", because he hung onto Esau's foot, trying to exit first. This seemed to fit him because throughout his life he was always trying to work out some kind of a deal in order to get ahead. As the two grew, Esau became a rugged individual who loved to hunt game and to carouse with the Canaanite (Canaani) women. Jacob (Yaacov/YAHacov), on the other hand, was quiet, reserved, considerate, compassionate, and gentle—but very crafty. He regarded the firstborn's heritage to be something of great value, but was unable to enjoy its privileges because of the circumstances of his birth. On one particular occasion, Esau had been hunting while Jacob (Yaacov/YAHacov) had been preparing a stew of lintels. When Esau returned, he saw his brother's red stew, and because he was famished and had little regard for his birthright, he gladly traded it for a bowl of the lintel stew (another reason why he was nicknamed Edom/Red—he thought more about the red stew than he did about his birthright). Nowhere in Scripture is Jacob (Yaacov/YAHacov) rebuked for this act of manipulation to gain an undeserving birthright. Later on, his mother, Rebekah, would also use her manipulative talent in a different and more daring plot in order to elevate her youngest son's position (this trait seems to be quite prevalent on her side of the family, as we will soon see).

ROGER W. FEARING

YAHveh's Fourth Covenant with Mankind

What seems so surprising is that Isaac (Yitzhak) wasn't more aware of Esau's attitude toward spiritual matters or family heritages, especially since he married two pagan women, which was totally contrary to YAH's instructions. Then again, Isaac (Yitzhak) was no prize either. Even though he displayed faith when he was a young man on Mt. Moriah (Moreeah), he faltered when confronted by the Philistine king, Abimelech; he lied saying that his wife was his sister in order to avoid a confrontation, just as his father Avraham had done earlier. In spite of all of his shortcomings, YAH saw in Isaac (Yitzhak) a heart of obedience. (YAHveh always judges by the heart and is ready to overlook our actions if we walk in obedience.) Just prior to his encounter with Abimelech, Isaac (Yitzhak) received the fourth covenant for mankind from YAHveh, which reaffirmed His plan to bless all of the nations through him and His people, the Hebrews.

Now when Rebekah remembered that YAHveh had said that He was going to pass the "Promised Seed" through Jacob (Yaacov/YAHacov), she felt just as her mother-in-law, Sahrah, had felt—that YAH needed a helping hand now and then. When Isaac (Yitzhak) was beginning to lose his eyesight, he felt the time had come for him to pass his blessings on to his eldest son, Esau, but Rebekah had a different plan. She pulled a switcheroo on Isaac (Yitzhak) by devising a way to get the blessing transferred to Jacob (Yaacov/YAHacov) instead. It resulted in Jacob (Yaacov/YAHacov) having to hightail it out of the camp in order to save his own skin, especially when his brother, Esau, found out about what he had pulled (There's always a consequence to our actions). Rebekah and Isaac (Yitzhak) both agreed that Jacob (Yaacov/YAHacov) needed to go and stay with Rebekah's brother, Laban, until things cooled down.

YAHveh's Fifth Covenant with Mankind

On his way to Laban, Jacob (Yaacov/YAHacov) had a dream in which YAHveh appeared to him and pronounced the same promise to him as he had given to his father, Isaac (Yitzhak), and to his grandfather, Avraham—that through them He planned to bless all of the Gentile/Goyim nations. This would be the last time that YAHveh would make this particular covenant with any of Avraham's descendants, although Jacob (Yaacov/YAHacov) would pass this on to one of his own twelve sons. When he does, the promise will become divided, with the blessing of the promise going to one son and the birthright going to another.

As soon as Jacob (Yaacov/YAHacov) reaches Haran, the land of his uncle, Laban, he meets his cousin Rachel (Rahkal), and like his father, Isaac (Yitzhak), and his mother, Rebekah, it was love at first sight for both of them. Because he had no dowry for her, when he asked Laban for her hand, he agreed to work for a period of seven years to earn it. At the end of that seven years of labor, Uncle Laban pulled a switcheroo of his own (What comes around, goes around.). After Jacob's (Yaacov's/YAHacov's) wedding night and too much wine and celebrating, he discovered in the morning that his wedding bed had been switched with (SURPRISE!) Leah, Rachel's (Rahkal's) older sister. As Laban explained later, it was not the custom of his people for the younger to marry first. After the customary wedding week, Laban gave Jacob (Yaacov/YAHacov) Rachel (Rahkal) also, but he had to agree to work for another seven years for his true love.

Jacob (Yaacov) Builds a Family

Speaking of customs, YAHveh seems to have one of His own—Rachel (Rahkal) is also found to be barren, and Leah is the first to bear children. Her firstborn is a son, Reuben, which means *"see, a son"*. Leah comes through again with a second son, Simeon (Seemehon), which means *"I've been heard"*. Then she produces a third son, Levi (Lehvee), which means *"to be attached"*. Finally, they have a fourth son, Judah (YAHuda), which means *"praise"*. Then she stopped for awhile. In the meantime, Rachel (Rahkal) became frustrated and gave Jacob (Yaacov) her maidservant, Bilhah. By her, he produced two more sons, Dan (Dahn), which means *"judge"*, and Naphtali, which means *"this is my wrestling"*. Not to be outdone by Rachel (Rahkal), Leah gave Jacob (Yaacov) her maidservant, Zilpah. (How does this guy keep up???) She in turn bears him two more sons, Gad (Gahd), which means *"a troop"*, and Asher (Ahsher), which means *"how happy am I"*. After this, we see a little horse trading going on between the two sisters (wonder where they learned that?), and Leah hires Jacob (Yaacov) from Rachel (Rahkal) for an evening of romance. Lo and behold, Leah turns up with a fifth child, another boy, Issachar (Yitzsakar), which means *"I'm for hire"* or *"this is a reward"*. Then Leah had son number six, Zebulun, which means *"he will dwell"* or *"for honor"*. Leah produces one more time, but this time it's a girl, and they name her the feminine equivalent to *"Dan"*, Dinah (Deenah), which means *"judgment"*. Finally, YAHveh remembers Rachel (Rahkal) and opens her womb to give her their first son, Joseph (Yosef), which means *"will add more"* or *"one of compassion"*.

We find some very important symbolism here. Jacob's (Yaacov's) family consisted of twelve sons and one daughter from four different mothers, but only two wives. When we look at the pattern of four in Scripture, we find that it usually refers to something geographical about the Earth. Whatever term is used, it is usually referring to the four compass-reference points (N, S, E, and W) and means the "Whole Earth". This pattern could be making reference to something affecting its occupants, who dwell on its face, or their nations and is usually found in such terms as the four corners of the Earth or the four winds of the Earth. As we continue our pilgrimage through the Scriptures, we will find that YAHveh did scatter His people, Israel (YisraEL), over the whole face of the Earth (the four corners) in order to keep His promise to Abraham (Avraham).

YAH's pattern of two and twelve is demonstrated in Jacob's (Yaacov's) two wives, or brides, and his twelve sons who were birthed by them or their handmaidens. When we look at these two brides, we see one who is older and wiser and one who has captured his heart. As we continue to watch these twelve sons develop into a nation and become known as Israel (YisraEL), we also see strife come between the descendants of Leah's fourth son, Judah (YAHuda), and Rachel's (Rahkal's) first son, Joseph (Yosef), that will divide them several different times throughout history. However, at the same time, Rachel's (Rahkal's) second son, Benjamin (Ben-yah-meen), will join with Judah (YAHuda) to form a bond, and these two together will become known as the Jews (YAHudi). We will also see Joseph (Yosef) receive the firstborn rights of the family through the laying on of hands by his father, Israel (YisraEL), upon his own youngest son, Ephraim (Efraeem). Then, in the book of Exodus, we will see YAHveh make a marriage covenant with His bride, Israel (YisraEL), who will, within a few hundred years, become divided for the last time into the two brides/houses, Judah (YAHuda) and Israel/Joseph (YisraEL/Yosef). YAHveh will commission the oldest and wisest bride, Judah (YAHuda), to take on the responsibility of keeping His Torah (Instructions) throughout the coming centuries and to bring forth the Seed of Promise. The younger bride, Israel/Joseph (YisraEL/Yosef), who had captured His heart, will receive the commission to go into the entire world and tell of His love for all mankind in order for them to receive salvation through His only begotten Son.

Jacob (Yaacov) Wrestles with God's Angel

Jacob (Yaacov) then makes plans to return to his father's land, Canaan, but first he makes one more deal with his uncle to raise livestock for his final wages. Over another seven years and with YAH's help, he was able to accumulate twice as many herds as Laban. After some more wheeling and dealing and more manipulation by both parties, Jacob (Yaacov) secretly sets out with all of his possessions to return home. Soon after their departure, Laban takes after them because of some stolen artifacts. There is more bickering until, finally, an oath is taken by the two, and they go their own separate ways.

In preparing to enter his homeland, Jacob (Yaacov) divided his family into two groups in order to protect them, just in case his brother, Esau, still had bitterness in his heart. In anticipation of meeting Esau, he sent a gift of reconciliation to him, hoping to obtain peace (shalom) between them. The night before the two clans were to meet, Jacob (Yaacov) found himself in a wrestling match with a stranger. This match went on all night before he realized that this was no ordinary man—this was an angelic being in the manifestation of a man. During their struggle, Jacob (Yaacov) insisted that the angel bless him. The angel asked him his name, and when he replied, "Jacob (Yaacov)", the angel said, "no longer will you be called Jacob (Yaacov), but Israel (Yis-raEL)". In other words, no longer would he be called "the supplanter" or "the replacer", but Israel (YisraEL), which means "one who struggles with ELohim", "the Prince of ELohim", or even "YAH's Hero". Haven't we all struggled with God at one time or another? If you have and He won, it is because you have accepted His Son as your Redeemer, and you too are now called Israel (YisraEL), YAH's Hero, an Overcomer, or a Conqueror. Jacob (Yaacov) named the place where this happened, Peniel (PeneeEL), which means "I saw ELohim and lived". He may have lived, but he was left with a reminder of his encounter—the angel had touched his hip during their match and left him with a permanent limp. To Jacob's (Yaacov's) surprise, his reunion with his brother, Esau, proved to be peaceful, and they departed somewhat reconciled. Unfortunately, that didn't prove to be the case for their descendants. Esau's descendants married several of Ishmael's (YishmaEL's), and they later became the archenemies of Jacob's (Yaacov's) descendants.

By the time he finally settled his family back into the land of Canaan, his sons ranged in age from forty on down. Dinah (Deenah), Jacob's (Yaacov's) only daughter, was about twenty when a man by the name of Shechem, son of Hamor (Shehkhem ben Hahmor), spotted her. He first raped, or seduced her and then told his father that he desired her as his wife. Hahmor went to Jacob (Yaacov) in order to negotiate a deal to exchange their sons and daughters in marriage. Jacob's (Yaacov's) sons were outraged and in their plan of revenge, told Hahmor that the only way they could agree was if all of the men in their clan would become circumcised, just as they were. He agreed, and three days after all of Hahmor's men had become circumcised and before they could heal, Simeon (Seemehon) and Levi (Lehvee) took swords, entered the city, and slew all of the men. After retrieving their sister, the rest of Jacob's (Yaacov's) sons followed behind, looting everything in sight. By the time Jacob (Yaacov) had discovered their plan, it was too late; they had already begun to plunder the city. He was outraged at their plot because they had disregarded his counsel and had done this thing on their own. He admonished them for their misguided deed and informed them of the consequence—they had just made all of the people in the land their enemies.

YAH then directed Jacob (Yaacov) to return south to where he had the dream in which he saw the angelic beings ascending and descending the ladder, when he was first fleeing his brother, Esau. Before they left the area, he told his sons to rid themselves of any idols or artifacts that they may have acquired in their looting of Shechem (Shehkhem), including any that they may have picked up in their travels, because ELohim required them to do so. After he arrived, he sanctified the area with a drink offering and poured oil upon the very place where he had laid his head that strange night years before, and he called the place Bethel (Biet-EL, "the house of EL"). YAHveh again spoke to Jacob (Yaacov) and confirmed that his name was to be "Israel (YisraEL)" from that time on. There are many places in the TaNaKh (Old Testament) where Israel's (YisraEL's) descendents are referred to as either Israel (YisraEL) or Jacob (Yaacov). If you look closely at their content, you will see that whenever YAH used the name Jacob (Yaacov), He used it in the context of their behavior when it was not pleasing to Him, whereas when He used the name Israel (YisraEL), it was when He saw them as His obedient sons.

Tragedy continued to plague Jacob (Yaacov) when Rachel (Rahkal) gave birth to their second son, Benjamin (Ben-yah-meen, "son of my right hand"), because she died in the process. If that wasn't enough, his firstborn, Reuben, had defiled his bed when he had sexual relations with Bilhah, the mother of Dan (Dahn) and Naphtali. What was the consequence for Reuben's behavior? He lost his firstborn birthright. It normally would have gone to the second born or the third, but both Simeon (Seemehon) and Levi (Lehvee) had already forfeited their chance to gain the birthright when they usurped their father's authority and slaughtered the city of Shechem (Shehkhem). So now the responsibility moved to Judah (YAHuda), the fourth-born son. Jacob's (Yaacov's) sorrow continued with the death of his father, Isaac (Yitzhak). The only consolation that he received was the short reunion that he had with his brother, Esau, at their father's funeral. This would prove to be the last time that they would see each other. Esau's descendants continued their mixing in marriage with not only the YishmaELites (Yishmali), but also with the Hahmites (Hahmi), the Moabites (Moabi), and the Ammonites (Ammoni). His direct descendants became known as the Edomi. Most of the people in the Middle-Eastern countries today are the mixed descendants of Ham (Hahm), Ishmael (YishmaEL), Moab, Ammon, and Esau. That does not mean that their descendants actually stayed in the Middle East—some mixed with the Japhethites (Yafethi), the descendants of Noah's youngest son, and migrated north into Europe. The migration and the mixed marriages of all of Noah's descendants have been a part of a very intricate plan of YAHveh's. He has used it throughout history to fulfill His promise to Avraham. This is no small matter, and we will refer to it many times throughout this book. We all may have a little Kaeen (Cain), a little Ishmael (YishmaEL), a little Moab, a little Ammon, a little Esau, and a little Israel (YisraEL) in us. The question is, which one of these have we patterned our own lives after without realizing it?

WHAT WE WEREN'T TAUGHT ABOUT THE BIBLE AND ITS HISTORY

Israel's (YisraEL's) Favorite Son Joseph (Yosef)

Most of us who have a family usually have one son or daughter that seems to cause us to be the most proud. We love all of our children, but one just seems to shine a little more than the others. Israel (YisraEL) was no exception; Joseph (Yosef) and then Benjamin (BenYAHmeen) seemed to garner his attention the most. I'm sure their being the sons of his beloved Rachel (Rahkal) and their being born in his old age had a lot to do with it, but whatever the reason, he really loved them and showed them favor. Of course, this did not go unnoticed by the rest of the family. As with most families, there is always some rivalry, but with Israel's (YisraEL's), it became a dividing force. Envy and jealousy began to manifest themselves among the brethren, which allowed hatred and strife to rise up. Joseph (Yosef) didn't help matters any because he was a dreamer, and he was spoiled. He was also blessed with an abundance of charisma from YAHveh, and he had been given the gift of being a seer. Because of his youth, he had not yet developed the proper self-discipline or received the proper guidance in the use of these gifts. Consequently, when YAH gave Joseph (Yosef), at about the age of seventeen, two different prophetic dreams, one about sheaves of grain and the other about stars, he, in his excitement, shared these dreams with his family. Unfortunately, they were not received in the same spirit as they were given. The dreams spoke prophetically of a time when he would be in an exalted, authoritative, and prophetic position, how he would save his family from certain destruction, and how this would determine their future. They also spoke of another "One" who would someday restore the house of his father, Israel (YisraEL). But Joseph's (Yosef's) brothers could only see an arrogant little brother who was trying to rob them of their position with their "dad" (abba).

To make matters even worse, Israel (YisraEL) had a garment made for him that resembled a robe for a prince. It was made of many bright colors and fabrics that were usually used to denote a prince or a ruler. Israel (YisraEL) saw his beloved son as someday being a ruler and this would also prove to be prophetic, in reference to the "Promised One" who would be "the King of kings". When the right opportunity arose, Joseph's (Yosef's) brothers decided to kill him and rid themselves of this dreamer. But the oldest, Reuben, advised against it. When some Ishmaelites (YishmaELi) came along, Judah (YAHuda) suggested that they sell him instead. The price that they received was twenty pieces of silver. Now they needed a story to convince their father of Joseph's (Yosef's) whereabouts, so they dipped his robe (garment) in some goat's blood and told Israel (YisraEL) that he had been slaughtered and eaten by some kind of a beast.

Can you see the prophetic story here? Later in history, another Judah (YAHuda), Judah (YAHuda) Iscariot (Yiscariot), sold the Son of the Father to an enemy for thirty pieces of silver. Many were convinced that He was dead, but He came back from the grave in order to rule and reign over all of the nations of the world. But instead of goat's blood, it was lamb's blood, the blood of the Lamb of YAHveh that covered the garment that He wore. His was not a garment to just proclaim His authority—it was one that would bring praise to His Father (Abba). His was not a robe of many colors; it only had one, which was the color of His blood that was offered to the nations of the world as the evidence of the price that He had paid for them—His death.

Joseph (Yosef) was transported to the nation of Egypt, a shadow or forerunner of today's world system, and sold into slavery. Egypt was known by the Hebrews as Mitsrahyim, which means "a place of bondage" or "a place of temptations and trials". It was settled by the descendants of Ham's (Hahm's) son, Mitraim. There, Joseph (Yosef) was put in charge of the house of his master, Potiphar, a high official of the Pharaoh of Egypt (Mitsrahyim). It was there that he was tempted by the wife of his master to have sex with her, but he refused. After being falsely accused of trying to rape her, he was cast into prison by Potiphar. (He was about twenty-three at the time.) Because of his steadfast faith in YAHveh, his ELohim, not only was he able to cope with his situation, but he also found enough favor with the prison officials that he was put in charge of governing prison activities. Two of Pharaoh's servants were also cast into prison, and both confided in him about dreams that they were having. YAHveh revealed their interpretation to Joseph (Yosef), which showed that one would be restored to his original position, and the other would lose his life. Later, these interpretations would prove to be accurate. Then, seven years later, YAH gave Pharaoh two dreams that his wise men and magicians could not interpret. The first one was about corn and the other about cows. His servant remembered that Joseph (Yosef) had correctly interpreted his dream and told Pharaoh about his ability. So Pharaoh had Joseph (Yosef) brought before him in the hope that he would be able to do as well for him. Joseph (Yosef) correctly interpreted his dreams. They warned of a coming famine that would last for seven years, but would be preceded by seven years of plenty in all of Egypt (Mitsrahyim) and the surrounding lands. Joseph (Yosef) gave Pharaoh his advice on how to survive the upcoming famine, so Pharaoh put him in charge of all things that were within his kingdom in order to accomplish this plan. He also gave Asenath, the daughter of the priest of On (Heliopolis), to Joseph (Yosef) as his wife. He was able to accomplish everything that was required of him by the grace of YAHveh. He was also blessed with two sons as his heirs, Manasseh (Mahnahseh), which means *"to help forget"*, and Ephraim (Efraeem), which means *"twice fruitful"*. Once more, we see the mixing of the seed of a Hebrew with the seed of an Egyptian (Mitsrahyim), but, as I said earlier, this time under and with YAH's complete guidance and blessing. The seven years of plenty and the seven years of famine, I believe, may be speaking prophetically about the events that lead up to the beginning of the millennium of peace (also known as the restoration of the Tabernacle of David), when Yeshua sets up His Kingdom reign in the great and final day of YAHveh.

In the meantime, his father, Israel (YisraEL), and his brothers were also experiencing the effects of the area-wide famine. They heard of the provisions in Egypt (Mitsrahyim), so Israel (YisraEL) sent all of his sons, except Benjamin (BenYAHmeen), to purchase enough grain for their survival. When they arrived, they presented themselves to Joseph (Yosef) in order to make their request for grain. Joseph (Yosef) knew who they were immediately, but they did not recognize him. When Joseph (Yosef) saw that his brothers failed to recognize him, he devised a plan that he hoped would bring his brothers to repentance for their sin against him and YAH, which might restore his family.

Joseph's (Yosef's) plan included accusing them of being spies. They emphatically denied the false charges and pleaded for an opportunity to clear their name. After they told him of another brother whom they had left behind with their father, Joseph agreed to accept his testimony if they could produce him. After a family meeting, they agreed to leave one of their brothers behind as a guarantee of their return, so Simeon (Seemehon) volunteered to be the one. They gathered their belongings and provisions and went back to their father to retrieve their youngest brother in order to present him as the proof of their story. When the brothers arrived back at their father's tents, he was infuriated with their agreement. He couldn't bear the thought of the possibility of losing his beloved Rachel's (Rahkal's) second son to this madman in Egypt (Mitsrahyim). Finally, because the famine was threatening to eliminate everyone, Israel (YisraEL) relented to the proposal, but only after Judah (YAHuda) guaranteed Benjamin's (BenYAHmeen's) safe return.

When they arrived for the second time in Egypt (Mitsrahyim), Joseph (Yosef) was overjoyed to once again be able to lay his eyes upon his younger brother. He called for a feast to celebrate the occasion. His brothers were still unaware of his identity and thought it rather strange for such a high official to pay so much attention to them. The next day, Joseph (Yosef), who was still trying to put fear into their hearts, sent them back to their father. Before they were able to go very far, he sent soldiers to accuse them of stealing a cup, a silver cup that he said he used for the purpose of divination. He threatened to send them back without their youngest brother, but for his father's sake, Judah (YAHuda) stepped forward and offered to be a substitute for Benjamin (BenYAHmeen), just like Yeshua offered to be our substitute. When Joseph (Yosef) saw this unselfish act, he knew for certain that repentance had finally entered the hearts of his brothers. It is at this time that he revealed his true identity to them. He assured them that they should not feel guilty for what they had done because YAHveh had used it not only for their survival, but also to provide a place for them to raise their future generations. This whole situation was a glimpse into the future, when Judah (YAHuda) would also fail to recognize the promised Messiah, Yeshua. This failed recognition will continue until the right time and circumstance, when Yeshua will open their eyes and reveal His full identity to them, just as Joseph (Yosef) did. At the end of the age, we will also see the descendants of these two brothers, Judah (YAHuda) and Joseph (Yosef), be reunited for the final time in order to fulfill YAHveh's Torah plan.

After much rejoicing, his brothers returned to their father, Israel (YisraEL), and brought him the good news. The years of anguish were finally over, Israel's (YisraEL's) prayers had been answered, and his family was reunited. YAHveh reassured him that this was all a part of His plan in order to fulfill His prophecy to Avraham, that the Hebrews would reside in Egypt (Mitsrahyim) for a total of four-hundred years and become a mighty nation. Some of Avraham's clan had already been there for over two-hundred years, ever since the first time that Avraham visited the land and took some Egyptians (Mitsrahyim) with him (including Hagar), bringing them halfway to its fulfillment. When Joseph's family had finally arrived in Egypt (Mitsrahyim), Pharaoh sent them gifts and settled them as shepherds, along with the other Hebrews, in the land of Goshen, the best grazing land in all of Egypt (Mitsrahyim).

Seventeen years later, Israel (YisraEL) called for his sons to be brought before him so that he might bestow his blessings upon them. He summoned Joseph (Yosef) first and made him swear that his body would be taken back to the land that had been promised to his fathers, Abraham (Avraham) and Isaac (Yitzhak), and be buried there with them. Later, after Joseph (Yosef) was told that his father's health had become worse and that he was near death, he went in to see him, bringing his two sons with him. Israel (YisraEL) then called all of his sons to his side, and disregarding tradition, he called Joseph (Yosef) forward first before his older brothers. He then called Joseph's (Yosef's) sons forward to receive their father's blessing. Joseph (Yosef) placed his oldest son, Manasseh (Mahnahseh), at his father's right hand—for that is the symbol for strength, wisdom, and authority—and his youngest son, Ephraim (Efraeem), to his left. Israel (YisraEL) then purposely crossed his hands so that Ephraim (Efraeem) would receive the firstborn blessing. Joseph (Yosef), thinking that his father's eyesight may have failed him, corrected him. But Israel (YisraEL), being quite aware of his actions because he was being directed by YAH, told Joseph (Yosef) that he knew what he was doing. He then proceeded to place his name Israel (YisraEL) upon both of them, but it would be Ephraim (Efraeem) who would be the head of the House of Israel (YisraEL) from that time on. This was when he proclaimed the younger son, Ephraim (Efraeem), to be the greater of the two. In the TaNaKh, the tribes of Joseph (Yosef) and Ephraim (Efraeem) are referred to as Israel (YisraEL)—all three are one and the same.

Then Israel (YisraEL) called his other sons forward and began to bestow his blessings upon them. He began with Reuben, which means *"see, a son"*, and reminded him that he had lost his firstborn rights because he had defiled his father's bed. He went on to Simeon (Seemehon), which means *"I've been heard"*, and Levi (Lehvee), which means *"to be attached"*, and reminded them of their angry outburst that had led them to the slaying of Shechem (Shehkhem). Therefore, because of their disregard for their father's authority, they too had forfeited their right to the firstborn inheritance. Then he came to his fourth son, Judah (YAHuda), which means *"praise"*, and he told him that he would be equal to a lion (a symbol of power) and that he would receive the scepter (a symbol of kingship) of the family until the Promised One, "Shiloh" (Sheeloh), arrived. He remarked that Judah (YAHuda) would tie his donkey and its colt to a vine (a symbol of the Messiah). Then he said that he would wash his garment, or tallit (tahleet), in wine, the blood of grapes (a symbol of the Messiah's death). He continued on by telling Dan (Dahn), which means *"judge"*, that he would live up to his name and judge many, while Naphtali, which means *"this is my wrestling"*, would become a freedom lover and orator. He prophesied that Gad (Gahd), which means *"a troop"*, would find himself being harassed and constantly in turmoil, and that Asher (Ahsher), which means *"how happy am I"*, would find his contentment as a farmer. His ninth son, Issachar (Yitzsakar), which means *"I'm for hire"* or *"this is a reward"*, would have sluggards as descendants, and Zebulon, which means *"he will dwell"* or *"for honor"*, would have seamen as his descendants. Finally, his youngest, Benjamin (BenYAHmeen), which means *"son of my right hand"*, was told that his descendants would be warriors and swordsmen. Soon after Israel (YisraEL) gave these blessings, he breathed his last and was taken to be buried with his fathers, just as he had requested.

When Joseph (Yosef) was one hundred and ten and was about to die, he too made the same request as his father, Israel (YisraEL)—that his bones would be taken back to the land that was promised to them by YAHveh.

Conclusion

YAHveh has made five covenants with mankind (Adam/Ahdom) up to this point by simply renewing each from the previous one. He will continue to do this throughout history because He never nullifies one by replacing it with another—He just increases his grace. He has also shown us all of His beginnings, including the one that divided Israel's (YisraEL's) firstborn rights between Judah (YAHuda) and Joseph (Yosef) so that He might fulfill His promise to make Avraham a father and a blessing to many nations. His goal has always been the same—to redeem His creation from its fall. Starting from

Adam (Ahdom) and continuing through Noah, Shem, Abraham (Avraham), Isaac (Yitzhak), and Israel (YisraEL), He has been faithful to His promise to build for Himself a people who will worship, honor, and love Him as their ELohim.

CHAPTER 2
...about Exodus

We enter into a time when YisraEL had grown into a population of nearly two-million people. They had basically been kept separated from the Egyptians (Mitsrahyim), not losing their culture completely, but still never knowing self-government. In spite of being isolated, they still had become knowledgeable about the culture and religions of their masters. They didn't possess any written records that they could fall back on—only a few clay tablets that their ancestors had been faithful to keep. Most of their history was handed down by word of mouth or through legends. We will soon learn how YAHveh used this situation to deliver them out of bondage and into a position of dependency upon Him for their basic needs. He was going to cause a messianic-type deliverer to rise up who would be another forerunner of the Promised One—Joseph (Yosef) being the first. YAH would then offer them an opportunity to enter into a nuptial agreement with Him—a sixth covenant. And if they would be willing to surrender their lives to Him, He would provide them with the laws and ordinances necessary to lead them into a life of complete fulfillment and joy—a type of heaven on Earth. YAHveh would give them the design for a portable dwelling place for His Presence, a type of Eden, complete with articles of worship that would reveal the identity of the coming Messiah. However, because of their sinful nature, they would rebel against this dependency.

Over two-hundred years had passed since Joseph (Yosef) had brought the House of Israel (YisraEL) into the land of Goshen in Egypt (Mitsrahyim). A new Pharaoh sat on the throne, who became quite concerned about the growing population of the Hebrews. Recent archeological and anthropological finds have revealed the identification of the Pharaoh who reigned at that time as possibly being "Seqenenre Tao II". He saw them as a potential threat who might side with his enemies in case of a war. His solution was to turn them into slaves and to have them build him a city, but the harder he worked them, the more they seemed to multiply. Finally, he gave an order to all of the midwives to kill the sons born to the Hebrew women, sparing only the daughters. It's hard to say what kept these midwives from carrying out that command. Some speculate that they feared the Hebrew's ELohim; others say that they admired the Hebrew people because of the compassion that they had for others. Whatever the reason, they gave Pharaoh the excuse that the Hebrew women were so hardy that they delivered their children before they could even get there. So Pharaoh gave the order to have all of the Egyptians (Mitsrahyim) go and carry out this horrible deed.

Moses (Mosheh), the Deliverer and Prophet

Meanwhile, one of Levi's (Lehvee's) descendants, Amram, had a son that his wife, Yochebed, kept hidden for three months. She built an ark (container), made it waterproof with pitch and asphalt, and placed it among the reeds near the Nile River. She set it afloat and told her daughter, Miriam (Meeryahm), to follow it until it reached its destination. To me, this is reminiscent of Noah and the ark being watched over by YAH's Ruach (Spirit) until it came to rest in a renewed World. While bathing, Pharaoh's daughter discovered the child and decided to raise it as her own. The child's sister persuaded her to choose their mother to be its nurse. Then Pharaoh's daughter named him Moses (Mosheh), which means *"drawn from the water"*. Throughout Scripture, we are taught about the spiritual part that water plays in our lives because of its cleansing properties.

The TaNaKh is rather quiet about Moses' (Moshehs') growing-up years, only that he had a kindred compassion for his fellow Hebrews. As a prince of Egypt (Mitsrahyim), he was raised in luxury with all of its perks and was quite familiar with all of their traditions, superstitions, and religions, but somehow he knew that he had a responsibility to the Hebrews.

One day, when Moses (Mosheh) was about forty-years old, he observed an Egyptian (Mitsrahyim) mistreating a fellow Hebrew and attempted to come to his aid. In the process, he accidentally killed the Egyptian (Mitsrahyim) and then tried to cover it up by burying him in the sand. The next day, he also saw two Hebrews fighting, and when he stepped in to settle things, one of them confronted him about the incident that had taken place the day before. Moses (Mosheh) knew then that he had been discovered, so he took refuge in the wilderness. While wandering there, he met a Midian priest by the name of Reuel, who was also known by the name of Jethro (Yethro), and his seven daughters. Soon after, he married Zipporah, one of Reuel's daughters. Moses (Mosheh) became a shepherd for his father-in-law and tended his sheep for a period of forty years. Being an Egyptian (Mitsrahyim) prince had become just a faded memory to him by this time. YAH seems to do that to those he chooses—He gets rid of all that he can't use in their lives. Moses (Mosheh) more than likely received a full education on the spiritual beliefs of the Midians from his father-in-law.

Then one day, while tending his father-in-law's sheep near the Arabian mountain range of Sinai, he came to the foot of the desolate mountain of Horeb.

WHAT WE WEREN'T TAUGHT ABOUT THE BIBLE AND ITS HISTORY

There, he saw something rather strange—a shrub ablaze. That in itself wasn't strange because bushes and shrubs often caught on fire in the heat of the deserts as they dried out, but this one wasn't consumed—it just kept burning. When Moses (Mosheh) went to investigate the cause of this, he heard a voice speaking to him. The voice introduced Himself as YHVH (YAHveh), which means I am who I am/I was who I was/I will always be whom I will always be. It also means that He is the Alpha and Omega (in Hebrew: the Aleph and Tav), the first and the last/the beginning and the end. He told Moses (Mosheh) that He was the ELohim of Avraham, Isaac (Yitzhak), and Jacob (Yaacov)/YisraEL—that meant that He was also Moses' (Mosheh's) ELohim. YAHveh then revealed to Moses (Mosheh) that He had chosen him to be a deliverer (savior) of YisraEL in order for them to receive the inheritance that He had promised to their fathers.

At first, Moses (Mosheh) resisted because he didn't feel qualified. This seems to be a problem that plagues many of those whom YAH chooses. *"For you see your calling, brethren, that not many wise according to the flesh, not many mighty, not many noble, are called"* **(I COR 1:26)**. YAHveh assured him that He would always be there with him. He then gave him a few supernatural signs to convince him of this promise. He was to use these same signs to convince his brethren that he had truly been sent by YAH. Convincing the elders of his people would only be the beginning of the difficult struggle that he would experience in the deliverance of His people, YisraEL.

YAH told Moses (Mosheh) that He was going to strike down all of the firstborn of Egypt (Mitsrahyim) because Pharaoh had dared to mistreat His firstborn, YisraEL. Notice that YAHveh calls YisraEL His firstborn. He also refers to both Joseph (Yosef) and his youngest son, Ephraim (Efraeem), even though he was half Hebrew and half Egyptian (Mitsrahyim), as being His firstborn. Finally, He also calls Yeshua, His only begotten Son, His firstborn. All of these references are important to remember while we are discovering **"WHAT WE WEREN'T TAUGHT ABOUT THE BIBLE AND ITS HISTORY"**.

YAH told Moses (Mosheh) that on the day of their deliverance, the Egyptians (Mitsrahyim) would be so overjoyed at their departure that they would give the people of YisraEL much of their personal wealth to encourage them not to return. On the other hand, there were some who were so awed by the power of YisraEL's ELohim that they decided to leave with them. This was just another example of YAH's mixing of the nations in order to fulfill His promise to Avraham. Then, once again, Moses (Mosheh) tried to talk YAH out of sending him by making the excuse that he was slow in speech (or had a speech impediment) and would not be capable of confronting Pharaoh. So, YAH promised him that he could use his own brother, Aaron (Aharon), to be his spokesperson. Moses (Mosheh) then gathered his family and left for Egypt (Mitsrahyim).

While they were on their way to Egypt (Mitsrahyim), YAH had become angry with Moses (Mosheh)—nearly enough to take his life. The exact circumstances are not revealed; perhaps YAH had struck him down with a serious illness. Whatever it was, Moses (Mosheh) had definitely lost favor with YAH. He may have brought YAH's wrath down upon himself due to an act of neglect because even after YAH had revealed to him the importance of the firstborn son's position among the Hebrews, he still had not honored their customs by circumcising his own son. Moses (Mosheh) had apparently taken on the customs of his father-in-law, a Midiani who was a descendant of Avraham through his second wife, Keturah. These descendants followed the customs of the Arabs and circumcised their sons at the age of thirteen rather than at the age of eight days, like the Hebrews. Zipporah seemed to sense the reason for YAH's wrath because she took it upon herself to circumcise their firstborn for him. Afterwards, she touched Moses' (Mosheh's) feet with the foreskin and declared to him that she too was now a Hebrew. Since nothing further was said about this incident, this must have delivered Moses (Mosheh) from his encounter with death.

The Reunion of Two Brothers

At the same time that Moses (Mosheh) was on his way to seek his brother, YAH gave Aaron (Aharon), Moses' (Mosheh's) brother, instructions to meet him in the desert at Mt. Horeb. These two brothers were strangers due to the circumstances in their lives—Aaron (Aharon) had been a slave during the time that Moses (Mosheh) was a prince.

After confirming to each other what they had both been instructed by YAHveh to do, they set out to tell the House of YisraEL the good news. They were both excited in their anticipation of the people's response to the news that their deliverer had finally arrived. But one problem was going to have to be resolved before they could leave Egypt (Mitsrahyim). Their tribes had become mixed, and YAH wanted them to be separated by clans so that He could invoke the blessing of their father, YisraEL, upon them after they entered the land that He had promised him. This was there first experience in losing their identity, but throughout the Scriptures, we see YAH constantly having to develop plans to keep YisraEL from becoming mixed with the nations around them, or their tribes becoming divided between themselves. He would one day mix them among the nations Himself, causing them to again lose their identity until the right time in history—then He will bring about the final reunion of all of these brothers.

WHAT WE WEREN'T TAUGHT ABOUT THE BIBLE AND ITS HISTORY

The Testing Begins

Even though YAH had warned Moses (Mosheh) ahead of time that the Pharaoh who now reigned would resist his request to let His people go into the wilderness to worship Him, he didn't expect this Pharaoh to increase the people's burden because of it. And, of course, the people of YisraEL then blamed Moses (Mosheh) for trying to be a do-gooder. We all may at one time or another experience some peer pressure or rejection that may cause us to doubt ourselves or our mission—Moses (Mosheh) was no exception. Moses (Mosheh) returned to God in fear and had to be reassured of his calling. YAH reminded him that His people had to be in Egypt (Mitsrahyim) for four-hundred years in order to grow to be a mighty nation, and now, since that time was nearly up, he was to be His instrument to deliver them, thereby fulfilling His promise to their fathers. Moses (Mosheh) may have been quite familiar with this particular Pharaoh—he may have been his step-brother. Records show that "Seqenenre Tao II" had a grandson by the name of "Ahmosheh" (which, by the way, means "the brother of Mosheh"). Was this the son of the Pharaoh's daughter who rescued Moses (Mosheh) from the river and gave him his name?

Moses (Mosheh) and his brother, Aaron (Aharon), appeared before the Pharaoh (Ahmosheh?) for a second time, but now they were accompanied by YAH's signs and wonders to confirm His words. Pharaoh laughed at their attempt to persuade him and had his pagan magicians duplicate their signs, which they did through the art of illusion. Because of this, YAHveh began to strike down some of Egypt's (Mitsrahyim's) elohim by sending plagues upon the land. He singled out ten of Egypt's (Mitsrahyim's) most predominate elohim. The number "ten" is the number that YAHveh uses to denote fulfillment. The first "el" (mighty one) that He demonstrated His power over was the "Nile River", which was supposedly ruled by the el "Hapi". Here, He had Moses (Mosheh) touch the river with his staff, and it immediately turned into blood, which caused the fish to die. Pharaoh once again turned to the magic of his magicians, who were able to duplicate this sign also. In doing so, they may have even invoked some of the spirits of darkness to do their bidding. Now, what powers did YAHveh give to Moses (Mosheh) to invoke these ten plagues upon Egypt (Mitsrahyim)? Is it possible, since YAHveh is Adonia of all Creation and can move events in heaven and on Earth at His will, that a sequence of catastrophic events could have produced such a domino effect that it caused these plagues in Egypt (Mitsrahyim) to take place at that very moment in history? Is there such an event? In 1500 BCE, a volcanic eruption did occur on the island of Santorini, which is located in the Mediterranean Sea, just south of ancient Greece, which was so devastating that it nearly destroyed the whole island. The aftereffects of such an eruption could have caused these types of events to occur in the same sequence as the plagues that Egypt (Mitsrahyim) experienced.

After denying YisraEL permission to go out into the desert to worship their ELohim for a third time, YAH attacked the second of Egypt's (Mitsrahyim's) "els"—He sent "frogs" out of the Nile River to overrun the land. Frogs and toads were ruled by "Heka", the frog and toad goddess. Once again, the magicians were able to duplicate the plague. But this time, Pharaoh feigned his consent and agreed to let YisraEL go out into the desert to worship their ELohim. Once the frogs had been cleaned up, he denied their request.

The third plague involved the el of "gnats" coming up out of the el of the "dust" of the Earth. Now, whether that represented the worship of the insects or the worship of the soil and agriculture, I'm not sure—both were elohim to them. But, since the fourth plague was definitely against insects and because the soil or the dust became a plague of gnats, I would think that this third plague was against "Geb", the el of the "soil/dust". When the magicians tried to reproduce this phenomenon, they failed miserably and admitted that it must have come from YisraEL's ELohim.

A forth plague that was cast upon Pharaoh and the people of Egypt (Mitsrahyim) involved "Khepfi", the el of "flies". This one appeared to be YAH's judgment against the worship of all flying insects. The one unique thing about this plague was that it did not affect the Israelites (YisraELi) or the land that they inhabited, Goshen. YAHveh was establishing a pattern to show His people that even though they may experience a portion of His wrath, He would provide them with a means of escape from His complete anger. His YisraEL would only be an observer of the final seven plagues. This mirrors His final judgment of the Earth, when He sends His last seven bowls of plagues.

Once again, Pharaoh summoned Moses (Mosheh) and his brother, Aaron (Aharon), and asked them to call upon their ELohim to release Egypt (Mitsrahyim) from this plague. This time, he gave them his permission to go into the desert to worship YAH, but with the stipulation that they could only go a few miles. Moses (Mosheh) told Pharaoh that they needed a distance of at least three days because of the types of sacrifices that they would be required to offer. He explained to him that sheep and goats had to be used, which might prove to be offensive to Pharaoh's people because these too were elohim of the Egyptians (Mitsrahyim). He agreed, but once again it only proved to be just more rhetoric from Pharaoh because the next day he decided against it.

As a result of the hardness of Pharaoh's heart, YAHveh chose to pronounce His fifth plague of judgment upon "Khnum, Hathor, and Apis", the Egyptian's (Mitsrahyim's) elohim of "livestock". This in turn only hardened Pharaoh's heart even more, and he refused to let YAH's people go for the seventh time.

Apparently, Pharaoh and the people of Egypt (Mitsrahyim) looked to their magicians as being elohim because of all of their incantations for healing and their appearance of knowledge. It was thought that they were servants of "Thoth", the el of wisdom and medicine. Therefore, YAH, as His sixth judgment, struck everyone with boils, and the magicians were helpless to do anything. Once again, Pharaoh asked Moses (Mosheh) to go before his ELohim and ask for deliverance from the plague. Then, just as before, after they were delivered, his heart was hardened, and he refused to let the people of YisraEL go for the eighth time.

Like most of the nations in that region, Egypt (Mitsrahyim) also worshiped "Nut" (Noot), the el who ruled the hosts of heaven, the weather, and the seasons. Remember, YAHveh's enemy, Satan (hasatan), is also known as the prince of the air. So, YAHveh judged Egypt (Mitsrahyim) the seventh time with the worst hailstorm in their history for not releasing His people at His request. Their fields and property were destroyed by the storm. YAHveh also instructed Moses (Mosheh) to be sure to teach all of the future generations about the things that He had just done in order to remind them to always look to Him and not to His provisions as their ELohim. *"But seek first the kingdom of ELuah and His righteousness, and all these things shall be added to you"* (**MATT 6:33**). *"And my ELuah shall supply all your needs according to His riches in glory by Messiah Yeshua"* (**PHIL 4:19**). This time, Pharaoh agreed to only let the men of YisraEL go to worship. This, of course, was unacceptable to Moses (Mosheh) and Aaron (Aharon) because YAHveh had said ***all of His people***.

This answer released YAH's eighth judgment upon them—the plague of locusts. "Anubis" had dominion over the insects and was also an el of agriculture, which included the fields. (Many artifacts with beetles, locusts, or other forms of insects engraved on them have been discovered throughout the region of the Middle East.) So, what remained of their crops that the hailstorm hadn't already destroyed, the locusts then ate. Once again, Pharaoh pleaded for mercy from Moses (Mosheh) and Aaron's (Aharon's) ELohim. And once again, YAHveh relented—once again, Pharaoh reneged.

When YAHveh's ninth judgment came, He again included the host of the heavens, but mostly on Ra/Amon-Re/Zeus, the sun el, and declared its light to cease upon the Earth. Now, whether this came about through a combination of a dust storm and heavy rain clouds or perhaps a heavy fog, Scripture doesn't say, but everywhere in Egypt (Mitsrahyim), and only in Egypt (Mitsrahyim), there was darkness. The only light that could be found was in YisraEL's land of Goshen. This plague lasted for three days. Pharaoh then told Moses (Mosheh) that he and YisraEL could leave, but they couldn't take their livestock with them. Moses (Mosheh) explained that they must take their livestock because they had not yet been given the instructions for their sacrifices—all of their livestock would have to be at the ready. Their eleventh request was made, and the eleventh denial was given.

The people of Egypt (Mitsrahyim) were petrified with the fear of Moses (Mosheh) and the Israelites (YisraELi) because of the demonstrated power of their ELohim. So, when YAH told Moses (Mosheh) to ask the Egyptians (Mitsrahyim) to give them gold and silver for their exodus, they gladly obliged. Moses (Mosheh) made his twelfth and final request to Pharaoh to let YAH's people go. Egypt's (Mitsrahyim's) greatest elohim of all was Pharaoh himself. He was considered to be the incarnation of "Ra" as well as "Osiris", the giver of life and the chief elohim of them all. If he refused this time, he and all of the Egyptians (Mitsrahyim) would be required to pay for their sin of disobedience to YAHveh with the life of their own firstborn males. (This is, of course, the price that YAHveh Himself paid for our sins).

There were twelve requests—one request for each of the twelve tribes of YisraEL. There were ten plagues—one for each of the ten nations of the world (the ten horns in the Book of Revelation) who will look to themselves as their own elohim at the "end of days", causing YAHveh to bring all things together for the final judgment of the age.

The First of Many Feasts that Point to the Messiah (PASSOVER/PESACH)

YAHveh calls Moses (Mosheh) and Aaron (Aharon) to instruct them to prepare the people to be delivered from the bondage of Egypt (Mitsrahyim). He gave them special instructions on how to prepare a meal that would be used as a metaphorical memorial of their deliverance, as well as a rehearsal for their deliverance from sin through the Promised One.

YAHveh gave Moses (Mosheh) and Aaron (Aharon) instructions for a calendar, so that His people, YisraEL, could keep track of all of their future celebrations. This would also be the beginning of their countdown to the promised Millennium of Peace (Shalom). The first month of their first year of the countdown would be called "Abib", or "Aviv". Abib is the Hebrew word that means "the budding of the barley grain", which is used to determine the beginning of the spring season. A month (originally "moonth") always began in ancient times at the sighting of the first crescent of the "new moon". This is how a Hebrew is supposed to keep track of his appointed seasons (moedim), months, and years. When the twelfth month (Adar) ended, certain designated people would go out into the land and gather in barley samples. If the barley had budded by the time the new moon crescent was sighted, then the new year had begun; if not, then an additional month, called "II Adar", would be added to the year, and it would be considered a leap year. YAHveh uses His moon to direct His monthly and annual scheduling; we use a manmade calendar that is based upon a Roman timetable. Roman months were named after Roman deities. Man loves being in charge of the outcome of everything; that's why he likes his own calendar to be constructed in such a way that it makes everything predictable. You know how it goes, thirty days has September, April, June, and November. With a Hebrew calendar, it's completely different; the first month of the year, or any given month, may have twenty-eight days this year, thirty or twenty-nine days next, and so on—it is not as predictable. This way, YAH has the say as to when things are to be scheduled. As I explained before, the first month was to be called Abib/Aviv; it was also known as "Nisan", a Babylonian name. The second was called "Iyar". The third month is "Sivan", the forth is "Tammuz" (a Babylonian-elohim name), the fifth is "Av", the sixth is "Elul", the seventh is "Tishri", the eighth is "Heshvan", the ninth is "Kishlev", the tenth is "Tevet", the eleventh is "Shevet", and the twelfth is "Adar". If a thirteenth month is necessary, it is called "II Adar".

Next, they were to do as Ahdom's second son, Abel (Ahbel), which was to choose an unblemished male lamb or goat from their flocks and was less than a year old. They were to do this on the tenth day of their first month. They were to take it into their house to live with them for four days in order for it to become like a member of the family, making it more of a sacrifice when they had to slay it on the fourteenth day, just before sunset. They were to take its blood and symbolically cover their household with it by spreading it on the doorframe of the entrance to their house. They were to take special care not to break any of its bones. This describes Yeshua because He rode into Jerusalem (YAHrushalayim) on the tenth day of Abib. He was examined for four days by all of His brethren. Then, on the fourteenth day, He was crucified and not one of His bones was broken. Whosoever believes this to be true and calls upon Him to be their Lord (Adonai), they will be saved from their sins and will receive the gift of eternal life.

After this, they were to roast it—not boil it or eat it raw. They were to try to eat all of it before morning and burn what they couldn't. They were to eat it with bitter herbs and bread that was not made with yeast. On the evening of their meal (which would now be the fifteenth of Abib), the final and worst plague of them all would come upon each residence in Egypt (Mitsrahyim). If there was blood on the doorframe, the plague would pass over that house. It made no difference whether they were Hebrew or Egyptian (Mitsrahyim), if they believed YAH's words and followed His instructions, they would be spared—this is faith in action. But if the destroyer (hasatan) did not see the blood, he would enter in and take the life of the oldest (firstborn) male child of the family who lived in that house. This curse even included the livestock. YAHveh ordained that day to be commemorated as YAHveh's Passover (death of the firstborn) and Pesach (feast of the lamb)—these are to be one and the same. Today, the meal is known as the Pesach or Seder meal. Although it originally was to be celebrated by each individual family, it would later be changed into a national celebration. It would eventually evolve into a tradition consisting of four phases, each being preceded by a cup of wine to be drunk as a drink offering to YAH, acknowledging what He had done for them. The cups of wine represent the blood that was spread on the doorframes; they also represent the blood that the suffering Messiah would shed for mankind's sins. The first phase of the Seder meal commemorates the family and its importance to the people of YAHveh. This phase of the meal is sanctified with the first cup of wine known as the "Cup of Sanctification". YAHveh always began His seven annual festivals with His Passover.

Passover launched the beginning of the second festival, which was to be celebrated for seven days. This would be known as the Feast of Unleavened Bread (Chag HaMatzot) because YisraEL would not have the time to make bread with yeast and wait for it to rise before their exodus from Egypt (Mitsrahyim). In Scripture, bread represents the basic substance of life, and yeast is usually a symbol of sin because it spreads so easily into each lump of dough. Therefore, unleavened bread, or bread without yeast, represents the absence of sin in one's life. The first day and the seventh day of this feast were to be consecrated as holy (kedosh) days (Sabbath days) with no ordinary work being done on them; they were to be completely separate from the weekly Sabbaths (LEV 23:3). They were set aside as Sabbaths because YAHveh wanted to establish the importance of this feast to His people, YisraEL. All of YAH's feasts, or appointed times (moedim), were to be His teaching tools for all future generations to come. They were to help His people recognize the Messiah when He arrived on the scene, and after He arrived, they were to be celebrated as a reminder that He had come. YAHveh also gave special instructions that no one except those who obeyed His Torah and were circumcised could partake of these celebrations. In other words, these festivals were to be for only those who were of the blood covenant. Believers today are not required to be circumcised in order to be saved, as were the ancient Israelites (YisraELi) before the Lamb of YAH came into the world—Yeshua became our blood covenant and met those requirements for us. These feasts were given to all generations to keep forever as a memorial to YAHveh for His mercy and grace that He has shown His people. Why we, His believers today, insist on changing His appointed times (moedim) and appoint our own, such as Christmas, Sunday Sabbaths, and Easter, smacks of rebellion to me. *"You shall not add to the word which I command you, nor take anything from it, that you may keep the commandments of YAHveh your ELohim which I command you"* (DEUT 4:2).

After the Israelites (YisraELi) heard all of Moses' (Mosheh's) instructions and had obeyed them, the midnight hour arrived, and the Angel of Death entered into the city of Pharaoh. Not one family, from Pharaoh on down, was left unaffected that night. There was death everywhere, except in the houses where the lamb's blood had been placed upon its door mantel. When dawn came, Pharaoh called for Moses (Mosheh) and Aaron (Aharon) and gave them the order to leave Egypt (Mitsrahyim). Moses (Mosheh) called for the people to gather all of their possessions, along with whatever they could obtain from the Egyptians (Mitsrahyim), and prepare to leave the land. Moses (Mosheh) then gathered Joseph's (Yosef's) bones, as he had requested, to take with them back into the Land of Promise. The Exodus consisted of about 1,800,000 people (600,000 men, plus women and children).

YAHveh gave more instructions to His people concerning the necessity of keeping this Feast of Passover after they had entered into the land that He had promised Avraham's descendants, the land of the Canaanites (Canaani). Then He commanded them to dedicate the firstborn male from each family and flock to YAHveh for His service. This was to remind them of the acts of grace that He had bestowed upon them when He took the Egyptians' (Mitsrahyim's) firstborn, which resulted in their release. He reminds them, and us, that knowing Him involves much more than just acknowledging His Majesty—it also requires us to be participants in His words through His feasts. *"But be doers of the word, and not hearers only, deceiving yourselves"* (**JAM 1:22**).

YAHveh had a plan through which He would demonstrate His power to meet all of their needs. He avoided taking them by the shortest route (the route we would all prefer) into the land that He had promised. Instead, He led them to a dead-end at the Red Sea. A pillar-type cloud of dust led them during the daytime (dust tornados are common in the deserts of the Middle East, but not one that is continuous). A pillar of fire led them by night. YAHveh explained to Moses (Mosheh) that He was going to harden Pharaoh's heart one more time and cause him to repent of his decision to let YisraEL go.

When the YisraELi saw Pharaoh's army pursuing them, they lost faith and began to complain about their situation. (YAH hates complainers; refrain from doing it or a much worse problem could arise.) *"Nor murmured, as some of them also murmured, and were destroyed by the destroyer"* (**I COR 10:10**). YAHveh caused His dust tornado to move from the front of YisraEL to the rear, where it would separate His people from Egypt's (Mitsrahyim's) army. YAHveh instructed Moses (Mosheh) to raise his rod toward the waters of the Red Sea and to hold it there all night. (Sometimes YAH's instructions are really demanding in order to test whether or not we trust Him.) When dawn broke, the waters of the Red Sea began to separate, with one wall on one side and a second wall on the other, allowing the people to cross over on dry land. When Pharaoh's army pursued, it was swallowed up in the sea. (If we follow His instructions, He will deliver us from the enemy—if not, we're on our own.) Both Moses (Mosheh) and his sister,

Miriam (Meeryahm), sang a song and danced before YAHveh as a celebration of praise for His salvation. (YAHveh loves music, singing, and dancing as an expression of worship.)

In spite of the wonderful signs and miracles that YAHveh had just demonstrated, the people of YisraEL continued to grumble and complain about the minor hardships that they were called to endure. It had only been three days since their deliverance from the Egyptians (Mitsrahyim) when they began to complain about the lack of water. In response, YAHveh led them to a place where He changed bitter water into sweet (contaminated into fresh). Then YAHveh set forth a decree among the people, that if they would obey all that He commanded them, He would protect them from all harm. In the second month of their journey, the month of Iyar, YAH guided them onto an oasis. Though they had plenty of water there, they were beginning to lack food, so they began to grumble again. YAH promised them that they would have meat and bread within twenty-four hours. First, He sent them quail that very night. The next morning, bread came to them in the form of creamy-white flakes, like snow, and was sweet to the taste. They called it "manna", which means "What is it?" YAH instructed them to gather this "manna" each morning according to each family's need. They were to gather twice as much before the evening of the seventh day and were not to do anything on the seventh day, except rest. YAH was establishing His first weekly Sabbath rest. They were also instructed to take some of the manna and keep it in a jar as a memorial to this miracle.

As they continued their desert journey, water became less and less available, and they began to complain and grumble again about their conditions. This time, YAH instructed Moses (Mosheh) to take his staff and strike a particular rock, and when he did, water began to flow from it. Now, was this a true miracle? In the Middle East, it is not unusual for water to be trapped in above-ground cisterns after the rainy seasons. Rain runs down into crevices and becomes trapped, and if struck in a weak spot, it will release the trapped water. Even so, how would Moses (Mosheh) know which rock would produce a sufficient amount of water for such a great number of people, and how would he know where to strike it unless he were divinely guided? As was said before, all of these events were meant to be teaching tools and examples for generations to come. *"Moreover, brethren, I do not want you to be unaware that all our fathers were under the cloud, all passed through the sea,...all were immersed into Moses (Mosheh) in the cloud and in the sea,...all ate the same spiritual food,...and all drank the same spiritual drink. For they drank of that spiritual Rock that followed them, and that Rock was Messiah"* (I COR 10:1-4). *"Now all these things happened to them as examples, and they were written for our admonition, on whom the ends of the ages have come"* (I COR 10:11).

YAHveh's Sixth Covenant with Mankind, the Covenant of Marriage to YisraEL

In the third month, the month of Sivan, YAH led His people to Mt. Sinai (Seenahee), also known as "Mt. Horeb", in the Sinai (Seenahee) mountain range. There, He instructed Moses (Mosheh) that when His people entered the land that He had promised their fathers, they were to celebrate their first wheat harvest. Every year after that, they were to count off fifty days to determine "Shavuot" (the waving of two loaves of wheat bread), starting from the first Sabbath after Passover. They would do this by counting and setting aside an omar of barley grain each day to be burnt as an offering by the priests until Shavuot; this would determine their next wheat-harvest celebration. This wheat harvest would always fall on the anniversary of their arrival at Mt Sinai (Seenahee). YAHveh spoke to Moses (Mosheh) again from this mountain and began to lay out his sixth covenant for mankind. His plan was to make the nation of YisraEL His bride; all that she was required to do was to agree to be His people and obey His Torah. Then He would make her a holy (kedosh) nation above all the other nations, and He would be her ELohim. He then told them to consecrate themselves and return to the mountain in three days. The people of YisraEL agreed to these conditions, and for the next three days, they washed themselves and their clothes and abstained from sexual relations with their spouses. This washing was the first form of baptism, or immersion (mikvah), that they would experience. It would become an eternal symbol for consecration, which means to be set apart or holy (kedosh). The people were then given the first instruction from a set of many instructions. They were not to touch this mountain that YAHveh was about to descend upon from heaven. YAH manifested Himself in smoke, fire, and lightning that was accompanied by the sound from the blast of a shofar (ram's horn). The sound of His voice was in the shofar blast as He spoke forth His first basic instructions to His newly betrothed. These became known as the "Ten Commandments of YAHveh". The people became terrified upon hearing His awesome voice and asked Moses (Mosheh) to be their intercessor. So Moses (Mosheh) approached YAH on behalf of the people of YisraEL, and once again, He emphasized the absolute necessity of their looking only to Him for their guidance, protection, and provisions. He also warned them not to become like the other nations who relied upon their own intelligence, wisdom, and experiences for guidance. They, out of ignorance, were actually following after demons, making them their elohim and allowing them to direct their spiritual lives. But, He foreknew that He would have to eventually scatter His people, YisraEL, into these nations because they too would not obey His commandments.

He also told Moses (Mosheh) that He was going to send them a special Angel who would lead them into the land of their inheritance. He warned them that other nations were dwelling there now and that they would have to be driven out because they had defiled the land with their abominations and worship of demons. He told them that it must first be cleansed because it was holy (kedosh) to Him, just as they were, and that the land was to be theirs for eternity. He even gave them the geographical description of the territory that each tribe would eventually be assigned to. Moses (Mosheh) began to record all of these instructions, creating the five scrolls of the Torah. He explained all of YAH's requirements to the people, and they agreed to them. In essence, they said "I do" to YAHveh's proposal. YAH referred to this gathering of His people as His assembly, or congregation. The word that He used here for congregation is the Hebrew word "kahal" and is the equivalent to the Greek word "ecclesia", which when translated into English, is the word "church", or really "assembly/congregation". So, in all actuality, YAHveh really established His Kahal/Church on the first Feast of Weeks, called Shavuot or Pentecost (Greek for fifty), fifteen-hundred years before His Son, Yeshua, said, *"And I also say to you that you are Peter (Kefa), and on this rock I will build (continue to build) My Church/Ecclesia/Kahal and the gates of Hades shall not prevail against it."* It was upon the rock of the truth from Peter's confession—*"You are the Messiah, the Son of the Living ELohim"* (**MATT 16:16**)—that He was going to build up His *"Kahal"*. His "Kahal" was *not* birthed on the Pentecost after Yeshua's death and resurrection, but fifteen-hundred years earlier. But on this particular Pentecost/Shavuot, Yeshua was establishing two things: first, this would be His Bride's opportunity to renew her vows to Him, and second, He was giving them the gift of His Ruach (Spirit) to impower His people to go and witness to the world that the Messiah had come and was now going to begin to restore the House of YisraEL, just as He had promised. He was sending them to gather in the lost sheep of YisraEL from the four corners of the Earth, where he had scattered them, in order to accomplish this restoration.

YAHveh called Moses (Mosheh) to come up on Mt. Sinai (Seenahee) to receive all of His instructions for His people, YisraEL. Moses (Mosheh) took with him the commander of YisraEL's army, Joshua (Yoshua), from the tribe of Ephraim (Efraeem). I find this significant because the name "Joshua" (Yoshua) is a derivative of Yeshua, which means "Savior of YAH". YAHveh's only begotten Son, Yeshua, was from the tribe of Judah (YAHuda), was a prophet like Moses (Mosheh), and was the Savior of the world. Joshua (Yoshua) was from the tribe of Ephraim/Joseph (Efraeem/Yosef), was a leader and prophet like Moses (Mosheh), and was also a savior of YisraEL. These two tribes (YAHuda and Yosef) would be separated and restored several different times before their final restoration in the end times.

WHAT WE WEREN'T TAUGHT ABOUT THE BIBLE AND ITS HISTORY

YAHveh Establishes a Replica of Heaven on Earth, a Second Eden

YAHveh gave Moses (Mosheh) the blueprints for His second Eden in the form of a "Tabernacle in the Wilderness". The "Tabernacle" (Mishkahn) was to be the courtyard and dwelling place for YAH's portable sanctuary. Notice the word "kahn" within the word "Mishkahn". It is a derivative of the word Kahal/Congregation. Both are places where YAH intends to establish His residence. There, He would meet with His prophet, Moses (Mosheh), and Moses' (Mosheh's) brother, Aaron (Aharon), along with the priests and the elders of YisraEL. YAH instructed Moses (Mosheh) to collect all of the materials needed for the building of His sanctuary from the people.

YAH then gave them instructions for the design of a special wooden chest called the "Ark of the Covenant", which was to be overlaid with gold inside and out, including gold-plated poles that would be used to transport it. He told Moses (Mosheh) that it would later be used as a container for the Testimony that He would provide for him.

Next, Moses (Mosheh) was given the design for the "Mercy Seat", which was a covering for the Ark and a place where YAHveh would manifest Himself while speaking with Moses (Mosheh) and the high priests. It was to be hammered out using a solid piece of pure gold and was to have two cherubim sculptured on its top. Most illustrations of cherubim that we see today are little babies with wings or winged women or men. These illustrations actually come from ancient Babylonian and Greek art and are not true depictions of cherubim. Cherubim from biblical times are usually depicted as four-legged animals, such as horses or lions—these symbolized both power and strength. They were adorned with the head of a lion, a man, an ox, or an eagle. In the book of the prophet Ezekiel and in the Apostle John's Book of Revelation, they are depicted as having all four faces. They also possessed wings, demonstrating their spiritual ability to mount up as eagles.

Next, he was given the design for the "Table of the Bread of Presence". It too was to be made of wood, overlaid with gold, along with gold-plated carrying poles and gold utensils. Displayed on the table would be twelve loaves of unleavened bread, symbolizing the twelve tribes of YisraEL. They were set in two rows of six; this may have been a representation of the two houses of YisraEL, Judah (YAHuda) and Joseph (Yosef), who would one day become divided. These loaves were called the "Showbread".

Next was the design for the menorah (a multiple-branched oil lamp). It was designed after the tree of life in the Garden of Eden and had seven branches. It too was to be hammered out of solid gold. Its purpose was to perpetually light the Sanctuary of YAH's tent of meeting, using the oil from olives—the olive tree also represents the whole House of YisraEL. The menorah symbolized

YAHveh's eternal light to His people, and the olive oil represented His Ruach HaKedosh (Holy Spirit). Yeshua, in the Book of Revelation, was in the midst of a similar menorah that He said represented seven different congregations in Asia. In all actuality, they symbolized the ongoing condition of all of His people throughout history. *"Then I turned to see the voice that spoke to me. And having turned I saw seven golden lampstands"…"The mystery of the seven stars which you saw in My right hand, and the seven golden lampstands: The seven stars are the angels of the seven congregations, and the seven lampstands which you saw are the seven congregations"* (**REV 1:12 & 20**). The seven angels that are mentioned here are also identified later: *"And I looked, and behold in the midst of the throne and of the four living creatures, and in the midst of the elders, stood a Lamb as though it had been slain, having seven horns and seven eyes, which are the seven Spirits of ELohim sent out into all the earth"* (**REV 5:6**).

Then YAH showed His servant, Moses (Mosheh), the dimensions of the Tabernacle (Mishkahn) itself. He was commanded to write down the specifications so there would be no mistakes. He was given the length, width, height, and type of material to be used in the making of the outside curtains that were to surround the courtyard, along with the design for the hardware that would fasten everything together. He was given the size and the type of material that was to be used in the construction of the box-shaped tent of the Tabernacle (Mishkahn). The colors that were to be used for the dye for the materials and the description for the designs used in the embroidery work were also given. The clothing that the priests were to wear was described, along with the material that they were to be made from. Finally, specific instructions were given for the ordination and the consecration of the priests.

All of the utensils and furniture that were to be used inside of the Tabernacle (Mishkahn) were to be made from pure gold or were to be gold-plated. The items used outside, within the courtyard, were to be made with either silver or bronze. The courtyard posts were bronze over wood. Gold and silver are natural elements that only need fire to refine them for use and are rare and valuable—they are symbolic of spiritual wealth and strength. Bronze, on the other hand, is a combination of copper and tin and has to be smelted by men through hard labor before it can be used. Bronze, as well as iron, wood, and clay, are symbolic throughout Scripture of man and his limited ability to create.

A bronze laver was to be constructed for the purpose of ceremonial cleansing. The inside of the laver was to be lined with polished mirrors that were donated by the women of the congregation (kahal) of the Children of YisraEL. The purpose for the mirrors was for the priests to be able to see their own reflections whenever they came to wash and be reminded that they were originally created in the image of YAH. *"For if anyone is a hearer of the word and not a doer, he is like a man observing his natural face in a mirror;...for he observes himself, goes away, and immediately forgets what kind of man he was. But he who looks into the perfect law of liberty (the blessings promised in the Torah) and continues in it, and is not a forgetful hearer but a doer of the work, this one will be blessed in what he does"* (**JAM 1:23-25**).

The purpose for surrounding the courtyard with curtains was to prohibit a view of the Tabernacle (Mishkahn) by any approaching visitor—the privilege of seeing the Tabernacle (Mishkahn) was to be exclusively for YAH's people. For anyone else, they would have to be willing to climb up on a hill or a mountain, if available, and view it from an elevated vantage point, which would provide them with a heavenly perspective of it. The interior of the Tabernacle (Mishkahn) itself was prohibited for anyone, except for the priests, to see. Inside the Tabernacle (Mishkahn) was the holiest place of all, the Holy of Holies, where the Ark of the Covenant was placed. It was to be hidden by a specially-designed veil that only the high priest could enter through once a year.

The high priest, in this case Aaron (Aharon), was to be especially adorned in linen of white and blue. He was to wear a turban as a head covering to show both his headship and his submission to ELohim. The priests, who were Aaron's (Aharon's) sons, were to wear tunics of white linen, along with hats or small caps instead of turbans. Today, the Jewish (YAHudaim) male wears a small cap that is known as a yarmulke or kippa. The high priest was also to be adorned with an ephod and a breastplate. Two onyx stones were to be on the shoulder straps of the ephod. The names of six of the tribes of YisraEL were to be engraved on the one and the remaining six to be on the other, according to the order of their birth. When placed in this manner, the head of the high priest divided the tribes. Later, when the tribes had received their inheritance in the land, the territory of the tribe of Benjamin (BenYAHmeen), which contained YAH's city, YAHrushalayim, would divide the two main tribes—Judah (YAHuda) to the south and Ephraim (Efraeem) to the north. This also symbolized the coming division of the whole tribe of YisraEL. Yeshua is our High Priest and our Head. It is He who will bring the divided houses of YisraEL together as His last and final mission. *"For He Himself is our shalom, who has made both one, and has broken down the middle wall of division between us,...having abolished in His flesh the enmity, that is, the law of commandments contained in ordinances, so as to create in Himself one new man from the two, thus making shalom,...and that He might reconcile them both to YAHveh in one body through the crucifixion stake, thereby putting to death the enmity"* (**EPH 2:14-16**).

On the breastplate of the high priest, there were twelve precious stones with the names of the twelve tribes engraved on each one. It was worn over the breast near the lungs and heart, where the breath and life of man are located. Also worn near the heart were the Urim and the Thummin. They were used by the high priest to receive direction from YAHveh for YisraEL—these are referred to many times throughout the TaNaKh. The Urim was a prism-type stone that when taken into the presence of YAH in the Holy of Holies, it would refract His Shchinah Glory, reflecting it off of the letters of the names of the tribes that were on the high priest's breastplate. The Thummin was the interpretation device used to decipher the message that was reflected off of the letters. It's interesting to note that white stones will be used by Yeshua to identify each member of the tribes of YisraEL when they stand before Him at His judgment. *"He who has an ear, let him hear what the Ruach (Spirit) says to the congregations. To him who overcomes I will give some of the hidden manna to eat. And I will give him a white stone, and on the stone a new name written which no one knows except him who receives it"* (**REV 2:17**). A white stone signifies purity.

YisraEL Committed Adultery

Moses (Mosheh) had been on the mountain and out of the sight of the people of YisraEL for forty days while he received the instructions from YAHveh. The people began to suspect that the worst had happened to him, so they called upon Aaron (Aharon) to fashion an image for them—they needed something that they could see that would take Moses' (Moshehs') place as their Adonai (master) and leader. Aaron (Aharon) fashioned a golden calf in order to satisfy their lust for another el (mighty one). Bulls and calves represented strength in Egypt (Mitsrahyim), just as they do in our stock market today. They believed that this image could go before them and lead them into the new land. (YAH's people lose faith so quickly when they are faced with a real challenge, and more often than not, they will begin to look to themselves for guidance.) YAHveh instructed Moses (Mosheh) to go back down the mountain because the people were in the middle of the act of committing spiritual adultery. YAH wanted to destroy them and make Moses' (Mosheh's) descendants His people instead, but Moses (Mosheh) interceded for them and reminded YAH of His promise to Avraham, Isaac (Yitzhak), and Jacob (Yaacov). Moses (Mosheh) threw down the two stone tablets and smashed them before the people of YisraEL. Most people picture Moses (Mosheh) breaking two large tablets of stone, but most archeologists agree that they were probably not much larger than the palm of the hand. It was common in those times to keep records on clay or stone tablets of that size. Moses' (Mosheh's) tablets were more than likely stone and not granite because they were so easily "broken" before the people.

Moses (Mosheh) called for those who would be faithful to YAHveh as their ELohim to step forward, and the whole tribe of Levi (Lehvee) responded. He then gave the order for them to kill, at random, neighbors and friends in order to demonstrate YAHveh's wrath—three thousand were killed that day. Because of the obedience of the Levi (Lehvee), the whole nation of YisraEL was spared. YAH honored the tribe of Levi (Lehvee) for their obedience by making them His special servants and priests, who would minister to Him from that time on. The Levi (Lehvee) would now be His personal servants instead of the firstborn of every tribe, although the firstborn were still to be dedicated for the purpose of remembering what He did in Egypt (Mitsrahyim).

YAHveh promised to always keep His Presence among them in the form of His Angel. *"And all drank the same spiritual drink. For they drank of that spiritual Rock that followed them, and that Rock was Messiah"* (**I COR 10:4**). He also called Moses (Mosheh) to come back up the mountain for an additional forty days, where He revealed Himself physically to him. He dictated the remaining Torah to him and gave him a second set of His commandments—perhaps they were cut from granite this time, for longevity's sake.

The Tabernacle (Mishkahn) is Completed and the Articles Arranged

The artisans and the craftsmen were assembled, the materials were collected, and the work began on the construction of the Tabernacle (Mishkahn). This mobile Tent of Meeting would continue to be the place where YAH would meet with His people until he chose a more permanent structure. After the cloud would lift and move and the people would follow it to its next destination, the Tabernacle (Mishkahn) would always be erected again in an east-west direction. The entrance faced east, just as the Garden of Eden had faced east. When an individual faced east, it symbolized their turning their face away from ELohim, while facing west represented their approaching Him. In Scripture, the four directions (north, south, east, and west) represented the four corners of the Earth and the four winds upon the Earth. This symbolism usually referred to the inhabitants of the whole Earth and usually spoke to the fact that He was available as ELohim to all of the nations of the Earth if they would just submit themselves to Him and to His Torah. The geographical arrangement of the Tabernacle (Mishkahn) caused all who wished to meet Him or desired to become a part of His nation, YisraEL, to approach Him from the east. YAH is "The Light" and the light of day rises in the east and sets in the west. He has always offered only one way into His presence and that is by faith in His Promise (which is His Messiah), who is also "The Light". After entering the Tent of Meeting, the first thing that was required of them was to have the high priest, who acted as their representative, offer the blood of an innocent, clean animal upon the altar of burnt offerings for their "unintentional" sins and as a substitute for their own blood. "Intentional" sins required the shedding of their own blood by death or the blood of an innocent person who would act as their substitute. This presented a problem since no one could qualify as innocent. *"For all have sinned and fall short of the glory of ELuah"* (**ROM 3:23**). Yeshua is both our substitute Blood Offering and our High Priest.

The priests would then go to the bronze laver and wash themselves before entering the Tabernacle (Mishkahn). The priests were the representatives of the people. After we accept Yeshua as our sacrifice, we become priests and members of a nation of priests, and we can now represent ourselves. We then must go through a second step, the cleansing of our lives, before entering into His dwelling place. This is done through the "washing of the water by His words". *"Husbands, love your wives, just as the Messiah also loved His congregation and gave Himself for it,...that He might sanctify and cleanse it with the washing of water by the word,...that He might present it to Himself a glorious assembly (kahal), not having spot or wrinkle or any such thing, but that it should be holy (kedosh) and without blemish"* **(EPH 5:25-27)**. Upon entering the sanctuary of the Tabernacle (Mishkahn), there on the south side is the menorah representing the Seven Ruachs of YAHveh, shining and lighting the way into His very presence. On the north side is the Table of Presence containing the twelve loafs of unleavened bread that represent the twelve tribes of YisraEL, who have the responsibility of feeding the word of YAH to all of the nations so that His promise to His servant, Avraham, (that he will be a blessing to all of them) can be fulfilled. On the far west end of the sanctuary is the altar of incense that is burning continuously before the veil that shields the way to the Most Holy Place. The burning incense represents the prayers of YisraEL ascending up into the nostrils of YAHveh. The veil that prevents everyone, except the high priest, from entering into YAH's presence, will do so until the crucifixion of Yeshua, when it will then be torn from top to bottom, allowing complete access to Abba YAHveh forever. Behind this veil sat the Holy Throne of EL Shaddia that was now made approachable by the very blood of His only begotten Son, Yeshua HaMashiach. YisraEL can now come face to face with her Eluah and submit her own petitions before Him.

Conclusion

The book of Exodus, the second book of the Torah, begins to reveal to us how we are to worship YAHveh, our Elohim, in both spirit and in truth. *"ELuah is Ruach (Spirit), and those who worship Him must worship in spirit and in truth"* **(JOHN 4:24)**. The five books of Torah reveal to us the dual purposes of judgment—to punish disobedience and to bless obedience. Simply put, obedience brings blessings, while disobedience brings curses. We have been taught that we are no longer under the Law of the Torah. What we are not under is the curse of the Law, not the Law itself. That's because the Law also contains blessings—that part was purchased for us by the blood of our Messiah, Yeshua. We are told by YAH in His TaNaKh and by Yeshua in the Renewed Covenant to be holy (kedosh). Yeshua said, *"If you love Me, keep My commandments"* **(JOHN 14:15)**. His commandments and His Abba's commandments (the Torah) are the same. The Torah is good for making us holy (kedosh), through the keeping of His Sabbaths, New Moons, Feasts, and all of His 613 commandments. Yeshua fulfilled most of them, but He has left some for us to keep until He returns—they are our form of worshiping Him. Failure in the keeping of them only grieves our Heavenly Abba and deprives us of His desire to bless us. *"He who has My commandments and keeps them, it is he who loves Me. And he who loves Me will be loved by My Abba, and I will love him and manifest Myself to him"...."If anyone loves Me, he will keep My word; and My Abba will love him, and We will come to him and make Our home with him. "He who does not love Me does not keep My words; and the word which you hear is not Mine but the Abba's who sent Me"* (**JOHN 14:21, 23&24**). Keeping His words and obeying His commandments in order to gain salvation amounts to dead works because there is no spirit involved. Receiving His gift of grace through faith in His Son's sacrifice and then walking in that faith by doing His works is our sacrifice of praise and amounts to worshiping Him in spirit and in truth. *"For by grace you have been saved through faith, and that not of yourself; it is the gift of YAHveh not of works, lest anyone should boast"* (**EPH 2:8&9**). Now we are able to keep His Sabbaths, New Moons, and His Festivals without the fear of stumbling. *"Therefore let no one judge you in food or in drink, or regarding a festival of a new moon of sabbaths which is a shadow of things to come, but the substance is of Messiah"* (**COL 2:16&17**).

Now we will begin to study the purpose of the construction of the Tabernacle (Mishkahn), the sacrifices connected to it, and the ordinances surrounding it. We will begin to see why it was necessary for YAH to distinguish between clean and unclean and His purpose for putting restrictions on certain behavior and attitudes. The Torah was given to cause us to focus on our own sinful nature and the things that separate us from Him. *"But we know that the law (Torah) is good if one uses it lawfully"* (**I TIM 1:8**).

CHAPTER 3
...about Leviticus, Numbers, and Deuteronomy

The next three books that we will examine are the final three writings of the Torah. They contain both the history of YisraEL for the next forty years and the instructions to Mosheh on how to exercise, or implement, all of YAH's commandments and ordinances. The book of Numbers contains the accounting of YAHveh's two censuses that He ordered—one at the beginning of their journey and the other at the end. Deuteronomy is a review that Mosheh shared with YisraEL about YAH's guidance, protection, and provisions that He had supernaturally provided for them over the forty years in the wilderness. Leviticus lists most of the instructions that were given to the tribe of Levi (Lehvee) for their execution of His ordinances. Other ordinances for the Levi (Lehvee) can be found scattered throughout Exodus, Numbers, and Deuteronomy. These were all of the ordinances that were given to YisraEL in order to guide her into becoming a holy (kedosh) nation unto Him.

We will first look at the book of Numbers, which describes the first time that the Tabernacle (Mishkahn) was erected in the wilderness. It took place on the first day of the first month, Abib, in the second year after they were delivered from slavery in Mitsrahyim. With everyone aware of the instructions for the ordination of the priests and the high priest, Mosheh consecrated Aaron (Aharon) and his sons for service in the Tabernacle (Mishkahn).

YAHveh Prepares YisraEL to March into the Promised Land

YAHveh gave the order for Mosheh to begin a census of the tribes in order to determine the number of men who were twenty years and older for the purpose of establishing warriors for His army. The land that He was giving them was not unoccupied, and they were going to experience resistance—they would have to do battle in order to conquer it. It was His gift to them as their inheritance, but it was going to be necessary to spill blood. But He assured them that He would be with them in their conquest. The census was also taken in order to establish each tribe's position in the encampment around the Tabernacle (Mishkahn). However, He did not include a census of the tribe of Levi (Lehvee)—they would have a separate census to determine their duties and encampment placement later.

YAHveh reminded Mosheh once more about His decision to take all of the tribe of Levi (Lehvee) as His own for the purpose of ministering to Him in the Tabernacle (Mishkahn). But He was still to have all of the firstborn of YisraEL dedicated to Him because they were to become the future spiritual heads of each house, after their fathers. This established YAH's patriarchal order for families in the House of YisraEL. The age for service to Him as priests was to be from twenty-five years to fifty; this would include five years of apprenticeship before actually entering into a full ministry at the age of thirty. King David (Dahveed) later reduced the age of apprenticeship to twenty. Those over fifty were to retire from service to Him and become the elders (overseers). This should help us to understand YAHveh's instructions in the Renewed Covenant that pertain to our selection of both elders and deacons for His congregations (kahals) since we have now become His priests.

Mosheh was then instructed by YAHveh to craft silver trumpets to be used for the calling of His army into battle and for the calling of the House of YisraEL to congregate before Him. They were also to be used for announcing the sighting of the new moon in order to begin each month, as well as announcing the beginning of the appointed feasts. These silver trumpets were to be used only at the Tabernacle (Mishkahn) and then later at the House of YAH. After they settled in the land of Canaan, the shofar would be used as well.

After the Tabernacle (Mishkahn) was completely assembled and the Kahal of YisraEL was finally able to use it to meet with YAH, He then called them to celebrate their first Passover since they had left Egypt (Mitsrahyim). He also established, at this time, the ordinance stating that if for any reason they were unable to gather in the first month to celebrate Passover, they could celebrate it on the same day one month later.

In the second month of their second year, in the month of Iyar, the cloud over their encampment began to move. Mosheh repeated YAH's instructions to them, that whenever the cloud that covered them began to move, they were to disassemble the camp and follow the cloud. As long as they were under the cloud, they would be under YAH's protection and within His provisions, but if not, they would be susceptible to any and all attacks from their enemies. These instructions applied to all of His people, YisraEL, and as a believer in His promises and His Messiah, you are His YisraEL. Therefore, if we seek His face and His kingdom and submit ourselves to His instructions that are in His Torah, we too will remain under His protection and within His provisions. Whenever He says to change, to go, or to stand, and we obey Him, He will bless our obedience.

Once again, YisraEL complained about not having the same diet that they were used to eating in Mitsrahyim. They were no longer satisfied with bread from heaven—they wanted meat. Mosheh also began to complain to

YAH that he was unable to govern these stiff-necked people any longer. So YAHveh instructed Mosheh to choose seventy elders from among the congregation (kahal) of YisraEL to assist him in future spiritual matters and that He, YAHveh, would send His Ruach upon them in order to help them rule with him. He also promised the Kahal of YisraEL that He would send them quail to eat for thirty days and that they would soon become sick of it. So Mosheh did as he was instructed and chose the seventy from among the tribes of YisraEL. When the seventy appeared before Mosheh and ELohim in front of the Tabernacle (Mishkahn), the Ruach fell upon them, and they began to prophesy (speaking ecstatically). This is the phenomenon that was manifested many times throughout the Scriptures, including on the day of Pentecost (Sukkot). *"And they were filled with the Ruach and began to speak in tongues, as the Ruach gave them the utterance"* (**ACTS** 2:4). *"While Peter (Kefa) was still speaking those words, the Ruach fell upon all those who heard the word...And those of the circumcised (the YAHudi) who believed were astonished, as many as came with Kefa, because the gift of the Ruach had been poured out on the Gentiles (Goyim) also...For they heard them speak with tongues and magnify God (ELuah)"* (**ACTS** 10:44-46). *"And when Paul (Shaul) had laid hands on them, the Ruach came upon them, and they spoke with tongues and prophesied"* (**ACTS** 19:6).

Miriam (Meeryahm) Became a Leper

Mosheh decided to take another bride for himself, an Ethiopian woman. Nothing is mentioned here, but Zipporah, his first wife, must have died sometime along the way. Miriam (Meeryahm), Mosheh's sister, displayed her prejudice when she rebuked him for it and, at the same time, challenged his right to have authority over the Kahal of YisraEL. If that were not enough, Mosheh's brother, Aaron (Aharon), also chimed in with their sister. YAHveh became so outraged at their spirit of rebellion that He brought the plague of leprosy upon her for seven days as a warning to the others not to repeat this. This was the second time that Aaron (Aharon) had displayed his weakness in times of peer pressure and had shown that he feared men more than he feared YAH. It was only because he was Mosheh's brother and had been appointed as high priest that he had not yet felt YAHveh's wrath.

The Judgment of Forty Years in the Wilderness

The Children of YisraEL finally reached the edge of the wilderness, just outside of the land that was promised to their fathers, Avraham, Isaac (Yitzhak), and Jacob (Yaacov). YAHveh instructed Mosheh to choose leaders from each of the tribes to go in and to see for themselves the goodness of the land that He had promised them. Mosheh chose the twelve chief elders of the tribes to covertly seek out the land and to bring him back a report of its condition. These twelve included Caleb from the tribe of YAHuda and Joshua (Yoshua) from the tribe of Ephraim (Efraeem). The name Joshua (Yoshua), which means "the salvation of YAH", was given to him by Mosheh—he was previously known as Hoshea, which means "salvation". They entered and spied out the land for forty days. Ten of them returned with a mixed report, admitting that it was an excellent land, but that the present occupants appeared to be too mighty for them to overcome. Only Caleb and Joshua (Yoshua) came back with a positive report. It is important to remember that these two were descendants of the same two tribes that the patriarch, YisraEL, had chosen to be the heads over the houses of YisraEL.

The report that was brought back by the ten angered YAHveh, and once again, He desired to strike down the Children of YisraEL for their stubbornness and make Mosheh and his descendants His people. Once again, Mosheh interceded for the people and reminded YAH not to do this because of the mighty work that He had already done for them. YAH conceded, but promised that none who had left Mitsrahyim, except for Caleb and Joshua (Yoshua), would ever enter the land that He had promised. Instead, it would be an inheritance for their children, and their fathers would have to wander in the wilderness one year for every day that they had spied out the land of Canaan. This one-year-for-every-day-punishment pattern will appear several more times throughout the Scriptures. YAHveh also promised that it would be mostly Caleb's descendants who would eventually be the ones to settle the land permanently. Upon hearing this, the Children of YisraEL confessed that they had sinned, but decided that the punishment was too great to bear. Therefore, they decided that they would go in anyway and possess the land, as was originally planned. Mosheh warned them not to because YAH's decision was final. They didn't heed Mosheh's warning, and as a result, they were soundly defeated, and all of those who had spied out the land, except for Caleb and Joshua (Yoshua), died in the process.

This has been a lesson that the entire House of YisraEL has had a difficult time in learning. We dare not start something that we on our own have decided is what ELohim wants us to do and then ask Him to bless our mess. Instead, we must always seek His plan, His way, His method, and not our own, or as the Scriptures say, we must work out our salvation with fear and trembling. If we are not sure that the direction we are going is His plan, then we should stop and wait upon Him. Test the plan first, and then throw out what is not working. *"Test all things; hold fast what is good....Abstain from every form of evil"* (I THES 5:21&22). To assure your success, you can't be a novice in the things of ELohim. *"For everyone who partakes only of milk is unskilled in the word of righteousness, for he is a babe...But solid food belongs to those who are of full age; that is, those who by reason of use have their senses exercised to discern both good and evil"* (HEB 5:13&14). So learn through experience to use the word of the Father properly and learn to be patient. If you do, He will provide your needs according to His riches in glory through HaMashiach (the Messiah), Yeshua (Jesus).

Forty Years of Bickering

Sometime during the forty years of wandering in the wilderness, a Levi (Lehvee) by the name of Korah, along with two hundred and fifty rebels from the other tribes, questioned whether Mosheh and his brother, Aaron (Aharon), were the only two who had the anointing of leadership. Mosheh reminded them that YAHveh Himself had blessed the tribe of Levi (Lehvee) with the honor of being the only tribe chosen out of all of the tribes to minister to Him and that Aaron (Aharon) and his sons were chosen to be His priests. They argued that they were not satisfied with his answer, so Mosheh told them to appear at the door of the Tabernacle (Mishkahn) the next day with censers of fire. When they did, the Earth opened up and swallowed Korah and his family. After that, YAH sent fire down and consumed the other two hundred and fifty. Then, if that weren't enough, the multitude blamed Mosheh and Aaron (Aharon) for the death of the rebels. YAHveh responded to that with a plague that killed fourteen thousand and seven hundred more. Mosheh and Aaron (Aharon) once again intervened in order to stave off YAH's wrath against His people. Finally, YAHveh called Mosheh to settle this spirit of rebellion once and for all. He had Mosheh call for all of the princes of each tribe to assemble before the Tabernacle (Mishkahn). They were to bring with them their rods, or walking staffs, that had their names engraved upon them. Mosheh placed all twelve rods inside of the Tabernacle (Mishkahn). The next morning, he went in and found that the rod with Aaron's (Aharon's) name on it had budded with leaves, almond blossoms, and fruit. This brought great fear upon the people of YisraEL, and Aaron's (Aharon's) priesthood was absolutely confirmed. Aaron's (Aharon's) rod was then placed in the Ark of the Testimony as a witness and a sign not to rebel against YAH's anointed.

It was at this time that YAH established the tithe for the Levi (Lehvee). A tithe from the entire congregation (kahal) of YisraEL was to be given to the Levi (Lehvee) for their livelihood and for servicing and maintaining the Tabernacle (Mishkahn), as well as for ministering to YAHveh on behalf of the Kahal. At the same time, all other offerings, including the Levi's (Lehvee's), were to go to the priesthood because neither the priests nor the Levi (Lehvee) were to receive any land for an inheritance—their inheritance was the privilege to serve YAHveh. Today, the House of YisraEL and its priesthood are one and the same. There is no Tabernacle (Mishkahn) or House of YAH to maintain, so the offering and ***not the tithe*** is to be used for the growth and maintenance of the Kahal of Yeshua. Church buildings, synagogues, and temples are not Houses of YAH. He never ordained their use—men have ordained them.

The Last Days of the Forty-Year Wandering

Near the end of the forty years in the wilderness, YAH began to bring about His final judgments upon those who challenged His Torah. This included Miriam (Meeryahm), Mosheh's sister, for her part in the golden-calf incident and for exalting herself above her brother by questioning his authority. She died before entering the Promised Land, and YisraEL mourned her passing.

After the forty years had passed, nearly all of those who had been a part of the original exodus had either died off or had been killed, and only their children were left. Few of them had any recollection of the original miracles and manifestations of YAHveh. But the spirit of their fathers had not yet been fully extracted from their midst because when water became scarce, they too resorted to murmuring and complaining. Mosheh found himself consulting YAHveh again, wondering what he should do to provide for their needs this time. He was instructed to glorify YAH and His ability to meet His people's needs by taking them to the rock where YAH had originally provided the Children of YisraEL with water. This time, he was to bring forth the necessary water by speaking to it. But when Mosheh and Aaron (Aharon) had gathered the people at the rock, in his anger toward them for their constant complaining, he struck it instead—it still gave forth its water supply. But because he reacted to his own fleshly anger toward the people, Mosheh took away the impact of the importance of ELohim's ability to meet His people's needs with just His words.

Shortly after this, the Kahal of YisraEL approached the land of Edom, where the descendants of Esau lived. They requested permission to cross, but their request was denied. Instead, the Edomi came out to do battle with this new, young YisraEL. YAH told them not to respond to the challenge, but to retreat instead and that He would show them a different passage into the land.

Now came the time for YAH to carry out His judgment upon His chosen leadership. YAH was already angry with Aaron (Aharon) because of his display of weakness in fearing men more than he feared Him in both the golden-calf incident and in agreeing with his sister's challenge of Mosheh's authority. Adding to this, he was also a participant with Mosheh in robbing ELohim of His glory at the rock, so he was sentenced to die on Mount Hor. Mosheh too was deprived of being allowed to enter the land that was promised to YisraEL because of his disobedience there. Soon the time came for Mosheh, Aaron (Aharon), and his son, Eleazer, to go up Mt. Hor to exchange the headship of the priesthood. The exchange involved the putting on of the robe, the turban, and the ephod of the high priest by Eleazer. When they returned, Mosheh and Eleazer were carrying Aaron's (Aharon's) remains, and the Children of YisraEL cried and mourned for thirty days.

Finally, after forty years in the wilderness, the Kahal of YisraEL had gotten most of Mitsrahyim out of them. They no longer had a slave mentality—now they had one of freedom. At the same time, this relatively young YisraEL had little or no experience in war. That soon changed when a king of the Canaanite (Canaani), Arad, felt threatened by their presence. After seeing them back down from a confrontation with Edom, he was confident that they would be no match for his army either and that they would flee again. But this time, YAH told them to stand and fight because He would give them victory. Arad's army was crushed, and YisraEL burned their cities; they had obtained their first military victory over the Canaanites (Canaani). After that battle, they asked permission to cross through the land of the Amori on their way to Canaan. King Sihon refused to let them pass, so YAH told them to crush them, and they did. Then King Og of the Bashanite (Bashani) came out against them because they appeared to be a threat to him. They too were defeated with YAHveh's blessing. It was about this time in YisraEL's history that Mosheh began recording their travels in what we call the book of Numbers.

Balaam, an Unworthy Prophet of YAHveh

YisraEL was about to gain more experience in warfare as Balak, the king of Moab, saw them approaching his land. King Balak had received reports about these people known as YisraEL and the power of their ELohim. He didn't want a confrontation with them, so he called upon the elders of Midian to consult their prophet, Balaam, about placing a curse upon them. The land of Moab and the land of Midian shared the same border. These two kingdoms also shared the same basic religious and political views. If you remember, Mosheh's father-in-law, Jethro (Yethro), was a Midianite (Midiani) priest. Some of the Midiani apparently recognized YAHveh as being the one true living ELohim over all of creation because of the things both Jethro (Yethro) and Balaam had said about Him. They were also descendants of Avraham through his second wife, Keturah, who knew YAHveh as ELohim. Balaam practiced both divination and the worship of YAHveh (a mixing of religions, not unlike some of the western religions of today).

After Balaam sought YAH's counsel on this matter and was told not to go, he informed Balak's messengers of YAH's answer. Balak asked him again, but this time he sent some princes from both Moab and Midian with an offer of wealth and power if he would do it. Apparently Balaam thought that YAH would change His mind now that there was money involved because he went to Him a second time. YAHveh knew Balaam's heart, so He decided to use this situation to bring both His Name and the name of His Children, YisraEL, respect and honor among the nations. YAH told Balaam that he could go this time, but that he must only speak the words that He would give to him. On his journey to Moab, Balaam's donkey began to behave strangely. Unaware that the Angel of YAH had appeared to his donkey and had blocked its path, Balaam struck her twice with his hand for balking. When this phenomenon occurred a third time, he struck her with his rod, and to Balaam's surprise, she spoke to him and rebuked him for his treatment of her. Then Balaam's eyes were opened and he saw the Angel for himself. Balaam sought forgiveness and repented of his perverse heart for wanting the personal gain that had been promised him by Balak. He vowed to speak only the words that YAHveh gave to him for Balak, no matter what.

So instead of cursing YisraEL, Balaam blessed them, and Balak rebuked him for it—this occurred three times. Then Balaam blessed YisraEL with a fourth prophecy saying that they would defeat all of their enemies and that their ELohim would establish an "Eternal Kingdom" for His "King of the Universe" who would someday come through them. He also prophesied the inevitable destruction of Moab. Balak left in frustration still unconvinced, but he would later return to try again.

Balak and Balaam Try a Second Scheme to Destroy YisraEL

YisraEL had not heard the last from Moab and Midian. King Balak hadn't given up on destroying YisraEL, so he returned to Balaam looking for a new scheme. Balaam suggested that they should try to corrupt them from within by sending in their women to seduce the men of YisraEL into marriage. The women of Moab and Midian were worshipers of Baal of Peor, a fertility god (eluah). Their form of worship to Baal included prostitution, infant sacrifice, and all types of perverse sexuality. As the men began submitting to their seduction and began listening to them about their pagan practices, they started to join with them in those practices, causing them to turn away from their faith in YAH and His Torah. When YAHveh saw this, He gave Mosheh the order to have all of the men who were involved in these practices gathered up and executed. At the same time, a sudden plague (perhaps gonorrhea) broke out among all of the tribes of YisraEL, and when a member of the tribe of Simeon (Seemehon) wanted to marry a Midiani woman, Phinehas, the son of Eleazer, killed them both. The plague then stopped, but not before twenty-four-thousand YisraELi had died from the disease. After that, YAHveh gave Mosheh orders to have YisraEL attack the Midiani for their horrendous tactics. YisraEL responded with obedience and annihilated the Midiani in that area, including their five kings and their prophet Balaam.

Some may question whether Balaam was a prophet or just a soothsayer. To answer this, we need to go to the Scriptures to see what it says on the subject. We find these words pertaining to prophets in the TaNaKh: *"When a prophet speaks in the Name of YAHveh, if the thing does not happen or come to pass, that is the thing which YAHveh has not spoken; the prophet has spoken it presumptuously; you shall not be afraid of him"* (**DEUT 18:22**). *"Formerly in YisraEL, when man went to inquire of ELohim, he spoke thus: "Come, let us go to the seer"; for he who is now called a prophet was formerly called a seer"* (**I SAM 9:9**). *"And I have seen folly in the prophets of Samaria: They prophesied by Baal and caused My people YisraEL to err"…"They continually say to those who despise Me, "YAHveh has said, "You shall have shalom"'; and to everyone who walks according to the imagination of his own heart, no evil shall come upon you"'* (**JER 23:13 & 17**). In the Renewed Covenant (Brit Chadashah), we find this: *"But the manifestation of the Ruach is given to each one for the profit of all:"…"But one and the same Ruach works all these things, distributing to each one individually as He wills"* (**I COR 12:7 & 11**). Some may disagree with my conclusion, but I believe that the Ruach of YAH gives these gifts to many different individuals while they are still in their mother's womb. When that individual discovers that he or she has this gift, it is left up to them to choose how they will use it. They can use it for their own gain, turn it over to the Prince of Darkness, or if they come to know YAHveh through His Son, Yeshua, they can use it to profit all who are within the body of Yeshua. Today, these gifts have many different names: clairvoyance, mental telepathy, fortune telling, faith healing, etc. I have seen the Church demand that when an individual possesses one of these gifts and becomes a born-again believer, they renounce the gift and then promise never to use it again. If I am correct in my observation, then the enemy of YAH has won another victory in keeping the Kahal of Messiah crippled. I don't believe that hasatan has the power to give any gift to anyone. The servants of hasatan do have the ability to call upon the powers of darkness to perform counterfeit miracles to make it appear as though they possess supernatural gifts. But we need to remember that *"Every good gift and every perfect gift is from above, and comes down from the Abba of lights, with whom there is no variation or shadow of turning"* (**JAM 1:17**). It is up to us to choose how we use them—either for or against the kingdom of YAH, or for our own personal gain. We have the free will to make that decision.

The Final Census and the Exchange of Leadership

After the plague, YAHveh called for the final census of YisraEL to be taken. Again, it was to determine the number of available men of fighting age who could make up YisraEL's army because they were going to have to fight for the land that had been promised to them. YAHveh told them to dispossess the inhabitants because they had defiled the land with their detestable practices. He also knew that the only way YisraEL would feel that it was their land was to fight for it. The census revealed that YisraEL's fighting force had diminished by about eighteen hundred. Mosheh knew that he would not be the one to lead them into the land of promise, so he asked YAHveh whom He had chosen to succeed him. YAH told him that Joshua (Yoshua) from the tribe of Ephraim (Efraeem) would be his successor.

After Mosheh had laid his hands upon Joshua (Yoshua) to commission him to the immense task of being YisraEL's overseer, the heads of the tribes of Rueben, Gad (Gahd), and half of the tribe of Manasseh (Mahnahseh) approached him. They had come to request that the land on the east side of the Jordan (Yarden) River be given to them as their possession. At first, Mosheh thought that they were tempting YAH, just as their fathers had done forty years earlier, and that they were showing their cowardliness. They reassured him that this was not the case. They agreed to cross over the river and help their brothers conquer the Promised Land before returning to their families on the east side of the river.

These two-and-one-half tribes displayed the first sign of a desire to be independent of the others. The land of Canaan was the Promised Land, but they desired the land east of the Jordan (Yarden) River. Remember, it was Rueben who showed his independence and his lack of fear of losing his right to the double portion that was due the firstborn by defiling his father's bed. Here, he is displaying his unwillingness to be a part of the promise to his ancestral fathers. Gad (pronounced God or Gahd), on the other hand, had always shown his aggressive attitude and independence by living up to his name, "troop". And Manasseh (Mahnahseh) was not only willing to separate himself from the rest of YisraEL, but was also willing to be separated from the rest of his own tribe by insisting on having land on the Jordan's (Yarden's) east side.

YAHveh directed Mosheh on how the territories of the new land were to be allotted. He told him that the land was to be divided into twelve parts; the size of each part would be determined by the population of each individual tribe. The drawing, or casting of lots, would determine the boundaries of each allotment. YAH used the casting of lots many times as the means by which YisraEL would make her decisions; He also used the Urim and the Thummin to show His will to them. Today, we do not have the Urim and Thummin to use in order to make decisions regarding spiritual matters or to help us determine YAH's will for or lives. But the casting of lots could still be used, and it certainly would be biblical. Maybe the members of Yeshua's Body ought to consider using it again.

Mosheh Reviews the Torah Before YisraEL

Now we will take a look at the events surrounding the writing of the fifth book, the book of Deuteronomy, which means "a second law", "a second look at", or "a review of the law" in Greek. Mosheh began to review the instructions, as well as the events that YisraEL had experienced over the past forty years of their short existence as a nation. He admonished them to never add to or take anything away from YAH's instructions (**DEUT 4:2 & 12:31**). He reminded them of the horrific evil and threat to their continued existence if they followed any form of idolatry. He reminded them that they were a chosen nation—YAH chose *them*, they didn't choose *Him*. He also reminded them that YAH had given them covenants to insure His plan for them and that it was He who gave them His Torah face to face on the mountain—it did not originate from the imaginations of men. We see these same instructions in the Renewed Covenant (Brit Chadashah). *"Knowing this first, that no prophecy of Scripture is of any private interpretation,...for prophecy never came by the will of man, but men spoke from ELuah as they were moved by the Ruach HaKedosh"* (**II PET 1:20&21**). *"All scripture is given by inspiration of Eluah* (God), *and is profitable for doctrine, for reproof, for correction, for instruction in righteousness,...that the man of ELuah may be equipped for every good work"* (**II TIM 3:16&17**).

It was here in **DEUT 6:4&5** that the YisraELi creed was introduced. (Yeshua called it "the greatest commandment" of them all.) *"Hear, O YisraEL: YAHveh our ELohim, YAHveh is Echad* (One)*!" You shall love YAHveh your ELohim with all your heart, with all your soul, and with all your might"*. In other words, love Him with your whole triune being—the image that you were originally created in. He continued by instructing them that they were to diligently teach YAH's instructions to their children and to their children's children. This is where the term "bar (son) mitzvoth (commandments)" or "bat (daughter) mitzvoth" comes from. It literally means "the son or daughter of the commandments." He reminded them that if they did this, they would perpetually possess the land as their inheritance. He also reminded them not to test YAHveh by disobeying His Torah. As long as they continued in His Torah, He would continue to bless them; if they began to abuse His Torah, He would vomit them out of the land, just as He did the previous inhabitants. He warned them not to become proud of their inheritance because they hadn't earned it—it was a gift to them because of YAH's promises to their fathers. It was also during this time that Mosheh once again reviewed the Ten Commandments with the Children of YisraEL.

We too will now take a closer look at YAH's Ten Commandments in conjunction with many of His other 613 that are found in the texts of His books of Leviticus, Numbers, and Deuteronomy. The first four of these commandments pertain directly to their fear and love for their ELohim. They were not to seek or serve any other elohim in any way, form, or fashion. Nor were they to fashion any image as a substitute for His presence, or the image of any elohim of the nations around them, or an image of anything that He had created. They were not to speak of Him or use His name in any way except with the utmost respect. And they were to honor the one day of the week that He had designated to be set apart from the rest of their workweek.

Service to Another ELuah

Let's begin with the first commandment where YAH says unequivocally that He is a jealous ELohim and will have no other elohim before Him. Remember, the Hebrew word for God, or god, is "el" and means the "mighty one" and that "elohim" is simply the plural form of "el". Any being, supernatural or natural, or thing that can take possession or precedence over our lives ahead of YAHveh can be considered an "el". That includes our careers, our hobbies, our talents, our intellect, our religion, our denominational traditions, or even our families. Whatever we put first in our lives and whatever occupies our thoughts and our plans over everything else will manifest itself as the "el" of our lives if we allow it to. The first priority in our life should be YAHveh, then our family, and then everything else after that. Even Yeshua said, *"He who loves father or mother more than Me is not worthy of Me. And he who loves son or daughter more than Me is not worthy of Me"* (**MATT 10:37**).

Well then, how do we follow and serve Him? He tells us we are to be like Him in justice. *"YAHveh stands in the kahal of the mighty; He judges among the elohim;...How long will you judge unjustly, and show partiality to the wicked?... Selah (which means "pause" and "ponder")...Defend the poor and fatherless; do justice to the afflicted and needy...Deliver the poor and needy; free them from the hand of the wicked...They do not know, nor do they understand; they walk in darkness; all the foundations of the earth are unstable...I said, you are elohim, and all of you are children of the Most High...But you shall die like men, and fall like one of the princes'"* (**PSALM 82:1-7**).

YAHveh warned YisraEL over and over again not to mix their worship of Him with the worship of the elohim of the nations around them. If they did, He knew it would eventually result in their serving them. What or who were the elohim that He referred to? They were the evil and malignant mighty ones that the KJV translation calls "devils" and the other translations call "demons". The word "demon" is a derivative of the Greek word *"daimonion"* and means "an evil deity or god". YAHveh forbids His people to have anything to do with these elohim who manifest themselves through diviners, sorcerers, omen interpreters, witches, spell-casters, mediums, spiritists, familiar spirits, or astrologers. Notice that He doesn't refute their existence, but, instead, forbids their practice. All of these are those who have submitted themselves to the evil side of the supernatural. He condemns to death those who are involved in such practices for these are not small things to Him. He also warns of the false prophets who speak in His name when He has not sent them—they too will meet the same fate. Of course there are the tricksters, the hucksters, and those who practice the sleight of hand to deceive naive and gullible people, but these are not they to whom He is referring. As I have mentioned before, YAH, through His Ruach, distributes these gifts to whomever He chooses—it is up to us to choose how we'll use them (or abuse them).

But the question still remains—where do these devils, elohim, or demons come from? There are basically two schools of thought regarding this, neither of which I concur with. The first one is that they are the fallen angels that were thrown out of heaven when they sided with Lucifer in his rebellion against YAH. But as I have already explained in Chapter One, they couldn't be because in **JUDE: 6** it says that they were being kept in chains in reserve until the "great day", or "judgment day". The second theory is that there was a pre-Adamic (Ahdomic) race that had been judged as wicked and had also been punished with a flood. This race of people were suppose to have been thrown into the pit, and from there, they became hasatan's (Satan's) obliging servants. This theory has one main flaw and that is that death did not come until after the fall of Ahdom. Therefore, a pre-Adamic (Ahdomic) race couldn't have experienced death. I don't believe that it is necessary to go to the extreme regarding the existence of a pre-Adamic race in order to come up with the answer to demons or devils. Scripture tells us that the pit (deep pit or abyss), also known as "the grave", is identified as the place that demons or devils could enter and exit from. *"YAHveh kills and makes alive; He brings down to the grave and brings up"* (**I SAM 2:6**). *"O YAH, You have brought my soul up from the grave; You have kept me alive, that I should not go down to the pit"* (**PS 30:3**). *"To You I will cry, O YAH my Rock: Do not be silent to me, I become like those who go down to the pit"* (**PS 28:1**). *"Let burning coals fall upon them; let them be cast into the fire, into the deep pits, that they rise not up again"* (**PS 140:10**). *"For He had commanded the unclean spirit to come out of the man. For it had often seized him, and he was kept under guard, bound with chains and shackles; and he broke the bonds and was driven by demons into the wilderness....Yeshua asked him, saying, "What is your name?" And he said, "Legion," because many demons had entered him...And they begged Him that He would not command them to go out into the abyss"* (**LUKE 8:29-31**). *"Then the fifth angel sounded: And I saw a star fallen from heaven to the earth. And to him was given the key to the bottomless pit...And he opened the bottomless pit, and smoke arose out of the pit like the smoke of a great furnace. And the sun and the air were darkened because of the smoke of the pit...Then out of the smoke locusts came upon the earth. And to them was given power, as the scorpions of the earth have power."..."And they had as king over them the angel of the bottomless pit, whose name in Hebrew is Abaddon* (Destruction), *but in Greek he has the name Apollyon* (Destroyer or Satan)" (**REV 9:1-3, 11**). Couldn't those on Earth who have been wicked and have rebelled against YAHveh and have been sentenced to the pit until the judgment give themselves over to the Prince of Darkness for his bidding? Wouldn't they want to do anything to escape the pit, or abyss, rather than stay in that torment? *"There was a certain rich man who was clothed in purple and fine linen and fared sumptuously every day.*

"But there was a certain beggar named Lazarus, full of sores, who was laid at his gate,...desiring to be fed with the crumbs which fell from the rich man's table. Moreover the dogs came and licked his sores..."So it was that the beggar died, and was carried by the angels to Avraham's bosom. The rich man died and was buried. "And being in torments in Hades, he lifted up his eyes and saw Avraham afar off, and Lazarus in his bosom..."Then he cried and said, 'Father Avraham, have mercy on me, and send Lazarus that he may dip the tip of his finger in water and cool my tongue; for I am tormented in this flame.'...But Avraham said, 'Son, remember that in your lifetime you received your good things, and likewise Lazarus evil things; but now he is comforted and you are tormented....'And besides all this, between us and you there is a great gulf fixed, so that those who want to pass from here to you cannot, nor can those from there pass to us'" (LUKE 16:19-26). However, there seems to be no restrictions mentioned here about returning to the Earth and walking as a disembodied evil spirit, tempting or coercing the living in order to enter a willing vessel. Could this be? One more possibility: has the Prince of Darkness had the freedom to recruit other angelic beings to become his principalities, powers, or demons since the fall? Don't know—nothing said!

Graven Images

In the second of the Ten Commandments, YAHveh specifically commands "no graven images". He forbids sacred pillars that are carved from either stone or wood. The only pillars that He accepted were those set up to mark boundaries or memorials to Him and were to be erected only with stones that were not cut with a tool—they had to be natural. These later became places where cities were built. Throughout YisraEL's history, YAH tells them not to build high places for themselves (Babel was a high place). He instructed them to tear down any high place that they might find in the land that they were about to occupy. They were forbidden to copy any of the pagan religions and were not to sacrifice to Molech. (Remember, Molech was the name that the Chaldeans gave Nimrod after his death.) They were not to plant or cut down any tree for the purpose of making a wooden pillar that would later be dedicated to Asherah (Ashtoreth), which is another name for Nimrod's wife, Ishtar. (Ishtar was also called "the queen of heaven" and was worshipped as a fertility goddess. She surrounded herself with all types of symbols of fertility, such as eggs and hares, or rabbits. The eggs were usually dipped in red dye to represent the blood of sacrificed infants. It was her coronation that was celebrated as the day of Ishtar, or Easter, which is the English equivalent of her name.) These wooden pillars were an abomination to YAH because they represented the male genital organ. These pillars or their equivalent are still being found today in many archeological digs. Asherah poles have evolved over the years and are still seen today in many different forms, such as the towers at the mosques in the Muslim nations where the call for daily prayer is sounded. Unfortunately, they can also be found today in many contemporary architectural forms, such as the obelisks for the Masonic Order, in the courtyard at the Vatican, the Washington Monument in Washington, D.C., and even on the Christian cathedrals, or what we refer to as steeples. These have been innocently introduced into our culture out of ignorance, but are still no more acceptable in YAHveh's sight now than they were at the time of Mosheh. This is why it behooves us to keep seeking His understanding and not to remain ignorant. *"My people are destroyed for lack of knowledge. Because you have rejected knowledge, I will also reject you from being priest for Me; because you have forgotten the Torah of your ELohim, I will also forget your children"* (**HOSEA 4:6**).

Man for some reason does not seem to be able to resist the temptation of bowing down to ***things***. We just can't, or won't, ignore the traditions that our fathers began or followed—we continue to participate in their sins. Some brothers and sisters still pray to statues of Yeshua, His mother, angels, or images of saints. We build expensive buildings and pour tons of money into their maintenance in the belief that this is what the Father wants. We keep trying to please Him with the works of our hands. We need to repent from this foolishness and return to our first love, the works of Torah. *"Nevertheless I have this against you, that you have left your first love..."Remember therefore from where you have fallen; repent and do the first works, or else I will come to you quickly and remove your lampstand from its place—unless you repent,"* (**REV 2:4&5**). We need to learn how to worship Him in spirit and in the truth of the Torah.

YAHveh was very explicit about where He was to be worshiped. Man never had the privilege to pick or choose where it would be. YAH's first choice was a portable dwelling place, the Tabernacle (Mishkahn). After that, when His servant, King David (Dahveed), insisted, He gave His permission for His first permanent house to be built in Jerusalem (YAHrushalayim). YAH never wanted a temple (palace or public building) to be built for Him—temples were the places where pagan elohim were worshiped. He, like us, dwelt in a tent or a house. The word used in the Scriptures that is translated as "temple" is "Behyeit" or "Beth" in Hebrew and actually means "house". After YAHveh's Ruach left His House in Jerusalem (YAHrushalayim), it never returned. *"Then the glory of YAHveh went up from the cherub, and paused over the threshold of the **behyeit**; and the **behyeit** was filled with the cloud, and the court was full of the brightness of YAHveh's glory"..."Then the glory of YAHveh departed from the threshold of the **behyeit** and stood over the cherubim"* (**EZEK 10:4&18**). So, when Zerubbabel rebuilt YAH's House, or ***Behyeit***, His Ruach never dwelt there. It did, however, become a temple, or palace, where just some of the "symbols", or articles, of YAHveh were displayed. Today, if you have repented from your sinful, fleshly ways and you receive YAH's only begotten Son, Yeshua, into your heart as the Adonai of your life, then YAH's Ruach will come and dwell in you as His *Behyeit*.

The Test of a True Prophet

The Scriptures address the subject of false prophets from two perspectives that are both found in Deuteronomy. The first is a prophet that performs signs and wonders in order to seduce others into following after another elohim. The other is one who speaks presumptuously out of his own imagination and does not truly represent YAHveh. He is to be tested as to whether or not the thing that he has spoken comes to pass. If not, then those hearing him should not be afraid of his words and should not listen to him any further. Both false prophets are to face the same fate, which is death—the first because he has misused his gift and the second because he was speaking presumptuously.

The ministry of a prophet needs to be explained a little more thoroughly. A prophet of YAH has the responsibility to give His people inspired instructions through prophesying. A prophet may prophesy in three different ways. The first is "foretelling", or seeing into the future. Here, YAHveh will give His prophet a revelation, either through a vision or a dream, in order to show him a future event that will take place. The second is called "forth telling", which means to proclaim YAH's words or instructions in such a way that their meaning is brought into full light and understanding. The third is speaking His words in an "ecstatic manner". An example of this is found in **NUM 11:25** when the Ruach of YAH came upon Aaron (Aharon) and the seventy elders. Another example can be found in I Samuel, chapter ten, where King Saul (Shaul) joined up with the prophets near Gilgal and prophesied with them there. This third form, when used in the Kahal, is to be followed by an interpretation. In modern times, this "ecstatic manner" is known as "glossolalia", or "speaking in tongues". It is the same phenomenon that was heard at the Feast of Pentecost (or in Hebrew, Chag Shavuot), in the book of Acts. The Apostle Paul (Rav Shaul) tells believers to pray for the interpretation of tongues in order to edify others (I COR 14:5). Many mistake this instruction as referring to a direct translation. But interpretation means to interpret the meaning of the message—not to translate it word for word. Those who try to discredit this phenomenon say that glossolalia is just gibberish and that it is not an authentic language, but who can truly say whether a language is authentic or not. The Apostle Paul (Rav Shaul) speaks about the "language of angels". And then there are those languages that have been lost for centuries. What if the utterance was a combination of all languages—known and unknown? And what if the miracle was found in the hearing and not just in the utterance? Who can really say how this phenomenon actually works? But we do know that the release of one's tongue to be used for edification by the Ruach is just one of many works of faith that the Apostle James (Jacob/Yaacov) exhorts all believers to exercise (**JAM 2:17**).

Expressing Our Love for YAHveh Through His Provisions

Mosheh continues, at the direction of YAH, to warn the House of YisraEL not to use His name in blasphemous ways. He is the one true living ELohim above all others, and His Name is to be used with all love and compassion when referring to Him. He instructs them that as soon as they come into the land of their inheritance, they are to come up to the places where He chooses to be worshiped. He commands that the first of everything, whether animal, crop, or offspring, belongs to Him and is to be dedicated to Him. The firstborn of children or animals must be dedicated on the eighth day after their birth. A tenth (or tithe) of all produce is to be brought before Him each year at the place and time that He designates. It is to be taken from all of their grain, new wine, oil, and the firstborn of their flocks and herds. It is to be brought to the Tabernacle (Mishkahn) of Meeting, at the place He has designated, and there it is to be eaten in celebration before Him. He instructed them that if it is too great of a distance to travel due to the quantity of all of their tithes making it difficult for them to attend, then they are to sell their tithes for money and bring that to the Tabernacle (Mishkahn) of Meeting instead. There, they are to use it to buy anything that they want in order to celebrate the Feast of YAH. But, He also instructs them to use the tithe of their produce every third year to feed the Levi (Lehvee), the stranger, the orphan, and the widow in their own towns.

So, the tithe, or one tenth of our production, is to be used by us for celebrating what YAH has done for us. It is also to be used to feed those among us who are our fellow believers in YAHveh and are less fortunate than we are. "Tithing", as it is taught today, isn't a freewill offering—it has become a demand that we bring a tenth of our income to our man-made palaces for the purpose of their maintenance, as well as for providing the wages of those who continue to teach us in error. I don't mean to come down too harshly on the organized church or the many denominations that have evolved from it. However, haven't we in many cases lost sight of the Father's true meaning of worship? Haven't we let the political structuring of the organized denominations become more important to us than the actual inspiration of His presence? As I understand the Scriptures, we are called to bring freewill offerings—**_NOT TITHES_**—to be used to maintain the material necessities for those who are placed over us as our spiritual overseers and to meet the needs of those among us as they arise, offering them always with a cheerful heart. In that way, those of us who have had the works of our hands blessed by YAH can in turn bless and benefit others so that we may all rejoice together. We limit YAH when we limit our offerings to just tithes—He wants to bless us with abundance. Remember to always give according to the need.

Honoring YAH by Celebrating the Sabbath

Our Abba (Father or Daddy) *commands* us to rest on the Sabbath—He doesn't *just suggest* it. He wants us to keep it holy (kedosh) to help remind us that He is the Creator of all things visible and invisible and that He created everything in six days and rested on the seventh. (I have already shared with you what I believe took place regarding the length of days in the first chapter of this book.) We are also told that on the seventh day, we are to worship Him and keep it holy (kedosh). We call the seventh day Saturday, which is a Roman name that comes from the Roman pagan el, Saturn (Saturn's Day). In Hebrew, it is simply called the "seventh day" ("yom shabeeyee"). YisraEL is to corporately observe Sabbath on every seventh day after six days of working. They are to do no ordinary work, including even lighting a fire—because fire symbolizes the work of His Ruach. The seventh day is the seventh day and not the first day of the week. Nowhere in the Scriptures are we instructed, either by Yeshua or by any of His apostles (shelichim), to change the seventh day to the first. The organized church claims that they celebrate the first day of the week as the "Lord's Day" because Yeshua's resurrection took place on the first day of the week. That still does not make it the Sabbath. If they want to commemorate Yeshua's resurrection, they should do it right and celebrate it only one day of the year—the first day after the weekly Sabbath following Passover. This day is scripturally called the Feast of Firstfruits, and Yeshua fulfilled it when He rose from the dead. The organized church celebrates a day called "Easter" for this event. But in all actuality, "Easter" is an altogether different animal. (I have mentioned this earlier, and I will describe it in more detail later in Chapter Twenty-Seven.) More times than not, these two days do coincide by falling on the same day. But remember, we don't have the authority to change the feast days.

At the same time, YAHveh, in His wisdom, says, *"Remember the Sabbath day* (a Shabbat/resting day) *to keep it holy (kedosh). Six days you shall labor and do all your work"* (**EXOD 20:8&9**). Because YAH states it this way, it could also mean that those who find that they have to work on the seventh day of each week because of the demands of their employer, or just the nature of their vocation, and have no choice in the matter, they could still take the day after they have completed six days of work, honor that as their Sabbath, and still be scripturally correct—YAH is still the "ELohim of Grace".

The Sabbath is also a sign of His covenant with His chosen people, YisraEL. Just as the wedding ring is a sign of our covenant in marriage to our spouse, the Sabbath is the sign of our covenant in marriage with Yeshua, our bridegroom.

Along with the weekly Sabbaths, the House of YisraEL was commanded to keep the Sabbaths of His appointed feasts. YisraEL's failure to keep either the Sabbath years or the Jubilee years caused YAHveh to eventually dispossess them from the land that He had promised Avraham, Yitzyak, and Yaacov. And it was idolatry worship that brought them to the point of despising all of His Sabbaths. Let me again emphasize that idol worship is not necessarily limited to only graven images. As I have said before, there are also idols of the heart. Remember, an idol is anything that takes the place of YAHveh as our source and reason for being—that includes vocations, hobbies, wealth, physicians, medicine, science, or even families. When not put in their proper perspective or priority in our lives, they can become idols. I cannot repeat this enough.

Besides Sabbaths, YAH also commanded that YisraEL observe the New Moons. In the previous chapter, I named the twelve Hebrew months of the year, starting with the month of Nisan, or Abib/Aviv. The first day of each month was determined by the observation of the sliver of the new moon that appeared on the horizon at sunset and was referred to as Rosh Kadesh, the head of the month, or the new month. (This word should not be confused with the word kedosh/kadosh, which means Holy.) When the sliver was spotted, the witness would sound the shofar (ram's horn) to announce its appearing. Because the time of the appearing of this New Moon was never certain, it became known as the "day and hour that no man knows". This gives us a little insight as to what Yeshua meant when He said, *"But of that day and hour no one knows, neither the angels in heaven, nor the Son, but only the Father"* (**MARK 13:32**). The first day of the seventh month is also such a day. It is known as Yom Teruah (the Day of the Trumpets).

Honoring Him Through His Appointed Times (Moedim), the Annual Feasts

In the third book of the Torah, Leviticus, YAHveh told the Children of YisraEL what they should do after they entered the Promised Land. They were to come up three times a year to the place that He would show them in order to celebrate His Feasts. These were His appointed times (moedim). They were to do this throughout their generations because He intended for these annual celebrations to be continued forever in this land that He said belonged to Him. The first annual pilgrimage was for the purpose of celebrating their first barley harvest (Abib/Aviv), the second for celebrating their first wheat harvest (Shavuot), and the third for celebrating the final ingathering of all their harvest (Sukkot). The first two annual celebrations took place in the spring and the third in the fall.

The first appointed time (moedim) was the barley harvest. The barley-harvest celebration consisted of eight days of feasting. Within those eight days were two Feast Sabbaths and one weekly Sabbath. The first day was a Feast Day known as Passover (death of the firstborn) or Pesach (feast of the lamb). It was followed by seven days of feasting known as the Feast of Unleavened Bread (Chag HaMatzot). (These first two Feasts were explained more thoroughly in Chapter Two.) The first and the seventh day of Unleavened Bread were to be Feast Sabbaths. Remember, a Sabbath, regardless if it is a weekly or a Feast Sabbath, is a resting day when no ordinary work or merchandizing is to take place. However, a Feast Day is only a day of celebration – it is up to the individual whether he works or not. In order to recognize the actual harvest of the barley, there was within these seven days another Feast Day called the Feast of Firstfruits (according to the Scriptures, this was to be the day after the weekly Sabbath).

After celebrating the barley harvest, the Children of YisraEL were to count off seven more weekly Sabbaths. On the day after the seventh weekly Sabbath, a total of fifty days, they were to return to the designated place for His second annual celebration. They were to continue their celebration of harvest with the wheat harvest, called the Feast of Shavuot (a Hebrew word meaning Sevens or Weeks) or Pentecost (a Greek word meaning fifty). Within this celebration was another Feast Day that would also be a Feast Sabbath, and it would follow the seventh weekly Sabbath. Because of these fifty days, this feast would take place in their third month of Sivan.

Now, over the centuries, a controversy has arisen as to which Sabbath was to be used to determine the Feast of Shavuot. Was it the first Feast Sabbath, which was the first day of the Feast of Unleavened Bread (Chag HaMatzot), or was it the weekly Sabbath (Saturday) within the seven days of Unleavened Bread? I believe that it was the weekly Sabbath, taking into consideration the fact that the Scriptures say so, but also that Yeshua appeared to His disciples (talmidim), after coming out of the tomb, on the first day of the week (Sunday). This also tells us that the Feast of Firstfruits had to fall on the first day of the week, the day after the weekly Sabbath, because He had to fulfill all of the Feasts in order to be the Promised Messiah.

Others who count the first Feast Sabbath (the first day of the Feast of Unleavened Bread/Chag HaMatzot, the fifteenth of Aviv) as the Sabbath to be used, say that the Feast of Firstfruits would have been the next day, the sixteenth of Aviv, which could make the Feast of Firstfruits fall on any given weekday or on a weekly Sabbath (Saturday), because it would always be on the sixteenth of Aviv. If that were true, then in the case of Yeshua's resurrection, the beginning of Unleavened Bread (the fifteenth of Aviv) would have had to occur on a weekly Sabbath (Saturday, the seventh day of the week) in order for Him to have risen on the morning of the first day of the next week (Sunday) and Yeshua would have had to have been crucified on the fifth day of the week (the thirteenth of Aviv, Thursday in this case) in order for Him to have been in the tomb for three days and three nights. This would have been twenty-four hours before the time that the sacrificial lamb was to be slain – at the twilight of the fourteenth of Aviv (Friday) – that's bogus. Also remember that it was because it was the start of a Sabbath (the Feast Sabbath of Unleavened Bread which had to begin at sundown, the beginning of a Friday) that His body couldn't be completely prepared for burial. And since He was to be in the tomb for three days and three nights, it also means that there would have had to have been two Sabbaths in between (Unleavened Bread and the weekly Sabbath), keeping the women away for two days before they could return on the third day (Feast of Firstfruits) to complete their work. This means that He was crucified on the fifth day of the week, or Thursday (except this time it was the fifteenth of Aviv) and not on the sixth day, Friday (as the Church teaches), in order for Him to fulfill His own words. He was also to be the "firstfruit" of the resurrection, so that means that the first day after the *weekly Sabbath* had to be the Sabbath that was used to determine Shavuot. Don't become confused, remember that a Hebrew day always begins after a complete sundown and lasts until the twilight (just before a complete sundown) of the next day.

Their third and final celebration of YAH's feasts would not occur until the late summer or early autumn in their seventh month called Tishri. This feast was appointed in order for them to celebrate the ingathering harvest of all of their labors. It began on the first day of the month with the Day of Trumpets (Yom Teruah), which was another Feast Day as well as a Feast Sabbath, for the purpose of calling all of YisraEL to assemble. Later, this day would also become know as the Head of the Year (Rosh HaShanah). On the tenth day of Tishri was the Day of Atonement (Yom Kippur), which was their next to last Feast Day, which again was another Feast Sabbath. This is when the high priest would enter the Holy of Holies and bring the annual blood sacrifice to atone for the sins of YisraEL. This was the day that the people of YisraEL were to afflict themselves by fasting (due to their sins) and the only day that YAHveh ever commanded a fast from His people.

On the fifteenth day of Tishri, all of YisraEL were to set up booths (sukkoths) for eight days as a memorial to their forty years of wandering and testing in the wilderness because of their rebellion. (Without their being aware of it, it was also a rehearsal for their future wandering that would last two-thousand years after their total dispersion into all the nations of the world. This would come as the result of their not keeping the commandments, along with the necessity for YAHveh to vomit them out of the land because they would defile it, just like the pagan nations before them. It would also fulfill YAHveh's promise to Avraham, Yitzhak, and Yaacov, to bless all of the nations of the world through them.) This would be their final Feast and was called the

Feast of Ingathering, or Booths (Chag Sukkot). The first and the last day of this eight-day celebration would be their last two Feast-Sabbath Days of that year. This would also include one weekly Sabbath. After the final crops were gathered in and the celebrations were over, the nation would prepare for the upcoming rainy season called the early rain – these rains prepared the land for the next-year's yield. In the spring, the latter rains would come and start the cycle all over again.

All three of these annual celebrations are shadow rehearsals for future events and will eventually become anniversary celebrations. But the first two of these Feast Days, Passover/Pesach and Unleavened Bread, would also be changed in their meaning. Before they entered the land, the celebration was confined to just their immediate household and their own tents, but later it would become a national celebration that was held wherever YAH would choose. In Chapter Two, I spoke of the Seder meal and how it was made up of four parts, each preceded with a cup of wine. The first cup was called the Cup of Sanctification and used to sanctify the family Seder. Now there would be a second cup introduced into the Seder. It would remind them of their deliverance out of Mitsrahyim and of the plagues that Mitsrahyim suffered due to the different elohim that they worshipped—this cup would be called the Cup of Plagues. It was also a reminder of the promise that YAHveh made to YisraEL, that none of these plagues would befall them as long as they didn't bow down to any other ELohim. After the second cup, the Seder meal itself was eaten, and then the next two cups were celebrated, along with the Seder dessert—this concluded the ceremony. This pause between the second and the third cup that was caused by the eating of the meal/food (lechem) symbolizes the interruption that took place between the completion of the TaNaKh and the coming of the Promised Messiah, Yeshua (Our Heavenly Bread/Lechem).

There is a period of four months between the Spring Feasts and the Fall Feasts that is also significant. This pause represents two things: the forty-year period of YisraEL's wandering in the wilderness (forty being the number of testing) while waiting for those who rebelled against YAH to die, and the two-thousand-year period between Yeshua's birth, death, resurrection, and our present day. Yeshua had a three-fold ministry: Redemption, Sanctification, and the Restoration of all things. He has redeemed YisraEL to Himself through the shedding of His own blood on the Feast of Passover/Pesach. He is the Unleavened Bread that was broken for her. He rose from the tomb on the Feast of Firstfruits to be the firstfruits of the resurrection. He sanctified her by sending His Ruach on the Feast of Shavuot (Pentecost) in order to help her understand the full meaning of His hidden manna that was found in His Torah, making her holy (kedosh), and to provide her with the power of signs and wonders to confirm His Word. He also gave her the opportunity to renew her marriage covenant with Him by continuing to keep His Sabbaths and His Feasts in light of this new understanding. Now, after two-thousand years, He is still waiting for her to return to her first love, His Torah, because He is her Living Torah. When she does, He will be able to finish His ministry of Restoration. At the sounding of the trumpet on Yom Teruah, He will bring the people of YisraEL back to the Promised Land, thereby fulfilling this Feast Day. Over the following ten days, He will translate them up to be with Him, beginning with those who are in the grave and then those who are still living. He will then return them all to His land for the entire world to see. This will be the second and the "Greater Exodus". Then, on Yom Kippur, He will give the world a final opportunity to make the proper atonement for denying Him as the Messiah, thereby fulfilling this Feast Day. He will judge the Earth for five days, and then He will begin to celebrate a seven-day-wedding feast, the Feast of Sukkot, with His bride, thereby fulfilling this Feast. On the eighth day, there will be a New Beginning as He inaugurates His Millennium of Shalom and dwells with His people as King of kings and Lord of lords. May all of the Body of Yeshua return to His anniversaries and to His rehearsals—come quickly, Adonai Yeshua!

YAH assigned additional sabbaticals that were also to be observed, such as the Sabbath and the Jubilee years of rest for the land. He gave instructions for the land to have a Sabbath rest every seventh year. He told them to grow enough crops in the sixth year to see them through both the seventh and the eighth year. There was also to be a Jubilee year that was to be observed the year after seven Sabbath years, or every fifty years. In the forty-eighth year, they were to grow enough crops to see them through the next three years. YAH promised to bless their harvest in those years in order to sustain them, but only if they were obedient. The Jubilee year was to be a year of redemption, and all properties were to be returned to their original owners or their heirs. We can see the Jubilee year being mirrored in the fifty days of the counting of the omar of the barley grain between the Feast of Firstfruits and the Feast of Weeks, reminding YisraEL to keep this celebration.

YAHveh instructed Mosheh to have Aharon say a special blessing at the end of each gathering of the House of YisraEL—this included both the weekly Sabbaths and the Feast Days. This blessing is still being said today in the homes of the YAHudi on the Sabbath and at the synagogue on a Feast Day. Many Christian denominations are also reciting it at the end of their services. It is known as the Aharon blessing or the benediction and is found in **NUM 6:24-26**. "May the Lord bless you and keep you; may the Lord make His face shine upon you and be gracious to you; may the Lord lift up His countenance upon you and give you peace". In Hebrew it is said as follows: *"Yevarech'cha Adonai (YAHveh) v'ishmerech; Ya'er Adonai (YAHveh) panav eleycha viyechuneka, Yissah Adonai (YAHveh) panav eleycha veyasem lecha shalom".*

Establishing Clean and Unclean

Leviticus contained many other instructions that the Levi (Levee) were to use to teach YAH's people exactly what would be required of them in order to become a "set-aside/holy (kedosh)" nation. They must become a holy (kedosh) people because He was holy (kedosh) and no one could be in His presence and live unless they too were holy (kedosh). The book of Leviticus contained the majority of these instructions, but some were also scattered throughout all of the Torah. In order to be absolutely qualified to be holy (kedosh), He gave them 613 laws that were to be strictly followed without ever making a single mistake. This was impossible for any man or woman to accomplish, and He knew it. So, He promised, through His prophets, to send them His Messiah who would do it for them. This mandate is still in effect today, but Yeshua gave both Himself and His blood to purchase this holiness that is required and that the blood of animals could never provide. He made us clean in such a way that nothing we can do, outside of denying Him, can ever make us unclean again. The only requirement for us is just to have faith in Him alone and to confess our sins before Him, and He will cast them into the outer darkness where they will never be remembered again.

There were five different sacrificial offerings that were required to be presented at YAH's altar in order to purchase atonement. Three were free-will, or thanksgiving offerings, and two were to cover unintentional sins. The only atonement for intentional sin was death and that was reserved for the sacrifice of the Lamb of YAH. YAH explained to Mosheh everything that was required in order for the high priest and priests to maintain their holiness while presenting these sacrifices as atonement for the disobedience of His people. He explained the substitutes that could be used and the portions that were to be offered. He explained what it took to qualify or to disqualify anyone who attempted to make the atonement. He even explained the sacrifice itself as to what qualified or disqualified it as an offering.

He continued to describe the things that He considered to be clean and unclean and why. He pointed out that any type of human bodily discharge could invite communicable diseases, which could result in widespread sickness that could wipe out a small nation in no time at all. He was trying to inscribe upon their spirits the necessity of not socializing with others who do not adhere to such a strict set of hygienic, social, and political views. He was trying to instill in them the sense of responsibility that was necessary to survive in order to grow and become a great and mighty nation that was worthy of His blessings.

Along with the contamination that bodily fluids could produce, He also warns of contagious skin diseases and the contamination that comes from touching a corpse or the carcasses of dead animals. He introduces a proper cleansing procedure known as a "mikvah" (meekvah), the forerunner term for "baptism", to reestablish purification. A mikvah was usually done in the form of self-washing in either a private or in a public setting where mikvah pools were provided. At other times, a mikvah was done through the pouring on of spring water or by a sprinkling process. The procedure depended upon the type of contamination. The cleansing process had both a hygienic and a spiritual significance. An individual could become unclean, or contaminated, by a variety of causes. The cause could be mold or mildew in their personal belongings or within their habitation. Uncleanness could also be the direct result of disobedience to YAH's prohibition of the mixing of different breeds of animals, the mixing of textiles, or the consumption of forbidden foods. In any case, YAHveh was trying to establish in the minds of His people that they were a chosen nation that was unlike any other nation on the Earth. They were to have all appearances of being a separate and set-aside/holy (kedosh) people for Him and His purposes. He wanted to remind them and all the other nations of the world that He was the only Living ELohim and that there was no other like Him. Therefore, they could not participate in any of the other nations' indulgences. At the same time, He knew of a time when all of this would pass away (be paid for), and He would be able to pronounce all things clean through the blood of His only begotten Son. All the nations of the world would then be able to approach Him and become His YisraEL and be made kedosh (holy). He also knew of a time when He would provide mankind with all of the knowledge and wisdom that was needed to overcome most of the diseases and contaminating factions that could wipe out a nation.

Establishing YAH's Form of Government, Civil Justice, and Welfare

Just as the *Sh'ma* [*"Sh'ma YisraEL, YAHveh ELohenu, YAHveh Echad"* ('Hear O YisraEL, YAHveh Our God, YAHveh is One"...**DEUT 4:6**)] is the beginning of what Yeshua said was the greatest commandment, *"Love your neighbor as yourself"* (**LEV 19:18**) is the second. The first four commandments that are on the tablets that Mosheh brought down from Mt Sinai (Seenahee) pertain to the first greatest commandment, and the last six pertain to the second. The first of these last six, the fifth commandment, commands us to honor our father and our mother. Rav Shaul (The Apostle Paul) tells us in **EPH 6:2&3** that this commandment comes with a promise—*"That it may be well with you and you may live long on the earth"*. YAHveh does not speak idle words—He means what He says. If we cannot show honor and respect toward our earthly fathers and mothers, then there is something drastically wrong with our hearts, and our Heavenly Father looks at our hearts. We can give lip service in honoring, respecting, and loving our parents, but it is what lies within our hearts that reveals the truth to YAH. Yeshua says, *"A good man, out of the good treasure of his heart, brings forth good; and an evil man, out of the evil treasure of his heart, brings forth evil. For out of the abundance of the heart his mouth speaks"* (LUKE 6:45). And if our relationship with our parents is one of rebellion, it will eventually have an effect on our future relationships with others, including even our spouse and/or our children. Our parents do not have to earn our respect—they are due our respect. They are the ones whom YAH chose to be our parents. If they are abusive, it may damage our relationship with them, but we can never let it affect our respecting and honoring them. That respect and honor must manifest itself in our conduct toward them or it is without meaning. In Deuteronomy, YAHveh tells Mosheh what is to be done with a rebellious son. He is to be handed over to the elders and taken to the outskirts of the city, where he is to be stoned to death. He is told that any disobedient child is to be put to death in order to purge out the evil among them. If evil and rebellion is allowed to stay in the midst of the people, it will eventually spread to other parts of the community and will manifest itself in all manner of evil conduct. Today, such behavior must also be handled in a similar way. A rebellious child must be disciplined appropriately in order to discourage further evil, or it will grow to a point that he or she may have to be removed from the household in order to bring peace back to that home.

Mosheh goes on to other subjects, such as premeditated murder versus manslaughter and the need for cities of refuge for those who are responsible for accidental deaths. He covers the treatment of animals, which reveals whether or not a person has a compassionate heart. A compassionate heart is manifested in one's attitude toward the animal kingdom and toward others who are less fortunate than we are. Then He talks about the prohibition of stealing, cheating, or any other display of dishonesty toward others. He discusses debts, lending to others, and when or when not to charge interest. Debt always puts a person at the mercy of others. It even causes us to become the same as thieves if, due to no fault of our own, we are unable to meet that obligation. He discusses judges, courts, bribes, and perjury. And He talks about the punishments for dishonesty in weights and measures.

Mosheh covers adultery and unfaithfulness between husbands and wives as well as divorce. He goes on to include sexual misconduct among family members, neighbors, and harlotry. He emphasizes that YAH forbids any form of perverted sexual conduct, such as bestiality, homosexuality, or any other type of perversion, even cross-dressing. Some of the things that he doesn't directly address are things that we find unacceptable in our own society, such as bigamy and marriage to family members who are as close as cousins. YAHveh does not forbid these things. He does, however, encourage marriage within the tribes and clans. This is why arranged marriages were so prevalent. They do seem to promote lasting relationships when practiced within a society, if conducted fairly. However, YAH does discourage the practice of bigamy because He knows that more than one wife makes for an unstable marriage, as we have learned with Avraham and Yaacov. Throughout His Scriptures, YAHveh has addressed the harlotry of His people in their relationship with Him. That's because to Him, we are His bride, and prostituting ourselves with any other form of religion is totally unacceptable.

Finally, in the tenth commandment, Mosheh addresses our relationship with one another as neighbors. We are instructed not to speak evil of, or slander, or spread gossip about one another, and we are not to desire the possessions of others. These things encourage the evil thoughts that bring forth the evil words, which in turn bring about the evil deeds. Our objective in life should be about building a good relationship with Him and with others, and nothing or no one should be allowed to disrupt or discourage that relationship, especially our own self-centeredness.

YAHveh even gives Mosheh instructions on how to construct a proper warfare system. Warfare includes killing one's enemies. One's enemies are those who are either enemies of YAH, His will for His people, or His plan for His world. We are commanded to protect our families, ourselves, and our neighbors from these enemies because He has a purpose and a plan for all of us—we are not to allow anything to trample that plan under foot.

Mosheh commands us to keep all of YAH's statutes and ordinances in order to receive His covenant of blessings. He also warns us that if we fail and do not repent, He promises a sevenfold punishment until we do. This sevenfold promise of punishment plays a major part in where we are today in His timetable of events, which we will cover later in our study of His prophet, Ezekiel (YekezkEL). Once again, as He did in **DEUT 4:2** and in **DEUT 12:32**, He warns us not to do or to teach anything that is not written in His Torah. In addition, He instructs us to put tassels (tzitzits) on the corners of our garments to help us to remember His commandments. His instructions included the placement of a blue (the color of royalty) thread within the tassels (tzitzits)— the blue thread was to remind us that these commandments came from Him. Today, the men of Judah (YAHuda) wear a shawl known as a tallit (tahleet) over their shoulders as a modified version of the garments of their forefathers. Some wear an undergarment that allows the four tassels (tzitzits) to be exposed outside of their other clothing. Others tie four tzitzits to the belt loops of their trousers—a more modern expression that is practiced mostly among members of the Messianic Movement. As mentioned, it is practiced mostly among men, but YAH's instructions made no mention that it was restricted only to men. Through the centuries, the tzitzits have been tied in a specific way. Since the characters of the Hebrew language also have a numerical value, the numerical value of the word "tzitzits" is six hundred. Each tzitzit has eight cords that are tied with five knots, equaling thirteen. When this is added to the numerical value of the word "tzitzits", six hundred, we have six hundred and thirteen, which is the exact number of commandments that YAHveh gave to His children, YisraEL. The tzitzits were also referred to as "the hem of a garment". Their garment was their covering symbolizing the covering that YAH has provided for each of us with His Torah and His Ruach. The cloud that He used to lead His people in the Sinai desert was also His covering. The skin garments that He provided Ahdom and Eve (Cheva) were His coverings. The Tabernacle (Mishkahn) was His covering. His covenant with His people was and is His covering. The tzitzits are also referred to as being "His wings". The tallit (tahleet) with its tzitzits also represent this kedosh covering. Today, Messianics from both the House of Judah (YAHuda) and the House of Joseph (Yosef) wear this as a sign of His covenant promises. Even the small head covering known as the yarmulke or kippa is a version of this covering. "Kippa" comes from the root word in Kippur, which means atonement or covering. David (Dahveed) cut off the corner of King Saul's (Shaul's) garment and then later repented because it represented the king's authority. Later, as the King of YisraEL, he wrote a psalm that speaks of the protection that is found under YAH's wings. *"I will abide in Your Tabernacle (Mishkahn) forever, I will trust in the shelter of Your wings"* (**PS 61:4**). The prophet Malachi speaks of the Promised One who will have healing in His wings. *"But to you who fear My name, the Son of Righteousness shall arise with healing in His wings; and you shall go out and grow fat like stall-fed calves"* (**MAL 4:2**). And the Renewed Covenant speaks of the healing power in the hem of His garment. *"And suddenly, a woman who had a flow of blood for twelve years came from behind and touched the hem of His garment;...for she said to herself, "If only I may touch His garment, I shall be made well"* (**MATT 9:20&21**). *"And begged Him that they might only touch the hem of His garment. And as many as touched it were made perfectly well"* (**MATT 14:36**). It is also said that it was the corners of the tallit (tahleet) that Rav Shaul (Paul) made handkerchiefs out of and then sent out to be used for healing. *"Now Eluah worked unusual miracles by the hands of Saul (Shaul), so that even handkerchiefs or aprons were brought from his body to the sick, and the diseases left them and the evil spirits went out of them"* (**ACTS 19:11&12**). It is also suggested that the tallit (tahleet), when pulled over the head, became an individual's "prayer closet". Obviously, the tallit (tahleet) played an important part in the lives of the YisraELi, both then and now. I would like to see the wearing of the tallit become an important practice once again within the whole Body of Yeshua.

Mosheh's Last Days

After Mosheh finished admonishing and encouraging YisraEL with the commandments, along with its blessings and curses, He was told to bring his predecessor, Joshua (Yoshua), who was the son of Nun from the tribe of Ephraim (Efraeem), to the Tabernacle (Mishkahn) so that YAHveh could commission him to take over the leadership of His people. After Joshua's (Yoshua's) inauguration, Mosheh wrote a song that *prophesied* about YisraEL's unfaithfulness and the inevitable future of YAH's Children. He commanded the Children of YAHveh to keep the scroll that his song was written on with the Ark of the Covenant as a reminder of what was going to happen to them when they broke their covenant with YAH. Mosheh summoned all of the tribes of YisraEL to come before him so that he might bless them before he died.

When Mosheh pronounced his blessing upon the Levi (Lehvee), he saw himself as the Levi (Lehvee) who had had the responsibility of being their leader and teacher. He recognized their responsibility in carrying out his teachings to future generations. He acknowledged the skills that YAH had given them to discern the Thummin and the Urim correctly, and he put a curse upon any who would come against them. He confirmed Judah's (YAHuda's) departure from the Torah, their being dispersed, and then their returning to the Torah and once again becoming YAH's own people in His own land. He saw Benjamin (BenYAHmeen) being wedged between the two territories of Judah (YAHuda) and Joseph (Yosef). Later, it will be Benjamin (BenYAHmeen) who will join Judah (YAHuda) and be an ever-present remnant in the land until our present day. Both King Saul (Shaul), YisraEL's first king who was chosen by the people, and the Apostle Paul (Rav Shaul), Yeshua's thirteenth apostle, came from the tribe of Benjamin (BenYAHmeen). Mosheh pronounced a special blessing upon Joseph (Yosef), who was represented by his two sons, Ephraim (Efraeem) and Manasseh (Mahnahseh). They were to become the blessings to all of the other nations. They would be prosperous in all that they would do, and they would be strong in all of the nations into which they were sent. They would be more than conquerors—they would be overcomers unto the ends of the Earth. To Zebulun and Asher, he hinted of oil to bathe their feet in and treasures hidden in the sand. Could a great oil reserve be hidden under the territories of these two tribes? Some think so.

Before Mosheh was to be gathered onto his fathers, but after he had given his blessings over the twelve tribes, YAHveh took him up to the top of Mount Hor to survey the land that the Children of YisraEL were about to inherit. Then, after Mosheh's death, all of YisraEL mourned for thirty days, and Joshua (Yoshua) became the new leader and the first judge of YAH's people.

Conclusion

This finishes the five books of the Torah. The groundwork has been laid, and we can now venture into the books of the Prophets (Ne'vim) and the Writings (Kethuvim) to complete our research of the TaNaKh. The Ne'vim (pronounced Neh-veem) consists of twenty-one books, while the Kethuvim (pronounced Keh-too'-veem) consists of thirteen. Our having a good grasp on the TaNaKh, along with its hidden meanings, will give us a clearer understanding of the teachings of Yeshua and his apostles that are found in the Renewed Covenant. I want to once again emphasize the enormous need for us to understand the difference between being under the Law (Torah) with its curses and being under its blessings through grace. Therefore, we need to understand what it is that we are to continue to keep that was instructed by our Abba/Father. We do not have His authority or His permission to alter or change the keeping of it. We do have the responsibility, however, to research it in order to better understand it. *"My people are destroyed for lack of knowledge. Because you have rejected knowledge, I will also reject you from being priest for Me; because you have forgotten the Torah of your ELohim, I will also forget your children"* (**HOSEA 4:6**).

CHAPTER 4
...about Joshua, Judges, and Ruth

The books of Joshua (Yoshua) and Judges are part of the twenty-one Books of the Ne'vim (Prophets). Ruth is one of the thirteen books of the Kethuvim (Writings). The books of Joshua (Yoshua) and Judges are considered to be a part of the writings of the Ne'vim because YAHveh spoke to and through them on how YisraEL was to take possession of the land that He had promised their fathers.

What is the purpose of the books of the Ne'vim? It is through His Ne'vim that YAHveh speaks to His people regarding how they are to follow His instructions. It is through His prophets (ne'veem) that He confirms His words through signs and wonders. It is through His prophets (ne'veem) that He demonstrates His end-time metaphors. The circumstances that He puts His people through and the experience they gain by the way they succeed or fail in following His instructions are for the purpose of teaching and training them to recognize both near and far events. This training prepares them to receive their inheritance. The receiving of their inheritance tells us something about the final restoration of the whole House of YisraEL in the last days. The Scriptures are designed to do two things: to bring us into holy (kedosh) living and to bring us into our inheritance, the land of YisraEL. YAHveh never does anything without first revealing it to His Kahal through His prophets (ne'veem). *"The secret things belong to YAHveh our ELohim, but those things which are revealed belong to us and to our children forever, that we may do all the words of this Torah"* (**DEUT 29:29**). *"Surely Adonai YAHveh does nothing unless He reveals His secret to his servants the prophets"* (**AMOS 3:7**).

The scriptures point out that Joshua (Yoshua) was Mosheh's predecessor; he was also the first judge of YisraEL. He was raised up to be both their judge and a deliverer from their enemies. A judge's purpose is to interpret the laws for the people and then to instruct them on how they are to be applied to their society and culture. Having judges and elders is YAHveh's preferred form of government and was His form of leadership that He had given to Mosheh. Mosheh shared his authority with the elders from all twelve tribes, those proven to be wise and disciplined in YAH's Torah. We can see this same delegation of authority being taught in the Apostle Paul's (Rav Shaul's) letter to Titus. *"For this reason I left you in Crete, that you should set in order the things that are lacking, and appoint elders in every city as I commanded you"* (**TITUS 1:5**). The books of Joshua (Yoshua) and the twelve judges precede the final judge, SamuEL, who was also a prophet (ne'vee).

Joshua (Yoshua), YisraEL's First Judge

Joshua (Yoshua) experienced YAHveh's guidance and counseling in much the same manner as did Mosheh. YAHveh instructed Joshua (Yoshua) to carefully follow His instructions in the Torah and to meditate on them both day and night. He promised him that if he did, he would be prosperous in everything and would always be successful in all of his endeavors. This is the true prosperity message that is found in the Scriptures. One of the first things that YAH instructed him to do was to send spies into the city of Jericho (Yaricho). He was also given specific instructions on how to cross the Jordan (Yarden) River, which resulted in miracles that were similar to those that Mosheh had experienced at the Red Sea. The spies that he sent out came into contact with a local prostitute, Rahab, who hid them from the king of Jericho (Yaricho). She struck a bargain with them and was promised immunity, along with her family. Later in Scripture, we find Rahab joining YisraEL and becoming the bride of Salmon, a descendant of YAHuda, and in turn becoming the great-great-grandmother of David (Dahveed), the king over all of YisraEL. This is a good example of YAH's grace that He demonstrates over and over again throughout the TaNaKh. It shows us His desire to make all who are willing to obey His instructions His YisraEL. He accepts a person as His, not because of their "blood relationship", but because of their "faith relationship" from Avraham.

Before crossing the Jordan (Yarden), the two tribes of Reuben and Gahd, along with the half tribe of Manasseh (Mahnahseh), reaffirmed their commitment to help their brethren secure the new land before they would return to the east side of the Jordan (Yarden) River and take possession of their own inheritance. After crossing the Jordan (Yarden), Joshua (Yoshua) built a monument constructed from twelve uncut whitewashed stones (one for each of the twelve tribes of YisraEL), just as Mosheh had instructed him to build. YAH had instructed Mosheh to have Joshua (Yoshua) engrave all of the writings of the Torah on them and to set them up as a memorial of His promise to His people. Remember, twelve was also the number of precious stones that were used on the breastplate that the high priest wore over his ephod, each one engraved with a name of one of the twelve tribes. We see this number twelve, as well as stones, being used many times throughout the Scriptures to represent the Children of YisraEL. We also see the believers in Yeshua, the Messiah, referred to as living stones (**I PET 2:5**). They are to be given a white stone with a new name on it that no one knows its meaning, except the one who receives it

(**REV 2:17**). Then, in **REV 21:12**, we are told that there will be twelve gates at the House of YAHveh in the New Jerusalem (YAHrushalayim) that will have the names of the twelve tribes written on them. What does all of this mean? We have called ourselves "His Church", but He still sees us as His Kahal, His Son, His Firstborn, His Children, His Bride, and His YisraEL.

Joshua (Yoshua) then encountered the Angel of YAHveh, who assured him that He would go before them, just as the cloud and the pillar of fire had preceded them in the wilderness. This Angel of YAHveh could be no other than the Living Word, the Rock of YAH, before He became flesh and dwelt among us.

The crossing of the Jordan (Yarden) into the land of Canaan took place in the first month, the Hebrew month of Aviv. After the crossing, the same rite of circumcision that was commanded of Avraham was to be performed on this new generation of Hebrews before they could partake of Passover. Remember, circumcision was the physical sign of being kedosh (holy or set-aside). None of the males who were born in the forty years of wandering had been circumcised, so they were commanded to do so as soon as they entered the land. Because an uncircumcised person was not permitted to partake of the Passover celebration, it must not have been kept during the forty years of wandering, except for the two that were recorded at the very beginning. After entering the land, they began to enjoy the produce that was found there; it also enabled them to celebrate the three annual feasts that they were commanded to keep. Then YAHveh caused the manna from heaven to cease on the day after they celebrated their first Feast of Unleavened Bread (Chag HaMatzot) in the new land.

YAHveh commanded Joshua (Yoshua) to go in and possess two of the cities west of the Jordan (Yarden) River, Jericho (Yaricho) and Ai (Ahee). He gave very precise military instructions on how to achieve victory and told them not to keep any of the pagan articles as spoil. But after the fall of the city of Jericho (Yaricho), one of the YisraELi took some of these accursed things for himself. Therefore, when YisraEL tried to besiege Ai (Ahee), three-thousand of YisraEL's army were routed out by the men of Ai (Ahee), and thirty-six of YisraEL's men of valor were killed. When Joshua (Yoshua) heard of this, he tore his clothes, or garment/tallit (tahleet), as did the elders who also sprinkled dust on their heads in their grief. Joshua (Yoshua) prayed to YAH and asked Him how this could be. YAH told him of the sin that had been committed within their camp. The guilty party, a man by the name of Achan, was promptly dealt with. He and his family were led outside of the camp to be stoned and burned. He was made an example of so that YAH's people might understand that this kind of sin could not be tolerated. Joshua (Yoshua) was then assured of complete success in taking the city of Ai (Ahee).

The military tactic that YAH gave Joshua (Yoshua) to achieve victory over Ai (Ahee) was different from the one that He gave for Jericho, but it still was a familiar one because He had given it to Mosheh before, and He would use it again in the future. The tactic consisted of luring the enemy's army out of the city with a fake retreat. This would be followed by a flanking maneuver as they charged. The flanking army could then besiege the city and burn it. When their charging army would realize that they had left the rest of the inhabitants of the city vulnerable to attack, they would try to return to defend it. This would be followed by a rear attack from the previously retreating forces.

The crossing of the Jordan (Yarden) River and the taking of the two cities, Jericho (Yaricho) and Ai (Ahee), caused five of the kings in the land of Canaan to take action against what they thought was an invasion. They planned an attack against the people of YisraEL, but YAH intervened and sent a hailstorm, just like the one that He had sent down upon Mitsrahyim during the time of YisraEL's bondage. In addition, YAHveh caused the Earth to stop its rotation at the command of Joshua (Yoshua) in order to bring about a defeat of the Amori (Amorites). The five kings sought refuge in a cave, but were ousted by Joshua's (Yoshua's) men. They were tried for their crimes against YAHveh, found guilty, and executed. Kings from the north also came down to defend their territories, and they too were soundly defeated.

The point where YisraEL crossed over the Jordan (Yarden) River became the dividing line between the northern territory and the southern territory in the land of Canaan. The southern portion went to YAHuda, with Caleb receiving a special inheritance, the city of Hebron. The northern portion was given to the two tribes of Yosef, Ephraim (Efraeem) and the other half tribe of Manasseh (Mahnahseh), with Joshua (Yoshua) receiving a special inheritance, the town of Teemnath Serah. In one way or another, this phenomenon of a divided YisraEL has always manifested itself both physically and spiritually down through history.

When YAHveh assigned the specific territories to each of the other seven tribes, lots were drawn to determine who would be the first to receive their inheritance. The tiny tribe of Benjamin (BenYAHmeen) was first and was given the land immediately surrounding the area where YisraEL had first entered Canaan. This included the cities of Jericho (Yaricho), Ai (Ahee), Bethel (the House of EL), and the city that was occupied by the Yebusi (Yebusites/Jebusites) called Jebus (Yebus). After many battles, Jebus (Yebus) became known as Jerusalem (YAHrushalayim), the City of David (Dahveed). How appropriate that Benjamin (BenYAHmeen), the smallest of all the tribes, would have within its territory not only the city known as the House of EL (BethEL) but also the city which would one day be known as YAH's city of Peace (YAH-ru-shalom). Considering the fact that Jerusalem (YAHrushalayim) eventually became the capitol (the head) of YisraEL, the spiritual significance is evident. With YAHuda (the tribe that the patriarch YisraEL pronounced as the one from whom the scepter would never depart) to the south and Yosef (named as the tribe to receive the birthright) to the north, we can once more see the importance of the placement of the onyx stones upon the shoulders of the high priest, as was mentioned in Chapter Two. This is just another example of the symbolism that YAHveh used throughout His Scriptures to reveal His mysteries of restoration to His Children who follow His Torah.

The second lot fell to the tribe of Simeon, who shared its territory with YAHuda in the southern portion. After that, the other five tribes were given territories north and west of Ephraim (Efraeem) and Manasseh (Mahnahseh). Six cities were designated as cities of refuge—three were east of the Jordan (Yarden) and three were west of it. The tribe of Levi (Lehvee) was divided into three main clans, and each one was given a town with surrounding pasturelands to dwell in.

With the territories assigned, but not yet completely conquered, Joshua (Yoshua) blessed the two and one-half tribes before they returned to their territories east of the Jordan (Yarden). Before crossing the river to their side, they erected a monument as a perpetual reminder that it was twelve tribes who made up the House of YisraEL and that the Jordan (Yarden) River was not a border between them. The tribes west of the river misunderstood the gesture to be a pagan altar and became determined to punish the two and one-half tribes for erecting it. The altercation was avoided when the eastern tribes explained their full intent.

Joshua (Yoshua) served as the chief judge of YisraEL for a total of thirty years before he died at the age of one hundred and ten. YAHveh told him that YisraEL would not take the land as He had commanded them and that he was to remind them of what would take place as a result. It was just before he died that he made this commitment: *"And if it seems evil to you to serve YAHveh, choose for yourselves this day whom you will serve, whether the elohim which your fathers served that were on the other side of the River, or the elohim of the Amori, in whose land you dwell. But as for me and my house, we will serve YAHveh"* **(JOSH 24:15)**. After Joshua's (Yoshua's) death, ELeazar, the high priest and son of Aaron (Aharon), also died. Both were buried in the hills of Ephraim (Efraeem), along with the bones of Yosef, just as he had requested. Their tombs are there to this day in the land of YisraEL.

YisraEL Continues to Conquer Their Inheritance—But not Completely

For the next three-hundred-plus years, YisraEL failed time and time again to completely conquer the inhabitants of Canaan in spite of the fact that YAH had made the covenant that He would always be with them. Because of their fascination with paganism and their lust for the Canaanites (Canaani) women, they nullified that covenant. They not only began to intermingle with pagan religion and pagan society, but they even began to intermarry. A few accomplishments can be accredited to them, such as Ephraim's (Efraeem's) conquest of BethEL in Benjamin's (BenYAHmeen's) territory. But neither YAHuda nor Benjamin (BenYAHmeen) could completely drive out the people in Yebus/Jerusalem (YAHrushalayim). Instead, they would capture a pagan city and gather their plunder, including the foreign idols and articles of gold that had pagan artistry engraved on them. They would also make slaves out of those residing within the cities instead of executing them as commanded. Eventually, both the political and the religious influence of this plunder began to erode the social and spiritual fiber of YisraEL. Because of this, YisraEL began to commit apostasy from all that they were supposed to stand for as YAHveh's nation. Only a remnant remained faithful, and YAH used them to keep His people from completely rejecting His covenants with them.

After Joshua's (Yoshua's) death, his appointed elders ran the affairs of YisraEL for the next one-hundred years until they all eventually died. YAHveh then gave YisraEL four more judges: OthniEL, Ehud, Shamgar, and Deborah, who was YisraEL's only female judge. OthniEL was a nephew of Caleb and from the tribe of YAHuda, Ehud was a Benjaminite (BenYAHmeeni), and Deborah was a prophetess from Ephraim (Efraeem). Then YAH gave them their sixth judge, Gideon (Geedehon), the son of Yoash from the tribe of Manasseh (Mahnahseh), to help save YisraEL from the hands of the Midiani. Remember, Mosheh's father-in-law was a Midian priest, and Balaam, the seerer who was supposed to curse YisraEL for Balak, a king of Moab, was also a Midiani.

Gideon (Geedehon) was a hard man for YAH to convince because he was humble and just couldn't believe that YAH would choose him to save YisraEL from its enemies. YAHveh already knew this about him because He knows everything about everyone before He chooses them. And just like Avraham, He knew that once Gideon (Geedehon) was convinced about something, nothing could change his mind. This same attitude would be found in many of Avraham's Hebrew descendants. So YAHveh first introduced Himself to Gideon (Geedehon) by having one of His angels perform a few signs and wonders in order to convince him that he truly was His choice. Then Gideon (Geedehon) put YAHveh to the test with his famous "placing of the fleece". After Gideon (Geedehon) was convinced, he conquered the many troops of Midian with just three-hundred men. In reality, though, the physical advantage truly belonged to the Midiani because they were the first people to use camels in battle, and their number was like the sands of the sea—even so, they still were no match for the Living ELohim.

WHAT WE WEREN'T TAUGHT ABOUT THE BIBLE AND ITS HISTORY

The people of YisraEL tried to make Gideon (Geedehon) a king over them, but because of his humility, Gideon (Geedehon) refused the honor. However, a short time after his death, Gideon's (Geedehon's) son, Abimelech (Ahbeemelech), killed his brothers, usurped his authority over the people of YisraEL, and set himself up as their king. It didn't take too long for YAH to see to it that he was killed in battle.

YAHveh ordained Tola, from the tribe of Issachar (Yitzsakar), to judge His people for the next twenty-three years, who was followed by Yair, of Gilead (Geelead), for the next twenty-two. It was during the time of Yair's term as judge that a young Moabi maiden by the name of Ruth became a central figure in YisraEL's history.

The Story of Ruth

Only two of the sixty-six writings of Scripture are named after women, yet women played a vital role in almost every aspect of biblical history—remember too that the Ruach is YAHveh's feminine side, the woman was given the role of helpmate, and YisraEL is YAHveh's beloved bride. Therefore, it is important for us to examine the story of Ruth and find out how she affected YisraEL's history. We will do this once more with the story of Esther (Ester), the second book about a woman, and the part that she played in rescuing YAHuda from certain destruction.

One day, a man from the house of YAHuda by the name of ELimelech, from the town of Bethlehem (Beit-lechem/house of bread) in YisraEL, left the land of his people because of a famine. He moved his family to Moab, the land of YAH's enemy. There, his two sons mixed in marriage with the Moabi women who had been schooled in the belief of the pagan eluah, Molech. This was in total disobedience to YAHveh's commandments. Then, one of the reasons for His commanding them not to mix with the strangers in other lands became evident. The YisraELi died and his wife was left to tend to the affairs of her sons and their wives because there was no kinsman redeemer there for her. The woman's name was Naomi (Nahohmee), and because of her faithful attitude and her being faithful to her husband's work, she stayed in the pagan land for another ten years. Then, her two sons met an untimely death and she found herself not only a widow, but also shouldering the responsibility for the welfare of her two daughters-in-law. After hearing that the famine was over, she finally decided to return to the land of YisraEL and release her daughters-in-law from any obligation that they felt toward her. But the one named Ruth refused to leave her, while the other, named Orpah, decided to stay in Moab. Ruth loved and honored both Naomi (Nahohmee) and her ELohim and said that if Naomi (Nahohmee) would let her return with her, she would obey the Torah and make Naomi's (Nahohmee's) people her people.

One day, after their return to the land of YisraEL, one of Naomi's (Nahohmee's) relatives, Boaz, saw Ruth gleaning grain in one of his fields and inquired about her because he saw how beautiful she was. Boaz extended special privileges and grace to her and won her favor. At day's end, Ruth told Naomi (Nahohmee) about this handsome young man's favor that he had shown toward her. After Naomi (Nahohmee) learned that the man's name was Boaz, she recognized him as being one of her kinsmen and after a period of time, devised a matchmaking plan that would invoke the kinsman-redeemer statute. She told Ruth to go down to the threshing floor on a particular night and slip under the wings (or tzitzits) of the corner of Boaz's tallit (garment/prayer shawl) for security and submit herself to his safe keeping. Later, after Ruth told him of her situation, Boaz agreed to be her redeemer, but he first had to offer her to another kinsman who had the first legal obligation as a redeemer for a kinsman's widow. When the second relative refused to meet this obligation, Boaz gladly married Ruth and fathered a son whom they named Obed. Obed married and fathered a son named Jesse (Yesseh), who was the father of David (Dahveed), who became the king of YisraEL. Most of us, like Ruth, are descendants of pagan ancestors. We too can join the House of YisraEL after we decide to obey and serve YAHveh, the ELohim of YisraEL. But like Ruth, we also need a kinsman redeemer—we have one in Yeshua, if we accept Him by faith as our Messiah (Mashiach) and accept the price that He paid for our redemption.

The Last of the Judges

While this was going on in Ruth's life, there were two men in Bethlehem, one from the tribe of Dan (Dahn) and the other from the tribe of Ephraim (Efraeem), whose wives were barren. The one from Dan (Dahn) had the Angel of YAH come to him and announce that his wife would bare him a son whom they were to dedicate to YAHveh under the Nazirite vow. The wife of the man from Ephraim (Efraeem) also made a Nazirite vow to dedicate her son to YAHveh during a celebration of the Feast of Tabernacles (Sukkot/Succoth). The Nazirite vow is usually temporary, but because this one was being made by the parents, it would last the lifetime of the child. We find other participants of this Nazirite vow in Scripture. There was John the Baptist (Yochanan the Immerser) from the Renewed Covenant (New Testament), who was also dedicated by his parents for life, and then the Apostle Paul (Rav Shaul), who became a Nazirite, but only for a short period of time. The child from the tribe of Dan (Dahn) was given the name of Samson, who became one of YisraEL's judges and would be known for his supernatural, physical strength. The other was named SamuEL and would become YisraEL's final judge. A Nazirite was not to cut his hair, eat or drink anything made with grapes, and couldn't have any contact with the dead. Though Samson's parents had made this vow for him, Samson himself ignored it completely, except for the cutting of his hair—this was both his strength and his weakness. His character was that of a wild man concerning everything in his life, and he loved being promiscuous with the pagan women in the region, especially the Philisti women. In his final moments, he rededicated his life and rescued YisraEL from their enemy, the Philisti. Samson was unlike Yeshua in that he didn't live a completely sinless life, but at the same time, he was much like Him in that he sacrificed himself in order to save YisraEL. Yeshua was willing to do this so that all men, who would, could become His brethren.

As was said, Samson was from the tribe of Dan (Dahn), but the people of Dan (Dahn), as of yet, had not settled into a permanent piece of land as their portion of their inheritance. While spying out the city of Laish (Lah-eesh) as a place to settle, they came upon a man from the hills of Ephraim (Efraeem) named Micah (Meecah). They discovered that he had hired a Levi (Lehvee) to be a priest for his household and that he had provided him with an ephod to wear. He also had made for himself molten idols to worship. This was a good example of how the people of YisraEL were falling further and further into paganism and further and further away from the Living ELohim, YAHveh, because they had no king or leader. *"In those days there was no king in YisraEL; everyone did what was right in his own eyes"* (**JUDGES 17:6**). The people of Dan (Dahn) decided that they wanted Micah's (Meecah's) priest as their own, so they told the priest to come and bring the carved images and idols with him; he agreed. They then attacked the city, burned it, slaughtered the inhabitants, and renamed the city, Dan (Dahn). Eventually, even Mosheh's grandson, Jonathan (Yochanan), and his sons after him continued to serve the inhabitants of Dan (Dahn) as priests until their captivity by Assyria, even though the Mishkahn was still at the city of Shiloh (Sheeloh) during this time.

The land of Canaan continued to be corrupt, even with the presence of the people of YAH, because they did not drive out the inhabitants. Another example of the corruption is the story of another Levi (Lehvee) who had purchased for himself a concubine from Bethlehem of YAHuda. She became unfaithful to him by leaving him and returning to her father's house. To leave one's mate and return home is considered to be the same as harlotry. He went after her to bring her back, and on his return trip, he stopped for the night in Gibeah in the territory of Benjamin (BenYAHmeen). There, he encountered a situation not unlike that of Sodom and Gomorrah. Homosexuals tried to engage him in a perverted act after he had been invited to spend the night at the home of a hospitable old man. He struck a bargain with them by offering his concubine as his substitute. They raped her all that night, causing her death. To declare the repulsiveness of the actions of these men, he dissected her body into twelve pieces and sent one to each of the twelve tribes. This enraged the people of

YisraEL and provoked them into demanding not only retribution from the inhabitants of the city of Gibeah, but also the scoundrels who were responsible for this hideous behavior to be turned over to them. But instead of retribution, the people of Benjamin (BenYAHmeen) decided to defy their brethren and rebel instead. They were a very resilient people, so it took the fighting men of YisraEL three attempts before they were able to conquer the small tribe, and in the process, they nearly annihilated the people of Benjamin (BenYAHmeen). Because of this and due to a foolish oath that they had previously made, the rest of the tribes of YisraEL were forced to come up with a scheme to repopulate the tribe of Benjamin (BenYAHmeen) (**JUDGES 21:1 & 18**). All of this was a result of the tribes of YisraEL not honoring the covenant that they had made with YAHveh—instead, they did what was right in their own sight.

Conclusion

The YisraELi are the chosen people of YAH, but even they will cast off restraint when they have no revelation (**PROV 29:18**). They did not honor the Torah nor did they fear YAHveh. To them, it was more important to fit in. Having no discipline, they submitted themselves to the lust of their eyes and their flesh and yielded to the immorality of the pagan elohim. They longed for the monarchy of sinful man rather than the majesty of YAHveh. When they got into trouble, they ran to YAH; after He delivered them and they found peace, they ran back to the Baal's and the Asherah poles. In the final millennium, YAH will have His way and will establish His King over His people, YisraEL. Yeshua will be both King and High Priest of the order of Melchizedek. He will rule and reign from His Holy House in Jerusalem (YAHrushalayim), in the land of YisraEL, where all believers/saints will reside with Him as His Bride. He will assign those who have obeyed and have been faithful to His words as overseers/bishops/elders and judges over all of the Earth. We who are on this Earth at this time in history are experiencing the same sinful attitude among the nations as did the people of the Earth back in the days of YisraEL's rebellion. His people, both the House of YAHuda and the House of YisraEL, are still resisting the true lessons and instructions of His Torah. And the shofars of YAHveh are about to sound, calling His Kahal to gather before Him to return to the land that He had promised to Avraham and his descendants. Are we ready? If you are, Baruch HaShem! (Blessed be His Name!)

CHAPTER 5
...about I Samuel

Within the writings of the Prophets (Ne'vim), you will also find the books of I SamuEL and II SamuEL. I SamuEL records both the reign of Saul (Shaul) and the early years of David (Dahveed), YAHveh's chosen king for YisraEL.

Here, the tribe of Ephraim (Efraeem) will take center stage once again through the birth of SamuEL, who was the last judge of YisraEL. It is he who will ordain both the first and the second king of YisraEL, Saul (Shaul) of the tiny tribe of BenYAHmeen and David (Dahveed) from the tribe of YAHuda. As was said in the previous chapter, from his childhood on, SamuEL was dedicated as a Nazirite to serve YAHveh. His mother would come to see him every year on the Feast of Sukkot (Tabernacles) and bring him a tiny new robe to wear with the small ephod that she had given him when she first left him in the care of ELi (ELee), the high priest of YAHveh. YAHveh called SamuEL to be a prophet (ne'vee) for Him because His people had not heard His voice for many years—not since Mosheh and Yoshua. They now needed His direct instructions since they had all but forgotten His Torah.

ELi (ELee) proved to be an unworthy high priest. He allowed his sons to minister to YAH in spite of the fact that they were sleeping with the women who served at the door of the Mishkahn. They were also practicing extortion regarding some of the sacrificial meat that was brought there. Instead of chastising or replacing them for their repulsive behavior, ELi (ELee) only rebuked them. As a result, YAHveh brought judgment upon ELi's (ELee's) house. Both of his sons died on the same day that the Philistines (Philisti) defeated YisraEL and captured the Ark of the Testimony. When ELi (ELee) received the news that the Ark had been captured and that his sons had been slain in the process, he also died.

After capturing the Ark, the Philistines (Philisti) brought it to their city of Ashdod. But alas, it proved to be nothing but trouble for them. Whenever they placed it in the temple of their eluah, Dagon, the image of Dagon would fall over and eventually became dismembered. It has been said that Dagon was an amphibian eluah because "Dagon" comes from the Hebrew root word "dahge", which means fish. Some dispute this, but in some of the ruins of the pagan temples, images have been found that appear to be half man and half fish. And the priests who served them wore crowns that resembled the open mouth of a fish. These crowns are quite similar to the headgear that is worn by some of the clergy who are serving in Christian churches today. The crowns that are worn today are supposed to be symbolic of the tongues of fire that came upon Yeshua's disciples on the Feast of Shavuot (Pentecost). Is it just a coincidence or are they? I'll let you be the judge.

The people of Ashdod also became plagued with hemorrhoids, so they decided to send the Ark away. It was shipped off to another Philistine (Philisti) city, and its residents soon suffered the same plague. No matter where it was transported, the results seemed to be the same. Finally, the Philistines (Philisti) decided to send the Ark away from their land and back into the land of YisraEL, carried on a cart that was pulled by two heifers that had recently given birth to calves. They reasoned that if the plagues were caused by their possession of the Ark, the ELohim of YisraEL would guide the heifers back into YisraEL in spite of the braying of their offspring. This proved to be the case, and the two heifers carried the Ark back into the land of YisraEL. When the people saw the return of the Ark, they rejoiced and celebrated, but in their zeal, seventy souls decided to look into the Ark and were struck dead. This took place at Beth Shemesh, and after it happened, the residents there called for the people of Kiriath Yearim to come and take the Ark to their town. That is where it remained for the next twenty years.

In the meantime, the judge and prophet (ne'vee) SamuEL called upon the people of YisraEL to repent of their rebellion and return to following and worshipping YAHveh as their ELohim. He told them to rid themselves of the Ashtoreth poles, as well as the other pagan idols that also represented the elohim of the previous peoples of the land, and for them to gather at Mizpah to rededicate themselves to YAH. This is what a prophet (ne'vee) is called to do—they are to call the people of YAHveh to repentance and then instruct them in His words. The Philistines (Philisti) heard about the gathering and saw it as their opportunity to attack them and rid the land of these foreigners once and for all. But YAHveh fought the battle for YisraEL with thunder and lightning that day, which sent the Philistines (Philisti) into a panic. The YisraELi took advantage of the situation and began slaughtering them instead.

YisraEL desired to be like the other nations, so they called upon SamuEL to find them a king to rule over them. After consulting with YAH on the matter, he was told to grant them their request. YAH assured him that they were not rejecting him as their judge—they were rejecting YAHveh as their King and ELohim. YAH told SamuEL that He would choose a king for YisraEL, and when the time was right, He would point him out to him. YAHveh also told SamuEL to remind the people of all the freedoms that they would have to forfeit by having a mortal king reign over them. But they wouldn't listen and still insisted upon having a king to lead them, just like all the other nations in the land. To make matters worse for SamuEL, he soon discovered that his sons were no better then ELi's (ELee's) sons—they too were corrupt in their ways and not righteous like their forefathers.

King Saul (Shaul)

YAHveh chose the tiny tribe of BenYAHmeen, or what was left of them after the civil war with their brethren, to find YisraEL their king. Out of the house of Kish, He chose an unusually tall and handsome son named Saul (Shaul). YAH created the circumstances that caused some of Kish's donkeys to wander off, and he sent his son, Saul (Shaul), to recover them. After searching for them for three days, Saul (Shaul) became more concerned about his father's welfare than about the whereabouts of the donkeys and decided to return to his father's house. But his servant persuaded him to first go up and seek out the seerer of ELohim, who was supposed to be visiting in the next town, and request his help. When they arrived, they sought the whereabouts of the seerer and learned that he had indeed just arrived, but was on his way up to one of the high places that YAHveh had assigned to the region. This high place was a place where His servant, SamuEL, could go to fast, to pray, to eat, or just to worship Him. (YAHveh normally condemned high places that were found in the land of YisraEL because men had set them up for themselves.) Upon seeing Saul (Shaul), YAH told SamuEL that this was the one whom He had chosen for now to be anointed as the monarch over His people. So SamuEL invited Saul (Shaul) to a banquet, along with thirty other guests who were to be witnesses to Saul's (Shaul's) coronation. SamuEL placed him in a seat of honor and anointed his head with oil.

Saul (Shaul) spent the night with SamuEL and then was told where to find his father's animals. He was also told that he would encounter three men who would be carrying certain items and that he was to follow them to a particular Philistine (Philisti) outpost. He was also told that before he reached that outpost, men who would be playing on musical instruments, dancing, and prophesying (speaking ecstatically) would come down a hillside to meet him; he was to join in with them as the Ruach of YAHveh came upon him. In the morning, all of these things took place just as SamuEL had said. And, just as he also said, this experience would give Saul (Shaul) a new heart toward YAHveh. After his experience, Saul (Shaul) returned to the high place to worship YAHveh.

SamuEL again summoned all of YisraEL to come up to the city of Mizpah. He once more reminded them that they were the ones who wanted to have a king instead of YAHveh to govern over them. He then called out the tribe of BenYAHmeen, then the clan of Matri, then the house of Kish, and finally, He called out the son of Kish, Saul (Shaul). He then declared to all of YisraEL that Saul (Shaul) was now their king.

Not everyone wanted to accept Saul (Shaul) as their king at the beginning of his reign—he had to prove himself. Then, when an Ammonite (Ammoni) by the name of Nahash threatened to take the city of Jabesh (Yabesh) Gilead in YisraEL captive, Saul (Shaul) and some of his men went down and rescued them by slaughtering all of the Ammonite (Ammoni) raiders. As a result, the people were then ready to proclaim him as the king over all of YisraEL and asked SamuEL to reaffirm Saul (Shaul) as their king. While doing so, SamuEL again reminded them that YAHveh had been the one to choose their leaders in the past, but now they wanted that right and YAHveh was granting their request. He again warned them that they would soon have second thoughts, but then it would be too late.

Saul (Shaul) had several children, but two in particular stood out from the rest—his son, Jonathan (Yochanan), and his daughter, Michal. Saul (Shaul) reigned in YisraEL for forty years and proved to be worthy of YAH's warning about their desire to have their own king. In his first test of obedience to YAHveh, he failed miserably. Saul (Shaul) was about to have an encounter with the Philistines (Philisti), but was told to be patient and wait for SamuEL to arrive and offer up the proper burnt sacrifices and prayers before making the attack in order to insure them of YAH's blessings. But Saul (Shaul) began to lose his nerve when some of his troops became afraid and began to desert their posts, so he offered up the sacrifices himself. SamuEL rebuked him when he discovered Saul's (Shaul's) act of rebellion and lack of trust in YAH's timing. (This is a classic reaction—we pray, we ask, then we begin to doubt, and instead of waiting for YAH's timing, we act on our own.) Because of Saul's (Shaul's) double-mindedness, YAHveh denied him the right to continue his position as king over YisraEL and was told as much by SamuEL. It was at this time that YAHveh began to reveal the beginning of His plan of redemption for His people by proclaiming, through the prophet (ne'vee) SamuEL, His choice for their next king. His choice would be a forerunner of His Messiah, His "Beloved", and would be a man after His own heart. One of the Hebrew words for "beloved" is da'vid (dahveed)—His choice would be named "David (Dahveed)".

Now, in their oppression of YisraEL, the Philistines (Philisti) had not allowed anyone to practice the skill of a blacksmith to keep them from forging any weaponry. As a result, Saul (Shaul) and his son, Jonathan (Yochanan), were the only ones to have a sword or a spear in their possession. While Saul (Shaul) and his men were devising a plan to overthrow these Philistine (Philisti) oppressors, he pledged that all of the fighting men of YisraEL would fast until they tasted victory. But Saul's (Shaul's) son, Jonathan (Yochanan), was not present when the oath was made. In the meantime, Jonathan (Yochanan) had decided that he, his armor-bearer, and YAHveh already possessed all of the power needed to overcome these uncircumcised enemies of the Most High.

YAH gave him a plan, and when it was executed, the Philistines (Philisti) were routed. When King Saul (Shaul) saw the Philistines (Philisti) in disarray, he summoned his captains to find out who was responsible for it. It was determined that it was his son, Jonathan (Yochanan), who had initiated the attack that sent the Philistines (Philisti) into confusion. Then the rest of YisraEL joined in the attack and overthrew their oppressors, the Philistines (Philisti), that very day.

Before rejoining the fighting forces, Jonathan (Yochanan) and his armor-bearer found a vast amount of honeycomb lying on the ground in the woods, and because they were hungry, they helped themselves to it. One of Saul's (Shaul's) soldiers came upon them while they were eating it and told Jonathan (Yochanan) about the oath that his father had made the people take before entering the battle. Jonathan (Yochanan) said that his father was foolish for making the people take such an oath. Jonathan's (Yochanan's) observation proved true because later, the soldiers, in their weakened state, took some of the bounty of sheep and oxen, slaughtered them, and ate the meat along with the blood. When Saul (Shaul) was told about this, he built an altar and sacrificed burnt offerings for the sin of the people. Once more, Saul (Shaul) had become presumptuous before YAHveh and assumed the duties of the priest. He then consulted YAH as to what plans they should follow next, but he received no reply. He immediately assumed that sin had entered the ranks of the people and called for the drawing of lots to find the guilty party. When the lots were cast, it fell upon Jonathan (Yochanan). Saul (Shaul) asked him what the sin was that he was guilty of committing. Jonathan (Yochanan) acknowledged that he had eaten some honey and that he had considered the oath to have been a foolish one in the first place. Saul (Shaul) then insisted that his son had to pay with his life because of the oath. But the people refused to carry out the judgment on him because of his heroic deeds of the previous day. Saul (Shaul) relented, and Jonathan's (Yochanan's) life was spared.

Saul (Shaul) continued to conquer the enemies of YAH's people and was considered to be a mighty king for YisraEL. One day, YAHveh sent SamuEL to Saul (Shaul) to tell him that it was time to rid the land of the Amalekites (Amaleki), who had ambushed the Children of YisraEL on their journey out of Mitsrahyim. As a part of his instructions, he was told to destroy all that the Amalekites (Amaleki) possessed and that YisraEL was to take no bounty for herself. They failed to obey and kept the best of the livestock for themselves, and Saul (Shaul) took King Agag as his prisoner. When SamuEL discovered Saul's (Shaul's) disobedience, he was again infuriated and informed him that YAHveh had now completely rejected him as the king of YisraEL. As he turned to leave, Saul (Shaul) grabbed SamuEL's tallit (tahleet) and tore off a piece in the process. SamuEL informed Saul (Shaul) that in the same manner that he had torn his tallit (tahleet), so the kingdom would be torn from him and given to a man after YAH's own heart. Then SamuEL did what Saul (Shaul) was supposed to do—he took a sword and killed King Agag.

The Early Years of David (Dahveed)

SamuEL never saw King Saul (Shaul) again, but he mourned for him because of his foolishness. One day, YAHveh came to SamuEL and told him to go to the house of a man named Jesse (Yesseh) in the little town of Bethlehem (Beit-lachem /house of bread), in the territory of YAHuda, and to take a horn of oil for anointing. He was about to show him the one whom He had chosen to be King over YisraEL forever.

As soon as SamuEL entered the town of Bethlehem (Beit-lachem), the elders in the town came to him trembling with fear because they knew about the signs and wonders that accompanied him. SamuEL called for Jesse (Yesseh) and his house to accompany him while he sacrificed to YAHveh. While there, he told him that he had been sent by YAHveh to choose a new king for YisraEL, one whose kingdom would have no end. Jesse (Yesseh) then paraded seven of his sons before SamuEL, and he chose none of them. When asked if these were all of his sons, he confessed that his youngest was still out tending his livestock. When his youngest son, David (Dahveed), was summoned and SamuEL saw him, he immediately knew that he was the one. David (Dahveed) was handsome like Saul (Shaul), but unlike Saul (Shaul), he was humble and unassuming. He was strong in body and had a reputation of being brave and not backing down from lions or bears when his father's flock was threatened. He was also known to be gentle and spiritual, always writing songs and psalms about the ELohim of YisraEL.

After YAHveh removed the anointing of His Ruach from Saul (Shaul), an evil spirit (demon/devil) came and entered him. We need to remember that the Prince of Darkness, Satan (hasatan), was once a cherub. He oversaw or covered the throne of YAH, and all the praise from the heavenly host, before it was allowed to enter into YAHveh's presence (**EZEK 28:11-19**), had to first pass through him. He was a created being that was created for a specific task that he abandoned for a self-seeking one. Therefore, he was and is never allowed to do anything unless it is first ordained by YAHveh. YAHveh directs all of the affairs of the father of lies and grants only those activities of the demons that are according to His plans and purposes. YAH sent this tormenting spirit to humble Saul (Shaul), but because of his rebellious spirit, Saul (Shaul) became enraged instead and would throw fits of anger toward anyone who came near. His personal attendants noticed that music seemed to sooth him during these outbursts, so they suggested a fulltime musician as therapy for him.

Remember, YAHveh creates scenarios in all of our lives to test our response to them and to Him. In this case, He saw to it that Saul's (Shaul's) attendants received word about the talent and abilities of the young shepherd boy, David (Dahveed) ben Jesse (Yesseh) ("ben" means "son of"). After making their suggestion to Saul (Shaul), David (Dahveed) was summoned to play for the king. David (Dahveed), because of his gifts of music and his personal charisma, quickly became very close to Saul (Shaul) and was even made a personal armor-bearer to the king.

In the meantime, the Philistines (Philisti) were up to their old tricks of harassing YisraEL, so three of Jesse's (Yesseh's) other sons also joined the army to help drive them out of the land. During one of David's (Dahveed's) leaves of absence, his father sent him up to the front lines of battle where his brothers were stationed in order to check on their welfare. After arriving, he heard the ranting of one of the Philistine (Philisti) warriors bragging about slaying anyone who would dare to do personal battle with him. He stated that if anyone of the YisraELi men of war could defeat him, the remaining Philistine (Philisti) army would submit themselves to them. No one would take that challenge because he was a giant of a man, over nine feet tall, and intimidated everyone in the camp of YisraEL. David (Dahveed), when he heard this boast, was highly insulted by this uncircumcised blowhard and was embarrassed that none of the army of the ELohim of YisraEL would stand up to meet his challenge. So, he made the decision to do it himself on behalf of YAH, who was being blasphemed by this dog (dog is a slang term that the Hebrews used for any Gentile). His confidence was based upon the experiences that he had had in using his sling in successfully warding off or killing the wild beasts that would attack his father's flocks. So, David (Dahveed) saw Goliath (Goh-leeahht) as being just another beast (wicked people or nations are many times referred to as beasts by the Hebrew people) trying to threaten the House of YisraEL, YAH's chosen flock. And with YAH's power and David's (Dahveed's) sling and stone, this dog would also become a victim of YAH's judgment. That day, Goliath (Goh-leeahht), the Philistine (Philisti) champion, was defeated by this brave young lad, causing the army of YisraEL to find new courage in routing out the rest of the Philistines (Philisti) from the territory.

David (Dahveed) and Jonathan (Yochanan), King Saul's (Shaul's) son, had become like one (echad) in their friendship with each other. David (Dahveed), in a very short time, was promoted to a high-ranking officer in Saul's (Shaul's) army. But the more successful David (Dahveed) became in each military endeavor, the more jealous Saul (Shaul) became of his abilities. At the same time, David (Dahveed) continued to be a man of humility before Saul (Shaul). He always saw himself as being unworthy of anything that would exalt him above the king. Even when Saul (Shaul) offered him one of his daughters as a wife, he didn't feel deserving to be the king's son-in-law. All the while, Saul (Shaul) was trying to arrange for David (Dahveed) to be placed in the thick of a battle with the Philistines (Philisti) in order for him to be killed [a trick that David (Dahveed) would himself employ for selfish reasons later in life], but instead, he would achieve a fabulous feat of military victory and gain even more favor with both his fellow soldiers and the citizens of YisraEL. Finally, Saul's (Shaul's) younger daughter, Michal, who had fallen in love with David (Dahveed), spoke to her father about arranging their marriage. King Saul (Shaul) saw this as an opportunity to rid himself of this threat to his kingdom, so he told David (Dahveed) that he would accept the foreskins of one-hundred Philistines (Philisti) as his dowry for his daughter's hand. David (Dahveed), in his humility, felt that this was not really a sufficient dowry price for the hand of the king's daughter, so he brought back two-hundred foreskins. This infuriated Saul (Shaul) even more, so he coerced his daughter, Michal, into betraying David (Dahveed) in order to have him killed. But she loved him too much and helped him to escape her father's scheme instead.

It was during this time of persecution that David (Dahveed) wrote **PSALM 59**, telling of a time when he finds his life being sought for no other reason than for the favor that he has found in the eyes of YAHveh. He sees nations all around him having the same aggressive attitude toward YisraEL as King Saul (Shaul) has toward him and for the same reasons.

King Saul (Shaul) continued to pursue David (Dahveed), while his son, Jonathan (Yochanan), continued to defend him. In David's (Dahveed's) attempt to escape the king, he entered the city of Nob, a city of the Levites (Lehvee) and the high priest, Ahimelech (Aheemelekh). He stopped to inquire about food for his men, who had been faithful to him in his escape. The high priest gave him the daily showbread that had just been replaced with fresh, along with the sword of Goliath (Goh-leeahht), the giant. One of Saul's (Shaul's) Edomite (Edomi) servants, Doeg, witnessed the transaction. David (Dahveed) noticed that he was watching, and it troubled him as to what he might do.

Later, he tried to hide among the Philistines (Philisti) by pretending to be insane. When that failed, he hid in the mountains at the cave of Adullam. There, he was able to gather a troop of four-hundred men who were discontented with the king and had become dissidents of Saul (Shaul). It was also at this time that he wrote three more psalms: **PSALM 56**, a prayer for confidence—**PSALM 34**, a psalm of thanksgiving for YAH's encouragement—**PSALM 142**, a psalm in which he prayed for relief from those who were persecuting him without reason. David (Dahveed) then took his parents to his great-grandmother Ruth's land, Moab, for protection from Saul (Shaul). While he was there, he came into contact with another prophet (ne'vee) of YAHveh, Gad (Gahd), who warned him to return to the land of YAHuda to hide until YAHveh showed him what to do next.

David's (Dahveed's) fear for the priests at Nob was realized after Saul's (Shaul's) servant, Doeg, reported to Saul (Shaul) what he had witnessed. Saul (Shaul) sent for Ahimelech (Aheemelekh) and his family, who were serving as priests at the time, to question them about the matter. When they appeared before the king and were confronted about the incident, they denied knowing anything about David (Dahveed) being a fugitive. They said that they believed him to be a champion for both the king and YAHveh. Saul (Shaul), being blinded by his jealousy of David (Dahveed), accused them of conspiring against him, and he ordered his men to execute them. But because of their fear of YAH, his men refused. Doeg then volunteered, and he and his men slew the priests, along with the entire populace of Nob. One of Ahimelech's (Aheemelekh's) sons, Abiathar (Ahbeeahthar), escaped the massacre and ran to find David (Dahveed) to tell him the news. When David (Dahveed) heard it, he took full responsibility for the incident because he had seen Doeg that day. It was at this time that David (Dahveed), in his grief and anger, wrote **PSALM 52** about the destiny of evil men and their punishment, as well as the restoration and Shalom (Peace) for the whole House of YisraEL, which would take place someday. He would never see it, nor has it yet come to pass, except for brief periods of time throughout history.

YAH always kept David (Dahveed) and his men just one step ahead of Saul's (Shaul's) persistent pursuit. David (Dahveed) had complete trust and confidence in YAHveh's guidance and protection, and he expressed it in **PSALM 63**. But even when he rescued cities and villages, their inhabitants would many times reward him by betraying him to King Saul (Shaul) and his men. He expressed this dilemma in **PSALM 54**. At the same time, it seemed that whenever Saul (Shaul) was close to capturing him, the Philistines (Philisti) would attack some of his garrisons somewhere else and he would be called away to defend that city or town, allowing David (Dahveed) to escape once again. On one occasion, David (Dahveed) and his men were hiding in a cave, and it just so happened, out of all of the caves in the mountains that he could have chosen, Saul (Shaul) picked this one to use as his personal latrine. While he was there taking care of his personal needs, David (Dahveed) snuck up on him and cut off a piece of his garment (tallit). Afterward, he felt remorse for desecrating his king's tallit (tahleet) because of its great importance to Saul (Shaul), just as it is to all YisraELi because of its spiritual symbolism. So, David (Dahveed) called to Saul (Shaul) from the mouth of the cave and confronted him about his ability to take Saul's (Shaul's) life anytime he desired. But because of his anointed position as king over YisraEL, he had refrained from doing so and had spared his life instead. After hearing this, King Saul (Shaul) repented from any further persecution of David (Dahveed) and once more swore another covenant with him—not to continue in his jealousy. David (Dahveed) expressed his gratitude toward YAHveh this time in **PSALM 57**, praising Him for being his rescuer in times of great trouble.

David (Dahveed) took a woman named Abigail (Ahbeegaheel) as his second wife after YAH brought death to her husband, Nabel (Nahbel), for refusing to help David's (Dahveed's) men in spite of the fact that they had shown Nabel's (Nahbel's) own men much favor since they had arrived. David (Dahveed) took a third wife, Ahinoam (Aheenohahm), just before he became the official King of YisraEL. David (Dahveed) soon found himself in a situation where he had a second opportunity to slay Saul (Shaul), but again he refused, although he did confiscate the king's spear. Once more, King Saul (Shaul) found that he owed his life to David (Dahveed), and once more, David (Dahveed) explained that it was because of his loyalty to the King of the Universe that he had spared Saul's (Shaul's) life.

Because of the constant pursuit by Saul (Shaul), David (Dahveed) decided to try to feign his loyalty to the Philistines (Philisti) by joining them in a number of battles against YisraEL and their common enemies. During this time, some of the warriors from Saul's (Shaul's) forces defected and joined up with David's (Dahveed's). It is during these times that we see David's (Dahveed's) human side—even though he trusted in YAH completely, he still feigned some of his actions and tainted the truth. This revealed some of his frailties as well as his lack of faith in the King of kings at times—not unlike most of us. Yet YAHveh counted him as a man after his own heart. Our frailties should prove to us that we, just like David (Dahveed), have a need for a savior who can deliver us from these common pitfalls that plague us throughout our lifetime. However, this does not give us a way out of our own responsibilities to do what is right in His sight. For us to be guided as David (Dahveed) was, we must first search out the Scriptures for ourselves in order to learn YAH's ways. We must trust that His Ruach will reveal to us His truth that is found in His words. At the same time, we must be willing to set aside any ideas or concepts that we may have been previously taught. Finally, we must be willing to follow any new path or direction that He gives us.

The Final Days of King Shaul

In the meantime, Shaul acted out his life in just the opposite manner as Dahveed. He didn't look to YAHveh for his answers during his plight in life—instead, he trusted in himself to find the answers. At first, he prayed and hoped that dreams would guide him. After that failed, he turned to the prophets (ne'veem). He even called upon the priests to consult the Urim, but received no answer. He began to believe that he was the only one who could determine his destiny. But then, he remembered the experiences that he had enjoyed with his spiritual guide, SamuEL. Even though SamuEL had died, Shaul believed that the answers that he sought lay with him, even in the grave. So, he devised a plan whereby he would consult with the evil side of the supernatural through a seerer, a witch, in order to try to contact him. Even though Shaul had given a directive stating that anyone who practiced such divination would be prosecuted, he assured the witch that she would not if she would just arrange a meeting between him and the prophet (ne'vee) SamuEL. Just as the witch saw a spirit coming up from the hidden side, an evil one informed her that the person who had requested this encounter was none other than King Shaul himself. She became very frightened and accused him of trying to trap her through this divination, but he reassured her that this was not the case. When SamuEL was fully manifested (which could not have taken place without YAHveh's permission), he informed Shaul that all of this was allowed to take place in order to fulfill the prophecies that had previously been revealed to him and that now, because he had also turned to the spirits of darkness for direction, both he and his son would join him in eternity the very next day. Both King Shaul and his son, Jonathan (Yochanan), were indeed killed on the battlefield at the hands of the Philistines (Philisti) the very next day, with their bodies defiled by being beheaded and hung on a wall at Beth Shan.

Conclusion

A man judges by outward appearance, but YAHveh judges the heart of a man. Even those who sometime succumb to the desires of their flesh but are sincere in their devotion to YAHveh are judged righteous in His eyes. Some who say, "Don't judge me, God knows my heart", speak the truth to their own demise because He does know their heart. If you are honest with Him and are honest with yourself, if you truly desire His ways in your life and not your own, and if you are willing to give up the things of this world, He can and will use you, along with the talents and abilities that you may or may not even be aware that you have. Every human being that has ever taken a breath has an ordained purpose in life, whether it is for good or for evil—the choice is up to that individual. *"And if it seems evil to you to serve YAHveh, choose for yourselves this day whom you will serve, whether the elohim which your fathers served that were on the other side of the River, or the elohim of the Amori, in whose land you dwell. But as for me and my house, we will serve YAHveh"* (**JOS 24:15**).

CHAPTER 6
…about II Samuel, I Chronicles, and The Book of Psalms

In the first book of SamuEL, starting at chapter nine and through to its end, SamuEL recorded the reign of King Shaul. Many of these same events are also recorded by Ezra in I Chronicles, from chapter eight through ten. Both the first and the second book of Chronicles were written by either the prophet (ne'vee) Ezra or one of his scribes. Remember, however, that no matter who the writers or the scribes were, it was the Holy Spirit (Ruach HaKedosh) who authored all of the Scriptures. The Chronicles, even though inspired, were mainly written as historical records and are not to be considered prophecies. In the first nine chapters of I Chronicles, Ezra (Ezrah) recorded all of the genealogies from Ahdom through Avraham and included the genealogy of the sons of Yaacov up to King Shaul, who was from the tribe of BenYAHmeen. The two books of Chronicles and the Book of Psalms are just three of the thirteen books of the Writings (Kethuvim) of the TaNaKh.

I SamuEL ended with the deaths of both Shaul and Yochanan. The second book of SamuEL begins with Dahveed receiving the news of their death and continues by recording all of Dahveed's reign, including his exploits up until he reaches his advanced years at the end of the book. These same events are also recorded in I Chronicles, chapter eleven through to the end of the book. A question may arise as to who wrote the books of SamuEL if he died before the second book was written. More than likely it was written by the prophets (ne'veem) Gad (Gahd) and Nathan (Nah'thon), who included some of the things that SamuEL had written before his death. Dahveed will have more interaction with these two prophets (ne'veem) later in his life. When it comes to the Psalms, King Dahveed is credited with writing the majority of them, while those whom he had appointed as writers penned the others. And **PSALM 90** was written by Mosheh, which we have already discussed, while **PSALMS 72 & 127** were written by Dahveed's son, Solomon.

As was said, II SamuEL begins with Dahveed learning of the deaths of King Shaul and his son, Yochanan, from an over-exuberant Amalekite (Amaleki) messenger, who believed that he was bringing good news to Dahveed. Instead, Dahveed was horrified with this man's disrespect of the loss of YisraEL's king and ordered him to be executed. He expressed his grief and lamentation in **II**

SAM 1:17-27. At the same time, two more important characters in Dahveed's life emerged on the scene: Shaul's grandson, Mephibosheth (Mefeebohsheth), and another one of his sons, Ishbosheth (Yishbosheth). Mephibosheth (Mefeebohsheth) was only five-years old when all of this took place. Both of his feet were crippled due to a fall that was caused by his nurse's panic upon hearing of her master's death. Later on, Dahveed would show him great compassion because of the child's misfortune and because he was an heir of his king, King Shaul.

Dahveed is Made King Over the Tribe of YAHuda

After Dahveed saw these time-changing incidents take place, he inquired of YAHveh as to what he was to do next. YAH instructed him to go to the city of Hebron in the territory of YAHuda, where he would be made king over his fellow Jews (YAHudi). He took his two wives, Ahinoam (Aheenohahm) and Abigail (Ahbeegaheel), with him. At the same time, Shaul's army commander, Abner, took it upon himself to make Shaul's son, Ishbosheth (Yishbosheth), king over the House of YisraEL. This now caused the House of YisraEL to be divided. It would become Dahveed's responsibility as king, along with his descendants, to someday completely restore the House of YisraEL. Throughout history, even up to our present day, this has been the mission that YAH has given them. Over the next seven years, Dahveed would take on four more wives who, along with his first two, would give birth to a total of six sons. A young warrior by the name of Joab (Yoab) would also become an important character in Dahveed's life. Joab (Yoab) and his two brothers would have a confrontation with Abner, King Shaul's commander. During this confrontation, Abner would kill one of Joab's (Yoab's) brothers, which would later lead to a showdown between Joab (Yoab) and Abner.

After this incident, Abner was accused by Shaul's son, Ishbosheth (Yishbosheth), of sleeping with one of King Shaul's concubines. Abner became so outraged at this accusation by Ishbosheth (Yishbosheth), especially since he had just ordained him, that he decided to make a deal with Dahveed to hand the other eleven tribes over to him. Dahveed agreed, but asked for Michal (his former first wife and King Shaul's youngest daughter) to be returned to him. Abner agreed, and Michal was returned to Dahveed in spite of her present husband's protest and became his seventh wife. Abner conferred with the elders of the eleven tribes of YisraEL, and they all agreed to make Dahveed king over the entire House of YisraEL. The agreement was just about to be consummated when Joab (Yoab) almost killed the whole deal by murdering Abner in vengeance for his brother's death. When Dahveed heard of Abner's assassination, he was grieved and placed a curse upon all of Joab's (Yoab's) descendants from that day forward. This caused Ishbosheth (Yishbosheth) to become frightened that he and his whole house might be next on Dahveed's list. Soon after, two murderous traitors assassinated King Ishbosheth (Yishbosheth) and cut off his head because of his display of weakness. The two, thinking that they had done King Dahveed a great favor, presented their trophy to him. His reaction was the same to this news as it was when King Shaul had been killed—he had them both executed for their insolence.

Dahveed Becomes King Over All YisraEL

One of Dahveed's first accomplishments as King of YisraEL was capturing the city of YAH, Jerusalem (YAHrushalayim), from the Jebusites (Yebusi). When he did, Jerusalem (YAHrushalayim) became known as the city of Dahveed. The second mission that Dahveed set out to accomplish was to bring the Ark of the Testimony back to YAH's city of Shalom, Jerusalem (YAHrushalayim). He arranged for a party of YisraELi to go with him to help transport the Ark from the city where the heifers had carried it. But Dahveed did not consult with YAHveh about the mission, so it failed. Apparently, because the Ark had come into the city on a new cart that was harnessed to two oxen, he assumed that it would be appropriate to bring it back to Jerusalem (YAHrushalayim) in the same manner. But when one of the oxen stumbled and Uzziah (OozzeeYAH), one of Dahveed's servants, reached out to steady it, he was struck down by YAH and died. Dahveed became angry with YAH because of this, not realizing that it was through his own neglect that this curse had come. It was Dahveed's responsibility as king to consult YAH on every single one of his decisions because if he failed, others who were under his authority could be the ones who would fall victim to his neglect. When we are placed in a position of authority by YAH and we fail in that position, there will be consequences. It takes some of us a little longer to learn that lesson than it does others, but we all must learn it.

Not being sure of what to do next, Dahveed left the Ark for another three months at the house of Obed-Edom and returned to Jerusalem (YAHrushalayim). In the meantime, when the Philistines (Philisti) heard that Dahveed had been made king over all of YisraEL, they gathered their forces together to launch an attack. Dahveed made sure that he sought counsel from YAHveh this time and was assured of victory if he followed His instructions for doing battle. Dahveed consulted YAH twice about the battle, and twice YAH gave him two different plans to show the necessity of being precise in following His instructions. This is one of YAH's lessons that He wants all of us to learn—be precise in following His instructions, especially in His Torah. This is when Dahveed responded to his ELohim with **PSALM 18**. Dahveed then sought the proper instructions for bringing the Ark up to the City of YAH. He gathered the proper Lehvee of the house of Aharon and the priests, Zadok and Abiathar (Ahbeeahthar), to carry the Ark on its poles to a small, temporary mishkahn (tent) that he had prepared for it. A great celebration preceded the Ark, with many musicians and singers singing praises and worshiping YAHveh every step of the way. Thousands of bulls and rams were sacrificed along the route, and shofars were blown. Even Dahveed danced before the procession, stopping after every seventh step in order to sacrifice more animals. As they entered the great city of Jerusalem (YAHrushalayim), Michal, the wife of his youth, saw Dahveed dancing in his linen ephod and found it disgusting. Afterward, she demanded an explanation of his behavior because she thought that he was just showing off before the young maidens in the crowd. Dahveed rebuked her for her selfish jealousy and her lack of spiritual insight. He really wasn't surprised, though, considering that she was one of Shaul's daughters. A great celebration took place that day in the city of Shalom, and Dahveed appointed priests to minister regularly before the mishkahn (tent), where he had placed the Ark, and called for more praising, singing, and shofar blowing each and every day. This is when he wrote **PSALMS 96 & 105**, expressing his joy in once again having the Ark among YAH's people. In addition, he assigned Zadok to minister at the high place at Gibeon, where the Mishkahn that accompanied Mosheh in the Wilderness now stood. After reigning over YAHuda for seven years, Dahveed reigned over all of the House of YisraEL for thirty-three more years—a total of forty years as king.

YAHveh's Seventh Covenant with Mankind at the End of the Third Millennium

Three millenniums have now passed since creation, and Dahveed wondered why the presence of the Creator of the Universe, the Judge of all YisraEL, had remained in a tent. He turned to a newfound friend, Nathan (Nah'thon), a prophet (ne'vee) of YAH, with this question. His new friend responded with encouraging words, telling him that he should do whatever was on his heart because his ELohim was with him. Later, though, in a dream, YAH told Nathan (Nah'thon) to go back to Dahveed and tell him that the ELohim of the Universe could not be contained in a palace. Man has always tried to keep YAHveh in a box in order to have Him around whenever he needs Him. Ever since both of the houses that were built for Him were destroyed, man has tried to replace them with a church or a synagogue—YAH cannot be confined to a building made with our hands. But He does desire to dwell in our hearts and in our minds, and we should allow Him to be manifested in our lives through our speech and through the work that He assigns to us. YAH continued to bless Dahveed, though, by making a covenant with him and his house, promising him that there would always be one of his descendants upon the throne of

YisraEL and that one of his sons would have the right to build Him a house. YAHveh fulfilled that promise through Dahveed's son, Solomon (Shalomo), and then again through Yeshua. Yeshua will be the one to restore the House of YisraEL and construct the final House of YAHveh at the beginning of His Millennium Rest. This was YAHveh's seventh and final covenant that He would make with YisraEL until the Messiah would come.

YisraEL continued to do battle not only with the Philistines (Philisti) but also with the Ammonites (Ammoni) and the Syrians. After Dahveed retired from active duty as commander of the army, Joab (Yoab) became a key figure in defeating the enemies of YisraEL. At this time, Dahveed recognized YAHveh's hand in his struggles and acknowledged that the chastisement of His people was for the purpose of making them courageous and strong. He expressed this acknowledgment in **PSALM 60**. In this psalm, he mentioned three specific tribes: Manasseh, Ephraim (Efraeem), and YAHuda. Remember, Manasseh and Ephraim (Efraeem) both represented the tribe of Yosef and that Yosef was the brother who ruled in Mitsrahyim and was responsible for reuniting his whole family. Here, Dahveed calls Ephraim (Efraeem) a helmet. In Saul's (Rav Shaul's) letter to the Ephesians, he tells them to put on the helmet of salvation. *"And take the helmet of salvation, and the sword of the Holy Spirit (Ruach), which is the word of YAHveh"* (**EPH 6:17**). YAHveh uses the helmet as a symbol for salvation. The lost tribe of Yosef/Efraeem will one day take the Word of salvation to the entire world.

Bathsheba (Bathshe`bah)

Dahveed had seven wives but never fell in love with any of them as he had with a woman named Bathsheba (Bathshe'bah). Unfortunately for Dahveed, YAHveh forbade this love because she was the wife of a man named Uriah (UreeYAH). Dahveed saw her for the first time while she was bathing in what she thought was the privacy of her rooftop. The balcony that Dahveed was standing on at his palace was elevated higher than the rooftops of his subjects. Some say that Bathsheba (Bathshe'bah) wanted Dahveed to see her and desired to entice him because she would have been well aware of his vantage point. If so, it worked because Dahveed summoned for her to be brought to him so that he might lay with her that evening. And, of course, no one dare deny the king, so she submitted to him. Apparently, at that moment, Dahveed's' lust for her was stronger than his faithfulness to YAHveh because he committed adultery with her, and she became pregnant. After failing to manipulate an arrangement for copulation between this faithful soldier and his wife, Bathsheba (Bathshe'bah), Dahveed compounded the problem by having her husband, Uriah (UreeYAH), sent to the front lines of battle, hoping that he would be killed. Uriah was killed serving his king and his nation, YisraEL. YAH instructed Nathan (Nah'thon), the prophet (ne'vee) and friend of Dahveed, to tell him that this abominable thing had not escaped the eyes of his ELohim. He was told that the child, a son, had been conceived but would die shortly after birth. He was also notified that there would be continual strife within his household because of his sin and that one day one of his own sons would lie with some of his wives. Upon hearing this news, Dahveed sat down and composed **PSALM 51**. In verse ten, he confessed his uncleanness with these familiar words: *"Create in me a clean heart O'ELuah"*. Dahveed married Bathsheba (Bathshe'bah) because in spite of his sin of adultery and murder, he was still deeply in love with her. Shortly after the birth of their child, Dahveed was notified that his son was near death, so he prostrated himself before his ELohim and prayed and fasted, hoping that YAHveh would show mercy, change His mind, and let the boy live. After seven days of this, the child still died, and after Dahveed was told, he immediately rose up and went to make himself presentable before the people. He resumed his responsibilities to both his ELohim and YisraEL and continued his pursuit of YAH's enemies in order to bring shalom (peace) to the land. He gathered thirty-three mighty men to command all of his troops and brought down those who opposed the ELohim of YisraEL.

During this time, Bathsheba (Bathshe'bah) was still in deep depression about their loss, so Dahveed went into her to comfort her and she became pregnant again. YAHveh gave them another son, and He told them to give him two names: Solomon (Shalomo), meaning "peaceable", and Jedidiah (YAHdee-deeYAH), which means "loved of YAH". Dahveed had thirteen sons and one daughter with his eight wives, plus other sons and daughters from his concubines, while he lived in Jerusalem (YAHrushalayim). He was blessed by YAH, and his heirs grew in number.

King David's Son, Absalom

One of King Dahveed's favorite sons, Absalom (Avshalom), had a sister named Tamar. She was raped by a half brother, Amnon, a son by one of Dahveed's concubines. After Absalom (Avshalom) discovered who was responsible, he waited two more years for the right opportunity to take revenge. When that opportunity came, he arranged to have Amnon killed at a feast that he hosted for his friends and family. Afterwards, Absalom (Avshalom) fled into the wilderness in anticipation of his father's probable wrath. After three years, Dahveed's army commander, Joab (Yoab), devised a scheme that brought Absalom (Avshalom) back to Jerusalem (YAHrushalayim). But it took another two years before he and his father were finally reconciled.

In time, Absalom's (Avshalom's) ambition caused him to become desirous to be king over YisraEL, so he went to Hebron, where he devised a bloodless coup in order to proclaim himself as king. Rather than oppose his son, who might be killed in the process, King Dahveed went into temporary exile with the tribe of YAHuda following him. He drew up a counter plan that would reestablish his throne without harming his son. Once more, the House of YAHuda and the House of YisraEL were divided. More trouble besieged Dahveed when Ziba (Zeebah), who was a servant of Mephibosheth (Mefeebohsheth), the crippled son of Yochanan, discredited his master by telling the king that Mephibosheth (Mefeebohsheth) was going to use this situation to take back his grandfather's throne. Dahveed now felt betrayed by Mephibosheth (Mefeebohsheth) and granted to Ziba all of Mephibosheth's (Mefeebohsheth's) belongings. Later, after discovering Ziba's evil plot, he restored everything back to Mephibosheth (Mefeebohsheth). Then Dahveed came to the house of Shimei (Sheemehee), one of King Shaul's cousins, who, after hearing about the king's dilemma, came out to curse and throw stones at him and his army. When one of his commanders asked for permission to kill this arrogant dog, Dahveed refused. He reminded them that YAH may have sent him out to do this and that they should not be too quick to kill a possible servant of the ELohim of YisraEL. But Dahveed kept these things in his heart just in case any of this came from wickedness. Remember the words that Yeshua spoke when He taught on the hillside near Capernaum, *"But I say to you, love your enemies, bless those who curse you, do good to those who hate you, and pray for those who spitefully use you and persecute you, that you may be sons of your Abba in heaven; for He makes His sun rise on the evil and on the good, and sends rain on the just and the unjust"* (**MATT 5:44&45**).

Whenever Dahveed found himself in an adverse situation, he would turn to his ELohim for comfort. This was probably what motivated him to write **PSALM 3**. To make matters worse, Absalom (Avshalom) entered the city of Dahveed, went into his father's concubines and defiled his father's bed. His main purpose for doing this was to confirm to the rest of the tribes of YisraEL that he had taken over both his father's house and his crown. The inevitable happened—King Dahveed was forced to use his troops to fend off the attack that was led by Absalom (Avshalom). Even though Dahveed gave explicit orders not to harm his son, Joab (Yoab) ignored the king's command and personally took Absalom's (Avshalom's) life because of his own ambitions and dark heart. Joab (Yoab) had become quite angry over Absalom's (Avshalom's) decision to choose Amasa over him as his commander of YisraEL's army when the coupe began, and he wanted revenge. When the news of Absalom's (Avshalom's) death arrived, Dahveed was extremely distraught and mourned his death, but Joab (Yoab) rebuked the king for what he implied was a sign of weakness. Dahveed gathered himself together and decided to rededicate himself to the restoration of the House of YisraEL. So, he granted Shimei (Sheemehee) mercy, restored his relationship with Mephibosheth (Mefeebohsheth), the son of his friend Yochanan, and appointed Amasa to replace Joab as commander over the army of all YisraEL in spite of the fact that he had at first taken Absalom's (Avshalom's) side. This further outraged Joab (Yoab) against King Dahveed.

Another rebel, by the name of Sheba, continued the insurrection against Dahveed by encouraging some of the men of YisraEL not to resubmit themselves to the king. Therefore, King Dahveed sent his new army commander to go into the land of YAHuda and rally his troops to go after this rebel. When Amasa failed to return in the length of time designated, Dahveed sent Abishai (AhbeesYAHi) with Joab (Yoab) and his men to see if they could track down this Sheba fellow before he could gain any momentum in creating another coup. Joab (Yoab) used this opportunity to catch up to Amasa and by assassinating him, created the vacancy of the commander of the YisraELi army. Joab (Yoab) and his men then continued to pursue Sheba until they cornered him in the city of Abel, where an elder-woman in the city delivered Sheba's head to Joab (Yoab). When Joab (Yoab) returned to Jerusalem (YAHrushalayim), Dahveed made Joab (Yoab) the commander of his army again.

Dahveed Causes YisraEL to Suffer Because of His Poor Judgment

Famine and plague struck YisraEL, brought on by a wrong decision that Dahveed had made, along with a previous responsibility that was left unfinished. First, YAHveh pronounced a three-year famine on YisraEL because King Shaul had attempted to ethnically cleanse the Gibeoni and no retribution had ever been made for it. This was in violation of a covenant that had been made between the people of Gibeon and YisraEL, when Mosheh swore to spare them after the YisraELi were allowed to enter the land. YisraEL's solution to this dilemma was to have seven members of Shaul's house given over for execution as the atonement, or retribution price. So Dahveed agreed to this arrangement because he felt that this was the least he could do considering the thousands of Gibeoni that Shaul had exterminated while he was king.

Now, the plague came because of Dahveed's personal ambition when he ordered a military census to be taken without first consulting YAHveh. YAHveh informed Dahveed of his sin through his seer/prophet (ne'vee), Gad (Gahd). Dahveed was given three choices in making atonement for his sin of presumption. Instead, Dahveed chose to place himself and YisraEL in the hands of YAH and submit to His mercy. YAH sent a plague of death to cleanse the land of those who were found to have evil hearts and intent, and He even considered destroying His city, Jerusalem (YAHrushalayim)—but He recanted when His servant, Dahveed, interceded for it. Dahveed then built an altar to YAH upon the very site where Yaacov wrestled with the Angel of ELohim and where Avraham was willing to sacrifice his son, Yitzhak. It was currently being used as a threshing floor by a man named Araunah. Dahveed determined that this would be a good place to build a house for his ELohim, YAHveh. He had already received the plans for its construction from YAH and now all he needed to do was to decide upon its location and accumulate the needed materials. If he was not going to be allowed to build it himself, at least he would have made all of the necessary arrangements for its final assembling by the one whom YAHveh did choose. After this, He summoned his son, Solomon (Shalomo), and commissioned him to carry out its construction. He explained to him that YAHveh had disallowed him this privilege because he was considered to be a man of blood and the commission had to go to a man of shalom (peace). This was why he was given the name Solomon (Shalomo) even before he was born—it means a "peaceable man". Dahveed, keeping to his character, wrote a song for the dedication of the House of YAH—**PSALM 30**.

Dahveed Appoints the Leaders to Serve in the House of YAH

In the final years of King Dahveed's life and his reign, he gathered together the tribes of YisraEL in order to appoint those of the tribe of the Lehvee, according to their three clans, to serve in the House/Palace of YAHveh after it was built. The clan from which Aaron descended would serve as the priests and high priest, while those from the other two clans would help them in the service of YAH's House. Some were to be gatekeepers, while others were to be musicians. The musicians and the singers were to be divided into classes of twenty-four. The priests were also to be divided into divisions of twenty-four. The order for service for the priests was to be determined by the casting of lots. After this was accomplished, Dahveed also had to choose who would serve as military commanders, judges, and officials from each tribe, treasurers and officers for each tribe, as well as those who would serve as overseers. Dahveed made sure that all of these positions were assigned before he turned the plans over to his son, Solomon (Shalomo).

An interesting fact that we can glean from these twenty-four divisions of the clans of the sons of Aaron concerns the tribe of Abijah (AbeeYAH), the eighth tribe in the order of priests, as listed in **I CHRON 24:10**. Here, it is revealed that from that time on, a descendant from the order of Abijah (AbeeYAH) would serve in the House of YAH during the eighth week of any given Hebrew year. (It may help to refer to Chapter Two and its subtitle **"The First of Many Feasts that Point to the Messiah"** and review the twelve Hebrew months.) Remember, the first Hebrew month is Aviv, which coincides with our month of March or April. The eighth week would have fallen near the Feast of Weeks at the start of the third Hebrew month of Sivan, which would coincide with our month of May or June. When we begin our study of the Messiah's life in Chapter Nineteen, we will learn about Zacharias, the father of John the Baptist (Yochanan the Immerser), who was to serve as the high priest in the House of YAH during that time because he was a descendant of Abijah (AbeeYAH).

His wife, Elizabeth (ELisheva), who had been barren prior to this, conceived immediately following the time that he served. From this knowledge, we can now calculate the birth date of the Messiah, Yeshua. Elizabeth's (ELisheva's) cousin, Mary (Miriam), the mother of the Messiah, conceived when Elizabeth (ELisheva) was about six months pregnant. So, it would have been in the month of Kishlev, which is the ninth Hebrew month and coincides with our month of December or January. Nine months later, Mary (Miriam) would have given birth in the month of Tishri, the seventh Hebrew month, which coincides with our September or October—not in December. The birth would have taken place near the time of the Feast of Tabernacles. The tenth day of Tishri is the Day of Atonement. This would make it possible for the Messiah, Yeshua, to have been born on Yom Kippur, the Day of Atonement. Could it be that when He returns, it will again be on another Day of Atonement? It makes sense to me.

Solomon (Shalomo) Designated to be the Next King of YisraEL

Under the direction of YAHveh, ELohim of YisraEL, Dahveed commissioned his youngest son to be the heir to his throne. He admonished Solomon (Shalomo) to follow YAH's Torah and not to deviate from it. Then he delivered the plans for the House of YAH, which had been entrusted to him, to Solomon (Shalomo). He then solicited contributions from the Kahal of YisraEL to finance its construction and received a generous offering. The offering that was given was added to the bounty that Dahveed had already accumulated from his military victories. A full day of celebration followed, with YisraEL acknowledging King Dahveed's choice of his youngest son, Solomon (Shalomo), as his successor and Zadok as their high priest.

The Book of Psalms

There are 150 Psalms, either songs or poems of literature, that are written by several different composers but have only one Author inspiring them, as do all the books of Scripture. The book is compiled into five volumes, with each volume containing a variety of themes. If the Psalms were broken down into themes alone, you would find a total of five different themes.

The first theme speaks mainly about the promised Messiah, Yeshua, and starts with the very second psalm in the Book of Psalms. It says that He is coming to rule with an iron scepter and that the nations should both fear and respect Him. If they fail, they will feel His wrath and come under His judgment. Since Yeshua didn't fulfill this prophecy about Himself when He made His first appearance, His fellow Judean (YAHudaim) brothers rejected the authenticity of His being the Messiah. But they failed to remember that the promised Messiah would also come as a suffering servant. Their mistake was presuming that He would only come as the Lion of YAHuda. Others thought that there would be two Messiahs—one as a suffering servant and the other as a triumphant warrior. None of them had considered the fact that He might come as both, but on two separate occasions.

In **PSALM 22:1a**, Yeshua speaks His famous words, *"ELi (ELee), ELi (ELee), lama sabachthani?"* meaning, *"My ELohim, My ELohim, why have You forsaken me?"* In the rest of the psalm, He speaks of them cutting up His tallit (tahleet) and casting lots for His clothing. He speaks of His accusers as being dogs, lions, bulls, and evil men. (These are all metaphors that describe principalities and powers of darkness. Keep in mind that whenever the term "beast of the field" is used in Scripture, it is usually in direct reference to a king or a kingdom of this world.) He also refers to the great Kahal (Assembly/Congregation/Church) that is yet to come, which will be both YAHuda and YisraEL restored.

In **PSALM 27**, He speaks of dwelling in the House of YAHveh (the family of YAH) forever. Then He speaks of YAH's tabernacle (Mishkahn), or tent, which is really a metaphor of the tallit (tahleet) that YAH will give each of His redeemed ones (He is referring to our resurrected bodies). The land of the living is in reference to the Earth during the Sabbath Millennium.

PSALMS 45 & 47 speak of Him as the King of kings, and **PSALMS 48 & 87** speak of His relationship with Mt Zion (Zeeon) and with His people in His land. Finally, in **PSALM 110**, He speaks the words that He would later use to shut the mouths of the Pharisees when they challenged His claim to be the Son of YAHveh. *"And He said to them, "How can they say that the Messiah is Dahveed's Son?"..."Now Dahveed himself said in the Kethuvim of Psalms* (Writings of Psalms), *'YAHveh said to my Adonai, "Sit at My right hand, till I make Your enemies Your footstool."..."Dahveed therefore calls Him "Adonai'; how is He then his Son?"* (**MATT 22:41-46, MARK 12:35-37, LUKE 20:41-44**). He also refers to His Kingship as being of the order of Melchizedek—being both priest and king.

The second theme covers thirty-five psalms that speak of joy and praise. These consist of the exaltation of YAH's majesty, power, kindness, might, glory, judgment, righteousness, creation, instructions, blessings, purpose, love, deliverance, justice, salvation, holiness, compassion, faithfulness, and sensitivity. This theme is found in **PSALMS 8, 9, 16, 19, 21, 24, 29, 33, 65, 66, 67, 68, 75, 93, 94, 97, 98, 99, 100, 103, 104, 113, 114, and 117**.

PSALM 119 is the longest psalm in the Scriptures and is divided into twenty-two sections, each coinciding with one of the twenty-two letters of the Hebrew ahleph-bet, in their order. Each section is devoted to giving praise to YAH for the multiplicity of His insight and guidance in a Believer's life. **PSALM 122** praises YAH's city, Jerusalem (YAHrushalayim), and His House and instructs all people to pray for the peace (shalom) of His House. **PSALM 124** is another psalm of praise for deliverance, and **PSALM 133** (one of my favorites) is a psalm about all of the brothers of YisraEL, Jews (YAHudi) and non-Jews (non-YAHudi/Goyim) alike, celebrating YAHveh, His House, and His land (our inheritance) together.

PSALMS 134 & 135 speak to those who serve, or will serve, in the House of YAHveh. **PSALM 136** is a psalm of thanksgiving, which is something all of His people need to do every time they seek His face. **PSALMS 139, 145, 148, and 150** speak of His faithfulness to all of His creation, and His personal concern for each of us after we have been created in His image (born-again).

The third group consists of about seventeen psalms, which carry the theme of addressing those who are under the curse of the Law (Torah/Instructions) and those who are under the blessings. **PSALMS 1, 14 & 15** compare the characteristics of the wicked to the characteristics of those who are made righteous in the sight of YAH. **PSALMS 36, 37, and 39** remind us that those who appear to have riches and do not know YAHveh already have their reward here on Earth, but those who belong to Him have riches unspeakable because they have His Shalom. **PSALMS 40, 49, 50, and 73** compare man's religion to YAH's true spiritual realm that He offers by His grace through faith. Honor, respect, reverence, and the fear of YAHveh are emphasized in **PSALM 76** and **PSALM 82**, where YAH also refers to all men who are created in His image (born-again) as elohim (gods). Remember, before we were born-again, we were created in the image of Ahdom after his fall and not in the image of YAHveh. This was the psalm that Yeshua referred to when He once again had to rebuke the religious leaders for doubting His deity and displaying their religiosity. *"Yeshua answered them, "Is it not found in the writings of your TaNaKh, 'I said, "You are elohim"'? "If He called them elohim, to whom the word of ELuah came (and the Scripture cannot be broken), "do you say to Him whom the Av (Father) sent into the world, 'You are blaspheming,' because I said, 'I AM the Son of YAHveh'?"*(JOHN 10:34-36). **PSALM 84** compares YAH's house to the tents of the wicked—this is not a reference to dwelling places on Earth that are made with men's hands, but rather to the people, or families, who dwell within them. **PSALMS 92, 112, and 115** speak of the benefits received from following the Torah of the Living ELohim.

The fourth theme concerns the inner feelings of those who are in the middle of persecution and are crying out to YAHveh to rescue them from their enemies who range from political to betrayers of friends. These cries for deliverance, vengeance, protection, salvation, and refuge can be found in the following: **PSALMS 5, 6, 7, 10, 11, 13, 23, 26, 28, 31, 35, 41, 43, 46, 55, 61, 62, 64, 69, 70, 71, 77, 83, 86, 88, 91, 108, 109, 120, 121, 140, 143, and 144**. As you can see, this is the second largest theme out of the five, and it's probably because most of us find ourselves crying out to YAHveh like this—Dahveed being no exception. When you are trying to be a person after YAH's own heart, this is where you will find yourself most of the time. But at the same time, there are more psalms of praise and joy because of His mercy and grace toward us.

The fifth and last theme covers sixteen psalms and addresses other situations that we find ourselves in where we need His guidance. **PSALM 4** speaks of YAH's mercy for those who seek Him. **PSALM 12** tells us to trust only YAH's words and not those that come from men. **PSALMS 20 & 25** remind us to look to YAHveh for our protection, healing, deliverance, and teachings, according to His instructions in His Torah. **PSALMS 32 & 38** instruct us that if we confess our sins and seek His face, we will find His forgiveness and His deliverance. Many of our infirmities are the results of sins that we have not confessed. And if we wait too long before confessing them, they may leave us permanently stricken as a consequence. **PSALM 42** reminds us to look to YAH when our troubles become too heavy of a burden and we become depressed. YAHveh promises to shut the mouths of scorners and doubters when He finally restores the House of YisraEL. **PSALM 53** points out the consequences of refusing to acknowledge YAHveh as ELohim. In **PSALM 58**, YAHveh rebukes those teachers and leaders who do not show His justice to those whom they are responsible for—to Him, they are as wicked men. In **PSALM 81**, YAH expresses His frustration with His people who, because of their stubbornness in wanting to do things their own way, were not following His instructions for celebrating His New Moons and Feasts. His simple instructions regarding dancing, singing, praising Him with musical instruments, and blowing the shofar on His Feast days were being ignored; therefore, He was forced to forsake them. If His people will just learn to be obedient in the small things first, He promises that He will show them greater things. Those with a contrite, reverent, and humbled heart toward YAHveh, ELohim of YisraEL, will be the ones who will receive the rewards that He has in store for them because they fear Him, as expressed in **PSALMS 101, 111, 130, and 131**. Finally, in **PSALMS 141 and 146**, we find that if we, His people, offer the incense of our lips and the sacrifice of our hands raised to Him, if we trust Him to guard our lips and our ways, and if we walk uprightly before Him by trusting in His teachings rather than those of mere men and their philosophies, He promises to keep us from the snares and the errors that are found in them.

Conclusion

Even Dahveed, the one whom YAHveh points out as the man after His own heart, failed in his relationship with his ELohim. Yet YAHveh chose him to be the king over His people and to bring forth His Branch, Yeshua, as the one descendant who would be the King of kings and the King of the Universe. This should bring hope to all of us who seek His face, His mercy, His forgiveness, and His redemption for our unfaithfulness. He promises to be faithful to us even when we fail to be faithful to Him—*if* we seek His forgiveness according to His Torah.

Notice that all of the psalms that are written in the Scriptures, along with their promises, are given as blessings to His people, YisraEL. In order to receive these promises, you must be His people, YisraEL. Who then are His people, YisraEL? All of those who believe, do His words, and accept His Messiah, Yeshua, as their own personal Savior—whether they are a Jew (YAHudi) or a Joe/Christian (from the tribe of Yosef)—they are YisraEL.

CHAPTER 7
...about I Kings 1-11, II Chronicles 1-9, the Book of Proverbs, Song of Solomon, and Ecclesiastes.

The two books known as Kings are considered to be prophetic and, therefore, are credited as belonging to the twenty-one books of the Prophets (Ne'vim). The first eleven chapters of I Kings and the first nine chapters of II Chronicles cover the reign of Dahveed's only living son by Bathshe'bah, Solomon (Shalomo). Proverbs, Song of Solomon (Shalomo) (also known as Song of Songs), and Ecclesiastes are all considered part of the Kethuvim (Writings) of the TaNaKh. "Ecclesiastes" is the Greek word for "Teacher", which has its root meaning in the word ecclesia. This word "ecclesia" is used in the Brit Chadashah (Renewed Covenant/New Testament) and means assembly or congregation. With that said, we will now begin our study of the final division that takes place between the two houses of YisraEL, YAHuda and Yosef /Efraeem.

The time is somewhere around one-thousand years before the coming of the Messiah Yeshua, and King Dahveed's health is beginning to deteriorate in his advancing years. One of the treatments that they used to help maintain his body temperature was to bring in a young woman to share her body heat with him. Her name was Abishag (Ahbeeshag). Meanwhile, trouble continued in Dahveed's family when another son, Adonijah (AhdoneeYAH), in order to prevent his father from naming Solomon (Shalomo) as his successor, attempted a coup. Adonijah (AhdoneeYAH) had convinced the king's commander, Joab (Yoab), and the priest Abiathar (Ahbeeahthar) that the kingdom rightfully belonged to him. But Nathan, the prophet (ne'vee), informed Queen Bathshe'bah of the situation so that she might relay it to the king. King Dahveed took charge immediately and called upon the prophet (ne'vee) Nathan, his trusted friend, along with the priest Zadok and one of his mighty men of valor, Benaiah (BehnaheeYAH), to take his son, Solomon (Shalomo), place him on Dahveed's own donkey, and anoint him as king. When the people saw Solomon (Shalomo) on the king's personal donkey, they immediately abandoned Adonijah (AhdoneeYAH) and rushed to Solomon's (Shalomo's) coronation. In YisraEL, a donkey was considered a far nobler animal than a horse. Horses were the choice of Gentile kings because to them they represented power and strength and were suited to be used in battle. The donkey, to the YisraELi, represented nobility and strength and was best suited for servant-hood.

Solomon (Shalomo), the New King of YisraEL

King Solomon (Shalomo) showed mercy to his brother and vowed not to take vengeance if Adonijah (AhdoneeYAH) would behave himself in the future. But in his arrogance, Adonijah (AhdoneeYAH) made another attempt to gain power through the back door in a similar manner as did Absalom (Avshalom), when he asked Bathshe'bah to go before King Solomon (Shalomo) and request that he be given Abishag (Ahbeeshag) as his wife—he thought that she had actually been his father's concubine. King Solomon (Shalomo) recognized the ploy and had his brother executed. King Dahveed gave his son, Solomon (Shalomo), his blessings and instructions on how to secure the House of YisraEL from any further attempts to undermine YAH's purposes for them. Soon after this, Dahveed joined his fathers in death, and Solomon (Shalomo) began his own reign. One of the first things that Solomon (Shalomo) did was to remove Abiathar (Ahbeeahthar) as priest and assign Zadok to serve as sole priest over the House of YisraEL. Then he had Benaiah (BehnaheeYAH) remove Joab (Yoab) as commander by executing him with the sword. Finally, he confined one of his father's old enemies, Shimei (Sheemehee), to his house in Jerusalem (YAHrushalayim) at the price of his life if he disobeyed his confinement—he disobeyed.

Solomon (Shalomo) Makes Plans to Carry Out the Construction of the House of YAHveh

The Ark of the Testimony was still in a tent in YAHrushalayim, while the Mishkahn remained in Gibeon. So, King Solomon (Shalomo) went up to the high place at Gibeon and sacrificed a thousand burnt offerings at the bronze altar that was there. It was there that he had his first real encounter with YAHveh, ELohim of YisraEL. YAH appeared to Solomon (Shalomo) in a dream and told him that He would grant anything that he requested of Him. Solomon (Shalomo) chose to ask for wisdom so that he might best serve the ELohim of his fathers and guide the House of YisraEL. YAH granted him his request, and because he expressed a humble heart in serving as king, He also said that He would bless him with power and riches and shalom as long as he reigned *if* He would keep all of His instructions that were in His Torah. Immediately upon his return to YAHrushalayim, he demonstrated his newly-given wisdom in a dispute over a maternal matter.

When Solomon (Shalomo) began the construction of the House of YAH, he made a contract with King Hiram (Heerahm) of Tyre in Syria to supply him with the building materials that were needed. He also hired another man named Hiram (Heerahm), an artisan who would be responsible for all the intricate work and designs of YAHveh's house. Then he hired a mighty man of valor from the tribe of Ephraim (Efraeem), Jeroboam (YAHroboam), as foreman to oversee all of the construction of YAH's house. Throughout Scripture, I continually see YAHveh's House being incorrectly translated as "temple". This deserves repeating: temples were made for pagan idols and elohim. Our ELohim, YAHveh, had a house/palace built for Him—not a temple.

The place where the House of YAH was to be constructed was on the threshing floor that had once belonged to Araunah the Jebusiti (Yebusi), on Mt. Moriah (Moreeah). This was where Dahveed had the encounter with the *Angel of YAH* when YAH had sent a plague on the people of YisraEL. It was here that Dahveed had prayed and made sacrifice to his ELohim, who then recanted his judgment and removed the plague. The location of this construction site has been disputed throughout history as to whether or not it is where the Temple Mount is located today—at the Dome of the Rock or somewhere nearby. I have read several theories as to its possible location. I tend to lean to the one that places it west of the old city of YAHrushalayim and in an area that used to be the city dump, where the Gihon Spring now flows. The Gihon River was one of the four rivers that flowed out of Eden, and Eden was an Earthly model of Paradise. The Mishkahn was always erected near a flowing natural spring in order to provide a washing pool or reservoir (mikvah/meekvah in Hebrew) for the washing of the House utensils, as well as for the cleansing of the priests. Therefore, I tend to believe that the construction site of the House of YAH was more likely to have been closer to the Gihon River than the other sites—just a thought.

King Solomon (Shalomo) ordered all of the material for the House of YAH (olive, acacia, and cedar wood, as well as all quarry stone) to be cut before it was brought to the construction site in order to produce a near-silent atmosphere—thereby showing reverence to the Holy site. The palace for YAHveh was to be three-stories high with two bronze pillars at its entrance—one was called Boaz (Strength) and the other, YAHchin (YAH establishes). When the construction was finished, Solomon (Shalomo) brought all of the items that had been dedicated to the House of YAH by his father Dahveed to the treasury, along with the items from the Mishkahn that had been located at Gilead (Geelead). And, of course, he also had the Ark of the Testimony brought up from the tent in YAHrushalayim, where Dahveed had last placed it. A great celebration was about to take place as the House of YAH was to be dedicated in the seventh Hebrew month, Tishri, on the fourteenth day. This was the day that was just prior to the first day of the Feast of Tabernacles (Chag Sukkot). Singers sang while harps, cymbals, and lyres played, and one-hundred and twenty priests blew shofars—it was a glorious time to praise YAHveh. While this was taking place, the Shchinah glory of YAHveh filled the sanctuary of His House; it was so strong that the priests could not continue their ministering to Him. After the cloud had lifted, Solomon (Shalomo) gave a benediction toward YAH's house that included a prayer, that all who would call upon the Name of Adonai, no matter what their former heritage, would also be included as part of the House of YisraEL. The next day began the Feast of Sukkot, and instead of the feast lasting only seven days, Solomon (Shalomo) extended it for an additional seven days because the people were so joyful.

Solomon (Shalomo) had rededicated all that he was and all that he had to YAHveh, King of all. But as time went on, all of his power and wealth began working on his pride. Like many of us, he focused too much on his blessings and soon forgot their source—his ELohim. It was easy to start trusting and relying on his own experiences and his own wisdom rather than the wisdom that YAH had granted him at his request. As an example, he thought that by marrying many of the daughters of the kings of the surrounding nations, this would provide him protection from foreign attack. He also started collecting horses and chariots, thinking that this would give him the military strength that he needed for protection. Eventually, the women he married began to be a negative influence on his spiritual life. We find Solomon (Shalomo) celebrating his blessings in **PSALM 72**, and even though his confession credits YAHveh, his actions and lifestyle say something else.

Shalomo's Proverbs

The Proverbs and poems of Shalomo begin with his understanding of wisdom and knowledge. *"The fear of YAHveh is the beginning of knowledge"* (**PROV 1:7**). It could be said another way—in the beginning of knowledge was the fear of ELohim. The first ten chapters are focused on the wisdom and the knowledge that are in the words of YAH, with warnings about unfaithfulness and foolish thinking. In **PROV 11-22** and **25-29**, He uses idioms about adultery and folly to point out to his readers just how easy it is to lose focus regarding their relationship with YAH and with His words that are found in the Torah. All of these sayings contain points of wisdom that are based upon his relationship with YAHveh and upon his own experiences. **PROV 23&24** contain the sayings of other wise men. The last two Proverbs (30 & 31) are attributed to a man named Agur and to the mother of King Lemuel—the latter being about finding the perfect wife. These wise sayings cover a variety of subjects. They range from repentance to the keeping of YAH's instructions regarding righteousness through faith to the ultimate punishment of the wicked—from self-discipline to the discipline of our children—from pride and its ultimate destruction to humility and its ultimate reward—from properly handling wealth to righteous justice, generosity, and greed. They also warn us about guarding our speech and our hearts from the words of others.

WHAT WE WEREN'T TAUGHT ABOUT THE BIBLE AND ITS HISTORY

In the **Book of Proverbs**, we can see Shalomo expressing the wisdom that was given to him by YAHveh, but because of personal defects in his character, we can also begin to see that wisdom changed into pride and into his eventual destruction. This is better illustrated in his writings as "The Teacher" in Ecclesiastes. He expressed both joy and hope in Proverbs, but in his writings as a teacher, he expressed his disappointment in life as a whole. In his final days, he began to see where he went wrong by not keeping the teachings of the Torah, but with his life being about over, he could not undo his failings. He could, however, give warnings to others about seeking after the things of this world rather than seeking after the things of YAHveh, as he did.

Being a man of many words, King Shalomo also wrote, under the inspiration of YAH's Ruach, the Song of Songs. This was apparently to one of his many wives—perhaps to his favorite—but it is a perfect example of the relationship between Yeshua, the Bridegroom, and YisraEL, His Bride. It was probably around this time, or perhaps in the final days of his life, that he also wrote **PSALM 127**.

The time has now arrived for the king to rest with his fathers. But just prior to his death, one of his faithful advisors, Jeroboam (YAHroboam), a man of valor and the main overseer of the construction of the House of YAH, had become dissatisfied with the king. He was ready to rebel against him for straying so far from YAH's instructions of the Torah, while misleading His people, YisraEL, in doing so. Jeroboam (YAHroboam) was approached by Ahijah (AheeYAH), one of YAHveh's prophets (ne'veem). Ahijah (AheeYAH) asked Jeroboam (YAHroboam) to hand him his new tallit (tahleet), which he took and immediately tore into twelve pieces, telling him that these represented the twelve tribes of YisraEL. He then told Jeroboam (YAHroboam) to keep ten of the pieces for himself and deliver the other two to the king. The ten pieces represented the tribes that YAH was going to deliver into Jeroboam's (YAHroboam's) hands, while the other two would remain under King Shalomo's rule in order to fulfill YAH's promise to His servant, King Dahveed.

Conclusion

King Dahveed, even though he was a man after YAH's own heart and would be designated (for his name's sake and through his descendants) to be the King of kings and rule YAH's Kingdom forever, was not allowed to build a palace for his ELohim. Even so, he was given all of the provisions, along with the design, for this magnificent edifice that his son, Shalomo, would later inherit. His son, who never really learned to appreciate the great honor of this task, started off by ruling with the appropriate attitude, but because of his own pride due to wealth, power, and glory, soon fell into sin. And because of his sins of indulgence, the whole House of YisraEL would experience a fall through strife and division. Two nations would emerge out of the ashes of this tragedy, and this would set the stage for the coming of another son of King Dahveed, the Savior of the world, who would eventually, by the working of the triune Echad of YAHveh (Father, Son, and Spirit), bring about the final restoration of the House of YisraEL.

CHAPTER 8
...about I Kings 12—II Kings 8 and II Chronicles 10—21

YAHveh had given a total of seven covenants to His people since the beginning of creation, renewing each over the previous, which were designed to unify His people and to set them apart from the nations around them. But the powers of darkness knew that if this were to happen, it would mean their end, so the Prince of Darkness began attacking YisraEL at their greatest weakness—pride. Power and wealth, or the love of money and what it purchases, feeds pride, and this had led King Shalomo to his own demise. The example that he had set for his own son, Rehoboam, while he was king, became his son's basic training for life. This is true for all parents; if we expect our children to become solid and honest citizens, then we have to become their role model or they will develop their own. Shalomo's wise saying, *"Train up a child in the way he should go, and when he is old he will not depart from it"* (**PROV 22:6**), will always come into play, even if it is in the negative. Rehoboam, having learned well by his father's example of wine, women, and song, became more of an oppressor of YAH's people than his father had ever been. This would eventually lead to ten out of the twelve tribes rising up against the new king's yoke of taxation. The ten then called upon a man who had been their overseer during the construction of the House of YAH, Jeroboam (YAHroboam) from the House of Yosef/Ephraim (Efraeem), to become their new leader. But the tribes of YAHuda and BenYAHmeen remained faithful by keeping one of King Dahveed's sons on the throne to lead their tribes. These two tribes became known in the TaNaKh as the southern tribes, while the rest of YisraEL became known as the northern tribes. This division later became permanent because it was a part of the overall plan that YAHveh had chosen to implement His promises to Avraham, Yitzhak, and Yaacov.

The Beginning of the Reign of King Jeroboam (YAHroboam)

Jeroboam (YAHroboam), not understanding YAH's ultimate plan, sought to devise a way to keep the ten tribes of YisraEL, those given to him by Ahijah (AheeYAH), under his control. He decided to set up two golden-calf idols in the northern cities of Dan (Dahn) and Bethel. This way, the people would not have to return to YAHrushalayim to celebrate the Feasts. Besides setting up his own places of worship, he also set up his own priest system to serve YAHveh. This, of course, was an abomination before the Almighty and a direct act of defiance against YAH's instructions in the Torah. His substituting YAH's words with his own to stay in control could be called "replacement theology". Today's "organized church" has done the same thing by saying that the teachings of the "New Testament" have replaced that of the "Old Testament" and that the "Church" has replaced "YisraEL", even calling itself a type of "spiritual Israel".

Even though YAH promised that He would always have a descendant of Dahveed sitting upon the throne as the king of His people, this would not be the case for the northern tribes of YisraEL. The tribes of YisraEL from that time on would be cursed with many wicked kings usurping the authority of others, and Jeroboam (YAHroboam) would always be referred to as the king who was responsible for the division of YisraEL.

The Northern and the Southern Tribes of YisraEL

Shalomo's son, King Rehoboam, decided to try to force Jeroboam's (YAHroboam's) northern tribes to return, but a prophet (ne'vee) by the name of Shemaiah (ShemaheeYAH) came forward and instructed the king not to go up against their brothers because Jeroboam's (YAHroboam's) action was a part of YAHveh's overall plan. King Rehoboam obeyed the word of YAH that was given to him by the prophet (ne'vee), and it was accounted to him as faith. Because of this, YAH showed the southern tribes of YAHuda and BenYAHmeen considerably more mercy in their later years than He otherwise would have. When the tribe of the Lehvee and those from the northern tribes who feared YAHveh saw how Jeroboam (YAHroboam) was leading YAH's people away from His Torah, they left and returned to the House of YAHuda in the south. From that time on, YAH's prophets (ne'veem), in their writings, would refer to the southern tribes as YAHuda and the northern tribes as YisraEL, Yosef, or Ephraim (Efraeem).

Not long after the division, Jeroboam (YAHroboam) had an encounter with two different prophets (ne'veem) who warned him against his rebellion, but he refused to listen, resulting in negative consequences. When he tried to arrest the first one, one of his hands withered and he became a cripple. Then he sent one of his wives to the prophet (ne'vee) Ahijah (AheeYAH) to inquire whether or not one of his sons who had become ill would survive. Remember, Ahijah (AheeYAH) was the prophet (ne'vee) who had told him that he would be the leader of ten of the tribes of YisraEL. But this time, Ahijah (AheeYAH) told him that because he had committed so many atrocities against YAH, his son, along with the rest of his family, were going to die soon.

Meanwhile, in YAHuda, King Rehoboam began to allow his people to be influenced by the sins of both YisraEL and the people of the nations around them. They had failed to drive out the foreigners, which allowed paganism to creep in and corrupt the people in the south as well.

After Rehoboam's reign, his son, Abijah (AbeeYAH), became king and wasn't any better than his father. He was followed by his son, Asa (Ahsah), who did bring about some reform and led YAHuda's people back to YAHveh. But, he had one shortcoming—he didn't tear down all of the idols and high places that had been erected throughout the land (these were elevated hills where false priests assembled to make sacrifices to their elohim). While Asa's (Ahsah's) father, Ahijah (AheeYAH), was king, he and Jeroboam (YAHroboam) entered into a short civil war. These skirmishes between these brothers would crop up from time to time and would continue even to this day between the Jews and the Christians. All of YisraEL eventually became so involved with the nations around them that they lost their identity and became just like them. So, as punishment from YAHveh, YisraEL and YAHuda have been persecuted by the Gentiles (Goyim/Gohyeem—the Hebrew word for nations) ever since.

When King Jeroboam (YAHroboam) died, he was succeeded by his son, Nadab, who was assassinated in a blood coup by a man named Baasha (Bahahsha). At the same time, Baasha (Bahahsha) had all of the king's family murdered and set himself up as king, thereby fulfilling the prophecy of Ahijah (AheeYAH). After this, he threatened YAHuda with a civil war, and King Asa (Ahsah) of YAHuda, instead of seeking the face of YAH for instructions, looked to the king of Syria for help. YAH immediately rebuked King Asa (Ahsah), through His prophet (ne'vee) Hanani, for his lack of faithfulness. King Asa (Ahsah) then compounded his problem by having the prophet (ne'vee) Hanani thrown into prison.

In the meantime, YAHveh sent His prophet (ne'vee) Jehu (YAH'oo) to warn Baasha, the new King of YisraEL, not to go up against His people, YAHuda. The king ignored the warning, which proved he did not fear YAHveh; therefore, he and his whole family would be destroyed. It wasn't long before Baasha died, and his son, Elah (EL'YAH), became king in his place. He soon was assassinated by one of his army officers, Zimri, along with all of Baasha's family. But the people of YisraEL opposed this coup and responded to it by appointing Omri, who had been the commander of their army, as their new king. When the news of what had taken place got back to Zimri, he became fearful and took his own life. After Omri was made king, he decided that YisraEL should have a capitol city of their own, just like the other nations around them, so he purchased the city of Samaria, which remained their capitol until the day of their assimilation. After this, he arranged the marriage of his son, Ahab (Ack'hav), to the infamous *Jezebel* (*Yezebel,* the queen of hell). Omri died eleven years later, and Ahab (Ack'hav) became king of YisraEL, with Jezebel (Yezebel) as his queen. Ahab (Ack'hav) and Jezebel (Yezebel) were the worst king and queen that YisraEL ever had throughout their history. During their reign, a man by the name of Heir rebuilt Jericho (Yaricho) and sacrificed his two sons when he laid the foundation with its two gates—one son for its foundation and the other for its gates—just as Joshua (Yoshua) had prophesied would happen (JOSH 6:26). After that, Ahab (Ack'hav) built a temple to Baal and set up an Asherah pole in Samaria.

A year later, King Asa (Ahsah) of YAHuda died from a disease of his feet because he sought the help of physicians and not YAHveh. YAH wants His people to first seek Him as their source for healing before going to physicians. He has given mankind physicians because of His grace, knowing that not everyone would come to know Him as their Great Physician. Remember, He has the final word as to who will or will not be healed. King Asa's (Ahsah's) son, Jehoshaphat (YAHoshaphat), became YAHuda's new king. He continued where his father left off by following after YAHveh. He also cleansed the land of most, but not all, of the shrines and high places. He saw to it that Torah teaching was reestablished, and because of this, YAH saw to it that he and YAHuda prospered and once again became a mighty nation to be reckoned with. King Jehoshaphat (YAHoshaphat) even managed to establish some shalom (peace) with King Ahab (Ack'hav) of YisraEL.

YAHveh Sent His Ne'vee, Elijah (ELeeYAHoo), to Warn YisraEL of Her Sins

YAH sent a very unique ne'vee named Elijah (ELeeYAHoo) to YisraEL to warn her of her sins and to tell her what the outcome would be if she didn't repent. He would be the first ne'vee, but not the last, to have this mission. His uniqueness didn't stop there. Just like Enoch ("the blessed one"), the seventh-generation son from Ahdom, he too would be translated into YAH's presence instead of tasting death. Later, he would appear with Mosheh the Torah giver at the transfiguration of Yeshua the Messiah. Some believe that he will appear once more with Mosheh in the End-Times and will confront the Antimessiah just before Yeshua's return. When the Messiah came the first time, His cousin, John the Baptist (Yochanan the Immerser), was the first to announce His arrival. John (Yochanan) is said to have been like the ne'vee Elijah (ELeeYAHoo), who was a predecessor of the Messiah. Elijah (ELeeYAHoo) also trained a second ne'vee by the name of Elisha (Eleeshaw) as his protégé. Between the two of them, they performed more signs and wonders than all of the other ne'veem combined, except for the Messiah Himself.

One day, Elijah (ELeeYAHoo) confronted King Ahab (Ack'hav) and told him that a drought was about to begin and that it would only cease when he, Elijah (ELeeYAHoo), gave the word. Right after announcing the upcoming drought, YAH told Elijah (ELeeYAHoo) to go to a certain brook and wait for further instructions and that He would send ravens there to feed him. (This was a "Goshen" type of hiding place, as well as a metaphor of YAH's protection for those who belong to Him. The United States has been a "Goshen" for immigrants from all of the nations/Goyim/Gentiles who have sought religious freedom—our forefathers founded this nation on Biblical principles.) After a period of time, even this little brook dried up from the drought. YAH then gave Elijah (ELeeYAHoo) another mission that took him to the gate of a small town, where a starving widow who feared YAHveh was gathering sticks to cook the last meal that she had for her and her son. YAH had already revealed this to him, so Elijah (ELeeYAHoo) told her to fix him the meal instead, thereby giving her an opportunity to express her faith in YAH's provisions. If she did, YAHveh would see to it that she would never run out of oil and flour. (This was quite similar to the two times that Yeshua fed the five thousand and the seven thousand with only a few loaves of bread and a few fish. This also demonstrates how YAH will do very much with very little if we would just trust Him.) Then the widow's faith was tested again when her son died and Elijah (ELeeYAHoo) raised him from the dead, demonstrating that it is YAH who has the power over life and death because He is both the resurrection and the life, just as His Son, Yeshua, later confirmed.

Three years later, Elijah (ELeeYAHoo) met a man named Obadiah (OhbedeeYAH) whose name means "a servant of YAH". Whether or not this is the same Obadiah (OhbedeeYAH) that later became a ne'vee of YAH and wrote one of the Books of the Ne'vim is somewhat controversial, but he may be. Anyway, because of the famine, he was sent out by King Ahab (Ack'hav) to find fodder for the king's animals and met Elijah (ELeeYAHoo) along the way. Elijah (ELeeYAHoo) told him to go to the king and tell him that YAH commanded the king to meet with Elijah (ELeeYAHoo). Obadiah (OhbedeeYAH) was reluctant because Queen Jezebel (Yezebel) had been slaughtering all of YAH's ne'veem in order to silence them. But Elijah (ELeeYAHoo) assured him that YAH would not let this happen, so he did as he was told.

After King Ahab (Ack'hav) agreed to meet with Elijah (ELeeYAHoo), the ne'vee challenged the king to gather together all of the priests of Baal in order to decide once and for all who the true ELohim was. After four-hundred and fifty false priests and ne'veem assembled, they were given the first chance to prove the power of their *eluah*. They were challenged to go up to Mount Carmel, where they were to lay a bull on an altar made from a pile of wood, and Elijah (ELeeYAHoo) would do likewise. Whichever eluah sent down fire to consume the offering would, thereby, be proven to be the true ELohim. They did as he instructed and called on Baal all that day, cutting themselves as a demonstration of their faithfulness (which, by the way, is what many of us have seen on television when the Muslims in the Middle East flog themselves with chains in order to show contrition), but nothing happened. Around midday, Elijah (ELeeYAHoo) began to taunt them, saying that maybe their el was asleep. When they finally gave up and it was his turn, he rebuilt YAHveh's altar that had once stood there, using twelve stones to represent the tribes of YisraEL, and placed his bull on the pile of wood. He even had the false ne'veem of Baal dig a trench around the altar and then pour enough water over the sacrifice to overflow the trenches. When he had finished, he prayed to the ELohim of Avraham, Yitzhak, and YisraEL, and YAH sent down fire and consumed everything on and around the altar. When the people saw this, they declared YAHveh to be the true ELohim. Afterward, Elijah (ELeeYAHoo) had the people bring the false ne'veem of Baal down to the Kishon Brook and had them executed there. Then, at Elijah's (ELeeYAHoo's) word, the drought ended. Jezebel (Yezebel) was furious and threatened to put Elijah (ELeeYAHoo) to death; he responded by hiding from her in fear. Then YAHveh sent an angel to summon him to go to Mount Horeb. It took him forty days and nights to get there (remember that forty is always a number for a time of testing). It was there that Elijah (ELeeYAHoo) stayed in a cave and experienced a number of dynamic visions that were given to him by YAH to show him that He is not always found in dynamic events, but mostly in the still, small voice of a person's heart.

Elisha (ELeeshaw), Elijah's (ELeeYAHoo's) Protégé

Elijah (ELeeYAHoo) was then told to go and anoint a man named Hazael (HazahEL) to be the king of Aram in Syria. He was then told to go to Samaria and anoint Jehu (YAHu) to be the new king of YisraEL. After that, he was to go to a place called Abel Meholah to find a man named Elisha (ELeeshaw) and anoint him to be a ne'vee for YAH. Then YAH revealed to him that all during the time that he thought that he was alone and was the last to be faithful, YAH had kept for Himself seven-thousand others. This both encouraged and confirmed to Elijah (ELeeYAHoo) that YAH always keeps a faithful remnant and never abandons His faithful.

Meanwhile, King Ben-Hadad, the reigning king of the territory of Aram, gathered thirty-two kings from the other provinces of Syria and devised a plan to invade Samaria, the capital of YisraEL. King Ben-Hadad gave King Ahab (Ack'hav) an offer to surrender, but he refused after being promised victory by a ne'vee of YAH named Micaiah (MeekaheeYAH). So, seven-thousand, two-hundred and thirty-two brave men marched against the Syrians and struck down King Ben-Hadad's vast army. But the king and his officers managed to escape and decided to regroup and attack them later in the spring. In the meantime, the king's officers suggested that the reason for their defeat was because YisraEL's ELohim was from the mountains—therefore, they should attack them on the plains the next time. The ne'vee Micaiah (MeekaheeYAH) returned to King Ahab (Ack'hav) and told him not to fear because YAHveh would once more deliver Ben-Hadad's vast army into his hands. But the king of Aram and his officers escaped again and fled to a nearby city; they were captured this time and brought back to Samaria. When King Ben-Hadad showed the king of YisraEL contrition, he was shown mercy and his life was spared. But the ne'vee Micaiah (MeekaheeYAH), on behalf of YAHveh, rebuked King Ahab (Ack'hav) for not executing the king of Aram and told him that it would now be his life in exchange for the life of the king of Aram.

To illustrate King Ahab's (Ack'hav's) and his wife's, Queen Jezebel's (Yezebel's) wickedness, the king coveted a certain vineyard for himself that belonged to a local resident, but when the man refused to relinquish it to him because the property was originally his father's, King Ahab (Ack'hav) sat around his palace and sulked. When the wicked Queen Jezebel (Yezebel) heard about it, she devised a plan to seize the land by treachery and had the man slain under a false pretense. When the ne'vee Elijah (ELeeYAHoo) heard of this diabolical act, he pronounced a cruel death sentence upon both the king and his wife, Queen Jezebel (Yezebel), along with their whole house, just as He had done to Jeroboam (YAHroboam) and Baasha. But then, quite out of character, the king repented for his part, and YAH showed him His mercy, gave him a stay of execution, and passed the sentence on to his son, Ahaziah (AhazeeYAH). A short time later, Ahaziah (AhazeeYAH) began to share the throne with his father as a co-regent. Then King Ahab (Ack'hav) entered into an alliance with King Jehoshaphat (YAHoshaphat) of YAHuda to help him take back the territory of Ramoth-Gilead that the king of Aram had seized earlier. Then King Ahab (Ack'hav) consulted a ne'vee of Baal, who encouraged him to go into battle by telling him that he would be victorious. King Jehoshaphat (YAHoshaphat) suggested that they should also consult with one of YAHveh's ne'veem, but King Ahab (Ack'hav) was reluctant because Micaiah (MeekaheeYAH) was the only one nearby, and he didn't care for his prophecies. Then, after some deliberation, they sent for Micaiah (MeekaheeYAH), who also confirmed the victory but added that King Ahab (Ack'hav) would not survive the battle. Just as Micaiah (MeekaheeYAH) had prophesied, King Ahab (Ack'hav) was wounded in battle and died, even though he had tried to evade the enemy by disguising himself. Then a ne'vee of YAHuda, Jehu (YAHu), rebuked King Jehoshaphat (YAHoshaphat) for making an alliance with the wicked king of YisraEL, Ahab (Ack'hav), in the first place.

After receiving his rebuke from YAH, King Jehoshaphat (YAHoshaphat) of YAHuda continued to try to turn the people back to YAHveh, their ELohim, by appointing righteous judges to judge the affairs of men, according to the Torah. But they were continually tested by the nations around them. The Moabites (Moabi) began to invade YAHuda after King Ahab (Ack'hav) of YisraEL had been killed and his son, Ahaziah (AhazeeYAH), began to reign. The Moabites

(Moabi) had been forced to pay tribute to YisraEL under King Ahab (Ack'hav), and they had decided that it was time to cast off this yoke from their neck. Upon hearing of the invasion into their territory, King Jehoshaphat (YAHoshaphat) immediately turned to YAH in His House and called out to Him for guidance. YAH answered him through His ne'vee, Jahaziel (YAHazeeEL), who told the king and the people to go out to meet the Moabites (Moabi) and not to be afraid because the battle would belong to YAH. Early the next morning, they went out with singing and praises, led by King Jehoshaphat (YAHoshaphat) and the priests. Because they did as they were instructed, YAHveh met their obedience and faith with victory. But Jehoshaphat (YAHoshaphat) was one of YAH's slower learners; he made a shipping alliance with King Ahab's (Ack'hav's) son, Ahaziah (AhazeeYAH), who, like his father, was a rebel against the ELohim of YisraEL. However, the ne'vee Eliezer gave a prophecy to the king and told him that his shipping endeavors were doomed.

Shortly thereafter, King Ahaziah (AhazeeYAH) had an accident and sent a messenger to one of the seers of the false eluah Baalzebub to find out if he would recover. But YAHveh sent Elijah (ELeeYAHoo) to intercept the messenger and to give him YAH's own message to take back to King Ahaziah (AhazeeYAH), that he was about to come to his end because he went to a false eluah for comfort. When the messenger returned, King Ahaziah (AhazeeYAH) asked him what the one who gave him this message looked like. He described him as wearing a leather belt and a tallit made of hair. The king knew immediately that it was Elijah (ELeeYAHoo). The king, in his defiance, tried to order Elijah (ELeeYAHoo) to come and stand before him. Three times he sent out troops of fifty men to arrest him, but Elijah (ELeeYAHoo) took no orders from mere men, so he called fire down upon the first two troops. But the third troop was different because the captain humbled himself before YAH and confessed his fear of Him. So, YAH spared his life and sent Elijah (ELeeYAHoo), along with the captain and his fifty men, to bring YAH's message directly to the king himself. Then, just as YAH's word said, the king died and his brother, Joram (Yoram), took his place as the king of YisraEL.

Elisha (ELeesha) Takes Over Where ELeeYAHoo Left Off

The ministry of one of YAH's ne'veem was about to come to an end, but not without it continuing on through the life of his faithful friend and colleague, Elisha (ELeeshaw). One day, when they were traveling together, ELeeYAHoo told Elisha (ELeeshaw) that he was going to take a journey to the city of Bethel and asked him to remain at Gilgal. But, YAHveh revealed to Elisha (ELeeshaw) that He was going to miraculously take ELeeYAHoo away. Upon learning this, Elisha (ELeeshaw) expressed to his friend his desire to stay with him. ELeeYAHoo told his friend three times to remain at Gilgal, but

Elisha's (ELeeshaw's) reply remained the same. This faithfulness is a reminder of the faithfulness that Ruth had shown Naomi.

YAH began to reveal this upcoming phenomenon to each company, or school, of the ne'veem in each city that they came to. When they would see the two coming, they would come out to greet them, but Elisha (ELeeshaw) would tell them to remain quiet about what they knew. Now, when the two came to the Yarden River, ELeeYAHoo removed his tallit (garment/shawl), rolled it up, and struck the waters with it; they parted, leaving dry land for them to cross. We need to remember the significance of this sign. It teaches us about the power that is in YAH's deliverance of His people. Avraham crossed over both the Euphrates and the Yarden Rivers. Mosheh crossed through the Red Sea, and Joshua (Yoshua) crossed through the Yarden in a similar manner. The dry land represents YAH's Highway to deliverance, while the water that was parted represents His word divided into the two main covenants. YAHveh always has an old, or earlier, covenant that is followed by a new, or renewed, one that updates and increases His grace to a higher plane. One day, all of those who believe in His promises will travel on that final Highway to Holiness either in the resurrection or the rapture at His coming.

Elisha (ELeeshaw) made a request to the senior ne'vee, that he might receive a double portion of his spirit after he leaves. ELeeYAHoo told him that if he was able to witness his departure, it would be the sign that YAH had granted his request. Upon his departure, Elisha (ELeeshaw) was able to see him being taken away by a fiery whirlwind of horses and chariots. This whirlwind was exactly like the one that separated the Pharaoh and his army from the people of YisraEL during the first exodus and the column of fire that led His people through the wilderness during the night, which was the Angel of YAH—the Rock—Yeshua. He also saw that ELeeYAHoo's tallit had fallen to the ground, so he retrieved it, rolled it up, struck the water, and was able to duplicate the miracle that his friend had performed. ELeeYAHoo was translated just as Enoch (the seventh son after Ahdom) had been and just as Yeshua's Kahal will be at His return.

Elisha (ELeeshaw) now picked up where ELeeYAHoo left off in proclaiming the words of YAH, with signs and wonders accompanying them. The works that ELeeYAHoo and Elisha (ELeeshaw) did are an example of the works that the Kahal of Yeshua (His Body) will do in the latter days. They both demonstrated the power and love of YAHveh to all and confirmed His desire for all men to walk in His ways. They also represented the former and the latter Houses of YAHuda and Yosef, the descendants of the two brothers who make up the whole House of YisraEL. It is YAH who chooses the ones He wants to use, and He does it according to their hearts. He did this both before and after the first Advent of His Messiah. Neither one of these two was able to keep the Torah, nor any of His ne'veem for that matter—they all fell short of YAHveh's glory and holiness. But their faith in His Torah provided them their righteousness. He is the same today, yesterday, and forever. Their faith in His Torah, whether it was His written one or His Living One, Yeshua, does not change this fact. Nor does the observance of them change—only men change. Therefore, which are we to follow—the imaginations of men or the instructions and commandments of YAHveh? As for me and my house, we will serve the Living ELohim.

The Miracles of Elisha (ELeeshaw)

Among the many miracles that Elisha (ELeeshaw) performed were: the purifying of contaminated water—causing a widowed woman's oil to increase enough to sustain her and her son—raising from the dead the only son of a widow who was once barren—feeding hundreds from only a few loaves of bread—and causing an axe head to float on water. All of these miracles paralleled miracles that were performed by the Promised Messiah, such as: turning water into wine—raising the dead—feeding thousands with only a few loaves of bread and some fish—and walking on water.

During Elisha's (ELeeshaw's) ministry of messianic proportion and after YisraEL's subduing the territories of Edom and Moab, the Moabites (Moabi) began to threaten war again with YisraEL. King Joram (Yoram) of YisraEL appealed to King Jehoshaphat (YAHoshaphat) of YAHuda, along with the king of Edom, for assistance in subduing this rebellion. King Jehoshaphat (YAHoshaphat) suggested that they first consult with one of YAHveh's ne'veem. One of King Joram's (Yoram's) officers suggested that they consult with Elisha (ELeeshaw). At first, Elisha (ELeeshaw) rebuked King Joram (Yoram) for consulting him because prior to this, his spiritual advisors had always been pagans. But out of his respect for King Jehoshaphat (YAHoshaphat), he gave them instructions on how to defeat the Moabites (Moabi). Not long after this, King Jehoshaphat (YAHoshaphat) died, leaving his son, Jehoram (YAHoram), to reign in his place.

Before Jehoram (YAHoram) began his reign, he ensured his monarchy by having all of his brothers murdered, along with some of the princes of YisraEL. Now, as king of YAHuda, he began to go down the same paths as the kings of YisraEL by worshiping false elohim. Soon after, a letter mysteriously came to him from YAH's ne'vee, ELeeYAHoo, which he may have written before he was translated into the presence of YAH, but was to be delivered when the time was appropriate. It foresaw King Jehoram (YAHoram) as the king of YAHuda, his rebellion against YAHveh, his reign ending, and it pronounced a curse of infirmity upon him. He was told that he would suffer from a disease of his bowels. Soon after, he began to experience this curse. Then the Philistines

(Philisti) and the Arabs attacked him and killed all of his wives and children, except for his son, Ahaziah (AhazeeYAH). He was apparently named after the son of the wicked king of YisraEL, Ahab (Ack'hav), whom his father must have admired. Seeing their opportunity, Edom and the people of the territory of Libnah also revolted against the king.

At this particular time in Scripture, we have a king in YisraEL named Ahab (Ack'hav) who had two sons—one named Ahaziah (AhazeeYAH) and the other named Joram (Yoram). They both served as kings in YisraEL—one followed by the other. At about the same time, we have a king in YAHuda named Jehoshaphat (YAHoshaphat) who had a son named Jehoram (YAHoram), who in turn named one of his sons Ahaziah (AhazeeYAH)—they both served as kings of YAHuda. I must admit that this can get a little confusing and may be hard to follow at times, but try to remember which king belonged to which tribe.

Conclusion

This is the beginning of the final division of the whole House of YisraEL into the northern and the southern tribes of YAHuda and YisraEL. They will not be reunited again until the Messiah Yeshua restores them at the end of the age. The time of the prophecies about the Diaspora of the Houses of YisraEL and YAHuda from the Ne'vim is about to begin; they will warn the two divided nations of their sins and of their need for repentance and renewal, but their words will fall on deaf ears. The eyes and the ears of YAH's people will soon be closed and stay that way for the next 2,800 years, until the time of the Gentiles (Goyim) has been fulfilled.

As has been mentioned before, YAH has always sent ne'veem to speak to His people before He moved among them. During the age of the Ne'vim, a ne'vee would give both a "near" and a "far" prophecy. The "near prophecy" would determine whether or not they were true ne'veem. A ne'vee, if he claimed to be a spokesperson for the Living ELohim, had to bring his prophecies before the school of ne'veem. There, they were recorded and kept in order to test their accuracy. They were not considered to be true ne'veem unless their words came to pass, as was designated in the Torah. If they did, then their far prophecies would be considered canon, or inspired, and thus equal to the truth. There are fifteen ne'veem named in the twenty-one books of the Ne'vim. Daniel (DahneeEL) was never considered one of them because his prophecies could not be confirmed—they didn't take place until after the arrival of the Messiah. Therefore, his writings were included only in the thirteen books of the Kethuvim, or Writings. But in the case of ELeeYAHoo and Elisha (ELeeshaw), their near prophecies were the actual lives that they lived and the wonders that they preformed.

CHAPTER 9
...about Obadiah, Joel, II Kings 8-14, and II Chronicles 21-25

As just mentioned, there are fifteen ne'veem who have had their prophecies recorded in Scripture as part of the TaNaKh, or Old Testament. Three of them, Isaiah (YishshaYAH), Jeremiah (YirmehYAH), and Ezekiel (YekezkEL), are considered to be the Major Ne'vim, while the other twelve are considered to be the Minor Ne'vim. Obadiah (OhbedeeYAH) and Joel (YoEL) are two of the Minor Ne'vim. According to their listings in the TaNaKh, Obadiah (OhbedeeYAH) is the fourth minor Ne'vee and Joel (YoEL) is the second, but not according to their appearance in the historical order of events.

Obadiah's (OhbedeeYAH's) Prophecy Regarding Edom

Most of Obadiah's (OhbedeeYAH's) prophecies chastised the nation of Edom, which consisted mostly of the descendants of Esau, YisraEL's twin brother, and the mixed descendants of Nimrod. YisraEL and his brother, Esau, had become reconciled back at the time of their father's, Yitzhak's, burial, but their descendants remained enemies. If you remember, Esau was attracted to the Canaanite (Canaani) women and had taken several of them as wives. This led to more mixed marriages with other men and women of the area, who eventually became a rival nation called Edom. In the case of Obadiah (OhbedeeYAH) and his prophecies, Edom represented the total of all of the mixed nations who were descendants of Noah's two sons, Shem and Ham (Hahm). This also included the cousins of YisraEL: Ishmael (YishmaEL), or the Arabs—Moab, or the Moabites (Moabi)—Ammon, or the Ammonites (Ammoni)—as well as the people of Mitsrahyim.

YAHveh singled out Edom to use as His example to show how He would bring the promise of His wrath upon those who would rebel against Him. Perhaps He chose them because of their refusal to grant YisraEL safe passage through their land during their flight from Mitsrahyim to the Promised Land in Canaan. Then again, it may be because of the timing of their rebellion against YAHuda; but whatever the reason, YAH pronounced His judgment upon this rebellious, small nation. They would experience His wrath immediately and again in the future when they would receive their final destruction due to their hatred of their brothers, the Jews (YAHudim). In modern times, they would become better known as the Palestinians because they would settle in the land of the Philisti, along the Gaza Strip. As Obadiah (OhbedeeYAH) described Edom's eventual fate, he also announced the final victory of both houses of YisraEL, YAHuda and Yosef, and their restoration.

YAHveh Continues His Attempt to Guide YisraEL Through Elisha (ELeeshaw)

Now Syria began to make plans to attack YisraEL, but every time King Ben-Hadad of Aram tried to carry out his plan, the king of YisraEL would manage to either escape or somehow thwart his attack. It became so frequent that the king of Aram began to suspect that there might be a mole within his ranks revealing his offensive. But later, he was told that it was the ne'vee Elisha (ELeeshaw) who was responsible for his military failures. So, King Ben-Hadad gave orders to capture the ne'vee and throw him into prison. When word of Elisha's (ELeeshaw's) whereabouts reached the king, he dispatched troops to apprehend him. In the morning of the attempted capture, Elisha's (ELeeshaw's) servant, Gehazi, discovered that they were surrounded by Syrian troops. But Elisha (ELeeshaw) did not become concerned because he saw an army of YAH's angels giving them cover. And when he asked YAH to reveal this to his servant, they both became filled with tremendous confidence. When the troops began their approach, they were struck with blindness by YAH's army and became lost and confused. Elisha (ELeeshaw) and his servant led the blind army up to the capitol city of Samaria, where they turned them over to King Joram (Yoram) of YisraEL. However, instead of putting them into prison, the king set a feast before them and then sent them back to their own king. This action stunned King Ben-Hadad so severely that it was a long period of time before he even thought of raiding YisraEL again.

After a period of time had passed, word got around about the mighty works that the ELohim of YisraEL had been performing through His ne'vee, Elisha (ELeeshaw). One day, this word came to the commander of Ben-Hadad's army, Naaman (Nahaman), who suffered from a severe case of leprosy. The commander went to his king and asked for permission to seek out this ne'vee who did these mighty works by the power of his ELohim. So, the king of Aram sent a letter, along with Naaman (Nahaman), to the king of YisraEL, requesting that Naaman (Nahaman) be healed of his disease. When the letter was presented to King Joram (Yoram) of YisraEL, he immediately thought that King Ben-Hadad was trying to incite another conflict between them, and he became distraught. When Elisha (ELeeshaw) heard of this matter, he sent for Naaman (Nahaman) to appear before him, in order for YAHveh to heal him. But, when Naaman (Nahaman) arrived, Elisha (ELeeshaw) did not come out to meet him—he only sent out a few instructions for him to follow. This angered Naaman (Nahaman), and because of pride, he refused to follow the instructions, which only told him to go and baptize (mikvah/immerse or wash) himself in the Yarden River. But his servant reasoned with him about the simplicity of the instructions and encouraged him to give it a try. He relented and was healed. When he saw that he was healed, he praised, honored, and worshiped the ELohim of YisraEL. He was so overwhelmed by the miracle that had just happened that he immediately wanted to express his gratitude to Elisha (ELeeshaw). So, he sought him out again and offered gifts to him, but Elisha (ELeeshaw) refused them. Now get this, Naaman (Nahaman) wanted to take some of the soil from the land of YisraEL back to Aram so that when he worshiped YAHveh, he would have YisraELi soil to kneel on. At the same time, however, whenever King Ben-Hadad went to worship his pagan eluah and he accompanied him, he would ask YAH to forgive him for this pagan action. Boy, does that remind me of some of our brothers and sisters in the Body of Yeshua! Why is it so hard to abandon our old ways, those that men have put before us, in order to worship our Adonai? Why do we find it so hard to follow simple instructions? Why do we feel it necessary to always consult our intellect, which has been instructed in error, as to our understanding of the Law (Torah)? It's a mystery to me.

Another lesson to glean from this incident has to do with the behavior of Elisha's (ELeeshaw's) servant, Gehazi, after Naaman (Nahaman) made Elisha (ELeeshaw) an offer of a gift for his healing. Gehazi ran after Naaman (Nahaman) with a concocted story, saying that Elisha (ELeeshaw) had changed his mind about the gift, and then he kept the reward for himself. But YAH revealed the incident to Elisha (ELeeshaw), and he rebuked his servant for discrediting the name of YAHveh by implying that His power was for hire. As a result, Gehazi received Naaman's (Nahaman's) disease of leprosy as his reward. Even though Gehazi had experienced the power of YAH on many different occasions, it apparently had not affected the greed that was hidden in his heart. We all need to inspect our own hearts and get rid of the leaven of sin that might still dwell there before we try to do His works and wonders.

A few years later, a famine struck the city of Samaria. King Ben-Hadad decided that this would be an opportune time for him to raid the land of YisraEL and its capitol, Samaria, thinking that they would be unable to retaliate due to their weakened state. When King Joram (Yoram) got wind of this, he ran to Elisha (ELeeshaw) for YAHveh's instructions. Elisha (ELeeshaw) assured him of victory. Meanwhile, four lepers who were living outside of the city of Samaria decided to go into the camp of the Syrian troops and surrender to them, hoping to get some food to sustain them. But when they arrived at the camp, they discovered that it was empty and that there were all sorts of booty lying around. They immediately hurried to tell the king about their discovery. What had taken place before they arrived was that YAHveh had confused the Syrians during the night with what had sounded like a mighty army approaching their camp, and the fear of YAH had fallen upon them, causing them to flee. After the lepers made their report to the king, he suspected a plan for an ambush, so he sent out some troops to investigate the scene. They discovered that everything was just as the lepers had reported. In addition, they found a long stream of equipment that had been left behind by the retreating army—it led all the way to the Yarden River. They then plundered the abandoned Syrian camp, which sustained them until the famine was over.

Meanwhile, things weren't going very well in YAHuda either. Just as the mysterious letter from ELeeYAHoo had predicted, King Jehoram (YAHoram) of YAHuda died of a disease of his bowels and his son, Ahaziah (AhazeeYAH), ruled in his place. Ahaziah's (AhazeeYAH's) queen mother, Athaliah, encouraged him to follow after the eluah of King Ahab (Ack'hav) of YisraEL, so he sought the counsel of some of King Ahab's (Ack'hav's) advisors.

YAHveh sent Elisha (ELeeshaw) to complete another mission of his predecessor, ELeeYAHoo. He was to reconfirm that Hazael was to be the king of Aram in Syria in place of Ben-Hadad. YAHveh had arranged the circumstances for this to take place. King Ben-Hadad had become ill and heard that Elisha (ELeeshaw) was in Damascus. The king sent one of his advisors, Hazael, to find him and ask whether or not he would recover from this illness. When Hazael found the ne'vee, he was told that the king would surely recover from the illness but would soon die from another cause. Hazael returned to the king with the message that he would recover, but then he assassinated the king by smothering him the next day with a wet cloth and usurped his throne.

After this, Elisha (ELeeshaw) called upon one of the students from a school of the ne'veem to go and anoint Jehu (YAHoo), an army officer of King Ahaziah (AhazeeYAH) of YAHuda, to be the next king of YisraEL. This was the same Jehu (YAHoo) that ELeeYAHoo had anointed at the beginning of his ministry. With confidence in his heart, Jehu (YAHoo) took some of his soldiers and went to the city of Jezreel (YezrehEL), where King Ahaziah (AhazeeYAH) of YAHuda had gone to visit King Joram (Yoram) of YisraEL, who was recovering from wounds that he had received in battle. Upon arriving, he was challenged by two of King Joram's (Yoram's) horsemen as to his intent in coming. After the horsemen heard Jehu's (YAHoo's) answer, they joined his forces and rode with him. When the horsemen didn't return, the king of YisraEL, along with the king of YAHuda, mounted up and went out themselves to meet Jehu (YAHoo) and his troops. But when King Joram (Yoram) came within earshot of them, he was met with a slur against his mother, Jezebel (Yezebel). Jehu (YAHoo) immediately took his bow and fired an arrow into the king's heart and killed him; he also wounded King Ahaziah (AhazeeYAH) of YAHuda as he tried to flee. Jehu (YAHoo) then continued up the road to Jezreel (YezrehEL). Upon entering, Jezebel (Yezebel) saw him from her window in the king's palace and cast jeers at him. He called out to those who were with her on her balcony to throw her down. They did, and immediately upon impact, the dogs ran to lick up her blood, which fulfilled ELeeYAHoo's prophecy about her gruesome end. Jehu (YAHoo) continued on with his crusade and had all of the princes of the house of Ahab (Ack'hav) executed. When he came upon the princes of King Ahaziah (AhazeeYAH) of YAHuda, who were in the land of YisraEL visiting the house of King Joram (Yoram), he also had them executed. He searched out King Ahaziah (AhazeeYAH) of YAHuda and found him hiding in Samaria, where he put him to death with his sword. While in Samaria, he searched out all of King Ahab's (Ack'hav's) relatives and put them to death also, fulfilling ELeeYAHoo's prophecy regarding King Ahab's (Ack'hav's) whole family. Then, when Jehu (YAHoo) assumed the throne as YisraEL's new king, he began to destroy all of King Ahab's (Ack'hav's) and Queen Jezebel's (Yezebel's) Asherah poles, along with the temples and altars of Baal.

When Queen Athaliah heard of her son's death, she gave orders to have all of the heirs of the king slain so that she herself could gain the throne. All of King Ahaziah's (AhazeeYAH's) sons were put to the sword, except for one—Joash (Yohash). But later, she in turn was executed by the priests and the Lehvee of the House of YAHveh. The child Joash (Yohash) was then crowned king at the age of seven. They trained him up to love YAH and his Torah and to rule YAHuda in righteousness.

The Ne'vee Joel (YoEL)

While young Joash (Yohash) was serving as the king of YAHuda, the land was overrun by a supernatural swarm of locusts. YAHveh used this to teach the House of YAHuda an important lesson regarding their future captivity and His plan to restore them, along with the House of YisraEL, back into the land that He had promised Avraham.

Joel (YoEL) was sent by YAH to warn the House of YAHuda about an empire that would invade their land, just like this swarm of locusts. It would empty the land of its inhabitants, much like the locusts had emptied the land of its vegetation. This disaster would come upon them because of their neglect in following the Torah's ordinances and statutes concerning giving the land its due Sabbaths, and also because of the lack of their care for His House. He called for repentance and for a rededication to their responsibility on these matters—because without it, there would be no holding back His wrath. He told them that a mighty army was looming on the horizon that desired to gobble them up. But, YAHuda didn't feel the threat because of the buffers she had established for herself. She had subdued her enemies to the east, making them subject to her—to the west was the Great Mediterranean Sea—to the south, she had the Sinai (Seenahee) Desert—and to the north, the territory of YisraEL. YAHveh warned them not to put their confidence in their geography because He could change those buffers overnight. He told them that this would also be their same dilemma in the last day, that "Great Day" just before the restoration of all things.

He also promised them that if they repented and served Him and His Torah, they would in turn receive His blessings and prosperity. He promised that in the final days, He would bring the armies from the nations of the north to His land for a final judgment. He would pour out His Ruach HaKedosh (Holy Spirit) upon all of those whom He had scattered throughout the nations around them, and they would become His own.

The "near prophecy" of their captivity came to pass when Babylon captured YAHuda, while the "far prophecy" would occur when all of the nations of the world would converge on the land of YisraEL for the final battle. The "near prophecy" of the outpouring of His Ruach HaKedosh (Holy Spirit) began when He sent Him on the Feast of Shavuot (Pentecost), forty days after Yeshua's resurrection, and offered Him to all who would seek His righteousness, and the "far prophecy" will occur at the Millennium Sabbath/Rest. YAH also reminded them that the whole House of YisraEL was His inheritance and that the land of YisraEL was theirs. The fact that He spoke about the sun and the moon being darkened tells us that He is directing the majority of the impact of these things to occur in the last portion of the final days. He promised that YAHuda and YAHrushalayim, His city, would be restored just before all of these final judgments would come upon them.

YAHuda's confidence in the land of YisraEL as their buffer against the nations of the north began to be shaken when King Hazael of Damascus in Syria stormed the northern tribes, thereby diminishing their size. King Jehu's (YAHoo's) monarchy lasted for twenty-eight years before he died. His wicked son, Jehoahaz (YAHohahaz), assumed his throne and reigned for the next seventeen years. But, YisraEL never completely recovered from Syria's attack, nor did they recover all of their losses, even though King Jehoahaz (YAHohahaz) eventually repented for his rebellion against YAHveh. Then his son, Jehoash (YAHoash), reigned for the next sixteen years with no regard for YAHveh or His Torah. He did, however, turn to the ne'vee Elisha (ELeeshaw) for guidance once, while the ne'vee was on his deathbed, and was told that he would defeat the army of Hazael of Syria three times. After this was accomplished, he took back some of the cities, those that had been lost in previous battles, from King Hazael's son, Ben-Hadad (this was the third Syrian ruler named Ben-Hadad). Then, this King Ben-Hadad turned his attention to the tribe of YAHuda in the south and threatened to wage war against them.

During these times, young King Joash (Yohash) had begun to make some changes in the land of YAHuda. The chief priest Jehoiada (YAHoeeada) had arranged two marriages for him, and he began to repair the House of YAH, just as he had been directed to do so by the Ne'vee Joel (YoEL). But these things were short-lived because the chief priest died and his influence upon the king was soon forgotten. King Joash (Yohash) began to listen to the reasoning of his political advisors and abandoned the care of the House of YAH. He began to incorporate the Asherah poles, along with the idols of Baal, into the nation's form of religion, just as YisraEL had done. Then Zechariah (TzahkarYAH), the son of the chief priest Jehoiada (YAHoeeada), was murdered by King Joash (Yohash) because he dared to speak out against him about his forsaking both YAH's Torah and His House.

When King Hazael of Syria prepared to bring war to the land of YAHuda and King Joash (Yohash) found out, he bought him off with gold and silver from the House of YAH. Then two of his officials, one a descendant of Moab and the other of Ammon, assassinated him for murdering Zechariah (TzahkarYAH), the son of the chief priest Jehoiada (YAHoeeada). King Joash's (Yohash's) son, Amaziah (AhmahzeeYAH), took the throne for the next twenty-five years and had the two assassins of his father brought to justice and executed. He also restored the people back to the Torah, but still did not completely cleanse the land of the high places. He put together a war campaign against the rebels of Edom who had broken away from YAHuda years earlier. In his planning, he hired some troops from YisraEL to fight along with him, but decided to release them from their oath after a ne'vee of YAH warned him that he would lose the campaign if he were to use them—YAH was no longer with the people of YisraEL. King Amaziah (AhmahzeeYAH) took heed to this advice and easily overcame the Edomites (Edomi), completely destroying them, just as the Ne'vee Obadiah (OhbedeeYAH) had prophesied. But, after defeating them, he acted just like all of the other conquering nations around him—he brought back the idols of the Edomites (Edomi) as trophies and soon began worshiping and honoring them. In his arrogance and drunkenness of power, he threatened his YisraELi brothers to the north. To King Amaziah's (AhmahzeeYAH's) amazement, YisraEL attacked him first by breaking down a section of the wall of YAHrushalayim and then ransacking the House of YAH. They stole many of the gold treasures that were there and then returned to their land. Not long after this, King Jehoash (YAHoash) died and his son, Jeroboam II (YAHroboam II), another evil king, began his reign in YisraEL.

Conclusion

Obadiah (OhbedeeYAH) reveals to us the fate of the descendants of YisraEL's brother, Esau (now referred to as Edom), and any nation that makes itself an enemy of YAHveh's chosen people. Both ELeeYAHoo and Elisha

(ELeeshaw) demonstrated the works that would be manifested by Yeshua and His bride, YisraEL, through their lifestyles. And Joel (YoEL) tells YAHuda that she and her sister, YisraEL, are going to be snatched out of the land that had been given to their forefathers and that He will one day return them. However, before He does, He will send the Messiah, who will redeem them from their wickedness and will sanctify them with His own Ruach, so that they will not be unfaithful anymore. In the meantime, these servants of YAH are warning His people, YisraEL, that they are becoming more exceedingly wicked and that YAHuda is beginning to follow in their footsteps.

CHAPTER 10
...about Jonah, Hosea, Amos, II Kings 14&15, and II Chronicles 25-27

History continued to record the rebelliousness of both houses, the ten tribes in the north (YisraEL/Yosef/Efraeem) and the two tribes in the south (YAHuda and BenYAHmeen). There seemed to almost be a spirit of competitiveness between YAH's people as to who could defy His commandments the most aggressively.

Now we will look at the prophecies of the fifth, the first, and the third ne'vee, listed in that order, among the Minor Ne'vim. They are being called to warn the northern ten tribes of the House of YisraEL about the impending threat of an upcoming invasion that will sweep them away into all the nations of the world, where they will eventually become Gentiles (Goyim).

Jonah (Yonah)

It was sometime near the reign of King Amaziah (AhmahzeeYAH) of YAHuda and King Jeroboam II (YAHroboam II) of YisraEL that YAHveh called Jonah (Yonah) to be His ne'vee to speak to the people in Nineveh, the capitol city of Assyria. He was to proclaim to them that YAHveh was the one true ELohim. Most of us remember the story of Jonah (Yonah) and the whale. He tried to run from the responsibility that YAH had given him because he hated the fearsome Assyrians. (Sometimes we are given ministries that are not always to our liking.) YAH did not want the Assyrians to miss having a chance to repent of their wickedness before He pronounced judgment upon them. Assyria was the nation that would eventually become a threat to all of its neighboring nations. YAH would choose her to punish the House of Yosef/ Efraeem, the northern tribes of YisraEL, for their refusal to return to His covenant that He had made with them and their YAHudi brothers in the south. Both the nation of Mitsrahyim and the nation of Assyria represent all of the nations of the world system. This is why He continually speaks about His wrath and judgment falling upon them, symbolizing the end-times.

Instead of going up to Nineveh, Jonah (Yonah) tried to run away to the city of Tarshish (the city of true capitalism of his time) by the way of a ship from Joppa (Yoppa). While on board, a fierce storm began, which threatened to destroy the ship. Jonah (Yonah) was asleep in the rear of the ship when it was about to break up—not unlike the time that Yeshua was with His disciples on the Sea of Galilee. Jonah (Yonah), by the way, was originally from the territory of Galilee in the land of Canaan. After casting lots among the sailors to determine if there was anyone on board who could be responsible for this unusual storm, the lot fell on Jonah (Yonah). He confessed to them that he was a Hebrew serving the ELohim of the heavens who had made the land and the sea, so if they wanted to survive, they needed to throw him overboard because he was trying to run away from obeying Him. They were reluctant, but they did as he said. At that very moment, YAH saw to it that a great fish was feeding there (probably a whale that was scooping up plankton), which inadvertently swallowed him. Jonah (Yonah) prayed, and YAHveh delivered him by causing the fish (whale) to vomit him out onto some dry land—just as YAHveh was going to vomit YisraEL out of His land if she didn't repent after He sent out His ne'veem to warn her. Jonah (Yonah) spent three days and three nights in the fish's belly—the same length of time that Yeshua spent in the grave.

YAHveh then gave Jonah (Yonah) another chance to reconsider his mission—he wisely proceeded on to Nineveh. He proclaimed the words of YAHveh to them for three days. (This was the same number of days that Yeshua proclaimed the kingdom in Hades before releasing the saints from the Bosom of Avraham. They became the Firstfruits of the Resurrection after His Crucifixion, fulfilling that Feast.) He told them that they would have a forty-day-testing period, which would determine whether they were going to believe him and repent of their wickedness or suffer the wrath of the Judge and Creator of all things. Nineveh, from the king to the beggar in the street, put on sackcloth, sat in the dust, and repented for a time. Jonah (Yonah) was still angry with YAH for sending him to such a wicked people who did not deserve His mercy. YAHveh then explained to him that He did not desire to bring His wrath upon anyone who was ignorant of His grace and that He would always give those who were made in the image of the first Ahdom a chance to be born anew into *His* image, through knowledge and faith in Him.

Hosea (Hoshea)

The Ne'vee Hosea (Hoshea) became a voice for YAHveh to YisraEL during the reign of four kings of YAHuda: Uzziah (UzzeeYAH), Jotham (Yotham), Ahaz, and Hezekiah (HezehckeeYAH). This was during the same time that King Jeroboam II (YAHroboam II) reigned in YisraEL. YAH called upon Hosea (Hoshea) to be obedient in a most unusual way—He instructed him to betroth himself to a known prostitute of the community, Gomer, in order to relay a very important message to His people, YisraEL. (Gomer represented the northern tribes of YisraEL, YAHveh's bride who had prostituted herself to other elohim.) He was to purchase her for his own and then put her away (divorce) for her harlotry. YAHveh told him that they would have three children—two sons and one daughter. Hosea's (Hoshea's) firstborn would be a son, to whom the family inheritance belonged, and was to be named Jezreel (YezrehEL), which means *"YAH sows, or scatters"*. This was YAHveh's intention—to scatter YisraEL among the nations. His second child would be a daughter and was to be named Lo-Ruhamah, which means *"no mercy or love is to be shown"*. His third and last child would also be a son and was to be named Lo-Ammi, which means *"not My people"*. YAHveh was making a proclamation that through this marriage and family, He was going to divorce His bride because of her unfaithfulness, but only temporarily because of His promise to Avraham. He would not put her unfaithful sister, YAHuda, away at this time, however, because of His promise to His servant Dahveed. He continued to proclaim that He would in the last days send out His reapers (angels) to gather in His seeds—those that He had scattered throughout the nations of the Earth. He would at that time gather them back to Himself and to the land that He had promised to their fathers. In that "Great Day", He would reunite the two houses and make them one—the "Whole House of YisraEL". He would then call them *"His people/His loved ones"* (Ammi), and He would show them *"His mercy"* (Ruhamah). He would appoint them one king—Dahveed's son, "King Yeshua", and YAHveh's only begotten Son. In the meantime, they would forget the Torah, the Sabbaths, the New Moons, and the Feasts. YAHveh then gave instructions to His Ne'vee, Hosea (Hoshea), to take Gomer back as his bride, just as YAHveh would do for YisraEL.

YAHveh renounced the House of YisraEL for her unfaithfulness and proclaimed that the land was going to vomit her out because of her wickedness. The land was holy (kedosh) and could not withstand her adulterous behavior with idols and her setting up false priests and ne'veem. He charged her for not teaching her descendants the Torah, along with YAH's statutes and ordinances; therefore, they were being "destroyed because they lacked this knowledge". This kingdom principle stands eternally as a testimony to anyone who ignores YAH's principles. He goes on to say to all of those who claim to be teachers of His Torah that if they fail to properly instruct His children, He would forget their descendents as a result. He named YisraEL specifically to be the first to feel this curse because the responsibility for keeping the Torah was solely upon the shoulders of the one who had received the rights of the firstborn, Ephraim (Efraeem), and they failed. At the same time, He also acknowledged YAHuda as being just like her sister, YisraEL, but her chastisement would be delayed because they had the responsibility of being the Royal House, the one in whom His kingship would remain—they were the keeper of the Royal Seed.

YAH continued warning His YisraEL about more judgments that would befall them. He reminded them that when He chastised them for their unfaithfulness, He would also give them every opportunity to repent, but He knew that they would turn to the Assyrians for their help instead. And because of that, He would make them the Assyrian's inheritance. He still assured them, though, that they would one day return to Him, but not until after they had tried looking to all of the other elohim, idols, and religions of the world for their salvation. He even told them about one of the signs that would appear, but added that they would not comprehend its full significance until much later. He was speaking about His own death through His Son, Yeshua, who would be revived in two days and restored to life on the third. His death and resurrection would be the sign of the coming of their own revival and restoration. He would be their kinsman redeemer, redeeming them from their sins after they acknowledged Him and His Torah. He would then make them holy (kedosh), sanctifying them through His promised mikvah/baptism/washing by providing the outpouring of His early and latter rains of His Ruach, just as His Ne'vee, Joel (Yoel), had said that He would do. The time between the early and the latter rain signifies the time that the "Body of Yeshua/YisraEL/Kahal/Church" would remain in darkness, not having the full knowledge of His Torah. For two-thousand years they would not fully know Him, but the fullness of the knowledge of Him would come to light in the third millennium. The three days in the grave also hints of the three seven-year periods before the restoration of all things. In the first seven years, Ephraim (Efraeem/Church/Kahal) would begin to recognize itself as the invisible YisraEL. In the second, there would be a great revival. In the third, there would come a great falling away, leading to judgment and the second appearance of the Messiah, the King of kings.

He tried to explain to them that His Torah ordinances and statutes were merely vehicles for them to use to express their faith in Him. What He really desired from them was their acknowledgment of Him through their faithfulness and obedience—not through ritual sacrifices and burnt offerings. He pointed out how Ephraim (Efraeem) always seemed to turn to Mitsrahyim and Assyria (the systems of the world) and not to Him whenever they found hardship in their midst. He would consider them as though they were aliens because they would consider His Torah as alien to them. He sentenced them to wander among the nations because they would no longer possess a land of their own. But, He would still continue to exhort them with His promise to eventually cleanse them and return them to their original land. He spoke of causing them to be snatched, or raptured, back from the west, like birds out of Mitsrahyim and like doves out of Assyria, where He had driven them— *"They will come trembling"* (HOS 11:10&11). During this time, He declared His judgment of assimilation upon Ephraim (Efraeem), and He continued to reprimand YAHuda for her own misconduct. He noted that Ephraim (Efraeem) would become very wealthy while in her exile and would begin to think that her wealth could purchase her righteousness. In spite of their arrogance, He said that they would one day acknowledge Him once more as their ELohim and Savior. He promised that it would be He who would devour them like a leopard, a lion, and a bear. This three-beast description is the same one that He used in the book of Daniel (DahneeEL) and in the Apostle John's (Yochanan's) writings regarding his "Revelation" of Yeshua HaMessiach. These three beasts represent the three powerful nations that they would be assimilated into. He promised them that in spite of their sins, He would provide them with the opportunity to be resurrected from the grave. He called for them to repent from their rebellion, and eventually they would. He also promised them that they would return to His Torah and to His ways and that they would finally come to realize that these were truly right and good.

Amos (Ahmos)

Amos (Ahmos), just as Obadiah (OhbedeeYAH) had done, began his prophecies against not only YisraEL but also the surrounding nations for the part that they had played in the downfall of YAH's people. He declared His judgment upon the nations of Syria, Philistia, Edom, Ammon, Moab, the city of Tyre, and, finally, upon both the House of YAHuda and her sister, the House of YisraEL. He promised that He was going to destroy them completely unless they repented from their ways. He said that He would tear down the altars of the golden calves that were in Bethel and in Dan (Dahn), where they pretended to serve Him. He had sent ne'veem to warn them and armies of weaker nations to plunder them. He sent them famine and pestilence, but they still refused to submit to His Torah. Then, after He had poured out His wrath and expelled them out of His land, He promised to go into all of the nations, where He had sent them, and bring them back. He said that He would shake them as though they were being shaken through a sieve in order to separate those who had returned to His Torah from those who had continued to rebel. He swore that He would call all of the Gentiles (Goyim) who were also called by His name (those who would call themselves the "Church") and bring them back into the land of promise and to rebuild the tabernacle of Dahveed, which had fallen down. It had fallen down because His people were no longer one house but had become divided into two houses—the "House of Yosef" and the "House of YAHuda". Those who sought Him would find Him, but those who chose to lust after their own eyes would suffer the sword. He said that when that time arrived, all of these things would take place so rapidly that no one would have time to contemplate the hour or the day. But, He also said that He would let His people know when it was about to happen. *"If a shofar is blown in a city, will not the people be afraid? If there is calamity in a city, will not YAHveh have done it? Surely Adonai, YAHveh does nothing, unless He reveals His secret to His servants the ne'veem. A lion has roared! Who will not fear? Adonai, YAHveh has spoken! Who can but prophesy?"* (AMOS 3:6-8).

During this time, King Jeroboam II (YAHroboam II) of YisraEL died and was succeeded by three more kings in rapid succession: Zechariah, Shallum, and Menahem. Just prior to the third Ne'vee, Amos (Ahmos), being sent to YisraEL, King Amaziah (AhmahzeeYAH) of YAHuda was assassinated when he tried to escape to the city of Lachish after learning of a plot to kill him. His sixteen-year-old son, Uzziah (UzzeeYAH), was made king in his stead. King Uzziah (UzzeeYAH) remained faithful to YAHveh and to His Torah and saw very much success while he was on the throne of Dahveed. His domestic policies and his military might and strength brought prosperity back to the people of YAHuda. But, just as those before him, he neglected to remove the remaining high places that were built to the other deities. YAHveh will not tolerate compromise—it will always eventually bring down His wrath upon those who participate in it. Even though His people worship Him and serve Him, they must purge out the leaven within their midst. Then, like many of those before him, King Uzziah (UzzeeYAH) became prideful of his success, turned away from YAHveh, and began to see himself as the reason for his power. One day, he decided that he would burn incense at YAH's altar and bypass the priests, but YAHveh struck him with leprosy until he could no longer perform any of his duties as king, and his son, Jotham (Yotham), had to take over his duties. Meanwhile, the people in YisraEL, in spite of all the warnings, continued to fall deeper and deeper into iniquity and further and further away from YAHveh.

Conclusion

YAHveh is very clear in His description of things to come in both the near and the far future. He has to punish the northern tribes of YisraEL for their worship of false elohim and for their contrived worship of Him and His Torah. He even tells them what nation He has chosen to do this through. At the same time, He gives that nation an opportunity to repent from their wickedness before using them. But, because He knows that they won't, He also pronounces His judgment upon them. At the same time, He knows that His words that have been given through His ne'veem will not turn His people, YisraEL, from their headlong plunge into sin. He knows that He will have to pour out His wrath upon them. He also knows that He will one day restore them back into the land that He promised to their fathers—but only after He has mixed them into all the Gentile (Goyim) nations throughout the world. He will do it in the latter days through His Messiah, who will be chosen from the tribe of YAHuda.

CHAPTER 11
...about the Ne'vee Micah, the Beginning of the Prophecies of Isaiah, II Kings 15-18, and II Chronicles 27-31

Just as YisraEL was warned about her unfaithfulness to YAHveh through His ne'veem, YAH is also sending ne'veem to warn her sister, YAHuda. The first of these two are Micah (Meecah), who is listed as the sixth Minor Ne'vee in the TaNaKh, and Isaiah (YishshaYAH), who is listed as the first Major Ne'vee. These two appeared on the scene about the same time that Hosea (Hoshea) and Amos (Ahmos) were prophesying against YisraEL. Both Micah (Meecah) and Isaiah (YishshaYAH) will bring the same message to YAHuda.

Micah (Meecah)

Micah (Meecah) pointed to YisraEL and Samaria as an example for YAHuda so that they would avoid the same mistakes. He tells YAHuda that she and her capitol, YAHrushalayim, have not yet learned from YisraEL's chastisements. Like YisraEL, they were trying to follow after the religions of the nations around them in order to fit in. But, YAHveh had told them not to try to fit in—they were to be separate because this was to be their witness that YAHveh was their ELohim. (Believers, because they do not fear YAHveh as their ELohim, have changed His ordinances and statutes to please themselves in order not to appear different. YAHveh will only put up with this for a period of time—eventually He will demand accountability for their actions. Just as He did with both YisraEL and YAHuda, He will tolerate it for awhile until He has accomplished what He wants to do through it and then He will foreclose on the debt that is due Him. Those who choose to ignore His Torah and decide to celebrate Him in their own way are rebellious; they will have to face His judgment and suffer the consequences for their insubordination.) Micah (Meecah) reminded them that YAHveh will always send His ne'veem to warn His people of His impending wrath before He carries it out. They should learn to whom they need to listen. He reminded them of their tendency to listen to only false ne'veem because they tell them what they want to hear. He assured them that those who prophesy falsely and recklessly lead YAH's people astray will one day face His judgment.

Yet once again, as He did with YisraEL, YAH promises to bring YAHuda back into the land that He promised Avraham. He also promises to reunite and restore the whole House of YisraEL. He promises that YAHrushalayim, like Samaria, will fall, but unlike Samaria, she will be restored beyond her former glory. That's because she will have, dwelling within the House of YAHveh, the Messiah Himself, sitting on Dahveed's throne as King of kings and Lord (Adonai) of lords (masters). There, He will teach both His Torah and the proper way it is to be kept to all the other nations. He will end all conflicts between the nations and bring peace (shalom) to the whole Earth.

YAHveh intends to show several signs that will prove the accuracy of His words so that all the Earth will know that He is ELohim. To begin with, YAHuda will be led into captivity for a short period of time. YAH will then bring a remnant of His people back from this captivity and give them the responsibility of maintaining His Torah and occupying the Promised Land until the Messiah comes. His Messiah will come from the tribe of YAHuda, just as He promised, and from the city of the "house of bread", Bethlehem (Beit-lechem). He pointed out that when He sends His Messiah, YisraEL will no longer exist as they once did—they will have become invisible, absorbed by the surrounding nations. Only YAHuda will remain as a visible remnant. But, He also promises that His people, YisraEL, will begin to be restored as soon as the mother of the Messiah gives birth to Him. This will be His main ministry—to restore the whole "House of YisraEL". *"But go rather to the lost sheep of the House of YisraEL"* (**MATT 10:6**). *"But, He answered and said. "I was not sent except to the lost sheep of the House of YisraEL"* (**MATT 15:24**). When that day arrives, YAH will deliver His people not only from their desire to worship any other deity but also from the influence that those nations, which He had scattered them into, might have had on them.

He continued His rebuke against YAHuda for her false worship toward Him. He explained to her once again that He is not interested in her burnt offerings and sacrifices. Obeying His ordinances regarding burnt offerings and sacrifices means nothing to Him if, at the same time, they show no mercy toward others. His desire is for them to show mercy, grace, and love, just as He does, and to have an upright heart. Following all of His ordinances to the letter without understanding the spirit of them is unacceptable. He says that she has insisted on following after the traditions and examples that were laid out by her leaders rather than seeking Him and following after His instructions. Because of this, if He is to be a righteous ELohim, He must drive them out and punish them or they will never return to Him, and they will never again belong to Him. They have been destroying themselves with their own behavior, which will eventually lead to rebellion within their own families, which in turn will bring about their own national destruction. When the family unit itself begins to break down, this is a sure sign of disloyalty and disobedience to Him. But, as before, YAH continues to promise that He will not let His people come to a full end. He will bring them back much like He did the first time, when He delivered them out of the hands of Mitsrahyim. He will deliver them with mighty signs and wonders so that the inhabitants of the whole Earth will tremble with fear of the Almighty One of YisraEL. All of His people can have confidence in His words because of His promise to Avraham, Yitzhak, and Yaacov/YisraEL. YAHveh then goes on to pronounce His judgment upon the nation of Assyria for the part that she had played in the scattering of the northern tribes.

Isaiah (YishshaYAH)

Like Micah (Meecah), Isaiah (YishshaYAH) began by rebuking YAHuda for her insistence on rebelling against the Holy (Kedosh) One of YisraEL. He equated them to Sodom and Gomorrah. If YAHveh hadn't shown YAHuda His mercy, she would have been consumed in the same manner as they. YAH told them that the form of religion that they had chosen for themselves would never gain them His righteousness. He told them how He hated their Sabbaths, New Moons, and Festivals because they had become theirs and not His. (Believers cannot just go through the motions—they must celebrate His appointed times/moedim and not their own. Even if you do keep the right times and the right seasons, if you don't observe them with the proper attitude, they are still an abomination to Him.) He pointed out that they had been blinded to the truth of His Torah by indulging in the practices of the nations around them. They looked to the power and intelligence of mere men, to charms, superstitions, astrologers, mediums, and soothsayers. He judged them for their pride and arrogance because of what they thought that they had accomplished by the works of their own hands. Their leaders and shepherds were going to be held to an even higher standard because they had greater access to His instructions, ordinances, and statutes and should have known better. The men of the cities had neglected their duties by turning over the responsibility of instructing their sons to the women. Consequently, their youth no longer respected their elders, and their women had lost respect and honor for their husbands or for that matter, any other authority. They had learned to be manipulators of their men by flirting and tempting them instead of submitting to them and working alongside of them as their co-workers and helpmates. He warned them how all of these things could lead to greed, drunkenness, injustice, and all sorts of abominations. He told them that if they did not repent, He Himself would put a stop to this in less than one year. And, if they were to show any signs of ignoring His warnings, He would begin to stir up a flame in the hearts of their enemies, and a force mightier than they had ever experienced before would come upon them and flush them from the land. He continued to warn them that their idols, their false deities, and their armies were incapable of saving them—He was the only power that could.

Only repentance and redemption could purchase their right standing with Him after their hearts had been so rebellious. He would send His Spirit (Ruach/Breath) to sanctify them if they would circumcise their hearts and become born anew, thereby returning to Him and His grace. Building a fence around His Torah in order to be able to keep it to the letter wouldn't help them either. They must die to self and be raised afresh into a renewed life by His Ruach and by the washing (mikvah) of His word. But, because they wouldn't do these things for themselves, He would do it for them through the Messiah and, at the same time, provide this same grace toward anyone who would seek Him and His righteousness.

Then, just as Micah (Meecah) had spoken, Isaiah (YishshaYAH) also spoke to YAHuda about the promise of a final restoration, when YAHrushalayim will have a new House of YAH established within her gates and His Son, the Branch, will be their king. All of the nations will come up to YAHrushalayim to be taught the Torah by His Son, who will also be the Judge of the whole Earth, bringing peace (shalom) throughout the land.

On the political side of the events during this time, King Menahem of YisraEL died and his son, Pekahiah (PekaheeYAH), became king in his stead. However, his reign didn't last very long because he was assassinated by one of his chief officers, Pekah. While Pekah took over as king in YisraEL, the king of Assyria began to whittle them down by taking a little land here and a little land there. So, the near prophecies of Hosea (Hoshea) and Amos (Ahmos) were beginning to take shape.

At the same time, the disease of leprosy finally took its toll on King Uzziah (UzzeeYAH) of YAHuda and he died; his son, Jotham (Yotham), became the sole ruler. King Jotham (Yotham) continued with the rebuilding of YAH's house and was successful in defeating YAHuda's lifelong enemy, the Ammoni. But, in spite of his following after YAHveh and attempting to keep His Torah, the people continued to sin and wouldn't tear down the high places. In time, King Jotham (Yotham) died and his son, Ahaz, took his place. Ahaz also turned his back on YAHveh, ELohim of YisraEL. While Ahaz was still king in YAHuda, King Pekah of YisraEL had allied himself with King Rezin of Aram in Syria to take up arms against the southern tribes of YAHuda. But in the twentieth year of King Jotham's (Yotham's) reign, King Pekah was assassinated by a man named Hoshea, who then became the new king of YisraEL.

It was during the year that King Uzziah (UzzeeYAH) died that the Ne'vee Isaiah (YishshaYAH) was called by YAH to be one of His spokesmen. And when YisraEL and Syria began to threaten YAHuda, YAH sent Isaiah (YishshaYAH) to comfort King Ahaz, even though he did not follow after YAHveh. He told King Ahaz not to be afraid because both Efraeem/YisraEL and Syria would be scattered in another sixty-five years by Assyria. Isaiah (YishshaYAH) told him to ask YAH for a sign to confirm the word of comfort that was brought to him. King Ahaz refused, so YAH said that He would give him one anyway. However, the sign would not be forthcoming until a later time; it would be the birth of a son, who would be YAHveh Himself in the flesh, to a virgin. He would be called ImmanuEL, which means "ELohim is with you". YAH told Isaiah (YishshaYAH) not to be like the people of YisraEL or YAHuda, but instead, to look only to Him for his guidance. He said that He would use Isaiah (YishshaYAH) to cause both houses of YisraEL to stumble and fall because YAH would make him like a stone and a rock to them. He told him that if His people did not turn to Him and to the word of His testimony, His Torah, but continued to consult the dead on behalf of the living instead, He would cast them into darkness until they repented. But, at the same time, He promised that there would come a time when He would send forth a Light to both houses of YisraEL, and through Him, He would become a blessing, even to the Gentiles (Goyim). In the fullness of time, when all seems to be lost and there seems to be little hope, He will send them a child, a son, who will reign on Dahveed's throne, and His Kingdom will have no end. He will be called Wonderful Counselor, Mighty God (ELuah), Everlasting Father (Av/Abba), and Prince of Peace (Shalom).

He then reemphasized that it will be the House of YisraEL who must first pay the price for their wickedness, followed by the House of YAHuda. He once again promised to bring His wrath upon the nation of Assyria because of their glee in carrying out His judgment when He sent her as His rod to punish YisraEL. Here again, He assured both houses of YisraEL that He would save a few of them to reoccupy the land from which they were being expelled. He exhorted them not to be afraid because His anger would not last, but would subside in His timing. Once more, He reiterated His intention to send His Messiah from the lineage of Dahveed. He identified Him as having His Ruach upon Him and that He would have all of the attributes of His Ruach: wisdom, understanding, counsel, power, and knowledge. He would have and delight in the fear of YAHveh. He would defeat the powers of darkness by His words and instructions. He would restore not only the whole House of YisraEL to a state not unlike the original Garden, but also the whole Earth and the Universe. This not only speaks of a universal salvation, but also of a personal one for any individual who is willing to submit their life to His authority. A great celebration with singing, dancing, and much joy will take place on that "Great Day of YAHveh", when all things will be restored to Him.

Even after all of these words of prophecy from Isaiah (YishshaYAH), King Ahaz still would not relent, so YAHveh sent the kings of Syria and YisraEL into YAHuda to defeat her and to take many of her people into captivity. The army of Syria took some of the captives to Damascus, while the king of YisraEL,

King Pekah, took his share of captives to Samaria to make them slaves. But, he was stopped by the people from the tribe of Ephraim (Efraeem), who refused to take their YAHudaim brothers as slaves. Then the ne'vee Oded gave a warning from YAHveh, reminding YisraEL of the impending judgment already upon her head. He warned them not to add to it by taking their brothers captive. Then King Ahaz wanted revenge, so he turned to Assyria for assistance, only to be refused. In the meantime, Edom and Philistia attacked YAHuda and took away more captives. Once more, King Ahaz went to Assyria for help, but this time he bribed King Tiglath-Pileser with silver and gold from YAH's house, which finally convinced him to come to his aid. The king of Assyria quickly defeated the city of Damascus in Syria, and King Ahaz of YAHuda went up to pay tribute to him there. While in Damascus, King Ahaz noticed a pagan altar that was set up in one of their temples. He admired it so much that he had a duplicate made of it, which he brought back to YAHrushalayim to replace the one in YAH's house. Then he shut the doors of the House of YAH and had altars built upon the high places of YAHuda. There, he burnt sacrifices to the eluah of Damascus rather than to the Living ELohim.

After his death, a more righteous king took his place—his son, Hezekiah (HezehckeeYAH), who began to undo what his father had previously done. He cleansed the House of YAH and reopened it, instructing the Lehvee and the priests to reinstate their duties and to rededicate their lives to YAHveh, the ELohim of YisraEL. King Hezekiah (HezehckeeYAH) even sent an invitation to Ephraim (Efraeem), Manasseh, and all the other tribes of YisraEL to join them in the celebration of the Passover (Pesach) and the Feast of Unleavened Bread (Chag HaMatzot)—the first in many years. They celebrated it in the second month rather than in the first because not all of the necessary sanctification could be completed in time. The Torah allows for this under certain circumstances, which is a testimony to YAHveh's flexibility regarding His appointed times (moedim)—but not to their exclusion. The response was very good in that many from all of the tribes of YisraEL came to YAHrushalayim for the celebration. In fact, it was so successful that it was extended for an additional seven days. Afterward, many of them were so spiritually inspired that they went out into all of the land of YAHuda and YisraEL and began to tear down the high places, the Asherah poles, and the shrines to Baal. Many who had come from the northern tribes decided to repent from the adultery that they had committed against YAHveh in the past and to remain in the land of YAHuda. There, they could not only worship Him but also be taught in His house, learning to once again obey the ELohim of YisraEL.

Throughout Isaiah's (YishshaYAH's) prophecies, he, like all the other ne'veem, pronounced judgment upon all of the surrounding nations. But, he doesn't stop there; he also includes the nations of the world, with apocalyptic revelation not unlike the revelation that was given to John (Yochanan) by Yeshua. Pronouncements of judgment and wrath were dealt out to Assyria, Edom, Moab, Philistia, and Arabia, as well as to the cities of Damascus and Tyre. Babylon, with all of its wickedness, worldly lusts, and its many religions, was singled out for being controlled and manipulated by none other than Satan (hasatan) himself. This was only done to point out how the religious spirit of Babylon will spread throughout the world in the last days leading up to the "Day of the Lord" and that YAH's Messiah will be the one to judge it and bring it to its end. Babylon also represents all of the countries of the Middle East that oppose YAHuda and YisraEL—in other words, the Islamic nations. But, the religious spirit that accompanies this Babylonian idea reaches far beyond the nation of Islam—it also embraces any religion that is practiced from an ideology of narcissism (self indulgence), which sadly includes many aspects of today's Church with its practice in secularism.

Conclusion

Both Micah (Meecah) and Isaiah (YishshaYAH) spoke out against the false religious practices of His people, who had either begun to worship other elohim or were incorrectly observing His Torah. YAH is no respecter of persons; there is only one way—His Way. He is the one who created and designed all things, and all of His creation will operate only one way—His Way. He has laid out kingdom principles that empower the universe in its function—both physically and spiritually. Not following the instructions that He has laid out for us so simply and plainly will only lead to our frustration and confusion. He demonstrated this over and over again when He sent His ne'veem to warn His people, YisraEL. He laid the responsibility of observing and instructing His Torah on both the spiritual and the political leaders. When they refused, both they and the people under them suffered the consequences. Even so, it is still the responsibility of each individual to seek YAH and to serve Him on a personal level, which in turn will determine his or her personal destiny. We must learn from the mistakes of our ancestors in order to avoid making them ourselves. Yeshua came to fulfill all of the prophecies about Him and to do for us what we cannot do for ourselves, which is to save us from the curse of the Torah. But, even though He kept the Torah for us and then even died our death for us, we still need to keep that part of the Torah which produces the blessings that He has purchased for us. Not keeping it will only bring about sorrow and frustration. The instructions are really quite simple. And when or where we fail or stumble, He is always there to dust us off and to encourage us to try again and again. Yeshua came bringing with Him the "Good News" of how to understand the Torah so that we might do it—do it in spirit and in truth.

CHAPTER 12
...about Isaiah Continued, Nahum, II Kings 18-23, and II Chronicles 31-34

We now continue with the last half of the Ne'vee Isaiah's (YishshaYAH's) admonition and exhortation to YAHuda. He continues to speak more about the Messiah and His mission and ministry regarding the restoration of the whole House of YisraEL. We also hear from the Ne'vee Nahum, the seventh on the list of Minor Ne'vim. He too warns Assyria and her capitol city, Nineveh, about the destruction that will come upon them for being the cause of the assimilation and dispersion of YAH's people, YisraEL/Yosef/Efraeem. The Ne'vee Jonah (Yonah) had been sent earlier to bring this nation to the knowledge of YAHveh, and they responded favorably, but only for a season—the many centuries of wickedness engrained into their society soon brought them full-circle back to their cruel abominations. The ten northern tribes would be dispersed by them into the nations of the world, where they would become Gentiles (Goyim) and referred to as the ten lost tribes of YisraEL. But, they were never really lost because YAHveh knew the number of the hairs on their heads, or in today's terminology, their DNA. He never lost track of them, even though they lost track of themselves and forgot their ELohim and His Torah. But, the day will come when He will send His Ruach and plant the seed of remembrance in their spirit, and they will respond by returning to the love and the grace found in His Torah.

We begin this chapter where we left off in the previous one: with Isaiah (YishshaYAH) continuing his vision of the punishment of all the nations of the Earth in **ISA 24**. He described YAHveh as making the whole Earth a wasteland. Remember that the legitimacy of a prophecy is always determined if a near event occurs—then its future climax will be assured. But, all true prophecies will also contain two manifestations—a spiritual one and a physical one. For instance, we can see that YAH is speaking here about both the spiritual destruction of everything evil and the destruction of the Earth's physical surroundings. He is promising that everyone who refuses to acknowledge Him and fear Him in their heart will one day be swept from the Earth because everything that is good will become corrupted. At the same time, because everything has been corrupted, He will have to literally cleanse and recreate the Earth (make a new heaven and Earth). He says that those who have become rebellious have changed His Torah and its meaning, breaking His everlasting covenant that He made with mankind and the Earth. Only those who have not transgressed His Torah will be rescued. He says that the Earth will be burned and that only a few will be left. They are the ones whom He, for His own reasons, spares. The wicked will be gathered and shut up in a prison (The Pit) for a period of time, until the end of the Millennium of Peace (Shalom).

ISA 25 reveals that during that time, all of those who look to Him and His Messiah will experience eternal life and will feast and celebrate His Kingship. ISA 26 is a song to YAH stating that those who are trusting in Him will find refuge and peace (shalom). They sing about what they will learn through seeking His righteousness. They ask Him to show the wicked mercy, even though they still will not acknowledge Him. They sing that all of their suffering was for the purpose of learning about their own iniquity and about the surety of their resurrection. But, for those who choose unrighteousness, they will never find peace (shalom). Instead, they, along with the one whom they have chosen to follow, the Prince of Darkness, will find His wrath.

In ISA 35, Isaiah (YishshaYAH) tells about the beginning of the return of YAH's people who will reoccupy their land in the latter days. YAH says that He will provide a Highway to Holiness into His land. In other words, unlike before when every attempt to return was thwarted, it will not be so this time. Before this time, spiritual eyes and ears were hindered from understanding His plan—this will no longer be the case. The land will begin to bear fruit for its inhabitants, and the cities will flourish once again.

In ISA 28, YAH acknowledges that Efraeem will ignore His admonishments and His encouragements because they will be too busy indulging themselves with the fat of self-satisfaction that the world has to offer. The ones responsible, though, are the spiritual leaders who have put forth their own selfish agendas; therefore, they have no real compassion for the ignorant. They themselves have no understanding because they have relied upon the teachings of men rather than YAH and have become corrupted and drunk in their own hunger for power. All of this will begin to end because He will send His justice to annul all that men have done. He will send the One who will be the Cornerstone upon whom His ne'veem and apostles (shelichim) will lay the foundational teachings of YAH.

In ISA 29, Isaiah (YishshaYAH) tells all who will listen that YAHrushalayim will fall but will be raised up again in the latter days. He tells them that even though no one will listen because they will become blind and deaf and that all of these things will come upon them suddenly, YAH will one day restore all things to be just as they were before this calamity. (Notice that here YAH refers to YAHrushalayim as AriEL, which means "Lion of ELohim", and by the way, this is also the name of the prime minister of the land of

YisraEL at the time of this writing.) He promises to trample down the enemies of YAHuda even though she has forsaken Him. They had put their trust in the wisdom of men and not in Him; therefore, they had fallen from His grace. Even so, He will once more give them wisdom and understanding because of His love for His people and His City and because of His promises to their fathers.

In **ISA 33**, YAH refers to events that will take place after He has punished His people for their unfaithfulness toward Him. He speaks of when He will once more hear their cry of distress, just as He did when they were slaves in Mitsrahyim, and He will once more come to their rescue. When He does, those who have been their oppressors will themselves become the oppressed. He will come to both lift up and strengthen His people—He will send them their Messiah. They will witness all of this from all of the nations, where they have been scattered. They will see their glorious city and the appointed feasts being celebrated there once more. They will then be brought back to dwell there—never to leave it again.

The warnings and the exhortations did not seem to faze the people of the ten northern tribes of YisraEL because they seemed to be bent on their own destruction. King Hoshea (the one who assassinated King Pekah of YisraEL) was apparently a coward and yielded to King Shalmaneser of Assyria by paying him extortion money, or tribute, to keep him from carrying off the rest of the inhabitants of the ten northern tribes. Then, behind the king's back, he tried to double-cross him by making an alliance with King So of Mitsrahyim, but his plot was discovered and he was put into prison. Then, the king of Assyria fulfilled YAH's prophecies against the northern tribes of YisraEL/Yosef/ Efraeem by laying a siege against her capitol city, Samaria, for three years and then assimilating them into all of the nearby nations. These events took place around 720 BCE, which is a very significant date, as we will learn later when the Ne'vee Ezekiel (YechezkEL) pronounces the length of time of the captivity for the tribes of YisraEL.

The Assyrians then resettled Samaria, and to this day it has been a mixture of religions—there is even one that resembles a form of Judaism (YAHudaim). These inhabitants are a symbol of what Efraeem would become throughout the world over a period of time. Now the only thing that was visibly left of YisraEL was the tribe of YAHuda, who would take on the name of YisraEL to this day; but even they are only a remnant until the days of the Gentiles (Goyim) are fulfilled. Then YAH will restore the whole House of YisraEL and re-establish the tabernacle of Dahveed, which had fallen down (**AMOS 9:11**).

Then Isaiah (YishshaYAH) gave a very strange prophecy to YAHuda about Mitsrahyim. First, he warned them not to rely on Mitsrahyim to be of any help against Assyria when she began to threaten to do to them what she had done to YisraEL/Efraeem. Second, he told them that YAHveh planned to reveal Himself to both Mitsrahyim and Assyria and save many of His people who were within them. He said that He was going to send them a Savior—this could be no other than Yeshua Himself. Then He said that He was going to join them to YisraEL and that the three (YisraEL, Mitsrahyim, and Assyria) would be aligned together and would one day join YAHuda. They would all come together as the "Whole" House of YisraEL in the land that was promised to Avraham, Yitzhak, and Yaacov. This has to be one of His explanations of the restoration ministry of the Messiah Yeshua. Since we already know that Mitsrahyim represents an encapsulated form of the world system and that Assyria represents the Gentile (Goyim) nations who were responsible for the dispersion of the people of YisraEL/Yosef, this then has to be a metaphor that represents Christianity, which is really YisraEL hidden, or camouflaged, among the Gentile (Goyim) nations.

ISA 30 & 31 tells us that YAHuda, like her sister, YisraEL, was stiff-necked and would not listen to Isaiah's (YishshaYAH's) warnings. Instead, she went ahead and pledged her alliance to Mitsrahyim. YAHuda no longer looked to YAH and His Torah, nor feared Him, but instead looked to the wealth and weaponry of Mitsrahyim. Mitsrahyim, on the other hand, saw YAHuda as a buffer between her and Assyria, so she agreed to aid them in case of an attack. It didn't matter because YAHveh had a different plan. He would use Assyria to bring down the haughty Mitsrahyim and to chastise YAHuda at the same time. But, YAHveh still exhorted them—He told them that there would come a day when He would restore them back into the land and that they would again gladly follow all of His instructions in His Torah. He also assured them that He would bring Assyria down for her wickedness against His people; He would not restrain His wrath against them either. In His perfect timing, they too would come to their end.

King Hezekiah (HezehckeeYAH) brought some reform to YAHuda, as was pointed out earlier, but not enough to turn aside YAH's wrath—they still needed to be chastised for their insolence. The Assyrian king, Sennacherib, captured some of YAHuda's walled cities and demanded that YAHuda pay him tribute. King Hezekiah (HezehckeeYAH), like King Pekah of YisraEL, relented and took some of the gold and silver from the articles in YAH's house to pay the extortion. Soon after that, King Hezekiah (HezehckeeYAH) became ill and was told by the Ne'vee Isaiah (YishshaYAH) that YAH had told him that he was about to go the way of his fathers. King Hezekiah (HezehckeeYAH) immediately prayed to YAH, who then relented and gave the king another fifteen years to rule. Still, like so many before him, King Hezekiah's (HezehckeeYAH's) pride caused him to sin even further. For instance, the king of Babylon sent his condolences because of King Hezekiah's (HezehckeeYAH's) illness. King Hezekiah (HezehckeeYAH) showed those who had been sent from Babylon (they were actually spies) all that YAH had blessed him with and then took all of the credit for acquiring them. When the Ne'vee Isaiah (YishshaYAH) heard of the king's foolish act, he sent word and told him that because of his misdeeds, Babylon would one day come and plunder YAH's house, ravaging it and carrying off the rest of the articles that the king had put on display. King Hezekiah (HezehckeeYAH) repented once more, and YAH prospered YAHuda all the rest of his years as king. Even so, the words that Isaiah (YishshaYAH) spoke did come to pass as the consequence of this king's foolishness. Even though we may ask YAH for forgiveness and repent for our rebelliousness and our sins are forgiven, there still may be a consequence left that can affect us and/or our loved ones.

King Sennacherib once again threatened YAHuda and King Hezekiah (HezehckeeYAH) while mocking YAHveh, the Living ELohim. Once again, King Hezekiah (HezehckeeYAH) asked Isaiah (YishshaYAH) what YAHveh would have him do. YAH answered him by delivering the people of YAHuda in a most unusual way. During their attack, every Assyrian soldier became confused and wound up slaughtering his own countrymen as the result, and King Sennacherib returned to Nineveh, where he himself was struck down by his own sons and killed in the temple of one of his eluah. At the end of the fifteen years that were promised to him by YAH, King Hezekiah (HezehckeeYAH) died and was buried with the other kings of YAHuda. His son, Manasseh, succeeded him on the throne and quickly led the people back into paganism. This time, there would be no escaping YAH's wrath for the people of YAHuda—they would be overrun by the Babylonians and sent into captivity.

Isaiah (YishshaYAH) would no longer warn the people of YAHuda about any impending danger. It was too late for them now because the stage had already been set—it was just a matter of time. His new ministry would be to tell YAH's people about the days after their captivity, when they would return to the land that was promised to them.

In **ISA 40**, YAH reminded YAHuda that it was He who determined all things; He was the Creator of all things, and if He said something would happen, it would happen. He also reminded them that there had never been a single person who was ever created or who ever would be created that He was not mindful of. He knows the needs of everyone, and He has a plan for their life if they will seek Him and follow His lead. He hints again of His Messiah whom He will send, who will reveal to them His overall plan. He said that He will also send a voice crying in the wilderness, who could be no other than John the Baptist (Yochanan the Immerser), as the voice of ELeeYAHoo, ushering in the ministry of the Messiah. The people of Efraeem will also be the voice of ELeeYAHoo, but will be ushering in the *second* coming of Yeshua in the last hour.

In **ISA 41**, YAH rebuked His people for looking to idols and to other deities for guidance and protection. He rebuked them for depending upon their own ideas or upon the imaginations of men for their strength, for their destiny, or for their future.

In **ISA 42**, He once again promised to send them His servant, "the Messiah" (HaMashiach), whom He would cause His Ruach to rest upon. He would not come as a raging conqueror, but as one who does not look for recognition—His recognition would come through the love that He would show the people of the Earth. His blessings would be upon all of those who would heed His words, humble themselves like children, and receive His instructions concerning the "Good News," which is the fulfillment of the Torah in Him. He will make the blessings that come from following the Torah apparent to those who will hear, and He will take away the curse of the Torah from those who will put their trust in Him to pay the penalty for their sins. The curse came due to their inability and their lack of power to follow the Torah. Now when they fail, the curse will be covered with His blood. Their life will be renewed because of the hope that He brings—the curse will have been done away with. The enemy of YAHveh will finally be defeated, and all of His people will be able to sing and celebrate His feast days with true joy for what He has done. He will send this "Good News" throughout the Earth, even to the coastlands (which also means the isles across the seas, including the Americas). He says, though, that not all will receive this news with gladness; many will reject it because they love ruling and commanding their own lives and being their own judge and savior. They cannot save themselves, but enjoy thinking that they can by doing good works. Those who are religious and love their religion will not hear for they too are deaf to the truth because they love their religion. They cannot see with their own eyes the mighty works that He performs through His ne'veem; their hearts are too cold and hard because of their rebellious spirits. He reminds all who will listen that He removed His people, YisraEL, from their land because they would not keep His Torah. Likewise, He will remove anyone from His House who will not keep His commandments (Torah). *"If you love Me, keep My commandments"* (**JOHN 14:15**). *"If you keep My commandments, you will abide in My love, just as I have kept My Father's commandments and abide in His love"* (**JOHN 15:10**). *"Not everyone who says to Me, 'Lord, Lord,' shall enter the kingdom of heaven, but he who does the will of My Father in heaven. "Many will say 'Lord, Lord, have we not prophesied in Your name, cast out demons in Your name, and done many wonders in Your name?' "And then I will declare to them, 'I never knew you; depart from Me; you who practice lawlessness* (or, who are outside of the law/**"Torah"**)*.'"* (**MATT 7:21-23**).

In **ISA 43**, YAHveh reveals Himself as being both the Creator of all things, including His people, YisraEL, and the Redeemer of YisraEL. He tells us that He is both the Father and the Son, who is His Messiah. He is the Savior; there is and can be no other. He says that He is the one responsible for the extraction of YisraEL from the land, and also the one who will bring them back from the Four Corners of the Earth, where He has scattered them. He also says that He will bring them from the four winds back to their land. Since wind always refers to His Breath (Ruach or Spirit), then, by His Ruach, He will snatch them out and return them to their land. Here again, He promises that He will do this through a new thing, a renewed covenant—an eighth covenant that brings His other seven to fruition.

In **ISA 44**, YAH promises, through Isaiah (YishshaYAH), to pour out His Ruach upon His people, just as He did through His Ne'vee Joel (Yoel) (**JOEL 2:28&29**). This came to pass in his "near" prophecy recorded in **ACTS 2:1-4**. His "far" prophecy began in 1948 at a prominent Catholic University and is still spreading throughout the world, and it will not stop until the Millennium reign of Yeshua and beyond. He goes on to say that when this comes to pass, those who are called by His Name will declare with joy their inheritance and their being known as YisraEL. Once again, He refers to Himself as the "Rock", the same name that He gives to Yeshua, the Messiah (HaMashiach); He also declared Himself to be the "First and the Last" and that "there is no other", which again is who Yeshua says *HE IS*. Again, we can see more evidence that Yeshua and YAHveh are separate, yet One (Echad) and the same. YAHveh is the *"Almighty One"*, and He can be any place or every place at the same time (omnipresent); therefore, it is no challenge for Him to be the man Yeshua, His Son, and be the Father and still continue to be the ELohim of the universe at the same time. He declared that He will never forget His YisraEL or His promise to restore her, along with YAHuda, to His land. He also mentions here the name of the Persian king, Cyrus, and says that he will be the one whom He will raise up as His instrument to begin the restoration of YAHuda back into the land that He had promised to their fathers.

In **ISA 45**, He again declares King Cyrus to be the one whom He has chosen for this task. He repeats it here so all will know that when it happens, He is the ELohim that causes things to happen and that every event in history is a portion of His plan. He even calls Cyrus the king, even though Cyrus hasn't yet been born. He reminds all who have ears to hear that no one is born by accident. If anyone has breath in them, it is not because of their father or their mother, but because He has ordained it. Each individual that takes breath has a destiny to perform in His overall plan regardless if they ever come to realize it or not. That means, instead of seeking our own niche in the world, we should be seeking the part that we are to play in His kingdom (**MATT 6:24, MATT 6:33,** and **LUKE 16:13**). He declares Himself as being the only Savior and that He is the Savior of the "Whole" House of YisraEL. (We must come to this truth and begin to serve our ELohim in that capacity. We *are not* something created out of the finite minds of men. We *are* the people of YisraEL regardless of our genealogy. We *are* His from the ancient of times. We *are not* the Church!)

In **ISA 46 & 47**, YAHveh admonishes all of those who trust in the work of their own hands. They may be able to manufacture anything that they can conceive of in their minds and then build it with their own hands, but these things still have to be made from those things that YAH has already created. Man in his foolishness looks to what he can create as his hope and deliverance from death, sickness, and poverty. But YAH calls these things idols and says that only He can provide true and lasting salvation. He once again reminds us that Babylon is only a passing power, but her spirit, one of darkness, continues in the hearts and minds of men. Babylon declares herself as the one true religion, but she is just another whim of the Prince of Darkness, hasatan. She is a symbol of false religiosity and cloaks herself in a man-made substitute for true spirituality.

In **ISA 48 & 49**, over and over again YAHveh stressed the fact that YisraEL was His Servant and all that had taken place was just a part of His plan to make her the fulfillment of His promises to His sons: Ahdom, Noah, Avraham, Yitzhak, Yaacov, Mosheh, and Dahveed. But in order to prepare them to accomplish His purpose, they had to first go through a process of refinement. His plan was not only that they were to be a blessing to His sons, but also a blessing to the Gentiles (Goyim—the nations of the world) so that no man need suffer His wrath at the final hour of judgment. All of these events were going to lead up to the arrival of His only begotten Son, Yeshua, the Messiah (Yeshua, HaMashiach), who is the Holy (Kedosh) One of YisraEL. His ministry and objective was to bring the "Good News" that no one would any longer have to carry the yoke of trying to keep the "letter of the Torah". This yoke had carried with it a curse that no man could bear. But instead, they would now be able to enjoy the "spirit of the Torah", which is "love". He promised that He, by His Ruach, would pour this spirit out on any individual who would believe and confess Him as their Messiah. It would be His ministry and objective to bring the lost sheep of YisraEL back to the land of promise. He went on to say that the land of Zion (Zeeon), the land that He had declared as being His and the inheritance for His people, would no longer be barren and desolate but would once more blossom with His people. And the sign that this was about to be completed would be when Zion (Zeeon) began to see His people returning—this began in 1917.

In **ISA 50 & 51**, YAH promises to send the "Redeemer" to rescue all of those who have been oppressed by YAH's enemies. They were once given a divorce decree, but now their marriage to Him will be renewed because what they were unable to do for themselves, His Servant, His Right Arm, will do for them. He will keep the Torah, which they couldn't do. He will live the Torah, which they couldn't live. He will die their death in order for them to inherit both the land and eternal life. All of this is to be offered to all men because all have come short of the glory of YAHveh. He assures them that He is able to do this because it was He, their Salvation, who led them through the wilderness and split the waters in order for them to escape their captors. It was He who fed them with manna and gave them water from the rock. Because He was able to do that for them then, He will be the one to accomplish all of these promises now. He promises that the whole Earth, from Zion (Zeeon) to the coastlands/isles (the nations across the great seas), will see these things take place and will be a witness to the might of His Right Arm.

In **ISA 52 & 53**, He promises that when He begins to reestablish His city, YAHrushalayim, in the final days of her restoration, He will not let anyone possess her gates again, except those whom He has chosen. No matter what man tries to do to divide His land or His City, nothing will come of it because He has decreed it not to happen. The United States, the Palestinians, the United Nations, the European Union, nor anyone else will be able to divide His City again.

Then He identifies His servant by describing His appearance. He says that He will be a man who does not appear to be of any great stature. Instead, He will appear as a humble, but determined, man. He will be rejected by His peers and the religious leaders as being a false teacher. His claim to be the Messiah will be considered laughable, and He will be falsely accused of blasphemy. The multitudes will reject Him and call for his end. But even so, this is still a part of YAHveh's overall plan. His plan is to present Him as the Lamb of YAHveh to be the sacrifice for all mankind, the true Passover Lamb. This is what Avraham's near sacrifice of his son, Yitzhak, represented, except YAH's Son will be the Pesach without blemish, the firstborn of His flock, the Bread without leaven (sin), the Firstfruits of the resurrection, and the One who will purchase eternal life for all who believe.

In **ISA 54-56**, YAHveh promises that there will come a day when His wrath will subside against His bride, YisraEL. He will have brought forth a plan to redeem her from her sin; YisraEL will not sin against Him any longer. In that day, YisraEL's descendants will grow so numerous in the land that it will seem as though there isn't enough room to hold them all. He assures them that this will be a promise within a renewed covenant, like the one that He made with Noah when He promised that the waters would never cover the Earth again. He promises that He will provide her with a new holy (kedosh) city, one that will be built out of precious stones; she will share it with Him, and He will teach her His ways for eternity. He promises her that no one will form a weapon that can succeed against her. This renewed covenant will be for anyone who will put aside his own desire to please himself and come with an attitude to please Him. If that becomes their goal in life, He promises that they will find Him and that He will give them all of the other things that they would otherwise have been searching for. He reminds them again of who He is and of His ability to bring either rain or drought at His command. He assures those who are serious about listening that if He says it, it will come to pass, just as sure as the coming and the going of the seasons. He tells them that His words are like seeds and that they will produce exactly what He says, just as surely as the seeds of a certain fruit will reproduce that identical fruit. He also reminds them that what He has promised through His ne'veem is not restricted to just them—He says that His words are for all nations, even the Gentiles (Goyim). Anyone who will listen, believe, and trust in His words will also become His people, YisraEL, regardless of their race or heritage. Those who belong to Him will have a desire to please Him through their complete devotion to Him, having an attitude of submission to do whatever He has commanded them; they will keep His Sabbaths, His Festivals, and His Torah. He will judge His appointed shepherds as to whether or not they teach His Torah and His kingdom principles.

In ISA 57-59, YAHveh keeps reiterating the fact that YisraEL continually practices idolatry. She wants to have it both ways—she wants a relationship with the ELohim of the Universe, but at the same time, she wants to create Him in her own image. He reminds her that He is jealous of her and that she must turn back to Him; He created her for Himself, and He will not share her with the elohim of her vain imaginations. He explains that any of those among her who are willing to repent and come back to Him, He will heal and forgive and will lead them into full righteousness. Those who are stiff-necked and stubborn have been warned, and if they refuse to turn from their wicked ways, there is only one judgment left for them. They have been fooling themselves with their pretense of sincerity and their religious activities may have convinced others, but He knows their hearts. They make up their own feast days and fasting days, but His fasts are those that He has called—mere men do not have that authority. His fasts consist of doing for those who cannot do for themselves. To deprive oneself of comfort in order to bring comfort to others comes from a compassionate heart and not from a self-seeking one. By making these sacrifices out of a contrite heart, He will see and reward openly for what they have done in secret. He is not a stranger to the wickedness of men's hearts—He knows all of the secrets that hide in the dark corners of the minds and hearts of men. He promises that there will come a time when He will say "that is enough" and He will bring it all to an end. He is slow to anger, and He will give all of the nations who mock Him and His people enough time and rope to hang themselves because of their self-righteousness and their own good works, or they could repent and seek Him instead. There will come a time when they will answer to Him for their deeds that they thought went unnoticed. When that day arrives, those who have persevered will find that they have been delivered into His sanctuary, where no one will be able to torment and persecute them any longer. In that day, He will send forth His Ruach for the final time in order to fill to overflowing those who have remained faithful, and His words will go forth from their mouths like a sword and a fire to consume those who have mocked His truth. They will be the voice of ELeeYAHoo.

In ISA 60-66, YAHveh talks about His beloved city, YAHrushalayim, and the land that He has given His people, Zion (Zeeon). He talks about the condition of the land of Zion (Zeeon) in the final days before He brings judgment upon the nations of the Earth. He tells of how the darkness of sin shall come upon the whole Earth and into the minds of its people. But Zion (Zeeon) and YAHrushalayim will be a light, a place of hope. The darkness seems to be YAHveh's judgment coming upon the nations and Zion (Zeeon); the light seems to be the activities that are going on there because of YAH's blessings. This seems to be drawing their attention to His glory that is being magnified there. He also seems to be referring to the fact that the whole House of YisraEL has returned from all the nations where they had been scattered. At this time, YAH has seen to it that the wealth from all the nations has been distributed among His people. He mentions that they arrive in clouds, and like doves—which seems to hint of their return via the rapture (the resurrection and snatching away). Other sons come by ships from the faraway coastlands—perhaps they are those who have survived the judgment and have become convinced that YAH's Yeshua is truly the King of kings, or those who have returned to the land because of the prophecies.

Then, in a reflective manner, He speaks of His wrath that was once upon them as now being replaced with His mercy. He tells of how any nation that will not show Zion (Zeeon) favor will be doomed to failure in their existence. YAHrushalayim will be known as the city of Salvation (Yeshua), Praise (YAHuda), and Peace (Shalom). He will be the light of her glory, and she shall never know war or trouble again. But, before these things take place, her inhabitants will have the same ministry of salvation as their King, Yeshua; they will go into the entire world to proclaim the Torah's truth to all who have ears to hear, just as He did in His days. YAH says that He will begin this mighty work after He has sent His Right Arm (His Son, Yeshua) out with the gift of His Ruach. They will seek out the lost sheep of YisraEL and teach them of His ways, bringing them back to Him so that they might inherit the land of Zion (Zeeon), the land that He had promised to their fathers. Those who are gathered will be known as "His YisraEL". He will make a new covenant (by renewing the original) and make them His priests. He will gather them from among the Gentiles (Goyim), where He has scattered them, in order to fulfill what He told His servant, Avraham. His people, YisraEL, will be His bride—He will be their bridegroom. He has prepared a place for her in His Zion (Zeeon) since before the foundation of the Earth was laid. The land will bud, just as it did when He set up the Garden of Eden. He says that everything that He has promised will come to pass for His sake and for the sake of His Word. These things will also take place for the sake of His people, YisraEL, and His city, YAHrushalayim. It will take place for all the Gentiles (Goyim) to see and to marvel. His city, YAHrushalayim, will receive a new name; it will be called Hephzibah (My delight is in her), and the land, Zion (Zeeon), will be called Beulah (married or bride).

He admonishes and encourages all not to keep silent about His promises, but instead, to pave the way for His coming—they are to be the voice of ELeeYAHoo. He continues to say that His redeemed will come out from all of the nations and will be referred to as: "The Holy (Kedosh) People (Amee)"—"The Redeemed of YAHveh"—"The Sought Out"—"A City Not Forsaken". He speaks of how the "Angel of His Presence" will save His "Children" who are the "House of YisraEL". He recalls how He saved them the first time by the hand of Mosheh and how they rebelled against Him. He remembers how He had to punish them to bring them to repentance in order for them to be restored. He says that YisraEL will then acknowledge Him as their Father (Abba) and will finally come to Him, along with those who had never known Him before and hadn't been called by His Name.

Isaiah (YishshaYAH) confesses that YisraEL has sinned and deserves punishment for her wickedness, but at the same time, he recognizes that only YAHveh can be her Savior. He admits that any good thing that mere man can contrive as good works are nothing but filthy rags to the ELohim of YisraEL. He professes that all men are but mere clay and that YAHveh is the potter. He is the one who determines each man's work and place in the great tapestry of creation. He professes that YAHveh is the only ELohim and Father (Abba) of us all. He tells of YAH's plan for His people, that they will lose their identity as YisraEL and will become as the Gentiles (Goyim), no longer to be called by His Name. He explains, though, that at a particular time in history, and only YAH knows it, they will begin to seek Him, and they will find Him; He will reveal to them that they belong to Him and that He has kept them hidden. He says that up until the time that He calls them, they will worship other elohim and be unclean (unholy). But once they begin to seek Him, He will make them clean/holy (kedosh), and they will forsake their false idols and elohim and worship Him. And at His appointed time (moedim), He will bring them back to the land that He promised their fathers. He will set up a new heaven and a new Earth and will restore all things, just as they were in His Garden before the fall. Finally, He declares that as sure as He is the one who has created all things, He will do all that He has promised. He will send His truth through His words to all the nations; He will swiftly bring destruction upon the heads of those who refuse to hear it and continue to remain unclean. But, those who hear His voice, return to His Sabbaths and New Moons, and worship Him according to His Torah instructions, He will whisk away to receive the reward that He has prepared for them. Then, those who are left behind will see the destruction that He brings upon them for refusing to heed His many warnings. This ended the prophecies of Isaiah (YishshaYAH) to YAHuda. The people continued to ignore his message.

Meanwhile, in the land of YAHuda, Manasseh, the son of King Hezekiah (HezehckeeYAH), was only twelve-years old when he began to reign as king. He did not follow his father's final legacy, but instead, brought back all of the pagan idol worship that his father had destroyed and re-established the high places. After Assyria's king, Sennacherib, was assassinated, YAH sent the commanders of his army to YAHuda to capture King Manasseh and put him in prison in Babylon—a prelude to the coming events. While in Babylon, King Manasseh repented of his wickedness, so YAHveh restored him to his position on the throne of YAHuda. King Manasseh responded to YAH's grace by undoing all of the evil that he had done at first. This again was a rehearsal for what the whole nation of YAHuda would experience in about another two-hundred years.

The Ne'vee Nahum Declares the Ruin of Assyria and the City of Nineveh

Nineveh, the city where the Ne'vee Jonah (Yonah) was sent, knew the great ELohim, YAHveh, for only a short time. Apparently, too many centuries of worshiping other elohim had taken its toll on Nineveh for any revelation of the Living ELohim to last because about 125 years later, Nineveh of Assyria had fallen into deep, deep wickedness. Assyria had become a horrendous threat to the entire region and had been solely responsible for scattering the northern tribes of YisraEL into all of the roundabout nations. She had become totally ruthless in the way she responded to her enemies and was responsible for the slaughter of many, including some of YAH's own little ones. So, YAHveh declared their destruction with no chance of rebuilding. Babylon loomed on the horizon, and YAHveh decided to use her to both destroy Assyria and to take His beloved YAHuda into captivity for seventy years. Why seventy years? Because ten times seven equals seventy—ten always dictates completeness and seven, of course, is His number for holiness (kedosh) and cleansing. They hadn't given the land its Sabbath rest for its cleansing, which brought forth His wrath. Nevertheless, in spite of all of this, He would once more bring about holiness to the House of YAHuda at the end of the seventy years. No one would grieve the Assyrian destruction because of their barbarism. None of the countries that YAHveh pronounced His complete wrath upon have ever survived or were ever raised up again; most of their cultures have been buried in antiquity. Only the great nation of Mitsrahyim has actually survived intact; the others have completely disappeared or have evolved into a totally different culture. Babylon, Syria, and Persia became only a shadow of what they once were. Greece and Rome would still remain, but not as the countries that they once were. The cultures of Babylon and Persia would evolve into the religious nations of Islam (which means to surrender or to be submissive). The politics of Greece and Rome would remain only as an ideology that would evolve into a one-world-type of republic, having a system within it known as democracy and financed by capitalism.

After King Manasseh of YAHuda died, his son, Amon, reigned as king, but only for two years. He was assassinated by some of his own officials. But the people of YAHuda rose up quickly and brought those who were responsible to justice and executed them; they were not going to allow anyone, except a descendant of Dahveed, to sit on the throne. King Amon had a son who was only eight years old; they made him the new king of YAHuda. His name was King Josiah (YosseeYAH), and he ruled for thirty-one years. He restored YAHuda back to their worshiping the ELohim of the House of YisraEL.

Conclusion

YAHveh warned YAHuda through His Ne'vee, Isaiah (YishshaYAH), that the same fate awaited her as had come upon her sister, YisraEL; but just like her sister, she ignored all of the warnings. YAH then turned His attention to establishing His hope for future generations—He painted His picture of the promised Messiah, who would bring about the restoration of the whole House of YisraEL. He foretold of His future Millennium reign and the filling up of the land of YisraEL with His people, Zion (Zeeon). He described Yeshua's birth, ministry, physical appearance, His death, and His resurrection. He explained how He would use all of these coming events to spread His word throughout the Earth in order to make it possible for all mankind to become a part of His House. He also explained the coming work of His Ruach, who would accomplish all of this, which would include His bringing forth the revelation that would be needed in order to understand the spirit of the Torah, along with the confirming of His teachings through signs and wonders. He also sent his Ne'vee, Nahum, to warn YAHuda of His impending judgment, but she still refused to listen and repent, so He used Nineveh of Assyria to show her an example of His extended mercy. Even though Assyria had shown no mercy toward His people, YisraEL, He still gave her a chance to repent. But she too refused, and He sent destruction and doom upon her to show the certainty of His judgment. YAH is willing to forgive and bless anyone, no matter what their previous wickedness has been—this also is as certain as His judgment. This was both YisraEL's and YAHuda's only hope for redemption.

CHAPTER 13
...about the Ne'vim Zephaniah, Jeremiah 1-24, and II Chronicles 35

Zephaniah (TzefenYAH) is the ninth Minor Ne'vee listed in the Books of the Ne'vim and an uncle to King Josiah (YosseeYAH). He may have been the one responsible for the king's spiritual training and guidance that caused him to follow after YAHveh, the one true ELohim. Soon after, another Ne'vee, by the name of Jeremiah (YirmehYAH), the second Major Ne'vee listed, was sent to continue the admonishment of YAHuda in order to bring her back to the Torah so that she wouldn't go down the same path as YisraEL. Jeremiah (YirmehYAH) was a humble man, quite similar in character to King Dahveed. He showed his humanity when he questioned YAH about His purpose in using him to speak curses upon YAHuda for her ignoring YAH's warnings.

Zephaniah (TzefenYAH)

Zephaniah (TzefenYAH) began his prophecy by confirming that YAHveh had determined to bring about a Day of Judgment upon all mankind for their wickedness. His chosen ones, YAHuda, would experience firsthand His wrath for rebellion. This would be YAHveh's "near judgment" of the House of YAHuda, which would mean that there would someday be a final one. He described both days in detail, telling about the devastation that would take place; the first one would only be temporary and would last seventy years, but the final one would last for 2,000 years.

YAHveh called His people to repentance and gave them hope by saying that they could be hidden from His wrath if they would just turn back to Him. YAHveh has always promised to shelter those who have come into His righteousness—they may see His wrath, but not experience it. After this, He reminded them of His promise to destroy all of their oppressors who had harassed them over the years and to reestablish them in their inheritance. As did the spokespersons before him, Zephaniah (TzefenYAH) began to name the nations who had oppressed YAH's people and to pronounce either their complete or their partial destruction as the result. He promised to destroy all of the false hopes, dreams, and trust that men had placed in the elohim that they had made with their own hands and from their own imaginations.

He confirmed the destruction of Nineveh and the entire nation of Assyria. At the same time, He also confirmed that His judgment would come upon His holy (kedosh) city, YAHrushalayim. He reminded her that if He had brought destruction upon the nations that surrounded her for their wickedness, He must also do the same to her. He knew, though, that some would heed, and for their sake and for the sake of their fathers, He would reestablish her. He said that one of the signs that the "final day" was near would be when His pure language would once more be spoken within her gates. Then they would be able to understand His words and instructions, enabling them to humble themselves before Him and to serve Him properly. In that day, they would trust in the name of YAHveh, and in that day, even though they would be but a remnant, they would be the ones to inherit His promises. He promised that in that day, they would finally be able to rejoice and celebrate their final triumph over all evil and wickedness. He would be in their midst once again as their King, the Mighty One of YisraEL, and there would be singing and gladness. He would have dealt with all of their oppressors once and for all time.

Jeremiah (YirmehYAH)

Jeremiah (YirmehYAH) began his prophetic writings by describing the timeframe from the reign of King Josiah (YosseeYAH) to King Zedekiah (TzedkehYAH) of YAHuda. He, being a humble man, was reluctant to be a spokesman for YAHveh because of his youth. Humility seemed to reverberate among YAH's servants; Isaiah (YishshaYAH) claimed to have unclean lips, and Mosheh felt limited because of his speech impediment. But, of course, we know that YAHveh examines the heart and not the personality or human abilities. He knows us much better than we know ourselves. That was what He was telling Jeremiah (YirmehYAH) when He showed him the vision of the almond branch; it symbolized His choice, just as it did when Aaron's (Aharon's) rod budded. It said that "I AM" can cause life to blossom anywhere at anytime. After this, He showed him a boiling pot that represented the calamity that would soon be coming upon the House of YAHuda out of the north from Babylonia. He also told him that he would not bring any favor to himself among the people by telling them these things, but in spite of this, he was to stand firm because YAH was with him.

As with His other ne'veem, YAHveh used Jeremiah (YirmehYAH) to point first to the sins of YisraEL, then to YAHuda's. He admitted that He was bewildered as to why His people were so stiff-necked and refused to honor Him. He pointed out that even those of the other nations were more faithful to their false elohim, which profited them nothing, than were His children for whom He had moved mountains and had delivered from their bondage in Mitsrahyim. YisraEL had been an unfaithful bride and had lusted after the things that pleased her eye and her fleshly cravings. But, at the same time, because she knew YAHveh had done mighty things for her, she still wanted what she could get from Him. She was like a spoiled, rich maiden with too much wealth and too much time on her hands. She wanted her cake and to eat it too. She yearned to be her own master, so YAH told her that she had made her choice and that He would not hear her pleas or prayers any longer. He told her to look to her lovers to meet her needs in the future. He said that she would deny her faults, and because she felt she was without guilt or sin, she would slay the ne'veem He would send to warn her. YAH told her that the way in which she had chosen to walk had led her into the waiting arms of Assyria. She would once more be a slave, just as she had been in Mitsrahyim, only this time He would not save her as He did then—this was the result of her rebellion. But if she would repent, He would change His mind and restore her. At the same time, He knew that she wouldn't—at least not until just before the judgment of the whole Earth had come.

Then YAHveh turned His attention to her sister, YAHuda. He pointed to the fact that while YisraEL was playing the harlot and was experiencing His wrath and calamity for it, it didn't seem to leave an impression on YAHuda at all. She ignored her sister's punishment even though the Assyrians had carried her away. She refused to learn from the example that YAH had placed right before her very eyes. And because she had not learned from her sister's mistakes, He saw YisraEL as being more righteous than YAHuda.

YAHveh continued to call out to His bride, YisraEL, even though it had already been nearly two-hundred years since she had been taken captive by the Assyrians and led away into the nations of the north. His cry would extend out to all of the generations to come, who would one day hear the voice of His Ruach and finally answer. And when she did, He would restore her, along with her rebellious sister, YAHuda, and they would once more be reunited to be His people, and they would leave their inheritance of the land no more. They would humble themselves and return to His voice calling to them from His holy (kedosh) mountain. They would recognize Him as their Salvation (Yeshua) and return to His ways and to His Torah.

He said that if they would do this, they would bless the nations out of which they had come, and He would protect them from any harm that could come upon them. He would restore them to their former glory. They would be His people, and He would be their ELohim. He then turned His attention and words to the men of YAHuda and told them of their uncircumcised hearts, revealing that the circumcision of the flesh guaranteed them nothing. At the same time, He knew that they wouldn't repent and that He would again be forced to pour out His wrath upon them and upon His city, YAHrushalayim.

Therefore, He warned them that their plight was now before them; their destruction and exile was soon to come from the north, just as He had said.

At this time, Jeremiah (YirmehYAH) spoke up in defense of YAHuda and questioned YAH's fairness in promising them shalom (peace) and then delivering them to destruction. YAHveh assured Jeremiah (YirmehYAH) that His word was always true and that not just YAHuda, but all of YisraEL would one day experience His promise of shalom (but not before His judgment because of their harlotry). YAHveh lamented because of the destruction that He was about to bring upon His land and His people. This was the last thing that He desired to do, but they left Him with no choice—they were like a rebellious child or an unfaithful bride. It caused Him great pain to bring down His mighty arm upon them. To Him, the land was going to be empty once more, just as in the day of *"In the beginning"*. There would be nothing left of what He had originally planned for *"His Beloved"* (Dahveed). It would once more be *"void and without form."* Again He lamented because it grieved Him to have to do this to His YisraEL.

Jeremiah (YirmehYAH) tried to give them the benefit of the doubt; he pointed out to YAH that it was because of their ignorance that they had transgressed against Him, and he suggested that he could go to their leaders and plea YAH's case. YAH granted his request, and to his dismay, he discovered that they were more corrupt and ignorant than even the poor. He found out for himself that it was truly rebelliousness and wickedness in their hearts that caused them to do these things. There were none in the streets of YAH's city, YAHrushalayim, who were guiltless. They laughed at correction and grieved YAHveh's heart with their lewdness. They refused to believe that they had done anything wrong. Even their ne'veem prophesied out of a spirit of pride and vain imagination. They prophesied *"Shalom—Shalom"*, but there was no Shalom. They had brought this calamity upon their own heads, but He still promised not to utterly destroy them—there had to be some seed left in order to replant His harvest to come. Once again, He expressed His deep grief that both the House of YAHuda and the House of YisraEL had done this to Him.

YAH admitted that His people were very shrewd in their religiosity, but their ears were dull and they wore blinders. They listened to their leaders and false ne'veem because they told them what they wanted to hear. They had created YAHveh in their own image. He tried to encourage them to return to their old ways, the original ways of the Torah, but they refused to heed His instructions. He said that they had become like bronze and iron (in other words, they relied on the power of their own hands for their well being. YAHveh was no longer needed; He was old-fashioned). Although the nations around them would remember that they were once like silver (a very spiritual people), this was no longer the case—their ELohim had brought destruction upon them.

Now their enemy would come upon them like a beast of the field, and they would show them no mercy.

Next, YAH commissioned Jeremiah (YirmehYAH) to go and stand at the main gate of His House and pronounce all of His words, exactly as YAH had given them to him, to the people of YAHrushalayim. He was to tell them that if they failed to heed those words, He would bring down His House, which He had ordained to be built, just as He had destroyed the city of Shiloh, where His Mishkahn had once stood. He told him to tell them that they had made His House into a den of thieves instead of a house of prayer. If they failed to do just as He had commanded them, He would destroy them, just as He had destroyed their brethren, Efraeem/Yosef/YisraEL. He told him to declare to them that they were idolaters and pagans because they baked cakes to the queen of heaven, Ishtar, and poured out drink offerings to other elohim. He instructed Jeremiah (YirmehYAH) not to pray for these people because they had transgressed too much for Him to turn His wrath back now. He reminded Jeremiah (YirmehYAH) of His purpose for burnt offerings. He did not desire burnt offerings; they had no value to Him. They were merely the vehicles that He had chosen to use in order to teach them about the importance of their being obedient to Him. In their religiosity, they had come to believe that burnt offerings would mystically do away with their sins. But YAH knew that all of these words that He had given to Jeremiah (YirmehYAH) would not change their minds or their ways, but they still had to be forewarned because YAHveh was a *"just"* ELohim. YAHveh also forewarned Jeremiah (YirmehYAH) that he too would be rejected, just as all of the other ne'eveem before him had been.

His people had become worshippers of the heavenly hosts: the sun, the moon, and the stars. They even desecrated the tombs of their fathers by digging up their bones and spreading them before their false elohim. Once again, He declared that because of their insistence on serving other elohim and their not walking in His Torah, He would scatter them among the Gentiles (Goyim), just as He did the northern tribe of YisraEL. But even so, He would still keep a remnant in the land until the final restoration of the Whole House of YisraEL. He called for them to clothe themselves with sackcloth and ashes and to send for skillful wailing women because of the lamenting that would take place in the land. He reminded them that if they would just repent and not trust in their own wisdom, might, or riches, but trust in their knowing Him through His Torah instead, He would forgive and heal them and their land. Then, once again, He reminded them that being circumcised in the flesh did not make them His, but being circumcised in the heart would.

He rebuked them for following the customs of the Gentiles (Goyim). They would go out into the fields, cut down trees, bring them into their houses, and decorate them with silver and gold. They would then fall down before them and worship the elohim of the forest. (This became a custom that has been revived within the past 150 years, and it has been made a part of the celebration called Christmas. It was an abomination to YAHveh then, and I don't think it has received a reprieve since.) He went on to declare YisraEL as being the tribe of His inheritance. We who mistakenly call ourselves the "Church" are really His inheritance, YisraEL, and the land of YisraEL is our inheritance to be shared with our sister, YAHuda.

Jeremiah (YirmehYAH) again began to lament for YAHuda. He pleaded with the inhabitants not to resist YAHveh's judgment, but rather submit to His decision and learn from the lessons that He was teaching, or they would have to go through the fire again. He exhorted them to trust in Him rather than in their own vain imaginations. He condemned the nations who had come up against the apple of YAH's eye. Jeremiah (YirmehYAH) called for YAHveh to pour out His fury upon all of the nations and families who would not call upon His name.

Once more, YAHveh commissioned Jeremiah (YirmehYAH) to invoke His curse upon anyone who refused to keep His Torah and who walked after the imaginations of their own heart. (This is why Yeshua had to come and keep the Torah for us—to lift the curse placed upon us because our forefathers wouldn't or couldn't.) He explicitly pointed out that both the House of YAHuda and the House of YisraEL were refusing to keep His covenant with Him. He commanded Jeremiah (YirmehYAH) not to pray for them any longer because He had waited long enough, and it was now time for them to reap what they had sown. It was here that YAH first referred to the House of YAHuda and the House of YisraEL as a "Green Olive Tree", but now He was about to destroy it with fire. Of course, with a young green tree, even setting fire to it would not completely destroy it—the roots would still remain, allowing it to grow again.

Jeremiah (YirmehYAH) learned of a plot against him by those who wanted to take his life, but YAHveh reassured him that nothing would take place because he would live to see their deaths. Jeremiah was surprised that it was his own friends and neighbors who had been the ones to plot against his life, and all because he spoke the words of YAH. Then, YAH rebuked him for being so naïve; if YAH's people had turned against Him because of His words, even after He had blessed them since their bondage in Mitsrahyim, why should Jeremiah (YirmehYAH) be surprised that his friends had turned against him for his?

In YAHveh's compassion, He was even willing to give Babylon, the nation that would be taking YAHuda into captivity, a chance to follow Him. If they would, then after YAHuda had learned their lesson, YAHveh would show His mercy to them. But if they wouldn't, He would utterly destroy them.

YAHveh continued to rebuke what was left of His people and assured them that it was too late. He would send them into captivity for a time, and even if they prayed to Him with a fervent heart, He would not hear them. It was just too late—they must pay the consequences for their rebellion. He said that even if Mosheh and SamuEL stood before Him, He would not change His mind; His people must go through His purging. He said that they would all suffer His judgment through four different means: they would either die by diseases, by famine, by the sword, or be taken into captivity. This was all due to their accepting the abominations of their king, Manasseh. He said that if He were to pardon them, they would just backslide again. No, these judgments would be the best thing to happen to them because it would finally bring them into full repentance.

Then YAHveh informed Jeremiah (YirmehYAH) that he was not to marry and have sons or daughters as long as he was in the land of YAHuda because of His curses on its inhabitants. He was ordered not to mourn for those who were the victims of this curse—it was His chastisement. He was instructed not to celebrate or feast with any of those who had fallen under this curse because even in their mourning and feasting, they would be doing so according to the practices of idol worship. He told him that if they were to inquire of him as to why all of these things had come upon them, he was to tell them that it was because of the sins of their fathers, along with the training in corruption that they had received so well through their example.

It was at this same time that YAHveh instructed Jeremiah (YirmehYAH) to tell them that a time would come when the great exodus from Mitsrahyim would no longer be marveled. Instead, there would be an exodus in the final days that would be greater and would dwarf the first. He told him to tell His people of a time that was coming when He would send out fishermen to fish for men. [Yeshua called His disciples (talmidim) to be fishers of men.] He said that these men would be gathered from every nation because He knew them and everything about them. [Yeshua said that His Abba (Father) knows the numbers of the hairs on our heads.] Not one of YisraEL's descendants is hidden from Him—no matter how much intermarrying they may have done with the Gentiles (Goyim). He will not lose track of any—He knows their DNA. He said that they would come out from all of the Goyim nations that they had mixed with, turn from their former practices that they had learned from the Goyim, confess their sins, and repent. This is how YAHveh will make Avraham a blessing to all believers within the Goyim nations—they will learn that they are really YisraEL.

Jeremiah (YirmehYAH) faced the same nagging taunt as all of the other ne'veem before him had, and that was: "Oh yeah and when is all of this supposed to happen? We've heard that before!" They refused to listen because they didn't see immediate judgment. When Jeremiah (YirmehYAH) spoke out on behalf of YAHveh, he testified that YAH places a curse upon those who trust in man's ability to save himself by the works of his own hands, but puts a blessing upon anyone who puts their trust in Him for their well-being. So it is with anyone who puts up a front of trusting in YAHveh but looks to himself or others for his welfare—YAHveh knows the heart and motive of each person. YAHveh pointed out one other important neglect that YAHuda was guilty of, as He did with the House of YisraEL—desecrating the Sabbath. YAHuda was to do no work or any kind of merchandising on the Sabbath, but she also ignored His Word. He admonished them about that because it is the observance of the Sabbath (the seventh day—not the first) that is the testimony and the sign that distinguishes His people from all of the other nations.

The priests and the elders of YAHuda were put under conviction by all of Jeremiah's (YirmehYAH's) words of judgment from YAH, and because it was tormenting their ears, a son of one of the priests and chief governors had him arrested and put in stocks. This was Jeremiah's (YirmehYAH's) first encounter with real persecution and physical abuse since he began to pronounce YAHveh's prophecies of judgment upon YAHuda. It was then that he began to really regret becoming a spokesman for YAH, and he vowed not to speak anymore in His Name. He had no sooner made that decision when he realized that YAH's words burned in his own heart, and he knew that he had no choice but to speak them. When he acknowledged that, he became overjoyed and began to praise YAH again.

The Final Days of YAHuda,

Before Their Captivity

While Isaiah (YishshaYAH), Zephaniah (TzefenYAH), and Jeremiah (YirmehYAH) had been giving these warnings to the House of YAHuda, it had begun to cause even the kings to rethink their own relationships with the ELohim of their fathers. King Josiah (YosseeYAH) had begun trying to restore YAH's people back to their original worship at the House of YAH by first restoring and refurbishing its structure from the years of its neglect. During the remodeling, they discovered the Torah scrolls that had been hidden away, so the king had them brought out and read to him. He immediately recognized just how far YAH's people had fallen away from their ELohim and ordered the Lehvee to find someone who could give them instructions as to what they could do to make amends for their neglect. The priest Hilkiah (HeelkeeYAH) sought out a prophetess (nev'eeYAH) named Huldah (HuldYAH), who told them the same thing that all of the other ne'veem had said—that YAHveh would punish them for going after other elohim. But, YAHveh told her that

He would spare King Josiah (YosseeYAH) from seeing this calamity because of his faithful heart.

It was at this time that the king had the Torah read to the remnant of the House of YisraEL – those who had come down earlier from the north before the first Diaspora (the assimilation of YisraEL) and to the House of YAHuda. He then ordered all of the idols, along with their remnants, to be demolished and burned. His sweeping reform even extended north to Samaria. Then, in the first month, Nisan/Aviv, of the following year, he commanded the greatest Passover celebration ever, since the time of the judge and ne'vee SamuEL, to be observed.

After all of this reform, the people began to return to YAHveh, but just as was said by all of the ne'veem, it was too late. The first event to take place that began a domino effect was when Babylon invaded Assyria and utterly destroyed it, just as was prophesied. In the process, Neco, the Pharaoh of Mitsrahyim, tried to come to the aid of Assyria because he knew that he would probably be next. King Josiah (YosseeYAH) of YAHuda was concerned that if Mitsrahyim were to be successful in defending Assyria, both nations would soon squeeze them into submission, so he went out to do battle against Pharaoh. In the process, King Josiah (YosseeYAH) was fatally wounded in the battle and died.

His oldest son, Jehoahaz (YAHohahaz), was made king, but he reigned for only three months because Neco, Pharaoh of Mitsrahyim, made his younger brother, Eliakim (ELeeahkeem), king instead. Eliakim (ELeeahkeem) was also known as Jehoiakim (YAHoeeahkeem). Then the Pharaoh took Jehoahaz (YAHohahaz) captive, imprisoned him in Mitsrahyim, and made King Jehoiakim (YAHoeeahkeem) pay him protection money.

Conclusion

YAHveh is slow to judge. His desire is for all to repent and turn away from sin and its consequences. This is why He has allowed so much evil to continue and has not brought about His wrath over these past two-thousand years since the first coming of His Son, King Yeshua. His desire is that none should perish. But just as the timing was ripe for Him to send His Messiah the first time, so the timing seems to be ripe now. Just as He had promised, YAHuda *has* returned to the land of their fathers, and the rest of YisraEL is soon to follow. Zephaniah (TzefenYAH), in his warning to them, said that one of the signs that YAHveh's final restoration was about to take place would be when He had restored His pure language among His people. Today, the Jews (YAHudi) are in the land and are speaking their native tongue, Hebrew, for the first time in eighteen-hundred years. The language is being researched more and more all the time, and His people are rediscovering its importance in bringing about a fuller understanding of His instructions, especially in His Renewed Covenant.

Jeremiah (YirmehYAH) pointed out several other things to YAHuda as to why she must undergo YAHveh's chastisement. He pointed to their arrogance toward YAH and their wanting things both ways—to worship Him and, at the same time, other elohim. They had adopted many of the pagan practices, such as bringing in evergreen trees and decorating them in an attempt to please the eluah of nature. He says that *they* were meant to be a "Green Olive Tree", and they were not to corrupt this by worshiping another eluah. He couldn't understand why they hadn't learned anything from the example of what had happened to the tribes of the north. He also reminded them of YAH's promise to Avraham, along with His promise to King Dahveed, and told them that this was the only reason that YAH wasn't going to utterly destroy them. He pointed to a time in the future when YAH was going to cause the Whole House of YisraEL to once again experience a "Greater Exodus"—one that would dwarf the first. This means that it will have to not only include more people but also have more and greater miracles accompanying it. That sounds like a description of the rapture to me.

CHAPTER 14
…about Lamentations, Habakkuk, Job, Jeremiah 25&26, Daniel 1&2, II Kings 24: 1-7, and II Chronicles 36: 1-7

The days of calamity were quickly coming upon YAHuda, and Jeremiah (YirmehYAH) was a witness to it all and could do nothing about it. He lamented over the death of King Josiah (YosseeYAH) because he knew that he was trying to lead YAHuda back to Torah observance; but as YAHveh had told him several times, the mechanism for their destruction was already in motion. Jeremiah (YirmehYAH) wrote a poem about YAHuda's destruction known as Lamentations. The eighth Ne'vee of the Minor Ne'vim, Habakkuk (Chabahkook), presented his prophecies in a poetic form while writing about YAHrushalayim's destruction and the promise of her restoration in the last days. Job (Yov) was a man who lived about the same time as Avraham, and his dissertation is said to be the oldest of all of the Writings (Kethuvim). His story of personal prosperity, destruction, and restoration parallels the heart and despair of both Jeremiah (YirmehYAH) and Habakkuk (Chabahkook). Although the book of Daniel (DahneeEL) is only considered as being one of the Writings (Kethuvim) in the TaNaKh, I believe that it would have qualified as one of the Books of the Ne'vim if there had been sufficient enough time for his "near prophecies" to have manifested themselves. While compiling the Septuagint, however, the Hebrew/Greek scholars did deem it worthy enough to insert his writings between the three Major Ne'vim and the twelve Minor.

Lamentations

Jeremiah (YirmehYAH) is referred to as the weeping Ne'vee mainly because of his poetic writings of Lamentations. Although these writings have all the indications of being penned after the siege of YAHrushalayim, I will include them here due to the lamenting that he expressed at the death of King Josiah (YosseeYAH). In his writings of Lamentations, Jeremiah (YirmehYAH) expressed his personal anguish after seeing the City of Dahveed, as it was frequently referred to, so desolate and in ruins. He expressed his lamentations in a variety of ways: sometimes as a personal eyewitness, sometimes in the vernacular of the passion of YAHveh, and sometimes as a third party in being the voice of the city itself. He began by remembering the way the city had appeared before the occupation of foreigners and compared it with what he was now witnessing. He began to lament as though the city had taken on her own voice and he was her interpreter. He spoke of his observations and the conclusions that he had drawn as a surviving witness. YAHrushalayim was no longer the place that was bustling with children in her streets, elders, priests, or rabbis (teachers) at her gates, or filled with people coming to and from the appointed times (moedim) of Feasts and Sabbaths. He saw the House of YAHveh in ruins as a testimony against YAHrushalayim because the Torah was no longer taught or practiced within her. But, Jeremiah (YirmehYAH) was not allowed to console them by command of YAH. He reminded her that she had accepted the words of false ne'veem and teachers. He confirmed the fact that the warnings that she had ignored from YAHveh had now come to pass. Once again, he spoke as though this entire calamity had come upon the city just to torment him with grief. He said that he felt as though he himself had been abandoned. Then, it was as though he had come to his senses because he began to remember YAH's faithfulness of the past and how He had rescued him from his enemies in his time of need. He remembered that YAHveh had also promised that restoration would come to His people at the time of their repentance. He remembered YAH's compassion and promises of deliverance. He began to cry out in his indignation toward the nations who were responsible for the destruction that he had witnessed. He called upon YAHveh to avenge the people of YAHuda because their enemies laughed at them for trusting in their ELohim. Finally, he called out for YAHveh to complete His words by causing them to repent and restoring them, just as He had promised.

Habakkuk (Chabahkook)

Habakkuk (Chabahkook) also began his prophecy by lamenting the destruction that was about to come upon the land of YAHuda and upon YAHveh's city, YAHrushalayim. YAHveh responded by reiterating the fact that He had allowed Babylon to become as powerful as she had become for His purposes—He planned on using her to punish His people for their arrogance. Again, Habakkuk (Chabahkook) made his inquiry of YAH concerning what seemed to him unfairness toward His own people. He referred to the enemies of YAH's people as fishermen who captured them with nets and hooks and who saw them as having no more value than mere fish. Afterwards, they would bow down to their nets and worship them. Here again, we can see YAHveh's people being compared or referred to as fish.

It was at this time that YAH told Habakkuk (Chabahkook) to write these things down on tablets (most of the writings of the ne'veem were first put down on clay tablets and then later transferred to scrolls that were made of animal skins or papyrus, but only if the ne'vee was recognized as being a true ne'vee). YAHveh said that those who had found true righteousness would continue in it by faith, but those who were of the flesh would look to the works of their hands. He condemned those whose only thoughts were to acquire things for themselves and would stop at nothing in trying to quench a never-ending thirst for power and wealth. He promised that those who would wait patiently for His provisions and deliverance would not be disappointed. Evil, He said, would be overcome with the knowledge of YAHveh, and He compared it with the water that covered the sea. Habakkuk (Chabahkook) then prayed for salvation for YAH's people and for vengeance upon the wicked, those who oppressed YAH's people. He confessed by faith that no matter how bad things seemed on the surface, he would still trust, believe, and joy in his salvation and deliverance.

Job (Yov)

Job (Yov) was another man after YAH's own heart, which is understandable when you consider Job's (Yov's) overall attitude toward YAH. We can assume that he lived sometime between Noah and Avraham because of the different times and events in the Scriptures that he made reference to. It is written that he lived one hundred and forty more years after his struggle in life, so this would have put him in a time period where that kind of longevity was common. He lived in the land of Uz that was located near Ur, the land from which Avraham and his family journeyed. He was a prosperous individual who had gained enormous community respect and admiration. The account of his life was recorded in order to show that evil can come upon anyone at anytime for no apparent reason. Sometimes it comes as a direct result and consequence of our fleshly activities in life. Other times, they come to test our credibility, faithfulness, and trust in our Adonai and ELohim, YAHveh, and are used by Him to build us up for a future call that He may have on our lives; He may even desire to display us as a model for others to emulate. Whatever the reason, we must persevere as did Job (Yov) until we reach the other side.

Job's (Yov's) story began when those who were referred to as the "sons of ELohim" came to present themselves before YAHveh. Who were these "sons of ELohim"? Some believe that they were angels, but I can't find anyplace where there is a direct reference to angels as being YAHveh's sons. Therefore, my understanding is that they were the ones who were referred to in the first book of the Torah, Genesis, as being those who sought after the things of YAHveh. After their fleshly death, they would come into His presence in "Paradise" (in other places it is referred to as the "Bosom of Avraham"—they are one and the same). But, at the same time, YAHveh's archenemy, hasatan, also had access to His throne. Twice hasatan presented himself before YAH, and twice YAHveh challenged him to discredit Job (Yov). YAHveh knew Job's (Yov's) character, and He was going to hold him up as a role-model for all mankind to see. No one else would ever again have to face tragic circumstances like that in their lifetime. Believers should stop and contemplate Job's (Yov's) challenges before complaining about their own circumstances.

Out of all of the friends and acquaintances that he had acquired over his many years as a man of achievement, there were only four who cared enough to come forward to advise him of the different recourses that he might take to redeem himself. Eliphaz, Bildad, and Zopher were the first three who tried to reason with Job (Yov) concerning the cause as well as the effect of his deplorable state of affairs. Their counsel resulted in faultfinding and criticism, which did nothing to comfort him in his dilemma. Job (Yov) was only looking for a little compassion, understanding, and encouragement while he tried to find the strength to endure his pain until the trial ended. But all they managed to do in their ignorance of the ways of YAH was to make matters worse. Their accusatory way of questioning him began to tempt him into losing his faith and patience in waiting upon YAHveh's mercy. Eliphaz came to him three times, while Bildad and Zopher came twice, but none brought comfort—only non-resolutions. After learning how Job's (Yov's) other, more elderly, friends were approaching the problem with narrow insight, a fourth fair-weathered friend, Elihu, came to him offering additional empty advice. Even though many of the principles that they offered up as reasons for his dilemma seemed on the surface to be sound, they just did not grasp YAHveh's wisdom, nor did they have the understanding of His will for those He counted as being righteous.

After having all of this dialogue with one another and Job (Yov) just barely hanging in there, YAH finally came to Job's (Yov's) defense and admonished the four for presuming that they understood His purpose. He then spoke directly to Job (Yov) and both admonished and exhorted him for his reasoning. YAHveh had tested Job (Yov) in order to determine his patience and his faithfulness, and he passed. He then rewarded Job (Yov) for his patience by restoring him back to his original state, and then, for his faithfulness, He doubled his worth. This paints still another picture that helps reveal His reward system to us, as well as His plan for the restoration of His people at the end of the age.

Jeremiah (YirmehYAH) 25 & 26

During the reign of King Jehoiakim (YAHoeeahkeem), YAHveh sent two of His ne'veem to YAHuda for the purpose of denouncing their behavior in rebelling against the Living ELohim. The first was YAHveh's faithful servant, Jeremiah (YirmehYAH), and the second was Uriah (UreeYAH). YAH did this to confirm His word in accordance to His Torah, by providing them with two witnesses. First, Jeremiah (YirmehYAH) was to declare to YAHuda that YAHveh was sending His servant of judgment, King Nebuchadnezzar of Babylon, down from the north to take YAHuda into captivity for a period of seventy years in order to give the land its Sabbath rest, as was commanded.

Then, Jeremiah (YirmehYAH) was told to stand at the gate of the House of YAH and prophesy against their abominable behavior. While YAH's hand of protection was upon Jeremiah (YirmehYAH) at that time, it wasn't so for Uriah (UreeYAH); the king had him extradited from Mitsrahyim, where he had fled, and returned to YAHuda, where he had him executed.

After eliminating Assyria as a regional power, Babylon continued to gain strength under King Nebuchadnezzar's reign. And while in captivity, YAHuda would rededicate herself to following most of the commandments of the Torah, but would add traditions of her own, which would eventually affect their effort to be obedient to YAH's statutes and ordinances. Jeremiah (YirmehYAH) was then commanded to go and prophesy to the other nations, those neighboring the land of YisraEL, about the impending danger that they too were facing. He told them that they should not resist King Nebuchadnezzar and Babylon because they would be annihilated if they did. YAHveh was using her to punish all of the nations that had previously oppressed the apple of His eye, YisraEL, including her sister, YAHuda.

Up until this time, Jeremiah (YirmehYAH) was not keeping written records of the historical events that were taking place in YAHuda. So, YAH sent a scribe by the name of Baruch (which means "blessed") to record all of YAHveh's words for him. Then He told him to go and read them to the people at His House. After hearing the words of condemnation from YAHveh, King Jehoiakim (YAHoeeahkeem) had the scroll burnt.

YAHveh told Jeremiah (YirmehYAH) to have a second set of scrolls written and to pronounce judgment upon the king, telling him that he would be taken captive by Babylon. The words of YAHveh would not return to Him void, and the king was made to pay tribute to King Nebuchadnezzar for three years. King Jehoiakim (YAHoeeahkeem) was eventually taken to the land of Babylon, where he did indeed die. King Nebuchadnezzar also began to systematically dismantle the House of YAH and take the articles from it to Babylon. YAHuda began to look to Mitsrahyim for help, but the Pharaoh didn't dare try to respond.

Daniel (DahneeEL) 1 & 2

Among those being taken to Babylon was a young man by the name of Daniel (DahneeEL). He was a captive, along with his three friends, Hananiah (HahnahneeYAH), Mishael (MishahEL) and Azariah (AhzahreeYAH). They were all given Babylonian names that we are more familiar with: Shadrach, Meshach and Abed-Nego—Daniel (DahneeEL) became Belteshazzar. All four had made a solemn pledge to YAHveh that they would not defile themselves with anything that was even remotely connected to idols, even if it were to cost them their very lives. Because of this, YAH gave them special favor before the king of Babylon, Nebuchadnezzar.

Night after night, YAHveh sent dreams into the king's spirit, disturbing him until he was unable to rest. In desperation, he sent for his magicians and wise men to interpret his dreams. Prior to their appearing before him, he decided that he didn't want anyone trying to be presumptuous about its meaning. So, when they came in, he told them that if they were genuine seers, they would be able to tell him what his dream was before they attempted to interpret it. Out of his desperation, he promised that he would show his gratitude by handsomely rewarding the person who could do this, but if they failed, he would have them executed. When his wise men pleaded with him that only an eluah could do such a thing, he ordered the destruction of all of those who held the seat of a magician, wise man, or soothsayer.

Upon hearing of the king's outrageous decree, Daniel (DahneeEL) decided to step forward and take on this challenge in order to save the lives of these innocent men. But, before going into the king's presence, he asked his three friends to pray and ask for guidance and wisdom from YAHveh, ELohim of the Universe. Then, when he came before King Nebuchadnezzar, he immediately revealed to him his knowledge of the contents of his dream, just as the king had demanded. He told him that his dream came from the only true Living ELohim, the ELohim of his people, YAHuda of YisraEL. He told him that YAHveh, the ELohim of YisraEL, had shown him an image, or a statue, made up of four elements: gold, silver, bronze, and iron. Its head was of gold; its arms and chest were of silver; its belly, its hips, and its thighs were of bronze; its two legs were of iron, and its feet were a mixture of clay and iron. Then he told him that a huge stone came hurdling out of the sky and struck the feet of the statue, and because of the frailty of the foundational material, the whole thing collapsed into nothing but dust. Then the stone that struck the feet of the statue became a great mountain and filled the whole Earth. The king was amazed and convinced that surely YAHveh must be the true and mighty ELohim if he could show a mere man these things.

Daniel (DahneeEL) then gave the interpretation. The head of the image represented King Nebuchadnezzar and his kingdom in Babylon. And since it had been YAHveh who had given him the power to conquer all that he had and put everything under his authority, the head was made of gold. But in time, after the king's reign, another kingdom would be raised up and would overcome the Babylonian kingdom, even though it would be a lesser kingdom. This kingdom was represented by the silver arms and chest. The two arms of authority meant that it would share its power with another kingdom. Then a third kingdom would rise up. It too would be a lesser kingdom in importance, but more powerful in strength, and would overcome the second kingdom. This was represented by the bronze belly and thighs. Then a fourth kingdom would rise up and overcome the third, again of lesser spiritual importance, but still more powerful militarily. It too would become divided, as represented by the two iron legs and the feet that were mixed with iron and clay. Even though each kingdom was overcome by the next, the conqueror would always be influenced by the previous kingdom's cultural and spiritual sins, setting up heavenly principalities. However, in the end times, YAHveh will set up a kingdom that will crush all of these principalities. His kingdom will cover the whole Earth, and He will reign forever.

What Daniel (DahneeEL) described has proven to be true in history—right up to our present day. As I have said before, Daniel (DahneeEL) was never considered to be a ne'vee in his time because not all of his prophesies had a chance to be completely fulfilled; in other words, there were no near fulfillments that could be recorded as a test of the accuracy of his words. Yeshua, on the other hand, quoted him as being a ne'vee when He was describing the end times to His disciples (talmidim) in Matthew's Gospel (**MATT 24:15**).

As Daniel (DahneeEL) said, the gold head represented King Nebuchadnezzar and the kingdom of Babylon. The element of gold has always been connected with religion; we can see it as the material most often used, even in idol worship. YAHveh Himself commanded that both His House and His Ark be made of gold. Silver, though being of a lesser value, also has a direct connection with religion and deity; we can see this in the construction of the Mishkahn, with silver being used as a companion to the gold utensils. The Medes and the Persians, led by King Cyrus, were the kingdoms that eventually overcame the power of Babylon. Both nations were highly motivated by their polytheism and the power of their elohim (gods). These were represented by the silver chest and arms. Eventually, they too were conquered by another empire, lesser in religious influence, but more powerful in military strength, led by Alexander the Great of Greece. Instead of religion, the Greek Empire was motivated by human philosophy, art, science, and political power. It introduced mankind to both democracy and secular humanism. Just as bronze is manufactured as a direct work of man's ingenuity through the mixing of copper and tin, the third kingdom is represented by the mixing of religion and politics, producing secularism. After the Greek Empire, the Roman Empire took over, ruling and conquering its enemies with an iron rod and sword and spreading its power over the entire continent of Europe. It embraced all of the elements of the previous kingdoms, including their elohim and their politics. The Roman Empire introduced into the mix the political idea of a republic with its congressional and senate rule. Rome also became a divided empire with two capitols, one in Rome and the other in Constantinople—thus, the two iron legs. It too, like iron, was the direct work of men's hands. Now what about the feet made with clay and iron—what does that represent? Many who study eschatology today say that in the final days, a government with its base in Rome will be raised up, and through it, a world leader will come to establish himself as the king and eluah (god) of this world—then Yeshua will return. I believe that that government is already here. Remember the two feet? Today, the world is embracing both the Roman and the Greek Empires with their ideology of democracy and capitalism, mixed with secular humanism. Clay, or pottery, is described in allegories throughout the Scriptures as representing man and his frailties. Iron represents today's form of Roman democracy that the world is beginning to embrace. The highly-influential religion of Catholicism, with its base in Rome, also directs many of the world's decision-making. Does this not describe the feet of iron mixed with clay? If this is an accurate analogy, then the stage is already set for the final events to occur at most anytime.

There is one more thing to take note of here, and that is, by saving the lives of the wise men and magicians of Babylon, Daniel (DahneeEL) became highly esteemed as being one of the greatest Magi (magicians, or elders) of Babylon. This would prove to be very important some six-hundred years later when the Magi from the east (old Babylon) journeyed to the land of YAHuda, seeking the "King of the Jews (YAHudi)".

Conclusion

YAHveh is setting the final stages of His plan, continuing the countdown to the restoration of all things in order to fulfill His prophecies. He will complete His promise to Avraham, making him the father of many nations, by using the succession of these empires to affect the affairs of men, which will set the stage to bring forth Avraham's seed, the Messiah (meaning Yeshua). This will make Avraham the blessing to the Gentiles (Goyim), just as He promised. He has already scattered the ten northern tribes into all the nations through the Diaspora of Assyria, and now He is about to send YAHuda, who is also made up of the tribe of BenYAHmeen, into exile for seventy years before bringing them back to their land in order to possess it until the time of the Gentiles (Goyim) is fulfilled. YAHveh scattered His sheep in order for them to become lost throughout the nations so that when Yeshua sends out his fishermen, they will be able to fish for those "lost sheep of YisraEL" for the next two-thousand years.

CHAPTER 15
…about Ezekiel 1-33, Jeremiah 27-52, II Kings 24&25, and II Chronicles 36&37

Another Ne'vee, Ezekiel (YechezkEL), the third Major Ne'vee, begins his ministry near the middle of Jeremiah's (YirmehYAH's). These two men of YAH watch in horror and disbelief as their beloved city, YAHrushalayim, is destroyed and all of its people are either destroyed or captured. The last of the descendants of Dahveed have reigned as the kings of YAHuda. Even Ezekiel (YechezkEL) has experienced this foreign captivity.

After King Jehoiakim (YAHoeeahkeem) had Jeremiah's (YirmehYAH's) scroll burned, which was his way of showing his lack of fear of YAHveh, he then showed his defiance against King Nebuchadnezzar of Babylon. YAHveh responded to this defiance by sending bands of raiders from all of the surrounding territories to plunder the cities of YAHuda. Within a short time, King Jehoiakim's (YAHoeeahkeem's) reign ended in his death, and his son, Jehoiachin (YAHoeeakheen), was made king at the young age of eighteen. He had only reigned for three months when King Nebuchadnezzar took him and his mother as prisoners and brought them into Babylonia. After this, he made King Jehoiachin's (YAHoeeakheen's) uncle, Mattaniah (MattahneeYAH), king in his place. Sometime during the seventy years of their captivity, King Nebuchadnezzar besieged YAHrushalayim, slaughtered many of the inhabitants, burned the House of YAH, and took the rest of the citizens into captivity.

Ezekiel (YechezkEL) 1-33

Ezekiel (YechezkEL) was a priest from the tribe of Lehvee when he was called to be a ne'vee by YAHveh. He had already been in exile in the land of Babylonia for five years, along with King Jehoiachin (YAHoeeakheen), when he received a vision of the Angel of YAH, who had come to tell him many things about the future and the fate of both the people of YAHuda and the people of YisraEL. Daniel (DahneeEL), the ne'vee, and John (Yochanan), Yeshua's beloved disciple (talmid), will later have their own visions of the Angel of YAH. They will witness the glory of Adonai (the Lord), and although their visions will not be identical in appearance, they will be identical in nature and symbolism.

He described the vision as a whirlwind of fire, not unlike the pillar of fire that led Mosheh and the children of YisraEL through the wilderness for forty years or the chariot that swept ELeeYAHoo away. Within this whirlwind, he could see what appeared to be four living creatures. This symbolism is the same as what the disciple (talmid) John (Yochanan) described in the vision that he had on Patmos Island. As was pointed out earlier, the number four usually refers to the four directions, winds, or seasons, which in turn depict the regions of the whole Earth. So, this vision involved the whole Earth and its destiny.

Each creature had four faces: a man, a lion, an ox, and an eagle. [These coincide with the characterizations of the Messiah, Yeshua. The four writers of the Good News described Him in this manner: as a "man", Luke described Him as the Son of Man and wrote about His human side—as a "lion", Matthew described Him as the King of kings and the Lion of YAHuda—as an "ox", Mark described Him as one who came to be a suffering Servant of His Father to all mankind—finally, as an "eagle", John described Him as the Son of ELohim, who was every bit as much ELohim as He was a man. Some people have trouble with understanding how He can be a man and at the same time be ELohim. This understanding can only be accomplished through faith and faith alone. Isn't ELohim omnipresent? It takes faith to believe that. So, if He can be omnipresent, then He can be both a man and ELohim at the same time. Consider this also—Yeshua called His followers to go and spread the Good News, using signs and wonders to confirm His words. Only Elohim can do these wonders, and only by faith in His words can we manifest these works of His Spirit into this material world. He was calling us to be like Him in order to accomplish the mission that He had given His Messiah. He said we were to be His Body until He returns to reconcile all things to Himself. As His Body, we are to perform His ministry, which will eventually bring this event of reconciliation about. This ministry of reconciliation consists of: the Teacher (pastor/teacher) as the "man"—the Apostle (leader/guide) as the "lion"—the Evangelist (servant/exhorter) as the "ox"—the Prophet (spiritual interpreter/orator and/or seer) as the "eagle".] These creatures were awesome to behold in their overall appearance. They were mounted on a chariot with wheels, not unlike the vehicle that swept Elijah (ELeeYAHoo) away into heaven. The eyes that he saw covering the rim of the wheels are symbolic of the ever-seeing omnipresence of YAHveh. A glowing firmament was above their heads, and a voice came from within the firmament, both being symbolic of the Ark of the Testimony (Covenant) with its Mercy Seat.

Ezekiel (YechezkEL) was then given the commission to go to the children of YisraEL and speak all of the words that he was given to say. For now, only his fellow captives in Babylonia would be able to hear him, but there would come a day when all of YAH's people would hear and understand these words—when the Ruach of YAHveh revealed His mysteries to them through His written Word. He was then shown a tiny scroll and told to eat it, just as John (Yochanan) was instructed to do in his vision in the Book of Revelation. In both cases, the scroll tasted like honey (King Dahveed said in **PSALM 119:130** that YAH's words and the Torah tasted like honey). This vision reveals the coming days when Yeshua will redeem and sanctify the House of YisraEL and bring about its total restoration. Then YAH's Torah will once more be like eating the manna from heaven, with its taste of honey, to all who see and understand it like Dahveed.

YAHveh's immediate instructions to Ezekiel (YechezkEL) were for him to go to his brothers and share with them all of these warnings. YAH gave a specific order to him, that as a minister of ELohim, he was to warn all of those who were in a wicked state of evil that they would die if they remained there. If that warning was given and the person did not heed it, the guilt was to be upon that person's head—but if he wasn't told and he died, then the guilt was to be upon the head of the one who was sent to tell him. He told him that the same would apply to a righteous man who has stumbled—if he was told and failed to heed the warning, then he bore his own guilt. This is YAH's message to all who are sent to spread His words and the Good News of the coming of His Living Torah, Yeshua.

After this, YAHveh told Ezekiel (YechezkEL) that he was to be a living sign to the House of YisraEL. He was to take a clay tablet and draw the likeness of the city of YAHrushalayim on it. He was to depict it as a city under siege. He was also told to lie on his left side and face the diagram and to put an iron plate between the diagram and himself. This probably represented the fact that the Roman Empire would always be an obstacle between YAH and His City because iron represents that empire. Lying on his left side was the symbol that anything at the left hand of YAHveh was under His curse. He was to stay that way for three hundred and ninety days, each day representing one year. He was to stay in this position for over one year—not an easy task. At the end of this time, he was to turn to his right side for another forty days. The right side depicted YAH's favor. He was told that the time that he spent on his left side was to be a prophecy to the House of YisraEL, who for over the past two-hundred-plus years had already been assimilated and dispersed into the nations of the north. The time that he spent on his right side represented the forty years that the House of YAHuda would remain in exile in Babylon before any of the captives would begin returning. This, added to the thirty years already spent there, would give them a total time of seventy years in exile. Does this mean that YisraEL would be returning to the land one hundred and twenty years after YAHuda? No, because it didn't happen, not even for the remnant of the House of YisraEL who were with YAHuda when she was taken into

Babylonia. (Only a small portion of the House of YisraEL was with them; by then, the rest of the house was already dispersed throughout Africa, Asia, and upper Europe.) Then what about the prophecy—how was it to be fulfilled? To fully understand the prophecy, we need to return to the Torah regarding YAH's curses. They are found in **LEV 26:18, 21, 23&24, 28,** and **33.** Here, YAHveh promised four different times that He would punish His people seven times if they refused to obey Him and that He would also scatter them among the nations. That would mean seven times the three hundred and ninety years depicted by Ezekiel (YechezkEL), which would equal 2730 years. If we subtract the 723 years BCE from that figure, we will mathematically be brought to the year 2007 CE. Does this mean that the rest of the House of YisraEL, the tribes of Yosef who represent the ten northern tribes, will have the curse of their blindness lifted from them at that time? Only that date will reveal this—after the fact.

While he is performing these signs before YAH's people, he was instructed to make certain provisions for himself. For food, he was to make bread from a particular list of grains. For drink, he was to provide for himself a particular measure of water. He was told to bake the bread by using human excrements as fuel. Ezekiel (YechezkEL) rejected the idea, and YAH relented and allowed him to use animal excrements as a substitute. Why would YAH test Ezekiel (YechezkEL) with such a detestable command and then change His mind? I believe that He was using this as a symbolic metaphor to point to the time when the idea of clean and unclean, or holy and unholy, would not be determined in the same way as it had been from the beginning. I believe that it was to show that what had been considered unclean would one day be accepted as clean, when done in faith. Yeshua would make all things clean through His blood, thereby making Gentiles (Goyim) clean before YAHveh in order to draw all nations to Himself. I believe that this was what the Apostle Paul (Rav Shaul) was trying to tell the Goyim in his different letters to the Kahal of YisraEL. He explained to them that there was no difference between Greek and Jew (YAHudi), circumcised and uncircumcised, or what you ate or didn't eat, as long as you did it with thanksgiving and in faith toward Yeshua. He made all things pure and holy by the power of His blood and delivered all, if they would by faith believe His words, from the curse of the Torah. Many times we forget that He also purchased the ***blessings*** of the Torah for us by this same power of His blood. How are we to know the blessings that He purchased for us if we don't study and do the Torah?

After Ezekiel (YechezkEL) had finished his ordeal, he was told to take some of his own hair, which would represent the citizens of YAHrushalayim, and divide it into thirds. One third of it was to be burned, one third struck with a sword, and the final third scattered to the wind—but he was also told to hide a few strands in his tallit. This would mirror the prophecy of Jeremiah (YirmehYAH) regarding the fate of all of the city's inhabitants. He was then told to go and prophesy to the mountains, to the hills, and to the land of YisraEL, pronouncing judgment upon the land because His people had defiled it.

A year later, YAHveh caught Ezekiel (YechezkEL) up in another vision while he was in council with a group of elders. He was spiritually translated to the city of YAHrushalayim, to the House of YAH, where he was shown the detestable practices of idolatry that were being done there in secret, including the worship of the sun eluah (god), Zeus. After this, Ezekiel (YechezkEL) saw the same living creatures that were in his first vision (but this time he referred to them as cherubim); they had come to the House of YAH to remove the Shchinah glory from the mercy seat and to depart with it. This was YAHveh's judgment upon His Own Palace (it was not His House any longer, just an edifice built by men). Then, He promised Ezekiel (YechezkEL) that He would return His Shchinah glory to His Palace when He brought back the whole House of YisraEL to their land (His Son, Yeshua, would be the builder then). He also said that He would now become their sanctuary, through His Ruach, while they were in the nations where He had scattered them; in other words, He would make Himself known to them wherever they were so they could find a way to worship Him. When the vision was finished, the Ruach returned Ezekiel (YechezkEL) back to where he was sitting among the elders. Remember, this was a vision given to Ezekiel (YechezkEL) and not an actual event. It was to show Ezekiel (YechezkEL) exactly what kind of judgment He would place upon His own house/people/family.

Once again, YAHveh visited Ezekiel (YechezkEL) with even more instructions that required him to act out another prophecy before the people. One of the enactments depicted King Zedekiah (TzedkehYAH) of YAHuda during his capture. YAH reminded Ezekiel (YechezkEL) that the people had hardened their hearts toward all ne'veem because of the lies of the false ones. But some did believe Ezekiel (YechezkEL) to be a true ne'vee, although they thought that his prophecies pertained only to events that would take place in the distant future. But they were shaken into reality when they saw the king actually being captured and their beloved city ransacked and destroyed over the next five years. YAH then placed a curse upon all of the false prophetesses (nev'eeYAHeem) and ne'veem who, out of their own imaginations, prophesied lies in His Name, reassuring His people that there would be no destruction. This is a clear message to overzealous people who are looking for spiritual recognition and admiration not to become too ambitious. If YAH has called you to be a seer, you will know it because *all*, not just most, of your words will come to pass. A ne'vee, like a teacher, will be judged more severely. He also told Ezekiel (YechezkEL) to warn all of those who had set up idols within their hearts not to expect words of wisdom, knowledge, or prophecy to come to them because of their insincerity. People have a tendency to set up all kinds of idols in their hearts by seeking after the lust of their eyes (I'm not referring to just sexual lusts, I'm also referring to material pleasures) in order to satisfy and fill the void that YAHveh has placed within the hearts of all men that can only be filled up with Him. He makes it possible to fill that void through faith in His Son, Yeshua HaMashiach. However, many who have come to His Son have later returned to lusting after things because they have failed to follow His voice or because they have never learned how to hear it. To those who have experienced the need to repent and return to seeking Him, He has promised that He will be found when He is sought with a sincere heart.

YAHveh began to speak to Ezekiel (YechezkEL) about His city, YAHrushalayim, how He founded her and nurtured her before she became the beautiful and famous city that she was and how she had become a harlot and unfaithful to her Creator, YAHveh. A city is more than just buildings, parks, roads, and houses—it is its inhabitants who bring it to life. The spirit of its citizens gives it its character, personality, glory, and splendor. The character of its people determines its charisma. YAHrushalayim had many different cultures occupying it over the centuries. It was once the seat of the king/priest Melchizedek. After that, the Hittites (Hitti), the Amorites (Amori), the Jebusites (Yebusi), and finally the Judeans (YAHudaim) occupied her. In the end, her inhabitants had brought her down, and YAH compared her to her corrupt sisters, Samaria and Sodom. Therefore, He was forced to bring judgment and destruction upon her walls and gates. But, He will not leave her in this condition forever. He promises to restore her back to her original state on the Last Day, when He will bring back the House of YisraEL, along with the House of YAHuda, to dwell within her walls and gates once more.

Once again, YAH, through His Ne'vee Ezekiel (YechezkEL), reaffirms the kingdom principle that each man is responsible for his own actions and decisions; a father will not be punished for his son's sins or a son for his father's. Wicked men will be recognized as righteous if they repent and turn toward YAH, and righteous men will be punished if they turn away from Him. He established these principles after He had to pronounce His judgment upon YisraEL, when her citizens turned away from Him in masses. They all had to face assimilation because the righteous did not rebuke and correct the wicked.

A year later, the elders came before Ezekiel (YechezkEL) to ask him for YAHveh's direction, but, instead, they received a rebuke for coming. YAH had previously instructed them not to come, but because of their rebelliousness, they ignored His command. YAH had Ezekiel (YechezkEL) remind them of the story of their forefathers and the hardness of their hearts. YAH had warned them time after time what would lay ahead for them if they continued in their steadfastness in doing what was wrong. He reminded them how they had equated keeping His Sabbaths to being a small thing and refused to see it as a sign of their covenant with Him. He told them that they still had not changed. He knew their hearts and that they were still filled with indignation and wickedness—therefore, He would not hear their request for guidance. He reminded them that there would come a time when He would bring them back into the desert of YisraEL, where He would separate for Himself those who had stood fast with Him and walked with Him in faith from those who hadn't. (Yeshua referred to this as being the "Judgment Seat of the Messiah".) He reminded them that just before that time came, they would turn to Him with a new heart, one that would be faithful and willing to serve Him in gladness.

Then YAHveh had Ezekiel (YechezkEL) warn the people of YAHuda again of the coming disaster to their beloved city, YAHrushalayim, and that it would be the Babylonians who would lay siege to it and utterly destroy it. YAHveh was going to commission Babylon to be His sword to accomplish this. When it happens, King Zedekiah (TzedkehYAH), their final king, will be captured and brought into exile there.

YAHveh then began to speak to Ezekiel (YechezkEL) about the capitol cities of the House of YisraEL and the House of YAHuda, Samaria and YAHrushalayim, as being two promiscuous sisters. He gave the name of Oholah to Samaria and Oholibah to YAHrushalayim. They had learned the trade of prostitution while they lived in Mitsrahyim, but He still considered them to be His daughters. The first to enter into prostitution was Oholah, who gave herself to the Assyrian warriors after they had left Mitsrahyim. YAH then gave her up to her lovers; they in turn took away her sons and daughters, but killed her. Her sister Oholibah, who witnessed all of this, didn't learn a thing from it—she not only prostituted herself to the Assyrians, but to the Babylonians as well. They both lusted after Mitsrahyim, Assyria, Babylon, and their elohim. They thought that if they would become like them and serve their elohim, they would be accepted into their societies and would feel as though they belonged. But these nations saw how they had already been blessed abundantly with power and riches from their ELohim and were jealous, envious, and, at the same time, fearful. YAHveh's daughters reached out in fellowship to them and said, "Let's be friends, let's trade, exchange sons and daughters, share cultures, and elohim". Mitsrahyim (world system), Assyria (future empires), and Babylon (religious system) said, "Sure, why not; sounds good to us"—and then they raped, plundered, and exploited them. They feared these sisters because they were different and blessed, but the sisters themselves were unaware of their own blessings. Today, believers go through the same thing—they are in the world, but they are not to be of the world. But the world and what it has to offer seems so tempting, and, at the same time, what YAH has to offer seems so restrictive. And why not—we're just dumb sheep, and our shepherds have continued to raise us on milk and not on the hidden manna, which is supposed to be our meat. We haven't been taught how to walk in the Ruach and the Torah. That's why when we cry out to our Abba in a moment of despair, we don't have the discipline to endure. YAH has us for only that moment—the world has us the rest of the time. We're just too weak, having milk as our only diet. YAHveh sees this, and His heart is broken because of it; but He promised that one day He would change all of this. In the meantime, we will have to suffer tribulation until we learn the lesson of faithfulness to Him. Oholah (Samaria of YisraEL) was punished by His letting her have her way, and she became one of them and lost her identity. Oholibah (YAHrushalayim of YAHuda) was punished for a shorter period of time, but was allowed to return because of YAH's promise to Dahveed. After YAHuda returned, she added so many extra ordinances and statutes (the Oral Law) to the Torah in order to prevent her from ever missing the will of her Elohim again that she caused herself to miss the Messiah instead.

It had been five years since YAH had said that He was going to send King Nebuchadnezzar of Babylon to capture King Zedekiah (TzedkehYAH) of YAHuda, bring him into Babylonia, and destroy YAHrushalayim. On the tenth of Tevet, the tenth month, in the ninth year of captivity, YAHveh told Ezekiel (YechezkEL) that He was now going to fulfill all of the prophecies that He had given to His ne'veem regarding YAHrushalayim.

To Ezekiel's (YechezkEL's) horror, YAHveh does the unthinkable to His faithful servant, just to show him and his brethren what He Himself had been enduring. He told him that he should prepare himself to endure a lot of pain and that no one should be allowed to see his pain when it happens. His test came when YAHveh took Ezekiel's (YechezkEL's) wife in death. I can't imagine his pain. How would I be able to keep my faith after being told that I was going to lose the love of my life in order to provide a lesson for an unworthy and ungrateful people, who would just brush it off and ignore it anyway? YAH told him that this lesson was because He was about to take from them their most cherished possession, the House of YAH. They too were not to mourn; instead, they were to follow Ezekiel's (YechezkEL's) example.

When the siege came upon YAHrushalayim, YAHveh directed Ezekiel (YechezkEL) to speak forth condemnation against all of the past enemies of YAHuda and YisraEL. This was further confirmation of the impending destruction upon the enemies of YAHveh and His people that had been spoken of by all of His ne'veem throughout the centuries. Ezekiel (YechezkEL) pointed to Ammon, Moab, Edom, Philistia, and even the Pharaoh of Mitsrahyim as being the recipients of YAH's wrath. He then pointed to the wealthy cities of Tyre and Sidon as being the perfect example of what serving wealth instead of YAHveh could eventually do to either a nation or to an individual. They had been the epitome of success to the world around them, but He was about to bring them to their knees. Serving the eluah of wealth (money or mammon) seems logical and natural to those who feel that their personal treasures are the result of their own ingenuity and skills, but they are really only a part of YAH's plan to bring about His result and will for the lives of those He desires to touch through that wealth. All good gifts come from Him (**JAMES 1:17**). YAHveh described the deluge of His judgment that He was going to rain down upon them through King Nebuchadnezzar. Tyre was a capitalistic system, not unlike the United States, and because they were the central source of wealth in the region, her fall would cause all of the nations who had looked to her for their resources to suffer complete economic failure. This same fate will come to our country in time. The only thing that has saved us so far is our geographic location and our confession of "In God we trust". Once the latter changes (and it will), the power of darkness will be unleashed, and we will suffer the same loss.

Then YAH began to compare the city of Tyre with Hell when he spoke about the Pit and its king, hasatan—the king of Tyre had also proclaimed himself to be an eluah (god). YAHveh told Ezekiel (YechezkEL) to lament over the king because his foolish idea of making himself equal to YAH was setting himself up for sure destruction. YAH then began to describe the king as being like hasatan, who was once in His Garden (Paradise) and had "all beauty" before his fall. At that time, his name was Lucifer (meaning the morning star), and YAH compared his beauty with many exquisite gems and stones. His position was that of "a cherub of covering" over YAH's throne until his rebellion. YAH referred to him as being a merchandiser because of his ability to persuade one-third of His angels to join him in a coup against Him. He was covered with many instruments of music, and since he was a covering for YAH's throne, it seems to indicate that the praise of music, which was intended for YAH, had to first pass through Lucifer. Apparently, Lucifer wanted to keep a little of that praise for himself and to make himself *"as the most High"* (**ISA 14:11-15**). The result was banishment from YAH's throne. From all indications, YAH compared the destruction of Tyre and her king to what He had planned for the Pit and hasatan at the end of all things. Tyre and her wealth was a false Paradise, and her king wanted the exaltation and praise that was given by those he had wooed with his songs of wealth and power.

ROGER W. FEARING

YirmehYAH 27-52

We pick up where we left off with YirmehYAH—at the beginning of the siege of YAHrushalayim. King Zedekiah (TzedkehYAH), the final king of YAHuda, refused to listen to YirmehYAH's warnings from YAHveh and had him confined to the courtyard of the king's palace. YirmehYAH had warned the king not to resist the army of Nebuchadnezzar, king of Babylon, who was YAHveh's instrument of punishment for their sins. He told the king and the people the same thing that Ezekiel (YechezkEL) had told the captives who were already in Babylon, that one third of the inhabitants of YAHrushalayim would die by the sword and one third by famine and plague. The other third, those who did not resist and allowed themselves to be led captive, would survive, for this was the will of YAHveh. He told the king that he was going to be taken captive and that he would die while in captivity. Upon hearing these words, King Zedekiah (TzedkehYAH) had YirmehYAH arrested. Once again, as he had done in the past, YirmehYAH tried to comfort YAHuda, those who would listen, with the assurance that the captivity would not last forever and that they would one day return to the land. YAH would always keep a remnant for the sake of His promise to King Dahveed. He would also one day return *all* of the people of YisraEL to their land, the land that He had promised Avraham. In that day, there would be a time of Jacob's (Yaacov's) trouble like nothing ever before. This will take place sometime near the very brink of what will seem to be the final destruction of both houses of YisraEL, but He will come and save them and destroy all of their enemies.

Has the time of Jacob's (Yaacov's) trouble already begun? An interesting event has taken place in recent years. On the Day of Atonement (Yom Kippur) in 2000 CE, Ariel Sharon, just before becoming the prime minister of YisraEL in 2001, went up to the Temple Mount in YAHrushalayim to pray and was attacked by a Palestinian (Edomi) crowd in protest. While there, he read from the book of Ezekiel, chapter thirty-seven—we will discuss this in the next chapter. Since that time, the Palestinians have been relentless in their determination to deny YisraEL's right to exist. Their desire is to once again drive them out of the land. Some of the Jewish (YAHudaim) Rabbis (Rabboni— teachers of the Torah) have declared this to be what YirmehYAH prophesied— "the time of Yaacov's Trouble". Many who study eschatology believe that "Jacob's (Yaacov's) Trouble" and the "Seven Year Tribulation" are one and the same. My study of the Scriptures has given me a different perspective that I believe also has merit. While Yosef was in Mitsrahyim, there was a seven-year period of plenty just prior to seven years of famine. Could this be a metaphor of a period of time that will follow "Yaacov's Trouble"? If Yaacov's trouble did begin in the year 2000, this would mean that it should end around Yom

Kippur in 2007. This would coincide with the approximate time that the curse on Efraeem would end, according to Ezekiel (YechezkEL). Another thing to consider is that since the year 2000, more Christians have been turning back to their Hebrew roots than at any other time in recorded history and more Jews (YAHudi) have acknowledged Yeshua as their Messiah. The latter has been going on since 1967, which coincides with the Jews (YAHudi) retaking possession of YAHrushalayim—their city had been ruled by the Goyim since the destruction of the House of YAH in 70 CE. Another interesting fact is that in 2007, YisraEL will have occupied YAHrushalayim for *forty* years—a time of testing. Yeshua said, *"Assuredly, I say to you, this generation will by no means pass away till all these things take place"* (**MARK 13:30**). A generation was considered to be anytime between 40 and 70 years. One more thing to consider is that Yaacov's trouble would also include the House of Yosef. One year later, on Sept. 11, 2001 and also near the time of Yom Kippur, the United States of America was attacked by some of the descendants of Esau and Ishmael (YishmaEL). The United States of America has always been the melting pot of nations (goyim). That means that most of the descendants of the tribes of Yosef and many from the tribe of YAHuda have settled here. So, could this time of Yaacov's trouble also include the USA, along with YisraEL? Is it possible that these events will draw these two nations closer to one another, even spiritually? Will there be a second period of seven years following, and could it be the time when the two houses of YAHuda and Yosef will finally recognize each other as brothers and become the two witnesses who proclaim that YAHveh, the ELohim of all YisraEL, and His Son, Yeshua, as His Messiah, are also the true ELohim of all the Earth? Could this also be the time of plenty that comes just before the seven years of famine (the tribulation)? Time, as usual, will be the judge.

After reiterating all of the past prophecies that He had given to both houses, YAHuda and YisraEL, about the sins they had committed that had brought this great calamity upon them, YAHveh was now going to once more attempt to give them further hope in His promises of the coming Messiah. He also told them that He would one day make a new covenant with YisraEL (this would renew and complete all seven of His covenants that He had made down through the centuries since the beginning). He spoke of a Branch of Dahveed who would sit on His throne forever. He spoke of the restoration of the "Whole House of YisraEL", when they would return to the land in an exodus that would be greater than the one out of Mitsrahyim, because this time, they would be coming out of *many* nations where they had been scattered. He said that they once had shepherds who led them all astray with false teachings, but now, He will raise up righteous teachers who will lead them back into knowing Him through a correct teaching of the Torah. He said that all will know YAHveh in those days; they will all have an intimate relationship with Him. They will not have any of their sins counted against them—if they repent. In other words, they will never sin again in YAHveh's eyes—the price will have been paid once and for all time for those who belong to Him. He will accomplish this by writing His Torah upon their hearts and in their minds. This will commence when He sends His Messiah, who will remove their wickedness from them. He also promised that all of these things are as sure to come as is night and day, summer and winter. The Messiah will come to teach and to be a living testimony of the Torah, and YAHveh's Ruach (Spirit) will be the one who will accomplish all of this through Him, just as He did in "The Beginning" of all things. Yeshua the Messiah (Yeshua HaMashiach) said this very same thing: *"Do not think that I came to destroy the TaNaKh (Torah and the Ne'vim/Law and the Prophets), I did not come to destroy but to fill up (fulfill)."For truly, I say to you until heaven and earth pass away, one yod or one stroke will by no means pass from the Torah until all is filled up (fulfilled). "Whoever therefore breaks one of the least of these commandments, and teaches men so, shall be called least in the kingdom of heaven; but whoever does and teaches all these commandments, he shall be called great in the kingdom of heaven."* (**MATT** 5:17-19). He then goes on to tell about a New YAHrushalayim, one that will never belong to anyone but YAH and His people, YisraEL.

YAHveh, being the King of the Universe and Creator and Judge of all things, says, through His prophecies, to those who believe that He exits and that He is a rewarder of those who diligently seek Him (**HEB 11:6**), that He has a specific plan for them that cannot be changed. Those who are of the seed of Avraham by faith, not necessarily by DNA, are called Hebrew (crossed over) by YAHveh because they have "crossed over" from death to life. He also calls them YisraEL because they have struggled with ELohim and persevered until they were blessed. They have believed His testimony through the ne'veem and now also through His only begotten Son, Yeshua HaMashiach. He would come to walk among us as both the Son of ELohim and the Son of Man, teaching us how to understand His TaNaKh, how to do it properly while still honoring His Torah, and finally, how to teach it to our children and to others. He would teach us how to keep His Sabbaths, New Moons, and Appointed Feasts. He would teach us how He had become the Pesach for us, how the shedding of His blood would purchase our righteousness, and that our eternal life would come through His resurrection. He became the curse of the Torah for us, and He would send His Ruach to renew in us our betrothal vows to Him. He would also give us the power to witness these things to all who are hungry and thirsty for a personal relationship with Him in order for them to also receive the Blessings of the Torah. After this, He would commission us to go and search out all of the lost sheep of YisraEL and preach these things to them. This would include both the House of YAHuda and the House of Yosef (also known as Efraeem). *"They shall come with weeping, and with supplication I will lead them. I will cause them to walk by the rivers of waters, in a straight way in which they shall not stumble; for I AM an Abba to YisraEL, and Efraeem is My firstborn"* (JER 31:9). YAH's final goal is to restore the Whole House of YisraEL, the Kahal (congregation/church). All of these events are to occur in the final days of the "latter days", which would begin the day after Yeshua's crucifixion. But before YAH could set these wheels into motion, He would have to scatter His people throughout the nations so that they might become His living witnesses, showing them that His people were set-apart (holy/kedosh) to Him.

Just before YAH's city, YAHrushalayim, was captured by King Nebuchadnezzar, a group of rebels, including some of the sons of the priests, threw YirmehYAH into a deep well and left him there to die because of the words that he had proclaimed in YAHveh's name to King Zedekiah (TzedkehYAH) of YAHuda and to the people. When the king heard of this through a trusted eunuch, out of his fear of YAH, he had YirmehYAH pulled out and brought to him. He then made a bargain with him so that he could set him free. Soon after this, King Nebuchadnezzar laid siege to YAHrushalayim, ransacking and burning the city, along with the House of YAH, but he spared YirmehYAH out of his respect for him as a ne'vee of YAHveh, the ELohim of YisraEL. After the capture of the city and the deportation of what was left of its inhabitants to Babylon, King Nebuchadnezzar appointed a man named Gedaliah as governor of YAHuda. When many of the Jews (YAHudi) heard about this, they returned to YAHuda from the cities where they had fled during the siege. This lasted for only a short time because a descendant of King Dahveed by the name of Ishmael (YishmaEL) gathered a small army together and assassinated the governor for taking the throne of their father, Dahveed. But afterward, they became fearful of the army of King Nebuchadnezzar and decided to flee into Mitsrahyim; however, before going, they went to YirmehYAH for spiritual advice. There, they made an oath with YAHveh to obey whatever He said they should do. But when the word of YAH came to them through His Ne'vee YirmehYAH, telling them not to go, they rebelled and went to Mitsrahyim anyway, forcing YirmehYAH to go with them as their hostage. But they could not escape YAH's wrath for their insolence and rebellion; they all eventually died, either by the sword at the hand of the Babylonians after escaping, or by famine and pestilence.

While in Mitsrahyim, the word of YAHveh came to YirmehYAH to speak against all of the nations that had oppressed His people, including Mitsrahyim and Babylon—they would suffer destruction under YAH's wrath. Both of these mighty nations began striking out at all of the countries around them, trying to outmaneuver one another for the most advantageous and strategic position, in preparation for a final showdown between them. Eventually the two would clash, and Babylon would emerge as the victor and would rule the whole region for the next thirty years. Then, finally, Babylon would suffer defeat by the hand of the Mede-Persian Empire. It would also be this Empire, through King Cyrus' decree, that would resettle YAHuda back into the land of YisraEL, as was prophesied by Isaiah (YishshaYAH) in **ISA 44:28**. YirmehYAH's ministry seems to end here in Mitsrahyim because there is no mention of his returning to the land of YisraEL.

Conclusion

YAHveh says that all prophecy, all testimonies, and all words of instruction must be confirmed in the mouths of two or more witnesses. This is a kingdom principle that guarantees us truth and accuracy. The Ne'vim has confirmed time and time again that the descendants of the Middle East will be judged for all of the atrocities that they have committed against YAHveh's people over the centuries. These descendants have brought with them a culture of Babylonian and Persian false religions that were represented by the head and upper torso of the edifice that King Nebuchadnezzar saw in his vision. YAHveh promised to destroy them at the end of the age. Greece and Rome, the lower torso and legs, represent the false kingdoms that will fall with them. Only their repentance and confession that YAHveh is ELohim and that His Son, Yeshua, is Adonai will ever deliver them.

All of YAH's Ne'vim also repeatedly pointed to the House of YisraEL as being divided into two houses, the House of YAHuda and the House of Yosef/Efraeem/YisraEL. This all began when Yaacov, who later became YisraEL, fathered twelve children from four mothers—Leah and her concubine and Rachel (Rahkal) and her concubine. Remember, the number four tells us that this will have something to do with the whole Earth; YisraEL's descendants were eventually spread throughout the whole Earth. His first wife, Leah, gave birth to YAHuda, and his second wife and true love, Rachel (Rahkal), gave birth to Yosef, who in turn fathered Efraeem. It would be the responsibility of the tribe of YAHuda to carry the Royalty for the House of YisraEL, but Efraeem, being named as the firstborn of the House of YisraEL by his grandfather, Yaacov/YisraEL, would carry its Headship (**GEN 48:11-20**).

YirmehYAH confirmed what Isaiah (YishshaYAH) proclaimed, that YAHveh was going to write a new covenant in the minds and on the hearts of His people, YisraEL, and would remember their sins no more. How exciting it is to see all of these things come together and begin to happen right before our very eyes. If only YAH's people would stop wasting their time being religious and would instead allow their eyes and ears to perceive what is actually taking place all around them, they would quit playing church, become the Army of Elohim, and begin to conquer His enemies.

CHAPTER 16
...about Ezekiel 34-48 and Daniel 3-9

Now we will take a look at the remaining chapters of the Ne'vee Ezekiel (YechezkEL) and some of the visions and dreams that YAHveh sent to Daniel (DahneeEL), who then recorded them for future generations. We will examine their meanings.

Ezekiel (YechezkEL) 34-48

YAHveh came to Ezekiel (YechezkEL) and told him to speak to all of the shepherds of His flock, YisraEL, because they hadn't given proper care to His sheep. Instead, they had used their positions for their own personal advantage and had not shown the proper compassion for those He had placed in their care. At the same time, He also warned His sheep that they were still responsible for their own actions and would be judged individually for the way they handled what they had learned from their shepherds. In other words, even if they were taught incorrectly by their shepherds, they would still be held accountable for what they did with what they understood, correctly or incorrectly. Each sheep is still responsible for seeking for themselves the correct knowledge from the Great Shepherd, YAHveh, and should not rely upon someone else to educate them. (This is one of the many places in Scripture where YAHveh identifies His people as "the flock of His pasture"—synonymous with being "the House of YisraEL, His people".)

Ezekiel (YechezkEL) is told to focus his attention upon the surrounding mountains, where the enemies of His people have dwelt, and to prophesy against them. He is to pronounce YAH's judgment upon them—in the last days, they will become desolate and will be given over to His people. But then the mountains will be blessed with an abundance of flocks, herds, and crops—a land overflowing with milk and honey.

Now YAHveh directed Ezekiel (YechezkEL) to prophesy to the mountains of YisraEL, telling them of a time that would come when they would be inhabited by all of those who had remained faithful to His words and had become His YisraEL, causing all the other nations to become envious of their prosperity. He told Ezekiel (YechezkEL) to remind His people that He was not doing this for their sake but for the sake of His Name. He wanted them to know that He was the one who had scattered them throughout the nations in order for them to thoroughly mix with the Gentiles (Goyim) so that He could extend His grace to them also. Then He said that He would make Himself known to their mixed descendants in order to fulfill His promise to Avraham. He went on to say that even though they would profane His Name before all of the nations where He would send them (referring to the Goyim Church during the Crusades and during the Inquisition), He would still bless them for the sake of His Name. Once again, He promised to place them in their own land and cause them to walk in all of His Torah, but not before giving them a new heart and putting His Ruach within them. This promise was to take place after they were brought back into the land. He doesn't relate this transformation to a new or a renewed covenant as He had at other times—this seems to be different. This change seems to take place in relationship with another promise—an end-time promise that He was about to make.

In another vision, Ezekiel (YechezkEL) was taken to a second place and shown a valley of dry bones. Even though the valley is not mentioned here by name, it may have been mentioned by another ne'evee. *"It shall come to pass in that day that I will break the bow of YisraEL in the Valley of Jezreel."..."Yet the number of the children of YisraEL shall be as the sand of the sea, which cannot be measured or numbered. And it shall come to pass in the place where it was said to them, 'You are sons of the Living ELohim.' Then the children of YAHuda and the children of YisraEL shall be gathered together, and appoint for themselves One Head (Yeshua); and they shall come up out of the land, for great will be the day of Jezreel! Say to your brethren, 'My people,' and to your sister, 'Mercy is shown'"* **(HOSEA 1:5 & 1:10-2:1)**. It was here that he was asked whether or not these bones could come alive, and Ezekiel (YechezkEL) responded to Him by saying that only He, ELohim, could know for sure. He is told to prophesy to the bones and cause them to come to life. Many have said in recent years that they believe this represented all of the Jews (YAHudi) coming from all over the Earth to settle back into the land. But in all honesty, the Jew (YAHudi) never really completely left—YAHveh promised that He would always keep a remnant there. No, I believe that these are the faithful who have died over the centuries and who have looked for the "Promised One", or "Messiah", to come and resurrect all of those who have been made righteous in YAH's sight through their faith by His grace. Then he was told to call for breath to come into them from the four winds. Breath and spirit are synonymous with YAHveh's Ruach (Spirit). And wasn't Ezekiel (YechezkEL) told earlier that YAH would put a new spirit within them? He then told him that this was the Whole House of YisraEL (not just the YAHudi) and that He was about to return them to their land. Then He confirmed the fact that they shall live because He is putting His Own Spirit (Ruach) within them. This can be seen in two different ways: He had put His Ruach within them when they were alive, which gave them the assurance of the resurrection; now He puts it in them again, this time *at* the resurrection, in order to complete His promise that they would never taste death again.

Following this, He immediately told Ezekiel (YechezkEL) that he was to take up a stick and write on it *"For YAHuda and for the children of YisraEL, his companions"*. Then he was told to take a second stick and write on it *"For Yosef, the stick of Efraeem and for all the House of YisraEL, his companions"*. After this, he was instructed to join them together in his hand to represent the two sticks becoming one. The explanation that he was to give to anyone who might ask what this meant was: *"Tell them that this represents both of the Houses of YisraEL, YAHuda and Yosef, and that they will be made into one stick (or tree) in the land that YAHveh had promised Avraham"*. (These are a few of the verses from **EZEK 37:15-28** that Ariel Sharon read at the Temple Mount on Yom Kippur in 2000, commencing what has been called the beginning of "Yaacov's Trouble".) They will have one king, Yeshua, the descendant of Dahveed, as their Shepherd, and He will teach them how to keep the Torah forever. Then all of the nations of the Earth will come against YAHveh's vast army of saints, and they will be defeated and put under the foot of the King of kings. YAH will fight this final battle using all of the plagues of Mitsrahyim upon the armies of the Earth in the final judgment. Then, at the end of His judgment upon these nations and the Earth, those who remain will finally understand all of His words, those He had spoken through His Ne'vim.

Then YAH took Ezekiel (YechezkEL) and showed him a vision of the return of His Shchinah glory to His House. But, of course, Ezekiel (YechezkEL) wasn't aware that YAH's house would be rebuilt, renovated, and destroyed once more before all of these visions could be completed. This vision presents a mystery, though, to all of those who have studied it. Is this an actual house of worship or is it symbolic with a deeper meaning? The dimensions that were given were much larger than the house that Zerubbabel built for YAH, or even the one that King Herod had renovated later; but, at the same time, it was too small to be the one that Yeshua is to build during the Millennium. Some believe it to be the instructions that will be used for building a house of worship for YAH just before the final "Great Day". It seems that YAH may be giving the Jews (YAHudi), those who have still not accepted Yeshua as the Messiah, another opportunity to try to keep the Torah, in order to settle once and for all that the blood of His Lamb is the only sufficient sacrifice to cover their sins. All Jews (YAHudi) have been looking for an opportunity to rebuild the House of YAH. When this takes place, they say that the Messiah will come. Today in YAHrushalayim, they are gathering and crafting all of the necessary items to fill the House of YAH when it is rebuilt. They have even gone so far as to search, by the means of DNA, for some of the descendants of the tribe of Lehvee in order to reestablish the priesthood. They have also cut the cornerstone of the house—just waiting for it to be laid.

Ezekiel (YechezkEL) is then led out into the waters of a river which is flowing out from under this House of YAH and then going down to the Dead Sea, causing it to become fresh once again and teeming with all sorts of fish. He is shown trees growing on both banks of this river that will have both fruit for food and leaves for healing on its branches. This seems to be the same vision that was given to John (Yochanan) when he was shown the Book of Revelation. This part may be symbolic, referring to the House from which Yeshua will rule during the Millennium. This House is to have twelve gates, three on each side of its four walls, with each gate named after one of the tribes of YisraEL. This is identical to the description of the city that is to come down out of heaven at the end of the Millennium. There are certainly a number of similarities between the two, but at the same time, plenty of differences. Again, more will be made known as time reveals the truth about these visions. The last thing that is revealed to him is that the name of YAHrushalayim will be changed to "YAHshammah" (YAHveh is there).

Daniel (DahneeEL) 3-9

King Nebuchadnezzar decided to honor himself by erecting a colossus that was to be nine-feet wide by ninety-feet tall—probably to replicate the one that he saw in the dream that he had Daniel (DahneeEL/Belteshazzar) interpret. He called for all of his leaders to come and help him dedicate it to himself and to the land of Babylon. Apparently, he wasn't aware of the restrictions that Daniel (DahneeEL), Hananiah (HahnahneeYAH/Shadrach), Mishael (MishahEL/Meshach), and Azariah (AhzahreeYAH/Abed-Nego) were committed to in their faithfulness to YAHveh, their ELohim, because he sent out a decree requiring all of his subjects to bow before the edifice to show homage to him; if anyone refused, they were to be executed by being thrown into a fiery furnace. Even though Daniel's (DahneeEL's/Belteshazzar's) friends, Shadrach, Meshach, and Abed-Nego, had been made overseers of the affairs of Babylon, their positions could not save them from King Nebuchadnezzar's pagan decrees. So, when Shadrach, Meshach, and Abed-Nego were ordered to bow down before the colossus, they refused—they were then ordered to be thrown into the fires. Shadrach, Meshach, and Abed-Nego declared to the king that their ELohim was able to deliver them even from death, if it so pleased Him. This was an "in-your-face" challenge to King Nebuchadnezzar because he saw himself as a god (eluah). In his anger, due to what he considered insolence, he had the fires in the furnace stoked to seven times its normal heat. It became so hot that those who were commanded to throw the three into the furnace were themselves consumed by the heat in carrying out the orders. To the king's amazement, he saw another form, a man, manifested in the midst of the flames, together with the three. The Angel of YAHveh had taken on the form of a man and protected the three from the heat to the point that not even the smell of the furnace was on them. As a result, King Nebuchadnezzar promoted the three to an even higher position of authority, and he confessed YAHveh as being the Most-High ELohim.

Daniel (DahneeEL/Belteshazzar) is once again summoned into King Nebuchadnezzar's presence to interpret another dream that he had because, as before, his magicians and wise men could not. Here again, Daniel (DahneeEL), the great Babylonian soothsayer, as the other wise men referred to him, came to their rescue. This dream consisted of a giant tree that filled the Earth. This mirrored the mustard tree, or plant, that Yeshua described in one of His parables that represented the growth of His Kingdom on Earth, which was the result of His disciples (talmidim) spreading the "Good News". But this tree had lovely leaves and abundant fruit, just like in the vision that both Ezekiel (YechezkEL) and John (Yochanan) had regarding the trees that bordered the banks of the river that flowed out from under the House of YAH. Then he saw an angel come down and order the tree to be cut down, but the stump was to be left bound with a band of bronze and iron. Remember, bronze and iron also represent the Greek and Roman Empires (or a type of) which will emerge in the latter days and will try to oppress the works of the Messiah. Then he saw the stump covered with the wetness of dew and heard a proclamation from the angel that the person represented by the stump was going to join the beasts of the fields for seven years. Daniel (DahneeEL/Belteshazzar) submitted the dream to YAH and was given the following interpretation: the tree represented the Babylonian Empire, and the angel was the word of YAHveh, proclaiming that Nebuchadnezzar's kingdom would be cut off for seven years while he roamed the fields like a beast. At the end of the seven years, he would have his position restored to him, and he would then confess YAHveh as being the one True ELohim of Heaven and Earth. All of these things came to pass, and as a result, King Nebuchadnezzar did come to know YAHveh, the ELohim of YisraEL, as the true ELohim of Heaven and Earth and as his ELohim. Further examination of this dream seems to indicate that this was the "near prophecy" that did come to pass. The "far prophecy", however, seems to indicate that YAHveh's Kingdom will someday be cut off again for a determined period of time and will be bound up with the Greek and Roman ideology; but it too will be restored once more in order to proclaim YAH as ELohim—but this time for all eternity.

Much later, after King Nebuchadnezzar's reign, one of his grandsons, Belshazzar, took the throne of Babylon. [It is interesting that King Nebuchadnezzar would have one of his grandsons with a name so near the name that he had given Daniel (DahneeEL).] In the first year of King Belshazzar, Daniel (DahneeEL) had a dream that troubled him. He saw four beasts coming up out of the Great Sea (the Mediterranean), which had been stirred up by the four winds. Remember, the four winds represent the four corners of the whole Earth and also represent the move of YAHveh's Ruach (Breath/Spirit). Beasts usually represent kingdoms or empires. The first beast was a lion with eagle's wings. The second was a bear with three ribs in its teeth. The third was like a leopard with four heads and four bird-like wings. Then Daniel (DahneeEL) describes a fourth beast more terrible than the other three. It had iron teeth, bronze claws, and ten horns. He also saw an eleventh, but smaller, horn rise up and pluck out three of the other horns. Horns usually symbolize individual kings or rulers. The smaller horn seems to be unique in that it shows much charisma in its ability to speak great things. Then he saw the throne of YAHveh (the Ancient of Days) appear and giving the dominion of the Earth over to His Son, who then came out of the clouds of heaven to set up His never-ending kingdom. The books were opened by the Ancient of Days, and the fourth beast and the great-speaking horn was cast into the fire of judgment. Daniel (DahneeEL) was very troubled by the vision and asked for its interpretation from a being standing nearby within the vision. He was told about the four kingdoms that are to rule over the Earth until the last days. Then the fourth beast will make war with the saints and will be delivered up for judgment. The Kingdom of YAHveh will then be established forever. The four beasts in Daniel's (DahneeEL's) vision are synonymous with the four empires that were described in King Nebuchadnezzar's first dream: Babylon, represented by the golden head, is the lion with the eagle's wings—the Medes and Persians, represented by the silver arms and chest, is the bear with the three ribs between its teeth—the Greeks, represented by the bronze hips and belly, is the leopard with the four heads—the Romans, represented by the iron legs with iron feet mixed with clay, is the most terrible beast of the four, along with its charismatic leader, who blasphemes the Most High and persecutes the saints.

In the third year of King Belshazzar, DahneeEL had another troubling vision. This time he saw two creatures, a ram and a goat. The ram had two horns, which stood for two kings and their kingdoms—he later learned that they were the Medes and the Persians. The goat, which eventually overcame the ram, had one horn that represented the Greek Empire. Four horns came out of the goat's single horn and represented the four divisions of power that the Greek Empire would evolve into. A little horn came out of one of the four and represented a spirit of darkness, a representative of Satan (hasatan), who possessed one of the future Greek kings, King Epiphanies/Antiochus IV. He was the cruelest of any of the previous kings and a forerunner of the Antimessiah of the final days. He was responsible for the sacrifices to cease and for the sanctuary within YAHveh's second House to be desecrated. Gabriel

(GahbreeEL), an angel of proclamation for YAH, proclaimed that in the latter days, this same spirit would possess another leader, who would then make war with the Prince of princes (the Messiah) and His saints, but who would also be defeated. This second *possessed one* is said to come about 2300 days after the first. Since all of this is to take place after the Greek Empire establishes itself in the land of YisraEL in 300 BCE, and if we exchange days for years, the 2300 days, or 2300 years, will bring us right up to our present time.

King Nebuchadnezzar had taken many of the golden vessels from the House of YAH when he besieged YAHrushalayim. One day, while his grandson, King Belshazzar, was arrogantly using many of these vessels during a time of feasting and celebrating, he suddenly became alarmed as he witnessed the phenomena of a man's hand writing a message in Hebrew on the wall. After none of his magicians or astrologers could decipher this message, he sent for DahneeEL to come and interpret it after learning that he could speak this language. DahneeEL gave the king the following interpretation: because he had not followed the example of his grandfather by not recognizing YAHveh as being the true ELohim of Heaven and Earth, he was going to lose his kingdom to the Medes and Persians. That very night the king was slain, apparently by Darius, a Mede, who took the throne and appointed three governors to oversee his newly acquired kingdom. He appointed DahneeEL to be one of them. Other leaders within the kingdom became jealous of DahneeEL's new position and designed a plot to get rid of him. They knew that DahneeEL prayed regularly to YAH, so they convinced King Darius to send forth a decree stating that no one could pay any tribute or call upon any deity for the first thirty days after his coronation. Because of his faithfulness to his ELohim, DahneeEL did not cease his supplications. Those who plotted against him were able to apprehend him while he was praying and took him before the king and accused him there. The decree that the king had put into irreversible law had a penalty of death by the mauling of lions. When the evidence was clear that DahneeEL was guilty of ignoring the decree, the king reluctantly had him thrown into the den with the lions. At the same time, he showed a spark of faith by expressing some degree of confidence that DahneeEL's ELohim could deliver him, even in this dire situation. Then, at the very moment that the king spoke his faith of deliverance, YAHveh shut the mouths of the hungry beasts. Realizing that this had been a scheme to destroy DahneeEL, King Darius had all of those who had participated in this plot thrown into the den, and they were immediately attacked and devoured by the lions. Seeing the hand of YAHveh deliver his servant DahneeEL from the mouths of hungry lions, King Darius became a believer in the Living ELohim, just as had his predecessor, King Nebuchadnezzar.

Sometime during DahneeEL's captivity, he gained access to a copy of one of YirmehYAH's scrolls and learned of the prophecy regarding the number of years that YAHuda was to spend in the land of Babylon, as well as the many warnings that she had received before her exile. The time of this discovery was apparently in the sixty-third year of his captivity. DahneeEL was so compelled by his own sorrow for YAH's people and the destruction of the beautiful city of YAHrushalayim that he began to pray for its restoration. During his prayer, Gabriel (GahbreeEL), the angel of proclamation, was sent to him to reveal a prophecy regarding the coming of the Messiah and the end of the age. He told him about a period of seventy weeks of years that had to occur before the restoration of all things could take place, but not before the decree to rebuild YAHrushalayim had been given. This decree was given sometime between 450 and 445 BCE when Nehemiah (NehchemYAH) was commissioned to return to YAHrushalayim to complete its reconstruction. This reconstruction would take forty-nine years to complete, the time of the first seven weeks of years (7 X 7), and would be completed between 401 and 396 BCE. Then a period of sixty-two weeks of years was to take place, ending with the Messiah coming and then being cut off (crucified). All of this would take place over the next 434 years (62 X 7), which would end sometime between 33 and 38 CE. He then tells DahneeEL that a ruler will come once more to destroy the city, along with YAH's House, which takes place in 70 CE by a Roman general named Titus. But there still remains one more week of years (seven years) that is not accounted for—where is it? The answer to this lies in what Gabriel (GahbreeEL) tells DahneeEL next. There will come a time when the same one who was responsible for the destruction of YAHrushalayim in 70 CE, who was actually the "Destroyer" (hasatan), will manifest himself again, but this time as a prince of shalom/peace to the people because of a treaty of shalom in YAHrushalayim that he establishes. In order for this to take place, some of YAH's people will have to be in the land again and living in YAHrushalayim with threats of trouble all around them. The House of YAH will also have had to have been rebuilt and the sacrificial system reinstituted. This prince of shalom will then put an end to the sacrificial system after only three and one-half years into this treaty (in the middle of the seven-year period), thereby revealing who he really is. This is where you'll find the final seventh week.

There is still one more hidden morsel to consider. Because all of these figures were given to DahneeEL and he recorded them, those who considered him to be one of the great Magi of Babylon were able to calculate, almost to the exact year, when the *"King of the Jews (YAHudi)"* (**MATT 2:2**), who would be *"like the Son of Man/Son of God (ELuah)"* (**DAN 3:25 & 7:13**), should appear. When this time neared, the Magi from the East (Babylon) began to look for the signs in the heavens (**GEN 1:14 & JOB 38:31**). When His star appeared

(NUM 24:17), they sought out this King and found Him in Bethlehem (Beit-lechem—House of Bread).

Conclusion

The focus of Ezekiel (YechezkEL) and DahneeEL has been on the latter days and the restoration of the Whole House of YisraEL through visions and declarations of prophecy. The reconstruction of a third House of YAH is suggested, along with the reinstatement of its services in the form of offerings and sacrifices. It seems that this could possibly occur sometime after both YAHuda and Yosef have been reunited as the Whole House of YisraEL. The coming of four empires were revealed in sequential order of dominion to DahneeEL, as well as the length of time before the coming of the Messianic reign, when the covenant with Dahveed would be fulfilled through his son, who would also be the Son of YAH, Yeshua.

CHAPTER 17
…about the Remaining Twenty-One Psalms, Ezra, Daniel 10-12, Esther, Nehemiah, and the Ne'vim: Haggai, Zechariah, and Malachi

This will be the final chapter that will cover the events that lead up to the end of the writings of the TaNaKh and the beginning of the twenty-three-hundred years of rule by the Greek and Roman beast empires. This chapter will also include the last twenty-one Psalms, as well as the remaining books of the Writings (Kethuvim), which are: Ezra (Ezrah), Esther (Ester), Nehemiah (NehchemYAH), and the last two chapters of DahneeEL. It will end with the last of the Minor Ne'vim: Haggai (Hagahee), Zechariah (TzahkarYAH), and Malachi (Mahlakhee).

The Last Twenty-One Psalms

Of the last twenty-one Psalms not previously covered, the first nine are about the cry of YAH's people in exile, and the remaining twelve are about their rejoicing because of their return to their land. We begin with **PSALM 44**, where the writer confesses the shortcoming of YAH's people and sends out a cry for the promised restoration. In **PSALMS 74 & 79**, the writer asked YAH to remember the days of old, before His enemies destroyed His House and sanctuary, and how they showed no regard for His Name. The writer asks Him to respond once more with miracles in order to show the nations His power over the Earth and its inhabitants. In **PSALM 80**, the writer recognizes that YAHveh is his Savior and Redeemer and that all of His promises of restoration are meant for His divided house, which is made up of YAHuda and BenYAHmeen of the southern tribes, and Yosef, made up of his sons, Efraeem and Mahnahseh, who represented all of the northern tribes. In **PSALM 89**, the writer reminds YAH of His covenant with His firstborn, Dahveed, and His promise to him that one of his sons would always occupy the throne of the House of YisraEL and that His people are still looking to Him to restore them to the land, as He had promised. **PSALM 102** declares that YAHveh is the Creator of all things and that His promises cannot fail. Even though the writer and his fellow prisoners seem to have no hope, they still cling to His promises of restoration. They acknowledge the fact that His promises extend not only to them, but also to generations yet to come. In **PSALM 106**, the writer recalls all that YAHveh has done for His people, YisraEL—from their deliverance from Mitsrahyim by Mosheh, to the sins that have brought them to their present captivity. He reminds YAH of His promises of restoration and that only He is their deliverer. **PSALM 122** is a short psalm asking YAHveh to show His people mercy and grace. Finally, **PSALM 137** calls upon YAH to avenge His enemies, Edom and Babylon, because of what they did to His people and because they did it with glee and joy.

These last twelve psalms are YAH's people, YAHuda and BenYAHmeen, singing songs of praise and joy as they are being restored back into the land—their prayers were beginning to be answered. Here in **PSALM 78**, the writer recalls all of the marvelous works that YAH did in order to preserve His people, YAHuda and Efraeem, who time after time limited Him by continually tempting Him with their rebelliousness. He recalls how YAH continually warned them through His ne'veem, but they continued to return to their iniquities until He had no choice but to send them all into exile. The writer makes a pledge that he will never forget all of YAH's wondrous works and that he will declare them among His people and teach them to his children, just as the Torah commands. In **PSALM 85**, the writer calls upon YAH to remember to restore the blessings to the land that He has returned them to, just as His Torah and Ne'vim had declared that He would do. Here in **PSALM 107**, the writer encourages all men to give praise and thanks to YAHveh because He opens His hand of plenty for all mankind to partake from. He blesses the just and the unjust alike because He is a Good ELohim. He blesses the just so that they might see His grace, compassion, and generosity and the unjust so that they might turn away from their self-destruction and finally recognize their source. In **PSALM 116**, the writer gives thanks for his redemption after recognizing his sinfulness and his own inability to do anything to rectify it. But, he remembers the Cup of Salvation that he partakes of at the annual Feast of the Passover Seder. He remembers all that was promised to him if he will but submit his heart to the instructions of the Torah, along with all of its benefits. In **PSALM 118**, the writer speaks out as the voice of YAH's chosen ones, YisraEL. He begins with the edifying words that are recorded in **PSALM 136** (the psalm recited during the Passover Seder): *"That His mercy endures forever"* (mercy and grace are synonymous and are not limited to just the New Testament). He speaks of how YisraEL gained her strength and salvation from Him and how the prophetic voice of rejoicing and salvation are found in the tents of YisraEL. The gates of YAH and His House are mentioned here, as well as the prophetic words regarding the Messiah Yeshua being rejected as the cornerstone of His House. Also mentioned here are the words spoken by Yeshua as He entered the gates of YAHrushalayim on the tenth day of the month of Aviv before being inspected by the priest as the perfect Passover Sacrifice Lamb without spot or wrinkle. In **PSALM 125**, the writer reflects on the sureness of the promises of the ELohim of YisraEL. **PSALM 126** is one of gratefulness for YAH's showing YAHuda mercy in returning them once again to their land. In **PSALM 128**, praise goes to YAH for the mercy He shows to all who call upon His Name for deliverance and salvation and who find rest and comfort in His words, along with the promise that those who do will become His people, YisraEL. In **PSALM 129**, the writer becomes the voice of YisraEL and speaks of YAH's vengeance upon those who hate Him and His people; he then warns YisraEL not to ask for YAH's blessings upon any of those who curse them. The writer in **PSALM 132** reiterates YAH's covenant to always have a son of Dahveed upon the throne of YisraEL until the promised Messiah comes. YAH also promises to provide them with the teachings of His testimony (His Torah) so that they might have His words to follow and obey. He acknowledges that it is YAH who has chosen the people of Zion and not the other way around. **PSALM 147** is a song of praise, worship, and gratitude toward YAH as the Creator of the Universe and His mindfulness toward man, but especially His concern for His chosen people, YisraEL, whom He is gathering back under His wings of protection. His pleasures are not in His creation but in those whom He has created and who respond to Him with praise, hope, and fear. Finally, in **PSALM 149**, the writer exalts YAH and encourages His people to celebrate Him with dance, instruments of music, and songs of joy and praise because this is what He finds His delight in.

Ezra (Ezrah)

Ezra (Ezrah) is a scribe, historian, teacher, and priest from the tribe of Lehvee. As was said earlier, He is credited with the historical writings of the books of the Chronicles of the kings of YAHuda and YisraEL, as well as the particulars of his own testimony, which was named after him. He describes the events surrounding the beginnings of the first exodus from Babylon back to Judea (YAHuda), the homeland, even though he himself did not appear on the scene for another one-hundred years. His writings came mainly from others who kept records—he just continued them in more detail. He records that not everyone was anxious to return; after all, many who had left Judea (YAHuda) died and only their stories remained. Others were born and died while in exile; while still others, those who were born there, knew it as their only home. If they left, they would have to learn the ancient language, which by this time had been mostly forgotten. They had not practiced the Torah, and those who had had mixed its instructions with the customs and religious practices of the Babylonians, Medes, and Persians. But others felt the tug of the Holy Spirit (Ruach HaKedosh) and were ready to pull up and return to their promised land—mostly those who had come at an early age and could still remember the original splendor of both YAHrushalayim and the House of YAH.

The king of Persia, King Cyrus, was the one responsible for the decree that began the first part of this temporary restoration, which included the tribes of YAHuda and BenYAHmeen, along with a small remnant of the other tribes of YisraEL. King Cyrus had been named by YAH through the Ne'vee Isaiah (YishshaYAH) to be the one to begin this restoration two-hundred years before he was even born. Remember, Darius of the Medes and King Nebuchadnezzar of Babylon both confessed YAHveh as the only Living ELohim. They were His instruments for both chastising and blessing His people. Only 49,897 Jews (YAHudi) and YisraELi combined returned on this first attempt to restore this nation back into its land.

An overlapping of historical events takes place at this time. DahneeEL remained in Babylon and probably died there, and a young Jewish (YAHudaim) maiden by the name of Esther (Ester) married one of the Persian kings and became a queen of Persia. Then YAH called upon the last of His ne'veem to direct His people to push forward in the reestablishing of His Torah and His House, to be His witness that YAHveh is Lord (Adonai) and that He keeps His covenants.

The first of these overlapping events was the first return to the land, and it was led by a Jew (YAHudi) named Zerubbabel, YAHrushalayim's first governor, and by a Lehvee named Yeshua, who would become the first high priest of the new House of YAH. The expedition was financed through the freewill offerings from all of the exiles in Babylon.

Before the beginning of the reconstruction of YAH's House in the seventh Hebrew month of Tishri, Zerubbabel (the governor) and Yeshua (the high priest), along with other Lehvee, built an altar and offered burnt offerings before YAH. This seems to be when Yom Teruah also became known as Rosh HaShanah (the Head of the Year). After this, they also reestablished the celebrations of the Feast of Ingathering/Tabernacles (Chag Sukkoth), New Moons (Rosh Kadesh), and the other appointed feasts/times (moedim), which included Passover/Pesach and Pentecost/Feast of Firstfruits (Chag Shavuot).

Then the actual construction of the new House of YAHveh began with great anticipation and excitement. Before long, the surrounding neighbors, who were descendants of the enemies of YAH and His people, became fearful that the returnees would become a powerful and compelling force again in their territory, so they began trying to discourage and disrupt the rebuilding. This continued from the reign of King Darius until the reign of King Artaxerxes. The House of YAH was finally finished and dedicated, but many were discouraged because it did not compare in splendor to the one that King Shalomo had built for YAHveh.

Ezra (Ezrah) arrived on the scene one-hundred years later after learning, practicing, and teaching the Torah of YAHveh and after training to become a well-versed and qualified priest for his ELohim. Ezra (Ezrah) was then sent on an expedition to reinforce the Torah teachings in the community of the Holy City of YAHrushalayim. He didn't try to accomplish all of this on his own—he took with him fifteen-hundred other descendants of the House of YAHuda and some Lehvee, along with some of the articles from the House of YAH that had been taken by King Nebuchadnezzar. When he arrived in YAHrushalayim, he discovered a dilemma that he had not anticipated. Just as their fathers had done before them, the people of YAH had become careless in their self-discipline and had mixed themselves in marriage to pagan wives. Ezra (Ezrah) knew the consequences of such carelessness (the falling away from the Torah and the wrath of YAH upon them), so he began to fast and pray to YAHveh, the ELohim of YisraEL, for the forgiveness of the foolishness of his brethren. While he was praying and mediating for his brethren, conviction fell upon the Kahal of YAH's people, and they came to repentance and were willing to make a covenant with YAH, voluntarily putting away all of their foreign wives.

DahneeEL 10-12

These three final chapters of DahneeEL took place after Zerubbabel had finished building YAH's second House. DahneeEL had another troubling vision regarding the final days before the Messiah's reign and judgment. An angel came to him in the form of a man, who told him how he had to struggle with the powers of the air over Persia and that he had to receive help from MichaEL, the Archangel, in order to finally reach him. He told him that three more Persian kings would rule after King Darius and then a king from Greece would come and conquer his foes and reign over all of the existing nations. He told him that this Grecian Empire would become divided into four territories and an uprising between Syria and Mitsrahyim would occur. Mitsrahyim would eventually be defeated and never again historically rise to any real power, fulfilling the prophecies about her that came through the mouths of YAH's ne'veem. Then the king of the north seemed to take on a new characteristic of overwhelming power, which seemed to point to the end times because of the content in which the angel spoke to DahneeEL. This seemed to mean that a ruler would come from the north (which could mean from Europe, the Middle East, or any nation north of the Holy Land) at an appointed time to oppose the "covenant people". He would persecute them and show favor to any who would forsake or deny them. He would exalt himself above all elohim, even the ELohim of all the Earth, YAHveh. It was told to DahneeEL that this ruler would not have any regard for even the ELohim of his forefathers. The angel said that he would honor an eluah (god) of fortresses (military might) who would be an eluah (god) that even his fathers did not know (a foreign eluah) and who would possess great riches—perhaps Allah (which means "the god" in

Arabic) of the wealthy Arab nations of Islam. Could this be a person who has embraced Allah just for convenience and who was a former professing YAHudi, Messianic, or Christian, but was really serving the eluah of self ambition and mammon—in other words, a secular humanist posing as a follower of one of these great religions? History will tell. At that time, MichaEL, the Archangel, will take charge over the principalities of the air and of darkness and cause the saints to begin to prevail over them. This time is described as a time of trouble that is like no other that has ever taken place on Earth before. During this time, the resurrection seems to be described as taking place. The length of time seems to point to a particular period known as a time, times, and half a time (three and one-half years), when the power of YAH's people will be shattered. Some say that this phrase means an undeterminable length of time, but that doesn't fit the overall context of the message. This would also coincide with Gabriel's (GahbreeEL's) message about the event that takes place in the final week of the seventy weeks.

DahneeEL was told that the meaning of the message that the angel brought would be revealed just before all of these things would take place, which is described as a time when the Earth would become a place of abundant education, wealth, and extensive travel. He also saw two individuals standing, one on each side of the Tigris River. They are not identified here, but could they be the two witnesses that are described in the Book of Revelation—possibly Mosheh representing YAHuda, the Torah keepers, and ELeeYAHoo representing Yosef/Efraeem/YisraEL, the Brit Chadashah keepers? Will they be the ones who will proclaim both Advents of the Messiah? Finally, DahneeEL is told: *"And from the time the daily sacrifice is taken away, and the abomination of desolation is set up, there shall be one thousand two hundred and ninety days. Blessed is he who waits and comes to the one thousand three hundred and thirty-five days"* (**DAN 12:11&12**). One thousand, two hundred and ninety days from one thousand, three hundred and thirty-five days leaves forty-five days. The angel here is saying that those who wait an additional forty-five days will be exceptionally blessed. Using the days of the Hebrew calendar, there are three hundred and sixty days in one year. Three and one half years (the time that both GahbreeEL and MichaEL referred to) times this would equal one thousand, two hundred and sixty days. But the angel said one thousand, two hundred and ninety days—thirty additional days. If Yeshua's Second Advent commences on Yom Kippur (Day of Atonement), as I believe it will, there will be five more days before Chag Sukkot (the Feast of Tabernacles) begins, which lasts another eight days—a total of thirteen days. These eight days, I believe, will be the time of "The Judgment Seat of the Messiah", when He will separate the lost from the redeemed and there will be an Ingathering of all who belong to Him (the rapture). Seventeen more days will need to elapse in order to total the thirty-needed days before the promised one thousand and ninety days has expired. This is probably the length of time needed for the setting up of the image of the Antimessiah in YAH's House, causing the abomination of desolation—this would be one Hebrew month after Yom Kippur. These thirty days, when added to the forty-five days that the angel said to wait, will equal three and one half years plus seventy-five days. Seventy-five days is the average time between Yom Kippur (Day of Atonement) and Chanukah (the Feast of Dedication/Lights). Will the House that Yeshua rebuilds, spoken of in the Book of Revelation, be sanctified and dedicated on the twenty-fifth day of the ninth Hebrew month, Kishlev, which is the Feast of Lights/Chanukah and which is also the anniversary of the dedication of YAH's other two Houses that He had built? If this is so, then surely those who wait the additional forty-five days will be abundantly blessed because they will witness Yeshua's dedication of YAH's *eternal* House of Worship.

Haggai (Hagahee)

Remember, we read in the book of Ezrah that the construction of the House of YAH had gotten bogged down. In response, YAH sent two of His Ne'vim, Haggai (Hagahee) and Zechariah (TzahkarYAH), to encourage the continuation of the project. YAHveh prompted Haggai (Hagahee) to write a letter to the governor of YAHuda, Zerubbabel, and to the high priest, Yeshua, stating that YAH had kept back His best from the people because they had allowed their own selfish desires to come before the finishing of YAH's work, the rebuilding of His House. The power of the Ruach of YAHveh was in the words of this letter, and the people's desire to finish the work was rekindled on the twenty-forth day of the sixth Hebrew month of Elul. On the twenty-first day of the seventh Hebrew month of Tishri (the last day of Sukkot, Hoshanah Rabbah), Haggai (Hagahee) spoke the words of YAHveh to Zerubbabel and Yeshua and told them not to be dismayed, for they had become discouraged because the House of YAH, which they had just built, did not seem as glorious as the first. Haggai (Hagahee) then told them that YAH's Shchinah Glory would one day return and that His House would then be more glorious than all the others combined. YAH also promised that His Shalom would abide there forever—He was not referring to the material structure that they had just finished, but to the one that His Son, the Messiah, would eventually build. The dedication was scheduled for the twenty-fifth of the ninth Hebrew month of Kishlev, the anniversary of the dedication of the one that Shalomo had built. On the twenty-fourth, Haggai (Hagahee) was sent to remind everyone of how up until that time YAHveh had withheld His blessings from the works of everyone's hands, but from now on, because of their obedience, He would see to it that the blessings would again flow until He brought the Goyim nations to judgment.

ROGER W. FEARING

Zechariah (TzahkarYAH)

Zechariah (TzahkarYAH) was actually Hagahee's young protégé. He began to speak out just two months after Hagahee with a warning to the people not to make the same mistake as their forefathers did by disobeying YAHveh. Three months later, he received eight visions from YAH regarding events that were to take place in the latter days, the days between the Messiah's first and second advents, which were glimpses of the Book of Revelation.

In his first vision, he saw three horses of various colors that he was told represented the nations that had persecuted his brethren in YAHuda and YisraEL. The Angel of YAH (who was actually Yeshua) told him that the nations were at ease after dispersing the Houses of YisraEL into captivity and that YAHveh was angry with them because even though He used them to perform His chastisement, they had evil intent in doing so. He will not let their arrogance go unpunished. Here, YAH sends comforting words through Zechariah (TzahkarYAH), saying that He still had every intention of blessing Zion (Zeeon) once again.

His second vision consisted of four horns and four craftsmen (remember that the number four represents the whole Earth and that horns represent the heads of nations or kings). These four are the ones who were responsible for scattering YAH's people—therefore, they represent Babylon, Persia, Greece, and Rome. The craftsmen are more than likely the spirits of the four living creatures found in the prophecies of YechezkEL and in the Book of Revelation.

His third vision was of a man measuring YAH's city, YAHrushalayim. This appears to be the same man, or being, who measured the city for YechezkEL in his writings and again for Yochanan in the Book of Revelation. He signifies that YAH is preparing His city to receive His YisraEL, those who had been scattered throughout the Earth, so that they might come and dwell with Him there forever. But first, He will assign the task of the stewardship of His Holy Land, the inheritance of YisraEL, to YAHuda until that day comes.

His fourth vision included Yeshua, the present high priest, who will be used by YAH to represent the ministry of the Messiah, Yeshua, His only begotten Son. He sees Yeshua, the high priest, standing in filthy garments (a soiled robe and tallit). He is then given fresh, clean ones, inferring that he will now represent YAH's Son, the *"BRANCH"*, whom He has promised to send. His Messiah will keep His statutes and commandments and will become the Cornerstone of His House, and He will be filled with the seven angels of His Ruach. Hasatan, who wants YAHrushalayim for himself, will oppose Him, but YAH will rebuke him for even considering it. During Yeshua's reign on YAH's throne, He will bring peace (shalom) to each man who has been obedient to His Torah and who has received His promised inheritance.

His fifth vision was of two olive trees, a menorah (an oil lamp with seven branches), and a bowl with seven pipes used for feeding oil into the lamps. In the Angel's explanation, He referred to Zerubbabel as being the one He was addressing. This time Zerubbabel represents the **BRANCH**, Yeshua the Messiah, because here Zerubbabel is the governor, or ruler, of YAHrushalayim. Both Zerubbabel, the governor, and Yeshua, the high priest, represented Yeshua, the Messiah, because He is both YAHveh's King (governor) and High Priest forever (in the order of Melchizedek). He speaks about Him bringing down the mountains (or high places) and being the capstone (the crown of His House), as well as the one who lays its foundation. The two olive trees that supply the oil to the menorah are His witnesses, Mosheh and ELeeYAHoo, the same ones who are in the Book of Revelation who represent the House of YAHuda and the House of Yosef. The lampstand/menorah represents His Kahal, the congregation of His people, also found in the Book of Revelation (**REV: 2&3**).

His sixth vision was that of a flying scroll above him that was thirty-feet long and fifteen feet in diameter. He was told that the scroll (or book, as we would understand it) contained the curses for all of those who opposed YAHveh, who were described as either being thieves or perjurers. In the Book of Revelation, Yeshua is described as the only one worthy of opening the scroll that has the seven seals. The scroll (or book) with the seven seals is actually the Book of Revelation itself. The seven seals explain the curses that will fall upon an unbelieving Earth and its inhabitants of thieves and liars (those of wickedness). The seventh seal reveals the seven trumpets (shofars) of salvation that await those who have been faithful and the seven bowls of judgment that await those who have been unfaithful.

His seventh vision was that of a woman in a basket with a lead lid on top. From the description of her, it would appear that she could possibly be the "Queen of Babylon" (Ishtar), "The Mother of Harlots" (Yezebel), or "The Woman on the Scarlet Beast" referred to in the Book of Revelation, or all three. Whoever she was, she was carried away to await judgment in the land of Babylon by two other women with wings—perhaps the two redeemed daughters of Zion (Zeeon), YAHuda and YisraEL.

Finally, he had an eighth vision of four chariots drawn by four pairs of different colored horses. They appeared to be similar to the three horses that he saw in his first vision and the four horses that were described in the first four seals of the scroll in the Book of Revelation. If I am correct, then they and their riders are the ones who have been commissioned to carry, throughout history, the Word and the Will of YAHveh over the face of the Earth.

Then YAHveh gave Zechariah (TzahkarYAH) instructions to make a golden crown that was to be placed upon the head of Yeshua, the high priest. Once more, it was to demonstrate how YAH plans to anoint His Promised

One, the **BRANCH**, and how He will be the one to build His permanent House and sit and rule there forever. At the same time, He is commissioning the rebuilding of His second House in His city, YAHrushalayim.

Two years later, some of YAHuda's leaders came to Zechariah (TzahkarYAH) and requested YAH's instructions on whether or not they should continue their fasting rituals as they had done in captivity. They thought that by embracing these religious activities they were pleasing YAHveh. But YAHveh gave instructions in His Torah to fast only once a year—in the seventh month of Tishri, on the tenth day known as Yom Kippur (Day of Atonement). They were not to follow after the pagan fasting rituals that called for a fast whenever they felt guilty about something. The only fasting, burnt offerings, and sacrifices that pleased Him consisted of following what Yeshua said was taught in the Torah: *"You shall love YAHveh your ELohim with all your heart, with all your soul, and with all your mind'"* (**DEUT 6:5**)...*"This is the first and great commandment... ."And the second is like it: 'You shall love your neighbor as yourself'"* (**LEV 19:18**) *"On these two commandments hang all the Torah and the Ne'vim"* (the TaNaKh) (**MATT 22:37-40**). Similar instructions are given in **ISA 58:6-8**. In other words, fasting on your own does not please or impress YAHveh, but following the essence of His TaNaKh does. He reminds those who came to inquire of Him through Zechariah (TzahkarYAH) that it was because of YAHuda's and YisraEL's religiosity and their not following His instructions in His Torah that caused Him to judge them and find them guilty. They followed after the eluah of their own imaginations and interpreted His words their own way. This is why they were dispersed into exile in the first place. Then He goes on to remind them of the day when He will remember their sins no more and will once again restore both houses back into the land and into His city, YAHrushalayim. He promises to restore all things to be even better than they were before, to fill her streets with children, and to cause the men and women there to live to a great old age. It seems that YAHuda will be the first to see the beginning of this blessing, but He assures all of the House of YisraEL that those who were scattered into the nations (Goyim/Gentiles) will, just before that great day, take hold of the garment (tallit) of a Jew (YAHudi) and ask him to teach them the way of YAHveh.

Ever since 1967, after the Jews (YAHudi) stormed their city and reoccupied YAHrushalayim, YAH has opened the hearts of the YAHudi all over the Earth, convincing many that Yeshua is their Messiah, thus beginning the Messianic-**Jewish** movement. Since the year 2000, when Ariel Sharon went up to the Temple Mount on Yom Kippur (Day of Atonement) and prayed, many non-Jews/Goyim and Believers/Christians began to more earnestly seek their own Hebrew roots—this was the beginning of the Messianic-**Israeli** (Two-House) movement. They did just as the Scriptures foretold—they took hold of the tallit of a Jew (YAHudi) and began to learn the ways of the Torah.

YAH confirms through Zechariah (TzahkarYAH) that those who have taken part in oppressing His firstborn, YisraEL, will see their own demise. He also confirms through Zechariah (TzahkarYAH) that His Promised Messiah will come at the beginning of these times and that His people will be able to identify Him when He arrives in YAHrushalayim riding on a colt, a foal of a donkey.

After identifying the Messiah, YAH goes on to speak about what He intends to do with His people, YisraEL. He says that He will make the House of YAHuda His bow and the House of Efraeem, meaning the tribes of Yosef, His arrows and that He will make both of them His weaponry against Greece, or the Greeks (another name for Goyim/Gentiles). He continues to exhort His people by promising them that the shepherds who have misled them in the past will be punished. He will replace them with leaders that He will raise up from the House of YAHuda, and it is also from there that He will send to them the cornerstone of His new House, a tent peg, and His bow for battle (all metaphors for YAHuda). He promises that He will *strengthen* the House of YAHuda and *save* the House of Yosef. He says that He will whistle for them and gather them, which is a metaphor for the sounding of the shofar and the ingathering at the end times (or rapture). He reaffirms their being sown into far countries, where they will remember Him and return to Him (and His Torah). He says that He will bring them into the land of Gilead and Lebanon, where there will not be enough room to contain them. Zechariah (TzahkarYAH) continued to admonish the shepherds for their not truly caring for YAH's flock. He said that he had two staffs in his hand, one called Grace and the other Unity. He broke both of them into two pieces because both grace and unity would be broken between the two, the House of YAHuda and the House of YisraEL. He said that YAHuda would lose the land once more, but would return in the last days to never leave again. YAHveh had used this same idea before—when He had YechezkEL take two sticks to represent YAHuda and Efraeem being reunited into the Whole House of YisraEL.

YAH promised that He was going to make YAHrushalayim a heavy stone for all people to bear, but would ordain the people of the House of YAHuda to be the stewards of it. She would always be a mystery to other nations in her ability to withstand their endeavors to oppress her. YAHveh would bring salvation to the tents of YAHuda first. He said He would defend the city that they were to maintain and that no one would be able to overcome them when they tried. He promised that in the "Great Day", all of her inhabitants would have their eyes opened and would recognize the one whom they had *pierced* and would mourn for Him as though they were mourning for their only *son*. In that day, He would bring forth a fountain of knowledge, and all of the false ne'veem, false teachers, and those with unclean spirits would be cast from the land. So much fear would fall upon the people that anyone caught prophesying would deny doing it and point instead to his chosen vocation as proof of not practicing spiritual things. He tells of the time when the Shepherd that He sends them will be struck down because He came speaking the truth of YAH's words and they were convicted through them. Because of this, He will strike two-thirds of YAHuda with judgment, but will save the other third, along with those He tests through fire.

On that day, YAH will gather all of the nations of the Earth to come against His city, YAHrushalayim, and His Shepherd, whom they pierced, will return and stand once more on the Mount of Olives, where He had ascended. The mountain shall split in two from east to west. Fresh spring water (called living water) from within the Earth will flow into the Dead Sea, connecting the Mediterranean Sea to the Dead Sea, which will once more team with life. In that day, YAH, through His Son, Yeshua (Dahveed, His beloved), will be King over the whole Earth. On that day, it will be proclaimed that "YAHveh is Echad" and "His Name is Echad". He speaks of a dreaded plague coming upon anyone who fought against His city, YAHrushalayim. After that, the nations will have a mandate to come up before YAH once a year to celebrate the anniversary of the Feast of Ingathering/Sukkot/Tabernacles. Anyone refusing to honor the appointed time (moedim) will suffer drought in their land for one year.

Esther (Ester)

Esther (Ester) is the second book in the Writings (Kethuvim) of the TaNaKh that is about the life of a woman who was used by YAH to shape the events leading up to the coming of the Messiah. One of the unique characteristics of this book is that there are no direct references made to YAHveh, the ELohim of YisraEL, but His providential fingerprints are all through its contents.

During the time of the final rebuilding of the second House of YAH, a crisis arose in the land of Babylon that threatened the House of YAHuda and could have even thwarted YAH's plan for a partial restoration back into the land. It took place after King Darius reigned in Persia and his son, Xerxes (also known as Ahasuerus), inherited the throne. By this time, DahneeEL had come to his eternal rest with his fathers, and the work on the second House of YAH was slowly seeing its completion. YAH's Ne'vim Hagahee and TzahkarYAH had come on the scene, and the people of the House of YAHuda were beginning to respond to their words. Meanwhile, King Xerxes was celebrating his own greatness, as well as the greatness of Persia and Media. During one of his celebrations, after overindulging in wine and strong drink, he called for his wife, Queen Vishti, to come before him and his guests in order to flaunt her beauty. At the time, she was also entertaining the wives of the dignitaries, so when this insulting request came from her husband, she refused to be humiliated. This in turn was seen as an act of insolence toward the king and an embarrassment to his authority. His advisors suggested that he banish her from her royal position as queen through a decree so that it would not become a precedent among the rest of the women toward their husbands. Eventually, King Xerxes had many regrets regarding this decree but could do nothing about it because according to Persian law, once the king issues a decree, even he cannot revoke it. He soon missed Queen Vishti's charm and beauty and began to brood about his decision. His advisors then suggested that he send out another decree calling for all of the beautiful virgins in the land to be gathered and brought before him so that he might choose a new queen from among them. The king jumped at the idea and issued the decree.

Among the young women in the territory, there was a Benjamite (BenYAHmi) girl by the name of Hadassah who was the cousin of a man named Mordecai. Being concerned for her welfare because she was a YAHudi, he gave her the Median name of Esther (Ester) for her protection. As it turned out, her beauty surpassed all of the other maidens and she was chosen to wear the queen's crown. During the process of elimination of the maidens, which took a full year, her cousin, Mordecai, kept a close personal watch on her welfare because of his concern for her. After the king had decided on Esther (Ester) as his choice, he gave a great feast on her behalf. Her cousin, Mordecai, was among the guests, and while in the courtyard, he overheard a plot between two of the king's eunuchs, planning the king's assassination. Mordecai sent word to Queen Esther (Ester) to warn the king. Queen Esther (Ester) then relayed the news to the king about the conspiracy and that it had been uncovered by her relative, Mordecai.

As time passed, the king promoted a man by the name of Haman to a position of authority over the king's affairs. This guy was filled with himself—a true narcissist. He longed for recognition from all of the king's subjects in everything that he did. Now Mordecai, being a YAHudi, would not bow to any man because no man was worthy of such homage. Haman, being so arrogant, became furious when he saw Mordecai's insolence and demanded an explanation. When he was told that Mordecai was a YAHudi and that it was against his culture and theology to bow to any man, he acquired an immediate hatred toward all YAHudaim. From that moment on, Haman became obsessed in finding a way to commit genocide on all YAHudi. He cast lots (pur) in order to determine the most opportune time to carry out his diabolical plan. The lot fell to the month of Adar (the twelfth month). Haman went before the king and accused the YAHudi of insolence toward the king, convincing him that they were a threat to civil order and stability and needed to be eliminated. With the king's blessings, an official decree went out into all the land regarding the king's decision. After the decree went out and Mordecai learned of the plot, he traded his robe and tallit for sackcloth and ashes and went before the king's gate, where he wailed for mercy for his people. Esther (Ester) learned of her uncle's anguish and called for one of her servants to investigate as to the cause. Upon learning of the decree, she knew that she had to create a way to expose Haman's wicked plot and devise a plan to counter it. So, she decided to go before the king and request his presence at a private dinner. But first she requested that her uncle notify all of the YAHudi that they should fast and pray for three days for her success.

The main obstacle that she faced would be obtaining an audience before the king without being summoned first. If anyone, including the queen, were to enter the king's throne room without an invitation, they would be subject to execution. In order for this to be negated, the king would have to override the ruling by holding out his scepter to the one approaching, thereby acknowledging his approval. She knew that she was placing herself in grave danger, but because she knew the fate of all YAHuda could be at stake, she took on the attitude that if she perished, she perished. After the three days of fasting, she went before the king, and as YAH would have it, he held out his scepter to her so that she might have the audience she needed. She invited the king and his right-hand man, Haman, to a special banquet, saying that she wanted to prepare it for them in order to make a particular request. During this banquet, Esther (Ester) said that she would like to honor both the king and Haman at a second banquet the next day and that she would make her request known at that time.

Haman was overjoyed that the queen would honor him so in the sight of the king. He rushed home to his family to share the good news, but on his way, he once more encountered Mordecai who, as before, refused to bow to his presence, which once again infuriated him. Upon arriving home, he shared with his family both the good news and the humiliation that he had suffered before the people because of Mordecai's defiance. His wife suggested that Haman make a request to the king that Mordecai be hung for his rebellion. Haman had a fifty-foot gallows erected for just that purpose.

It seems that YAH sent a spirit of unrest, which kept the king awake that night, so he requested that a boring book of chronicles be brought and read to him to help alleviate his insomnia. In the reading, it was revealed that a plot to assassinate him had been foiled by an informant who had never been properly compensated for his loyalty. That informant was none other than Mordecai. In the morning, when Haman came into the court before the king to make his request for Mordecai's execution, the king asked him for his advice as to what should be done to honor someone who had been overlooked for his great loyalty? Haman, thinking that the king was referring to him, suggested that he be adorned with royal robes and led around by one of the king's nobles on one of the king's horses and for him to wear the royal crest. The king was delighted in the suggestion and ordered Haman to be the one to do so for Mordecai. After the parade, Haman ran home and cried on his family's shoulders. Shortly thereafter, he was summoned to prepare himself to attend the banquet that Queen Esther (Ester) had arranged.

After they arrived and had begun to feast, the king asked once more for the queen to make her request. She asked that she and her people be spared their lives. The king was shocked and inquired of her as to how such a thing could be? Queen Esther (Ester) revealed to him the plot and its perpetrator. In the king's wrath toward Haman, he gave the order for Haman to be hung on the very gallows that he had purposed for Mordecai. The king had Haman's house given to Queen Esther (Ester). The king then placed Mordecai in Haman's position and gave him his signet ring, along with the authority it carries. In the third month, Sivan, Mordecai had a decree of his own sent out, stating that all of the YAHudi were to be allowed to take up arms in order to defend themselves against any adversary. So, when the twelfth month, Adar, arrived and those who hated the YAHudi tried to carry out the first decree, the YAHudi were able, with the help of some of the king's men, to defend themselves—they killed 75,500 men and saved all of the YAHudi who were in the land. All of this took place on the thirteenth day of Adar, and on the fourteenth, they rested. Queen Esther (Ester) and Mordecai sent a decree out into all the land where the YAHudi were still captive, establishing that in the future, these two days were to be recognized as holidays for the purpose of lamenting and celebrating. These holidays were given the name Purim. This name was chosen in order to remind them of the lots (pur) that had been drawn, which had determined what day the YAHudi were to be destroyed. Today, Purim is still being celebrated on these two days. On the fourteenth day of Adar, the YAHudi fast and pray to YAH for saving them. On the fifteenth day, they celebrate with gift giving and partying. When II Adar (a leap-year month) comes, the fourteenth and fifteenth of that month are also celebrated. Our YAHudaim brothers love to party every chance they get.

Malachi (Mahlakhee)

The final Ne'vee on the scene is Malachi (Mahlakhee), the twelfth Minor Ne'vee. His message is one of both chastisement and exhortation. His ministry of bringing YAH's message comes sometime between the time of Queen Ester's encounter with Haman and her son's, King Artaxerxes I, commissioning of the rabbi and priest, Ezrah, to return with fifteen hundred more YAHudi to reestablish both the teachings of the Torah and true worship within the House of YAH.

Malachi (Mahlakhee) is sent by YAH to remind His people that all that He has said has come to pass. All of YisraEL's most powerful enemies, those who had plundered and pilfered them, have either been reduced to only a weak remnant or have been annihilated altogether. YAH uses Edom as His example of this punishment. He also admonishes the priests for performing their duties half-heartedly. Because they have done so, He promises to raise a people up (meaning the Gentiles/Goyim Nations) who will have a greater desire to worship Him—both in spirit and in truth. He promises to raise this new priesthood up with a new covenant—one where all men will come to know Him as the One True Living ELohim, the ELohim of His people, YisraEL. YAH was speaking of a time when His people, YAHuda, in their attempt to avoid the same mistakes as their forefathers, would add so many statutes and regulations to His Torah that it would become a burden to all who tried to obey it. These statutes were known as the Oral Law and would become known as the Talmud after they were written down some eight-hundred years later. The Oral Law was so burdensome that even the Messiah, Yeshua, denounced it as a yoke too heavy to bear and said for us to take His yoke instead—one that was easy (**MATT 11:29&30**—as does Rav Shaul in **ACTS 15:10**). This is where a lot of error in our *"churches"* has occurred. Because of these scriptures, they believe that we are no longer under the Law (Torah). They say that the Law (Torah) is a yoke that is impossible to bear and that it was just for the Jews (YAHudi) anyway—we are under His Grace, which does away with the Law (Torah). Their error comes from not understanding that there is a difference between the Law (Torah) and the Oral Law (Talmud). But hopefully after reading this book, you will have developed a deeper understanding of the Father's Torah and the purpose that it still has in our lives.

By the time Ezrah had arrived on the scene, nearly two-hundred years had passed since the Torah and worship in YAH's House had been practiced. Because of this, it was easy for their traditions to become mixed with the worship of the foreign elohim of Babylon. The true meaning of love and grace had been long forgotten and replaced with a false religion that was totally foreign to YAHveh. Ezrah reminded them of their marriage to YAHveh and also of the covenant that they had made with Him. Even though YAH had expressed His hatred toward divorce because of the lives it affects, alters, and sometimes even destroys, they had played the harlot and had divorced themselves from Him.

YAHveh made another appeal to His people, YAHuda, the only tribe that was left who carried His name and was the dominant tribe who now represented His people, YisraEL. His appeal was for them to return to the true teachings of the Torah and the Ne'vim because if they did, they would be able to identify His Messenger who would usher in His Promised Messiah—if they didn't, they would miss Him. He reminded them that if it weren't for the fact that He was the ELohim who never changes and for the promises that He had made to their fathers, Avraham, Yitzyak, Yaacov, Yosef, Mosheh, and Dahveed, they would have been consumed long ago. They asked Him how they could return to His ways, and He told them not to rob Him anymore. He pointed out that they had robbed Him by not putting Him first in their lives. Instead, they had made their own pleasures their first priority. They had expressed their trust in what their monies could purchase for them more than they had expressed their trust in Him for their provisions. They had neglected their tithes and offerings that were to be used to maintain His House and for those who ministered there. Tithes, offerings (peace and freewill), sacrifices, and everything that was to be an expression of their thankfulness and gratitude toward His mercy, grace, redemption, sanctification, and restoration were being completely neglected. So, in order to begin to show their recognition of their sins, He wanted them to express their restitution by first restoring their giving with a cheerful heart. They had been reaping what they had sown in their greed by holding back what was required of them because they hadn't really trusted in YAHveh to meet their needs, and the result was their receiving the curse of the Torah instead. He told them to change their attitude, and if they did, the result would be that He would change their circumstances.

His final words to them were that He would send them their Deliverer, who would arise as "The Sun of Righteousness" and have healing in His *wings* (tassels/tzitzits on the hem of a tallit), and then they would be able to trample down all of their enemies. And once again, He reminded them to "Remember the Law (Torah) of Mosheh" and that He would send ELeeYAHoo to them. YAH was saying that He would send the spirit of ELeeYAHoo in the person of John the Baptist (Yochanan the Immerser), and in the last days, He would send him as the "House of Yosef". In both cases, ELeeYAHoo's ministry would be to turn the hearts of the fathers to their children and the hearts of the children to their fathers. Remember, sons and daughters, honor your parents no matter how much you may disagree with them—especially the sons toward their fathers. Family is what YAHveh commands to remain together as one (echad), and if they don't, He will have to strike (or judge) the Earth with a curse. The breakup of the family is why He is coming to judge the world and its system, which will take place before the coming of the great and dreadful day of **YHVH**.

Nehemiah (NehchemYAH)

The book of Nehemiah (NehchemYAH) is the thirty-ninth book that we will have examined from the TaNaKh, which completes its recorded writings. It is also the thirteenth book of the Kethuvim, the third section that makes up the TaNaKh. The geographic location of this final writing, or chronicle, is the territory of Susa, or Shushan, a place much like the land of

Goshen back in ancient Mitsrahyim. This land had also been set aside for the former inhabitants of the land of YisraEL. It was where Ezrah had set out from fourteen years earlier on his second return trip. It was also where Ester had the YAHudi people defend themselves thirty-five years earlier in order to escape annihilation. Nehemiah (NehchemYAH) held a very prominent position before King Artaxerxes I as his personal cupbearer.

One day, the king saw that Nehemiah's (NehchemYAH's) countenance had fallen, so he inquired as to the reason. Nehemiah (NehchemYAH) told him that he had learned a few months earlier that the city of his people and his ELohim, YAHrushalayim, had come into disarray because the people had lost hope and faith in the ELohim of YisraEL. Remember, King Artaxerxes I was more than likely the son of Queen Ester and knew YAHveh as the Creator of Heaven and Earth, so he too would have had compassion for his relatives, the YAHudi. He commissioned Nehemiah (NehchemYAH) to be seated as the governor of YAHuda and granted him everything that he would need to finish rebuilding the city.

By the Ruach, Nehemiah (NehchemYAH) spoke YAH's words to the people and encouraged them to rededicate themselves to the rebuilding of the walls and gates of the great city of their ELohim. But the revival to finish the rebuilding met with some resistance—the governors of the surrounding provinces, mainly Samaria from the north, mocked the people in their effort to rebuild. In all actuality, they were afraid that the YAHudi might become too powerful and pose a threat to the rest of the land. So, the YAHudi formed teams of workers who would both construct and guard the walls at the same time—they would place a trowel in one hand and a spear in the other.

Another problem they faced was that many people had been taken advantage of by the nobles and former governors of the land. These rulers had to be rebuked for their using politics for their own personal gain instead of helping their brethren and neighbors accomplish the task that YAH had given them. Nehemiah (NehchemYAH) himself tried to set the example by not extracting any of the expenditures from the people, but instead used only the funds that the king had put at his disposal.

Within fifty-two days after the project of rebuilding the wall around YAHrushalayim began, it was finished—but not until after many attempts had been made to discourage Nehemiah (NehchemYAH). He stood fast, knowing what YAH had sent him to do, and was not going to relinquish until it was complete. When the construction had ended, Nehemiah (NehchemYAH) called for the registration that had been taken when the people first began the restoration and made note of the names of those who had persevered. After reviewing it, he came to the conclusion that there were many more people needed in order to fill up the land.

WHAT WE WEREN'T TAUGHT ABOUT THE BIBLE AND ITS HISTORY

On the first day of the seventh month, the month of Tishri (Yom Teruah), Nehemiah (NehchemYAH) called Ezrah, the scribe and rabbi, to read the Torah before all the people. They assembled as the Kahal of YisraEL, even though they only consisted of the tribe of YAHuda and BenYAHmeen and just a small remnant of the other tribes, in the square at the Water Gate so that they might hear the words that YAHveh had spoken to Mosheh twelve-hundred years earlier. After they had heard the Torah read, they began to weep because of their iniquities and the iniquities of their fathers for not keeping YAH's ordinances and statutes. They vowed to honor all that was commanded of them regarding the Sabbaths, New Moons, and Feasts (appointed times/moedim). Once more, they proclaimed the day as being a holy day, a day dedicated to YAHveh, their ELohim, known as Rosh HaShanah (the Head of the Year), and it has remained the same to this day. From that time on, it was to officially be the head of their "civil" year, and Nisan/Aviv would remain as the head of their "agricultural and spiritual" year. It has taken on a more prominent position of importance than Yom Teruah (the Day of the "Sounding of the Shofar"), its original appointed time (moedim). They also consider it to be the anniversary of the first day of creation. They were told to count this as a festive day—a day of celebration, feasting, dancing, and the giving of gifts to one another. They also realized that their fathers had not been faithful in keeping the moedim (appointed times) every year since the time of Joshua (Yoshua). So they gathered branches from the four kinds of trees that were described in the Torah and built sukkoths (booths), just as they were instructed, in order to celebrate Chag Sukkot, the Feast of Tabernacles/Ingathering. Because of their understanding of its meaning, they set these up in the courtyards of the House of YAH and in the square at both the Water Gate and the Gate of Efraeem. (This Feast was discussed in more detail in Chapter Three.) The symbolism here is as follows: the number four represents the four corners of the Earth—the tree branches represent the sons of man—the different species symbolize YAH's provision for man—living under them in the courtyards of YAH's House for seven days symbolizes YAH's overall protection until the final ingathering—the Water Gate symbolizes the Living Water that He provides through His word—and finally, the Gate of Efraeem represents the re-gathering of the Whole House of YisraEL at the end-times.

On the twenty-forth day of Tishri, all of the people gathered in sackcloth with dust on their heads in order to show their contrition. They separated themselves from the foreigners who were in their midst and reviewed their heritages, along with their sins and the sins of their fathers against YAHveh, which reminded them of how He had shown them mercy in spite of their iniquities. After their words were written down and the covenant was sealed, they drew lots in order to determine how the territories were to be distributed to the different clans and who would dwell either inside or outside of YAHrushalayim. Chronicles and genealogies were compiled in order to determine the authenticity of each person's right of inheritance to the land. Strict guidelines for keeping the Torah were drawn up to help eliminate the possibility of anymore iniquity being committed against YAHveh, the ELohim of YisraEL. As I mentioned earlier, this became the Oral Law, which eventually became their downfall. Even though it may have led to a greater understanding of kingdom principles, it also became filled with the finite ideas of men that polluted the instructions from YAHveh. This eventually led to their inability to recognize the true Messiah when He came.

After this, Nehemiah (NehchemYAH) set up choirs, singers, musical instruments, and shofars for blowing in order to celebrate the dedication of the wall and all that it stood for. The people were back in the land of YisraEL, and the House of YAH was rebuilt. The House of YAHuda and BenYAHmeen, along with the Lehvee, had reestablished the Torah, its statutes with its ordinances, and once more the City of YAH, YAHrushalayim, was protected from her enemies by her walls and her gates. They were now prepared to receive their Promised Messiah—or so they thought.

Conclusion

These final six books, along with the final chapters of DahneeEL and the Book of Psalms, have guided us to the final and closing words of YAHveh, the ELohim of YisraEL, in His TaNaKh. All of the preparations have been made, and all of the evidence that was necessary has been revealed, preparing His people for the moedim (appointed times) of the first coming of His Messiah, which is also a rehearsal for His second advent. The tribe of YAHuda has been saved from annihilation, and the promised partial restoration of YisraEL and YAHuda back into their land is completed for now. The second House of YAH was built, which would later be refurbished by the Roman Emperor Herod for political reasons, and the plan regarding the events that will lead up to the last days of the judgment of the Goyim/Gentile nations has been revealed.

CHAPTER 18
…about the 400 Years Remaining Until the First Coming of the Messiah

There were 400 years from the time that the first Hebrews of Avram's clan had settled in Mitsrahyim until their deliverance by the Ne'vee Mosheh. There were forty years of wilderness wandering before the YisraELi Hebrews entered the land that YAHveh had promised Avraham. There were 400 years of YisraEL's independent rule before the division came between the two southern tribes, YAHuda and BenYAHmeen, and the ten northern tribes that were represented by Efraeem, the youngest son of Yosef. Then there were 200 years until the ten northern tribes were assimilated into Europe by the Assyrians and 200 more years before the Babylonians exiled the southern tribes into Babylon. There was an additional seventy years of captivity before they were returned to their homeland by the Persians. And now there will be 400 additional years of domination that will come at the hands of the Persians, Mitsrahyim, Greeks, and Romans. Between the time of their first judge, Yoshua, and King Shalomo's reign, the YisraELi had clung to YAH's promise of a land that He would one day give them. All during that time, their hope of possessing this land was always on shaky ground.

Beginning from the time that Ezrah and NehchemYAH began to get things organized and settled in YAHuda, the Greeks were beginning to rise in power with their mixed ideas of paganism and politics. These ideas consisted of democracy, philosophy, and art and would eventually evolve into a type of secular humanism. Men like Socrates, Plato, and Aristotle began emerging as great thinkers, which in turn began to elevate man to a god-like status. One of these men, Alexander the Great, became a conqueror of some of the nations in Asia, Europe, and northern Africa. He introduced the Greek form of democracy (nothing resembling what we're used to), which actually became a new form of religion, where man's ability to reason was equated to the elohim.

Alexander (who was schooled under Aristotle) found the YAHudi to be of no threat to him—after all, they had no army or king to conquer. He encouraged them to settle in Mitsrahyim, where he promised that they would have freedom to practice their religion. Greece had a different method of establishing its power over its conquered territories than the other YAHudi-conquering predecessors. For example, Mitsrahyim, when it dominated YisraEL, used them as slaves to build their cities and pyramids. Assyria assimilated them into other countries until they were so absorbed that they became unrecognizable. The Babylonians made them a part of their own society and used the scholars and educated populous to better their own culture. The Persians believed in keeping a remnant of those they had conquered in their own land so that they could continue to cultivate and preserve their cities and pay taxes and tributes to them. The Greeks on the other hand would simply change the culture, customs, and languages of their captives and then educate them through their arts and philosophies in order to make them think, look, and act like Greeks.

After Alexander the Great died, the territories that he conquered were divided between four of his generals, and many of the YAHudi were once more put under the authority of the Mitsrahyim. Mitsrahyim itself was now under Grecian rule and was experiencing its own form of cultural change. Even their capitol had been changed to a different city that Alexander the Great had named after himself, Alexandria. Some of the YAHudi still remained in Babylon, which was also now under Grecian authority, while others stayed in YAHrushalayim. The effect of intermarriage and the intermingling of cultures had both diluted and diminished the authority of the Torah in the eyes of many, except for the true orthodox believers. Because of the now wide dispersion of the YAHudi, access to the House of YAH had become impaired. Because of this, teaching houses known as synagogues became popular, and the teaching of the Torah was now being conducted by the rabbi instead of the priest.

As was said earlier, the Greeks re-cultured those they conquered through a process known as "Hellenism". The Hebrew language began to diminish and became replaced with Greek and with Aramaic, which was similar to Hebrew. The Torah became less and less relied upon for clear theology and began to be replaced by the Midrash and the Talmud. Judaism eventually came under the influence of sectarianism and became divided between the Pharisees, Sadducees, Herodians, and Essenes; eventually, the Zealots and the Nazarenes would be included. In about 280 BCE, seventy-two Hebrew scholars translated the TaNaKh into Greek and rearranged the thirty-nine books that were considered "canon", or "inspired", into what we now recognize as the "Old Testament". They named it the "Septuagint" (LXX), which means "the seventy". It is said that after comparing the two translations, the seventy-two individual scholars were amazed to find that they had all come to the exact same meaning of the words in the overall translation—it was as though they had been directed by an invisible hand. This was part of YAHveh's plan so that His words would now have a vehicle to reach the Gentiles (Goyim) in order to prepare the way for the coming of the news of His Son, the Messiah. All of these changes had come about due to the introduction of democracy and its widespread influence. Man became reliant upon philosophy and higher thinking, resulting in men

WHAT WE WEREN'T TAUGHT ABOUT THE BIBLE AND ITS HISTORY

equating themselves, as was said before, to the gods (elohim). Democracy in itself is a good thing because it gives people a voice. But because man is by nature sinful, it can become a tool that the enemy, hasatan, can use in getting him to believe that he is like a god—as he tried to do in the garden. But in time, YAH would use democracy to bring about the idea of freedom of religion to everyone in order to open up His instructions to all of the Gentile (Goyim) nations, who would eventually cross the oceans and develop a nation known as the United States of America.

While some of the YAHudi in Alexandria began to dabble in mysticism and the occult, a few books that were suppose to be "inspired" emerged and became known as the "hidden writings". They consisted of twelve additional books and were the beginning of the Hebrew "Apocrypha". Not all were born out of mysticism, but none were considered to be on the same level of inspiration as the TaNaKh. They never were accepted wholly by the YAHudi, but were later, 400 years after the Messiah's death and resurrection, included with other similar writings as being a part of the New Testament (Brit Chadashah). Included in these books was the story of Judas (YAHuda) Maccabeus (meaning "the hammer"), a type of savior (messiah) for the YAHudi. He delivered them out from certain annihilation by a type of "son of perdition", who had been prophesied by DahneeEL. This forerunner of the Antimessiah was named Antiochus Epiphanes, and he brought great persecution against the YAHudi and ridiculed their faith in YAHveh. YAHuda Maccabeus, along with two of his brothers, the sons of a Zealot named Mattathias, promoted an uprising among the YAHudi that caused reprisals from the Syrians, the Edomi, the Mitsrahyim, and the Greeks. Those who took part were later known as the Hasmoneans. The uprising began when Antiochus Epiphanes brought a statue of Jupiter (also known as Zeus, the Sun eluah) and set it upon the altar of YAHveh's House. Later, he sacrificed a pig upon this altar just to abominate the YAHudi house of worship and their religion, and then he proclaimed himself as being the true ELuah. With the efforts of Mattathias and his sons, especially YAHuda Maccabeus, they defeated the mighty army of Antiochus Epiphanes—not just once, but time and time again.

After the desecration of the altar in YAH's House, the menorah had to be re-lit in order for any worship to continue. It is said that only one jar of consecrated oil was found to fuel it and that according to YAH's instructions in His Torah, it would take another eight days to both formulate and consecrate the additional oil that would be needed to keep it lit. Miraculously, the oil didn't run out—the menorah stayed lit for the full eight days. This miracle has been celebrated ever since as the "Feast of Lights", or the "Feast of Dedication" (Hanukkah). It's important to remember that this feast, as well as the Feast of Purim, is not a part of the original appointed feasts (moedim) that are found in the Torah and that these two festivals were celebrated, or recognized, by the only tribe of YisraEL that was left, YAHuda. Today, however, some of the non-YAHudi Messianic believers in Yeshua are also celebrating these two feasts—they too want to commemorate the fact that YAH kept His promise to preserve the tribe of YAHuda. After all, they were the ones who were given the responsibility to both protect and preserve the Torah, and even more importantly, they were the ones through whom the Messiah would come.

The YAHudi and the Messianic/Christian actually agree on more things than they disagree. First of all, let me point out that they are the only two religions in the world whose members worship a Living ELohim—one who is Creator, Maker, and Judge of all things. Both the YAHudi and the Messianic/Christian know Him as a loving Eluah who is full of grace and mercy and desires to bless His people and not curse them. His relationship with us is based upon love and not fear. I would like to use this opportunity to point out something that I feel is important for you to understand. With other religions, their elohim rule by striking fear into the hearts of their followers and exist in the dark corners of their minds. These fears come from the father of lies, hasatan, the Prince of Darkness. He controls this spiritual atmosphere with demons that do his bidding. Those who follow after these elohim do so in spite of their fear, thinking that their worship will appease them and thereby ward off their destruction. Over the centuries, they have been given numerous names such as: Mars, the eluah of war—Neptune, the eluah of the sea—Venus, the eluah of love (she was only one of many fertility elohim). Instead of worshipping the Creator, they chose to worship His creation; they had elohim for the seasons, for trees, for different animals, as well as for the heavenly hosts. These hosts were known as Zeus (who manifested himself through the sun), Allah (which means the eluah—he was associated with the moon), and Jupiter (the son of Zeus—who was supposed to be manifested in the brightest planet in the heavens) to name just a few. In the past when nations who worshiped that way defeated an enemy, they would give credit to the eluah that they felt was the most responsible for their victory. Their mentality was to pit one eluah against another as though to say, "My eluah is greater than your eluah".

Even the Muslims claim to worship only one eluah, but their eluah is "Allah" of the moon, who supposedly controls its phases that determine both the time and years. They do this because Mohammed decided that *Allah* was supposed to be the greatest eluah—second only to Zeus of the sun, who supposedly ruled the seasons. Mohammed believed that the Messianics (also known as Christians), who were followers of the YAHudi Messiah, Yeshua, were also followers of Zeus. He came to this conclusion because the Roman Emperor, Constantine, who promoted Christianity, also worshiped Zeus. And since Mohammed hated the YAHudi, he therefore had no use for Zeus.

WHAT WE WEREN'T TAUGHT ABOUT THE BIBLE AND ITS HISTORY

Even today, the atheists, the humanists, and the secularists worship the eluah of Mammon, which Yeshua warned His followers not to do. Mammon, which represents the reward that the spirit of this world system (run by hasatan) offers, causes men to dedicate their whole lives (a form of worship) to serving what it promises to bring. But the truth is that what it promises is only temporal and will vanish with time. Only YAHveh and His Son, Yeshua, are eternal and offer true love, mercy, and acceptance. It is only He who heals broken hearts and provides happiness—exactly what mankind is hopelessly seeking for in "things".

As we turn our attention back to the Greek Empire, we see a new power emerging on the horizon from Rome. Province by province, the Roman army began to defeat the Greeks. Romans were like chameleons in that they adapted themselves to any society or culture that they admired, and they really admired the Greek culture and their democratic form of political rule. They themselves had a similar form of government that was run by a congress of senators and known as a republic. They had congressional territories with governors, called tetrarchs, controlling them. The Roman General, Pompey, invaded the land of YisraEL in 63 BCE, but was defeated in a power struggle over YAHuda by Julius Caesar, who was later assassinated by his friend, Brutus. After Caesar's death, one of his confidants, Mark Antony, appointed Herod as governor over the territory known as Galilee and gave him the title of "king". Herod later took on for himself the title of "King Herod the Great". Julius Caesar's son, Octavian, who would later be called Augustus and who was also credited as being the founder of the great "Roman Empire", retained Herod as "king" of YAHuda.

Mark Antony, because of his many military achievements, became an admired figure of Rome and had an influence on much of the Roman design within the city of YAHrushalayim. Some archeologists believe that because of his renown, the Roman government built a large fortress and garrison in the middle of YAHrushalayim and named it after him, calling it the "Fortress of Antonia". In the middle of this garrison, a palace was built for Herod, which later became a Roman temple of worship. These same archeologists believe that it was on this very temple site centuries later that a Byzantium cathedral was built, mistakenly believing it to be the site of the Temple Mount where the House of YAH once stood. Then later in history during the Muslim uprising, they too mistakenly thought that it was where the YAHudi had built their Temple and where the Crusaders (Christians) had erected their cathedral. So, they deliberately built their mosque, "Haram esh-Sharif" (Dome of the Rock), on it. This was a custom of the Muslims—after defeating their enemy, they would often erect mosques on the holy sites of those whom they had conquered. The reason that these same archeologists believe that the Muslims were mistaken is that the actual Mount Zion (Zeeon) was located at the southeast corner of the Old City of YAHrushalayim, as the TaNaKh points out, and not in the center of the city. If they are correct, then this would be the site that the original House of YAH was actually built on because it was recorded as being built on Mt Zeeon. Another thing that leads them into believing this to be correct is that the Gihon Spring empties into the Kidron River here, and it is believed by some that the House of YAH was built over the Gihon Spring in order to have a fresh supply of sweet water for sanctification and cleansing purposes. If all of these things are accurate, then the "Western Wailing Wall" is really the western wall of the "Fortress of Antonia" and not the western wall of the court that surrounded the House of YAH. And after all, Yeshua did say that *"Not one stone shall be left here upon another, that shall not be thrown down"* (MATT 24:2).

We will now focus our attention on three other territories in this region: YAHuda to the south, Galilee to the north, with Samaria sandwiched in between. This was the area in which the Messiah, Yeshua, would mostly minister. Fifty years prior to His birth, Herod befriended the YAHudi for personal and political gain. He financed the remodeling of the House of YAH and handpicked the high priest. The two main sects, the Sadducees and the Pharisees, began carrying most of the authority over all of the YAHudi in YAHrushalayim. The Sadducees were the more secular and liberal of the two, not believing in the resurrection and viewing miracles and anything supernatural as being witchcraft, charlatanism, or trickery. The Pharisees were the more orthodox, but had taken the Torah to new heights in legalism. The third group, the Essenes, believed in living a pure and sanctified life, neither marrying nor possessing any personal effects. The Catholic monks also designed themselves after this pattern. The Essenes were basically a society of hermits, as were many of the Catholic monks. It is thought that John the Baptist was originally an Essenian. The Zealots, the fourth group, were a more militant group and responsible for many uprisings against both the Romans and some of the YAHudi leadership who had aligned themselves with the Romans for political favors. At least one of Yeshua's disciples (talmidim), Simon, was once a Zealot. Another well-known YAHudi Zealot was Barabbas, who led an insurrection against the Roman republic and was later released in exchange for the crucifixion of the Messiah, Yeshua.

So, the stage is set. The YAHudi, in their zeal to not forsake the Torah, had legalized it through their Oral laws to the point that it was almost unrecognizable. They had developed a culture that was more political than religious in order to gain favor with their Roman occupiers. The time had now come for YAH to judge the final remnant of YAHuda—they too are to be assimilated into all of the nations over the next 2,000 years.

WHAT WE WEREN'T TAUGHT ABOUT THE BIBLE AND ITS HISTORY

Conclusion

Now is a good time for us to review the past ten-thousand years since the beginning of creation. In the first six-thousand years, YAH created the heavens and the Earth. For the next four-thousand years, man had dominion over His creation, but was under the bondage of sin for rebelling against Him. During the millennium rest that YAH had taken after His work of creation, man had become so corrupt that YAH had to set up a plan of destruction that would wipe out mankind and change the face of the Earth. He would start afresh with a new man of righteousness, Noah, through whom He would begin His plan of redemption and restoration. Within the next thousand years, He chose a second righteous man, Avraham, to start His chosen nation, the Hebrews, who would be used to bless all of the other nations of the renewed Earth by revealing to them the knowledge of Him and His plan. Avraham fathered two sons. The first would become the father of the Arab nations, and these would evolve into one final religious nation known as Islam. During the next thousand years, YAH raised up three more righteous men who would continue the implementation of His plan. First was Yitzhak, Avraham's second son and YAH's third righteous man, who would also father two sons, Esau and Yaacov, who would become two more nations that would rival one another until YAH's plan was completed. Yaacov, who was later called YisraEL, was YAH's fourth righteous man. He fathered twelve sons who became known as the nation of YisraEL, with its divided religious nations of the YAHudi and the Christians/Messianics. These two religious nations would be the result of the two different directions that would be taken by the descendants of two of YisraEL's sons, YAHuda and Yosef. The fifth righteous man was Mosheh, who would be used by YAH to give YisraEL His instructions known as the Torah so that all men, those who called upon the Name of YAHveh, could be saved from their sins. They were to follow these instructions in order for them to become mature enough to be able to discern His voice, thereby enabling them to understand the plan that He had designed for their individual lives. Then, finally, within the fourth thousand-year period, He raised up a king named Dahveed, YAH's sixth righteous man, who fathered the descendants that He would use to bring forth the seed of a virgin woman in order to bless the world with a Savior. This would be none other than YAH Himself in the flesh, coming as His only begotten Son, Yeshua, the Messiah (Yeshua HaMashiach—YAH's seventh, final, and *most* righteous Man). He also allowed His people, YisraEL, to become divided in order to fulfill His promise to Avraham, that he would become the father of many nations and bless the Goyim.

Now the time had come to usher in His Son, the Messiah, who would provide the redemption necessary for His people, who were called by His

Name, to come to the knowledge of His plan of redemption, sanctification, and restoration. And when He sends Him the second time, His people will finally be ready for the completion of their promised millennium rest.

CHAPTER 19
...about the Gospels of Matthew, Mark, Luke, John, and Acts 1

The last twenty-seven books of Scripture known as the New Testament or, as stated earlier, the Renewed Covenant (Brit Chadashah in Hebrew) had not even begun to be written for at least thirty years beyond the death and resurrection of Yeshua, the Messiah. It was another eighty or ninety years after that that they began to be put together and recognized as canon scriptures. So what did the apostles (shelichim) and elders teach up until then? They taught from the TaNaKh, just as Yeshua did. The idea that teaching the Torah from the TaNaKh was actually placing a person under the Law and that the Church had replaced YisraEL as YAHveh's choice of people is ludicrous and has never ever been hinted at in any doctrine of Scripture. This idea came about when men began to teach their own version of the Scriptures in order to control the religious thoughts of those who had placed their trust in them for spiritual guidance.

The Introduction to Yeshua, the Messiah

The main event that is recorded in the first portion of the Brit Chadashah is the life, ministry, death, and resurrection of Yeshua HaMashiach. As was mentioned in Chapter Fifteen, there are four eyewitness accounts recorded by four of His apostles (shelichim): Matthew, Mark, Luke, and John. In that chapter, I gave an explanation as to their relevance to the four-faced creatures that both the Ne'vee Ezekiel (YechezkEL) and the Apostle (Shelich) Yochanan saw in their visions.

In the eyewitness account and introduction by Yochanan, he saw Yeshua as the Son of God (ELuah) and described Him as being the Living Word (Torah) of YAHveh. Yochanan, by inspiration of YAH, credits Him as being the One who was responsible for speaking the words that brought everything into being. He goes on to describe Him as being rejected by His own people, the YAHudi—but this was for the fulfillment of what the Ne'vim had written about Him. He continued to reveal, by inspiration, that Yeshua came to bring man into a new-birth experience so that man might be born of YAH's Ruach, just as He had been, and not by natural birth alone, which had trapped man in the curse of sin.

Yeshua Qualifies as the Messiah

Through Birth

Both Matthew (MattatiYAH), who saw Yeshua as the King of YisraEL, and Luke (Lukas), who saw Him as the Son of Man, recorded His genealogy. Matthew (MattatiYAH) begins his record with Avraham and covers forty-two generations up to Yaacov, the father of Yosef, who was Mary's (Miriam's) betrothed and Yeshua's guardian-father. This was to show His qualification as being YAH's firstborn through the symbolic reference to His being a direct descendant of the tribe of Jacob/Israel (Yaacov/YisraEL), who was also called YAH's firstborn. Yosef was YisraEL's eleventh son, who had been given the firstborn status and the headship of the tribes of YisraEL from his father. Luke (Lukas), on the other hand, traces Yeshua's genealogy backwards from the seed of Mary (Miriam) to her father, also named Yosef, and then back to the first Ahdom—Yeshua would be referred to as the second Ahdom. Both of these genealogies pass through King Dahveed in order to qualify Him as the Promised Messiah.

The Birth of Both Yeshua and His Cousin, John the Baptist (Yochanan the Immerser)

John the Baptist (Yochanan the Immerser) was the son of a Lehvee priest by the name of Zacharias (TzahkarYAH) and his wife, Elizabeth (ELisheva), sister to Mary (Miriam), the mother of Yeshua. John the Baptist's (Yochanan the Immerser's) birth was six months before Yeshua's, according to the Apostle (Shelich) Luke's (Lukas') writings. As I explained earlier in Chapter Six, John the Baptist's (Yochanan the Immerser's) father, Zacharias, was a priest in the order of Abijah (AbeeYAH), which was the eighth order to serve as priests within the Holy of Holies at the House of YAH. The eighth order served in the first week of the third Hebrew month of Sivan. So, if Elizabeth (ELisheva) had become pregnant right after his week of service in the month of Sivan as the Scriptures state, which coincides with the Roman month of June, then it would have been in the ninth Hebrew month of Kishlev, near the Roman month of December, that Mary (Miriam) would have come to stay with her until Yochanan's birth, which would've had to occur in the twelfth Hebrew month of Adar, near the Roman month of March. If Mary (Miriam) had just become pregnant in Elizabeth's (ELisheva's) sixth month of her pregnancy, then Yeshua should have been born sometime in the sixth or seventh Hebrew month of Elul or Tishri, near the Roman months of September or October. The most likely date that His birth would have occurred would have been the tenth of Tishri, the Day of Atonement, since Yeshua is the atonement for the price of sin, the curse of the Torah.

Zacharias (TzahkarYAH) and his wife, Elizabeth (ELisheva), had been without children well into their advanced years due to the barrenness of Elizabeth (ELisheva). Other matriarchs in YAH's family had experienced this same barrenness—Sarah, Rebekah and Rachel (Rahkal). They all went without children until it was in YAH's timing and for His purpose. Gabriel (GahbreeEL), the angel of proclamation, announced that YAH's purpose this time was for their son to be the voice of ELeeYAHoo to usher in the Messiah. This was foretold in both books of the Ne'vim, YishshaYAH and Mahlakhee. *"The voice of one crying in the wilderness: "Prepare the way of YAHveh; make straight in the desert a highway for our Elohim"* (**ISA 40:3**). *"Behold, I will send you ELeeYAHoo the ne'vee before the coming of the great and dreadful day of YAHveh. And he will turn the hearts of the fathers to the children, and the hearts of the children to their fathers, lest I come and strike the earth with a curse"* (**MAL 4:5&6**).

As was mentioned earlier, another proclamation was made by the angel Gabriel (GahbreeEL) to Mary (Miriam), that she too was to conceive a child, but not by her husband, Yosef. Instead, her son would be born of the Ruach of YAHveh, not having sinful human blood within His veins, but pure and Holy (Kedosh) blood that would one day be shed for the sins of mankind, making it possible for anyone who would believe this to inherit eternal life. Yosef was also notified by the angel Gabriel (GahbreeEL) that he was to be the guardian of the Son of ELohim. After Herod had called for a census of the YAHudi, Yosef and Mary (Miriam) left for Yosef's place of heritage, the town of Bethlehem (Beit-lechem—house of bread) to register for it, just prior to Mary's time to deliver the child. They had to leave the town that they lived in, Nazareth, which was a city in Galilee, just north of the hated territory of Samaria. This also was to fulfill the prophecy of the Ne'vee Micah (Meecah). *"But you, Bethlehem (Beit-lechem) Ephrathah, though you are little among the thousands of YAHuda, yet out of you shall come forth to Me the One to be the ruler in YisraEL, whose goings forth have been from of old, from Everlasting"* (**MICAH 5:2**).

The Circumcision and Dedication of Yeshua and His Cousin, Yochanan the Immerser, and Their Early Years

On the eighth day after Yochanan the Immerser was born, he was to be circumcised according to the Instructions of YAH in His Torah. *"Speak to the children of YisraEL, saying: 'If a woman has conceived, and borne a male child, then she shall be unclean seven days; as in the days of her customary impurity she shall be unclean. 'And on the eighth day the flesh of his foreskin shall be circumcised"* (**LEV 12:2&3**). It was thought that he would be named after his father (abba), Zacharias (TzahkarYAH), but Zacharias (TzahkarYAH) told them no, that his name was to be Yochanan. Yosef too was told not to give his own name to the child that Mary (Miriam) bore, but to name Him Yeshua (the Salvation of YAH), which they did at the time of his circumcision. They were told that He would also be called ImmanuEL, *God with us*, by all who would come to know Him.

The proclamation angel, Gabriel (GahbreeEL), along with a host of others, visited shepherds who were out taking care of their sheep in the early autumn night and instructed them to go to a cattle shed in the side of a hill near Bethlehem (Beit-lechem). There, they would see the Messiah who was born to a virgin, as was told by the Ne'vee Isaiah (YishshaYAH), who prophesied this very event. *"Therefore YAHveh Himself will give you a sign: Behold, the virgin shall conceive and bear a Son, and shall call His name ImmanuEL"* (**ISA 7:14**). This was done as a sign that He would be a Shepherd to His people of both the House of YAHuda and the House of Yosef. Again, according to the Torah, Mary (Miriam) was to wait thirty days and then go to the House of YAH and present herself and the child for the purpose of purification, cleansing, and dedication. She was to bring a sacrifice of two turtledoves with her. *"Sanctify to Me all the firstborn, whatever opens the womb among the children of YisraEL, both of men and animal; it is Mine"* (**EXOD 13:2**). *"She shall then continue in the blood of her purification thirty-three days. She shall not touch any hallowed thing, nor come into the sanctuary until the days of her purification are fulfilled...'When the days of her purification are fulfilled, whether for a son or a daughter, she shall bring to the priest a lamb of the first year as a burnt offering, and a young pigeon or a turtledove as a sin offering, to the door of the tabernacle of meeting...'And if she is not able to bring a lamb, then she may bring two turtledoves or two young pigeons—one as a burnt offering and the other as a sin offering. So the priest shall make atonement for her, and she will be clean'"* (**LEV 12:5&6, and 8**). In the case of a poor person, two turtledoves could be presented—one as a freewill offering, or burnt offering, as a thanksgiving for the child and the other for the spilling of blood, the sin offering.

Remember, the blood of innocent animals was to be shed for the atonement of unintentional sins and for purification of any type of uncleanness. A woman was considered to be unclean in her monthly cycle or after giving birth (raw blood causes bacteria to form). Intentional sin could only be atoned for by the shedding of the blood of the guilty party. Yeshua's blood was to become the price of atonement for the sins of all who were guilty of both intentional and unintentional sin. His blood had to be free of sin in order to be the substitute atonement; no person born of a sinful man could ever qualify to do this. A human father could never procreate the Messiah—only the sinless ELohim, by His Ruach, could accomplish this.

Upon entering the courtyard of YAH's House, a ne'vee by the name of Simeon greeted Yosef and Mary (Miriam) with a prophecy regarding Yeshua's life. He said that He would bring revelation to the Gentiles (Goyim) and be the glory of YAH's people, the House of YisraEL and the House of YAHuda, and then he spoke about the Messiah's death. Mary (Miriam) kept these things in her heart and later shared them with Luke (Lukas), the writer who presented Yeshua as the Son of Man. Immediately after this, a prophetess by the name of Anna, a daughter from the tribe of Asher, proclaimed to all who were there that day that Yeshua was the Messiah. These things came from the mouths of two witnesses in accordance with the Torah. After this, Luke (Lukas) said that they returned to Nazareth.

The Coming of the Magi

They must have stayed in Bethlehem (Beit-lechem) for at least two more years before they returned to Nazareth because this is where they were when the Magi from the eastern nation of Babylon found them. These wise men had followed the writings of Belteshazzar (the Ne'vee DahneeEL, as we know him) and found them living there. These men were well versed in both the philosophy and the theology of many of the religions in the surrounding regions and were masters of astronomy. They were led to come to Bethlehem (Beit-lechem) because of the signs that they had read in the heavens and because of Belteshazzar's prophecies. (In the book of **JOB 9:9**, Job points out the fact that it is YAHveh who has named the stars and the constellations, and in **GEN 1:14**, YAH says that He made the stars for signs—but nowhere does He mention that He made them for soothsaying or fortune telling.) In their search, they came into YAHrushalayim, where they inquired of Herod as to the whereabouts of the new King of the YAHudi. The chief priest and scribes informed Herod the Great that according to the Ne'vee Isaiah (YishshaYAH), He would be born in Bethlehem (Beit-lechem). They left and later found Him in the house of his parents, where they presented Him with gifts of gold, frankincense, and myrrh (notice that there were three gifts, *not* three kings). They brought gold because they acknowledged Him as the "King" of the YAHudi. They brought frankincense and myrrh because they acknowledged Him as the "ELuah" of the YAHudi (not as a sign of His embalming at His death, as is taught in some circles—frankincense and myrrh were burnt at YAH's altar of incense). They knew from Belteshazzar's teachings that this king was to be the "Son of ELuah", therefore He would be both King and ELuah. After they left, Herod, out of his jealousy and fear of another king, ordered all male children two years and younger to be slain—two years of age because of the length of time that the Magi said that they had been observing the star, which seemed to be leading them. This also happened in order to fulfill the prophecy that was given by Jeremiah (YirmehYAH). *"Thus says YAHveh: "A voice was heard in Ramah, lamentation and bitter weeping, Rachel (Rahkal) weeping for her children,* *refusing to be comforted for her children, because they are no more"* (JER 31:15). Rachel (Rahkal) was the mother of Yosef, who was the father of Efraeem. Efraeem was the grandson of Yaacov, who gave him the firstborn birthright to carry the name of YisraEL. Herod, being the vessel of hasatan, could not thwart YAH's plan of redemption that easily. All of Rachel's (Rahkal's) children, the House of YisraEL, would be saved one day and would return to the land that was promised to them. *"Thus say YAHveh: "Refrain your voice from weeping, and your eyes from tears, for your work shall be rewarded, says YAHveh, and they shall come back from the land of their enemy....There is hope in your future, says YAHveh, that your children shall come back to their own border"* (JER 31:16&17). Yosef and Mary (Miriam) are told by an angel to go to Mitsrahyim, where it would be safe (many of the House of YAHuda were still in Mitsrahyim, where they had fled from the Greek invasion). They probably went to Alexandria because it was only about seventy-five miles away. This was also prophesied by Hosea (Hoshea) in his writings. *"When YisraEL was a child I loved him, and out of Mitsrahyim I called My son* (HOS 11:1). After Herod's death, they returned to the city of Nazareth, where Yosef raised Yeshua in the trade of carpentry. It was the Hebrew custom, based upon their teachings from Avraham and the Torah, that children were to be raised by their mother in order to teach them love and tenderness until they were weaned at about the age of three. For the next ten years, they were to be raised mostly by their father (abba) in order to learn discipline, a trade, and to be trained up in the ways of YAH and His Torah. Then at the age of thirteen, the age of maturity, the Hebrews would have a celebration called a bar (son) and bat (daughter) mitzvoth (child of the commandments). It was at this time, just before Yeshua's thirteenth birthday and while they were in the city of YAHrushalayim for the Feast of Passover, that Yeshua became separated from his parents and was not discovered until several days later. During this time, He remained in the city at the House of YAH, amazing the Rabboni (teachers) with His understanding of the TaNaKh.

Because Hebrew families are so close in their relationships and since Yeshua and Yochanan were cousins, they probably spent time together as youngsters, even playing together. When they were teenagers, they may have had quiet conversations about their unique births and future callings. Their hunger for the Torah may have only been surpassed by their desire to have a deeper walk with YAH. If so, these desires and thoughts would have taken place within a solid family atmosphere that was charged with love and support. As they began to approach the age of thirty and knowing that they would soon begin to experience their foretold ministries, their excitement must have really grown with anticipation that their relationship with YAH, their ELohim, would bring new revelation to any of the unanswered questions that they may have had.

WHAT WE WEREN'T TAUGHT ABOUT THE BIBLE AND ITS HISTORY

Yochanan the Immerser and Yeshua the Messiah Begin Their Ministries

For the next seventeen years after their Bar-Mitzvah, both Yeshua and Yochanan were preparing their lives for their ministries. While Yeshua was learning to be a carpenter like His guardian-father Yosef, His cousin, Yochanan, may have been studying the art of Torah-copying with the Essenes, but he never finished because YAH called him to be the voice of ELeeYAHoo.

According to the Torah, a man cannot enter into a ministry before the age of thirty. *"From thirty years old and above, even to fifty years old, you shall number them, all who enter to perform the service, to do the work in the tabernacle (mishkahn) of meeting"* (**NUM 4:23**). So, at the age of thirty, Yochanan came out from the wilderness in his wardrobe of camel hair, wearing a leather belt, eating a diet of locusts and wild honey, and preaching that everyone should repent from their neglect of the teachings of the TaNaKh. They were to prepare their hearts for receiving its true meaning, which would come to them through the coming of the Promised Messiah and His Kingdom. Yochanan would have appeared on the scene in the early spring of that year. For six months (since he was six months older than Yeshua) he articulated this message to all who would come out to hear him. Then he immersed them as a sign of cleansing from their sin of neglect and of their anticipation of the manifestation of their hope of the Promise. He told them that his ministry consisted of only cleansing them with water as a sign of their repentance, but the Messiah, when He came, would immerse them in YAHveh's Ruach in order to provide them with the power to become sons of the living ELohim. While Yochanan was ministering, he either heard in his heart or he saw in a vision YAH's confirmation about a dove descending down and alighting on his cousin, Yeshua, when he came to be immersed. This sign was to confirm that He was truly the Promised Messiah. Yeshua came to the Yarden six months after Yochanan, in the early fall, while the weather was still warm, and *not* in the winter, when it would have been impossible to be immersed outdoors because of the temperature. This would have been soon after His thirtieth birthday. When Yeshua finally arrived, Yochanan heard the voice of ELuah confirming that this truly was the Son of the Most High, just as he had been told when he saw the vision. Then he proclaimed Yeshua as being the sacrificial Lamb of ELuah. When the Messiah came on the scene, Yochanan inquired of Adonai Yeshua, just as He entered the Yarden River, whether or not the role of who should be immersing whom should be reversed. Yeshua reminded him that their ministries had been established by His Father (Abba) since the beginning of time, that this would serve as righteous obedience, and that this would also fulfill the prophecy regarding Him.

I want to reemphasis an important point that confirms my understanding that Yeshua's birthday is not in the winter near Dec. 25th. The Scriptures are clear that He was thirty years old when He began His ministry. They are clear about the difference in the ages between His cousin, Yochanan, and Himself. Logic tells us that when Yeshua appeared for His ordination, Yochanan would not have been immersing anyone if it were winter in YisraEL.

Yeshua Must Come Face to Face With His Father's (Abba's) Enemy, the Prince of Darkness

As soon as Yochanan saw and heard the confirmation that this was indeed the Promised Messiah, Yeshua was immediately led up by YAH's Ruach into the mountains of the wilderness to meet YAHveh's adversary, hasatan. The necessity for the anointing of the Ruach was because Yeshua, before that time, was like any other ordinary man, and to do the work of YAH, it first takes the anointing of the Ruach to bring about the power that is necessary to break the yoke of the curse of the Torah. Yeshua was alone with only His thoughts, faith, and the mandate from His Abba, to go into the mountains and wait. Trusting His Abba to sustain Him, He had nothing to eat or drink for forty days. Under normal circumstances, a human can live without food for about thirty days, but only three days without water. Don't ever try to do either of these unless you are convinced that you were told to do so by the Abba. After the forty days of fasting and testing (remember that forty is the number for testing), the first thing the adversary did was challenge Yeshua's authority, suggesting that He was not the Son of ELuah, and if He were, prove it by performing a miracle of changing stones into bread to end His hunger. But Yeshua answered him with a commandment from the fifth book of the Torah: *"So He humbled you, allowed you to hunger, and fed you with manna which you did not know nor did your fathers know, that He might make you know that man shall not live by bread alone; but man lives by every word that proceeds from the mouth of YAHveh"* (**DUET 8:3**). Then the adversary challenged Him again by taking Him to the highest point on the wall of the House of YAH and telling Him to prove His Deity by jumping without experiencing any harm—he even quoted from the Kethuvim in the Psalms (Tehillim): *"For He shall give His angels charge over you, to keep you in all your ways....They shall bear you up in their hands, lest you dash your foot against a stone"* (**PSALM 91:11&12**). Then Yeshua answered him again from the fifth book of the Torah: *"You shall not tempt YAHveh ELohim as you tempted Him in Massah"* (**DEUT 6:16**). The adversary was not yet finished with this second Ahdom—he took Him to a high mountain that gave a panoramic view of the surrounding land and told Him that all of it could be His if He would just give His allegiance to him, hasatan. Once more, Yeshua answered him from the fifth book of the Torah: *"You shall fear YAHveh your ELohim and serve Him, and shall take oaths in His (HeShem) Name"* (**DEUT 6:13**).

The testing finally came to an end after the forty days, which would mean that the trial ended between the middle of fall and the end of it. It would have been near the time for the Feast of Dedication (Chanukah). It says in Luke (Lukas) that the enemy departed from Him until another opportune time—the adversary wasn't going to give up that easily. Notice that Yeshua stopped hasatan with the Word of YAHveh. He knew His Abba's words, and He knew that He could use them to defeat the enemy who cleverly tried to use YAH's words to trip Him up. If you are a Believer and you are tempted by the adversary, you must know the Abba's Word, both His written and His Living Word, Yeshua—otherwise you'll lose. The Prince of Darkness knows Abba's words better than any of us, and he will try to use them against us in order to test our knowledge and faith. You must know all of the first thirty-nine books of the sixty-six—not just the last twenty-seven—and you must really know the first five, the Torah, in order to understand the heart of our Abba.

Yeshua Chooses His First Disciples (Talmidim) and Goes to His Hometown in Galilee

After Yeshua's victory in His first trial, He returned once more to where Yochanan the Immerser was still preaching his message to the hungry multitudes. When Yochanan saw Him approaching, he once more made the proclamation regarding His Deity. Andrew and Simon, two of Yochanan's disciples (talmidim), changed their allegiance and decided to accompany Yeshua in His travels instead. Yeshua saw something in Simon that caused Him to later rename him Peter (Kefa, the rock or pebble). Soon after, they came upon Phillip, and Yeshua invited him to follow them. Phillip in turn invited Nathanael to also go with them. The four traveled back to Yeshua's hometown, Nazareth in Galilee, where they were invited to a wedding of a friend of Yeshua's mother, Mary (Miriam), in the town of Cana (today it is known as Qana and is in Lebanon). Apparently, Yeshua's guardian-abba, Yosef, has left the scene of His life; he may have passed on to the next life sometime during the seventeen years of Yeshua's maturing because he is never mentioned again in all of Scripture. The wedding was so successful that somewhere in the middle of it they ran out of wine, and Yeshua's mother asked Him to intervene and solve the dilemma. Yeshua, of course, knew that His mother was aware of His calling, but wondered exactly what she wanted Him to do. He questioned her motive and assured her that now was not His time to reveal His Messiahship. She understood and told the servants to follow whatever instructions He would give them, but to do it quietly. Now Yeshua knew why He was there—it was all part of His Abba's plan to demonstrate His creative powers to His first four disciples (talmidim) because it was going to take a number of demonstrations to prepare them for their final commission. He told the servants to fill six empty water containers that were normally used for the purification ceremonies—they held between twenty and thirty gallons of water. He then told them to take the wine decanters, draw out some of the water, and present them to the master of ceremonies. When they did, it became wine of the highest quality.

Another purpose for this demonstration was to reemphasize the importance of YAHveh's first marriage proposal to YisraEL in the desert at Mt. Sinai (Seenahee). In the Hebrew tradition, the bride was offered a cup of wine in the bridegroom's proposal; if she accepted, the proposal was established. A second and final proposal would be a renewal of YisraEL's vows on its anniversary (Shavuot) three and one-half years later. The first had been sealed with the giving of His ordinance of keeping the Sabbath (see Chapter Three—Honoring YAH by Celebrating the Sabbath—and **DEUT 5:12-15**), and the second would be sealed by the washing of the *water* of His Word (the TaNaKh) and His *blood*.

Yeshua Attends His First Passover Celebration after Entering His Ministry

The wedding at Cana probably took place during the first Hebrew month of Aviv, in the first spring after His ceremonial cleansing (mikvah/baptism) and His trial in the wilderness. The reason I say this is because it is only mentioned in Yochanan's writings, where he says, *"On the third day there was a wedding"*, and he speaks of Passover as being at hand, immediately after the wedding incident. At any rate, when Yeshua entered the courtyard of His Abba's House after arriving in YAHrushalayim with His four disciples (talmidim), He saw sheep, goats, and doves being sold for sacrificial purposes and money being exchanged for them. He became outraged and began overturning tables, opening stalls and cages, releasing the animals and birds. He even began beating those who were buying and selling these items with a whip made from cords that He had found in the courtyard. When the priests and Levee heard what was going on, they came to investigate as to who this madman was and why He was doing this unthinkable act. When they asked Him, He answered them with a riddle—*"Destroy this house and in three days I will raise it up"*. They decided that He must be mad to be saying something as incredulous as this. But Dahveed had foreseen this in his heart and had prophesied, *"I have become a stranger to my brothers, and an alien to my mother's children; because zeal for Your House has eaten me up, and the reproaches of those who reproach You have fallen on Me"* (**PSALM 69:8&9**). But here again, it wasn't for their sake that He said this—it was more training for His disciples (talmidim) because they would need to remember both the writings that He taught them from the Kethuvim and what He had said about His raising up this House if it were destroyed (meaning His body after His death and resurrection).

WHAT WE WEREN'T TAUGHT ABOUT THE BIBLE AND ITS HISTORY

This incident and others not recorded at that time, along with His clear teachings of the TaNaKh, caused many to begin to believe that He was the Promised Messiah. Even a man by the name of Nicodemus, a priest, spiritual teacher, and ruler of the YAHudi, came to inquire about His masterful ability to understand the TaNaKh and also His ability to make it seem so clear on one hand and yet so mysterious on the other. Nicodemus may have also been at YAH's House when a young boy by this same name, Yeshua, was able to articulate the TaNaKh so well, eighteen years earlier. Yeshua asked him why it was so difficult for him to understand that no one can perceive spiritual things as long as they have only a carnal view of life as their perspective. A person must be born-again of the Ruach in order to understand spiritual principles. Nicodemus still didn't get it—he thought Yeshua was talking about reincarnation or something similar. Yeshua continued to expound on this kingdom principle by explaining that a person must first exercise his own faith in YAH's instructions in the Torah and then submit to the exercise of ceremonial cleansing (mikvah/baptism). If they believed in their heart and confessed with their mouth all that the TaNaKh had to say about the Messiah and His ministry of restoration and that He would also provide for them eternal life through the resurrection, they would then be born afresh. He reminded him of how Mosheh had lifted up the bronze serpent in the wilderness and told the people that if they would just merely look upon it, they would be healed. He said the result would be the same if YAH's people would merely look to Yeshua as the Messiah—eternal healing would take place, including the forgiveness of their sins. Next, they should tell others what had happened to them. If they follow these simple instructions, they too, regardless of their former heritage, would become citizens of the House of YisraEL. By doing this simple act of faith, they would no longer be merely flesh that was born with a destiny laden with sin—instead, they would be like Yeshua, spiritually born of the Ruach of YAHveh.

Those of you who may be reading this book and have never experienced this phenomenon might ask, "How can a person be sure if they are born-again?" I discussed this idea of the "new birth" earlier in the introduction of my book; if you don't recall what I said, then stop and go back now. YAHveh says that He will confirm His words with signs and wonders. The sign and wonder that follows the new birth will manifest itself in you, and you will begin to have a deeper desire to know more about your Abba and His Son, Yeshua. His Scriptures will take on a new appeal. The things you used to like to do that involved self indulgence will lose their intrigue—not all at once, but little by little. Being with other believers will become more and more important to you. You will begin to follow your new desires and, at the same time, let your old ones fade away. Your biggest enemy will be the discouragement that you will receive from those who won't understand what has happened to you—that's why it will be necessary for you to find a fellowship of like believers.

Yeshua Returns to Galilee and Calls Two More Disciples (Talmidim)

While in YAHrushalayim and the territory of YAHuda, Yeshua and His disciples (talmidim) continued sharing the good news of His coming and that He *was* the promised Messiah who was identified in the TaNaKh. They immersed (as described in the Torah for sanctification and cleansing) those who believed their words, for the remission of their sins and for their new life in Yeshua as their Messiah. In the meantime, Yochanan the Immerser acknowledged to his own disciples (talmidim) the necessity for his own short-lived ministry to diminish and end.

Yeshua follows His Abba's direction and proceeds to return to His own territory in Galilee. In their return, they pass through the desecrated territory of Samaria. Yeshua and His four disciples (talmidim) came upon their ancestor Yaacov's well in the land given to his son, Yosef. Yeshua sat down at the well while His disciples (talmidim) went into the nearby city of Sychar to purchase some food. This is where an unsavory Samaritan woman approached Yeshua and began to talk with Him. He told her all about herself and revealed to her that He was the Messiah who was promised in the TaNaKh. She believed without questioning and ran back to the city to tell everyone that the Promised Messiah had just spoken with her. In their astonishment, they all ran out to see for themselves. He introduced her and the citizens of Sychar to the meaning of the living water that was spoken of by the Ne'vim. He also told them that the YAHudi, their rival, would be the ones through whom salvation must come because they were to be the tribe who gave both the Living and the written Torah to all who would receive them.

While she was telling everyone she met about Him, His disciples (talmidim) returned with the food that they had purchased. When they asked Him to eat, He told them that He already had His portion. He was referring to the fact that He had just completed doing His Abba's work of adding more children to the kingdom. The town's people came out to them and requested that they stay a few more days, which they did. Afterwards, many of the Samaritans acknowledged that this truly was the Promised One, the Messiah. It was at this time that Yeshua pointed out to His disciples (talmidim) how the ne'veem are rarely received by their own, but how quickly the hated Samaritans had accepted the good news of His coming. After the two days at Sychar, they returned to Galilee to the city of Capernaum. It was here that Yeshua preformed His second miracle, that of healing a man's son who was dying, with just the words *"your son is healed"*. He stayed at Capernaum for awhile before going to His boyhood town of Nazareth. There, He went into one of the synagogues and as was customary, read from one of the scrolls from the Ne'vee Isaiah (YishshaYAH). *"The Ruach of Adonai YAHveh is upon Me, Because Adonai has anointed Me to preach good tidings to the poor; He has sent Me to heal the brokenhearted, to proclaim liberty to the captives, and the opening of the prison to those who are bound; to proclaim the acceptable year of YAHveh"* (ISA 61:1&2). When He stopped, He told all who were there that the prophecy that He had just read and that they had just heard was being fulfilled that very day in their presence. He proceeded to tell them that only a few would receive His words because of His hometown status. When a hometown boy steps out and begins to share what YAH has done for him, unless he can back it up with the proper "ordination" papers, he is mostly ignored and even ridiculed. I know from experience that family and friends are not always your best advocates. This seemed to be the case here. Yeshua's friends and neighbors became filled with the rage of hasatan and tried to take Him up to a high place with the desire to throw Him off. But Yeshua disappeared from their sight and merely walked away. No one could take His life—He was ordained to give it when His Abba deemed it so.

From there, He went back to Capernaum and once more began to preach from the book of the Ne'vee Isaiah (YishshaYAH). *"Nevertheless the gloom will not be upon her who is distressed, as when at first He lightly esteemed the land of Zebulon and the land of Naphtali, and afterward more heavily opposed her, by the way of the sea, beyond the Yarden, in Galilee of the Gentiles* (Goyim). *The people who walked in darkness have seen a great light; those who dwelt in the land of the shadow of death, upon them a light has shined"* (ISA 9:1&2). While Yeshua was teaching these things and more people were listening, learning, and believing, He came upon the fishing boats of His two disciples (talmidim), Peter (Kefa) and his brother, Andrew. They had been fishing all day on the Sea of Galilee and hadn't caught a thing. He got into Peter's (Kefa's) boat and told them to try one more time. When they did, they caught more than they could haul in, and once more, they were shocked as to whom this truly must be. He assured them that He was going to make them fishers of men (remember, the lost tribes of the north were many times referred to as fish in the TaNaKh). It was at this time that two more brothers, James (Jacob/Yaacov) and John (Yochanan—the one who wrote about the Messiah as the Son of YAH), after seeing this great miracle, also decided to join Him as disciples (talmidim). This increased His private following to six. On the next Sabbath, they went into a synagogue in Capernaum, and there, He delivered a man from demon possession. Then He went to Peter's (Kefa's) house, where He healed his mother-in-law of a fever. After that, He began to openly go from town to town in Galilee and into their synagogues, teaching the Torah and healing every kind of disease, including paralysis and leprosy. He even told others that their sins were forgiven, which is something that no one else was ever able to claim. His following grew as the people came from Galilee, Decapolis, YAHrushalayim, and from all the area of YAHuda to see these wonderful things.

Yeshua Chooses Six More Disciples (Talmidim) and Calls Them All to be Apostles (Shelichim)

While ministering healing to a paralytic man on a Sabbath, Yeshua told him that it was his sins that were the cause of his condition but that they were now forgiven. When the local rabbis heard of this, they accused Him of blasphemy. From the beginning, the religious community was His biggest opposition. Yeshua called His seventh disciple (talmidim), a man from the tribe of Lehvee named Matthew (MattatiYAH), who had gained much wealth and esteem from his vocation as a tax collector. Matthew (MattatiYAH), out of his joy of being called, immediately gathered some of his friends and fellow tax collectors and threw a great banquet in Yeshua's honor. It didn't take long, however, for the rabbis and the Pharisees to accuse Yeshua and His followers of socializing with sinners and not conducting themselves properly as teachers of the TaNaKh. His answer to their accusations came from one of the scrolls of the Ne'vim—*"For I desire mercy and not sacrifice, and the knowledge of ELohim more than burnt offerings"* (HOS 6:6). The animosity toward Him continued to grow within the religious community. After a year and a half into His ministry and while still in the region of Galilee, He learned that His cousin, Yochanan the Immerser, had been thrown into prison for daring to rebuke Herod Antipas, King Herod's son, for usurping his authority and unlawfully marrying one of his brother's wives.

The season for the second Passover is near, and we find Yeshua and His followers going up to YAHrushalayim for the celebration. The controversy regarding His teachings and the miracles that He had performed on several Sabbaths was now preceding Him. The first occasion for Him to test the hypocrisy of the religious leaders came on a Sabbath when He entered the city of YAHrushalayim and went to the pool of Bethesda, near the Sheep Gate of His Abba's House. His Abba had been performing miracles at certain times near Passover when the sick would find enough faith to enter the pool to be immersed (mikvah) in order to be healed. There was a man there that had for thirty-eight years used the excuse that no one would help him into the pool in order for him to receive his healing. Yeshua challenged his faith by asking him, *"Do you want to be made well?"* Instead of answering yes, he began using his same old excuses that were based upon human reasoning. Yeshua didn't want to hear his excuses, so He put it to him bluntly, *"Rise, take up your bed and walk."* Now, at the words of Yeshua, His faith kicked in, he tried, and lo and behold, he was walking. Afterwards, some fellow YAHudi saw him carrying his mat on the Sabbath and rebuked him for breaking the Torah. He told them about his healing and that the one who told him to rise and walk also told him to take up his mat. Later, when Yeshua saw him again in His Abba's House, He told him never to use a disability again to gain sympathy and live off of others. The man then began to tell his fellow YAHudi that it was this Man, Yeshua, who did this for him. When the YAHudi found out that it was Yeshua, they began to question His authority in having done this. He told them that both He and His Abba worked continuously to bring about everything that had been prophesied concerning the last days, when the Messiah would establish His Kingdom upon the Earth. He told them about the power that His Abba had given Him to raise the dead and the authority to judge and forgive sins. He told them that the TaNaKh had testified of His coming, but they had ignored its witness and the witness of Yochanan the Immerser. He testified that both His words and His working of miracles were also His witnesses. His words enraged them even more because He now had put Himself on the same plane of deity as YAHveh by referring to Him as His Abba.

Other similar incidents happened that enraged them, but what enraged them the most was His ministry of healing on the Sabbath. He told them that it was right to do good on every day, especially the Sabbath, and that the Sabbath was made for man and not the other way around. Yeshua then retreated back to the Sea of Galilee, where His message was more readily received and appreciated by the more common folk. It was not Yeshua's intention to bring attention to Himself, as was happening in YAHuda, but to bring everyone's attention to His Abba and His words in the TaNaKh. *"Behold! My Servant whom I uphold, My Elect One in whom My soul delights! I have put My Ruach upon Him; He will bring forth justice to the Gentiles (Goyim)....He will not cry out, nor raise His voice, nor cause His voice to be heard in the street. A bruised reed He will not break, and smoking flax He will not quench; He will bring forth justice for truth....He will not fail nor be discouraged, till He has established justice in the earth; and the coastlands shall wait for His Torah"* (**ISA 42:1-4**).

Much of Yeshua's ministry was setting people free from guilt and demon possession—many of the diseases and sicknesses were the result of these curses. As He went about teaching and confirming His Abba's words with signs and wonders, He gained more and more followers. He also added five more disciples (talmidim) to His group: Thomas—James (Jacob/Yaacov), son of (ben) Alphaeus—Simon from the sect of the Zealots—Judas, son of James (YAHuda ben Yaacov)—and Judas (YAHuda) Iscariot. This brought the total to twelve—a number that represented the twelve tribes of YisraEL because they were the ones to whom He was sent in order to restore YAH's Kingdom. Later, He would assign them to the position of apostles (shelichim).

In Yeshua's first year of ministry, He only had four confidant disciples (talmidim): Kefa—Kefa's brother, Andrew—Phillip—and Phillip's brother,

Nathanael/Bartholomew. By the end of His second year, He had added three more: James (Yaacov)—James' (Yaacov's) brother, Yochanan—and Matthew (MattatiYAH). So, His last five disciples (talmidim) were only with Him during the last year and a half of His ministry. Five more became notable apostles (shelichim) after His death and resurrection: Luke (Lukas)—Mark (Markus)—Paul (Shaul)—James (Yaacov) and Jude (YAHuda), Yeshua's brothers. Luke (Lukas) wrote two separate writings regarding the events that surrounded the Messiah's life and what happened to His disciples (talmidim) thereafter. His revelation and inspiration seems to have come after he began gathering facts that pertained to the Messiah's life from Yeshua's mother, Mary (Miriam). Mark (Markus) became a follower soon after Yeshua's arrest and then later became a disciple (talmidim) of Kefa. It seems that his account of Yeshua's life came from what Kefa had shared with him. Mark (Markus) and Luke (Lukas) came into a close relationship with the Apostle (Shelich) Paul (Shaul) while ministering with him.

Yeshua's Ministry Intensifies as He Teaches and Focuses on Kingdom Principles
Taught Through Parables

After Yeshua had gathered to Himself those who were to become his apostles (shelichim), He began teaching the true kingdom principles of the Torah to larger and larger crowds of people. At times, He would set them on one hillside and then preach to them from the opposite one, creating a natural amphitheater. A number of these teachings became known as the "Sermon on the Mount". The most popular of these were His "Baruch" (Blessed are/ Happy are) teachings. They consisted of nine teachings that contained words of encouragement to those who were truly interested in seeking righteousness. He taught them that those who desired and hungered after spiritual knowledge more than earthly possessions could achieve their goal if they would persevere in spite of any opposition. He told them that they were the equivalent of salt and light and that their perseverance would keep the wrath and judgment of their Abba from coming upon the Earth too soon, thereby preserving it. He told them that if it were possible, Heaven and Earth would have to pass away first before one of their Abba's commandments or even the smallest mark or stroke in His Torah would fail. He strongly denied that His purpose was to change anything that was written in the TaNaKh, but instead, He came to see that all of the curses were annulled and only the blessings of the Torah remained for all of those who dared to believe in Him. He reminded them that He came only to redeem, sanctify, and restore the Whole House of YisraEL. He explained the meaning of the sixth commandment, *"You shall not murder"* (**EXOD 20:13**). In Abba's eyes, murder is more than taking the life of another—it has more to do with the attitude of the heart. All of us have been guilty of murder, according to Abba's standard, and that is why if we claim to be without sin, we are liars and there is no truth in us. He goes on to point out that if we have only a *thought* of sexual desire for someone outside of marriage, we are guilty of adultery and are breaking the seventh commandment, *"You shall not commit adultery"* (**EXOD 20:14**). Here too, Yeshua was able to point out that there is no one without sin and that all are in need of salvation through redemption and a Savior. He tells us that our Abba hates divorce. *"When a man takes a wife and marries her, and it happens that she finds no favor in his eyes because he has found some **uncleanness** in her, and he writes her a certificate of divorce, puts it in her hand, and sends her out of his house"* (**DEUT 24:1**). There is no excuse for it, except for *marital infidelity*; everything else can be worked out if the couple would only try. He goes on to say that we must strive for honesty in our hearts and that any oath that we take need not be guaranteed by requiring ELuah to be our witness. Let your yes be yes and your no, no—anything else comes from the evil one.

He clears up the requirement for retribution about an eye for an eye. This commandment was only meant as a judicial sentence in a civil suit before a court—not between individuals. Our hearts need to be compassionate and forgiving toward others, and we need to approach confrontations with mercy and humility—not vengeance and anger. That doesn't mean we are to forgive unconditionally because forgiveness that is given without repentance first makes mercy cheap. We should be motivated to love unconditionally without expecting something in return. Our spiritual lifestyle regarding our giving, praying, and fasting should be done in all humility and kept private; but regarding our witnessing of Abba's mercy and grace that He has shown toward us, they should be boasted about, praised openly, and shouted from the housetops.

Yeshua taught that our Abba wants us to have money and riches but that they should not be allowed to have us. He says if we allow this, then the things of this world will become "idols" and "elohim" to us. Our goal in this life should be to be generous with the things our Abba has given us—this will be storing up treasures in His Kingdom. He says that our eye should be full of light—that's a Hebrew cliché which means we should have a generous, good heart and not a greedy, evil one.

He teaches that our primary goal in life is to seek our Abba's Kingdom and to understand its principles, and if we do, He will see to all our material needs. Anxiety will destroy our bodies, but faith in our Abba and His Son will give us life, health, and strength.

He says that judging is a very serious exercise, so when we judge, it must be done in a very loving and merciful way. Showing compassion and being merciful in judging will reap our Abba's compassion and mercy toward us.

That is what "pressed down, shaken together, and running over" means—it is not money that we will receive—it's His mercy and grace. That particular scripture is misused so often by preachers or others who want to justify asking for donations to keep their pet projects going, while trying to bring conviction upon those from whom they are soliciting—all in the Name of the Lord.

We are counseled by Yeshua to use wisdom when sharing what our Abba has done for us. We are to use the gift of discernment and share these things only with those whose hearts are ready and open, otherwise our witness may be used to mock our faith and cause others to doubt. We must be prepared for our witnessing not to be as effective as we might desire because only a few may receive it with joy—there may not be as many who will enter into the kingdom as we might have hoped for. But for those who do receive our witness, He assures us that they will also receive the gifts of the Ruach if they only ask their heavenly Abba expecting to receive them—He will grant anything that is asked for out of a heart of humility and selflessness.

Yeshua warns us not to be naïve—just because an individual claims to be a follower of Him doesn't make it so. He tells us again to use the gift of discernment and to test those who claim to be His shepherds to see if their temperament and lifestyle (their fruits) measure up to their confession. He says that many, both leaders and laymen, will come to Him at His Mercy Seat of Judgment and claim to be His, but He will send them away because they denied His teachings and commandments regarding the TaNaKh. He says that those who are truly His disciples (talmidim) will be those who hear His words, understand them, and then put them into practice. He compared them with someone building a house—He is its cornerstone, and the TaNaKh, along with the teachings of His Apostles (Shelichim) regarding the TaNaKh, are its foundation. If anyone builds his life and his family (his house) upon this foundation, it will not fall when the storms of this life or the adversary try to destroy it.

Many times, when Yeshua would return to Capernaum after spending a day on the hillsides teaching, He would be met by someone seeking a miracle. On one occasion, some YAHudi elders sought Him out on behalf of an "ELohim-fearing Goyim" (as they referred to them). This non-YAHudi was a centurion of Herod's army whose servant had become seriously ill. Having the love of YAH in his heart and concern for his servant's well-being, He sent for Yeshua to come and heal him. But before Yeshua could get there, he sent out other servants to stop Him and ask that He just give the command for healing instead—he knew that his servant would be healed because he understood the principles of authority. Yeshua held this Gentile (Goy) up as an example of true faith in His Abba's authority. Yeshua knew that in the future there would be many more Gentiles (Goyim) from all walks of life and from every nation that would do the same, while many of the citizens of YAHuda would deny Him. Another time, as Yeshua was passing through a town called Nain, an only son of a widow had died and was being carried out to be buried. Moved with compassion, Yeshua spoke just a word and the young man was raised from the dead.

Yochanan the Immerser sensed that his time on Earth was drawing to a close and he wanted to be reassured that Yeshua was the true Messiah, so he sent two of his disciples (talmidim) to question Him one more time. Yeshua sent them back to Yochanan to report all that He had been doing since Yochanan had been thrown into prison. He then turned to the crowd that had come to hear Him teach and reminded them about the prophecies in the TaNaKh concerning both He and Yochanan. *"Behold, I send My messenger, and he will prepare the way before Me. And Adonai, whom you seek, will suddenly come to His House, even the Messenger of the covenant, in whom you delight; Behold, He is coming says YAHveh of host"* (**MAL 3:1**). He told them that both the Torah and the Ne'vim had spoken of their coming and that Yochanan the Immerser truly had the spirit of Elijah (ELeeYAHoo). He pointed out the double-mindedness of those who opposed Yochanan's message, saying that he had a demon because of his sobriety and unusual diet but, at the same time, saying that He, Yeshua, was a drunkard for eating and drinking with the common people. When people presented the mighty miracles that Yeshua was doing for those who were poor and afflicted as proof that He must be the Messiah, the religious leaders accused Him of doing the works of the eluah, Beelzebub/hasatan, the ruler of demons. But Yeshua reminded them that if that were true, hasatan would be working against himself because YAHveh was being given the credit for all of these works and miracles; He reminded them that a house divided against itself will not stand. This kingdom principle holds true even with the divided houses of YAHuda and Yosef. When these two houses are once more reunited with Yeshua as its king, then and only then will the Earth have its promised peace (shalom). The religious leaders asked Him for more evidence that He was who He said He was, but Yeshua told them that the only sign that they would see would be the sign of Jonah (Yonah), referring to the time that He would be in the grave (three days and three nights). He warned them to watch their words because their accusation and condemnation were putting them in danger of crossing the line and blaspheming the Ruach for which there is no redemption.

During Yeshua's ministering, women who had become followers proved to be his most loyal and supportive advocates. Many times, He had come to their defense because He knew that they had been forced to do things against their will by the oppressive men in their lives. This was due to the overall attitude that had been acquired by men toward women over the centuries. Being the Son of YAH, He knew that women were more sensitive to the working of YAH's Ruach than men. On one occasion, a prostitute, who recognized Yeshua's pure compassion, followed Him into the house of a local Pharisee and began to weep and wash His feet with her tears, anointing them with expensive oil and then wiping His feet with her hair. When the Pharisee saw this, he was convinced that Yeshua couldn't be who He said He was because He would have known what kind of a woman she was. What I want to know is why was she allowed in this Pharisee's house in the first place if he knew what kind of a woman she was—hmm? Maybe Yeshua wondered this too when He rebuked him for being so inhospitable to her, especially since she had shown plenty of remorse and repentance. So, He forgave her for her sins. Here again, the religious leaders became infuriated over His audacity in thinking that He could forgive sins.

These accusations prompted Yeshua to begin teaching about the workings of demons and the chief demon, hasatan. He tells them how dangerous it is for someone to have tasted of the good things of His Abba, YAHveh, and then to turn away from His instructions in the Torah. He used the example of a demon being cast out of a man and it returning with seven more demons more evil than it had been. It was able to reenter the man, bringing its friends, because after being delivered from the lies that had been taught to him originally, which brought on his being possessed in the first place, he had failed to refill himself with the proper Torah teachings.

Another time while Yeshua was teaching, someone told Him that His mother and His brothers were outside and wanted to speak to Him. He answered them by saying that anyone hungry for the things of His heavenly Abba was His true family. He said this because He felt it was a perfect time to give them an example of the importance of being a member of YAH's family. Still another time, a Pharisee invited Him to dinner, hoping once more to entrap Him in His words or in His customs. When Yeshua didn't participate in their religious hand-washing ceremony (this particular ceremony was very pompous and precise), He was asked why. Yeshua first complimented the Pharisees on their tithing practices regarding the ordinances of the House of YAH (practiced as long as the House of YAH stood), but then He rebuked them for their overlooking the more important things, such as compassion, which should be practiced all the time. He continued to chastise the rabbis, who were also there, for their adding to the Torah with customs that were impossible to keep, thereby putting people into bondage with man-made rules.

He then began to teach the crowds that followed Him about the false teachings regarding the Torah that their religious leaders had put upon them. He reminded them that His teachings clarified the true meaning of the Torah and the TaNaKh and was a much easier yoke to bear. He reminded them not to fear men and their rules and regulations but to fear YAHveh—for men can only bring death to the body, but YAHveh can bring death even to the soul. He reminds them that someday all of the mysteries of YAH will be revealed to all of those who are faithful. He reminds them that YAH is aware of everything, even the lives of sparrows and the number of hairs on an individual's head (the DNA number of every person created). He tells them never to concern themselves about the words of their testimony because as long as they are committed to following YAHveh, His Ruach will give them the words necessary, when the time comes.

Yeshua spoke a parable to the crowds about a rich young ruler who had become so preoccupied with life, its abundance, and his desire for immediate satisfaction that he neglected to prepare for his position in eternity. He suddenly found himself facing the very thing that he had neglected—the end of his days. Now everything temporal that he had sought after had become someone else's who hadn't earned it, and he realized his foolishness too late. Yeshua was warning everyone to take inventory of their lives and not to squander it on things that will not last. Yeshua turned to His disciples (talmidim) and pointed out that life consists of more than just the seventy or so years that are spent here on this Earth, and there is no guarantee that you will even have that much time. No, life is forever, and where you spend it is determined by the decisions that you make during those few short years on this Earth. He reminds them that YAHveh, their ELohim, is the one who rewards those who seek Him and that He will meet their every need but not necessarily their wants. Having the desire to always possess things will only produce anxiety, which will in turn only bring disappointment and sometimes even death. Seeking YAHveh will always produce joy, love, comfort, and assurance when it is done diligently because He promises that He will be found. He continues to exhort them to always remain faithful once they have found YAHveh because they'll never know when He will come to test their faithfulness. If He finds them remaining in their faithfulness, they will be rewarded, but if He finds them returning to their old ways, they will be chastised. He then reminds them that those who have experienced many of His blessings by following His instructions and performing them will also be expected to continue in them without failing, more so than those who have not.

He also tells them that He understands His teachings will bring controversy and that they will divide families, including His own. He says the truth is always divisive because people, out of their pride, would rather follow traditions than the truth. He tells them that His teachings will even bring about His being immersed into a time of great suffering. It was for this reason that He came; He has to suffer in order to accomplish what His Abba sent Him to do. He admits that afterwards His teachings will set the world on fire with the controversy that they will cause.

He is amazed that what He has taught seems so new to them. He reminds them that all of these things were spoken of Him by the Ne'vim. He continues by reminding them that because they were unable to discern the times, there would be a consequence. They needed to learn to judge both the times and themselves. He tells them that if they judge themselves truthfully, they will repent of their willful ignorance. He says that He judges them for their judging others about their neglect but not themselves.

He gives them a parable about a fig tree that didn't bear fruit. It was given one more chance to produce by being fed properly, but if it still didn't produce, then it was to be cut down and burned. He taught all of these things so that they might see for themselves who they really were and would begin seeking His Abba's truth and eternal life.

During a Sabbath gathering, He finds Himself in another situation where He needs to extend His Abba's mercy by healing a woman who hasatan had bound with a stooped back for eighteen years. Of course, when He does, He is immediately challenged by the religious leaders who find themselves threatened by His teachings and works. Again, He has to rebuke and embarrass them for their lack of knowledge and compassion.

After this, Yeshua intensifies His teachings with parables that contain the hidden treasures that His Abba wants to reveal to His special chosen twelve. One of His parables is about a farmer sowing seed and how it applies to those who are exposed to His Abba's words. Some fell on the road and were quickly eaten by birds—this is when His words get snatched away because they are not understood by the hearers. Others fell on stony places and quickly sprang up, but just as quickly died because they had no root—this is when His words are joyfully received, but because life is hard, His words quickly lose their meaning and die in their heart. Others fell in places that contained weeds and thorns and lived for a short while and then withered—this is when His words are received and put to use, but the temptation of the world comes and they who heard them make poor choices and return to their old ways. But there are some that do find their way into good soil and grow and multiply themselves—this is when His words find their way into those who have faithful hearts and reproduce themselves by sharing with others the joy and the good treasures that they have found.

Yeshua's disciples (talmidim) question Him as to why He chooses to teach in this manner and not plainly. His answer comes from the TaNaKh. *"And He said, "Go, and tell this people: 'Keep on hearing, but do not understand; keep on seeing, but do not perceive.' "Make the heart of this people dull, and their ears heavy, and shut their eyes; lest they see with their eyes, and hear with their ears, and understand with their heart, and return and be healed"* (**ISA 6:9&10**). By teaching in this manner, even though this was the way that every rabbi taught, YAH was going to hide the true meaning from those who had not prepared their own hearts by humbling themselves and repenting. But these things would be revealed to those who have a true desire to seek Him. It's just like those around us who love the things of this world. They may own a Bible, but it is only for show—they have no desire to research its contents. Those of this world will never even crack it open because of its title. Only those who have a supernatural curiosity will begin to read it and ask questions.

Yeshua lays out another parable about wheat and weeds. After another farmer sows seeds of wheat in his field, he discovers after a period of time that someone else had thrown weed seeds in there too, trying to destroy his crop. When his servants desired to pull up the weeds, the wise farmer tells them not to because the wheat will be uprooted also. He lets them grow together until the wheat is mature and strong, then he separates them and burns the weeds. The farmer is Yeshua, the field is the world, the seeds are the sons of the kingdom, the weeds are the sons of hasatan, and the harvesters are the angels. When the day of accountability comes, the angels will gather up all those who do not practice the kingdom principles of the Torah and cast them into everlasting punishment. The sons of righteousness will enter into rest with their Abba.

He then shares a few more parables that are examples of the surety of the coming of His Abba's Kingdom. Like the parable of the lamp under the basket, He says YAH's words are not to be hidden. He promises that in time, every mystery that has so far been hidden will be revealed. He promises that those who diligently give light to His words will receive a greater reward when the time comes. He compares the Word once more to a seed that a farmer plants. The farmer's job is to plant and water—the growth is up to YAHveh. He compares the growth of the kingdom to the growth of a mustard seed—even though it is small, it will grow into one of the largest herbs on Earth. He compares it with yeast and how it grows and keeps growing from one batch to the next—it only takes a little to make hundreds of loaves of bread. He compares its value to something greater than any treasure or rare pearl that a man could find on Earth or in the sea—because its value is ***eternal life***. Then once more he describes His purpose and theirs as being like fishermen, fishing for men instead of fish, and their catch, along with those who follow them, will be gathered up by the angels to be sorted—the good will be kept and the bad will be cast into the fire at the end of times. They are to be His ambassadors and are to be those who proclaim the treasures from both the old and the new understandings of the TaNaKh. After this method of teaching, He told them that He was doing this to fulfill what was said about Him—*"I will open My* *mouth in a parable; I will utter dark sayings of old, Which we have heard and known, and our fathers have told us."* **(PSALM 78:2)**.

Yeshua Instructs His Apostles (Shelichim) on How to Minister Through Miracles to the Multitudes

On one occasion, after the crowds became so large that Yeshua was finding it hard to even move about, He told His disciples to get into their boat, cast off, and to go to the other side of the Sea of Galilee. After the motley crew shoved off, Yeshua found a comfortable spot in the boat and took a nap. A storm began to brew, and suddenly the crew found themselves in what they thought to be a very perilous situation. After waking up Yeshua and making Him aware of their possible fate, He rebuked the storm and then His talmidim for not understanding that nothing could happen to them as long as they had not yet fulfilled the mission that had been given to them by the Creator of the universe. (Remember, when you learn to hear the voice of your Abba and you seek and obey that which He places on your heart to do, nothing can keep you from accomplishing it, except yourself.) Then they suddenly found themselves on the other side in the land of the Gadarenes. This miracle of sudden movement is commonly known as "being translated".

Once on the other side, they were met by two naked men who were obviously out of their minds due to demon possession. They lived among the tombs of the dead and apparently had superhuman strength and couldn't be imprisoned. They approached Yeshua and immediately understood that He was the Son of ELuah and that He had authority over the unclean spirits within them. They begged Him not to send them back into the abyss (Pit or hell), but instead, send them into a nearby herd of pigs. When He did, the swine stampeded down the side of a hill and over a cliff into the Sea of Galilee. The pig herders ran into the nearby village, but they soon returned, bringing the residents with them, who immediately asked this intruder to leave because they were afraid of losing more of their livelihood. In the meantime, one of the men who had been released from these demons asked Yeshua if he could join Him in His travels, giving his testimony. Yeshua said he would do much better by staying where he was and testifying there.

Yeshua and His talmidim returned to their craft and sailed back to the land of Galilee. There they were immediately approached by a man named Jairus, a ruler of a synagogue, with a request for Him to come to his house because his daughter was on the brink of death. While on the way, a woman who had suffered from a female disorder for twelve years pushed through the crowd in order to touch the tassels (tzitzits) of His tallit. The tzitzits are also referred to as wings of a garment **(PSALM 94:1)**—symbolizing that she was under His wings. She instantaneously felt strength go into her body, and Yeshua felt strength leave His. When it was made known to Him who it was, He turned to her and told her that it was *her* faith that had made her well. He was telling her that it was the driving force of her belief in who He said He was that motivated her to press the crowd and not give up until she had exercised her faith by just touching His tallit. Before arriving at Jairus' house, they were told that the girl had already died. He entered with three of His talmidim at His side: Kefa, Yochanan, and Yaacov. He sent everyone else out except for the girl's parents because the others began to mock His efforts. (You cannot minister in an atmosphere of ridicule and doubt.) With only a word from Him, she arose from her death bed and rejoined her family.

From there, He went out and came across two blind men, along with a third one who was also unable to speak—all due to demons. He healed all three by casting out the unclean spirits. He continued to minister in both parables and miracles throughout Galilee until He returned once again to His home town of Nazareth, where He was unable to do much at their synagogues because of their unbelief. He made note that strangers who come into a community find it much easier to bring forth new revelation than one who lives there.

Yeshua felt that it was time to send out His talmidim on their first assignment as shelichim to emulate the works He had demonstrated to them and also to gain experience in their walk of faith. He instructs them to go only into the territory of YAHuda for now and to seek out those among the YAHudi who were descendants from all of the twelve tribes of YisraEL, those who have a heart for the truth of the Torah. He tells them that their trial must be one of true faith, where they only rely on their Abba to supply their needs and not on their own skills. He instructs them that if they and the message He sends with them are not received in any particular community, they are to leave the town or village and shake off the dust of their sandals as a testimony against them. He warns them that in time they will be scourged and beaten in the synagogues where they minister, but to count it as all joy because both He and the ne'veem before Him were treated the same way. He tells them and all of us who go out to do His work in His Name to be as crafty and wise as the enemy hasatan, the serpent, but as loving and gentle as the dove of the Ruach. He encourages them to look to their Abba for their words because He will supply them via His Ruach. He says that if anyone will confess Him as the Promised Messiah before other men, He promises to confess them before His Abba—but just the opposite if they deny Him. He says that a man's enemies will come from his own family, fulfilling what was said by the Ne'vim—*"For son dishonor father, daughter rises against her mother, daughter against her mother-in-law; a man's enemies are the men of his own house"* (**MICAH 7:6**). But, those who do receive them and their message will be treated the same as if they had received Him.

After He had sent them off, Yeshua received word that His cousin and friend, Yochanan the Immerser, had been beheaded while in prison, just for Herod's own pleasure. After this, Herod, in his paranoia and fear, began to fantasize that perhaps Yeshua was Yochanan reincarnated.

When His shelichim returned from their first mission and told Yeshua what had taken place, He tried to take them off to another location of solitude to rest, but the crowds followed. Yeshua has now been two and one-half years into His ministry and has reached His third Passover celebration. Just prior to this, He once more found Himself and His talmidim in the hills of Galilee, teaching before a multitude of about five-thousand men, along with their wives and children. Yeshua, seeing their hunger for His words, also noticed that there were many there who had nothing to eat, so He told His talmidim to feed them from what they had. But they told Him that they only had five loaves of bread and two fish. After they had distributed this meager amount, it was as though it had been a banquet because there were twelve baskets of leftover fragments. We can see something symbolic revealed through this miracle. He has given us a teaching on reciprocity and the restoration of the two houses of YisraEL. *The bread* represents a staple for life, but it is also a symbol for the words of YAH, His Abba. The five loaves would have to feed five-thousand (one loaf per thousand), but for YAHveh, it's more than enough. *The Fish* represent mankind—they were to be fishers of men. The number two equals the number for the divided House of YisraEL. Using this symbolism, the revelation equates as follows: the distribution of a small amount of bread (the word of YAH) and the fish (the House of YisraEL) are given to supply the need of an overwhelmingly hungry multitude (the lost sheep of YisraEL). The twelve baskets of leftover fragments represent the number of the invisible tribes who make up the Whole House of YisraEL—YAH will gather them to Himself in the end times.

Then Yeshua instructed His talmidim to get into their boat and sail back to Capernaum. He told them to go to the city of Bethsaida, a town close to YAHrushalayim, in order to prepare for the Passover celebration. As they were rowing out on the sea, a strong wind began to prevail, and they began to struggle against it. Yeshua had remained behind and secluded Himself to one of the mountains there in Galilee, but He could observe them in His spirit as they struggled. It was around ten o'clock in the evening, so He got up and proceeded to intercept them on the waters. By His powers of creation, He overcame the laws of physics and approached them by walking on the water. When His talmidim saw Him, they thought it must be a supernatural manifestation of some kind. Kefa recognized Him and called out for him to give a command that he also might have this power—Yeshua obliged him. But Kefa, being only a mere man, became aware of his human limitations and fear took over, so he began to sink. Yeshua rebuked him for his lack of faith, grabbed him, and then they both entered the little boat. The wind immediately ceased its tumult. They changed their course and headed back to the land of the Gadarenes, where He had previously cast out the demons from the two men. When they landed, many people came out to meet them, only this time with great anticipation because of the witness of one of the men who had been set free from the demons. There, He healed many—some of them by their only touching His tallit.

When Yeshua and His talmidim returned to Capernaum, the crowd was perplexed because they had seen His talmidim leave without Him, but now they were returning with Him aboard. After inquiring as to how He managed to accomplish His disappearing act, He told them that they were more interested in His feeding them rather than in whom He really was. Then they wanted to know what works they might do to please YAHveh. He told them to believe on the one He had sent. Then just as He had suspected, they challenged Him to perform more miraculous works, such as giving them bread from heaven to eat, as was done in the TaNaKh. *"Then YAHveh said to Mosheh, "Behold, I will rain bread from heaven for you. And the people shall go out and gather a certain quota every day, that I may test them, whether they will walk in My Torah or not"* (**EXOD 16:4**). *"You gave them bread from heaven for their hunger, and brought them water out of the rock for their thirst, and told them to go in to possess the land which You had sworn to give them"* (**NEH 9:15**). *"Yet He had commanded the clouds above, and opened the doors of heaven, had rained down manna on them to eat, and given them of the bread of heaven"* (**PSALM 78:23-25**). He immediately corrected their understanding by reminding them that it was His Abba that gave them the bread from heaven—not Mosheh. He explained to them that it is He that is the true bread from heaven and that He was sent so that they might understand and believe this in order for them to obtain the resurrection and everlasting life. Some of the YAHudi who were in the crowd began to mock His words and tried to cast doubt among those who were listening because He referred to Himself as the true bread from heaven. Then He threw them a real zinger when He reminded everyone that their fathers who ate of that manna died, but whoever would eat of His flesh would never die. Boy, this was over the top. Now they thought that He was suggesting cannibalism. Their becoming distraught over hearing this teaching didn't surprise Him, though, because He knew how they would react. Only those whom His Abba had chosen would understand the true meaning of His words because of what the Ne'vim had foretold: *"All your children shall be taught by YAHveh, and great shall be the shalom of your children"* (**ISA 54:13**). He continued with the idea of their not only eating His flesh, but also the drinking of His blood. No YAHudi would ever drink blood—it is absolutely forbidden. Yeshua was laying the groundwork for the interpretation of the cups of wine and the unleavened bread that were drunk and eaten at the Passover Seder. The cup He was referring to was the third cup of the Seder meal, which is called the "Cup of Redemption". I will discuss this cup later when Yeshua explains the full meaning of the Passover Seder. The result of this discourse that Yeshua was now introducing began to turn many of His previous followers away. He explained to those remaining that His words came from the Ruach and that they contained both spirit and life. The Scriptures remain silent as to when Yeshua and His talmidim actually partook of this particular Passover celebration.

The next turn of events took place a short time later when some of the leading Pharisees from YAHrushalayim once again approached Yeshua and questioned Him about the traditions His talmidim continued to disregard. The tradition they were referring to had to do with the special way the hand-washing ceremony was to be performed. If anyone didn't do it in this particular manner, their hands were considered still unwashed. This is a good example of how the spiritual leaders continued to twist scriptures to fit their traditions, disregarding its more important lessons. *"Therefore YAHveh said: 'Inasmuch as these people draw near to Me with their mouths and honor Me with their lips, but have removed their hearts far from Me, and their fear toward Me is taught by the commandments of men'"* (ISA 29:13). This was the second time Yeshua had to address this tradition. Yeshua immediately rebuked them with the truth from the TaNaKh. He continued to show them how they had misused YAH's words to nullify other commandments. *"Honor your father and your mother, that your days may be long upon the land which YAHveh your ELohim is giving you"* (EXOD 20:12 & DEUT 5:16). Also from the Torah, *"And he who curses His father or his mother shall surely be put to death"* (EXOD 21:17 & LEV 20:9). They mistakenly taught that anyone who gave to the House of ELohim could count it as being "Corban" and thereafter would no longer have any obligation toward the care of their parents. After His rebuke toward the spiritual leaders of YAHrushalayim, He then directed His attention to those who had gathered to hear His words with hungry hearts. He began to clarify His meaning regarding food being made unclean without washing. The purpose of the washing ceremony is to draw attention to our need to lead kedosh lives, which was the same purpose of the mikvah that Yochanan the Immerser taught. But food cannot defile a man—the food that is eaten is made clean by the digestive process. What does defile a man is what comes out of his mouth through his words because it is they that reveal what lies within his heart. He said these things to prepare them for even further teachings on how the Brit Chadashah would amend the understandings of the Torah.

Once more, Yeshua and His talmidim returned to minister in their familiar area of Galilee. The summer dragged on and while traveling near the region of Sidon, they came across a Goy woman who pleaded with Yeshua to cast a demon out of her daughter. He reminded her that the bread of salvation was meant for only the children of YisraEL. She confessed this as being true, but reminded Him that the family dogs (Goyim are commonly referred to as dogs by the YAHudi) are not forbidden to eat the leftover breadcrumbs that are dropped from the table. Because of her answer of faith and profound understanding, He granted her request.

He continued His journey throughout the region of Galilee and healed a deaf and mute man, which caused the crowds to begin to gather in larger and larger numbers. When the crowd grew to about four-thousand men, plus women and children, He decided to duplicate His miracle of reciprocity. This time they had seven loaves of bread and a few small fish. When this multiplication miracle was complete, they had seven basketsful left over—we already know the significance of the number seven.

It wasn't long until both the Pharisees and their religious rivals, the Sadducees, began to draw up an alliance against Yeshua; they must have deemed Him to be the biggest threat to their present status quo. They sought Him out and demanded that He present them with a sign as to His self-proclaimed Messiahship. His reply was again that of the sign of the Ne'vee Yonah (as if what He had already done was not enough). He again boarded one of the fishing boats and told His talmidim to push off and go somewhere else. While onboard, He commented to them about the leaven (sin) of the Sadducees and Pharisees (that of their false and misinterpreted religion), and how they must try to avoid following their example. His talmidim thought that He was referring to their not having brought any bread with them. He marveled at their blindness. Once they arrived on the other side, they went to Bethsaida and there began ministering the healing power of ELohim. One of their candidates for healing was a blind man who apparently needed a little boost in his faith. Yeshua first led him out of town and then applied some spittle on his eyes. He apparently received only a partial healing at first, so Yeshua laid His hands on him again and told him to look up. When he did, he received his sight. Not everyone who asks has enough faith to receive what they ask for—some need a little more encouragement than others.

While they were traveling toward Caesarea Philippi, Yeshua asked His talmidim what people thought regarding His true identity. They told Him that many of the people that they had spoken to had a variety of opinions. But He was more interested in what conclusion they had come to. Kefa, the most outspoken of the twelve, said, *"You are the Messiah, the Son of the Living ELohim"*. Yeshua said that He would use Kefa's confession as the key to build His Kahal upon. (He meant His Assembly, Congregation, Family, Nation, Kingdom, or the restored House of YisraEL—they all applied.) Kefa's statement, when spoken from the heart, would justify and redeem the one confessing that truth.

He said He was going to give them, as well as all believers in Him, the same authority that He had—to forgive sins. It was at this time that Yeshua gave Simon the name Kefa (the pebble). Yeshua then began to prepare His talmidim for His impending death. But Kefa rebuked Yeshua for talking about such a ridiculous subject as His death—how could He die, He was the Messiah. Yeshua in turn rebuked Kefa for thinking with his mind instead of his spirit, causing him to become a vessel for hasatan to speak through. He reminded all His followers that if they truly decided to follow after Him and do His works, they must abandon their own natural desires and comforts and focus on the needs of others. Their Abba's goal is restoration; this should be theirs also. Their focus should be on determining and establishing where their talents and abilities could best contribute to this goal and then perfecting them.

Six days later, Yeshua went up to a mountain with His three most faithful and dependable talmidim: Kefa, Yaacov, and Yochanan. After arriving, He went off by Himself to pray. Later they witnessed Him being transformed before their very eyes into all His majesty and glory (the Son of Man coming into His Kingdom). They also beheld the two great witnesses: Mosheh, who represented the tribe of YAHuda because they had the responsibility of being the custodian of the Torah, and ELeeYAHoo, who represented the tribe of Yosef because they would have the responsibility of being the proclaimer and revealer of the identity of the Messiah. Kefa, in his enthusiasm and thinking that they may be witnessing the beginning of the Messiah's Kingdom reign, began babbling about building booths (sukkots) for the three of them. He did this in his excitement because it was near the time of the Feast of Tabernacles (Sukkoth), the designated time of the ingathering and restoration of YisraEL. Suddenly, they all heard the voice of YAH speaking to them and confirming Yeshua's identity. Afterwards, when they were descending from the mountain, Yeshua instructed them to keep this to themselves until after His death and resurrection. He also confided in them regarding the second coming of ELeeYAHoo. He said that Yochanan the Immerser was the first symbolic coming of ELeeYAHoo and that there would also be a second, which would precede the promised restoration, just before He returned to usher in His Kingdom.

During Yeshua's ministering with His shelichim, a boy with a spirit of epilepsy was brought to Him. The father of the boy told of how his son had once thrown himself into a fire, being obsessed with suicide. He said that when His talmidim tried to deliver the boy from the demonic spirit, they failed. Therefore, He brought the boy to Yeshua, their teacher, for deliverance. Yeshua rebuked His talmidim because they still did not understand their position of authority and how that authority should be used through faith and not through their own righteousness. They still had not grasped the part that humility and trust played in doing the work of their Abba.

Shortly thereafter, Kefa was challenged with obeying a civil law regarding taxes paid for the upkeep of the House of YAH. Kefa wasn't sure what Yeshua's position was on this, so he went to inquire. Yeshua, already knowing what was on Kefa's mind, told him to go catch a fish and that in its mouth there would be the exact amount owed for the taxes. He followed Yeshua's instructions, and sure enough, there was the money, just as Yeshua had said. Imagine what YAHveh, our Abba, had to do to set up that set of circumstances. First, someone had to have lost a gold coin worth the exact amount needed. Second, at the same time, a fish would have had to be swimming by and swallowing it, thinking it was food. Third, that fish had to be swimming in a particular place at a particular time when, fourth, Kefa was at that particular place at that very moment to cast his net or spear into the water and catch that particular fish. When we speak of coincidences in our lives, maybe we better think twice and analyze the fact that what we may shrug off as just a coincidence may be Abba showing us a path or giving us a clue as to a decision He wants us to make.

One day, a discussion arose among Yeshua's shelichim about their concern as to what position each of them might hold in the coming kingdom. Yeshua pointed to a child and said that anyone who has the attitude of trust like this child is counted as great in the kingdom. Children have a heart of learning and a natural trust toward their parents. They are innocent because they begin with no knowledge of right and wrong—they only have emotions and curiosity. They look to their parents and their elders to show them how to conduct themselves in a world full of questions. He tells them that this is the kind of trust that all who are within the House of YisraEL are to have, and they are to conduct themselves accordingly. They need to seek the truth for themselves but have an attitude of trust for those whom Abba has raised up to help instruct them. So, if anyone who has been called to instruct instructs only to benefit himself instead of the kingdom and takes advantage of their subordinate's ignorance, they should be treated like a cancerous limb or body part and gotten rid of. He based this upon the last written words of the Ne'vee YishshaYAH—*"And they shall go forth and look upon the corpses of the men who have transgressed against Me; For their worm does not die, and their fire is not quenched. They shall be an abhorrence to all flesh"* (**ISA 66:24**). He goes on to tell them of a lost sheep and a faithful shepherd. He says the conscientious shepherd will go to any length to find any one of his flock that has wandered off and bring it back. So it should be among those whom He has set in charge of the lost sheep of YisraEL.

He says there is another thing that applies to any brother or sister among you: if that person does something against you, either intentionally or unintentionally, you are to go to him or her and make them aware of the offense.

It is best to settle things between the two of you in private. If the person who offended you refuses to settle the matter, you are to go to an elder or a deacon. They are to act as a mediator between the two of you by listening to both sides and then making a judgment in the matter, as taught in the Torah—*"One witness shall not rise against a man concerning any iniquity or any sin that he commits; by the mouth of two or three witnesses the matter shall be established"* (**DEUT 19:15**). If the person still will not repent, then it is to be made known to all the kahal of believers in that community to let them decide what the recompense should consist of. If the person will still not agree, they are to be put out of the kahal and treated as an unbeliever. He once more confirms to them the authority that they have been given to do the works of YAHveh, their ELohim and Abba, in His Name. He tells them that it will only take two witnesses in agreement with the TaNaKh, and whatever they ask of the Abba, it will be done for them in accordance to His plan. He goes on to say that it will only take two or three of them to make up a kahal, and He will be there with them, by His Ruach. Kefa asks Yeshua to clarify this a little more by asking Him how many times he's required to forgive someone—seven times? Yeshua told him a parable of a man who had been forgiven a tremendous debt and then turned around and threw one of his servants into prison for a small debt. When the one to whom he had been indebted heard of it, he had him thrown into prison because of his greed. He then told him that if a man sins against him and then realizes his error and repents of it, he is obligated to forgive him, even if it were seventy times seven (meaning without number).

Yeshua's Last Celebration of the Feast of Sukkoth Here on Earth

The summer is over, Tishri (the seventh month) has arrived, and preparations were being made for the Day of Trumpets (Yom Teruah), the Day of Atonement (Yom Kippur), and the Feast of Tabernacles (Chag Sukkoth). Yeshua was apparently visiting His family in Nazareth when His brothers began to chide Him about His ministry and were trying to urge Him to go up to YAHrushalayim with them to celebrate the Feast of Tabernacles (Chag Sukkoth)—even His own brothers doubted His claim of being the Messiah. Yeshua had not yet been given instructions by YAHveh on whether or not He should attend the celebration, so He told them that He was not going, but they should. It wasn't until after they left that He received the instructions from His Abba to go. He kept a low profile until sometime in the middle of the week of the Feast. It was then that He entered His Abba's House and began to teach that if He were seeking glory for Himself, He would only represent Himself and not try to give glory to ELohim. He questioned them as to why they were seeking to kill Him. Was it for His seeking glory for His Abba or for doing the works of His Abba on the Sabbath day—the day of His Abba?

WHAT WE WEREN'T TAUGHT ABOUT THE BIBLE AND ITS HISTORY

Those who heard Him began to question why He was accusing them of trying to kill Him, not realizing that there were some among the religious leaders who were planning to do just that. His words infuriated many who were there, those who did not believe that He was the Messiah, while others became more convinced that He was. Then, in their frustration, some tried to do Him harm, but since this was not a part of YAH's plan, He was able to slip past them in their confusion.

Then on the last day of the Feast, Hoshanah Rabbah, He entered His Abba's House and announced that the gift of the Ruach HaKedosh would come to any believer who would ask His Abba in His name. That gift would include an anointing on the words of those who received it so that when they witnessed on behalf of their heavenly Abba, they would change the lives of those who would hear them. This brought about a huge debate among those who were there regarding His claim of authority. Then the religious leaders sent some of their guards to arrest Him for stirring up the people. He told them that He was about to leave and where He was going they would not be able to follow. They again wondered what He was talking about. They began to speculate as to the meaning of His words and wondered if He meant that He was going to go among the Goyim to seek out new converts. The guards who had been sent out to arrest Him became frightened when they heard His words and saw that the crowd seemed to support Him, so they returned empty-handed. When they were asked why they had returned without Him, they began to tell them what they had heard Him saying. Nicodemus, the rabbi and priest who had spoken to Yeshua earlier and who had learned about the ***new birth***, agreed with the guards and warned the others about their possible impending error. They then began to accuse him of also being bewitched by Yeshua's words. That's when they began debating among themselves as to the possible authenticity of His claims; but things became more confused because they didn't have all of the facts regarding His testimony. Remember, Yeshua spent most of His time ministering to those near the area that He grew up in, Galilee, so very little was actually known about Him in YAHrushalayim.

The Pharisees decided to test His knowledge of the Torah again since He was teaching just outside of the House of YAH. So, they brought before Him a woman caught in the act of adultery. He knew their heart and the reason why they were doing this, so He ignored them. Instead of answering, He stooped down and began to write on the ground with His finger. Many have speculated as to what He may have been writing, so I'll put in my two cents. I like to think that He wrote, "Where is the man she was with—isn't he also guilty of this same act?" He then stood up and said, *"He who is without sin among you, let him cast the first stone."* They all left without anyone raising their hand against her.

Yeshua asked the woman where all of her accusers were. When she told Him that they had all left, He told her that He also forgave her, implying that they must have forgiven her too. Then He told her that she should go now and begin to lead a righteous life.

Yeshua continued to teach in His Abba's House and had mixed crowds within His audience. Some believed His claim to be the Messiah, while others accused Him of having a demon. He said to those who believed Him that they should stay true to the things He was teaching them regarding the meaning of the Torah. He said to the others that they were slaves, but His words and the truth that He taught would set them free. They said they were already free because they were sons of Avraham. He told them they were slaves to sin and that their father was not Avraham, but hasatan. He said if their abba had been Avraham, they would have received His words instead of wanting to kill Him. He told them that their father was the father of lies and a murderer and that was why they would not believe the truth and why they wanted to do *their* father's will and murder Him. When He judged them of these things, they retorted by accusing Him of being a Samaritan Goy or having a demon. Then He spoke some other words of life to them and said that if anyone would keep His sayings, they would never taste death. Their response was to say that all men down through the ages, both wicked and righteous, have tasted death. Then they questioned Him as to whether He thought Himself to be greater than the ancients. His answer to them was that Avraham, all the ne'veem, and their fathers had their hopes in seeing Him in His day, and they have. He said this to reinforce His teachings regarding life after death. They reminded Him that He wasn't even old enough to be an elder, so how could He claim to have known Avraham? He answered them by revealing His full identity in saying, *"Before Avraham was—I AM* (meaning YHVH)." When they heard this, they went into a rage and tried to stone Him, but He again miraculously walked past them without their even seeing Him.

When He rejoined His talmidim, they pointed to a man born blind and asked Him why he was born that way and if it was a result of some sin. He told them that this wasn't the case, but instead, it was so that His Abba would receive honor and glory for what was about to take place on this day. He then took some soil from the ground, spat in it, made little mud pies, and placed them on the blind man's eyes; He then told him to go to the mikvah of Siloam and wash his eyes. When he obeyed, he began to see for the first time in his life. When his friends and neighbors realized that he had been healed of his blindness, they asked him how it happened. He said that a man named Yeshua had done this and that was all he knew. Now, because it was done on the Sabbath, his friends took him to the Pharisees to share his good fortune with them. But when they heard about it and found out who was responsible for this act, they renounced it and said that Yeshua was a sinner because He worked on the Sabbath. Then the people asked how a sinner could do this wonderful thing. Others didn't believe that the healed man had ever been blind in the first place, so they called upon his parents to verify this miracle. They told everyone there that they couldn't account for what had happened to him, but they did know one thing for sure—he was definitely born blind. Then they asked them why they needed their verification—he was old enough to speak for himself. The Pharisees then began to accuse the man of being one of Yeshua's talmidim and that he was as much a sinner as Yeshua. He said that he didn't know if Yeshua was a sinner or not, but he did know one thing—he was born blind and now he was able to see. He reasoned that only a man from ELohim could have done this kind of work because no one had ever before performed this type of miracle that he knew of. Then the Pharisees excommunicated him from the local synagogue for having anything at all to do with such a person as this—one having all of these allegations against Him. Later, Yeshua came up to him and asked whether or not he believed in the Son of ELuah. The man wasn't sure of what he was being asked. Yeshua then told him that he was speaking with Him at that precise moment. When the man realized who it was that had just healed him, he worshiped Him. Yeshua shared with him the kingdom principle that many who are actually blind can see much clearer than many who claim that they can see. The Pharisees heard Yeshua's words and asked Him if He was referring to *them* as being blind?

Then Yeshua tried to explain to those who had come to hear His teachings that He was the good shepherd in search of His sheep and how His true sheep knew His voice and obeyed it. He said that He was the door to the sheep pen and the only way to His Abba. He said His sheep would follow Him wherever He would lead them, and anyone trying to enter the sheepfold by any other means was a thief and a robber. He told them that it is the enemy who comes to steal, kill, and destroy—He came to bring an abundant life to those who would follow Him. He told them that He came for the lost sheep of YisraEL—not just for the ones who were found in the tribe of YAHuda, but also the ones of Yosef—those who were scattered over the face of the whole Earth. They had no idea what He was talking about. He said He would lay down His life for His sheep and that no one could take it from Him—He would gladly give it away for their salvation. Many remained divided over His words.

After the Feast of Sukkoth, Yeshua returned to Galilee to resume His ministering there. As you can see, the majority of His ministry was performed in the hills of His boyhood home. This was the area where the original northern tribes of Yosef/Efraeem were located. I believe He did this to symbolize where His ministry in the future would be most accepted and received—in the nations of the Goyim. Many of the descendants of the nations of the Goyim have migrated to our county—the United States of America. The USA is where His ministry has most effectively been used by YAHveh. The Goyim in the USA have launched the most effective proclamation of His total Word ever in history—to the entire world.

Then, as autumn began to fade into winter, Yeshua knew it was time for Him to make His final journey to the city of both His Abba in heaven and His ancestral abba, Dahveed—YAHrushalayim. On His way, He and His talmidim came upon several different villages in the territories of Galilee and Samaria, but they passed through them because of His determination to reach YAHuda and minister there. But, as they were passing through a certain Samaritan village, the people there refused to allow them to stay overnight, so Yeshua's talmidim wanted to call fire down upon them, just as ELeeYAHoo once did. But Yeshua rebuked them and told them that He came to save men, not to destroy them. A little further on, they came upon ten men who were cursed with the disease of leprosy. They cried out to Him as He passed, *"Yeshua, Adonai, have mercy on us."* He stopped and told them to go and show themselves to the priest—this was to verify that they were no longer lepers according to the ordinance of the Torah. So, they by faith, even though they still had their leprosy, turned and began their journey to YAHrushalayim for their verification before the priest. Because they recognized that Yeshua was truly Adonai in the flesh, confessed it, and then began their journey by faith, they became healed on the way. In their excitement and joy as to what they were experiencing, they forgot to give thanks—all except one. He returned to Yeshua to show his gratefulness, and Yeshua blessed him. One thing for sure, if any of the others ever lost their healing, this one did not.

Before they reached YAHrushalayim, probably somewhere near Jericho (Yaricho) in YAHuda, Yeshua turned to those who had been following and learning from Him and commissioned them to go out and do His works. Just as He had sent out His twelve shelichim earlier, He now sends out seventy-two of His followers in groups of two so that everything would be established in the mouths of two or more witnesses. He assures them that anyone who would receive them would be in essence receiving Him and His Abba. When they returned, they were ecstatic with overwhelming joy at their success. Yeshua once again assures them that when they go and do His works and the works of His Abba, nothing will be able to harm them because they have been given all of His authority to accomplish His will and the will of His Abba. He did this to demonstrate that anyone, at any point in time, if they will participate in the faith walk that He offers, will also be able to perform these acts and bring glory to their Abba. He reminds them that they can be assured that their names have been written in heaven in the Book of Life and that this is a greater thing than any of the miracles that they have just performed.

WHAT WE WEREN'T TAUGHT ABOUT THE BIBLE AND ITS HISTORY

As He was teaching, an expert in the Torah stood up and challenged Yeshua's understanding of it. He wanted to know how one could receive eternal life. Yeshua reminded him of the two greatest commandments: *"You shall love YAHveh your ELohim with all your heart, with all your soul, and with all your might"* (**DEUT 6:5**), which comes from the *Sh'ma* (Sheh-mah') of the Hebrew creed, and *"You shall not take vengeance, nor bear any grudge against the children of your people, but you shall love your neighbor as yourself: I AM YAHveh"* (**LEV 19:18**). Then he asked Him to clarify who He meant by "neighbor". Yeshua responded by using the parable of the "Good Samaritan". In this example, a Samaritan man showed more kindness to a wounded stranger than did some of the self-righteous religious leaders who passed by, being more concerned about their defilement than the chance to show this stranger mercy. The purpose of the parable was to demonstrate to the Torah expert that the Torah is not understood through the mind or by its works, but rather it is understood with the heart and the mercy that it produces.

Soon, Yeshua and His talmidim came to a small village by the name of Bethany outside of YAHrushalayim. They stayed there for awhile with some friends by the names of Martha, Miriam, and their brother, Lazarus. Later, He and the twelve went on a little further to the Mount of Olives, where He taught them the fundamentals of prayer. It was at this time that He taught them what we have come to know as the "Lord's Prayer"; remember, it is His ***pattern*** for prayer and not necessarily to be said by rote. He went on to instruct them about personal prayer and how they must not give up until they have received their answer from their Abba. He taught them about the importance of praying within their Abba's will and to never think that they've come to know everything about Him. He said that they should keep knocking and keep seeking and that their Abba would teach them many things throughout their lifetime. Every gift that He has promised to those who seek Him, He will be faithful to give, including the gift of His Ruach HaKedosh. He is a good ELohim and Abba and would never give a counterfeit gift. But those who seek Him must be persistent—He rewards perseverance.

Yeshua Celebrates His Last Chanukah

When the celebration of Chanukah arrived on the twenty-fifth day of the ninth month, Kishlev, Yeshua was at His Abba's House. While there, He was approached by a crowd of YAHudi who doubted His claimed identity. Once more they asked Him whether or not He was the Messiah. He told them that nothing He could say would further convince them—it was a matter of faith and a personal decision. They apparently believed that it might be possible that He was the Messiah, but not the Son of ELuah or equal to Him. Therefore, when He once again made the claim that He and His Abba were One (Echad), they began to take up stones to execute Him. He challenged their reasoning when He reminded them of what YAHveh once said in the TaNaKh about those who belong to Him: *"I said, 'You are elohim, and all of you are children of the Most High'"* (**PSALM 82:6**). He said that they were equal to elohim because they were originally created in His image. So why did they now question whether or not the Promised Messiah, whom He referred to many times in the TaNaKh, was not equal to YAHveh. After saying this, they attempted to kill Him again, but once more He walked past them because they were helpless to harm Him.

After the celebration, Yeshua left YAHrushalayim and traveled with His talmidim east across the Yarden River to the territory of Perea (modern day Jordan). While in the province, many came to hear His teachings, but others wanted Him to leave because of their fear of Herod and the religious leaders. He taught about His coming kingdom and about those who claimed that they were of the tribe of YAHuda, but who would never be included in His Kingdom. He spoke of those who would be included, those who would come from many other nations and from every point on the Earth. Some tried to frighten Him off by telling Him that Herod was seeking to kill Him, but He retorted that claim by telling them that Herod had no power to do anything to Him until He had returned to YAHrushalayim. As Yeshua's time grew near, He began to more fervently lament over YAHrushalayim in His prayers because of her stubbornness. He knew, however, that one day soon they would praise Him when He entered her gates for the last time. They would finally cry out, *"Blessed is He who comes in the Name of YAHveh! We have blessed You from the House of YAHveh"* (**PSALM 118:26**).

Yeshua was invited to one the Pharisee's homes for a banquet, where He was given the opportunity to speak. There, He noticed a man among them who was suffering from a disease that causes a severe accumulation of water in the joints (known as dropsy). It was a Sabbath and knowing how the religious leaders felt about healing on the day of rest, Yeshua asked them point-blank whether it was a good thing to heal on the Sabbath or not. Afraid of looking foolish, they kept quiet—so He healed him. He then began to teach them how their traditions had gotten in the way of YAHveh's true meaning of His Torah. He taught them using a parable about not being so anxious to take a seat of honor before they had been invited to do so. Then He taught on how much more blessed they would be if they showed mercy and hospitality to those who could not repay. He went on to teach that many who expect to be invited to sit down at the great banquet in the kingdom will be disappointed when they are not because of the way they treated their fellow man while they were in this world.

After leaving the banquet, he continued teaching through parables as the people began to gather in larger multitudes to hear Him. He taught that those who want to follow after Him and the kingdom principles that He teaches may find themselves having to choose between following His instructions or those of their parents. They must be prepared to give up their families and their own lives if it proves necessary. He says that a person is like salt—if they lose their flavor (meaning what they were created to do), then they have lost their value and have no real purpose but to be cast aside. He goes on to teach other parables showing how YAHveh values the life of each individual because they belong to Him. For example: finding a sheep that was once lost—finding a lost coin—or having a prodigal son return. From a Messianic-Hebrew perspective, this parable of the prodigal son speaks volumes about the nation of YisraEL and its restoration. It begins with a young son wanting to go and experience what the world has to offer and demanding his father's inheritance even before his father has died. His father, because he loves his son so terribly much, gives him his inheritance, hoping that in time he will discover where happiness truly lies. (This represents the ten northern tribes of Yosef who broke away from YAHveh and His Torah to sample for themselves the riches and the elohim of the other nations.) Once he had spent all of what he had and realized how foolish he had really been, he returns, hoping to be accepted back—at least on the level of being a hired servant. (Just like the Goy looking for forgiveness on a level of less than that of a son because they knew that they had rejected YAH's Torah.) But, when the father realizes that his son has learned his lesson, he calls for a celebration because his son, who was once considered to be dead, has now returned. (The Goyim, or Yosefs, have returned to Abba YAHveh and are now born-again.) The older son becomes jealous and refuses to go to the banquet. He reminds His father that after all of the years that the younger son was out squandering his inheritance, he had remained faithful. (He represents the two southern tribes of YAHuda, who have kept the Torah intact and have remained faithful to YAHveh and His Torah.) The father reasons with him that he should also be rejoicing that His brother has retuned to the family and is once again alive. (Abba desires that YAHuda reconcile with his brother, Yosef, so that the Whole House of YisraEL is once again restored.)

Another parable that Yeshua taught them was about a shrewd steward of a rich man who had been dismissed because of dishonesty. Afterward, he devised a plan to recover the money owed to his rich employer while, at the same time, guaranteeing a livelihood for himself through the indebtedness of others to him. When the rich man heard of his shrewdness, he commended him for it. The lesson for His talmidim in this parable is that they need to learn to be wise in the handling of the riches of this world. They need to know how to make it benefit their calling and YAH's kingdom, but, at the same time, not allowing it to corrupt them. They are to learn to be good stewards of their riches and not slaves or servants to it. They can only serve one master at a time—either

YAHveh and His kingdom or the treasures of this Earth and its kingdom—it is impossible to do both.

After hearing these parable teachings, the Pharisees and the religious YAHudi mocked and laughed at their supposed meaning. Yeshua told them that the time was at hand for them to understand the full and true meaning of the TaNaKh. He rebuked them for not understanding its original meaning, even though Yochanan the Immerser preached it. He reminded them of how they and their fathers have divorced YAH and His Torah by chasing after and betrothing themselves to foreign elohim or to the riches of this world. By mixing the Torah with other religions, they have caused corruption among the Goyim nations as well. Yeshua was trying to teach them that all men can now become partakers of the tree of life and be married to YAH and His Son through the Brit Chadashah (Renewed Covenant), which is the fulfillment of the Torah and the Ne'vim (TaNaKh).

This leads Yeshua into telling the parable about a rich man and a poor beggar named Lazarus (not Yeshua's friend, Lazarus). Lazarus was poor but faithful to the commandments of YAH, but the rich man wasn't. After they both died, the rich man found himself in Hell and could see Lazarus over in Avraham's bosom (also known as Paradise). A deep chasm separated them, and neither could cross over to the other. The rich man begged for someone to go and tell his brothers about this place. Avraham told him that if they wouldn't believe Mosheh and the Ne'vim, they wouldn't believe someone rising from the dead (meaning Yeshua's resurrection).

The Pharisees and the Torah experts challenged Him as to when this kingdom that He spoke of would come, but Yeshua told them that they couldn't see it because it is found in the hearts of true believers. Knowing that this same question was in the minds of His talmidim, He told them that His kingdom would come to the Earth when it is least expected because the people who love this world will be so preoccupied with it that they will ignore the signs. He told them to study and know and understand the signs. One of the signs will be the swiftness of its coming—no one will be able to say it is here or there. He warns them not to allow themselves to become attached to material things. Those who do will be left behind when the angels come to the Earth for the ingathering of His people and their return to the Promised Land.

Then He taught them that they should be both patient and persistent while remaining humble to Him and their Abba. He did this through two parables: one about a persistent, but patient, woman and a judge—the other about a tax collector and a Pharisee. Then finally, in this list of parable teachings, He explained to them how some who thought they should come first in the kingdom will come last, and others who thought they deserved to be last will come first because our Heavenly Abba knows our hearts and is a just and loving

ELohim. He told them about a vineyard owner and about the men he had hired to work his vineyard. Even though he hired workers throughout the day and they worked for different lengths of time, he paid them all the same. When they asked him why this was, he asked them whether or not they had originally agreed to the amount that he would pay them. When they said yes, he told them that they had no argument because it was his vineyard and his money. Some who were first may have gotten less overall than those who came last, but it was for him to decide—no one got cheated.

Yeshua's Friend, Lazarus, Dies

While Yeshua was ministering beyond the Yarden in Perea, word came to Him that Lazarus, Miriam and Martha's brother, was sick. Immediately He proclaimed that this sickness had occurred so that YAH's Son could show the glory of His Abba to all. This was not unlike the time that He had healed a man who had been born blind. He said then that it was not because of any sin that was in this man's life but rather for YAHveh's glory.

Two days after receiving the news concerning Lazarus, He told His talmidim that they should go up to YAHuda once more. They reminded Him that there were those there who were waiting to kill Him. He answered them by saying that He had received instructions from His Abba to go. He also told them that their friend, Lazarus, was sleeping, but He was referring to Lazarus' body being asleep in death. They boldly proclaimed that if He wasn't afraid to go, neither were they.

By the time they arrived in Bethany, Lazarus had been in his tomb for a period of four days. When Martha heard that Yeshua had arrived, she ran out to Him and told Him that if He had come sooner, He could have healed her brother, but now it was too late because he was already dead. When Yeshua told her not to fear but that life would be restored to her brother, she told Him that she knew this to be true—in the resurrection. Yeshua then told her that it was their faith in Him that made the resurrection possible.

After speaking with Yeshua, Martha ran back to her home where she had left her sister, Miriam. When Miriam heard that Yeshua had come, she too, along with a number of YAHudi, ran out to meet Him with the same greeting as Martha had earlier. When Yeshua saw their mourning and unbelief, He wept and groaned within Himself. After reaching the tomb where they had laid Lazarus' body, He ordered them to remove the stone that was in front of it. Martha spoke up to remind Him that her brother had been dead for four days and that his body would surely be decomposing by then. Yeshua reminded her of the power of ELuah. As those who were there began to respond to His commands, He began to give thanks to His Abba for what was about to take place. In fact, His words of thanksgiving were for the sake of those who were witnessing this event so that they would also give thanks for His grace. It was at this point that He called out Lazarus' name and commanded him to come out of the tomb—he came out still wrapped in his grave linen. Yeshua told them to undo his bindings and set him free. Word of what had happened got out to the Pharisees in YAHrushalayim, and they became even more alarmed about the events that were taking place at such a rapid pace. This was going to cause more of the YAHudi to begin to follow Yeshua, and they would surely begin to lose their positions as being the spiritual leaders. At the same time, the Roman government would probably see this as the beginning of a possible uprising and put everyone in chains. Then the high priest, Caiaphas, not realizing that his position made his words potentially prophetic, said, *"It is right that this one man should die for the sake of everyone else, so let us bring it about."* The fulfillment of this prophecy would bring about salvation—not only for the YAHudi but also for the tribes who were scattered over the face of the whole Earth and for all others who would believe.

While Yeshua was in the area, He continued to give more teachings regarding kingdom principles. Some Pharisees from the community then came to ask Him a few questions regarding marriage and divorce, and Yeshua answered them from the Torah—*"So ELohim created man in His Own Image; in the Image of ELohim He created him; male and female He created them....Therefore a man shall leave his abba (father) and maw (mother) and be joined to his wife, and they shall become one flesh"* (**GEN 1:27 & 2:24**). They questioned Him as to why then had Mosheh granted the issuing of a certificate of divorce. Yeshua replied that Mosheh only did it because of the hardness of the hearts of their fathers and that it was not within YAHveh's plan or will for mankind to continue treating marriage in such a frivolous manner.

Yeshua continued to counsel His talmidim about the value of marriage and family and the proper attitude that should be shown toward children in general. He discussed wealth and its hold on men and how challenging it is for those who possessed it to be able to grasp kingdom principles. He reminded them, though, that with Eluah everything is possible. He counseled a rich man who asked how he might achieve righteousness, and Yeshua told him to obey the Torah. *"Honor your father and your mother, that your days may be long upon the land which YAHveh your ELohim is giving you. "You shall not murder. "You shall not commit adultery. "You shall not steal. "You shall not bear false witness against your neighbor. "You shall not covet your neighbor's house; you shall not covet your neighbor's wife, nor his manservant, nor his maidservant, nor his ox, nor his donkey, nor anything that is your neighbor's"* (**EXOD 20:12-17 & DEUT 5:16-21**). He then tells him to go and sell everything that he has and follow Him. The young man realized that this would be too much and turned away. He didn't own riches—they owned him. Yeshua told His talmidim that since they had basically done all of these things already, they would one day sit on thrones in His Millennium Kingdom and judge the Whole House of YisraEL. He taught them many other things during those few days. Then He told them for the third time about His death and how He would rise from the dead on the third day. Yochanan and his brother, Yaacov, spoke up and wanted to know if their thrones could be next to His in His Kingdom. He told them that it would be up to His Abba to make that decision. The other ten were very displeased when they heard this question. (Pride and jealousy emerged between these brethren that typified the power struggle that has existed among the YisraELi down through the ages. Yochanan and Yaacov were like YAHuda and BenYAHmeen in that they wanted special recognition from Yeshua. The other ten became offended because of their arrogance. YAHuda and BenYAHmeen have always been faithful stewards of the Torah and want recognition for this. The other ten tribes of Yosef/Church also want recognition because they have witnessed to the world about the identity of Yeshua as being the Son of ELuah.) Yeshua asked the two brothers whether or not they would be able to be immersed in His immersion—the immersion of rejection, persecution, and death. They said yes. He then confessed that one day they too would suffer His immersion, and they did. (Likewise, YAHuda and BenYAHmeen have also suffered because for two-thousand years they have been without a country. In 1947, almost one generation ago, their punishment for rejecting their Messiah was finished and their curse had passed—the time of the Goyim is nearly over.)

Yeshua slowly begins His final journey to YAHrushalayim, but first He enters Yaricho, where He meets a little man named Zacchaeus, a tax collector like Matthew (MattatiYAH). Zacchaeus is told by Yeshua that He will come and stay at his house that very day. When others heard about this, they accused Yeshua of having fellowship with sinners. But He knew Zacchaeus' heart and knew that when he said he would repent and give back all of his ill-gotten gain, he meant it (repentance begins with recompense). This is what He meant by claiming that Zacchaeus was being a true son of Avraham. While at Zacchaeus' home, Yeshua taught about those who would be judged as to whether or not they were true sons of Avraham. He told about a man who went away to inherit a kingdom. He gave three months' salary to ten of his servants (a picture of the ten northern tribes) and entrusted them to keep what was his. There were others who hated him and would not submit to his authority. When he returned after gaining his kingdom, he went to each one to see what they had done with what had been entrusted to them. One had gained ten times as much, another gained five times as much, and still another only kept it in a bag, doing nothing with it. He chastised the third one for not at least putting it into a bank to draw interest. He then took his portion away from him and gave it to the servant who had increased his by ten fold. Then he told the rest to slay all of those who had hated him because they were his enemies. This gives us a picture of the reward system that awaits His YisraEL in the millennium. On His way out of Yaricho, Yeshua came across two blind men along the side of a road who were acknowledging Him as being the Messiah, and because of their faith in Him, they were healed. Finally, Yeshua and His talmidim came again to the city of Bethany, where Lazarus lived—about two miles outside of YAHrushalayim.

From there, Yeshua and His talmidim decided to go to a city named Efraeem to stay and wait until the greatest Passover celebration ever would take place—His last. (Here again is a prophetic symbol that His message would be kept in stewardship by the children of Yosef/Efraeem until the appropriate time.) They stayed in Efraeem until just six days before Passover, the eighth of Aviv, which would have been on the sixth day of that week (Friday on the Roman calendar), before they returned to Bethany. While in Bethany, they again stayed at the house of His friends, Lazarus, Martha, and Miriam. But before going to their house, they stopped at the house of a former leper, Simon (perhaps the very one of the ten who stopped to give thanks to YAH for his healing). While there, Miriam, in her admiration of Yeshua, took expensive oil and anointed His feet and wiped it with her hair. YAHuda Iscariot objected to it because of its value, but Yeshua, knowing his heart and the real reason, rebuked him and said that without her knowing it, she was beginning to prepare Him for His burial. Some of the religious leaders found out where Yeshua was staying and decided to include Lazarus in their plot of assassination, hoping it would help squelch the stories of his being raised from the dead.

The Days Leading Up to Yeshua's Crucifixion

The meal that Lazarus and his sisters shared with Yeshua was the evening meal between the sixth and seventh day of the week, the beginning of Sabbath. This meal is known among the YAHudi as Erev Shabbat, or the Evening of Sabbath. Remember, a Hebrew day always begins at sundown and lasts until sundown the next day. No ordinary work or merchandising (buying and selling) is done on Sabbath—it is a true day of rest. On the morning of the first day of the week (Sunday on the Roman calendar), Yeshua began His final trip into the city of YAHrushalayim. This also was the tenth of Aviv, the day that all of the citizens of YisraEL were to choose their Passover/Pesach lamb to be slain for their Seder meal—one without spot or blemish (**EXOD 12:3**). Christians remember it as Palm Sunday. Before they entered the city, Yeshua sent two of His talmidim to a certain place to find a donkey and her colt. They were to untie the colt and bring it to Him so that He could ride into the city. As I said in Chapter Seven, this is how the king of YisraEL is identified—*"Rejoice greatly, O daughter of Zion (Zeeon)! Shout, O daughter of YAHrushalayim! Behold your King* *is coming to you; He is just and having salvation, lowly and riding on a donkey"* (**ZECH 9:9**). Remember, this was also how King Dahveed identified his son, Shalomo, as the one to succeed him as king, rather than his son, Adonijah (AhdoneeYAH).

When they had done this, His talmidim threw their tallits upon the colt, and Yeshua mounted it and proceeded to ride into His Abba's city. As He approached the city, He began to weep because He saw her soul in its people and He knew the fate awaiting her. When He entered her gates, the people who had heard that He was coming began cutting and throwing palm branches down before Him and shouting words from The Book of Psalms, just as He had said they would. They were shouting: *"Blessed is He who comes in the name of YAHveh! We have blessed You from the House of YAHveh"* (**PSALM 118:26**). Now it was customary at this time for the priests to bring all of the selected Pesach lambs into the city for inspection. They would be paraded into the city and ushered to the House of YAH. So, when the Pharisees saw Yeshua coming (YAHveh's Pesach Lamb) and heard the shouts, they told Him to silence the people, but He told them that if He tried, then the stones would cry out. The Pharisees knew that He had achieved their greatest fears and had won the people over to Himself. After going to His Abba's House with His talmidim for awhile, the time began to grow late, so He returned to Bethany with them.

The next day was the morning of the second day (Monday on the Roman calendar). Yeshua and His talmidim made preparations to return to YAHrushalayim, but first they stopped by a fig tree to see how much fruit it would produce that year. However, when they came to it, they found only leaves and no fruit buds for that season – so, Yeshua cursed it for its sterility. Upon reaching the city, Yeshua once again found merchants buying and selling animals and birds for sacrificing and exchanging money in His Abba's House. This is at least the second time that Yeshua witnessed this—the first being at the Passover He attended in the beginning of His ministry. Scriptures do not say, but He must have witnessed them following this practice even before He entered the ministry but kept silent about it because He hadn't yet received the authority to say anything. During His ministry there were two other Passovers in between these two recorded accounts. What about them—did He respond with violence then? Perhaps these were the only two times that He attended the Passover celebrations. The Torah does command that every YisraELi must attend at least one of the three annual appointed times (moedim), or feasts, every year—but not necessarily all. The Scriptures are quiet about other things too. Did He tithe? Did He bring sacrifices? Of course we know that He didn't need to bring sin offerings or guilt offerings because He was without sin. But what about freewill offerings or thank offerings? We need to stop and remember two other events that occurred earlier in history. First of all, we know that the

Ark of the Testimony had already been either stolen or hidden because the Holy of Holies was empty during Yeshua's ministry. Second, we also know that the Shchinah glory left during the time of the Ne'vee YechezkEL, who penned his account of these events; this means that YAH's presence was no longer there. Without His glory, His House was only symbolic. The inhabitants of the land of YisraEL were never completely faithful in their obedience to the Torah instructions regarding the House of YAH—the books of NehchemYAH and Ezrah are clear about that. His covenant had been broken too many times, and His Torah commandments had to be amended. This may be why Yeshua only referred to it as a house of prayer at that time—*"Even them I will bring to My holy mountain, and make them joyful in My House of Prayer. Their burnt offerings and their sacrifices will be accepted on My altar; for My House shall be called a House of Prayer for all nations"*.... *"Has this House, which is called by My Name, become a den of thieves in your eyes? Behold, I, even I, have seen it,' says YAHveh"* (**ISA 56:7 & JER 7:11**). Now His Abba's presence was only there when He was there because He and His Abba are One (Echad).

The Pharisees were reluctant to do anything at this time because they could observe for themselves His popularity. The blind, lame, and sick came to Him, and He healed them. The children praised Him to the point that the religious leaders complained. He reminded them of what The Book of Psalms said—*"Out of the mouth of babes and infants You have ordained strength, because of Your enemies, that You may silence the enemy and the avenger"* (**PSALM 8:2**). Among those who were hearing His teaching were some Goyim who were also seeking YAHveh and His Kingdom. They asked Phillip, who told Andrew, who in turn asked Yeshua if they could speak with Him. His reply was that His hour had come (in other words, the restoration was about to begin—the restoring of the House of Yosef with the House of YAHuda), and to accomplish this, He had to become like a seed that died in the ground—producing a harvest of souls for His Abba's kingdom. When He made this confession, a Voice came from heaven and said, **"I have glorified My Name and I will glorify it again."** He told them that they heard the Voice in order to strengthen their faith. Then He told them what was about to happen to Him—He was about to be lifted up for their sake. Some believed, while others didn't, even though they all heard the Voice. After His teaching, He and His talmidim left to return to Bethany for the night.

The next morning was the third day of the week, the twelfth of Aviv (Tuesday on the Roman calendar). When they came to the fig tree that Yeshua had cursed the day before, they were astonished that it had withered from the roots up and had died. Yeshua told them that when they are in YAHveh's will and learn to do what He is doing and say what He is saying, they too will be able to accomplish these works and even greater works. (This is an important lesson for all believers—all things are possible if we learn to be obedient to the training of His Ruach.)

As they arrived at YAH's House, the chief priests were there waiting to question Him. They challenged Him on what authority He had in doing the things that He had done and in teaching the things He had taught. He in turn put before them a catch-22 question about Yochanan the Immerser's teachings— *"I will also ask you one thing, and answer Me: "The mikvah of Yochanan—was it from heaven or from men?"* (**LUKE 20:3&4**). When they felt trapped, they refused to answer. Yeshua likewise refused to answer them as to His authority. He then went into His Abba's House and began to teach once more in parables. He taught about two sons: one son broke his word to his abba, while the other refused to give his word, but later changed his mind and did his abba's will. Another parable was about a man who owned a vineyard and leased it out to some vinedressers because he had to leave to take care of other business. But when he sent servants to gather the harvest of his fruit from those leasing it in order to turn over the profits, they beat up the servants. After this happened several times, the owner sent his son, thinking they would show him respect. Instead, they killed the heir, trying to gain ownership for their own benefit. Yeshua, of course, was pointing to the rebellion of the present religious leaders of the nation of YAHuda because of their greed to lord it over the people. He also referred to The Book of Psalms to make His point—*"The stone which the builders rejected has become the chief cornerstone. This was YAHveh's doing; it is marvelous in our eyes"* (**PSALM 118:22&23**). The religious leaders knew that all of this was in reference to them.

He continued to teach, this time about a wedding feast. He told of a king who was giving a wedding feast for his son and invited all of those he thought were his friends. But their response was to think little of the event, and some even beat and killed those who brought the invitations. When he learned of it, he sent his army to destroy those ungrateful subjects. Then he sent invitations to others he wouldn't have normally considered as friends. They responded with gratefulness and came celebrating, dressed in their best robes and tallits. But one who thought he too ought to be there came dressed casually, not wearing a wedding robe. When the king saw him, he had him thrown out because of his lack of proper respect. Yeshua's lesson was that being religious will not get you into the kingdom, but being sincere will. Here again, Yeshua was telling how the people of YAHuda would reject Him, but multitudes of the Goyim would gladly accept Him.

The Pharisees once again wanted to trap Yeshua both in His words and in His knowledge regarding Roman law, so they had the liberal sect of the YAHudi question Him. They asked Him about the religious approach toward paying taxes to Caesar. Yeshua answered, "What is made in Caesar's image, give to Caesar, but what is made in the image of ELuah, give to ELuah."

Then the Sadducees tried their hand. They were very secular in their approach to the TaNaKh and did not believe in the resurrection. They tried to trap Him by asking about marital responsibility when it came to the marriage of several brothers to one woman who had not conceived any children. He told them that there will be no marriage in the kingdom (all will be married to YAH's Son). Then He addressed their error regarding the resurrection and reminded them of what the Torah had to say about YAH being the ELohim of Avraham, Yitzhak, and Yaacov. He spoke of them in the present tense and not the past because they had only tasted physical death. *"Moreover He said. 'I AM the ELohim of your abba—ELohim of Avraham, the ELohim of Yitzhak, and the ELohim of Yaacov.' And Mosheh hid his face, for he was afraid to look upon ELohim"* (**EXOD 3:6**).

Then some experts in the Torah asked Him which commandment was the greatest. Yeshua didn't refer to any of the Ten Commandments but again referred them to the Hebrew *Sh'ma* (**DEUT 6:4&5**) as being the greatest commandment and the other being in **LEV 19:18**, which also is not one of the ten. The first is described in detail in the first four commandments of the ten, and the second is described in detail in the last six. He told them that every lesson and commandment, all 613 found in the TaNaKh, are built upon these two. Some leaders in the Body of Messiah today say that those two are the only commandments that Yeshua taught believers to follow. True students of Scripture know better—that simplicity of thought is ludicrous. At the same time, others teach that we are under grace and not under the law and that the TaNaKh (Old Testament) has been replaced with Yeshua's teachings, along with the rest of the Brit Chadashah (New Testament). They also teach that YisraEL, because of her not recognizing Yeshua as the Messiah, has been replaced with the Church. I may sound redundant when I say this, but it deserves repeating—and I will repeat it a few more times. The Law (Torah) is only one part of the TaNaKh; there are three parts: the Torah—the Ne'vim—and the Kethuvim. The Torah doesn't contain just two commandments, nor does it contain only ten—it contains 613. All 613 are just mini-particles of the ten, which can be summed up in the two. Just like elements are made up of molecules and are in turn made up of atoms, which are made up of electrons, neutrons, and protons, which are further made up of sub-atomic particles, and so on, so are the instructions of YAHveh. Another comparison would be that of the Brit Chadashah, which has over one-thousand laws within it, but yet we are still under grace. Then, when you factor in the rules and laws that the different religious denominations add, the figure gets astronomical. Remember what Yeshua said, *"Do not think I came to destroy the TaNaKh. I did not come to destroy but*

WHAT WE WEREN'T TAUGHT ABOUT THE BIBLE AND ITS HISTORY

to fulfill. 'For assuredly, I say to you, until heaven and earth pass away, one yod or one stroke will by no means pass from the Torah till all is fulfilled" (**MATT 5:17&18**).

What we are no longer under is the *curse* of the Torah—Yeshua paid that price for us by becoming that curse. We no longer have to carry that heavy, impossible yoke of fear in trying to follow and obey the Torah. We are now under His grace and His blessings and should have a heart that *wants* to follow and obey His Torah. We now know that even when we do mess up, that assuredness of His grace and mercy will lead us back into a life of joy and fulfillment. His Torah, however, still remains as our guide and tutor. His instructions are still the same yesterday, today, and tomorrow and will remain that way until *ALL* of His Torah is fulfilled. To teach that grace has substituted the need for Torah is like saying a particular degree can be achieved without attending any form of proper schooling or training in that subject. His Torah teaches and reveals who He is and who we are in Him. His Torah guides us in living a life that is righteous and pleasing to Him. To take on the attitude that His Torah no longer applies to our lives is irresponsible and prideful. What have **WE** done to deserve being exempt from doing what is pleasing to Him?—Nothing. We don't even deserve to be exempt from the curse of not following the Torah, but it is because of His love for us, through His Grace, that we are allowed back before the mercy seat of our Abba—through the shed and cleansing blood of His Son. Now it becomes an attitude of: "Abba, I love You, and I want to please You. I want to know You in the most intimate of ways. I want to follow everything that You have instructed, and I will follow joyfully. I know that when I fall down and fail, You will pick me up—the blood of Your Son will cleanse me again. Your Torah will no longer be a yoke upon my neck, too heavy for me to bear, but, because of the ultimate and final price that Your Son paid for me, it will be an adornment instead. I will know You deeper than ever before. I now obey You because I love and fear You, and not because I fear the curse of the Torah." Abba wanted to establish a relationship with us so much that He knew our own free will, pride, and self-centeredness would stand in the way. My daughter puts it this way: "No parent wants to have a relationship with their child based upon fear, and the only reason the child obeys you is because they are afraid of the consequences. It is so much better to have a relationship with your child when they obey you because they love you and trust that when they do fall down and fail, there is forgiveness and there is grace." It is the same with our Abba. As parents, we have rules for our children to help them grow and stay safe. We discipline our children because we love them. We instruct our children and have a relationship with them because we want them to have a relationship with us. It is the same with our Heavenly Abba.

It was now Yeshua's turn to ask questions, so He asked the Pharisees, who were standing there, from what linage will the Messiah come? They said that He will be the son of Dahveed. Then He asked them if that is true, why did Dahveed, while being inspired by the Ruach, call the Messiah Adonai. *"YAHveh said to my Adonai, "Sit at My right hand, till I make Your enemies Your footstool"* (**PSALM 110:1**). He was asking them that if the Messiah was the son of Dahveed, why then would Dahveed call Him Adonai. The obvious answer was that He would be both the Son of Man through Dahveed's linage and the Son of ELuah through the miraculous conception of the Ruach. They could not, or would not, answer Him.

From this point on, He began to strongly expose, rebuke, and condemn all of the religious leaders who opposed Him because of their desire to control their followers, keeping them subordinate to them. He points out all of the things that they love to do that draw attention to themselves. He says they may sit in the seat of Mosheh, but they desecrate its authority. He tells those who are under their authority to only follow their teachings as they apply to the TaNaKh and to what Mosheh taught, but not to embrace their examples. Men are spiritual teachers only as long as they teach the words of YAH. Likewise, men are fathers only as long as they emulate their Heavenly Abba. He says for them to remember that they only have one Teacher—the Ruach. They only have one Abba—YAHveh. He commends the Pharisees for tithing to the House of YAH but condemns them for ignoring justice, mercy, and faith. He also condemns them for spending too much time in trying to understand the smallest things about the Torah while forgetting its cornerstone and foundation—love and grace. He tells them that they are so caught up in their oral laws that they don't understand what is right before them; this is why they don't recognize Him as the Messiah. Because of this, they will soon be cast out of the land, just like their brothers, the tribes of Yosef, and they will not return until YAHveh's appointed time. He knows that when this happens, it will be when He returns to gather to Himself all that His Abba has given Him—on that last Great Day. Once more, Yeshua laments over YAHrushalayim (**PSALM 118:26**). Then He looks over at a widow who was placing the last of her possessions, two coins, unselfishly in the offering box and points to her as being a faithful, true believer who understands that she can always depend upon her heavenly Abba to provide for her. He knew that His Abba would respond to her humility.

He left His Abba's House with His talmidim, and as they were leaving, they began to remark about the beauty of YAHveh's House. Yeshua knew that it was time for Him to tell them about its future destiny. He told them that not one stone of their beloved structure would remain recognizable. Josephus, a YAHudi historian who was an eyewitness to General Titus' destruction of YAH's House and the city of YAHrushalayim, says that all of the walls were torn or burnt down in order to extract the melted gold from its interior. Not one stone was left standing upon another. All of this took place forty years later in 70 CE. Here again, Josephus' statement also puts the legitimacy of the Wailing Wall as being the only structure left of YAH's House in the shadow of doubt, as was mentioned in the previous chapter.

When His talmidim later pressed Him as to when they could expect to see the establishment of His Kingdom, He said that certain things would have to occur first. He said others would come to claim the messiahship, but they would be liars. Many wars would be fought within the land, and it would experience many environmental changes, as would the whole Earth. Many other great nations throughout the Earth would rise up and try to establish dominance, but they would fail. The Whole House of YisraEL would be persecuted, both the visible House of YAHuda and the invisible House of Yosef. False religions, false teachers, and false seers would spread their lies throughout the Earth. And because the Torah is not taught, the hearts of men will grow cold, and love will not be practiced. But the "Good News" of the Messiah and His Kingdom will be shared throughout the world. When all of this has been accomplished, He will return to set up His Kingdom.

Another sign that He said would take place before His Kingdom could be reestablished is when the same scenario that the Ne'vee DahneeEL wrote about occurs (notice that Yeshua calls DahneeEL a Ne'vee when the rabbim wouldn't). *"Then he shall confirm a covenant with many for one week; but in the middle of the week he shall bring an end to sacrifice and offering. And on the wing of abomination shall be one who makes desolate, even until the consummation, which is determined, is poured out on the treaty."..."And forces shall be mustered by him, and they shall defile the sanctuary fortress; then they shall take away the daily sacrifices, and place there the abomination of desolation."..."And from the time that the daily sacrifices is taken away, and the abomination of desolation is set up, there shall be one thousand two hundred and ninety days"* (**DAN 9:27** & **11:31** and **12:11**). This means that a man who will have great authority will make a treaty with the inhabitants of the land of YisraEL that will last for seven years. A new House of YAHveh will be standing in YAHrushalayim, where daily sacrifices will have been reestablished. In the middle of the seven years, he will by force cause the practice to cease. This practice will be forbidden for another three and one half years, at which time this man will defile the sanctuary of the House by setting up a false image as his eluah—probably one of himself. Yeshua says that when this takes place, to flee and not to think twice—just leave. (Many YAHudi, those who believed Yeshua's warnings, were able to survive the destruction of YAHrushalayim in 70 CE when they thought that these events, which occurred at that time, were the signs of the end—they fled to Masada, where they were safe for awhile.) He went on to tell them that other things would take place that would also confirm the true time. He said there would be worldwide tribulation so bad that if He didn't return, all mankind would be destroyed. He admonishes them to watch for the ones who would come in His Name but would not be teachers of the truth. He said that they would be very convincing with their false signs and wonders. Finally, He told them that the one true sign that He had returned would be when everyone on Earth would see His coming, all at the same time—His return would cover the sky. The deceivers can only be in one place at one time, and just like a dead carcass, that will be where the vultures (or deceived ones) will congregate—but not the true and informed believer.

Another sign to look for will be a catastrophic disturbance in the cosmos, which will affect all the lights that are mentioned in the Book of the Beginnings, Genesis—*"For the stars of heaven and their constellations will not give their light; the sun will be darkened in its going forth, and the moon will not cause its light to shine.—All the host of heaven shall be dissolved, and the heavens shall be rolled up like a scroll; all their host shall fall down as the leaf falls from the vine, and as fruit falling from a fig tree"* (ISA 13:10 & 34:4). In the natural, this happens to the sun and moon during a solar and lunar eclipse. What is interesting is that a solar eclipse can only take place during a new moon and a lunar eclipse only during a full moon. A new moon marks the beginning of a Hebrew month, and on the seventh new moon of a Hebrew year, the Day of Trumpets is celebrated. A full moon always marks the beginning of the Feast of Unleavened Bread (Chag HaMatzot) in the first month of any Hebrew year, and in the seventh month, it marks the beginning of the Feast of Tabernacles (Chag Sukkot). Could it be that a cosmic catastrophe will occur, such as the Earth being struck by an asteroid or comet, which would knock it so far out of kilter that both a solar eclipse and a lunar eclipse could occur in the land of YisraEL in the same month, the seventh month, which is the holy month? And could this event be followed by a meteor shower, created by going through a field of asteroids or the tail of a comet, like nothing the Earth has ever experienced since before the flood? This could cause an event that would seem as though the stars were falling from the sky. He says it will be at that moment when He will appear to everyone on the Earth at the same time, or at least during one rotation of the Earth (one full day). He describes another event that parallels the description of the rapture, when He says His angels will gather up His people after the sound of the great shofar.

There is still one more sign that He says will take place. Those in the world will not be aware of any of these signs, so He wants His people to understand them and be watchful. He says the population of the world, not His people, will be in the same blind attitude as were the people during the time of Noah. When He comes, it will be at a time when only a few will be expecting Him—even some believers will be surprised. But He does give another clue—He says, *"It will be on a day and in an hour that no one knows; no, not even the angels of heaven, but My Abba only."* Every month when the new moon appears, it is referred to among the Hebrews as coming "on a day and in an hour that no man knows, only YAHveh." That's because the coming of the new moon can only be approximated; it is not officially here until its crescent is actually observed. This is what He meant when He said that not even the angels know, but only His Abba. We might know when the Day of Trumpets is celebrated, but we do not know when the new-moon crescent will appear or which Day of Trumpets will be the right one. Even a Hebrew year can only start at the end of the month of Adar, the twelfth month, but only if the barley plant has shown its head. If not, a thirteenth month, II Adar, has to be declared, which makes the previous year a leap year. Many times the YAHudi are a whole month behind all year because they have followed the Rabbinic Calendar, which is published ahead of time, instead of following the ripening of the barley. He goes on to declare that not everyone will be taken at that time, only those who have learned the signs properly and are ready. Yeshua says that even though He has given many instructions, there will be some who will not be ready and will suffer the consequences—they will miss the rapture and the Wedding Feast because they weren't watchful. Then He told a parable of ten virgins (symbolic of the ten northern tribes of Yosef), five prepared themselves properly for the coming of the bridegroom and five didn't. Those who didn't were left outside and were unable to attend the bridegroom's wedding. This alone gives credence as to why we *must* know His Torah. We must know His Hebraic mind, His Hebraic calendar, His Hebraic months, and His Hebraic Feasts. We must know Him intimately with a Hebraic heart, a heart that has been grafted into us (**ROMANS 11**), or otherwise we may miss the most intimate part of Him. This is what hasatan wants—he wants us to be caught off guard and to be deceived. He has tried to keep YAHveh's people blinded and misinformed. This is just one more thing added to **"WHAT WE WEREN'T TAUGHT ABOUT THE BIBLE AND ITS HISTORY"**.

Yeshua said that afterwards there will be a reward system for those who have used what YAHveh gave them. He explains about the five, two, and one talent given to servants before the master went on a journey. This parable parallels the story of the salaries given to some servants. The results are also the same. We will receive in the same proportion as we have used what Abba has given us. These rewards could very well be cities, territories, or communities for us to oversee. Again, YAHveh has given us the Torah. Are we going to use the Torah—learn the Torah—practice the Torah—live the Torah? Our rewards depend on it.

Then He discusses the Judgment Seat of the Messiah with them and how He will have the duty of dividing those who claim to be His from those who truly are His. He describes them as sheep and goats, or two different flocks. These are the righteous and the wicked. The righteous will reign with Him in the Millennium. The wicked, however, will be destroyed, but they will be resurrected at the end of the Millennium to stand before the Great White Throne for judgment. This is described in Yochanan's Book of Revelation.

When Yeshua finished telling them these things, He told them that His time would come in two more days—this would be Thursday on the Roman calendar, which would be the fifth day, Aviv 14, on the evening of the beginning of Passover. He was going to be the Pesach Lamb. That's right, "mishpochah" (a Hebrew word for "family"), Yeshua was crucified on **Thursday and not on Friday**. Study the Scriptures carefully—you have been misinformed considerably.

In the meantime, the chief priests and elders were debating as to how they could trap Yeshua and kill Him. They didn't want to do it during the feast because they were afraid of the people. Then YAHuda Iscariot provided the perfect opportunity for them when He bargained a price, thirty pieces of silver, to deliver Him to them.

Yeshua and His talmidim spent that evening and the next (a camp meeting) on the Mount of Olives. The following morning was the fourth day, the thirteenth of Aviv (Wednesday on the Roman calendar), and He once again returned to His Abba's House to teach. He continues to be astonished at the people's unbelief but knows that this was what was prophesied about the condition of their minds and spirits. *"Who has believed our report? And to whom has the arm of YAHveh been revealed?"*—*"Make the heart of this people dull, and their ears heavy, and shut their eyes; lest they see with their eyes, and hear with their ears, and understand with their heart, and return and be healed"* (**ISA 53:1** and **6:10**). YAH's purpose is not to reveal who He is to the wicked, or they too might worship Him. In spite of popular belief, He doesn't want to scare people into heaven or out of hell. He wants people to recognize their inability to save themselves by acting righteous outwardly but remaining corrupt inwardly. He wants them to understand and recognize the sinful nature that is in their hearts, then to repent and turn to Him. When they do, their hearts will be ready to receive His message. Some of the leaders did believe that Yeshua was the Messiah but were afraid of being rejected by their religious colleagues if they confessed His identity. He was going to give them one more opportunity to confess Him as the Messiah—if they didn't, it would be their last. They needed to understand that His words were not His, but His Abba's—their Adonai. He told them that He didn't come to judge, but if they refused to heed His words, they would be their own judge.

Yeshua gave some of His talmidim instructions to go and make ready the essentials for celebrating the Passover Seder meal. He told them where to go, who to see, and what to say. When all was made ready, Yeshua reclined at the table and began to institute the Passover proceedings. If you notice, nothing is mentioned about the main entrée, the roasted lamb—only maror (a bitter-herb dip), wine, and bread. That is because this was not the actual Passover Seder. The actual Seder could not be instituted until the next evening on the fourteenth of Aviv (**EXOD 12:6**) at twilight, which is the beginning of the fifteenth of Aviv, the first day of the Feast of Unleavened Bread (Chag HaMatzot) (**LEV 23:5&6**). This was just a rehearsal—many YAHudi groups did this for the purpose of instruction and exhortation. The Church has identified this as "The Lord's Supper", "The Last Supper", or "Communion". He begins by telling them that He will not be able to keep the actual Passover because He will *be* the Passover Lamb. But He said He looks forward to the time when they will all celebrate it together with Him in the Kingdom of ELohim. I don't know about you, but I think it is a good idea to know how to participate in a Passover Seder. I wouldn't want to be like the guy who showed up at the wedding feast without the proper robe and tallit. How many churches even recognize the Passover? And mind you, Passover and/or the Feast of Firstfruits do not always agree with the Roman calendar's date that our churches traditionally celebrate as Easter Sunday. Many times a good month or even several weeks separate the two. Why is that? It's because of the Hebrew leap year, II Adar, which I explained earlier. Also in Chapters Two and Three, I explained that the first two cups are drunk before the meal is actually consumed. The first was the Cup of Sanctification and the second, the Cup of Plagues. It is this first cup that Yeshua offers after giving thanks that leads Him into telling them that He will not be able to partake of the actual Seder with them this time. He then takes the unleavened bread and, as tradition dictates, breaks it into two separate pieces and sets half of it aside.

Traditionally this set-aside half is to be wrapped in a napkin and hidden for the youngest child to recover later. He or she is to go and find it after the meal is eaten—it is seen as a type of dessert and is called the *afikoman*. This tradition is a training tool for the children of the household. I wish I could elaborate further on this Seder meal, but there are a multitude of symbols that would have to be explained. That's why I said we all need to learn how to participate in a Seder. The YAHudi instructions on how to prepare and celebrate a Seder, along with its comparison and symbolism to Yeshua, the final Pesach Lamb, allows the believer to know both the Abba and Yeshua even more intimately. This is also why I encourage you to study these things for yourself. What I will do, though, is give you a brief overview of the rest of a traditional Seder meal. The second portion is the eating of the meal itself, which Yeshua and His talmidim didn't do because it was only a rehearsal. The third portion of the Seder follows and consists of the partaking of a third cup of wine known as the Cup of Redemption. This portion now represents our personal Passover and helps us remember our own personal redemption. A final fourth cup remains before the Seder is complete. This cup is known as the Cup of Praise or the Kingdom Cup. It is not about remembering; instead, it is one of anticipation—a rehearsal cup. This was the cup that Yeshua was referring to when He said that He was looking forward to sharing it with His talmidim (and us) at the Seder (wedding feast) in His Kingdom. There is also a fifth cup known as ELeeYAHoo's Cup. It is never drunk—it remains untouched at an empty setting at the table. It is placed there in anticipation of the arrival of ELeeYAHoo because when He arrives, the Messiah will not be far behind.

Getting back to Yeshua's actions, He then divided the remaining portion and distributed it. He explained how this represented His body being broken for them and that the wine represented His blood being shed for them. He said that in the future, whenever they partook of the Passover Seder, if they would partake of it remembering what He had taught them that night, their eyes would be opened to the understanding of all of the mysteries in each step of the ordinances (Haggadah) of the Seder. By doing this, He was saying that the Passover Seder would now no longer be just the memorial of the Exodus from Mitsrahyim but also a memorial of the exodus from the curse of the Torah. After the distribution of the bread, Yeshua stopped to make the declaration that there was a betrayer among them. They immediately began to discuss who it might be that could do such a thing. This then led to a further dispute about who was the most worthy to hold a high position in His Kingdom. He interrupts and admonishes them to remain humble because that is what will determine greatness in His Abba's Kingdom. He did promise them again, though, that they would sit on thrones, judging the twelve tribes of YisraEL.

Yeshua then stood up, took off His outer robe, wrapped a towel around His waist, and proceeded to wash the feet of His talmidim. At this point in the Seder, the custom was for each person to wash their hands, but Yeshua changed the procedure. Kefa chided Yeshua not to wash just his feet, because that was too humiliating, but to give him a bath also if need be. Yeshua said it was only his feet that needed cleansing because they were the only thing that made contact with the earth and were always in need of washing—meaning that Kefa was no longer of this world but of His Kingdom. Yeshua did remark, though, that not all were clean—meaning YAHuda Iscariot. He told them that He did this to show them that they too were to always be ready to wash one another's feet, showing care and love for one another. He went on to say once again that there was one among them who must do what he must do to fulfill Scripture—*"Even My own familiar friend in whom I trusted, who ate My bread, has lifted up his heel against Me"* (**PSALM 41:9**). Kefa saw Yochanan leaning on Yeshua, so he motioned for him to ask Him to reveal who it was. Yeshua told him that it would be the one who would dip his portion of bread into the maror (the bitter-herb mixture) with Him. At that moment, YAHuda Iscariot dipped his bread into the maror with Yeshua. Also at that same moment in time, hasatan entered YAHuda, and Yeshua told him to go and do what he must do. When he left, the others thought that he went to take care of an errand for Yeshua.

Yeshua exhorted them once more to love one another to the point that others will thereby identify them as being one of His followers. Then He told them that He was going away and that they would not be able to come with Him. Kefa spoke up and asked Him where it was that He would be going that he wouldn't be able to follow. It was then that he told Yeshua that he would definitely be one of His followers and that he would follow Him even unto death. Yeshua told him that He knew his spirit was right, but because of his flesh, he would deny Him three times that very night before the rooster crowed twice at dawn. Then He told them that He was going to go to prepare a place for them and that He would return someday to take them with Him. Thomas spoke up and asked about the way to the kingdom, and Yeshua told him that He was the Way. Then Phillip asked Him to show them the Abba, and Yeshua told him that because they had seen Him, they had seen the Abba. He told them that when they went out to minister His message to others and found that they had a need to be met in order to carry out their mandate, they needed only to ask in His Name, and He would do it for them. He then reminded them that if they truly loved Him, they would do and keep all of His commandments, all 613 of them, because soon they would understand their full meaning. He is the Living Word and Torah—every commandment ever made throughout the Scriptures (TaNaKh) is His commandment. He promised them that He would ask His Abba not to leave them without help. He would send His Ruach to teach them and to remind them of His words. He told them He would manifest Himself to them, and He and the Abba would come and dwell within them if they would keep all of His commandments as He had taught them. Mind you, they didn't have the Brit Chadashah yet—they only had the TaNaKh. Yeshua instructed them on the importance of keeping the Torah and then added that *if* they truly loved Him, they would do and keep all of His commandments—not just ten—not just two—but all.

He told them that His time was very near and that when they went out this time on their own to fulfill their mandate, they were to take with them their moneybag, sack, sandals, and even a sword. This time it would not be a test as to the strength of their faith for their needs, but instead, it would be a test of their faith in His instructions that would see them through. He told them that if they didn't have a sword, then they should sell their tallit and purchase one (He really was referring to a Torah Scroll, not an actual sword). What they were now being called to do was to do battle against the power of darkness with the words of the Torah. Then He told them something else about His mission that they wouldn't understand until later. *"Therefore I will divide Him a portion with the great, and He shall divide the spoil with the strong, because He poured out His soul unto death, and He was numbered with the transgressors, and He bore the sin of many, and made intercession for the transgressors"..."Awake, O sword, against My Shepherd, against the Man who is My Companion," says YAHveh of hosts. "Strike the Shepherd, and the sheep will be scattered; then I will turn My hand against the little ones"* (**ISA 53:12** and **ZEC 13:7**). He would be hanging between two thieves when he gave up His spirit.

By now evening had begun, and they had entered the fifth day of the week, the fourteenth of Aviv (Thursday on the Roman calendar). At the next twilight of that day, the Passover lamb would be slain and eaten, and the first day of Unleavened Bread (Chag HaMatzot) would begin. Before leaving the upper room, they sang a hymn and then left to go up to the Mount of Olives. As I said before, they apparently didn't complete the last portion of the Seder because nothing is noted in this regard. On their way up, Yeshua tells them that they will all be put in a precarious position, and they will all forsake Him. He continued to teach them their final lessons before He was taken from them. One of the lessons that He taught was about His being the true vine and His branches being those who have faith in His words. They are His offspring and are pruned back if they fail to produce fruit. Those who refuse to abide in Him are cast off and burned. He continued speaking of their abiding in Him by abiding in His love. The way we are to express our love for Him is by keeping His commandments, meaning those that He taught both by His words and by the life that He lived as our example. He told them once more that they would have a new method of identification. It would be in the manner of how they loved one another. (I would say that this has been our biggest Achilles' heel—not loving one another. Christians have hated the Jews, Jews have hated the Christians, and we fight among ourselves on how to worship our Abba.) He told them that by living a lifestyle of obedience to His words, the world would hate them just as they hated Him. Once again, He reminds them that He would send the "Helper" (Ruach) to teach and strengthen them in their time of weakness, persecution, and trials. He went on to explain the ministry of the Ruach of YAH and how He would encourage them when they most needed it. He told them once again why He must go away, and once more they questioned Him as to the meaning of His words. He assured them that they would feel sorrow when He left, but their sorrow would be turned to joy. Once again, He told them that the hour was coming when they would be scattered because of a brief fear that they would experience due to their association with Him. Yeshua has to repeat, repeat, and then repeat it again because His people are dull of hearing. Then He stopped and began to pray for Himself regarding the work that His Abba had given Him to do. He also prayed for His talmidim and all future believers, that none would be lost and that all would be one (echad) with one another, just as He and His Abba are One (Echad).

After they finished praying, they crossed the Kidron Brook and entered a garden on the Mount of Olives known as Gethsemane. Taking the same three with Him that He did when they went up on the mountain, Kefa, Yochanan, and Yaacov, He went to pray and told them to keep watch. He began to pray in agony because His flesh desired not to have to drink this cup of sacrifice. He even began to perspire with drops of blood—He was in that much anguish. YAH sent angels to strengthen Him, which caused His divine side to take over, and He submitted to His Abba's will. He returned to find Kefa, Yochanan, and Yaacov sleeping because of their weariness. This occurred three times before He finally woke them up so that they could help Him meet His trial. It is then that YAHuda Iscariot brought the Roman guards, along with the guards from YAH's House, to arrest Yeshua. YAHuda Iscariot went up to Yeshua and kissed Him as the signal to the others that He was the one they wanted. When Yeshua asked them who it was they were seeking, they answered, "Yeshua of Nazareth." He told them that He was the one they were looking for. When He did, the power of the Ruach overcame them, and they fell backwards. (This phenomenon has been called "being slain in the Spirit". This is an authentic experience, but it has been counterfeited and abused in many religious circles, including many Charismatic gatherings.) When they ask again about His identity, He gives the same answer and then requests that the others be let go. Kefa, in a knee-jerk reaction, cuts off an ear of one of the servants of the high priest. Yeshua responds by commanding His talmidim not to resist and, at the same time, reaches out and restores the ear of the servant. At this point, just as Yeshua had said, His talmidim ran away to avoid His fate. Among them is a soon-to-become talmidim, Markus, who leaves so abruptly that the only garment he is wearing, a linen toga, is left behind in the struggle.

After binding Yeshua, they led Him away to Annas, the father-in-law of Caiaphas, the high priest. Kefa and Yochanan followed behind. Yochanan went into the courtyard because the high priest knew him, while Kefa waited outside. A short time later, Yochanan had Kefa brought in, and the girl who opened the gate for Kefa asked him whether or not he was one of Yeshua's followers—He denied it. (That was once.) Meanwhile, Yeshua was questioned by Annas about his teachings and after being struck for His answer, was taken before Caiaphas to answer the charges. When Kefa walked over to a fire within the courtyard to warm himself, someone else questioned him on whether or not he was a talmidim of Yeshua because of his Galilean accent. Again Kefa denied his association. (That's twice.) Then a relative of the servant who had his ear cut off spoke up and said, "Yes you are, you were in the garden with Him."

Kefa answered, "Man I am not—you are mistaken." At that very moment, the rooster crowed twice; it was dawn, and Kefa ran off to weep because he remembered Yeshua's words.

Meanwhile, Yeshua continued to be questioned all night by Caiaphas and by the elders of the Sanhedrin counsel, who used false witnesses who couldn't agree as to their testimony and their accusations. In their questioning, they asked Him whether or not He was the Son of ELuah, and after giving them His answer, they accused Him of blasphemy and then struck and abused Him even more until morning.

Apparently during the night, after realizing that his betrayal of Yeshua was going to cost Yeshua His life, YAHuda Iscariot tried to return the blood money to the chief elders. *"Then I said to them, "If it is agreeable to you, give me my wages; and if not, refrain." So they weighed out for my wages thirty pieces of silver. And YAHveh said to me, "Throw it to the potter"—that princely price they set on me. So I took the thirty pieces of silver and threw them into the House of YAHveh for the potter"* (JER 11:12&13). Upon their refusal to take back the price of betrayal, he threw it to the floor and went out and committed suicide.

At daybreak, they escorted Yeshua to the Praetorium to go before the governor, Pontius Pilate, and accuse Him of treason. They called for Pilate to come out to them and give them an audience because they could not enter the Praetorium (Goyim grounds), which would defile them, causing them not to be able to partake of the Passover meal that night. When Pilate came out, they made more false accusations against Yeshua, but He continued to keep silent. Pilate reentered the Praetorium and had Yeshua brought before Him there, where he asked Him if He truly was the King of the YAHudi. He acknowledged the truth to Pilate—He was a king, but not of this world. This is when Pilate asked Him the question, *"What is truth?"*, as I mentioned in the introduction of this book. The crowd outside told Pilate that Yeshua had been making trouble throughout the land, beginning in Galilee. Because Pilate could not determine if Yeshua could be held for anything, he decided to send Him to King Herod, who was in YAHrushalayim at the time because Galilee was under his jurisdiction.

Crazy Herod was anxious to see this Yeshua Man because of all the stories that he had heard. He hoped to get Him to perform one of His miracles, signs, or wonders before him. But when Yeshua refused to answer any of his questions, he had him dressed in a scarlet robe and sent back to Pilate.

Meanwhile, Pilate's wife warned him that she had had a disturbing dream about Yeshua the night before and that he should not harm Him. So Pilate once again sought to release Yeshua to the people, but they demanded the release of Barabbas, a dissident of the Roman occupation and an assassin, instead. What is rather ironic about this man Barabbas is his name. Bar means son, as in Bar-mitzvah, and abbas means fathers. So, Yeshua, the Son of the heavenly Father (Abba), was substituted for Barabbas, the son of the fathers. They not only demanded Barabbas' release, they demanded Yeshua's crucifixion. Pilate submitted to their demands and had Yeshua beaten with a flogging whip that consisted of lead balls with hooks on them that were attached to the ends of leather straps. After His beating, soldiers of the Praetorium jammed a crown of thorns down over His brow, put the scarlet robe back on Him, and mocked and paraded Him around. After being returned to Pilate, he took Yeshua and pleaded with the crowd to reconsider their demand. But they just screamed louder for Him to be crucified. They screamed out that He deserved to die because He proclaimed He was the Son of ELuah. This frightened Pilate even more, so he took Him back into the Praetorium. Pilate began questioning Yeshua again, hoping to find a reason to release Him, but Yeshua kept silent. Pilate vehemently begged Him to speak up for Himself and asked Him whether or not He realized that His life was in his hands at that time. Yeshua told him that he was not the one that held His life in the balance.

By this time, it was about noon, or the sixth hour, of the fifth day of the week, the fourteenth of Aviv. Pilate brought Yeshua out once more before the crowd and directed their attention to Him as he said, "Behold the Man" and "Here is your King". They replied, "We have no king but Caesar—crucify Him!" Pilate called for a bowl of water to be brought out, and he washed his hands symbolically of the whole incident. Afterwards, Barabbas was released, the scarlet robe was removed from Yeshua, and His own clothes were put back on Him. A crucifixion stake was given to Him to carry. (Whether this was a horizontal beam or a vertical one, the Scriptures do not say. Some have said that the YAHudi objected to a horizontal one because when it was attached to a vertical post, it resembled the Roman letter "t", which represented a sacrifice being given to honor a victory of the Roman war eluah, Thor. Therefore, because Yeshua was a YAHudi, it would be an abomination before YAHveh to do this.) Yeshua, being weak from His brutal handling, staggered under the weight of the beam, so a man by the name of Simon from the land of Cyrene in northern Africa was chosen to carry it for Him. When Yeshua saw the women following and weeping, He told them to weep instead for their children because there would be days coming when their own would be persecuted and ravaged ruthlessly. He reminded them of what the TaNaKh said, *"Also the high places of Aven the sin of YisraEL, shall be destroyed; The thorn and thistle shall grow on their alters; they shall say to the mountains, "Cover us!" and to the hills, "Fall on us!""* (HOS 10:8). He then posed a question to them—if they would do these things in the time of the coming of the Promised Messiah, what would they do to them in the time when all of this was but a faint memory or considered to be just a myth?

ROGER W. FEARING

The Crucifixion

They arrived on the outskirts of the city at a place known as "The Place of a Skull", where the Messiah, along with two criminals who were found guilty of robbery, would be crucified. It seems that capital punishment was the order of the day for anyone, regardless of the crime. Simon of Cyrene struggled up the hill carrying the heavy stake that the Messiah would soon be impaled upon. Once there, the soldiers nailed a declaration on Yeshua's stake proclaiming, "Yeshua of Nazareth, the King of the YAHudi". Pilate had ordered it, and when the YAHudi who were standing nearby saw it, they protested. The "Place of a Skull" must have been one of the many sites where crucifixions took place, but on that day, it appears that only three of them dotted the landscape—one on Yeshua's right and the other on His left. The Scriptures declare that the hour was the third hour of the day. This was more than likely the time-keeping of the Romans (three p.m.), when we consider the circumstances leading up to the actual events. As has been mentioned before, the Hebrew daytime starts at dawn, or around six a.m., so it is obvious this could not have taken place at nine a.m. (the Hebrew third hour)—it would have been too early for all of the other situations to have occurred by then. It would have been closer to the Hebrew ninth hour, or three p.m. This would also coincide with a more reasonable time when He would have been removed from the tree. Also, as we made note of earlier in the Scriptures, He was brought the second time before Pilate in the sixth hour, or noon. He could not have seen Pilate in the sixth (Hebrew) hour if He had already been hung on the tree in the third (Hebrew) hour.

While Yeshua was suffering under excruciating pain, the soldiers who had hung Him there cast lots for His clothing, which fulfilled another prophecy regarding Him—*"They divided My garments among them, and for My clothing they cast lots"* (**PSALM 22:18**). The soldiers, in their perverse and cruel humor, offered Him a sponge soaked in vinegar as a drink. Many who were there witnessed for themselves His humility during His punishment, while others began to mock and accuse Him because of His words. This included the elders, the priests, the scribes, and even one of the thieves being crucified with Him. The other one, however, recognized His innocence and out of faith asked to be remembered when Yeshua entered His Kingdom. Yeshua assured Him that they would be together that very day. Even without being immersed after conversion, Yeshua granted him salvation because of his faith and acknowledgment—so much for religious traditions and regulations. He and the Messiah were sharing in another type of immersion, though—the immersion of suffering. Then Yeshua, in His compassion, looked down at His mother, who was standing below Him, and commissioned His talmid, Yochanan, to care for her.

Yeshua hung there for three more hours until about six p.m., when He cried out the words from **PSALM 22:1**: *"ELoi, ELoi, lama sabachthani?—ELohim, ELohim, why have You forsaken Me?"* The psalm goes on to say, *"Why are You so far from helping Me, and from the words of My groaning?"* During that time, from three p.m. until six p.m., an unusual darkness came upon the Earth. Some have suggested that storm clouds, along with a solar eclipse, could have taken place at that time. This could not be the case as far as the solar eclipse is concerned because this was the fourteenth of the month of Aviv, the time of a full moon—a solar eclipse can only occur during a new moon. Again, Yeshua asked for something to drink, and they once more offered Him vinegar. Once He tasted the vinegar, He cried out in a loud voice, **"It is finished"**. He also said, *"Into Your hand I commit My spirit"* (**PSALM 31:5**). This psalm continues with: *"You have redeemed Me, O YAHveh ELohim of truth"*. At that very moment, the Earth quaked, the rocks split, and the thick veil that concealed the Holy of Holies at the House of YAH was torn in two from the top to the bottom, exposing the Holiest Place for all to see and enter. The way to YAHveh, the Abba of Heaven and Earth, was now revealed and made accessible for all mankind. Many of those destined for the resurrection came out of the tombs as a witness to His being the Adonai of all things. Although the Scriptures do not explicitly say so, those destined for the resurrection would have risen on the same day that Yeshua did, the day of the Feast of Firstfruits—they would have been the firstfruits of the resurrection.

At first the soldiers stood in awe at the sight, but then out of fear, they ran to break the legs of those hanging from their crosses in order to hasten their deaths. However, when they came to Yeshua, He appeared to be dead already. To make certain, they pierced His side and water and blood came out, which indicated that He was indeed dead. *"He guards all His bones; not one of them is broken"* (**PSALM 34:20**). *"And I will pour on the House of Dahveed and on the inhabitants of YAHrushalayim the Ruach of grace and supplication; then they will look on Me whom they have pierced; they will mourn for Him as one mourns for his only son, and grieve for Him as one grieves for a firstborn"* (**ZECH 12:10**).

The Burial

It was now twilight of the Preparation Day (Thursday, sundown of the fourteenth of Aviv), the day that the Pesach lamb was to be prepared. In this case, Yeshua was the prepared Pesach Lamb of ELohim. It was also the day before the feast Sabbath of Unleavened Bread, the end of the fifth day and the beginning of the sixth day of the week (Friday). Because this feast Sabbath, the fifteenth of Aviv, fell on the sixth day (Friday), the weekly Sabbath (Saturday) would be the following day. Because of this, Yeshua's body needed to be taken down and hurriedly placed into a temporary burial tomb and could only be partially embalmed. There would be two days in between before the embalming could be completed on the third day. Yosef of Arimathea, a member of the Sanhedrin Council, and Nicodemus, a priest and rabbi, both secret believers in Yeshua's Messiahship, asked and gained permission to remove His body for burial. Not all of the elders, priests, scribes, Pharisees, Sadducees, and everyday YAHudi denied Yeshua as being Messiah Adonai. But these two were bold enough to come forward and take charge of the situation. They took His body to a newly prepared tomb chamber owned by Yosef himself. They were accompanied by some of the women who had provided Yeshua and His talmidim with most of their material needs. When they arrived, they quickly prepared the body of our Adonai with enough embalming spices to preserve His body for the next three days and wrapped it in a burial shroud. The first night and day was the beginning of the Sabbath of Unleavened Bread. The second night and day was the weekly Sabbath. The third night and day was the Feast of Firstfruits, the first day of the following week—they could finish the embalming then because it wasn't a Sabbath. On the Sabbath of Unleavened Bread, the Pharisees and the chief priests requested that Pilate place a guard at the entrance to the tomb for three days. This would guarantee that Yeshua's talmidim could not come and steal His body in order to claim His resurrection—Pilate granted their request.

The Resurrection

Apparently sometime during the early hours of the third morning, perhaps even before the sun had risen, another earthquake took place, and an angel of YAHveh came down and rolled back the stone that covered the entrance to the tomb. The sight overwhelmed the guards, and they too were "slain in the Ruach of YAH" (fell down as though dead). The incident so frightened them that they ran for their very lives. Shortly after dawn, three of the women who usually ministered to Yeshua (Miriam, Yeshua's mother—Miriam of Magdala, a former prostitute who had seven demons driven out of her—Salome, also known as Joanna) came to finish the embalming process. When they arrived, the stone had been rolled away, and when they entered, they saw two men in shining clothing standing at both the foot and the head of the place where Yeshua's body had been placed. The two men reminded them of Yeshua's words about His resurrection and that His words had been fulfilled—*He had risen*. The women ran away in fear of what they had just witnessed. Miriam of Magdala ran and told Kefa and Yochanan first, who then ran immediately to the tomb to see for themselves. When they arrived, they found the linen burial cloths laid out just as Miriam had described. After Kefa and Yochanan had left to verify what they had seen, Miriam of Magdala stayed in the garden and wept because she didn't know what had become of her Adonai. Seeing who she thought might be the gardener, she asked whether he could shed some light on the situation.

Then Yeshua spoke to her, and she realized it was her Rabboni Messiah and not the gardener. She fell at His feet, but He told her not to touch Him because He had not yet returned to present His blood before His Abba. He instructed her to go instead and tell His talmidim what she had just witnessed. While the other two women were running to tell the remaining talmidim, Yeshua appeared to them also. He told them to tell the rest of His talmidim that He had kept His word and had overcome death for all of those who believe in Him and that they should wait in Galilee—He would meet them there.

While all of this was going on, the guards ran to tell the chief priests what had just happened. After meeting with the elders, they decided to pay the guards money to report that Yeshua's talmidim had stolen the body after they had fallen asleep. They assured them that they would take care of the necessary details in order to keep them from suffering any consequences. The Scriptures say here that this story would continue to be the one told, and it has been throughout the centuries.

When the women came to tell the other talmidim about what had happened, no one wanted to believe them. But that same day, two other talmidim, not of the Twelve, were on their way to the city of Emmaus, which was about seven miles away, when they met Yeshua on the road but did not recognize Him. One of them, Cleopas, shared with Him about the recent events and how it had left them all distraught. Then Yeshua began to remind them how the TaNaKh had revealed that all of these things must happen to the Promised Messiah, and if they had been astute, they would not have been beguiled. Later, when Yeshua accepted their invitation to break bread with them, their eyes became open to His identity. Then, as soon as He had said the barukh (blessing), He immediately disappeared from their sight. Apparently Yeshua had also appeared to Kefa because when Cleopas returned to YAHrushalayim and told his story to the Ten, they told him that Kefa too had seen Him. At that moment, Yeshua appeared to them, even though the doors were locked. He greeted them with "Shalom ahlekehim" (Peace be unto you). They were frightened at first, thinking they were seeing a spirit. Yeshua assured them that it was He because, unlike a spirit, He had flesh and bones. He then sat down and ate some fish and some bread to prove it. (Yeshua doesn't deny the existence of ghosts or the ability of spirits being able to move among the living. To me, this confirms that the spirits of the wicked can become demons and have the freedom to leave the Pit to haunt and torment the living.) After reassuring them that He was truly alive, He breathed on them the Ruach of ELohim. This was the giving of the gift of Redemption; they were now born of the Ruach and now officially made sons like Ahdom—in the likeness of YAHveh. Mankind (Ahdom) was made on the sixth day in the image of YAH. After sin, Ahdom's descendants were made in his (Ahdom's) image. Now, after Yeshua's gift of the Ruach, they were once more made (or born-again) in the image of YAH, through faith by grace. Now they were given the authority to forgive others of their sins. Not only that, but this gift had been made available to any who would believe on Him. This took place when only the Ten (talmidim) were there—the Eleventh, Thomas, was not with them on this evening of the Feast of Firstfruits. However, when he was told about the incident, he refused to believe unless he could see it with his own eyes. One week later, probably on the next weekly Sabbath, all of the Eleven were together this time, and Yeshua appeared to them and had Thomas place his hand and finger in His wounds. Yeshua appeared to them for a third time while they were fishing. He was on the shore and called out to them, asking whether or not they had caught anything. He then told them to recast their nets, and they caught one hundred and fifty-three fish at one time. When Kefa realized it was Yeshua, he jumped overboard and swam to meet Him. Once on shore, Yeshua asked Him three times whether he loved Him or not. Kefa answered each time, *"Yes, You know that I love You."* (This was done so that Kefa could pay recompense for denying Him three times on the night that He was arrested.) Yeshua responded each time by telling Kefa to feed His sheep. After that, He told him in what manner he was to meet his own fate. Kefa then asked Him what manner of death would Yochanan meet, and Yeshua told him that this was not his affair. Yochanan lived to be the last of the Shelichim and died in Ephesus after his imprisonment on the isle of Patmos, where he wrote the Book of Revelation. Kefa went on to be a Shelich to his fellow YAHudi and was crucified upside down at his request—he didn't feel worthy to die the same way as His Adonai. These things happened at the hands of the cruel Emperor Nero.

The Mandate and Ascension

Yeshua appeared to them many more times during the period between the Day of Firstfruits (which begins the barley season) and the fiftieth day (when the wheat season begins), which is called Shavuot and is the final day of the Feast of Weeks. Seven Sabbaths are to be counted before bringing the Feast of Fruits to a climax. His time with them would have been about forty days (remember, forty is a time of testing). Just before He left them, He gave them a mandate. First, they were to teach everything He had taught and demonstrated to them concerning the revelation of the TaNaKh to anyone who would listen. They were to begin their teachings in YAHrushalayim and from there take them into all of the surrounding YAHudi territory. After that, they were to go into the territory of Samaria and beyond to Galilee, to seek out the lost sheep of YisraEL from the twelve tribes, and then beyond to the Goyim nations in every direction. They were to immerse in water all who confess Him as Adonai, as a public sign of their confession. They were also to immerse them in the teaching of the TaNaKh by the washing of the water of His Words. They were to immerse them into the fullness of their Abba, into the fullness of the Messiah, and into the fullness of their Helper, the Ruach HaKedosh, through these teachings. He told them that whoever receives these teachings will be redeemed—whoever will not, will be condemned. He went on to tell them that whoever receives these teachings will also receive power from the Ruach to heal the sick, cast out demons, and speak in the languages of men and angels (languages they have not learned in the natural). They will have the power to overcome any attempt on their lives until they have accomplished that mission for which they were created to accomplish.

Acts 1

After giving them all of these promises, He then continues with His instructions for them to wait in YAHrushalayim until they receive the power to fulfill His mandate on the Day of Shavuot, a few short days away—about ten. When He had given them all of these final instructions, He led them up toward Bethany, to the top of the Mount of Olives. They then asked Him if He was going to restore the Whole House of YisraEL at that time. He told them only His Abba knew the appointed time for this to take place. He told them that they should just concern themselves with following the instructions that He had just mandated to them. After this, they saw Him ascend into the clouds, and an angel told them that they would see Him return in the same manner that they saw Him leave, when He returns to set up His Kingdom. This was the climax of the seven earlier covenants that had been given to the people of YisraEL—this was now the beginning of the eighth and final covenant, the **"Brit Chadashah"** (the number eight stands for new beginnings). They stayed for awhile and worshiped Him and then returned to YAHrushalayim. They all went up to the upper room, probably the one where they had the Seder rehearsal, and cast lots to determine who would replace YAHuda Iscariot. This was done because Kefa recognized what the TaNaKh had prophesied about this situation. *"Let their habitation be desolate; let no one dwell in their tent"* (**PSALM 69:25**). *"Let his days be few, and let another take his office"* (**PSALM 109:8**). The lot fell to Matthias (another Mathew) and he became the Twelfth Shelich.

Conclusion

The life of Yeshua HaMashiach demonstrates one very important thing—He was the Living Torah and at the same time YAHveh our ELohim in the flesh. He fulfilled all prophecy regarding the Promised Messiah. He lived a life of sinlessness because we can't. He paid for our redemption with His sinless blood—the only atonement eligible. He gave us understanding of the truth of the TaNaKh. Now He expects us to be able to live it since there is no more curse left in the Torah to be paid. He sent the gift of the Ruach to redeem, sanctify, and teach us, while bringing to our remembrance all the things that He taught. He has given us eternal life in the promised resurrection. He has promised us a millennium period in which to rest, rule, and reign with Him, followed by a new Heaven and Earth. What more do we need? Why have we changed what He has given us into something that He wouldn't recognize as being anything that He taught regarding the Torah and the TaNaKh? Why Sunday Sabbaths—why Easter and Christmas—why church buildings—why images of saints and images of Himself to fall down and pray to? This wasn't what He taught, and this certainly wasn't His will for us. Why do we make it so hard when He made it so simple? Why don't we just allow ourselves to be conformed into His image instead of our trying to create Him into ours?

CHAPTER 20
...about Acts 2—15

The book of Acts, or the ministry of the Shelichim, is really just part two of Lucas' writings regarding the life and ministry of Yeshua. Many of the things that he records in this second set of writings are about events that he personally witnessed. Others were the accounts that were passed on to him from other eyewitnesses, including the shelichim, when he later joined up with them during their travels.

The first event pertaining to the twelve shelichim involved Yeshua's promise that they would receive power, granted to them by YAH, through His Ruach HaKedosh. He described it as being similar to Yochanan's immersion, except that this time it would be an inward immersion from YAH's Ruach, who would saturate their entire being, including their spirits. He had told them to wait in YAHrushalayim until they received it. They patiently waited in the upper room and prayed, not knowing what the authorities might try to do to them because all of Yeshua's followers were suspect in a recent revolt against Rome. But when the Feast of Shavuot arrived on the day after the forty-ninth Sabbath following Firstfruits, they gathered into one place in the Courtyard of YAH's House and joined the multitude of YAHudi who came from the surrounding nations to celebrate the feast. Then everyone who had come to the House of YAH witnessed a startling phenomenon. They saw fire coming down out of the sky and heard the sound of a violent wind—but they felt neither breeze nor the heat from the flames. What they did see was the fire dividing into smaller flames and hovering over each of the one-hundred and twenty followers of Yeshua who were there in their midst. These were similar sounds and sights to those that their ancestors had witnessed on this anniversary during the giving of the Torah on Mount Seenahee (Sinai) fifteen centuries earlier. Then another phenomenon occurred almost immediately following the first. All one hundred and twenty went throughout the crowd and began to speak to those who would listen—they spoke about the wonderful works of YAH and His Son, Yeshua HaMashiach, in the languages and dialect of each individual person. Some who just could not accept this miracle began to mock and accuse them of being drunk, even at that early hour of the day.

Kefa grabbed the crowd's attention and began to teach them from the TaNaKh, out of the book of the Ne'vee YoEL. *"And it shall come to pass afterward that I will pour out My Ruach on all flesh; your sons and your daughters shall prophesy, your old men shall dream dreams, your young men shall see visions; and also on My menservants, and on My maidservants I will pour out My Ruach in those days. "And I will show wonders in the heavens and in the earth: Blood and fire and pillars of smoke. The sun shall be turned into darkness, and the moon into blood, before the coming of the great and terrible day of YAHveh. And it shall come to pass that whoever calls on the Name of YAHveh shall be saved. For in Mount Zeeon and in YAHrushalayim there shall be deliverance, as YAHveh has said, among the remnant whom YAHveh calls"* (**JOEL 2:28-32**). Kefa was confirming that they were witnesses of this partial fulfillment of one of the many prophecies regarding the coming of the final days that would commence at the arrival of the Messiah. This was the early fulfillment—its climax would come just before His return and after the remnant of the Whole House of YisraEL had been restored. He continued to preach using the words of King Dahveed: *"I have set YAHveh always before me; because He is at my right hand I shall not be moved. Therefore my heart is glad, and my glory rejoices; my flesh also will rest in hope. For You will not leave my soul in Sheol, nor will You allow Your Holy One to see corruption. You will show me the path of life; in Your presence is fullness of joy; at Your right hand are pleasures forevermore"* (**PSALM 16:8-11**). Kefa reminded them that King Dahveed could not have been speaking of himself because of what he said later: *"YAHveh said to my Adonai, 'Sit at My right hand, till I make Your enemies Your footstool"* (**PSALM 110:1**). After Kefa's sermon, the followers of Yeshua were increased by three thousand in that one day. Each one was immersed in water afterward, as a sign of their commitment, and received the infilling of the Ruach HaKedosh.

Then, just as Yeshua had promised them, *"They went out and preached everywhere, Adonai working with them and confirming the word through the accompanying signs. Omien (Amen)"* (**MARK 16:20**). After this, they sat under the teachings of the shelichim and began to receive insight as to the full meaning of the TaNaKh. Many sold their possessions to support this new community, or kahal. They gathered daily at the House of YAH, shared their bread with one another at each other's home, and continued in the growth of the Body of Messiah. Was this a New YisraEL? No, it was the original beginning to be restored—YAHudi, Samaritans, Galileans, and Goyim (these were descendants from all of the tribes).

Later, Kefa and Yochanan went up to the House of YAH to pray during the time of the evening prayer, around six p.m. While approaching the gate called Beautiful, they took notice of a beggar asking for alms. Now they had seen this man many times before, as had Yeshua, because he had been there begging daily. But the Ruach caused them to take notice because YAHveh wanted to do something for this man on this particular day. But instead of giving him any alms, Kefa tested his faith by saying to him, *"Silver and gold I do not have, but what I do have I will give you: In the name of Yeshua HaMashiach of Nazareth, rise up and walk"* (**ACTS 3:6**). Now I'm sure this man had seen Yeshua going in and out of the House of YAH many times with His talmidim, so he knew Kefa and Yochanan by mere sight. But when he heard these words, faith for healing rushed into his body, soul, and spirit, and as Kefa took him by the hand, he stood up and began leaping and running into the House of Worship, praising ELuah. When the people standing about saw this miracle, they began wondering what they had just witnessed. Kefa rebuked them for their unbelief and declared that this had happened because the ELohim of Avraham, Yitzhak, and Yaacov wanted to glorify His Son, Yeshua, whom they were responsible for putting to death, but who had risen from the grave. He continued to remind them of what all the Ne'vim had prophesied about these things, even Mosheh, the giver of the Torah—*"YAHveh your ELohim will raise up for you a Ne'vee like me from your midst, from your brethren. Him you shall hear."*—*"I will raise up for them a Ne'vee like you from among their brethren, and will put My words in His mouth, and He shall speak to them all that I command Him. 'And it shall be that whoever will not hear My words, which He speaks in My Name, I will require it of him"* (**DEUT 18:15** and **18&19**). Kefa stood amazed at them for their blindness, especially since they were descendants of the fathers of YisraEL. They had been taught these things from their youth, but they couldn't seem to make the connection. *"In your seed all the nations of the earth shall be blessed, because you have obeyed My voice."*—*"And I will make your descendants multiply as the stars of heaven; I will give to your descendants all these lands; and in your seed all the nations of the earth shall be blessed"* (**GEN 22:18, 26:4**). Because the talmidim were teaching these scriptures regarding Yeshua to the people in YAH's House, the priests and the Sadducees had them arrested and put into prison. Even so, five-thousand other men heard these truths and believed, and they too were added to the Kahal.

The next day they had to appear before the Sanhedrin Council and explain themselves. When asked, they proclaimed that they had done and taught these things in the Name of Yeshua, the Son of YAHveh, and even dared to remind them of the words of the TaNaKh—*"The stone which the builders rejected has become the chief cornerstone"* (**PSALM 118:22**). The rulers became afraid of what the crowd might do if anything severe were done to these men because the people had seen their works and heard their words, so they just commanded them not to teach or speak in the Name of Yeshua again. Kefa and Yochanan responded by saying that they could not do that; they must continue because it was their commission as servants of YAHveh.

After being let go, they went immediately to the others and told them of the incident. They all began to praise YAHveh, ELohim of YisraEL, and asked Him once again to confirm His words with signs and wonders as they took His word forward. They reminded themselves of King Dahveed's words:

"Why do the nations rage, and the people plot a vain thing? The kings of the earth set themselves, and the rulers take counsel together, against YAHveh and against His Messiah" (**PSALM 2:1&2**). Once again, the Ruach of YAH came down and shook the place where they were gathered and refilled them with His Power. YAHveh still longs to do all of these things for His people, YisraEL, but they first have to return and be in harmony with His Torah and His TaNaKh. Over the centuries He has manifested some of these things in order to encourage His people, but they would walk in His truth for awhile and then return to their old ways. We are now living in the final days before the return of His Son to take His rightful place as King. I believe that YAH is Reforming His Kahal for the last time—so be ready.

There was a man named Yosef whom the shelichim called Barnabas (Son of Encouragement). He was a generous man who loved YisraEL and Yeshua. He decided it best to sell all that he had and give it to the benefit of the House of YisraEL. Another man, named Ananias, along with his wife, Sapphira, had either jealousy or admiration toward Barnabas' generosity. In either case, they harbored greed in their hearts, so they conjured up a scheme. They would sell their land as Barnabas did, but they would only give a portion of it to the support of the Kahal of YisraEL. They wanted to impress everyone and cause them to think that they too were on the same spiritual level in their generosity as Barnabas. But the Ruach was not going to allow this type of corruption to begin to plant its seeds in the hearts of these new believers, so He revealed their plot to Kefa. Kefa was outraged and prophesied their deaths as they came forward one at a time, trying to deceive those in authority and lying to the Ruach. (This is a lesson for us all. Don't try to deceive those who are truly in spiritual authority—it won't work. If the Ruach of YAH is truly in the midst of a kahal, He will expose those who are wrongdoers, as well as the plans of deception that are in their hearts. Those who are self-seekers and come into His presence with motives of greed will soon become uncomfortable among true worshipers and will either come under conviction and repent, or leave. His concern is for the spiritual health and well-being of His family.) Because of the sincerity of their commitment to furthering the growth of the kingdom, the shelichim continued to work in the Power of the Ruach by healing and delivering many sick people who were brought to them.

Once more the chief priests and Sadducees took council and ordered the shelichim to be arrested and thrown into prison. While in prison, an angel came and opened the prison doors and told them to return to the House of YAH and to witness to any who would receive the full truth of the Torah. In the morning, the rulers of the Council gave orders that the shelichim be brought out to appear before them, but when the guards got to the prison, they found that they were all gone and had returned to Shalomo's Porch to preach their new doctrine regarding the Torah. They were arrested the second time for their insubordinate actions and brought again before the Sanhedrin. When they were told that they were not to teach in Yeshua's name any longer, the shelichim asked them whom they should obey, ELuah or men. This time the high priest and those who were with them wanted to take them and have them killed. But a very well-known Pharisee by the name of Gamaliel spoke up and warned them that if this phenomenon, which was being manifested within YAHuda, was of just mere men, it would soon disappear, but if it were from ELuah, no one could stop it. He recommended leaving them alone, so they had them beaten and then released. The shelichim continued to teach from house to house and in the courts of the House of YAH, accompanied by signs and wonders.

There were two Messianic sects within the Body—those who spoke mostly Hebrew and those who had adopted the more common language of Greek. Those who spoke the original language of the Torah (Hebrew) began to neglect the needs of the widows of the ones who spoke Greek. When these types of disputes began to occur, the shelichim decided that it was time to have others appointed who could take care of such matters so that they could concentrate on the spiritual needs of the Kahal. This was when the office of deacons was created. This first office consisted of seven men, chosen by the shelichim, who were full of the knowledge of the TaNaKh and filled with the Power of the Ruach.

One of these men, Stephen, had become well-known among the brethren because of his spiritual understanding and because of the signs and wonders that confirmed his words. His fame and the fame of all of those who followed the teachings of Yeshua continued to spread throughout the land of YAHuda and even among the Orthodox YAHudi. Those of the Orthodox doctrine began to refer to them as the sect of the Nazarenes. One of the Orthodox synagogues gathered together false witnesses to say that Stephen was one of those who taught that the Torah was no longer to be followed, or that no one was under the Law any longer, and that the teaching of Mosheh had been made obsolete. He was brought before the high priest and asked whether or not these things were true. He gave his answer by appealing to their knowledge of the TaNaKh. He reminded them of their abba, Avraham, and the words that YAH had spoken to him: *"Now YAHveh had said to Avram: "Get out of your country, from your kindred and from your abba's house, to a land that I will show you"* (**GEN 12:1**). He went on to remind them that when Avraham obeyed His words and went to Haran, he remained there until he was seventy-five-years old. Afterwards, YAH took him to the land of Canaan, where He promised him that after his descendents had dwelt in a foreign land for four-hundred years, they would eventually come into bondage and be oppressed. But He promised them that He would deliver them and bring them back into the land that He had promised Avraham. *"Then He said to Avram: "Know certainly that your descendants will be strangers in a land that is not theirs, and will serve them, and they will afflict them four hundred years. "And also the nation whom they serve I will judge; afterward they shall come out with great possessions"* (**GEN 15:13&14**). Stephen continued speaking about the covenant of circumcision and how Avraham had begotten Yitzhak, who begot Yaacov and his twelve sons, the patriarchs. Then, how Yaacov's sons sold their brother, Yosef, into Mitsrahyim (Egypt), where he found favor with the Pharaoh and eventually became governor. After this, Yosef died and the descendants of YisraEL increased, and another Pharaoh put them into slavery because he was afraid of their great numbers. He told of how Mosheh was born to be a deliverer, or savior, for them and how he was raised in the Pharaoh's courts until he was forty-years old, but left because he had struck down another Mitsrahyim while defending a fellow Hebrew. The next day, when he saw two of his kinsmen fighting, he tried to separate them, but found out to his dismay, their attitude toward him—*"Who made you a ruler and a judge over us? 'Do you want to kill me as you did the Mitsrahyim yesterday?"* (**EXOD 2:14**). So he fled. Then after another forty years of being a shepherd, He saw and heard the Angel of YAHveh speak to him out of a burning bush at Mt. Seenahee—*"Then He said. "Do not draw near this place. 'Take your sandals off your feet, for the place where you stand is kedosh (holy) ground." Moreover He said, "I AM the ELohim of your abbaim (fathers)—the ELohim of Avraham, the ELohim of Yitzhak, and the ELohim of Yaacov." And Mosheh hid his face, for he was afraid to look upon ELohim. And YAHveh said: "I have surely seen the oppression of My people who are in Mitsrahyim, and have heard their cry because of their taskmasters, for I know their sorrows. "So I have come down to deliver them out of the hand of the Mitsrahyim, and to bring them up from that land to a good and large land, to a land flowing with milk and honey, to the place of the Canaani and the Hittitim and the Amoritim and the Parizzim and the Hivitim and the Yebusi. "Now therefore, behold, the cry of the children of YisraEL had come to Me, and I have also seen the oppression with which the Mitsrahyim oppress them. "Come now, therefore, and I will send you to Pharaoh that you may bring My people, the children of YisraEL, out of Mitsrahyim"* (**EXOD 3:5-10**). Then Mosheh returned, succumbing to YAHveh's persuasion, to deliver his brethren, thereby bringing to fruition YAH's promise to Avraham. Stephen then reminded them of some other words that Mosheh had written in the Torah that YAHveh had given him—*"YAHveh your ELohim will raise up for you a Ne'vee like me from your midst, from your brethren. Him you shall hear"* (**DEUT 18:15**). But even though it was this Mosheh who gave the oracles of YAHveh to us, our abbaim (fathers) rejected him also. *"Now when the people saw that Mosheh delayed coming down from the mountain, the people gathered together to Aharon, and said to him, "Come, make us an eluah that shall go before us; for as for this Mosheh, the man who brought us up* *out of Mitsrahyim, we do not know what has become of him"* (**EXOD 32:1**). Stephen continued to remind them what the Ne'vim had to say about YisraEL. *"Did you offer Me sacrifices and offerings in the wilderness forty years, O House of YisraEL? You also carried the tabernacle of Moloch your king and Remphan your idols, the star of your elohim, which you made for yourselves. Therefore I will send you into captivity beyond Damascus to Babylon for seventy years," says YAHveh, whose Name is the ELohim of hosts"* (**AMOS 5:25**). He reminded them that they were just like their abbaim in that they were stiff-necked and would not obey or listen to their heavenly Abba. They desecrated the tabernacle in the wilderness and insisted on building a dwelling place for the ELohim of Yaacov, who does not live in a house made with hands like the temples of foreign elohim. But because they were a stiff-necked people, He relinquished to their appetites and allowed them to build Him a palace anyway. *"Thus says YAHveh; "Heaven is My throne, and earth is My footstool. Where is the house that you will build Me? And where is the place of My rest?"* (**ISA 66:1&2**) Upon hearing his words, the crowd came under conviction, went wild, took up stones, and stoned him to death. In the meanwhile, they laid their clothes at the feet of a rising new star among the Pharisees named Rav Shaul (Rabbi Saul/Paul).

The religious leaders apparently did not heed the words of the great teacher/rabbi and Pharisee, Gamaliel, because they refused to leave the Nazarenes alone. Instead, the persecution grew worse, and Gamaliel's star pupil, Shaul/Saul, joined in, relishing the idea of dragging the followers of this sect of blasphemers from their homes and putting them into prison. As a result, this new commune began to seek refuge in other regions of YAHuda and in Samaria. Then Shelich Philip, one of Yeshua's first talmidim, went into the territory of the Samaritans and witnessed to the people there about the Messiah. He, like Stephen, did many signs and wonders confirming YAHveh's truths regarding the TaNaKh. Samaria, being full of people who practiced all types of religions because of their ancestors, had many practicing soothsayers, magicians, and others of the black arts. Among them was a sorcerer named Simon the Great, whose powers were credited to YAHveh, ELuah/the Mighty One, but he used them for personal gain. But when this Simon heard the words of Philip and saw the miracles that he did, he too believed and was immersed into the Body of Believers. Kefa and Yochanan heard about the great work that Philip was doing for the growth and restoration of the Whole House of YisraEL, so they went up to Samaria to assist him in administering the immersion of the Ruach HaKedosh. After they arrived, they told the multitude of new believers about receiving the Ruach, and when they began to lay hands on them and the manifestation of speaking in an unlearned language emerged, Simon the Great offered to purchase this gift from Kefa with money. Kefa discerned that Simon had a spirit of bitterness deep within him that had deceived him for many years. It caused him to have such a high regard for the power of money that he had taken the gifts that YAHveh had given him and had given them to hasatan for personal profit. Kefa commanded him to repent from this attitude, and when he did, he asked Kefa to pray for him to be forgiven for his sin.

One day, Philip was told by the Ruach to go down to the Gaza strip, along the Mediterranean Sea, where he would find an Ethiopian eunuch of the queen's court, studying and trying to understand the TaNaKh. The eunuch was reading where it said, *"He was oppressed and He was afflicted, yet He opened not His mouth; He was led as a lamb to the slaughter, and as a sheep before its shearers is silent, so He opened not His mouth; He was taken from prison and from judgment, and who will declare His generation? For He was cut off from the land of the living; for the transgressions of My people He was stricken"* (**ISA 53:7&8**). When Philip found him, he explained that it was Yeshua, the Promised Messiah, who was being described here and how He came and died so that the curse of the Torah might be lifted. Upon hearing this, the Ethiopian eunuch believed that Yeshua was the Son of ELuah. They found some water nearby, and the eunuch asked if he might be immersed in the Name of Adonai Yeshua. As soon as the eunuch was immersed, Philip was translated away out of the eunuch's sight to the city of Ashdod.

Another name that the Nazarenes became known as was "The Way". Young Rav Shaul, in his ambition, desired to pursue this cult of blasphemers, as he saw them, and bring them back to YAHrushalayim for trial—all the way to Damascus in Syria, if necessary. But Yeshua had other plans for this zealot; He was going to use him to take His message to the lost tribes of YisraEL, who were scattered among the Goyim throughout the Roman Empire. So, just before Shaul arrived in Damascus, he was met with a blinding light that was accompanied by a voice that told him about the error of his ways. Yeshua knew Shaul had a hungry heart for the Torah and the things of YAHveh, but he, as were so many others, had been terribly misguided. The voice of Yeshua penetrated his heart, and he repented of his errors. He was now convinced that Yeshua was the Promised Messiah whom the TaNaKh had spoken of as being YAHveh in the flesh. His ELuah had come down to dwell with man, making it possible for him to fellowship with his heavenly Abba. The brightness of the Shchinah glory that beamed from Yeshua had left Shaul blind, so Yeshua told him to go into Damascus and ask for a man named Ananias, who would lay hands on him to restore his sight. Shaul was now born-again and did as he was commanded. He went to a man's house, whose name was YAHuda, where he fasted for three days. Meanwhile, Yeshua appeared in a vision to Ananias and told him to go to YAHuda's house on a street in Damascus that was named Straight and minister healing to a man named Shaul. At first Ananias was reluctant because he had heard of Rav Shaul's reputation for persecuting the Kahal, but he went anyway.

WHAT WE WEREN'T TAUGHT ABOUT THE BIBLE AND ITS HISTORY

When Ananias arrived, he laid his hands on Shaul, called him brother, and he received both his sight and the infilling of the Ruach. Afterwards, they went out to a place where Shaul could be immersed in the Name of Adonai. He then ate and spent time with the kahal at Damascus. After gaining his strength, he went into the local synagogues and told of his experience and how Yeshua had fulfilled the prophecies of the TaNaKh as the Messiah. Upon hearing this, the Orthodox devised a plan to kill him, but the talmidim in Damascus heard of the plot and helped him escape by letting him down over the city wall in a large basket. After returning to YAHrushalayim, it was only Barnabas who believed the story of his experience on the road to Damascus, while the rest of the talmidim were afraid. Barnabas introduced Shaul to the other shelichim, and it was only then that he was accepted and could begin to teach throughout the city of YAHrushalayim. When the religious leaders of the city heard of this, they too began to arrange a plot to assassinate this traitor turncoat. This time the shelichim took him and sent him on to Tarsus, his place of birth.

For a short period of time, the Kahal throughout the territories of YAHuda, Samaria, and Galilee experienced a certain amount of growth and shalom. It was during this time of shalom that Kefa continued to take the "Good News" to his fellow YAHudi who had not yet decided whether to accept this new doctrine of the Torah or not. While in a town called Lydda, he healed a paralytic man named Aeneas who had been bedridden for eight years. There was another town close to Lydda called Joppa (Yoppa), where a woman named Gazelle, who was a talmid, had died. When some of her friends heard that Kefa was in Lydda, they asked him to come and minister life back into her. Kefa went immediately and prayed for her, and she was raised from the dead. Many came to believe in Kefa's witness regarding Adonai and were immersed in Yeshua's Name. Kefa stayed in Yoppa several more days at the home of a tanner named Simon.

Not far from Lydda and Yoppa was the city of Caesarea, where a Goy soldier and officer of the Roman Army, Cornelius, lived with his family. He and his whole house were "ELohim Fearers" (as they were called) of YAHveh, the ELohim of YisraEL, who supported the YAHudi people financially and prayed to YAH daily. One afternoon an angel appeared to Cornelius and gave him instructions to send for Kefa, who was boarding at Simon the tanner's house in Yoppa. The next day he sent some men to Yoppa to request Kefa's audience at his home. Meanwhile, Kefa was up on the rooftop of Simon's house, having lunch and praying, when he fell into a trance and saw a vision that repeated itself three times. The vision consisted of a very large four-cornered sheet (remember what the number four stands for) with all kinds of unclean animals trapped in it. Kefa heard Yeshua's voice repeat, "Rise Kefa, kill and eat." Three times Kefa responded, "No way, I have always been obedient and never eaten anything that wasn't kosher." Yeshua replied, "Don't call something that I have now deemed kosher, non-kosher." Kefa couldn't quite grasp what Adonai was trying to tell him at the time, but he would later. While he was contemplating the meaning of the vision, the Ruach spoke to him through a word of knowledge, telling him that he was to go with three men who were down stairs seeking him and wanting him to accompany them to the house of Cornelius, one of the prominent Goyim in Caesarea. Kefa invited them to spend the night—he would go with them in the morning. The next day, when he entered Cornelius' home, it became clear to him what the vision meant. The vision was given to him three times in order to confirm it as a permanent ordinance—just as his three-time denial of Yeshua had separated him as a talmidim and his three-time confession of his love for Him had reinstated him. Kefa understood that YAHveh was now willing to make a covenant with anyone who accepted Yeshua as the Messiah, thereby granting them citizenship to YisraEL. He now understood that what made something either clean or unclean was YAHveh's word and that the dietary ordinances had been YAH's way to distinguish them as a separate/holy/clean people from the Goyim/unholy/unclean and not just because of hygienic or purity reasons. But now Yeshua fulfilled or filled up that ordinance because *"For ELohim so loved the world (clean and unclean) that He gave His only begotten Son, that whoever believes in Him should not parish but have everlasting life"* (**JOHN 3:16**). Kefa was a devout Orthodox YAHudi himself, and unless he heard directly from Yeshua, there was no way that he was going to deviate from what he understood the Torah to teach. This was going to require a complete change in his thinking regarding the Goyim. It was going to be hard for him to accept Yeshua's ministry of the restoration of the Whole House of YisraEL to include the previously unclean Goyim. (The dietary ordinances were not the only thing that Kefa would have to struggle with—later it would be the ordinance of circumcision.) Cornelius told Kefa of his vision and how he had obeyed the instructions that he had received, so now he was ready to hear whatever it was that Kefa had to tell him. Kefa explained the plan of redemption and salvation to him, and he and his whole house accepted Yeshua as their redeemer. While he was explaining these things, the Ruach fell upon them, and they began to magnify YAHveh with ecstatic praise. When the Messianic YAHudi heard them magnifying YAHveh in this manner, they realized that ELuah had also accepted the Goyim into the House of YisraEL. Afterwards, they were all immersed in Yeshua's Name. Others who heard of this incident doubted its authenticity but came to accept it when they heard it from Kefa's own mouth.

There remained a certain amount of prejudice among the YAHudi toward those who were not of their descent or were not of the Hebrew speech. As a result, many who had gone out to share their testimony did so only with those who spoke Hebrew. There were some, though, who did share these things with the YAHudi who spoke Greek. Therefore, both Hebrew and Greek-speaking talmidim were being created daily, causing the "Good News" to spread even faster. When word of these things reached YAHrushalayim, the kahal sent Barnabas to Antioch to verify this exciting news. When Barnabas saw for himself how many were being added to the Whole House of YisraEL at Antioch, he stayed for awhile to minister in order to bring them to a greater level of maturity. He later went to Tarsus and sought out Rav Shaul to assist him with the ministry. They remained a year, and the kahal that developed were called "Messianics" by the Hebrews and "Christians" by the Greeks. Also while there, a ne'vee, or seer, by the name of Agabus came to them and gave a prophecy, that a famine was coming and for the people to prepare. So, some of the elders there took up an offering and sent it to the brethren in YAHrushalayim via Barnabas and Shaul.

It was about this time that a third King Herod, Herod Agrippa I, came on the scene; he was the nephew of Herod Antipas. Like both his grandfather, King Herod the Great, and his uncle, he too was insane with power. When he saw what was happening among the YAHudi and heard the discourse that seemed to be tearing at the very fiber of this hated religion, he chimed right in and added to the confusion by doing a little persecuting of his own. He had Yochanan's brother, Yaacov, one of Yeshua's first talmidim, slain. Then he went after Kefa and had him arrested during the days of the Feast of Unleavened Bread. Herod was planning to put him on trial after the celebration, but on the night before the celebration was over, another miracle took place. The kahal at YAHrushalayim were praying for Kefa's release when an angel appeared to Kefa during the night. Kefa thought it was a vision, but before he knew it, the shackles and chains had fallen from his hands and legs. Then the doors were flung open, and he found himself outside in the street. When he realized that the incident was for real and not just a vision, he ran to the house of Yochanan Marcus' mother, where he knew the kahal was meeting. Upon his arrival, he quickly knocked, and a young girl heard his voice and became so excited at their prayers being answered that instead of letting him in, she ran and told the others. They doubted her and couldn't bring themselves to believe what she was saying. Kefa persistently pounded, and they were amazed once more when they opened the door and there he stood. He told them to tell everyone, starting with Yaacov, Yeshua's brother, what Adonai had done and then he left. When crazy Herod heard what had happened, he had all of the guards who were on duty that night executed. Herod had become so obsessed with his power that he thought that he was an "el" (god) himself. But like hasatan, it became his demise—he met his death at the hands of an angel of YAH. The angel caused him to be eaten up by worms—probably from eating swine, a carrier of such pestilence at that time.

Barnabas and Rav Shaul had delivered the offerings that had been given to them by the kahal in Antioch and were about to return when it was decided that young Yochanan Marcus should accompany them on their return trip. When they arrived, many of the ne'veem and rabbim had been praying, and the Ruach told them that they were to send both Barnabas and Shaul out beyond the local territories. They began their ministry to the Goyim at Cyprus and from there, traveled to many of the surrounding cities. They, with Marcus as their assistant, would teach this new understanding of the TaNaKh every Sabbath in the synagogues to anyone who would listen. On one occasion, they had an encounter with a false ne'vee of Eluah, who was another one who had given his gift over to hasatan by practicing sorcery. Upon the arrival of Barnabas and Shaul, this sorcerer tried to discredit their ministry as well as the message that they had brought to the elders of the local synagogues. Rav Shaul rebuked him for his wickedness and pronounced blindness upon him by the power of the Ruach. This act convinced those, who had both witnessed the event and heard the message, that Yeshua was Adonai. They continued their mission to the Goyim at Perga in Pamphylia, where Marcus left to return to YAHrushalayim. After preaching there, they departed for another city called Antioch in Pisida, where they brought their message to the YAHudi in their local synagogues. On one of the Sabbaths, after the reading of the TaNaKh, the rulers of the synagogue gave them an opportunity to speak a word of exhortation. Rav Shaul began to share with both the Orthodox and the Goyim proselytes (ELohim Fearers) a brief message, starting from the time of the Exodus, through the Judges, and down through SamuEL to the part where YAH made Dahveed a promise. After that, he went on to the ministry that Yochanan the Immerser offered and then to Yeshua as the Promised Messiah. He explained how Yeshua became the complete fulfillment of the Messiah as was prophesied by the Ne'vim, how He was rejected by the Pharisees, given over to Pilate for crucifixion, and how YAHveh had raised Him from the dead, thereby fulfilling the Scriptures: *"I will declare the decree: YAHveh has said to Me, You are My Son, today I have begotten You"* (**PSALM 1:7**). As well as, *"Incline your ear, and come to Me. Hear, and your soul shall live; and I will make an everlasting covenant with you—The sure mercies of Dahveed"* (**ISA 55:3**). Also, *"For You will not leave My soul in Sheol, nor will You allow Your Holy One to see corruption"* (**PSALM 16:10**). Shaul explained how these things could not have applied to King Dahveed, but only to YAHveh Himself in the manifestation of His Son, Yeshua HaMashiach—Dahveed died, but Yeshua was raised from the dead as the Firstfruits of the resurrection. Then Shaul warns those who opposed this idea—it would bring the wrath of ELuah upon them because of what the TaNaKh had to say further: *"Behold you despisers, marvel and perish; for I work a work in your days, A work which you will by no means believe, though one were to declare it to you"* (**HAB 1:5**). Both the Goyim and the YAHudi were astonished at their words and asked that they might return on the following Sabbath to share more. Others of the Orthodox were offended and disputed what had been shared as being contrary to their belief. Barnabas and Shaul were not surprised at the mixed response and spoke once more from the TaNaKh: *"Indeed He says, 'It is too small a thing that You should be My Servant to raise up the tribes of Yaacov, and to restore the preserved ones of YisraEL; I will also give You as a light to the Goyim, that You should be My salvation to the ends of the earth"* (ISA 49:6). The Goyim were overjoyed that they had been included in YAH's plan, and all who believed were saved and filled with the Ruach HaKedosh. But the unbelieving YAHudi were outraged and told them to leave, so they left shaking the dust off of their sandals as a testimony against them and continued on to the city of Iconium. Their message wasn't accepted there either, and both the YAHudi and the Goyim tried to stone them, so they moved on to Lystra. Lystra was a city filled with many Goyim who worshiped a pantheon of elohim. Shaul saw a man there who had been crippled all of his life, listening intently to his message and being filled with faith at the same time. He spoke to the man and told him to stand up, and when he did, he walked. When the crowds saw this, they believed Barnabas and Shaul were elohim themselves and began to worship them. But they rebuked them and tried to explain how it was that YAHveh, the Living ELohim, was responsible for the work that had just taken place. They tried to explain that He was the same ELohim who was responsible for the seasons and the rain. When they heard this, they all the more wanted to make sacrifices to them out of their ignorance. When the YAHudi from Antioch and Iconium in Pisida heard that Barnabas and Shaul had gone down to Lystra, they followed. They began to tell lies about them in order to turn these confused citizens against them also. As a result, Shaul was stoned so badly that they thought he was dead, so they dragged him out of the city and left him there to rot. The Scriptures do not say whether he was dead or not, but when the talmidim gathered around him, he rose up and continued on with Barnabas to complete their mission. He and Barnabas went to another city called Derbe, where they had much more success with their message. After that, they began to return to the previous cities where they had already ministered in order to strengthen the new talmidim there. They also appointed elders in each community to further the teaching about the fulfillment of the TaNaKh through Yeshua HaMashiach. Then they returned to the kahal at Antioch to give a report of the results of their expedition.

It didn't take long before some error began to creep into the kahal in YAHrushalayim. Some Messianic YAHudi had come down from the region of YAHuda and had begun teaching that in order to be completely saved, Goyim, like the YAHudi, must be circumcised along with believing in Yeshua as HaMashiach. When the kahal in Antioch heard this, they sent faithful

Barnabas and Shaul to YAHrushalayim to help settle this dispute. Upon their arrival, they gathered the elders and the shelichim to hear all that YAHveh had done among the Goyim. Some of the believing Pharisees interrupted and said that the Goyim had to also submit themselves to the Torah and to the rite of circumcision before they could be accepted into the Kahal of YisraEL. Kefa stood up and reminded them that keeping the Torah to the letter never saved anyone and that this was the reason for Yeshua's coming to them in the first place. He reminded them of how the fathers never kept the Torah but abused it instead, yet YAHveh still showed them mercy by sending His Son to take away the curse of the Torah because it was too heavy of a yoke for them to bear. Yaacov, Yeshua's brother, spoke up to remind them of Kefa's experience with Cornelius and his household and how this agreed with the Ne'vim regarding the restoration of the Whole House of YisraEL. *"On that day I will raise up the mishkahn* (tabernacle) *of Dahveed, which has fallen down, and repair up its damages; I will raise up its ruins, and rebuild it as in the days of old; that they may possess the remnant of Edom* (the descendants of Esau), *and all the Goyim who are called by My name," says YAHveh who does these things"* (**AMOS 9:11&12**). Yaacov suggested that the only ordinances that the Goyim needed to abstain from in order to keep the Torah and the spirit of the Torah was not to follow after their former lusts. They should not compromise their worship of YAH with idols or have anything to do with idols. They should not have anything to do with fertility rituals, fertility elohim, or anything that has to do with perverted sexual practices. They should also abstain from anything that is not properly slaughtered or meat that is sacrificed to idols. They should also honor and show proper respect for the sanctity of life that is within the blood of animals and not to treat it as a delicacy to eat. All of these things pleased the shelichim, and so a letter stating these amended ordinances was sent out to all of the Kahal of YisraEL. When Shaul and Barnabas returned to the kahal at Antioch with their letter regarding the matter, they too were pleased. While staying at Antioch preaching and teaching, Shaul learned that this same controversy had also been raised in the kahal at Galatia, one of the towns that he had ministered in. So, he sat down and wrote them a separate letter to help them resolve their problem.

Conclusion

At this point, it should be obvious that the book of the Acts of the Shelichim was laying out a pattern for the Kahal of YisraEL to follow in conducting themselves as the doers of the true works of the Ruach of YAHveh. Shaul (who became the thirteenth shelich) and Kefa dominate the scene for a purpose. The commission and mandate for the Body of Messiah is to complete the work of Yeshua. They are to bring together the two houses of YisraEL,

YAHuda and Yosef, for restoration. Kefa was sent to proclaim the good news about the end of the curse of the Torah to the YAHudi. Rav Shaul was to let the Goyim know that they too could observe the Torah and believe the promises of the TaNaKh without reservation and become a part of the nation of YisraEL. But since the Goyim were not allowed to enter the House of YAH and practice the ordinances of the YAHudi, the ordinances of the House of YAH had to be amended and did not pertain to them. Besides, these ordinances were only necessary to point to the coming of the Messiah. Now the Messiah had come and He was with them and within them by the power of the Ruach. Within a few more years, the House of YAH would no longer be standing, and even the Orthodox YAHudi would not be able to properly exercise their faith. In the next few chapters, we will look at Rav Shaul's letters to the different kahal that he ministered to and how he instructed them regarding their conduct in the matters of the Torah and its observances.

CHAPTER 21
...about Galatians, Acts 16—19, I&II Thessalonians, and I&II Corinthians

In this chapter, we will cover Rav Shaul's first five letters to three of the kahal that he planted, and we'll do it in the order that he wrote them. Today's Bibles, other than chronological bibles, do not list them in the actual order that they were written. In order to better understand the problems that were occurring because of the birthing pangs that each of these fledgling kahal were experiencing, we will be looking at the circumstances leading up to the trials they faced.

Rav Shaul's Letter to the Kahal at Galatia

The controversies about how to obey the Torah, which included circumcision being combined with faith in Yeshua in order to be saved, were not confined to just the kahal in YAHrushalayim. Disputes on this particular subject, as well as others, had reached other kahal in the region of YAHuda and even beyond to Galatia. These disputes began to cause division among the brethren there. In the very beginning of Rav Shaul's letter to them, he chides them twice for listening to what he refers to as another gospel. He reaffirms to them that it is faith in Yeshua through YAH's grace alone that has redeemed them from the curse of the Torah and not by doing its works. He says that if anyone at anytime, even if it were he or an angel, were to preach to them anything else, those with such a message should be accursed. And yet, we are told today that YisraEL has been replaced by the Church. We are also told that Saturday Sabbaths have been replaced with Sunday worship, that the Feasts have been replaced with Easter and Christmas, and that now we are only required to follow the teachings in the New Testament (Brit Chadashah) and not the Old Testament (the TaNaKh). *This is another gospel.* I know I sound redundant, but this is not what Rav Shaul taught because it would have been impossible for him to teach such things since the Brit Chadashah had not been written and wouldn't be for another one-hundred years.

He continued by reminding them of his past and how he had been a meticulous scholar of the TaNaKh and zealous in his persecution of anyone who disputed its validity. He knew all about the wisdom of men and how in their ignorance, they missed the true meaning of its message, as did he. He told them how he had to be given a new understanding through supernatural means. First, he had to be born-again and filled with YAH's Ruach. Then Yeshua personally taught him through revelation. It was revealed to him that even before he was in his mother's womb, he was destined to experience all of the things that took place in his life. YAH knew ahead of time every decision and every path he would choose, so He arranged all of his circumstances beforehand. He was first called to be a Pharisee in order to equip him to be able to educate the Goyim in how to live the Torah in their lives, but by faith through grace. He said he learned through the personal teaching of the Ruach for a period of three years before he finally left Damascus and went up to the shelichim in YAHrushalayim. It was there that he met with Kefa and Yeshua's brother, Yaacov. He talked about the trouble he had in convincing the brethren of his new-birth experience because of his reputation regarding his persecution of the Kahal. After this, he told them how he had gone out and had begun to preach and teach for a period of fourteen years before he returned to YAHrushalayim with Barnabus and Titus.

Then Shaul used Titus as an example for not carrying out the rite of circumcision. Titus had been a Goy and was not under the original blood covenant. Under the Renewed Covenant (Brit Chadashah), Yeshua fulfilled this ordinance. Before, it was a sign of the promise that was given to YisraEL of the coming of HaMashiach—now that promise was complete. It was also no longer a sign that was to be used to distinguish between the clean and the unclean, YAHudi and Goyim, male and female, slave and free. It had served its purpose and was now completed/ fulfilled/filled-up. Even today within the Messianic kahal, the idea of circumcision has again become controversial. We need to recognize that circumcision no longer separates or distinguishes a Jew from a non-Jew—many other religions practice it too. It is also a medical procedure that is commonly used within most societies. It is just good hygiene, just as kosher eating is a good diet practice.

He goes on to denounce this teaching as one brought in by false brethren and being used for the purpose of establishing control over the lives of others. He writes about how he even had to rebuke Kefa at one point, when he showed preference toward his YAHudi brethren over the Goyim during a particular set of circumstances. Apparently even Kefa had forgotten about the grace that YAHveh was showing the Goyim and that they weren't required to obey certain rites that the YAHudi had chosen to continue to follow. These rites led to the denial of access to the House of YAH for the Goyim. Dietary ordinances, circumcision, and tithing were direct Torah ordinances pertaining to the House of YAH, and Goyim were forbidden access to it. But, of course, there was no way for the YAHudi to know that in another twenty years, even they wouldn't be able to enter YAH's House—it was going to be destroyed.

WHAT WE WEREN'T TAUGHT ABOUT THE BIBLE AND ITS HISTORY

He continued to expound on the truth of living by faith instead of by the works of the Torah. There is nothing wrong with works unless it begins to take the place of faith—that's the danger. The Torah does not become a burden unless following it to the letter is required in order to obtain salvation. If that were the case, we would all be condemned. Rav Shaul tried to point this important principle out in all of his letters. He reminded them that faith came long before the Torah was ever given. *"And he believed in YAHveh, and He counted it to him for righteousness"* (**GEN 15:6**). And it was through Avraham's kind of faith that YAH said He would bless all of the nations (goyim). *"I will bless those who bless you, and curse him who curses you; and in you all the families of the earth shall be blessed"* (**GEN 12:3** and **18:18** and **22:18**). Trying to follow the letter of the Torah brings a curse. *"Cursed is the one who does not confirm all the words of this Torah. And all the people shall say, Amen (Omien)"* (**DEUT 27:26**). No man has ever been able to keep all of the words of the Torah except one, Yeshua. That's why YAHveh gave us His Son—to become the curse for us. Now we can live and walk by faith in His Torah without the fear of breaking it. *"Behold the proud, his soul is not upright in him; but the just shall live by faith"* (**HAB 2:4**). Therefore, we are to humbly follow the Torah because it is good and right to do so, not because its works will bring righteousness. If a person still believes that it will, it is because he is proud, his soul is not upright in him, and he *will* continue to be under the curse. *"You shall therefore keep My statutes and My judgments, which if a man does, he shall live by them: I AM YAHveh"* (**LEV 18:5**). No man could do this, and YAH knew it; that is why He provided a sacrificial system to atone for men's failure. And, of course, Yeshua was the ultimate atonement. He paid for the curse once and for all. *"If a man has committed a sin worthy of death, and you hang him on a tree, "his body shall not remain overnight on the tree, but you shall surely bury him that day, so that you do not defile the land which YAHveh your ELohim is giving you as an inheritance; for he who is hanged is accursed of ELohim"* (**DEUT 21:22&23**). He tells them that all of these things had to come to pass so that YAH could send His Ruach to infill them in order to teach them these mysteries and so that the Goyim, who have the hidden descendants of the tribes of Yosef within them, could also receive the truths of the Torah. All of this was provided so that the promises to Avraham would be fulfilled. The promise made to Avraham was *"to your Seed"* (**GEN 22:18**), who was the Messiah. Rav Shaul reminded them that this covenant came four-hundred and thirty years before the Torah was given to Mosheh at Mt. Seenahee—the four-hundred years that His people would spend in Mitsrahyim (**EXOD 12:41**).

Rav Shaul continues to explain the reason for the giving of the Torah. He points out that YAHveh knew that man could not obtain salvation by trying to be kedosh (holy). Therefore, He appointed Mosheh to be their teacher and ne'vee who would guide them through His Torah. Mosheh would show them how trying to be kedosh on their own couldn't be done. In His Torah, YAH gave them His annual, monthly, weekly, and daily exercises to point to the "Seed of Avraham"—the one who could and would do it for them. By faith, they learned that obedience brought righteousness and that disobedience brought the curse for which atonement must be made. Now that the Seed has come, faith for His coming is no longer needed, but is replaced by faith that He has already come. Now we are to observe His ordinances as a memorial of His first coming and as a rehearsal for His second. Now He shows us His mercy so that faith is the only requirement needed by those who have not yet been immersed into His Son. The Torah is our guardian until the Abba's appointed time for that "Great Day". We will always be learning and receiving His revelation if we are continually seeking His face and doing the kingdom principles that are found in His Torah. The Torah reveals our sonship to us, which establishes our relationship with our Abba, and that this sonship is available for all men of all nations. What remains is our need to rehearse for the final coming of the King of Glory. After that, we can celebrate, for an entire millennium, the completion of all of His promises.

Rav Shaul warns them that they must ground themselves in his teachings regarding the freedoms that they have obtained outside of the curse of the Torah. If they begin to doubt, they will again find themselves trying to obtain these freedoms through the keeping of the Torah. Doing this would be no different than if they went back to their pagan practices from which they had been delivered. He asks whether or not they have forgotten what it was like when they had first learned the truth, when it was revealed to them by the Ruach HaKedosh, and the joy that they had felt after receiving it. He says that if they don't heed his warnings, they will be like the first son of Avraham, YishmaEL, who was conceived by the flesh, rather than like Yitzhak, who was conceived by the Ruach. He points out how this, like many of the Torah's teachings, is symbolic of YAHveh's work toward man's salvation. YishmaEL's mother, Hagar, was a bondswoman, whereas Yitzhak's mother, Sarah, though barren, was free. Hagar stands for the Torah that was given at Mt. Seenahee and the Earthly city, YAHrushalayim, but Sarah stands for the Promise that was given on Mt Moriah (Moreeah) and the Heavenly city, YAHrushalayim. *"Sing, O barren, you who have not borne! Break forth into singing, and cry aloud, you who have not travailed with child! For more are the children of the desolate than the children of the married woman," says YAHveh* (**ISA 54:1**). All of those who are born only of the flesh will be no more, but those who are born of the Ruach of the Promise will live forever. *"Therefore she said to Avraham, "Cast out this bondswoman and her son; for the son of this bondswoman shall not be heir with my son Yitzhak"* (**GEN 21:10**).

Once again he reminds them that keeping the ordinance of circumcision will not obtain for them any particular favor in YAHveh's eyes. If they take up the practice of keeping the Torah for their salvation, they will fall from their Abba's grace and will have made void the Messiah's sacrifice for them. What will gain them favor from the Abba is faith working through love. *"You shall not take vengeance, nor bear any grudge against the children of your people, but you will love your neighbor as yourself: I AM YAHveh"* (**LEV** 19:18). Faith working through love will also gain them liberty. It will bring true shalom and comfort in times of trouble and trials. He does caution them here, though, not to abuse their liberty by trying to please their fleshly desires.

He encourages them to learn to walk by the Ruach who is within them. Doing so will fulfill the spirit of the Torah. He encourages them to learn to recognize the fruits of the Ruach in their lives and the fruits of the Ruach in others. Fruits are the product or result of the seed of their origin. The fruits of the Ruach are love, joy, shalom, patience, kindness, goodness, faithfulness, gentleness, and self-control. If anyone walks in the lust of the flesh, he will reap corruption and eventually separation from the Messiah. If anyone walks in the Ruach, he will become one with his brethren and one with the Messiah. He says that each one of them has the responsibility of restoring any who have fallen away and of teaching the kingdom principles to all who are hungry and thirsty for the knowledge of righteousness and of Adonai. He finishes his letter by once more reminding them of the purpose for the rite of circumcision.

Acts 16—19

Near the time that Rav Shaul writes to Galatia, he has a disagreement with Barnabas regarding young Yochanan Marcus. Shaul felt that Marcus had abandoned the ministry because of his lack of commitment to the cause, while Barnabas felt it was only because of his youth. As a result, they departed from one another and pursued separate paths, with Shaul teaming up with Silas as his new companion. Soon the two of them met another young man by the name of Timothy, whose mother was a YAHudi and his father a Goy. Apparently, Timothy had made a personal decision to be circumcised, in order to honor his mother's heritage and to keep peace among the other YAHudi who lived in the communities that they were going to visit, because Rav Shaul preformed the rite of circumcision on him. This one-time act on Shaul's part did not change the position that he and the elders of the YAHrushalayim council had taken earlier regarding the rite of circumcision.

Now as they were about to enter the region of Asia to revisit the brethren there, the Ruach of ELohim redirected them, through a vision, to go to the Babylonian region of Macedonia instead. One of the first cities that they had established a kahal in was Philippi. The day they entered was on a Sabbath, and they met a woman there by the name of Lydia. She was a Goy who feared the ELohim of YisraEL and was open to hearing the message of the coming of the Promised Messiah. After hearing the message, she and her household desired to be immersed and to receive the Ruach. She requested that Rav Shaul and his company spend time at her house while ministering in the area. (Hospitality is a key attitude needed by all Believers to minister and grow the House and the Kahal of YisraEL.) While ministering, preaching, and praying among those of that community, a young slave girl with the gift of prophecy came among them and began to prophesy regarding Shaul's message. Unfortunately, she had given her gift over to the spirits of darkness and had become a soothsayer in order to profit her masters. In her confused state of mind, she was proclaiming Shaul's authenticity but disrupting his ministry at the same time. Rav Shaul's response was to discern the problem and then to cast out the controlling spirits in the Name of Yeshua HaMashiach. As a consequence, her masters, after realizing their loss, had Shaul and his company arrested and thrown into prison. But during the night, as they were singing and praising ELuah, YAH shook the prison with an earthquake that opened the gates of the jail, and they shook off the shackles that had bound them. Their jailer thought that they had all escaped and was just about to take his own life when Shaul discerned the man's fear of YAHveh and seized the opportunity to share Adonai's love and compassion with him. Upon doing so, he stopped the dastardly deed that the man was about to commit. Here again, the result was that the man believed on Yeshua as his Savior, and that night he and his household were saved. Fear also fell upon the whole city that same night, and the magistrates of the town sent word to Shaul that he and his whole company should depart from their community. Since they had been humiliated publicly, Shaul demanded a public apology and told them that they shouldn't have been treated in such a manner in the first place because he was a Roman citizen. When they heard that he was a Roman citizen, they obliged him and sent them on their way.

From there, Shaul and his company went to the city of Thessalonica, again at the direction of the Ruach. For three Sabbaths in a row, Shaul shared the TaNaKh with the YAHudi there regarding the Promised Messiah. A number of them, along with some Goyim, received the "Good News" with joy, while others rejected it. Those who rejected it hired some thugs to ransack the house of Jason (YAHson), where Shaul was staying. They dragged Jason (YAHson) off to the city leaders to accuse him of sheltering those who were declaring their allegiance to another king rather than to Caesar. After extorting some funds from Jason (YAHson), they released him. In spite of all of this, they still managed to establish a kahal there.

Rav Shaul moved on to the city of Berea, where the populace received them with more appreciation. Both the YAHudi and the Goyim received the Word that Shaul taught them with enthusiasm and tested it against the TaNaKh, which proved him true. But when the YAHudi in Thessalonica learned of their success, they sent more troublemakers to thwart it. Not wanting to undo what was accomplished by staying, Shaul moved on to Athens in Greece without Silas and Timothy, but later sent for them to join him there.

Athens was a city full of Greek scholars and followers of many pagan elohim. When Shaul began to seek out the few YAHudi who were there and to share with them what the TaNaKh had to say about the Promised Messiah, he also attracted many Goyim, who became intrigued after hearing about this "Almighty One (EL Shaddahee)" who was above all other elohim. When some scholars heard about this new doctrine, they immediately came to challenge what he taught. They insisted that he explain himself regarding these things that he proclaimed as truth and then took him to one of their coliseums on Mars Hill for him to do so. Among all of the monuments that were there commemorating their many elohim, he noticed that one was marked as the "Unknown ELuah". He began to convince them that the ELuah he spoke of was none other than the one whom they had acknowledged as this "Unknown ELuah". He explained to them that the ELuah he taught about was the Living ELohim above all others. He was not to be worshiped by making graven images to commemorate Him—He was to be worshiped in spirit and in truth as being the one who had created all things for His own use. After briefly explaining the foundation of the Torah and the "Good News" of the Messiah, many there came to faith in YAHveh and were saved.

Rav Shaul left Athens and moved on to another predominantly Goyim city, Corinth. Here again, he faced opposition from the citizens and the leaders of the pagan temples because of their customs and culture. While there, he became friends with Aquila and his wife, Priscilla, a couple of fellow YAHudi tent makers. He preached Yeshua as the Messiah in their synagogues every Sabbath, where he persuaded both YAHudi and Goyim of this truth, including Aquila and Priscilla. It was here that both Silas and Timothy finally caught up and joined him once more in the ministry. Even though many believed, still others opposed him, so he left the synagogues and continued to preach from house to house. He also vowed at that time, because of the opposition that he had received from his fellow YAHudi, that in the future, he would only take the message to the Goyim. Many of the Goyim believed Shaul's teachings and were immersed. Among them were rulers of two synagogues, Sosthenes and Crispus, along with his neighbor, Titus Justus (Yustus). An uprising among the Goyim led to Sosthenes receiving a beating. Gallio, the city's proconsul, ignored the incident because it had come about due to a religious dispute between YAHudi and the Goyim. Once more, Rav Shaul had accomplished what YAH had sent him to do among the Goyim, so he soon departed and headed back to Ephesus, taking Aquila and Priscilla with him. After arriving, he left them there while he prepared to go up to YAHrushalayim for the annual Feast of Unleavened Bread. On his way, he stopped in Antioch and Galatia in Asia to visit some of the kahal that he had established during his first journey to the region.

While staying in Ephesus, Aquila and Priscilla met a man by the name of Apollos of Alexandria in Mitsrahyim, who had been a talmidim of Yochanan the Immerser and had only heard of the coming of the Messiah but had not yet received the grace of Yeshua or His immersion. They shared with him Shaul's doctrine and their experiences, and he received it with faith and joy and was immersed in Yeshua's Name. Apollos went on to Corinth and proved to be most persuasive regarding the "Good News", which brought many YAHudi to the knowledge of Yeshua as HaMashiach, increasing and expanding the fellowship of the kahal there. When Shaul returned to the region of Ephesus, he ran across twelve talmidim of Yochanan the Immerser who Apollos had been affiliated with and asked them if they had yet received the immersion of the Ruach HaKedosh. They admitted that they hadn't even heard of such an immersion. After Shaul shared with them the fulfillment of the Torah through Yeshua and His promise of the Ruach, they received it with joy, were filled up, and prophesied in tongues, glorifying YAHveh and His Son, Yeshua. Unusual miracles began to take place in the region when Shaul began cutting up pieces of his tallit, blessing them, and then sending them out among the community—people began receiving healings and deliverance from evil spirits as a result of just touching them.

A story began to circulate in the region about a YAHudi priest who tried using the Name of Yeshua to cast out seven evil spirits from a man possessed. But without having the authority to do so, he was overpowered and attacked by this same man and severely beaten and stripped naked. This story proved to be so powerful that many confessed Yeshua as Messiah and either threw out their scrolls of magic and soothsaying paraphernalia or burned them.

More trouble arose in Ephesus when a silversmith by the name of Demetrius, who molded and hammered out silver images of Diana (one of the fertility goddesses whose temple was in Ephesus), accused Shaul of blaspheming Diana with his preaching of Yeshua as being the Son of the One True ELuah. His only real concern was the money that he was losing in sales of his product. When he had stirred up hatred toward Shaul, the crowds went to the homes of Gains and Aristarchus, two of Shaul's traveling companions, and dragged them out to stone them. But the city clerk came to their rescue by telling them that the two were innocent of the charges and that if they had committed a crime, it should be settled properly in a court of law. When things died down, Shaul went to see the two and exhorted and encouraged them to persevere. Then, just before his arrival in Ephesus, Shaul took the time to write two letters to the kahal in Thessalonica and two to the one in Corinth.

I Thessalonians

Rav Shaul knew that the kahal of both of these cities were just fledglings and were prone to the peer pressure of their pagan neighbors to return to their old ways. He also knew that many of the YAHudi who were among them would try to take advantage of their ignorance of the Torah's ordinances and persuade them into following the works of the Torah as their means of salvation.

In Thessalonica, disputes seemed to be arising about Shaul's teachings regarding the resurrection and the timing of the return of Yeshua to gather up His followers. He and his companions, Timothy and Silas, had experienced firsthand the resistance that the citizens of this community expressed toward these new spiritual ideas. So Rav Shaul wrote a letter to Thessalonica to exhort them regarding their hospitality and openness to the teachings about the "Good News" of the Messiah and His mission on Earth. He commended them for their faith and willingness to express that faith by the power of the Ruach HaKedosh. He commended them for their willingness to turn from their former practices and to boldly demonstrate to the region around them the power that the Living ELohim had over idols and even nature itself. He commended them on how they had received this message as though it was from Eluah Himself and not just from mere men. He saw how they went on to exercise their faith without allowing it to puff them up as though it were something they themselves possessed.

Shaul writes to them regarding his staying and continuing to minister to the kahal in Athens while sending Timothy ahead to be their shepherd in the things of faith because he was concerned about their ability to withstand the tribulation that was sure to come from their tempter and enemy, hasatan. Once more, he commends them for their steadfastness because Timothy had returned with a good report about them. He realizes that because of their former practices and the weakness of the flesh, he still has to be concerned about their lack of resistance to sexual sins. He encourages them to resist these temptations because it will result in their turning away from holiness and reentering into uncleanness, which will bring down the wrath of ELuah upon their heads. He encourages them to continue to practice their expression of brotherly love toward one another and toward all men. When they do this, it will prepare the hearts of others so that the Ruach might enter, helping them to accept Yeshua as their Savior. He encourages them not to be idle but to learn to work with their own hands to show how productive the children of YAHveh can be.

After these exhortations, Shaul reminds them of his teachings about the signs that will precede the return of Adonai. First, he reminds them that only those who truly believe that Yeshua died for their sins and rose again will experience the blessing and promise of the resurrection. He speaks of bodily death as being synonymous with sleeping—our bodies sleep, not our spirits. Upon death, our spirits will immediately be in the presence of Yeshua and in the mansions that He has prepared for us in Paradise. For those who are without that hope (or unbelievers), their bodies will sleep until the second resurrection, but in the meantime, they will be in the presence of darkness. He explains that this condition will remain until the Great Day of Adonai, when the sound of the Shofar of ELuah and a shout of the archangel are heard. At that time, when all who are with Adonai hear the sound, they will immediately receive their newly resurrected bodies that will be recreated from the elements of their old corruptible ones. At that same moment, all of the Believers who are still alive on the Earth will go through a molecular change within their existing bodies, making them identical to the resurrected bodies of those who had been asleep; they will then be caught up into the presence of Adonai. One thing that he doesn't reveal here is the length of time between these two events. The idea of it taking place in the twinkling of an eye could mean that the change will be quick but not necessarily all that sudden—it could take place over a period of several days.

He continues by telling them that when this happens, it will come at a time when the people of this world, because of their ignorance, will least expect it—just as suddenly as a thief in the night. This will not happen to those who have been taught the importance of the times and seasons of YAHveh. He has built into His appointed Feasts the signs, symbols, and metaphors that reveal His secrets about these events. Even with this knowledge, His YisraEL will still be like virgins awaiting their bridegroom—some will be ready, while others will not.

After these reminders that prove once again the importance of studying the TaNaKh, he goes on to exhort them to love one another, to be patient, and to hold in high regard those whom YAHveh has appointed over them. He goes on to list several attributes that they need to practice all of the time in order to keep them from stumbling. He exhorts them to always rejoice no matter what their circumstances, good or bad, because they don't know what their Abba might be using to bring about a blessing to any particular individual, family, or kahal. He reminds them that their conscious life should consist of practicing to keep Adonai first and foremost in their mind and praying always, or at least having an attitude of prayer at all times. He also tells them to have an attitude of thanksgiving toward YAHveh and toward their fellow believers. He warns them to be careful not to quench the Ruach when He is present and working among them by being either critical or doubting. That means being sensitive to His presence, which they should be if they have trained themselves in doing the other things that he had just mentioned. He exhorted them to be open to all prophecy, which could come through preaching, foreseeing, foretelling, or even including the use of tongues with interpretation. But he warns them to be sure to test all things against both the TaNaKh and their own experiences and to keep and use only those things that pass that test. He then closes his letter by reminding them to pray for him and the brethren who are in the ministry and to always express their love for one another with a traditional kiss.

II Thessalonians

Soon after Shaul wrote his first letter to Thessalonica, he finds it necessary to write to them again. They were still disputing about the time and the events that were to take place before Adonai returns. But this time, he explains to them that it will come after believers have experienced a certain amount of trials and tribulation for their belief. He also tells them that those who are guilty of bringing on those trials will be judged with fire for their disobedience.

Shaul also learned that there were a certain few who had come into the kahal at Thessalonica bringing false teachings, saying that Adonai had already returned and that the resurrection had already taken place. Shaul reassured them that this could not have happened because certain events leading up to the "Great Day" had not yet occurred. Even though Shaul doesn't mention the writings of DahneeEL directly, he does mention what he wrote regarding the final days when the son of perdition will appear on the scene. He reminds them that just before that great event takes place, there will be a great falling away from faith in YAHveh, Yeshua, and the Torah. Then the incarnate of hasatan will be manifested, who will be mostly responsible for this falling away. He will consider himself to be ELuah and will place himself in the House of ELohim as ELuah. (We know that the House of ELohim was destroyed in the year 70 CE and has not been rebuilt up to the present time, which means that it will have to be rebuilt first before these things can take place.) He reminds them that it is this single event that is restraining, or holding back, Adonai's return. YAHveh is patiently bringing these events into place. He will cause both the necessary faith and the unbelief to fill the hearts of mankind that will bring about that day. Then the incarnate of the Prince of Darkness will make his claim, ELuah will destroy him, and Adonai will return.

Shaul reminds them to always give thanks to YAHveh for His choosing them to receive both their salvation through the blood of Yeshua, His Son, and their sanctification through the immersion of and through the power of the Ruach of their ELohim. He goes on to exhort them to hold on to the good traditions that he has taught them—such as abstaining from sexual immorality, from eating blood, things strangled, or things polluted by idols—but to continue to keep the Sabbath, New Moons, and the Feasts. (Today this would also apply to the wearing of skull caps/kippas, tallits, and the blowing of the shofar on the feast days because these are all traditions that the Goyim should continue to keep to help remind them of their Hebrew roots and their relationship to their brothers, the YAHudi.) He exhorted the YAHudi to continue to keep all of the ordinances that pertained to the House of YAH, including tithing, eating kosher, and the bringing of sacrifices. Yeshua was the example, and He kept all of these ordinances because the House was still standing. He also prophesied that one day the House would not stand, so the ordinances that served the House would, of course, have to cease until it was rebuilt. However, all of the other traditions that pertained to keeping the Torah would always remain because they would continue to teach us of His promises. Shaul even goes on to say that they are to withdraw from any brother who refuses to keep these traditions. To do otherwise was to be considered disorderly and disobedient. He also directs them that if there is anyone who is lazy or refuses to carry his own weight by not working, they are not to allow him to even eat with them. Sluggards drain the brethren of strength and divert the attention away from those who truly need help—they also are usually the ones who become busybodies. He encourages them to keep the teachings that he has given them in his letters and to have nothing to do with those who ignore his instructions until they have repented from their rebellion.

I Corinthians

The kahal at Corinth seems to be much larger than those in Galatia or Thessalonica. Although it is predominantly made up of Goyim who have come out of the Roman/Greek culture with its pagan temples of polytheism, fertility cults, soothsaying, and the worship of demons, Shaul has shared the Kingdom of Yeshua and introduced Hebrew thought and customs to them. He begins his letter by commending them for their faith and works, but admonishes them for their tendencies to return to exalting men instead of Yeshua. He points out that this in turn can cause division because each one believes that their choice of leader is wiser than the others. They tend to hold the one who was responsible for their immersion in higher esteem than others, even though they all teach the same message. Shaul explains to them that no man is greater than another—all have an individual mission to accomplish, which is unique to that individual. He continues to admonish them for their foolishness and tells them they are falling victim to the plans of their enemy, hasatan. His plan is to divide and conquer—their mission should be to unite and restore the Whole House of YisraEL. Shaul understands that man's nature is to rely on his own understanding and intellect, but also knows that this leads to man's thinking too highly of himself. Shaul teaches that this can be a detriment. *"Therefore YAHveh said: "Insomuch as these people draw near to Me with their lips, but have removed their hearts far from Me, and their fear toward Me is taught by the commandments of men, therefore, behold, I will again do a marvelous work among this people, a marvelous work and a wonder; for the wisdom of their wise men shall perish, and the understanding of their prudent men shall be hidden"* (**ISA 29:13&14**). He reminds them that Yeshua said He would send signs and wonders to confirm His words because a YAHudi is taught to seek signs, but the Goyim depend on wisdom. Consequently, when Yeshua came as the sign promised in the TaNaKh, the YAHudi were so caught up in their own manmade traditions that the Messiah became a stumbling block, and to the self-proclaimed-wise Goyim, it was foolishness. Shaul points out that if YAHveh could be either foolish or weak, it would still be far greater than anything man could devise. He reminds them that YAH doesn't call the haughty, wise, or proud to serve him—instead, He chooses the meek, humble, and despised because noble men glory in themselves, and they should be avoided. *"Thus says YAHveh: "Let not the wise man glory in his wisdom, let not the mighty man glory in his might, nor let the rich man glory in his riches; but let him who glories glory in this, that he understands and knows Me, that I AM YAHveh, exercising lovingkindness, judgment, and righteousness in the earth. For in these I delight," says YAHveh"* (**JER 9:23&24**).

Shaul reminds them of the first time that he came to them to share the revelations that ELuah had revealed to him by His Ruach. He said it should have been obvious to them that what he shared did not come from him because he had no outward physical appearance that would have persuaded them. He reminds them that anything they receive from YAH is revealed to them by the power of the Ruach and not by persuasive words. He reminds them that all revelation comes this way so that men cannot glory in it. *"For since the beginning of the world men have not heard nor perceived by the ear, nor has the eye seen any ELohim besides You, who acts for the one who waits for Him"* (**ISA 64:4**). He exhorts them not to rely on the intellect of men but rather on the wisdom of the Ruach, who will reveal all the mysteries of YAH to them who wait. He reminds them that the natural mind cannot receive the things of YAHveh because they appear to be foolishness to them. Only those who have been born of the Ruach can understand the things of YAHveh's Kingdom and its principles. *"Who has directed the Ruach of YAHveh, or as His counselor has taught Him?"* (**ISA 40:13**).

Shaul admits that their tendency to act and think in a carnal way is because they still lack training in spiritual matters. So, he begins to lay out for them some of the kingdom principles that should help them understand how each person whom YAH has chosen has a particular mission to accomplish. He explains how those whom ELuah has chosen are like a field that belongs to Him. He sends one to sow the seeds of the TaNaKh in it and another to water it with the TaNaKh; they work as one (echad), but it is YAHveh who brings forth the abundant harvest by His Ruach. He gives another example. They are His building and Shaul, a shelich who teaches the TaNaKh, is the one who lays the foundation and is the chief master builder; Yeshua is the cornerstone. Someone else is the contractor who builds according to the blueprint of the TaNaKh, while others act as subcontractors under their supervision and lay out the stones (living stones—those who have been chosen to serve Him since the foundation of the Earth was laid by YAHveh). The material used is compared to silver, gold, and precious stones, which are the teachings of the Ruach—wood, hay, and straw, are the teachings of men. When that final "Day" comes, both the people and the principles that they lived by will be tested in the fire of the Ruach. Those who chose the proper materials (principles/teachings) will have endured and will receive the greatest reward—those who did not, though they may be saved, will receive less. Each Believer is YAH's building, or His House, and His Ruach desires to dwell there. He won't if that Believer has only been taught through the wisdom of men. The wisdom of men (their intellect) many times will negate the teachings of the TaNaKh because they contain traditions contrary to it. Following this so-called wisdom may carry with it negative consequences. Shaul points out that the teacher who uses these principles to teach by will be punished severely. Once more, Shaul warns them not to be caught up in the teachings and wisdom of men because it is pure foolishness to YAH and there will be a price to be paid by both the teacher and the student. *"He catches the wise in their craftiness, and the counsel of the cunning comes quickly upon them"* (**JOB 5:13**). *"YAHveh knows the thoughts of man, that they are futile"* (**PSALMS 94:11**).

Rav Shaul warns them to be careful in judging matters because they do not have the complete knowledge of YAHveh. Matters aren't always as they may seem to be on the surface. When Adonai returns, His true judgment will be revealed, along with all of His mysteries. Shaul tells his readers that he has given them all of these examples so that they won't pit one teacher, or instructor, against another—they are all used by ELuah to teach as though they were one (echad) in order to edify the Kahal of the Messiah. He points out that if those who had been appointed as their teachers were seeking to be exalted above others, they would have sought out the highest seat, but instead, they suffered persecution on their behalf and counted it as being a worthy cause.

He tells them that over time they may have ten-thousand others who will instruct them in the matters of the "Good News", but they need to remember that it was he who first came to them and begot them. He sees them as his children and loves them just as a father would. He only wants them to respect him as a child should his parent. He says his desire is to come to them as though he were their earthly abba, full of praise and compassion and not with a rod of correction. Instead, he is sending Timothy to remind them of all of these matters and to bring them this letter.

He also tells them that he has learned that there is a man among them who has committed the same sin that Rueben, the firstborn of Yaacov, committed by taking for himself his father's wife. He warns them that if they allow him to stay in the kahal, he will corrupt and encourage others to do similar things. He compares it with what happens to unleavened bread when a little leaven comes into contact with it and how it affects the whole loaf. He mentions Passover and how Yeshua was the sacrifice for them. He brings this up because it was apparently Passover season when he sent the letter. He instructs them that anyone committing blatant sin in their midst must be considered as one who is still in the world. He knows that they wouldn't have anything to do with those outside the confines of the kahal who would commit such abominations—therefore, they should have nothing to do with any within. He must be judged properly and then cast out of the community, denying him the enjoyment and protection of their fellowship. He needs to be sent out and treated as an outsider and an unbeliever. He refers to it as "delivering him to hasatan for the destruction of his flesh". *"Then you shall do to him as he thought to have done to his brother; so you shall put away the evil person among you. "And those who remain shall hear and fear, and hereafter they shall not again commit such evil among you"* (**DEUT** 19:19&20). Let me repeat once more—the Torah teaches that all blatant sin is worthy of death, while unintentional sin can be atoned for by the shedding of blood through an animal sacrifice, taking the place of the one who had sinned. Yeshua became our final sacrifice, paying the penalty for both types of sin for us. He lifted the curse, but we still must accept the consequences of our actions and decisions.

Shaul directs the kahal in Corinth not to take matters of dispute to the civil courts of men, but instead, they should settle matters within the kahal according to the Torah. He reminds them that one day they will be judging angels, so why shouldn't they be qualified to judge themselves. At one time they were of the world and were judged by the law of the world, but now they are of the kingdom, and the law (Torah) of the kingdom should be applied to their lives. Since they are no longer under the curse of the Torah, they are free to do all of the things that are good within the Torah without restriction. However, with freedom comes responsibility, and with responsibility comes accountability. Neglecting these two laws will result in individual independence, and individual independence is equivalent to making yourself your own eluah, which is rebellion that leads to sin and the loss of freedom. But if they commit unrighteous acts, like sexual immorality, they bring harm to themselves, their loved ones, and to the whole Kahal of YisraEL. He tells them that they are now betrothed to Yeshua and are of one (echad) flesh with Him. *"Therefore a man shall leave his father and mother and be joined to his wife, and they shall become one* (echad) *flesh"* (**GEN** 2:24).

Now anyone committing sexual immorality is sinning against Yeshua and the House of YisraEL as well as themselves—they are one (echad). He continues by giving an example. Except for spiritual reasons, such as fasting and praying, a married couple should not abstain from sexual activity, but should remain submissive to one another in order to promote fidelity. Neglect could lead to temptation, which in turn could lead to the sin of adultery or sexual immorality. He says that you are one flesh and do not belong to yourself. Shaul personally subscribed to remaining unmarried because of the responsibilities involved, but if a person is weak in their self-control, they should consider marriage. From here, he touches on the subject of divorce. If a divorce takes place between two believers, they are to remain unmarried for the rest of their lives in order to leave the door open for reconciliation. If two unbelieving couples are married and one becomes a believer, he or she is to stay with their spouse in case their lifestyle might convince the unbeliever to repent. Also, they are to stay so that they are able to bring up their children in the ways of Adonai—this keeps the children kedosh until they become accountable for their own sins. Now if the unbelieving spouse wants to leave, they are to be set free from their vows so that peace (shalom) might be allowed to remain in the family. The believing spouse, however, should still remain unmarried just in case the other becomes born-again and decides to return. But if the unbeliever remarries, he or she is guilty of committing adultery, which releases the faithful one from their vow—it is as though the former spouse has died. Shaul then encourages all widows and virgins to stay as they are if they can, making it easier to serve Adonai, otherwise they should marry, if they need to.

After this, Shaul goes on to discuss the subject of remaining as each is called. If you are a YAHudi, remain a YAHudi; if you are a Goyim, remain a Goyim; it is not important to YAH which you are just as long as you understand the importance of keeping the Torah the way Yeshua instructed. Being circumcised or remaining uncircumcised does not matter because that covenant was fulfilled by the shedding of the blood of the Messiah. Here again, he points out that circumcision is a good thing, but it does not save you one way or the other.

From here, Shaul touches on another very controversial subject—food. He points out that food offered to idols is nothing, but we are to abstain from it because of what it stands for. Idols are not elohim because we know that there is only one ELohim, and He is YAHveh, echad with His Son, Yeshua HaMashiach. Therefore, the meat that is offered to idols cannot defile us unless we believe that it will. YAHveh is the Creator of all things, including meats, and He made all things good originally—it is only unclean if He deems it so. But in the knowledge that we now have, all things are new and clean because of the blood of Yeshua. That means that all of the old things pertaining to the curse have now passed away and, therefore, can no longer be considered unclean. So, like circumcision, abstinence from different kinds of food has nothing to do with our salvation. But, if partaking of any kind of food might cause our brother to stumble because he does not have this knowledge and to him it is a sin, then we need to also abstain. He brings this out again a little later. If a person thinks that something is a sin, even if it isn't, because he thinks it is and rebelliously or recklessly partakes of it, to him it becomes a sin due to the condition of his heart.

After clarifying this point, Rav Shaul moves on to the responsibility of the Kahal of YisraEL, which is to support those who have been called into the ministry of Adonai and to help equip them for every good work. He explains that there are those who claim to have been called of YAH into this responsibility but who are really only there to take advantage of the naive. He assures them that this is not his intent or the intent of any of the shelichim who are affiliated with him. He prefers to support himself so that no one can lay that complaint against him, but others who have given up their vocations and sacrificed material gains in order to minister the truth of the Messiah should be properly compensated. *"You shall not muzzle an ox while it treads out the grain"* (**DEUT 25:4**). This is another lesson from the Torah. He goes on to remind them of his duty to be a role model for them to emulate. His duty is not to offend, but to encourage and to exhort. When sharing with his fellow YAHudi, he honors what they deem to be kedosh (holy), and when he's with Goyim, he does likewise because he knows he must first gain their trust in order to prepare them for the truth. This is far more valuable than the dogmatism of some doctrine. He has trained himself to do this without sinning or causing others to sin because of their ignorance. He encourages them to see life in the Ruach as though it were a race for a crown. Train hard, sacrifice, learn all that you can, gain experience, put everything together, and don't quit when the going gets tough. Then, when the race of life is over, you will receive a crown as a reward—not one that is temporal, made of earthly material, but an imperishable one that will last for all eternity.

Now Shaul turns back to the fundamental teachings of the TaNaKh. He points to the pattern YAHveh designed in the second book of the Torah, the book of the Exodus. This is the pattern for immersion into a kedosh life. First came the covering of the sea (this symbolizes immersion in water) and the covering of the cloud (being led by the Ruach). After this came the spiritual food of manna (this symbolizes the unleavened bread of Yeshua's body) and then the spiritual drink from out of a rock (the water of the teachings of the words of YAHveh through His Son, Yeshua HaMashiach, the Living Torah and the Living Rock). But he reminds them that those who were called out of Mitsrahyim rebelled and did not want what their ELohim offered. They decided that walking in faith and following an invisible ELohim was too burdensome. They wanted an el that they could see, so they had Aharon craft them a golden calf to go before them. *"Then they rose up early on the next day, offered burnt offerings; and the people sat down to eat and drink, and rose up to play. And YAHveh said to Mosheh, "Go, get down! For your people whom you brought out of the land of Mitsrahyim have corrupted themselves. "They have turned aside quickly out of the way which I commanded them. They have made themselves a molded calf, and worshiped it and sacrificed to it, and said, 'This is your el, O YisraEL, that brought you out of the land of Mitsrahyim!'"* **(EXOD 32:6—8)** When they did, they turned their back on YAHveh, so He turned His back on them. Shaul warns them not to complain, not to go back to their old pagan ways of worshiping through sexual immorality, and not to tempt the Messiah with blatant disobedience. He assures them that no form of temptation will come to them that hasn't already been overcome by the Messiah and that their heavenly Abba will not leave them without an escape route from any temptation that seems insurmountable. He reminds them that one of the temptations that they will find hardest to resist will be the pressure that they receive from family and friends to return to idolatry. But they dare not compromise or rub elbows with those who still practice such abominations—it will cause them to either stumble or backslide. Now they are in communion with those who have discovered the truth of salvation from their sins, and when they sit down to break bread with other believers at either Passover or Shabbat, they are partaking of the body of the Messiah. The bread represents His body, and the wine represents His blood. These elements are to remind them of the tremendous sacrifice that He made for the debt they couldn't pay—and the one He didn't owe. He tells them that even though idols are nothing, compromising and partaking in meaningless worship to them is equal to the partaking of bread at a table with demons. This is unacceptable.

Once again, Shaul brings up the subject of proper eating versus improper eating. He does so by first reminding them that knowledge of the purpose of the Torah is as important as the ordinances themselves. He reminds them that in the beginning, all things were made perfect by YAH, but they didn't remain that way because of the blatant sin of mankind (ahdom). *"The earth is YAHveh's, and all its fullness, the world and those who dwell therein."* **(PSALMS 24:1)** Then, after the Earth had received its judgment and its cleansing by the flood, YAHveh used animals to distinguish between that which was clean and that which was not. He instructed them that animals were to be an additional food source for man besides the fruits and herbs. Later, through Mosheh, He designated that only the clean animals were to be used as their food and for sacrifices as thanksgiving, or freewill offerings, to be their payment for unintentional sins. They were to be used in the ordinances of both the Mishkahn (Tabernacle) and the House of YAH to teach about the Messiah and His total sacrifice. They were not to remain after His coming and after the destruction of YAH's second House. It was prophesied that they would one day be reinstated, but only as a sign of the approach of His return. Then, after He came the second time, He would set up a whole new system that would contain a whole new meaning. The reason that Shaul gave for the continuation of eating kosher was in order to not offend those who still observed it. He pointed out that even though he had the freedom to do so, he also had the responsibility not to cause his brethren to stumble. He confessed that even though all things were lawful for him, not all things were helpful, and some things just did not edify. Eating and drinking should be done to the glory of ELuah. He exhorts them to imitate him as he imitates the Messiah.

While he was on the subject of eating, Shaul decided to comment on observing the proper conduct when coming before Adonai to worship or to partake of communion with the brethren on Passover or Shabbat. He reminds them again that they should not stray from the YAHudi traditions that he had taught them about the spiritual order of things. First, the Messiah was subject to Abba ELuah, then the patriarch of each family was to be subject to the Messiah, and finally, the wife was to be subject to the patriarch. They are not to come before Adonai dressed as they did when they came before their pagan fertility elohim. Therefore, the women, when coming before Adonai, were not to shave or uncover their heads, as do the prostitutes at the fertility temples. Men were not to cross-dress as women and wear veils or head coverings, as was the practice at the fertility temples, or to imitate a woman by wearing their hair the same length. All of these things could be confusing to others, besides being an abomination before YAHveh. They were not to come to communion as though it were a party. They were to come humbly and in awe of Adonai, showing respect for Him and for those who came with a contrite heart. Eating, drinking, and partying were to be kept within the confines of their own houses. He reminded them of the ordinances and the YAHudi traditions that were to be observed when they did come. The only changes in the YAHudi traditions were the ones that Yeshua implemented on the night that He was betrayed, when He took the bread and said, *"Take, eat; this is My body which is broken for you; do this in remembrance of Me."* Also when He took the cup of wine and said, *"This cup is the Renewed Covenant* (Brit Chadashah) *in My blood. This do, as often as you drink it, in remembrance of Me."* He warns that if any are careless or flippant about these ordinances and partake of them in an unworthy manner, they will be held guilty of sin, which could result in poverty, sickness, and even death.

Another abuse that the kahal at Corinth was guilty of was the abuse of the spiritual gifts. Rav Shaul first began his critique regarding spiritual gifts by defining their origin. They were already familiar with spiritual gifts and with their use and abuse because they had practiced their counterfeit when they were pagans. But there, the gifts came from the dark side of the spiritual world and were manifested by the prince of demons, hasatan. The Prince of Darkness tries to counterfeit every work of our Abba, and we need to be wise in the wisdom of the Abba's Ruach in order to tell the difference. First of all, any work or gift from Abba has only one fundamental function and that is to glorify Him and/or His Son, not the one the gift is operating through. All gifts are distributed and operate under the authority of His Ruach. The works of administration and ministries are under the authority of Abba's Son, Yeshua. And finally, all activities that occur on Earth (past, present, and future) are sanctioned by YAHveh. Shaul points out that the gifts that the Ruach manifests for the purpose of exhorting the Kahal of YisraEL and confirming the words of YAH are divided into three groups of three, or nine basic gifts. Any of these gifts can be exercised at any time by anyone who has been redeemed and sanctified, but only at the discretion of the Ruach HaKedosh. At times, the Ruach will issue these gifts on a very temporary basis to different individuals just to edify a local kahal for a specific reason. Some individuals have been predetermined before birth to be able to operate in certain spiritual gifts. Unfortunately, some of today's contemporary spiritual leaders do not recognize the validity of these gifts and accuse anyone who uses them as being an instrument of hasatan. They demand that these individuals repent and never use them again, thereby depriving the Body of Messiah of their benefits. At times, some individuals do use them for personal gain, and without realizing it, they have handed these gifts over to the powers of darkness.

Let's return to the three categories of gifts. The first category is the gifts of insight. These consist of wisdom, knowledge, and discernment. These are gifts that are given to an individual by the Ruach HaKedosh when there is no possible way for that individual to have had any prior understanding or knowledge of another person, place, or thing. The second category is the power gifts, which consist of faith, healing, and miracles. The third and final category of the three is the vocal gifts. They consist of prophecy, tongues, and interpretation of tongues. If you remember, we touched on this subject briefly in Chapter Three, where I discussed ecstatic speech, which is how the gifts of tongues are manifested. Tongues means languages, but these languages are given by the Ruach. They may be manifested as a single language, a combination of several languages, even languages spoken and known only by angelic beings, or all of the above combined. When manifested, they have been labeled by the natural man as glossolalia, or gibberish. Shaul warns his readers that the latter should only be practiced when there is someone who can interpret its meaning—interpret, not necessarily translate. He later discusses the private use of this gift for the purpose of self-edification.

WHAT WE WEREN'T TAUGHT ABOUT THE BIBLE AND ITS HISTORY

There are times when some individuals will innocently practice these gifts with very little knowledge of YAHveh or His Son, but they will use them in a very loving and compassionate way just because they are very loving and compassionate people. Some of these gifts have also been mistakenly referred to as extra-sensory perception, such as mental telepathy or clairvoyance. At the same time, on the dark side, these gifts have been counterfeited by soothsayers, mediums, witches, or just plain charlatans.

Shaul reminds them that all gifts are to benefit everyone and are to be used to edify the Body of Messiah. They are to operate in unison, just as the different limbs and organs of the human body do. They are to profit all, but when misused, they can divide, cripple, and even kill a kahal. He emphasizes the fact that, just like in the human body, there is no unimportant function of any member. Only men in their selfishness say otherwise in order to try to control or dominate others. He then points to the ten basic ministry gifts as an example of how this works, beginning with the ministries that carry the most responsibility, down to the least. But above all, if any gift or ministry isn't motivated by love, then the gift is useless.

Rav Shaul begins explaining the importance of love by giving examples of how each gift, beginning with the least and then going up to the one carrying the most responsibility, would fare without love as its motivation. He focuses on love as being the core of YAHveh's motivation for the "Gifts" of the Ruach, paralleling that of love being the core of the "Fruits" of the Ruach. He points out that when all of YAH's activities have come to an end, it will be His love that will prevail and remain. The gifts will no longer be needed because both he and we shall stand face to face with the Messiah, having all understanding of His hidden mysteries and basking in the fullness of His love.

He once again turns his attention to the least of the gifts, tongues, because its use had been so abused at Corinth. He desires to clarify its proper place within the House of YisraEL. He exhorts everyone to make use of tongues for personal edification, but not as a public gift unless there is someone present to interpret. He equates tongues used in public, along with the proper interpretation, to prophecy that is spoken directly in a known language. Tongues alone, given in an unknown language, edifies no one except the one speaking. Although he encourages everyone to seek the gift of pure prophecy, he does not want to discourage the use of tongues for personal edification. He exhorts them to use all of the vocal gifts when both praying and singing, making sure they bring glory to their Abba when they do. He reminds them that all of the gifts are to confirm YAHveh's words and purpose. *"For with stammering lips* (ecstatic speech or glossolalia) *and another tongue He will speak to this people, to whom He said, 'This is the rest with which You may cause the weary to rest," and, "This is the refreshing"; yet they would not hear"* (**ISA 28:11&12**). The gifts are to be signs for bringing unbelievers to repentance—not for scaring them away. Therefore, they must be used properly.

He then begins to instruct them in the proper use of the gift of tongues in ministering to others. He says that when they are gathered together, the order should be that no more than two or three people should exercise the gift and that each one should wait until the other has finished. For every tongue spoken, there must be at least one present who can interpret. He says that this rule must also apply to those who prophesy—only one at a time and no more than three. All then must wait patiently until the prophecy has been properly judged by the elders as to its accuracy and truth. At this time, he inserts in his instructions that the women who have been wailing and moaning, as they did in the pagan temples, are to conduct themselves in silence and reverence before YAHveh. If something was prophesied or taught that they did not understand, they were not to stand up and be disorderly, but were to be submissive and respectful to their husbands, just as the Torah teaches. They should wait until they get home and then ask their husbands to explain the meaning. YAHveh is the ELuah of order and not of confusion.

The kahal at Thessalonica apparently wasn't the only group made up predominantly of Goyim who were having trouble understanding the doctrine of the resurrection—so were the Corinthians. In both cases, there were two confusing doctrines that could have been the cause—either the Sadducees' belief that there is no resurrection or their previous polytheistic-pagan teachings regarding reincarnation. In either case, Shaul felt he needed to reassure them of its fundamental truth, so he took them step by step in progression from the Messiah's Passion, death, and resurrection to the time that Yeshua revealed Himself to Shaul. He explains that if none of these things had actually happened, then they should return to their old ways because all of their hope for salvation was useless. He further reassures them that all that they have believed in was not in vain. There is a resurrection, and their faith has not been futile—the Messiah does reign as King and does have authority over all powers. He will put an end to all other authority and powers and will return to finish off the last enemy—death itself. *"You have made him to have dominion over the works of Your hands; You have put all things under his feet"* (**PSALM 8:6**). He gives them another example by pointing to those who are still dead in their sins. If there is no resurrection and there is no deliverance from death and all things remain as they are, what good is there in being immersed into a faith that has no solution to death? If they have no solution for themselves or for others who are dead in their sins, what good is it? Why should anyone risk their very lives for such a lie? Why not just forget everything and have a good time—go out and party? *"And in that day Adonai YAHveh of hosts called for weeping and for mourning, for baldness and for girding with sackcloth. But instead, joy and gladness,* *slaying oxen and killing sheep, eating meat and drinking wine: "Let us eat and drink for tomorrow we die!"* (**ISA 22:12&13**). Then he admonishes them by telling them that they have to turn away from associating or keeping company with those who practice evil and return to the truth that he has taught them. They have no excuse—they have been given the knowledge of the True ELohim. He continues to explain what it means to experience the resurrection in order to encourage them to look toward this promise with hope. He explains the difference between the two Ahdoms—the first was natural, the second was spiritual. The first sinned and was separated from YAHveh—the second did not and is forever at His Right Hand. The natural man must come first before the spiritual can follow. Everything the Creator created has its own form and glory—whether it is terrestrial or celestial—whether it is man, beast, fish, or bird. Each creature has a soul, but man also has a spirit because YAH breathed into man His own Ruach. The changes between the two Ahdoms cannot take place until one dies so that the other may live. *"And YAHveh ELohim formed man of the dust of the ground, and breathed into his nostrils the breath of life; and man became a living being"* (**GEN 2:7**). Since we bear the image of the first Ahdom of dust, we will also bear the image of the heavenly Ahdom. He goes on to tell them that at the time of the resurrection, there will be some who will not have experienced the death in their flesh, but they too will go through a change because their natural bodies cannot inherit the kingdom. He continues to lay out the steps leading up to this change that will take place on that glorious day. First, there will be the sound of the seventh shofar, and all of those who have died as believers will be raised with new resurrected bodies, and then those who are still alive will also be changed. From that moment on, death will no longer be their enemy. *"He will swallow up death forever, and Adonai YAHveh will wipe away tears from all faces; the rebuke of His people He will take away from all the earth; for YAHveh has spoken"* (**ISA 25:8**). *"I will ransom them from the power of the grave: I will redeem them from death; O Death, I will be your plagues! O Grave, I will be your destruction! Pity is hidden from My eyes"* (**HOSEA 13:14**). Finally, Shaul points to the Torah as the source that reveals what sin really is, with its curse being death. Then he goes on to remind them that since they have been set free from the curse of the Torah by the shed blood of the Messiah, they have been set free from experiencing the sting of death, which is the separation from their ELohim forever.

After Shaul finishes his instructions regarding his concerns toward their spiritual welfare, he turns his attention to a request for their brethren in the kahal at YAHrushalayim. He suggests that on the first day of the week, before they do anything else, they lay aside a portion of their monetary offerings for that week in order to meet the needs of this matter. This is not to be interpreted as being a sanction for a Sunday Sabbath. Instead, it suggests that each individual, before anything else is accomplished, should first set aside some of his financial gain in order to benefit others. He closes his letter by encouraging them to show hospitality toward Timothy when he comes to deliver it to them. He tells them that he hopes to come to see them sometime after the Feast of Shavuot in the late spring and then to possibly spend the summer and winter with them. He continues with a few more salutations and greetings on behalf of others and finishes by telling them to greet each other with a holy kiss (this was a common Middle-Eastern custom and is still practiced today).

II Corinthians

After Shaul wrote his first letter to the kahal at Corinth, but before he wrote his second, he suffered as the result of a number of incidents that took place at both Ephesus and Athens. Timothy had already returned from his mission of exalting the truths that Shaul had previously shared with them. Now Shaul has become occupied with having to defend himself against a bombardment of false accusations, which were challenging his authority and were coming from many of the different cities where he had planted congregations. He opens his second letter to them by acknowledging their suffering, but he assures them that the testing of their faith was necessary. He reminds them that all who have received the revelation of redemption, justification, and sanctification must experience these things. However, he is still looking forward to being with them once more, in spite of the fact that he was prevented from coming to them earlier.

He begins to share with them his regret that he had to be so forceful and demanding in his previous letter regarding their conduct in spiritual matters, but it was necessary for their maturity. He says it is now time to reconsider and bring the man who had sinned in the area of immorality back into the fold and to nurture and minister to his needs. He says he grieves that he could not be in their presence, which to him is like a healing balm. He understands how they must have felt in looking forward to his arrival and then being disappointed when he was unable to be there as he had hoped. He also suffered disappointment when he was unable to be with his friend, Titus, after being called to Macedonia.

He reminds them of their overall calling—they are to be an example of life to those who are saved, and they are to remind those who are perishing in their wickedness of the death that awaits them. Just like his letters to them, they are to be living letters to others, being evident to those around them that they have been called to "live" the Torah in their sight. This is possible because it has now been written on their hearts and not just on tablets of stone or the parchment of scrolls. When Mosheh brought down the written Torah and its glory was displayed on his face, bringing glory to YAHveh even before the Messiah came, how much more glory would the Ruach of YAHveh bring when it is lived out in each of their lives. He continues to explain how Mosheh had to cover his face with a veil in order to hide it from YisraEL because they had been rebellious. Now YAHveh has lifted the veil by rending it from the top to the bottom in order to reveal Yeshua as His glory in them. He tells them that it takes more than reading the TaNaKh each Sabbath to be a witness for YAH—it takes being living letters before the whole world to establish His glory. But when those who have had a veil over their understanding accept Yeshua as their Adonai, that veil is also lifted from their eyes, and they can begin to live out the Torah in the Ruach. Living out their lives in the Ruach brings total freedom to them, compared to living it out only in the letter. Each person has the responsibility of returning to the written Torah so that the Ruach can use it as a mirror to reflect back to them how they used to be so that they won't return to their old lifestyle of living as though they were still under the curse. Those who insist on gaining their salvation through keeping the Torah will never understand the message until they have allowed the Ruach to prepare their hearts for its truth. He says they walk in deceitfulness—you walk in truth. Even though ELuah has the power to bring light out of darkness as He did at creation, *"Let there be light"; and there was light"* (**GEN 1:3**), He will not intrude on their will. They have a free will to choose—or not to choose.

He reminds them that because of the truth of this "Good News", they have the power of the Ruach over every circumstance in their lives. They cannot be beaten down like those who are perishing. *"For You have delivered my soul from death, my eyes from tears, and my feet from falling. I will walk before YAHveh in the land of the living; I believed, therefore I spoke, I am greatly afflicted." I said in my haste, all men are liars"* (**PSALM 116:8-11**). Our testimony is one of life through faith and not death because we live by the Ruach and not by circumstances. We are to live by that faith even though our bodies are perishing. We have the assurance that our spirits live on as though we are not perishing because we have the promise that when we are finished with these temporal bodies, another awaits us that is eternal. Inwardly, we groan to obtain that body which can never be destroyed because this body we now live in is limited. When we receive our eternal body, it will be without limits. We know these things to be true because the Ruach has guaranteed it in out hearts, and, therefore, we walk by faith and not by sight. The final test, if we have lived this way, will be when we all stand before Messiah at His Seat of Judgment, where He will review all of our works, whether they were of faith or of ourselves, and this will determine the extent of our rewards.

Now Shaul begins to expound on the main purpose and mandate of all of those who have been redeemed by the blood of Yeshua. They are to become ambassadors for the Messiah to reconcile those who are lost in their trespasses and sins against ELuah the Abba. Just as all of the shelichim have tried to be living examples of this to them, now they are to be living examples for others who are lost, just as they were at one time. They are to die to self and live for others, just as Yeshua did for them. His life, His death, and His resurrection were for them so that they could live out their lives for the purpose of sharing the reality of salvation to others. The old life of selfishness has passed away, and now the new life of selflessness should have taken its place. He reminds them that they are also called to bring restoration to the House of YisraEL in order to complete the work the Messiah has been sent to do. *"Thus says YAHveh: "In an acceptable time I have heard You, and in the day of salvation I have helped You; I will preserve You and give You as a covenant to the people, to restore the earth to cause them to inherit the desolate heritages"* (ISA 49:8). He reminds them that they are called to bring forth the manifestation of YAH's promise to the fathers, from Avraham to the present, and that no set of circumstances can be allowed to stand in the way. If this mandate is not carried out by them, then Abba will find a people who will carry it out, no matter how long it takes. *"I will walk among you and be your ELohim, and you shall be My people.—My mishkahn* (tabernacle) *also shall be with them; indeed I will be their ELohim, and they shall be My people"* (LEV 26:12 and EZEK 37:27). They can limit YAHveh only by their doubting—not because He failed to provide the necessary tools. They must exercise their own will by turning from their old ways and walking in the new ways of Adonai. *"Depart! Depart! Go out from the midst of her, be clean, you who bear the vessels of YAHveh.—"I will bring you out from the peoples and gather you out of the countries where you are scattered, with a mighty hand, with an outstretched arm, and with fury poured out.—"I will accept you as a sweet aroma when I bring you out from the peoples and gather you out of the countries where you have been scattered; and I will be hallowed in you before the Goyim"* (ISA 52:11 and EZEK 20:34 & 41). Also, *"I will be his Abba, and he shall be My son. If he commits iniquity, I will chastise him with the rod of men and with the blows of the sons of men"* (II SAM 7:14).

    Shaul then began to reflect back to the times when he had suffered trials, tribulations, and afflictions on the behalf of all of the Kahal. It was the report that Titus returned with that brought Shaul the most encouragement because it told him about the fellowship and love that they bestowed upon him. He was also strengthened to learn about the maturity they were showing by following the instructions that he had given them in his first letter. Titus was also encouraged by what he saw. But once again, Shaul finds that he needs to come to them for rest due to the continuous oppression that both he and the other brethren have experienced before writing this second letter. He tells them that he will be sending his friend, Titus, this time to receive their generosity when he delivers this letter to them.

    Shaul exhorts the kahal at Corinth to show their generosity to their YAHudi brethren in YAHrushalayim and in YAHuda because they are still in need. He commends them and all of the kahal throughout Macedonia for the generosity that they have shown in the past when asked. He once again uses this opportunity for them to give without reservation as a test of their sincerity and their generosity. Through this, he hopes to increase their understanding of what their Messiah Yeshua gave for them so they might have the opportunity to receive eternal life. He reminds them that their giving must be of a cheerful and eager heart and to do so willingly and not begrudgingly because any other attitude will not afford them their just reward. For what they sow, they shall also reap, just as the Torah teaches. *"So when they measured it by omers, he who gathered much had nothing over, and he who gathered little had no lack. Every man had gathered according to each one's need"* (**EXOD 16:18**). He encourages them to prepare their gift before Titus even gets there so that when he himself comes with both the Goyim and the YAHudi brethren to visit them, they will be an example of mature cheerful givers, just as he has boasted. He reassures them that their generosity will not go unnoticed by YAHveh because it was given in faith (that is, if it was given in faith) and because their Abba, YAH, loves to pour out his abundance upon those who act in the works of faith. *"He has dispersed abroad, he has given to the poor; his righteousness endures forever; his strength will be exalted with honor"* (**PSALM 112:9**). He also assures them that their giving furthers the kingdom in its growth and glorifies their Abba because of it.

Rav Shaul switches his attention to that of defending himself because he knows that some of his YAHudi brothers, those who deny Yeshua as the true Messiah, have spread lies about his authority. He admits that he is not mighty in appearance, but assures them that YAH does not choose his ambassadors by their physical appearance, as do men. As a matter of fact, He usually does just the opposite in order to confound the natural man. But his record speaks for itself. He reminds them that neither he nor they struggle against men of flesh and bone—they are but the vessels that their true enemy, hasatan, uses. He assures them that the letters he sends them, containing his instructions, carry the same authority as if he were in their midst and instructing them. He reminds them that all of the teachings he has given them, both in word and by letter, were confirmed by signs and wonders as to their authenticity. *"But let him who glories glory in this, that he understands and knows Me, that I AM YAHveh, exercising lovingkindness, judgment, and righteousness in the earth. For in these I delight says YAHveh"* (**JER 9:24**). Even so, Shaul is still concerned about their spirituality and that they might fall prey to other teachings brought to them by false rabbi and become deceived, as was Cheva (Eve) in the Garden. He warns the kahal at Corinth, just as he did in Galatia, because he knows their vulnerability. He admits to his not being the best orator, but reminds them that what he lacks in articulation, he more than makes up for in the knowledge of the Torah, YAHveh, and His Son, Yeshua HaMashiach. He reminds them that he has never charged any of the kahal for his ministry of teaching and would never accept any wages even if it were offered him. He warns them that those who come with enticing words come with the knowledge of men and not with spiritual understanding. One of hasatan's greatest means of deception is coming as an angel of light, full of knowledge and intellect.

He reminds them that he is no stranger to personal rejection from either the Goyim or the YAHudi because of the "Good News" that he proclaims. But in every case of persecution and physical abuse that he has personally received because of his message, YAHveh has protected, delivered, and saved him from any real harm. When trials came his way and he found himself in fear and weakness, YAH always gave him the strength to overcome. These are but a few of the things that he feels he can boast about.

He then tells a story of a man who fourteen years earlier had an experience of being caught up into Paradise, where he saw things that he could not describe. Shaul says that he wasn't able to tell whether this was an out-of-the-body experience or not. One thing he does know is that the story encouraged him to continue persevering in his mission of convincing others that there was a Paradise.

Shaul told them that he understands trials because of the struggle over one that he has been buffeted with for many years, an infirmity that he has pleaded with Adonai to remove on three different occasions. Adonai told him to endure and that if he did, he would also find the strength to overcome every other trial that would come his way. Once again, he apologized for not taking anything from them as a wage for his ministry, but he personally felt that since Yeshua had given them to him to nurture, he was as responsible for them as a parent would be. He admits that he could be criticized for seemingly having a double standard, but they needed to learn to support those who have taught them because this teaches responsibility.

At the same time, he knew there were still schisms within their ranks, such as between those who desired to continue participating in lewd behavior and those who desired to repent from their old habits. He told them that he was looking forward to visiting them for a third time, but was concerned that when he did, he would have to chastise them for not purging the leaven from their midst. He encourages them to do the right thing before he arrives because he will be obligated to judge them if they don't. He reminds them that he has spoken of these matters in his letters to them, through his instructions brought to them by others, and even personally while in their presence. This will be his third trip, and because of the kingdom principle established in the Torah, he must pass final judgment on their behavior. *"One witness shall not rise against a man concerning any iniquity or any sin that he commits; by the mouth of two or three witnesses the matter shall be established"* (DEUT 19:15).

After his final visit to Corinth and before he leaves to go up to YAHrushalayim, Shaul knows that he needs to also visit the kahal at Rome, where Priscilla and Aquila have established the "Good News" among the Goyim and the YAHudi. He decides to write them a letter that is to be read among the Believers there to inform them of his doctrine beforehand so that they will be ready when he arrives.

Conclusion

In all five letters, Rav Shaul expressed his frustration with the confusion that had been raised by others within the different kahal. Some of the YAHudi wanted to continue in their understanding of the old traditions of salvation by keeping the Torah, while the Goyim wanted to drag in pagan traditions, and still others wanted to compromise both. These problems have been dividing Believers for two-thousand years, but Yeshua prophesied that this would be the case until the fullness of the Goyim had been completed. This would also be the time when the scales would be lifted from spiritual eyes and the stops would be removed from spiritual ears because this would be YAHveh's appointed time.

CHAPTER 22
...about Romans, Acts 20—28, Colossians, Philemon, Ephesians, and Philippians

Rav Shaul begins to prepare himself for his final journey to YAHrushalayim, where he hopes to celebrate the spring feasts of Passover, Unleavened Bread, and Shavuot. But it is there that he will be arrested, just as he was forewarned through prophecy, and it will be there that he will write his letter to the kahal at Rome. He hasn't been back to Rome since the "Good News" had arrived there via other brethren, but he is anxious to share his testimony and teachings with them. He goes there by mandate from Adonai and is arrested for teaching his unorthodox doctrine. While in Rome, he writes letters of exaltation to the other kahal that he has planted, along with letters of exhortation to his friends, Timothy and Titus.

Acts 20

As Shaul continues to revisit as many of the Messianic communities that he has planted throughout Macedonia and Greece as he can, he continues to meet opposition from the Orthodox-YAHudi citizens who are located there. Sailing from port to port along the Mediterranean becomes his most convenient means of travel. After his visit to the kahal in Phillippi, he traveled to the town of Troas. There he met with several of the brethren on the Sabbath that followed after the week of the Feast of Unleavened Bread. While there, on the evening of that Sabbath, and at the beginning of the First day of the next week, Shaul began a teaching session that lasted until midnight with a number of the local talmidim. While sitting on a windowsill of a three-story house, a young man named Eutycyus was listening to the lesson, dozed off, and accidentally fell to his death below. Shaul ran down to him, picked up his body, and by revelation of the Ruach, pronounced that his life was to be restored—it immediately was. Shaul then returned to the upper room and finished his homily.

Shaul was disappointed that he was unable to attend the feast of Unleavened Bread at YAHrushalayim, but was determined to be there for the Feast of Shavuot. In his determination, he bypassed Ephesus, but called for a meeting with the elders of the kahal there instead. When they arrived, he tried to encourage them to stay the course by teaching the doctrines that he and the Ruach had entrusted to them regarding repentance from dead works and faith toward Yeshua HaMashiach. He tells them that he has feelings of trepidation because he has had several prophecies regarding his welfare if he travels to YAHrushalayim. In spite of this, he knows it is the will of ELuah, and he is ready to face what may lie ahead. He tells them that he does not expect to ever see them again. He then reminds them of what Yeshua once said, *"It is far better to give than to receive."* After praying with them, he began his journey to YAHrushalayim.

Romans

In his letter to the kahal at Rome, Shaul first establishes his credentials as a shelich of the Messiah and then exhorts them to follow the commandments of YAH that were spoken by the Ne'vee Habakkuk (Chabahkook). *"Behold the proud, his soul is not upright in him; but the just shall live by faith"* (**HAB 2:4**). He continues to encourage them to stay the course by pointing out the futile struggle that mankind has been indulging in while trying to find real meaning and happiness in life, yet ignoring what is evident before their very own eyes. He points out that nature itself gives evidence to the existence of a creator because it functions with perfect design, proving that there must be a perfect designer. But man has ignored this evidence and has chosen to worship the creation rather than the Creator. How absurd for mankind to make such a blatant mistake. The real reason for such insolence is man's sinful nature and his not wanting any accountability for his actions. Mankind, because of his sinful nature, desires to be his own eluah and doesn't want to be accountable to anyone but himself. This gives him the freedom to pursue all types of perversions, such as unnatural sexual activity, including bestiality, homosexuality, adultery, pedophilia, and other vile acts committed toward nature. It would also include other things such as talebearing, murder, pridefulness, self-love, showing lack of mercy, disobeying parents, and the list goes on. If he doesn't commit these acts himself, he ignores others who do by not renouncing them, which is the same as committing the acts themselves. He points out that all of these perversions and/or the approving of such actions is worthy of the judgment of death. He continues to show them how man has attempted to justify himself by judging others for these crimes against nature while secretly practicing these same things. When ELuah, out of His mercy and love, tries to bring man to repentance through chastisement, man kicks and screams and resists His correction. *"Also to You, O Adonai belongs mercy; for You render to each one according to his works.—If you say, "Surely we did not know this," does He who weighs the hearts consider it? He who keeps your soul, does He not know it? And will He not render to each man according to his deeds"* (**PSALMS 62:12** and **PROV 24:12**). These same attitudes are displayed daily in our own times, and the judgment remains the same.

WHAT WE WEREN'T TAUGHT ABOUT THE BIBLE AND ITS HISTORY

Shaul assures his readers that YAH is no respecter of persons—He doesn't see the YAHudi any differently than He sees the Goyim/Yosefs. The YAHudi are given the responsibility to keep the written Torah for all mankind for all time, and the Goyim/Yosefs are given the responsibility to share the free gift of the knowledge of the Living Torah, the Messiah. If either fails their responsibility, they will experience YAH's wrath—if they carry it out, they will enjoy His mercy. He continues to explain that those who have never been taught the Torah but sin against nature will be judged according to nature—Torah and nature are harmonious (The principles of the Torah are found in nature). But those who have heard the Torah and ignore its meaning by not doing the Torah will be judged according to the Torah. He gives a further explanation of these principles by pointing out that those who obey their own conscience, which is in harmony with the Torah, even though they are ignorant of the Torah, will be judged by what they do with what their own conscience understands as being right.

Then Shaul turns his attention to the scholarly YAHudi, those who are in the kahal in Rome. He asks them whether they obey the Torah based upon what they know as truth or based upon what was passed down to them through the traditions of their heritage. Do they teach one thing and do another, or have they dedicated their lives to obeying and doing the true works of the Torah? *"Now therefore, what have I here," says YAHveh, "That My people are taken away for nothing? Those who rule over them make them wail," says YAHveh, "and My Name is blasphemed continually every day.—"Therefore say to the House of YisraEL, "Thus says Adonai YAHveh; "I do not do this for your sake, O House of YisraEL, but for My kedosh Name's sake, which you have profaned among the nations wherever you went"* (**ISA 52:5** and **EZEK 36:22**). He then begins to speak to them, as he did to the Galatians and to the Corinthians, about what the YAHudi cherish so much—circumcision. Circumcision, he says, can be counted as nothing toward righteousness unless the Torah is obeyed to the letter by the one circumcised. Then he points out that this cannot be done by a sinful man and tells them that all men are sinful. But if an uncircumcised man obeys the righteous requirements that the Torah teaches, and he can if he has accepted the shed blood of the Messiah that covers his sins, then his uncircumcision is counted as though he were circumcised. It is not the physical act that is counted for righteousness, he tells them, but rather the spiritual condition of the heart, which can only be changed by the Ruach. He then asks if the YAHudi have any advantage at all by knowing and keeping the ordinances of the Torah. Of course they do, they were given the responsibility of keeping the Torah intact so that mankind could have the words which bring eternal life and provide knowledge of Him from whom those words came. *"Against You, You only, have I sinned, and done this evil in Your sight—that You may be found just when You speak,* *and blameless when You judge"* (**PSALM 51:4**). Then he asks if ELuah is unjust because he allows wickedness to abound and then judges those who commit it. Should we commit evil so that His mercy and goodness can abound? (Many had accused the Messianics of doing just that.) Of course not! YAHveh shall not be mocked! His Word, the Torah, reveals sin and exposes all men, both YAHudi and Goyim/Yosefs, who commit sin, and all are found guilty. *"The fool has said in his heart, "There is no ELohim." They are corrupt, they have done abominable works, there is none who does good. YAHveh looks down from heaven upon the children of men, to see if there are any who understand, who seek ELohim. They have all turned aside, they have together become corrupt; there is none who does good, no, not one"* (**PSALM 14:1-3**). *"For there is no faithfulness in their mouth; their inward part is destruction; their throat is an open tomb; they flatter with their tongue"* (**PSALM 5:9**). *"They sharpen their tongues like a serpent; the poison of asps is under their lips"* (**PSALM 140:3**). *"His mouth is full of cursing and deceit and oppression; under his tongue is trouble and iniquity"* (**PSALM 10:7**). *"Their feet run to evil, and they make haste to shed innocent blood; their thoughts are thoughts of iniquity; wasting and destruction are in their paths. The way of shalom they have not known, and there is no justice in their ways; they have made themselves crooked paths; whoever takes that way shall not know shalom"* (**ISA 59:7&8**). *"An oracle within my heart concerning the transgression of the wicked: There is no fear of ELohim before his own eyes"* (**PSALM 36:1**). The Torah reveals sin and shows that no one can escape it. Therefore, no one can be justified by the works of the Torah because that is not its purpose. It also bore witness that its justification comes from faith in the Promised One, Yeshua HaMashiach, revealed by both the Torah and the Ne'vim. It is only through the sacrificial blood of His Lamb, Yeshua, that the price that sin demands can be paid. So how are we justified by the Torah? By faith in what the Torah teaches about the Messiah. The YAHudi are justified by faith in the Words of the written Torah—the Goyim, by faith in the Person of the Living Torah. Does this nullify the Torah then? Absolutely not—it establishes its importance. If someone earns justification, it becomes a wage, but grace is a gift. Avraham did not earn his righteousness, but received it as a gift through faith. *"And he believed in YAHveh, and He accounted it to him for righteousness"* (**GEN 15:6**). King Dahveed also understood this kingdom principle. *"Blessed is he whose transgression is forgiven, whose sin is covered. Blessed is the man to whom YAHveh does not impute iniquity, and in whose spirit there is no guile"* (**PSALM 32:1&2**). Ask yourself this question, Shaul continues, when Avraham received this righteousness was he circumcised or still uncircumcised? Remember, he received the sign of circumcision only after he received YAH's grace. We are to walk in faith—this is true circumcision. Becoming an heir of righteousness is accomplished through faith and not through the Torah; the Torah is the result of our fathers walking in faith and is a witness to the faith of both Avraham and

Mosheh. As it has been said before, the Torah reveals sin and brings about YAH's wrath—therefore, there is no wrath when there is no Torah. Faith equals Torah keeping, and Torah keeping equals faith, when done in the Ruach and YAH's grace, and this equals the faith of Avraham. Therefore, Avraham becomes the abba of all—through faith. *"No longer shall your name be called Avram (exalted father), but your name shall be Avraham (father of nations); for I have made you an abba of many nations"* (**GEN 17:5**). *"Then He brought him outside and said, "Look now toward heaven, and count the stars if you are able to number them." And He said to him, "So shall your descendants be."* (**GEN 15:5**). Avraham believed, even though both he and Sarah were beyond childbearing years, and it was counted to them as righteousness. Shaul reminds his readers that these things were not written for Avraham's sake alone. They were also written for those who have faith to believe all of His promises about His Son and the price that He would pay for the justification of all who would believe over the centuries. All who seek forgiveness through the blood of the Messiah receive His shalom because they have been justified by His blood; but this does not deliver them from tribulation because Messiah also knows that tribulation produces perseverance, which produces character, which in turn produces hope—all by the power of the Ruach. However, Messiah's blood will deliver them, those who have been reconciled to Him, from Abba's wrath. His wrath will be poured out instead upon the ungodly, those for whom it was intended.

Once again, Shaul reminds his readers that sin and death came through the first Ahdom, who was made in the image of ELohim, but who lost his inheritance through sin. Now men can find righteousness through the shed blood of the second Ahdom and receive eternal life in the new birth. The second Ahdom was born a sinful man but was without sin because He was also the Son of YAHveh. Because of the first Ahdom's sin, sin abounds in the world, and the Torah reveals what sin is. But for those who try to walk an upright life even though they have never received the instructions of the Torah, sin is not imputed to them because they are ignorant of its instructions. Instead, grace is shown to them as though they had faith in the instructions of the Torah. The difference then lies in the knowledge of Torah. To know it and then to disobey it results in death. Not knowing it but still living a life that extends ELuah's grace to others will count as faith and will bring about the promises that are found in the Torah. Then he asks if this gives us a license to sin so that His grace might abound? Of course not, there is no way that living a sinful life should have any appeal to a true believer because they are dead to it. Our immersion into the Messiah is a good example of this. When we submit ourselves to this mikvah (immersion), we submit ourselves into His death. By partaking of this mikvah, we are identifying by faith that we are dying to self. After submitting to His death, we should thereafter walk in the newness of life that His resurrection has purchased for us. When we die to sin, sin is no longer our master (adonai). Instead, we have freely given ourselves over to be slaves to the Adonai of Life, Yeshua. But, we do have a free will, and because of that, we still can return to sin if we so choose. Therefore, we also need to submit our bodies as instruments created for the righteous works of YAHveh and His Son, Yeshua HaMashiach, our ELuah and Adonai. Sin and the curse of the Torah no longer have power over us—instead, we have the freedom to walk in the grace of His Torah. He says we must remember that we can only enjoy this freedom if we walk in the righteousness of His Torah through the shed blood of His Son, Yeshua, and not by doing the works of the Torah. To be truly free, we must become slaves of righteousness in our hearts, according to what we have learned, and not slaves to sin in order to complete the Messiah's mission. When we were in sin, we felt free, not knowing that we were recipients of the fruit of sin, which was death. Now, as recipients of grace, our gifts are justice, righteousness, kedosh living, and everlasting life. Doing the works of the Torah alone will only produce the wages of sin, which is death. Torah faith produces eternal life, which is the gift of grace from our Abba.

Once again, Shaul turns his attention to his YAHudi brethren, who should already have a grasp of the understanding of the Torah. A man who is born under the law of the Torah is married to YAH. He reminds them that the Torah teaches that as long as a person is under the law of the Torah, he remains there until he dies and then he is released, just as a person is bound to their spouse in their marriage vows. If either dies, they are released from that vow—but only then. So it is with those who believe the Torah. We are released from the law of the Torah when we die through immersion (a symbol of death). We can then begin to participate in the blessings of the Torah because we are now free from death and its curse. Then Shaul asks them if the law of the Torah causes them to sin or does it deliver them from it? The Torah is kedosh and reveals what sin is, and because it is revealed, we find ourselves embracing sin because of our rebellious nature. The Torah is spiritual, but we are of a carnal nature and live and act in the natural. Therefore, sin, when revealed, becomes natural to us. That means that all of us are in a constant war within ourselves, struggling between doing what is spiritual and right and what is carnal and evil. Our only salvation and deliverance is through Yeshua HaMashiach and our Abba's Ruach. Thanks be to YAHveh that He has provided us with His Ruach to walk in and His Messiah to walk with. Now we are able to walk in the Torah of His Ruach and live in the Life of His Messiah, who has made us free from the curse of the Torah and from sin and death. We were unable to walk in the fullness of the Torah because of the weakness of our flesh. But He has now enabled us to walk in the righteous requirements of the Torah by sending His Son to die in our place and to pay the price of sin for us. To subject ourselves to our flesh is death, but to subject ourselves to His Ruach is life and shalom. We must have the Ruach dwelling within us or we do not belong to YAH. If we do not belong to YAH, then we belong to hasatan. The indwelling of the Ruach guarantees us eternal life. Without Him, we are guaranteed eternal death. Therefore, we must live our lives in His Ruach, or we are not His sons and He is not our Abba. If we are not sons, then we cannot share in Yeshua's inheritance of the resurrection to eternal life. By walking in His Ruach, we become adopted in full sonship and delivered from the bondage of the "fear of death". We can then walk in the assurance that nothing in this life will ever be a threat to us. Even creation itself will be delivered from the curse of the Torah because of our faith in His promises. Creation, along with us, groans for the renewal and restoration of all things, both in heaven and on Earth. This was the hope of our ancient fathers, and even though we were still afar off at that time, it has become ours. By faith, this hope is assured. By faith, the Ruach will come to our aid to help us pray when we don't know what or how to pray. He will pray through us in our moans, groans, and unintelligible utterances (tongues). Our confidence is in the fact that He knows the will of ELuah and will pray the correct prayer when we are at a loss as to how to pray. We can also rest in the assurance that every event that has ever taken place in our lives, whether good or bad, will prove in time that it happened for our overall good because we love Him and know that we have been called for His purpose. He knew us before we were even conceived in our mother's womb, and He knew what decisions we would make, so He set up the circumstances that we would experience in order to fulfill His purpose for us. He is the ELuah of our circumstances—nothing is a coincidence. This means that we have nothing to fear because nothing can harm us as long as we seek His will and learn to do it. If He was willing to give His Own Son to die for us, then why would He not guard our footsteps? We must and will accomplish His will in our lives because even death cannot hinder us. *"Yet for Your sake we are killed all day long; we are accounted as sheep for the slaughter"* (**PSALM 44:22**). That makes us more than conquerors—it makes us YAH's Heroes (YisraELi), those who can overcome all obstacles.

Again, with much grief in his heart, Shaul turns his attention toward his YAHudi brethren who refuse to accept his message. He admits that if it were possible, he would trade his salvation for their unbelief so that the truth could reign in the hearts of the very ones to whom it was originally promised. The YAHudi are the last tribe left of the visible YisraEL; all of the other tribes have been obscured among the Goyim, not knowing their ancestry. So, because the majority of the YAHudi refused to accept the message that the shelichim had meant for them, YAH was sending Shaul out among the hidden tribes with the full message of the Torah. To be a true Hebrew, one does not necessarily have to come from Avraham's seed or Sara's womb, but from Avraham's faith. *"But*

ELohim said to Avraham, "Do not let it be displeasing in your sight because of the lad or because of your bondwoman. Whatever Sarah has said to you, listen to her voice; for in Yitzyak your seed shall be called" (**GEN 21:12**). YAHveh told Avraham this to establish through whom He was going to manifest the "Children of Promise". *"Is anything too hard for YAHveh? At the appointed time I will return to you, according to the time of life, and Sarah shall have a son"* (**GEN 18:14**). YAHveh sees the past, present, and future in one glance and knows the choices that each individual will make. It is our choice, but He knows the outcome of our choices, as He did with Yitzyak and Rebecca (Rebekah). *"Two nations are in your womb, two peoples shall be separated form your body; one people shall be stronger than the other, and the older shall serve the younger"* (**GEN 25:23**). *"I have loved you," says YAHveh; "Yet you say, 'In what way have You loved us? "Was not Esau Yaacov's brother?" says YAHveh. "Yet Yaacov I have loved; but Esau I have hated, and laid waste his mountains and his heritage for the jackals of the wilderness"* (**MAL 1:2&3**). Because of His ability to do this, He has already set the machinery in motion to bless those who will make the right choices. *"Then He said, "I will make all My goodness pass before you, and I will proclaim the Name of YAHveh before you; I will be gracious to whom I will be gracious, and I will have compassion on whom I will have compassion"* (**EXOD 33:19**). Just as He showers His blessings upon those whose hearts seek righteousness, He shows no mercy toward those whose hearts are full of malice. A perfect example of this was when He used the evil that was in Pharaoh's heart. *"But indeed for this purpose I have raised you up, that I may show My power in you, and that My Name may be declared in all the earth. "As yet you exalt yourself against My people in that you will not let them go"* (**EXOD 9:16&17**). In man's wisdom (or foolishness), he asks why it is that ELuah does this—is this fair justice? But should the creature be questioning its Creator as to what is justice when the creature is limited in comparison to the Creator's omnipotence? *"Surely you have things turned around! Shall the potter be esteemed as the clay; for shall the thing made say of him who made it, "He did not make me"? Or shall the thing formed say of him who formed it, "He has no understanding?"* (**ISA 29:16**). *"Woe to him who strives with his Master! Let the potsherd strive with potsherds of the earth. Shall the clay say to him who forms it, 'What are you making?' or shall your handiwork say, 'He has no hands?'"* (**ISA 45:9**). This is why the YAHudi can't understand why YAHveh would take His message to the Goyim, who were unclean. The reason lies within the promise that YAH made to the northern tribes of YisraEL, just before He scattered them among the nations of the Earth. *"Yet the number of the children of YisraEL shall be as the sand of the sea, which cannot be measured or numbered. And it shall come to pass in the place where it was said to them, 'You are not My people,' There it shall be said to them, 'You are the sons of the Living ELohim'"* (**HOS 1:10**). *"Then I will show her for Myself in the earth, and I will have mercy on her who had not obtained mercy; then I will say to those who were not My* *people!' 'You are My people!' And they shall say 'You are my ELohim!'"* (**HOS 2:23**). *"The remnant will return, the remnant of Yaacov, to the Mighty ELohim; For though your people, O YisraEL, be as the sand of the sea, yet a remnant of them will return; the destruction decreed shall overflow with righteousness; For Adonai YAHveh of hosts will make a determined end in the midst of all the land"* (**ISA 10:21-23**). Otherwise, the northern tribes of YisraEL would have become as Sodom and Gomorrah, and Avraham's promise would have been lost, making YAHveh a liar. *"Unless YAHveh of hosts had left to us a very small remnant, we would have become like Sodom, we would have been made like Gomorrah"* (**ISA 1:9**). Why is it that the YAHudi, who had attained the Torah, did not receive its benefit? Because they didn't seek it by faith—only those who do can receive it. That's why the Goyim, who didn't even know the Torah, were able to profit from doing it even though they didn't seek it. They received its truth by faith. *"He will be as a sanctuary, but a stone of stumbling and a rock of offense to **both houses** of YisraEL, as a trap and a snare to the inhabitants of YAHrushalayim"* (**ISA 8:14**). Therefore, thus says Adonai YAHveh, *"Behold I lay in Zeeon a stone for a foundation, a tried stone, a precious cornerstone, a sure foundation; whoever believes will not act hastily"* (**ISA 28:16**). It was Messiah who fulfilled the Torah and put away its curse. Therefore, He is the end or the completion of the Torah because there are no longer both blessings and curses—only blessings in the Messiah. Mosheh wrote the truth about the **letter** of the Torah and its type of righteousness. *"You shall therefore keep My statutes and My judgments which if a man does, he shall live by them: I AM YAHveh"* (**LEV 18:5**). But on the other hand, Mosheh also wrote about the **faith** of Torah and its type of righteousness. *"For this commandment which I command you today, it is not too mysterious to you, nor is it far off. "It is not in heaven, that you should say, 'Who will ascend into heaven for us and bring it to us, that we may hear it and do it?' "Nor is it beyond the sea, that you should say, 'Who will go over the sea for us and bring it to us, that we may hear and do it?' "But the Word is very near you, in your mouth and in your heart, that you may do it"* (**DEUT 30:11-14**). Therefore, if you just confess the Word, which is Adonai Yeshua, and believe in your heart that ELuah YAHveh truly raised Him from the dead, you will be saved. Any man, YAHudi or Goyim/Yosef, who does this by faith shall receive the same reward. Yeshua HaMashiach is both YAHveh in the flesh and the Living Torah. *"And it shall come to pass that whoever calls on the Name of YAHveh shall be saved. For in Mount Zeeon and in YAHrushalayim there shall be deliverance, as YAHveh has said, among the remnant whom YAHveh calls"* (**JOEL 2:32**). This "Good News" must be proclaimed to all men, it must be shouted from the housetops, and it must be preached in order for men to hear, believe, and call upon His Name. *"How beautiful upon the mountains are the feet of him who brings good news, who proclaims shalom, who brings glad tidings of good things, who proclaims salvation, who says to Zeeon, your ELohim reigns!"* (**ISA 52:7**). Of course, not all of those who hear will receive with hungry hearts. *"Who has believed our report? And to whom has the arm of YAHveh been revealed?"* (**ISA 53:1**). Who will believe our report? Those whose hearts are humble. Then they will receive faith by hearing the Word of ELohim, and He will see to it that it reaches the ends of the Earth. *"Their measuring line has gone out through all the earth, and their words to the end of the world"* (**PSALM 19:4**). Does YisraEL have any excuse for not hearing these things? *"They have provoked Me to jealousy by what is not ELohim; they have moved Me to anger by their foolish idols. But I will provoke them to jealousy by those who are not a nation; I will move them to anger by a foolish nation"* (**DEUT 32:21**). *"I was sought by those who did not ask for Me; I was found by those who did not seek Me. I said, Here I AM, here I AM,' to a nation that was not called by My Name. I have stretched out My hands all day long to a rebellious people, who walk in a way that is not good, according to their own thoughts"* (**ISA 65:1&2**). With all of these things said, did ELuah turn away from YisraEL then? No way; if He had, He would have been a liar, and He is not a man that He should tell a lie. Shaul points out that he is proof that YAH knows where all those of YisraEL are throughout the Earth at all times because he too is an YisraELi from the tribe of BenYAHmeen. YAH will always save a remnant no matter what happens elsewhere. ELeeYAHoo was a perfect example of one of His faithful who questioned whether or not YAH had forgotten His people. *"So he said, "I have been very zealous for YAHveh ELohim of hosts; because the children of YisraEL have forsaken Your covenant, torn down Your altars, and killed Your ne'veem with the sword. I am left; and they seek to take my life."—"Yet I have reserved seven thousand in YisraEL, all whose knees have not bowed to Baal, and every mouth that has not kissed him"* (**I KINGS 19:14&18**). By His grace, YAHveh has always kept a few who understood the difference between keeping His Torah by faith or by works. If a person keeps His Torah by works, then it is not of grace—grace is not grace if it has been done by works. But if he keeps it by grace, then it is not of works, and the works is no longer works because it has been kept by grace. So, all of YisraEL who have tried to obtain YAH's favor by works have missed His grace and were hardened against it, but others who sought it by faith have become His elect and have obtained His favor. *"Yet YAHveh has not given you a heart to perceive and eyes to see and ears to hear, to this very day"* (**DEUT 29:4**). *"For YAHveh has poured out on you the spirit of deep sleep, and has closed your eyes, namely, the ne'veem; and He has covered your heads, namely, the seers"* (**ISA 29:19**). *"Let their table become a snare before them, and their well-being a trap. Let their eyes be darkened, so that they do not see; and make their loins shake continually"* (**PSALM 69:22&23**).

Shaul was addressing the problem with the YAHudi head on. They thought that because they were of the seed of Avraham, they had YAHveh in their back pocket and that He would never give them up. He had put blinders on their eyes to the possibility that He could do such a thing. But what really happened was that they had given Him up. Even so, He would always keep an elect who would understand His grace. First, YAH sent the northern tribes of Yosef into captivity and dispersed them throughout the Goyim until they became so hidden that they couldn't even recognize themselves. Then, He sent the southern tribe of the YAHudi into captivity, for only seventy years at first, to wake them up so that they would take their responsibility of keeping the Torah more seriously. Then, out of a remnant of them, He brought forth His Son, Yeshua the Messiah, to give them an opportunity to repent from their pride and rebellion. But they ignored that too. Now He was sending shelichim out into the Goyim and gathering all who would receive the "Good News" regarding His Son, both the true Goyim and the lost sheep of YisraEL/Yosef. Eventually, He will cause His House/Palace to be destroyed and will then scatter the YAHudi out into all the nations of the Earth, but they will not entirely lose their identity like Yosef did. YAHveh's plan is to continue this pattern until the end of the sixth millennium, and then He will reveal His plan to the YAHudi and the Goyim/YisraELi who have believed. Then He will set up His Kingdom Millennium.

Shaul was able to see the House of YisraEL as an olive tree with some of its branches (sons) broken off. Then YAH grafted in some wild branches (Goyim/Yosefs), and they grew as though they were natural, enjoying the fatness of the roots. He warns the Goyim not to get too puffed up, though, because they can just as easily be cut off and replaced with the natural branches if they again decide to believe. But the days of the Goyim are only temporary because when their days have been fulfilled, or are completed, then the eyes of the YAHudi will be opened in order to fully understand the truth, and then the restoration will take place and the end will come. *"Therefore by this the iniquity of Yaacov will be covered; and this is all the fruit of taking away his sin: When he makes all the stones of the altar like chalkstones that are beaten to dust, when wooden images and incense altars do not stand up"* (**ISA 27:9**). *"The Redeemer will come to Zeeon, and to those who turn from transgression in Yaacov," says YAHveh. "As for Me," says YAHveh, "this is My covenant with them; My Ruach who is upon you, and My words which I have put in your mouth, shall not depart from your mouth, nor from the mouth of your descendants," says YAHveh, "from this time and forevermore"* (**ISA 59:20&21**). *"But this is the covenant I will make with the House of YisraEL after those days, says YAHveh: I will put My Torah in their minds, and write it on their hearts; and I will be their ELohim, and they shall be My people. "No more shall every man teach his neighbor, and every man his brother, saying, 'Know YAHveh,' for they all shall know Me, from the least of them to the greatest of them, says YAHveh. For I will forgive their iniquity, and their sin I will remember no more"* (**JER 31:33&34**).

Shaul reminds the Goyim that when the YAHudi refuse to believe their message of the Messiah and persecute them for it, they should count it as joy because it's still a part of YAH's plan—He allows it in order to build their character. They need to remember that the YAHudi are still His beloved because of the promises that He made to Avraham, Yitzhak, and Yaacov, and He cannot forget that. Shaul laments over both his brethren, the YAHudi and the Goyim, because their understanding of YAH's plan of redemption should be coming through faith instead of their trying to understand it with just their natural minds. *"Who has directed the Ruach of YAHveh, or as His counselor has taught Him? With whom did He take counsel, and who instructed Him, and taught Him in the path of justice? Who taught Him knowledge, and showed Him the way of understanding?"* (ISA 40:13&14). *"For who has stood in the counsel of YAHveh, and has perceived and heard His Word? Who has marked His Word and heard it?"* (JER 23:18). *"Behold, ELohim is exalted by His power; who teaches like Him?—Who has preceded Me, that I should pay him? Everything under heaven is Mine"* (JOB 36:22 and 41:11). None of us are able to understand the ways of YAH or why He allows certain things to take place in our lives, but we need to always remember that His ways are far above ours.

The main point that Shaul is trying to make to the kahal at Rome, which is made up of a mixture of former orthodox YAHudi and pagan Goyim, is that their lives and their bodies are not their own. They are to offer them up as vessels and instruments for YAHveh's use. The YAHudi are not to think that they are better than the Goyim, nor should the Goyim think of themselves as being special. The YAHudi are the visible remnant of YisraEL, and the Goyim/Yosefs have been chosen from among the nations to be the newest members of the House of YisraEL. Each one has something to offer the other. YAH will choose and equip those, from both houses, who are to be seers and ne'veem, others who will serve, others to teach, some to exhort, some to give from their abundance, and some to just show mercy to those who are downtrodden. But the key ingredient is love—YAH's kind of love, without reservation or end. Shaul exhorts them to stay clear of anything that even looks evil and grasp tightly unto all that is good. Show affection with brotherly type of honor. Be exuberant in your service to Adonai. Be patient, especially in times of trials, and always rely on prayer for deliverance. Show hospitality and generosity. Bless, don't curse. Try to agree and don't argue. Don't be tempted by riches or power. Find shalom with those who are less fortunate. Be above reproach. Treat all men, whether inside or outside the kahal, with respect in order to win favor among the unbelievers. It is not your place to repay the evil done to you—YAH will do the repaying. *"Vengeance is Mine, and recompense; Their foot shall slip in due time; for the day of their calamity is at hand, and the things to come hasten upon them'"* (DEUT 32:53). *"If your enemy is hungry, give him bread to eat; and if he is thirsty, give him water to drink.; for so you will heap coals of fire on his head, and YAHveh will reward you"* (**PROV 25:21&22**).

Then Rav Shaul turns his attention to instructing the kahal at Rome about submitting themselves to civil authority. He points out even corrupt regimes are used by YAHveh to keep order. It is not the business of the House of YisraEL to overthrow governments—YAHveh does that through the heads of nations. The business of the Kahal of YisraEL is to change hearts through the power of the Ruach. He encourages all to pay their taxes so that those in civil authority have the means to keep order within the masses. The world with its laws are governed by these authorities and are subject to them; all who are citizens of the kingdom are subject through submission to both the civil and the heavenly laws that are dictated in the ten letters (commandments) of the Torah. The first four speak about our love for YAH, which is the greatest commandment, the fifth is about our respect for our parents, and the last five are about our fellowman. *"You shall not murder. "You shall not commit adultery. "You shall not steal. "You shall not bear false witness against your neighbor. "You shall not covet—anything that is your neighbor's"* (**EXOD 20:13-17** and **DEUT 5:17-21**.) This fulfills the second greatest commandment. *"You shall not take vengeance, nor bear any grudge against the children of your people, but you shall love your neighbor as yourself: I AM YAHveh"* (**LEV 19:18**). Shaul hopes that all who read his letter will acknowledge that they have received some of the mysteries of the Torah through his words. The time of YAHveh's salvation is now at hand, and they should walk in the light of this revelation and not submit themselves to the temptations of the world around them.

He instructs the mature to be patient and to show mercy toward those who have not yet received complete instructions, like those who feel they must be vegetarians based upon their fears of eating any meat. He also tells them to refrain from judging those who fast and those who don't. These types of decisions are private and should be left up to those who feel led to do either. He warns them not to judge those who celebrate and observe certain days. Any day can be set aside for a celebration as long as it is not connected to idols, false elohim, or their holidays. Adonai is the one who judges our celebrations, and He does it based upon the attitude of our heart and not by the manner in which we celebrate them. If we begin to judge these matters, it will only cause division and strife and could cause our less-mature brother to stumble. These misdeeds could result in our having to stand before Adonai at the final "Judgment Seat of the Messiah" and give an account for those actions. And it is His judgment that can affect our rewards because He is the only one who is qualified to judge in these matters. *"I have sworn by Myself; The Torah has gone out of My mouth in righteousness, and shall not return, that to Me every knee shall bow, every tongue shall take an oath. He shall say, 'Surely in YAHveh I have righteousness and strength. To Him men shall come, and all shall be ashamed who are incensed against Him"* (**ISA 45:23&24**). Shaul is pointing out that the Torah they now walk in is one of tolerance and love, not of judgment and condemnation. The curse of the Torah has been lifted, thereby causing all things to become clean, including the food we eat and the days we observe, without doing away with the moedim (appointed times). The Torah has not been replaced but has been extended to embrace all things as being clean and kedosh before YAH. Even so, we must, at the same time, not become arrogant and reckless and offend those who choose to observe their traditional diets as they please—they too have that freedom. All things are to be done in faith because that which is not becomes sin to those who ignore their faith just to please themselves or men. Yeshua put aside His own human desire to remain alive, but submitted Himself to His Abba even onto death. *"Because zeal for Your House has eaten Me up, and the reproach of those who reproach You have fallen on Me. When I wept and chastened My soul with fasting, that became My reproach"* (**PSALM 69:9&10**).

Shaul reminds the YAHudi that the Messiah did not come just to confirm what the Torah, the Ne'vim, and the Kethuvim (TaNaKh) had to say about His being the suffering servant—He came to be Adonai to the Goyim as well. *"Therefore I will give thanks to You, O YAHveh, among the Goyim, and sing praises to Your Name"* (**II SAM 22:50** and **PSALM 18:49**). *"Rejoice, O Goyim, with His people; for He will avenge the blood of His servants, and render vengeance to His adversaries; He will provide atonement for His land and His people"* (**DEUT 32:43**). *"Oh praise YAHveh, all you Goyim! Laud Him, all you peoples! For His merciful kindness is great toward us, and the truth of YAHveh endures forever. Praise YAHveh!"* (**PSALM 117:1**). *"And in that day there shall be a Root of Jesse, who shall stand as a banner to the people; for the Goyim shall seek Him, and His resting place shall be glorious"* (**ISA 11:10**). He tells the YAHudi that they are to preserve the Torah, along with the rest of the TaNaKh, in order to instruct the Goyim in the ways of YAHveh. YAHveh's promise to Avraham was to make him an abba to many nations, not just to the House of YAHuda. His plan was to scatter the descendants of Yosef/Efraeem into the Goyim nations so that they too could become the seed of Avraham through both blood and faith, making them qualified heirs. Once more, Rav Shaul confirms that in the final days, just before the Messiah sets up His Kingdom, the Whole House of YisraEL will then be restored. This, Shaul confesses, is why Yeshua commissioned him to be a shelich to the Goyim. He is to help lay the foundation for the final restoration among the Goyim. His fellow shelichim were commissioned to take this same message and lay the foundation with their fellow YAHudi. It has been two-thousand years since they went out, and it is only today that Believers are seeing this come to pass. *"So shall He sprinkle many nations. Kings shall shut their mouths at Him. For what had not been told them they shall see, and what they had not heard they shall consider"* (**ISA 52:15**).

Shaul now turns his attention to closing his letter, explaining that his commission was the main reason for his not being able to visit them earlier. His plan is to go to YAHrushalayim to deliver the many contributions that he has received from the scattered kahal among the Goyim, which will help relieve the suffering of those in the Kedosh City of YAH. He asks them to receive a fellow servant by the name of Phoebe, who he is sending to them, and to show her the respect she deserves. He also sends his regards to those who have preceded him in ministry, such as Priscilla, Aquila, and a host of others. He sends the greetings of other teachers and ministers whom they are familiar with, including Timothy, his protégé. Finally, Tertius, the one who has scribed this letter for Shaul, sends his greetings also.

Acts 21-28

After finishing his letter to the kahal at Rome, Shaul prepared to return to YAHrushalayim—first by ship and then by caravan. Shaul continued to receive more warnings about his impending fate if he continued his trip to the City of Dahveed. He refused to be discouraged, even after he received a direct prophecy from Agabus, one of the ne'veem. Shaul was at the home of Philip, one of the original deacons appointed by the twelve shelichim, when Agabus arrived from his long trip from YAHuda. Agabus took Shaul's belt and said, *"Thus says the Ruach, 'So shall the YAHudi at YAHrushalayim bind the man who owns this belt, and deliver him into the hands of the Goyim.'"*

Upon arriving at the Kedosh city of YAHrushalayim, Shaul went to the house of Yeshua's brother, Yaacov, to lodge there. Some of the other brethren were there, so he began to share with them the mighty works that Adonai was doing among the Goyim. He was told that there were a number of Messianic YAHudi who were still insisting upon following the letter of the Torah. Apparently, there were still those who lacked a full understanding of Yeshua's fulfillment of the Torah through grace. They were saying that the lost sheep of YisraEL, who were found among the Goyim, were not exempt from the ordinances of the Torah. The debating continued to no avail even though these YAHudi had been informed as to what the council had already determined were the only obligations that the Goyim were to follow. Shaul was also informed that a false accusation had been raised against him claiming that he was teaching that the Torah was no longer to be observed. Shaul was advised by the elders to take those who had traveled with him, along with a group of four highly-esteemed men as their representatives, and go before the council regarding these false accusations. These four had taken a vow, had shaved their heads, and had served the seven days of purification. Shaul was told to pay their expenses and appear before the council humbly in order to assure them that these rumors were not true. But as soon as they came into the House of YAH, they were seized and falsely accused of defiling the House by bringing in Goyim. He was cast out of YAH's House, where the crowd outside tried to drag him off to kill him. Some Roman guards were sent to rescue him on the orders of their commander, who had heard about the commotion. But before he was taken into the barracks, he spoke to the commander and informed him of his credentials as a Pharisee. The commander then allowed him to address the mob who had previously tried to kill him. Most of those who were there didn't know exactly who he was until he began to speak to them in Hebrew (a forbidden tongue in YAHrushalayim at the time), informing them of his background as a leading Pharisee and a student of the renowned Gamaliel. He told them how he had been zealous in the persecution of those known as the "Way" and how he had been responsible for the death of many of those who had followed the teachings of this Yeshua who claimed to be the Messiah. He told them about his trip to Damascus in Syria to do more of the same when he encountered a vision of this Yeshua on his way there. Then he told them how he was blinded by a bright light that accompanied this vision and how he had received both his sight and his commission from this Yeshua through a man named Ananias. Even after the crowd heard his testimony, they refused to receive it and demanded his arrest. The Roman commander ordered him to be taken to the military barracks to be questioned further. Shaul spoke up to the centurion officer in charge and asked whether it was lawful to arrest a Roman citizen before he was even charged. The centurion immediately informed the commander of Shaul's statement that he was a citizen of Rome by birth rather than by purchase. The next day, the commander ordered the Sanhedrin Council to appear before him to present their charges against Shaul. The high priest, Ananias, ordered Shaul to be struck for his insolence after he began to defend himself. Shaul rebuked Ananias for going against the Torah by not allowing him to speak on his own behalf. Shaul was then rebuked for speaking in a disrespectful manner to the high priest. Shaul immediately apologized when he realized that Ananias was serving in that office at the time. He did this because the Torah taught that *"You shall not revile ELohim nor curse a ruler of your people"* (**EXOD 22:28**). When Shaul realized that both the Sadducees and the Pharisees from the Sanhedrin were present, he devised a plan. In his shrewdness, he brought up a point about the resurrection, knowing full well that the Sadducees didn't believe in it, but the Pharisees did and that this would cause a heated debate. It did, and immediately, dissension between the two began and a near riot erupted. When it elevated to that point, the commander sent soldiers down to retrieve Shaul and return him to the barracks. It was on that very night that Adonai Yeshua appeared to him and told him that He was sending him to Rome.

Some of the YAHudi decided that Shaul had to die for his blasphemy, so they designed a plan to kidnap and kill him. When the plot was revealed to the commander, he ordered that Shaul be taken to Felix, the governor of Caesarea, for questioning in order to decide his fate. The YAHudi hired a false witness by the name of Tertullus to accuse Shaul of being responsible for stirring up trouble among the YAHudi with his teachings. When Felix finally allowed Shaul to speak, he stated what he was really being accused of and how the YAHudi leaders had refused to even consider what he was proclaiming as truth. Felix had some knowledge of the doctrine of the "Way" and was married to a YAHudi woman who knew the Torah. He and his wife agreed to hear Shaul regarding his position on the Torah and the Messiah. When Shaul made his presentation, it caused Felix and his wife to become uncomfortable and under conviction. He continued to hold Shaul under his authority for two more years, all the while hoping that Shaul would offer him a bribe for his release. During that time, Felix was replaced by another governor by the name of Festus, who summoned Shaul to appear before him with his testimony. The YAHudi wanted Shaul to be returned to YAHrushalayim so that they could still carry out their plot to assassinate him. Festus asked Shaul if he would submit to standing before him in YAHrushalayim and be judged there. Shaul refused and demanded to stand before Caesar in Rome. During this time in Caesarea, King Herod Agrippa II came to visit Festus. Festus explained to him what had transpired regarding this prisoner Shaul and the events surrounding his case. The king requested that Shaul be brought before him so that he could hear for himself his defense. Shaul took advantage of the chance to speak to King Herod because he knew that he too had knowledge of both the Torah and the "Way". Shaul reflected on his earlier life as a Pharisee and then told him what had happened to him on his way to Damascus. He then shared the experiences he had while following his mandate and what had led up to his arrest. Festus accused Shaul of having too much learning and that it had driven him mad in the process. Shaul discerned that the Ruach was beginning to convict King Herod with his words and testimony, but there is no historical or biblical evidence that any conversion ever occurred. Festus, Herod, and his wife, Bernice, discussed Shaul's fate between them and determined that they could have released him if he hadn't appealed for an audience with Caesar.

Lucas, the writer of this account, has been traveling with Shaul during many of these events and describes their journey to Rome aboard two different ships, one from Adramyttium and the other from Alexandria of Egypt (Mitsrahyim). Autumn was approaching, which meant possible adverse weather conditions. Shaul warned his incarcerators not to venture out and sail against the winds because the Ruach had warned him that disaster awaited them if they did. Being seagoing craftsmen, the sailors ignored the words of this landlubber and proceeded anyway. An angel who was sent from YAHveh assured Shaul that his mission was to stand before Caesar and establish the "Good News" to him and to all of the Roman Empire—therefore, he was not to worry. YAH was going to bring His plan of salvation to all of the Goyim who were scattered throughout Europe and nothing was going to thwart it.

The result of man's wisdom was a shipwreck, but there were no casualties. They all washed up on an island called Malta. The natives there were somewhat primitive but friendly and showed hospitality toward the survivors. After the natives had built a fire to help the survivors dry themselves, a miracle took place. While gathering sticks for the fire, Shaul was bitten by a venomous snake and survived without incident. Because of this, Shaul was able to obtain an audience with a leading citizen of the island named Publius, whose father was about to die from a sickness. Rav Shaul was allowed to pray for him and through the laying on of hands, Adonai healed him. After this, others came to see the miracles and hear his words of salvation. He stayed and preached to them for the duration of the winter and departed for Rome in the spring.

After arriving in Rome, Shaul explained to the brethren all of the events that had led up to his coming to them as he had promised, but not quite as he had planned. The Kahal of YisraEL continued to grow while Shaul was there. Even some of the Orthodox YAHudi were persuaded in the validity of his message about the Messiah and the TaNaKh, but as usual, others rejected it. He made this proclamation from the Scriptures to those who were still stiff-necked after his testimony: *"And He said, "Go, and tell this people: 'Keep on hearing, but not understand; keep on seeing, but not perceive.' "Make the heart of this people dull, and their ears heavy, and shut their eyes; lest they see with their eyes, and hear with their ears, and understand with their heart, and return and be healed"* (ISA 6:9&10). He told them that YAH's plan was to include the Goyim—He knew that most of the YAHudi who heard this message would not receive it.

While in Rome, Shaul experienced total freedom to share his message to both the Goyim and the YAHudi for quite some time—about two years. He was only placed under house arrest with a Roman guard assigned to him. While under house arrest, Shaul continued to write letters to the kahal at Colosse, Ephesus, and Philippi. He also wrote a personal letter to Philemon. According to history, it wasn't until Emperor Nero came into power that both Shaul and Kefa were executed. He expedited this at the demand of the Roman citizens in order to enhance his own popularity.

Colossians

Rav Shaul wrote a letter to a kahal in Colosse, one that he wasn't responsible for planting. It was founded by a man named Epaphras, one of the shelich he had ordained. It seems that this shelich had planted other kahals in the cities of Laodicea and Hierapolis. All three of these kahals were predominantly Goyim and had pagan origins. Secular in nature, pagan religion was mainly practiced for the purpose of warding off demons and not for salvation or the changing of one's character. (Unfortunately some Christians have more or less taken on this type of mindset too—without even realizing it.) So, Shaul began to address this matter by reiterating the basic principles of the Torah and the purpose of having faith in the redeeming work of Yeshua and His Ruach.

He begins his letter by commending them for the faith that they had shown in the beginning, but then he admonishes them for turning away from that faith. He then reminds them of who Yeshua really is—YAH in the flesh and Creator of all things visible and invisible. He states that all powers, even demonic, were created by Him, for Him, and for His purpose and that He is the only Head of the Kahal of YisraEL. All who come to know Him in a personal way belong to Him regardless of their background. But even so, each individual has the responsibility to remain in His possession. Each one has the free will to follow or turn away—once saved does not mean always saved. When you allow your heart to be changed, it doesn't mean you will never let it become hardened again; any other idea is false and does not come from YAH but comes from the deceiver. Salvation came from YAH through His Messiah Yeshua and had been hidden from all flesh until His appearing. But now it has been revealed by His will and in His timing. Not all of the visible YisraEL has accepted this, so He has also offered it to the hidden and invisible YisraEL who are found among the Goyim.

He warns them of the cunning words of the pagan priests, who want them to return to the philosophies of men and to esteem them as though they were elohim. Faith is not found in philosophies and intellect. Most intellectuals reject and despise faith because it takes away from looking to one's inner self for the answers to life's challenges. This had become the practice of not only the pagan priests, but also the circumcised (the YAHudi). But Yeshua has preformed a new type of circumcision—a circumcision of the heart. He has provided a new type of mikvah that has taken them through death to the resurrection of eternal life. All of the things that were previously against them in the written curse of the Torah have now been lifted, and they are free to walk in the blessings without fear of reprisal. Now each person may walk in the freedom of celebrating the Sabbaths, the Feast Days, and the New Moons without fear of defiling them. He has made all things clean for those who trust in Him, and there is no longer a forbidding of certain food or drink.

He encourages them to concentrate on following only kingdom principles and not to return to the rules and demands of men who want to restrict them in order to have control and dominion over their lives. He tells them that seeking and understanding kingdom principles rather than worldly principles, which will only drag them back into bondage, will change their lives and provide them with all the freedom and love that brings true happiness. When they died in the immersion of the mikvah to their former life, they became dead to its lusts. He told them that when a person has died, they can no longer sin, so they should live as though they were dead to the lusts of this world. With His strength, they can overcome all of the temptations that this world can tempt them with. They should ask for this strength, and if they persevere, it will eventually come into their possession. He told them they have become a new person, and if they resist the old, they will experience the newness of being a new creature in Him through the power of His Ruach. In Him, there is no diversity—all are equal, whether YAHudi, Goyim, male, female, slave, or free. They should practice the fruits of the Ruach and be no respecter of persons, just as YAH is. They should practice and celebrate the whole TaNaKh with joy, singing, and dancing, doing so with all of the freedom that He has purchased for them through His death and resurrection. Husbands and wives should be submitted and loving to one another. They should build each other up and nurture strong families. YAHveh's House is a house of strength, where children respect and honor their parents, and parents love, encourage, and do not belittle their children. They should be good, responsible, and honest employees. Employers should also be good, fair, and honest with those who are under their authority. Above all, they should always give thanks to YAH for what He has provided for them, both materially and spiritually.

Finally, Shaul asks them for their prayers because he has been made a prisoner and is in chains in Rome for what he has preached. He informs them that he is sending this letter with Tychicus and Onesimus, who will minister and teach them all of the things that he has shared with the other kahal throughout the regions where he has traveled. He sends greetings from Markus, Demas, Lukas the physician, and their shelich, Epaphras. He closes by telling them to be sure to read his letter to the kahal at Laodicea.

Philemon

Rav Shaul follows up his letter to the kahal at Colosse with one to his friend and colleague, Philemon. Philemon is apparently an elder in a kahal that meets in the house of Archippus, near the city of Colosse. Shaul is sending a recent convert by the name of Onesimus to deliver the letter that he wrote to Colosse. He once was a servant of Philemon, who ran away, but is now ready to resubmit himself to his authority. Shaul pleads his case on Onesimus' behalf and is even ready to pay for any debt that he may still owe him if he would just find the grace in his heart to receive him back. He closes by sending greetings from Aristarchus, Markus, Lukas the physician, Demas, and Epaphras.

Ephesians

Tychicus is also the courier of Rav Shaul's letter to the kahal at Ephesus. Shaul is as much concerned about the growth of this kahal as he was with the one in Colosse. Here too, the leaders of the YAHudi who kept insisting that salvation can only be obtained by following the Torah to the letter, as well as those who were teaching pagan religions, were continually trying to influence the faith of this struggling kahal. This letter's format is more of a lecture for teaching purposes than one of encouragement and exhortation. Dealing with the kahal at Ephesus had been a real learning experience for Rav Shaul. He had suffered much persecution there by the YAHudi who continually challenged his teaching of the "Good News" and accused him of deviating from the Torah and its kingdom principles.

He begins by reminding all who believe in Yeshua as HaMashiach to count themselves as blessed for being chosen to be a part of His Body. Yeshua not only has redeemed them but has sanctified them through the Ruach HaKedosh. He reminds them that they, like all who are a part of the world system, were previously dead in their sins and trespasses. Now they have been made alive and have had the mysteries of the ages revealed to them. When they were part of the world system, they were sons of the prince of the air and slaves to the lust of their flesh. Now they are sons and heirs with Yeshua HaMashiach in the heavenly places. This was done by the gift of grace, through faith, from YAHveh and not by anything that they could have accomplished by following the Torah. He reminds them that they were once aliens to the Torah and to its blessings, which had previously been reserved for only the natural descendants of Avraham. But now they too have been made sons by adoption through the blood of Yeshua HaMashiach. Yeshua has now made all Goyim who would dare to believe and who were not originally of the House of YisraEL a part of the House of YisraEL. He has also broken down the wall that separated the two houses, YisraEL and YAHuda, making one new house. He abolished the curse of the Torah so that those who could not keep it (the YAHudi) would not be required to and those who were forbidden to keep it (the Goyim) could now come to know it and partake of its blessings without its curses. By doing this, He could make shalom between the YAHudi and the outcasts of YisraEL. Now all men could have access to the Abba—now all men could be of the House of YAH. The TaNaKh and the Brit Chadashah would be their foundation with Messiah Yeshua as their chief cornerstone; this would make them the true House of YAH where the Ruach of YAH could dwell forever. Shaul reminds them that this truth has now been offered to them through his ministry because of YAH's grace. He encourages them not to lose heart because he is in prison for what he has taught and preached. Instead, they should take heart because this was his destiny. Their destiny is to continue his work by spreading the "Good News" to the ends of the Earth to all who have ears to hear. He then says a prayer for them to be strengthened by the Ruach in YAH's grace and love.

Shaul exhorts the kahal in Ephesus to exercise the Fruits of the Ruach in order to sustain their strength and to do all things in love because love has the power of the Ruach within it. He exhorts them to always seek to operate in the gifts of the Ruach. They each should learn to operate within the gifts, talents, and abilities that were given to them through His grace, and they should work to maintain their unity (echad) in working toward their one (echad) goal of restoring the Whole House of YisraEL. *"You have ascended on high, You have led captivity captive; You have received gifts among men, even among the rebellious, that YAHveh ELohim might dwell there. Barukh be Adonai, who daily loads us with benefits, The ELohim of our salvation"* (**PSALMS 68:18&19**). Shaul explains that it was Yeshua who descended into the Earth after His death by crucifixion, and it was He who ascended on high to bring forth the gifts, talents, and abilities that were to be distributed among men. It is He who chooses and directs those who shall be shelichim, ne'veem, evangelists, or shepherds, teaching the "Good News". These are the ministries that were represented by the four-faced cherubs that YechezkEL and Yochanan saw in their visions. These four main ministries will continue until all who have spiritual ears and eyes have come to the full knowledge of the true meaning of the Torah. The work of Messiah will not be complete until all have matured into the one (echad) man, the Body of the Messiah. He exhorts them not to continue to walk in the ways of the other Goyim who are being deceived by their intellect and philosophies to the point that their hearts have become hardened to spiritual matters. He exhorts them to put away these former things, to become renewed in their minds with the principles that are found in the Torah, and to become regenerated by the Ruach in order to make them new men. He exhorts them to put away lying and to speak only the truth. They should learn not to sin when they become angry. *"Be angry, and do not sin; Meditate within your heart on your bed, and be still"* (**PSALM 4:4**). He tells them to put aside bitterness, wrath, corrupt communication, evil speaking, and malice because these things grieve the Ruach—grieving the Ruach will bring consequences. They are not only to refrain from practicing these abominations, but they are not to fellowship with those who do because it will bring shame upon them and their Adonai. They shouldn't even speak about such things because even that brings shame. Instead, they are to practice forgiveness, tenderheartedness, and kindness because these things glorify their Adonai, Yeshua. They are to walk in the light because they are children of the Light, and they are not of the darkness any longer because they have been shown the light of the truth about the TaNaKh. *"Arise, shine; for your light* *has come! And the glory of YAHveh is risen upon you. For behold, the darkness shall cover the earth, and deep darkness the people; but YAHveh will arise over you, and His glory will be seen upon you. The Goyim shall come to your light, and kings to the brightness of your rising.—Your dead shall live; together with my dead body they shall rise; Awake and sing, you who dwell in dust; for your dew is like the dew of herbs, and the earth shall cast out the dead"* (**ISA 60:1-3 and 26:19**). He exhorts them to learn humility and to be merry in their hearts with the Ruach, not with strong drink. They are to sing, be happy, celebrate, and give thanks for all the things that YAH has provided and, at the same time, remember that the world around them is evil and wants to drag them back into its activities.

Just as he did in Colosse and in Corinth, Rav Shaul admonishes the married men in the kahal at Ephesus to love and protect their wives, just as the Messiah does His own bride, the House of YisraEL. They are to teach her the words of Messiah, just as the Messiah washes His own bride in the Mikvah of the Torah. The wives are to submit to their husband's authority in the same manner that the Kahal is to submit to the Messiah. Husbands and wives are one (echad) with one another, just as the Kahal is one with the Messiah. *"And Ahdom said: "This is now bone of my bones and flesh of my flesh; she shall be called Woman, because she was taken out of Man." Therefore a man shall leave his abba and maw (mother) and be joined to his wife, and they shall become one flesh."* (**GEN 2:23&24**). He exhorts the abbaim (fathers) to train their children in the things of Adonai, which will bring blessings and happiness, and not in the things of the lust of the flesh and the abominations of darkness, which will bring Adonai's wrath upon them. He also exhorts the children to show honor and respect to their parents regardless of the circumstances because YAH promises both long life and happiness if they do. *"My son, keep your father's command, and do not forsake the instructions of your mother.—'Honor your father and your mother, as YAHveh your ELohim has commanded you, that your days may be long and that it may be well with you in the land which YAHveh your ELohim is giving you"* (**PROV 6:20, EXOD 20:12, and DEUT 5:16**). Shaul exhorts servants and employees to serve their masters and employers as though they were serving Adonai—they will be blessed by Adonai if they do. He exhorts employers to do the same for their employees.

Finally, before he closes his letter, he encourages all who are of the Messiah to always be prepared to do battle within the spiritual realm against the prince of the air, hasatan, and his demons. He reminds them of the fact that there are principalities and powers of darkness as well as of light. He also reminds them that they already possess the garments for this battle through their knowledge of the Torah, which is their armor. Their belt, which ties all of their armor together, is their understanding of the Torah's truths. Their breastplate is their love of obedience toward YAHveh. Their boots, or shoes, are the "Good

News" that they walk in regarding Yeshua HaMashiach's Kingdom and His Shalom. Their faith in the truth of His words is their shield against anything that hasatan's servants can throw at them. The knowledge of their redemption through the Messiah is their helmet, and finally, their revelation of the TaNaKh from the Ruach HaKedosh is their weapon of offense to use to destroy the works of the father of lies. But he warns them that even with the proper armor, they must always be watchful and pray for one another for guidance, all the while keeping one eye on what the Ruach is doing and the other on the tempter. This is how they are to protect one another from his schemes.

He asks them to not only keep all of their brethren in prayer but to pray for him also. He tells them that even though he is in prison and only able to speak to a few, he still needs the added strength of their prayers in order to boldly continue in his calling.

Philippians

Rav Shaul spent many days ministering in Ephesus and in Philippi and had established a very close relationship with the members of the congregations in each city. At Philippi, his main concern was with the interrelationships that were beginning to divide the kahal. This letter was written by Shaul and his close associate Timothy, who has been faithful to him and who had also ministered alongside of him to these same brethren.

Shaul is confident, even though he is in prison, that his circumstances are a part of a more elaborate plan of YAH's that will work for good for the Whole House of YisraEL. He reminds them that not all who preach do so out of their love for the family of Eluah but, instead, do it out of pride and selfish ambition. Even so, YAH will use their motives to further His plan and purpose. Shaul says that he has mixed feelings about his possibility of having to die for what he believes. He knows that if he dies, he will be with the Messiah and that would be a wonderful thing, but on the other hand, if he survives and lives, he will be able to continue to further the Kingdom among the Goyim. He says that he is excited about both possibilities. He assures them that if he lives, he will try to come and see them so that he can minister to them once more.

He exhorts them that no matter what may become of him, they should continue to conduct themselves in such a manner as to magnify the name of Yeshua. He reminds them that the enemy of their faith is always watching and waiting for them to misbehave. If by chance they do, he will be right there to accuse them of saying that they believe one thing while doing or living another. He reminds them to remain humble no matter what is being said about them in order to lift up the name of YAH. He pointed to Yeshua HaMashiach as their example—even though He was YAH in the flesh and could have used His power to escape His crucifixion, He took on the lowliness of a man and remained humble by submitting Himself to death for our sake. By being obedient to His Abba's will, Yeshua gained His Kingship, exalting Him above all else in the universe. If all Believers stand fast in their faith, they too can expect a just reward. All Believers must work out their own calling with a mind and spirit that overcomes their fears, and even though their flesh may recoil in trembling, they must learn to stand fast in their faith. If they live their lives in this manner, Shaul says that he will feel assured that he did not waste his time and effort when he delivered his words of salvation to them. He reminds them that the world is watching, so they should avoid all frivolous disputes and disagreements, which can only drag them down. He once more tells them that he hopes to be with them to reconfirm his words, but if not, he will be sending his trusted companion, Timothy, who will see to it that they have understood the importance of all the things that he has been sharing with them. The letter that he is writing to them now, he will be sending in the hands of Epaphroditus, his friend and theirs. He tells them that he would have sent it to them sooner but Epaphroditus had been ill, almost to the point of death, but because of YAH's mercy, he has miraculously recovered and is now ready for the task.

He warns them about being prideful and how it can destroy them through envy and covetousness. He holds himself up as their example. Even though in the flesh he could easily be proud, he counts all worldly things as being worthless. He was of the circumcised—a true Hebrew of the tribe of BenYAHmeen. He was an esteemed Pharisee in his faithfulness to the Torah and full of zeal for its adherence, even to the persecuting of Believers in Yeshua as HaMashiach. These things may have been considered as noble before men, but they stood in his way of grasping the full truth of the Torah because of his own pride. He thought of himself as being righteous because he thought he could obey the Torah for his own salvation. Like most, he didn't understand that no one, except for Yeshua, could keep the Torah, therefore condemning himself to be under its curse. But when he finally understood the purpose of Yeshua's sacrifice, he was able to obtain salvation by faith because the curse had been lifted. He also confesses that he can't obtain perfection and that he never will as long as he remains in the flesh. But his goal is to still strive for perfection and to bring glory to the Abba through the power of the Ruach and the shed blood of Yeshua. He exhorts them to take on this same mind and attitude, the one that the Messiah desires for all of us to have. By doing so, we become role models for others, and this is a worthy calling. He confesses to them that the task is not an easy one—many have attempted it but have fallen away because of pride. But if they use his example and do not waiver, they too can accomplish much through faith—just don't give up. He tells them to focus on the Messiah and not on anything that is of the Earth, and then they will succeed.

He tells them that he has also been made aware of the fact that some strife has arisen over frivolous things, which is dividing the fellowship in their kahal. He implores them to help the two women in their kahal settle their differences and not allow these things to cause this strife and division. All of them need to understand gentleness and not allow anxiety to tear them apart. They should learn how to settle things through patience and prayer and not allow pride and fear to rule their hearts and minds. They need to be content with what they have, be thankful and grateful for the good gifts from YAH, and not be jealous of one another. These things will bring true shalom from above into their hearts and love for one another as well. He tells them to labor at keeping their minds on the things promised to them by Yeshua and never on things promised to them by men. They should always think on the wonderful things that were taught to them about love, life, and shalom from the TaNaKh and not on the foolish philosophies of men.

Finally, he praises them for their generosity, love, and hospitality that they had shown him in the past and how grateful he has been for the sacrifices that they had made for him. He now exhorts them to heed all of his words so that they, as well as he, may be blessed by ELuah, and He would continue to meet all of their needs.

Conclusion

Shaul knew that his destiny was to go to Rome and from there preach the "Good News" to both the YAHudi and the Goyim. His mandate was to bring both the Torah and the "Good News" of the Messiah to them, especially to the Goyim. What he didn't know was that it would be from Rome that his message would become twisted and contaminated by future Roman Emperors, who would condemn his fellow YAHudi, destroy the House of YAH, forbid the teaching of the Torah, corrupt the "Good News" by compromising it with pagan religions in order to please the people, set up a counterfeit religion, and scatter the YAHudi throughout the Roman Empire. But an all-knowing ELohim would use all of these evil things to allow this distorted "Good News" to go out to all of the Goyim/Yosefs throughout the world. The Goyim/Yosefs would continue to sort out the truth from the lies for the next two-thousand years until the time of the Goyim is fulfilled. When this takes place, the full truth will be made known, and Yeshua will return to restore the Whole House of YisraEL and set up His Kingdom forever.

CHAPTER 23
...about I & II Timothy and Titus.

It is not clear when Shaul wrote these next three letters to his friends and fellow ministers. There are some who believe that he could have written them while he was making his way to Rome. Others think that he wrote them while he was in prison, after Timothy and Titus had been sent to minister to the already established Kahal that was scattered throughout the Empire. Still others think that Shaul was released for a period of time, and when he went back to visit many of the kahal, he wrote them from there. Whatever the case, it is evident from their content that he was concerned about false teachers and ne'veem infiltrating the flock of YAH and trying to corrupt the message regarding Yeshua setting all men free from the curse of the Torah. They were seeking to put YAH's people under their own control and leadership.

I Timothy

At the very start, Shaul begins to warn Timothy about those who would come into the Kahal of YisraEL trying to teach the Torah without any understanding of its basic principles. He warns Timothy that there are some who say that the Torah doesn't apply any longer because it has passed away with Yeshua's death. Shaul declares that this isn't true because the Torah is necessary to reveal what sin truly is.

He warns Timothy that some will come declaring themselves or others as being mediators between ELuah and men. But Shaul tells him that under no circumstances is there any mediator but one, Yeshua HaMashiach—not any man, woman, angel, or saint. He alone qualifies for He alone gave His life as a ransom for all others. He declares that all of the House of YisraEL should always acknowledge this. He tells Timothy to encourage the members of the Kahal to pray and worship their King by lifting kedosh hands in praise to the one and only Kedosh ELohim, YAHveh and His Son, Yeshua HaMashiach. He also addresses the manner in which the women of Yeshua's Body should adorn themselves—modesty is the byword. Gold and fancy apparel may impress the servants of the pagan elohim, but not YAH. They should show their submission to Messiah by being submissive to their husbands. They are to look to their husbands for their understanding of the Torah and submit to their direction regarding its instructions for the family. Women who understand these things will be blessed and will find protection from YAH during most birthing.

When Shaul wrote his letters to the kahal at Corinth, he gave them instructions telling them how to conduct the services in their synagogues. He now gives Timothy instructions on how to choose overseers to govern the synagogues. Remember, there weren't any church buildings when Shaul gave these basic instructions to the Kahal of YisraEL. Church buildings were designed and contrived in the minds of men much later in time, when the Roman government began dictating where and when Believers were to worship YAHveh and His Son. Shaul used the Torah as his model when he instructed Timothy to choose overseers or bishops (which are actually elders) within each kahal to govern the affairs of the members. Because they are of the eldership, they would have to be over the age of fifty, according to the Torah. A man was to have only one wife and not a harem. (One wife is the model that the Messiah and His bride portray.) They were to be even tempered, humble, kind, and hospitable. They had to have experience, knowledge, and practice in living the Torah. They had to have shown generosity and spirituality and not be influenced by what the world had to offer. They had to have earned the respect of their spouse, their children, and their community through their character. They could not be a new convert, but should be able to properly apply the teachings of the Messiah to the TaNaKh—otherwise, they could either fall into error or become prideful due to the abundant attention given to them. He also gave him similar instructions in choosing an overseer's apprentice, known as a deacon in the Greek (which means to serve). They were to be under the age of fifty, but over the age of thirty. They could minister in any of the pastoral ministries such as shelich, ne'vee, evangelist, or teacher after the age of thirty, but they could only enter the administrative office of elder or overseer (bishop) after the age of fifty. He reminds Timothy that since he is a shepherd of the flock of ELuah, he is to be their example by following the full instructions that are given in the Torah for ordaining overseers within the Kahal of YisraEL. He continues his instructions by saying that if Timothy sees to it that the proper government of YAHveh is set up to oversee the Kahal, the "Great Mystery" will be protected within the Body of Messiah. The Kahal has the responsibility of revealing this "Great Mystery" to those who are outside of the Kahal and still in the world. They are to proclaim to the world that: ELohim was manifested in the flesh in His Son, Yeshua—He was justified by the Ruach of ELohim—He was seen by angels—He was preached among the Goyim—He was believed on in the world—He was received up into glory.

Shaul goes on to warn him that the Ruach points to the fact that in the final days before Yeshua returns, some will deny their faith in His being the promised Messiah. They will submit to the teachings of men who have had their understanding confused by the lies of demons and seducing spirits. They will distort the basic teachings of both the Torah and the Messiah. They will teach men not to marry or partake of certain foods and will try to nullify or undo most of what Yeshua came to fulfill, using their confusing doctrines that are based upon the imaginations of mere men. As an example, Shaul points out that some will try to cause others to fall under the error that they should only eat kosher rather than receiving all foods with thanksgiving. But just like the Goyim, nothing is to be considered unclean because the Messiah's blood cleanses all things by faith. He points to the fact that conduct such as good hygiene, exercise, and diet is profitable but should never be taken to the extreme, where it could become an object of worship. Shaul continually exhorts Timothy to teach only from the TaNaKh regarding the ordinances that were renewed by the Good News that Yeshua revealed.

He exhorts Timothy to have courage and not to be intimidated by those who might despise him because of his youth, reminding him that the Torah teaches that the minimum age required to minister is thirty or older. He also reminds him that he was ordained by both Shaul and the elders who recognized that he had been called by YAH through prophecy and the laying on of hands. His experience and knowledge are being confirmed by the gifts of the Ruach, and he should rely on this to strengthen his faith. He goes on to instruct him on how elders, both men and women, are to be respected, how he should handle the affairs of widows who are both above and below the age of sixty, and how he is to keep strife and confusion to a minimum by nipping in the bud all rumors and gossip. Finally, he should see to it that the elders who are serving within each kahal are compensated for their time. *"You shall not muzzle an ox while he treads out the grain"* (**DEUT 25:4**). Any accusation of wrong doing that is brought against an elder can only be considered if it is brought by two or three witnesses. When ordaining leaders by the laying on of hands, make sure that they are properly qualified in order to avoid future problems that might cause damage to the rest of the Kahal. Shaul shows his concern for Timothy's health by advising him to consider using wine as an alternative beverage to aid his stomach's sensitivity and to ward off infirmities. He goes on to remind him to instruct employers and employees to serve each other as though they were serving the Messiah. Shaul tells him that those who ignore these sound teachings are not worthy of the blessings that they bring. They are driven by covetousness and only desire to make material gain from their fellow man. They care nothing about kingdom principles because they worship and love riches instead, bringing only evil into their lives. He warns Timothy to have nothing to do with these mischief seekers. He exhorts him to continue to seek the fruits of the Ruach as his earthly reward because when he does, he will discover what true happiness really is. He also tells him to encourage those who have obtained material wealth from this world to avoid the evil trap of loving their riches. They too will enjoy blessings from YAH if they are generous and share with those who have little or nothing. Before Shaul ends his letter to Timothy, he encourages him one more time to guard what he has been instructed in and to be wary of those who rely only on knowledge.

Titus

Rav Shaul's letter to his friend and companion, Titus, is quite similar to the first one that he wrote to Timothy. He begins by giving Titus instructions as to the qualifications for elders and the need for appointing them in every city. He was most concerned about YAHudi elders who were teaching fables rather than the unabridged Torah. As with Timothy, he gave Titus instructions on how both genders of senior citizens should conduct themselves in ministering to others. He also instructs the youth of the Kahal as to how they should behave. He includes instructions as to the proper conduct of employers and employees, just as he did with Timothy. He exhorts him to continue to encourage all believers to heed Yeshua's example by their giving of themselves in all manner of humility. They are at all costs to avoid disputes and divisions, which lead only to strife and evil conduct and will tear apart the Messiah's plan of restoration. Shaul ends his letter to Titus with the same basic exhortation and farewell as he has used in the past.

II Timothy

This second letter to Timothy appears to be the only one that may have actually been written from prison because it seems that Shaul now is no longer under house arrest but is being held instead in chains. Therefore, the time-lapse between the two letters may have been two or more years. He begins his letter by encouraging Timothy not to be discouraged by either the fact that he was now in prison or that persecution was coming to all Believers within the Kahal of YisraEL. He reminds him that YAH gives His people a spiritual attitude of love and a mind full of knowledge of Him—not a fearful or timid spiritual attitude. He reminds him that he was called for a particular purpose and plan designed by YAH—not one of men or from any personal ambition. Therefore, it cannot be thwarted or derailed as long as he keeps his eye on the goal. He tells him to remember all of the things that he taught him because they are sound and reveal the truth of both the Messiah and His Torah. Shaul expresses his thanks and gratitude to Timothy as well as to all of the brethren for their faithfulness to him and to their Messiah. He encourages Timothy to stay faithful to all the principles of the TaNaKh, practicing and sharing the outcome as a testimony and an example to others. He encourages him to shun fables and idle babblings and to test all testimony for truth and righteousness. He should avoid all quarrelling and gently correct those who challenge his doctrine by saying that it is in opposition to the Torah. He should teach the TaNaKh in the light of the Messiah's "Good News", establishing the fulfillment of the Torah.

Shaul warns him that as the time for the coming of the Messiah draws near, many will love sin more than life itself. He names off all the fruits of evil that will manifest themselves in the final days leading up to the arrival of Yeshua. He says that many will seek the knowledge of men but seldom will they seek the knowledge of ELuah, and those who seek righteousness will suffer persecution because they seek the absolute truth. He exhorts him to continue in the truth of the Torah that he has learned since his childhood. Shaul reminds him that all of the revelations that are found in the Torah and in the TaNaKh were given by inspiration of the Ruach of ELohim and not by men. Their purpose remains the same—they were given for teaching, reproof, correction, and instruction in righteousness to profit and equip all Believers in order to accomplish the plan and purpose that YAHveh has ordained for them.

He then charges Timothy to preach the truth of the Torah at all times—before, during, and after the Feasts—and not to deviate from these truths. He should shun those who only want their ears tickled. Shaul knows that his end is drawing near and is very concerned that after he has departed, the "Good News" that he has brought will be distorted and become unrecognizable. He knows that he has fought the good fight and run the race to its end, but he is concerned for others because he has already seen far too many falling away. Only a few like Lucas and Titus have remained faithful. He asks Timothy to bring Markus with him if he is able to come to visit him. Before he closes, he expresses his greatest concern and hope for the Goyim/Yosefs—that they may hear the truth and turn away from the false elohim and the philosophies of men. He closes his final letter with his many greetings to his long and closest friends.

Conclusion

Rav Shaul wrote all of these letters out of his personal concern for the purity of the Torah and its blessings. He wanted his fellow YAHudi brethren to be delivered from the false teachings about the Torah and the TaNaKh, which caused many of his brethren to miss the coming of the Messiah. He was also concerned that these same false teachings would somehow find their way into the understanding of the newly converted Goyim because of their vulnerability. The very thing that Shaul was concerned about happened. To this day, the YAHudi have continued to try to keep the ordinances of the Torah without the presence of the Ark or the House of YAH. They have been kept ignorant about Yeshua and His fulfillment of the prophecies within the Scriptures. In fact, they are still looking for the coming of the Messiah. However, many have given up hope and now only see the coming of the Messiah as just a metaphor and not as an actual event. And the Goyim/Yosefs have had the message twisted and perverted to the point that they no longer see the Torah and the TaNaKh as something relevant. It was replaced by a new set of teachings—the teachings of a Greek/Roman Messiah named Jesus, who came to do away with the Torah and replace YisraEL with the **Church**. I'm sorry, I know it seems to make sense—but it's wrong. Yeshua was a YAHudi from the tribe of YAHuda, which was the last tribe of the *visible* YisraEL. Yeshua came for the *lost* sheep of YisraEL (the *invisible* YisraEL), who were scattered among all of the nations of the world. He came to redeem, sanctify, and restore His Bride, all of YisraEL, back to His Kingdom. And He will—just as soon as she recognizes who she really is.

CHAPTER 24
…about James, Jude, and I&II Peter

These three shelichim address their letters to the lost sheep, or tribes, of the House of YisraEL. James/Jacob (Yaacov) and Jude (YAHuda) were the brothers of Yeshua. When Yaacov wrote his letter, he was the president of the synagogue in YAHrushalayim. At that time, churches were non-existent in the world—there were only synagogues, where both YAHudi and Goyim learned the teachings of the TaNaKh. There weren't any pastors as we know them; anyone in a position of authority was either an elder or a deacon. Those who were in positions of ministry were either shelichim, or teachers, or ne'veem, or evangelists—but all were considered to be pastors or shepherds. A synagogue was owned by an individual who was known as a ruler, and it was led by a president who could also be a ruler. The two letters that Kefa wrote were mainly to the YAHudi who were among the Goyim/Yosefs and who believed in Yeshua as the promised Messiah. Some have believed that Kefa was the first pope and the head of the Church, but this could not be because his ministry was to the YAHudi. Yeshua said that he was going to give the keys to the Kingdom to him, the authority to forgive sins, and that He was going to build His Kahal upon Kefa's confession that Yeshua was the Son of the Living Elohim—that was the rock, or pebble (Kefa), that He was referring to. If anyone qualified to be the first pope, it would have been Rav Shaul, whose ministry was to the Goyim of the Roman Empire. And if anyone qualifies to be the Head of the Church, it could only be Yeshua. But since there isn't any such thing as the Church, Yeshua is the Head and King of the House of YisraEL.

James (Yaacov)

Yaacov, a teacher and a chief elder, begins his letter by addressing it to the twelve tribes who were scattered abroad throughout the nations. He first pointed out the necessity of the patience that is needed because of the persecution that awaits all believers due to the intolerance of the world toward any religion outside of their own. Then he points to the importance of wisdom, knowledge, and faith, which can be obtained through prayer, but can be hindered through doubting. Yeshua is truth, and when truth is combined with faith, which is having trust in that truth, it can move mountains. When faith is lifted up in prayer without doubting, it moves Adonai to manifest His power. When knowledge and experience is combined with common sense and then added to faith, it produces true wisdom. These are the things that bring true happiness and joy—in other words, spiritual wealth. Worldly wealth, when compared, has no real value.

He goes on to point out that temptation comes from evil forces. These evil forces prey on us through the lust of our eyes, selfishness, and ignorance. When we submit to these temptations, we are led down a path toward wickedness. He explains that YAHveh never tempts—He only tests. He is love and will only give us good gifts, when we put our trust in Him and show our desire to please Him. Evil gifts come from the father of lies, and we receive them because of the lust of our flesh.

His good gifts come to us when we learn to be doers of His Torah and not just those who hear it. If we only learn and never do, we'll never gain experience and, therefore, never gain wisdom. We become like a man who sees his reflection in a mirror, either admiring or despising what he sees. Later he forgets what he saw and begins to remember only what he thinks he saw, deceiving himself in the actual truth. But if we use the Torah as our mirror and see ourselves as YAH sees us and do His words, we will gain true wisdom. Being doers of His Torah will also govern our speech and dialogue. If our speech only reflects worldly wisdom, then it will reveal the worldly lust that is still in our hearts. But if it reflects the wisdom that we've gained from being doers of YAH's instructions, then it will be our witness of the true Love of our Abba in heaven.

Yaacov points to his brother and Adonai, Yeshua, as being our example in our treatment toward our fellow man, showing no partiality between the rich and the poor—to Yeshua, all men are created equal. When we show this same kind of compassion, we fulfill the Torah, which he refers to as the "Royal Law of Liberty". *"You shall not take vengeance, nor bear grudge against the children of your people, but you shall love your neighbor as yourself; I AM YAHveh"* (**LEV 19:18**). Yaacov warns that if we disregard this command, we will have broken the Torah and can be subject to the punishment of banishment and death because we have stepped out of the mercy of our Abba—we are in sin. But when we show His mercy through obedience to His commands, it becomes the work of our faith. We are also working our faith when we celebrate the Feasts of His written Torah because when we do, we are celebrating the Living Torah and the mercy that He has shown us through His death and resurrection. When we minister to those who are poor in spirit with our substance and not just our words, we are extending Yeshua's mercy to them also. Believing that YAHveh exists and confessing His Name is not enough—even the demons know this. We must become His loving hands and arms, embracing others with His understanding—something the demons loath. We must become servants and serve Him in some capacity. Our faith must be active.

Yaacov points to Avraham as our abba of faith because he was willing to offer his only son, his son of promise, as a living sacrifice to YAH. He knew that YAH would not have lied to him about this son being the heir to the inheritance of the land of promise. If need be, He would raise him up from the dead in order to fulfill that promise. Because of his faith, Avraham was called a friend of ELohim. *"And he believed in YAHveh and He accounted it to him for righteousness.—"Are You not our ELohim, who drove out the inhabitants of this land before Your people YisraEL, and gave it to the descendants of Avraham Your friend forever?"* (**GEN 15:6** and **II CHRON 20:7**).

Yaacov warns those who desire to be teachers to expect a heavier judgment than others if they do not teach the Torah accurately. Again he points to the words that we speak as being the only witness to whether they are His truth or the fables of men. Our tongue is the most unruly member of our body because it reveals the content of our hearts. Our hearts must be under the control of the Ruach because He is in perfect harmony with the Torah. Only then can we bridle our tongue and speak the truth. Having bitterness and envy in our hearts will only bring destruction to ourselves and is demonic in nature. These things bear the fruit of selfishness, which will cause confusion in our thinking and will result in our doing the works of evil. The fig tree that only gives forth leaves and never any fruit is like the tongue that gives both curses and blessings—and we know what Yeshua did to the fig tree that didn't produce fruit. Our speech, which reveals our hearts, should always reflect our understanding of the kingdom principles of the Torah. Anything else brings only strife and warring within ourselves and causes division among us; the end result will be our desiring everything but receiving nothing. This attitude causes our prayers to be ignored because we desire selfish fulfillment. There is no compromising with the world; we are either spiritual or carnal, and if carnal, we are enemies of ELuah. *"Then YAHveh saw that the wickedness of man was great in the earth, and that every intent of the thoughts of his heart was only evil continually"* (**GEN 6:5**). Instead, bear the Fruit of the Ruach, which is from above. *"Surely He scorns the scornful, but gives grace to the humble"* (**PROV 3:34**). Therefore, with perseverance turn away from the gifts offered by the prince of this world. If you do, he will eventually give up and leave you alone, and then you will be able to submit your life to ELuah. Do the Torah without doubting because if you doubt it, you become its judge, and if you judge it, you cannot become a doer of it. Instead, you will be judged by it, and you will fall under its curse. Your life should be focused on only doing the Torah; then your footsteps will be guided toward true happiness, joy, love, and shalom. Failing to do this reveals a desire to do evil. If you have lived for riches, then repent because the riches of this world will escape your grasp. Instead, live for the true riches—live for YAH.

Finally, Yaacov ends his letter with his last list of instructions to all twelve tribes. Have patience until Adonai returns to restore the Whole House of YisraEL. Guard your speech and tongue. Do not swear by ELuah, but let your word be your pledge. Those who are patiently waiting for Him and are suffering should continue to pray. Those who are blessed should sing and praise Adonai. Those who are sick should confess any trespasses and then call the elders to anoint them with oil and pray the prayer of faith against the sickness—in doing so, they will be delivered. He gave the example of the ne'vee Elijah (ELeeYAHoo), who prayed a prayer of faith to hold back rain for three and a half years; then, when he prayed again, it rained. Finally, he makes a plea for them to go out to retrieve those who have wandered away from the truth and turn them back from their error.

Jude (YAHuda)

YAHuda (Yeshua's other brother), being a ne'vee to the Kahal of YisraEL, prophesied regarding the things that would befall believers in the times to come. He begins by addressing his letter to all who look to Yeshua for their redemption and sanctification. He warns them about men coming to woo YAH's people away from the knowledge of His grace in delivering them from the curse of the Torah. Then he exhorts them to remember the warning and the judgment that will come upon those who distort His Word. He points to those who opposed Mosheh and to the instructions that they received from YAHveh. He then reminds them of the angels who have been imprisoned in chains until the Day of Judgment for following hasatan and rebelling against YAH. He wrote about how sexual immorality brought swift judgment and annihilation to the cities of Sodom and Gomorrah. All of these examples were about those who had sold their very souls for recognition and had esteemed themselves above others, but only to their own shame and judgment. Then he quotes Enoch's prophecy about YAHveh coming with His Kahal in order to judge those who have taught and prophesied over the centuries from their own imaginations. These erred in their own words because they walked in the flesh and had not been sanctified by the Ruach. They were secular and religious and did not understand the truth of the Torah. But he exhorts those who have come to the true knowledge of Yeshua's message regarding the Torah to pray in the power of the Ruach in order to build them up in their kedosh faith. He also encourages them to be watchful among their brethren; they should attempt to warn those who might get caught up in the false doctrines of men, who have mixed YAH's Word with local pagan practices. After these brief warnings, he ends his letter.

WHAT WE WEREN'T TAUGHT ABOUT THE BIBLE AND ITS HISTORY

I Peter (Kefa)

Kefa begins his first letter by addressing his potential readers as those who have been dispersed throughout Asia. These are recognized among Hebrew-thinking people as being the ten northern tribes of Yosef, who were dispersed by Assyria eight-hundred years earlier. Many of the YAHudi who had come to the saving knowledge of their Messiah resided among them. The first thing he writes about is the price that Yeshua paid for their redemption. Then he speaks to them regarding the Ruach of the Messiah as being the Ruach of YAHveh, thereby endorsing the fact that the Ruach, YAHveh, and HaMashiach are One (Echad) and the same. (Some call this "The Trinity", a term that has been used to describe this union.) He reminds them that they are to conduct themselves in a kedosh manner, just as the Torah teaches. *"For I AM YAHveh your ELohim. You shall therefore sanctify yourselves, and you shall be kedosh; for I AM kedosh. Neither shall you defile yourselves with any creeping thing that creeps on the earth. 'For I AM YAHveh who brings you up out of the land of Mitsrahyim, to be your ELohim; You shall therefore be kedosh, for I AM kedosh."..."Speak to all the Kahal of the children of YisraEL, and say to them: 'You shall be kedosh, for I YAHveh your ELohim AM kedosh."..."Sanctify yourselves therefore, and be kedosh, for I AM YAHveh your ELohim"* (LEV 11:44&45, 19:2 and 20:7). Kefa is saying that what YAHveh has deemed unclean or unholy (such as the Goyim) remains in that state until the price of redemption is met. Insects, serpents, or any amphibious creature that lives close to the earth is symbolic of hasatan and, therefore, unclean. Anything unholy or unclean is outside of the House of YAH until it is pronounced clean by the high priest. Yeshua, our High Priest forever, has pronounced all who call upon His Name as holy (kedosh), and they are to remain that way by glorifying Him through their conduct and obedience to the Torah—this brings glory to His words and to His Name. He reminds them that this was accomplished when they were born-again of the Ruach. They are to express this fact through their love for their brethren as a witness that all who have been redeemed, whether Goyim or YAHudi, are now one (echad) in the Messiah. Now they are born of an incorruptible seed that will never taste death, but will endure forever. *"The voice said, "Cry out!" And he said, "What shall I cry?" "All flesh is grass, and all its loveliness is like the flower of the field. Because the breath of YAHveh blows upon it; surely the people are grass; The grass withers, the flower fades, but the word of ELohim stands forever"* (ISA 40:6-8). In order to perpetuate their redemption, a believer must first drink in the pure milk of the Torah (its basic teachings). Then, they are to exercise these basic teachings in order to gain experience, resulting in wisdom, which is spiritual meat.

Kefa's name, given to him by Yeshua, means a stone or a pebble. He points out the fact that all who confess Yeshua as their Messiah are also stones, ***living stones***. As living stones, who are doing the works of the Torah, we make up the *"House of YAH"*, with Yeshua as the cornerstone and the teaching of the TaNaKh as our foundation. To those who have hardened their hearts to this truth, it has become a stumbling block. This is what our Adonai meant when He said, *"Behold, I lay in Zeeon a stone for a foundation, a tried stone, a precious cornerstone, a sure foundation; whoever believes will not act hastily."..."The stone which the builders rejected has become the chief cornerstone."..."He will be as a sanctuary, but a stone of stumbling and a rock of offense to both the houses of YisraEL, as a trap and a snare to the inhabitants of YAHrushalayim"* (**ISA 28:16, PALM 118:22** and **ISA 8:14**).

Yeshua said that He would build His Kahal on Kefa's confession and that He would give him the keys to the kingdom (which was the power to forgive sin through binding and loosing) in **MATT 16:17-19**. This same shelich, Kefa, now describes what that Kahal would truly be. They would be a chosen generation, a royal priesthood, a kedosh nation, and YAH's special people who were called out of darkness into His marvelous light—those who were not a people, but are now the people of ELohim—those who had not obtained mercy, but now have obtained mercy (**HOS 1:9&10** and **ROM 9:25**). Kefa encourages all believers to live the Torah before men by submitting themselves to the laws of the land and to its governors, as long as those laws do not violate the Torah. He encourages all of those who are under the authority of an employer to do likewise. When they do this, they provide a favorable witness for Adonai because this too was His attitude. *"And they made His grave with the wicked—but with the rich at His death, because He had done no violence, nor was any deceit in His mouth"* (**ISA 53:9**). Kefa reminds all believers that Yeshua took our sins to the grave with Him, and by His wounds, He gave us healing for our bodies and deliverance from the second death (**ISA 53:5**).

He goes on to give instructions to believing wives, telling them to submit to their unbelieving husbands as the family head. He tells them that their willingness to do that will do more to attract their husbands to both themselves and to Adonai than any outward adornment. He also admonishes believing husbands to show honor to their wives as though they were the weaker vessel and to do so through love and understanding. Husbands should understand that they are no longer individuals but are, instead, one (echad) flesh with their wives. He also instructs all believers to honor and show respect for one another as though they were family members and tells them to refrain from foolish rivalry. *"Who is the man who desires life, and loves many days, that he may see good? Keep your tongue from evil, and your lips from speaking guile. Depart from evil, and do good; seek shalom, and pursue it. The eyes of YAHveh are on the righteous, and His ears are open to their cry. The face of YAHveh is against those who do evil, to cut off the remembrance of them from the earth"* (**PSALM 34:12-16**). He reminds them that "true" shalom does not come from the absence of evil but, instead, is experienced during times of evil. He encourages them to always be prepared to tell others of how and why it is that they have this kind of "true" shalom. *"Do not say, 'A conspiracy,' concerning all that this people call a conspiracy, nor be afraid of their threats, nor be troubled"* (**ISA 8:12**). The threats of people are designed to intimidate and are usually based upon lies. Never be afraid of expressing your testimony concerning what Adonai has done in your life. It is far better to suffer for that testimony than to suffer because of some evil that has come into your life. It was the Messiah who suffered and paid the price for our redemption because of the evil that we committed and for the debt we couldn't pay. After His death, He went into the prison of Hades as a testimony that He was the promised Messiah to those who had refused to heed the warnings of Noah and had been swept away by the flood for their evil. Now our Messiah is at the right hand of ELuah and is our representative, exercising all authority over all the angels, principalities, and the powers in the world of the invisible. The flood in the days of Noah was a forerunner of our mitzvah (baptism) in the Messiah, and our mitzvah is the substitute for our judgment and represents our testimony of faith in these truths.

No longer are we to walk in the ways of the Goyim or in the lust of the flesh. Now we are to walk in confidence and exercise the authority that our Messiah has purchased for us. We are to fulfill our commission by telling those who are in the world and dead in their sins the "Good News" of Yeshua HaMashiach, giving them the opportunity to choose life over death. We are to show them our works of faith by showing our love for one another. *"Hatred stirs up strife, but love covers all sins"* (**PROV 10:12**). Live the Torah before all men so that all men may see for themselves and understand the oracles of ELuah.

Kefa and the other shelichim, including Rav Shaul, were expecting the Messiah to return soon because of the evil that they were witnessing all around them. He encouraged them to hold on to their faith for just a little longer, even though they were experiencing harsh trials and persecution. He told them not to give up or to give in but to allow the testing of their faith to be for the good that they were doing and not for any evil work, which would bring disgrace to Yeshua's Name. When YAH's judgment comes, it will begin at His Own House and with His Own people, YisraEL, and it will climax with those who refuse to obey His commands. *"If the righteous will be recompensed on the earth, how much more the wicked and the sinner"* (**PROV 11:31**).

Kefa closes his first letter by exhorting the elders to use the wisdom and knowledge of the Torah to shepherd the Kahal and flock of the Great Shepherd, Yeshua, striving always to be His example of love and patience. He continues by exhorting the youth to submit themselves to the authority of the elders who have been appointed over them. *"Surely He scorns the scornful, but gives grace to the humble."* (PROV 3:34). He exhorts them not to ignore the teachings of the elders and the Torah because their enemy, hasatan, is like an old lion who seeks out the weak in order to lead them into destruction. Kefa sends greetings from Yochanan Markus and refers to him as his own son (He personally nurtured Markus and was probably responsible for the accuracy of the writing of the gospel of Markus). He also included greetings from "she who is in Babylon" (which could mean those of the House of YAHuda who had remained there since their original captivity). Kefa completes his exhortation to his readers by reminding them to greet one another with the Middle-Eastern tradition of a kedosh kiss.

II Kefa

There may have been a long period of time between Kefa's first letter and his second. And now it appears that he too has been imprisoned by the Emperor Nero and that Rav Shaul has already met his fate at this lunatic's hand.

He begins his second letter with overwhelming concern about Believers in Yeshua not practicing the Fruits of the Ruach. He encourages every one of his readers to rekindle these attributes in their daily lives. The lack of the evidence of such practice, he admonishes, will eventually lead to a backslidden lifestyle. It is at this time that he speaks of his own imminent death and in what manner he would suffer it, as told to him by Yeshua. He then reminds them that he was a personal witness to some of the incidents that Adonai Yeshua HaMashiach encountered during His time on Earth. He tells about the time that he personally heard the Voice of YAH announce that it was Yeshua who was His beloved Son and that the words of His Son were perfect in every way and prophetic in content. Kefa affirms that true prophecy will always come to pass and that it never originates in the imagination or the will of mere man. Both the Torah and the Ne'vim were inspired by the Ruach of YAHveh and were conveyed through chosen kedosh men who spoke of the many things to come that have been established since before the foundation of all creation. But just as there is the authentic, there is also the counterfeit.

Kefa now begins to reaffirm the words of Rav Shaul, Yochanan, and YAHuda regarding their warnings about other teachings and doctrines finding their way into the true teachings of Mosheh and Yeshua. Some will try to deny Yeshua's deity, others will say that the Torah is the only way to true salvation, and still others will say that it takes not only belief in Yeshua but also strict compliance to the Torah to obtain salvation. These, he says, are false teachers professing the doctrines of men and demons.

In many cases, the Shelichim, when writing instructions to the Kahal, would confirm certain kingdom principles without ever having knowledge of the writings of the others. This seems to be the case when Kefa reminded his readers, just as YAHuda had, that if YAH did not spare the angels who ignored His commands but placed them in chains until the final judgment for their rebellion, then He will certainly punish all rebellious men who do the same. He points to the first book of the Torah as evidence to this because of the judgment that had befallen those of Noah's generation who ignored his words of warning about repentance. Then he points to Sodom and Gomorrah and their destruction—with the exception of the few righteous who were allowed to flee. He says if angels, who have much more power than men, refrain from speaking any evil against others, knowing what their fate will be, then why do mere men think that they have a greater authority to do so? And why do they think they can follow the teachings of Balaam and ignore the Torah by mixing its teachings with the doctrines of men, thereby committing adultery against their Betrothed and ELohim? They do so because they are motivated by their sinful and selfish flesh and ignore Mosheh's instructions that were given to the House of YisraEL. He warns them that they, along with any who heed their words by following after them, will find themselves in a worse state than they were before they found their redemption. *"As a dog returns to his own vomit, so a fool repeats his folly"* (**PROV 26:11**). It would have been better for them to have never known or tasted the freedom that redemption brings.

Kefa, like Rav Shaul, warns his readers that just assuredly as they must face trials until Yeshua's return, impatience will overtake many while they wait. Scoffers will claim that He must have been a false ne'vee because He did not return as prophesied, forgetting the events that must take place first before His return. YAH's words shaped the Earth, His words destroyed the Earth, His words recreated the Earth, and they will once again bring it to judgment in His timing. It is at this time that Kefa reminds them of YAH's pattern of seven and that He works in the time frame of millenniums and not days. YAH knows exactly how many souls must come to repentance over the span of all the millenniums, and He will not end the age until the last one comes to redemption. Kefa tells them what the Messiah told him about the destruction of the heavens and the Earth and how the elements will be burnt up with fervent heat and fire when men are least expecting it. When these things begin to take place, those who believe His words should look with faith and hope to a new heaven and a new Earth.

Finally, he closes this second letter admitting that many will find both his words and the words of Rav Shaul hard to understand at times. He contends, though, that if they persevere to the end, they will come to the knowledge and understanding of all of the revelations that were given to the Children of YisraEL.

Conclusion

All of these letters that were directed to both Houses of YisraEL, Yosef and YAHuda, warn of a time when the teachings of the Torah will be challenged and distorted. They reemphasize the need to keep the basics alive and to persevere in resisting the teachings and philosophies of men becoming mixed with the truth of YAH. They encourage Believers to rely on the leading of the Ruach HaKedosh to guide and to teach them and to also be patient until the restoration of all things has been completed. These three shelichim, as well as Rav Shaul, found that their hardest job was to keep the Torah from being twisted by both their fellow YAHudi and the Goyim into something other than what both Yeshua and Mosheh had presented as the true meaning of YAH's heart.

CHAPTER 25
...about the Letter to the Hebrews, or Messianic YAHudi

The word "Hebrew", or "Ivrim", means to be a descendant of Shem's grandson, Eber, or Iver. Eber, or Iver, means "one who crosses over". Eber's son, Peleg, was present when the Earth divided (the splitting of the continents—**GEN 10:25**). Some of his family may have been caught in the Earth's splitting and were among those who were forced to cross over to the other continent when the split occurred (this is only a conjecture on my part). Avraham was called to come out of the land of his fathers' (avrim) and to cross over the Euphrates and Yarden River into the land of Canaan, the land of YAHveh's promise—he was, therefore, called a Hebrew.

Since YAHuda was the only visible tribe left and only a few of them accepted Yeshua as their Messiah, these few were the first to inherit the title "Messianic YAHudi". It is not clear which Shelich wrote this letter and still remains a mystery to this day. Some believe it may have been Rav Shaul or perhaps one of his protégés, such as Apollos, Barnabus, or even Silas. It may even have been Kefa since his primary ministry was to the YAHudi. One other theory that has been raised is that a Catholic bishop by the name of Jerome wrote it around 400 CE and then later added it to the Brit Chadashah. I can't even consider that because that would put all of the Scriptures in question as to their authenticity. If all Scripture is inspired, which I believe it is, then the Ruach would never have allowed it to become canonized. I believe whoever the writer was, it was written to reemphasize the basic kingdom principles of the Torah.

The writer begins by reminding the Messianic YAHudi that the source of their basic knowledge has come from the TaNaKh, but its clarification lies within the teachings of the Messiah, Yeshua. He points out that Yeshua was the only begotten Son of YAH and that He was born as a man, just a little below the angels, but exalted to be above them because He was also YAHveh ELohim. *"I will declare the decree: YAHveh has said to Me, You are My Son, today I have begotten You."..."I will be His Abba, and He will be My Son. If He commits iniquity, I will chasten Him with the rod of men and with the blows of the sons of men"* (**PSALM 2:7** and **II SAM 7:14**). He will be His Firstborn and will be worshiped as such. *"Let all be put to shame who serve carved images* (or things that come from the hands of men)*, who boast of idols. Worship Him, all you elohim* (or angels).".…"*Rejoice, O Goyim, with His people; for He will avenge the blood of His servants, and render vengeance to His adversaries; He will provide atonement for His land and His people*" (**PSALM 97:7** and **DEUT 32:43**). He declares to His angels that "*He makes His angels spirits* (or invisible ministers, messengers, and servants.), *His ministers a flame of fire*" (**PSALM 104:4**). But His declaration to His Son is: "*Your throne, O ELohim, is forever and ever; a scepter of righteousness is the scepter of Your kingdom; You love righteousness and hate wickedness; therefore ELohim, Your ELohim, has anointed You with the oil of gladness more than Your companions.*".…"*Of old You laid the foundation of the earth, and the heavens are the work of Your hands. They will perish, but You will endure; yes, all of them will grow old like a tallit; like a cloak You will change them, and they will be changed; But You are the same, and Your years will have no end.*".…"*YAHveh said to my Adonai, "Sit at My right hand, till I make Your enemies Your footstool*" (**PSALM 45:6&7, 102:25-27** and **110:1**).

The writer warns his readers to cherish their salvation, which was purchased for them with the blood of their Messiah and then confirmed with signs and wonders. He reemphasizes the fact that Yeshua qualified as being the Promised One. And as such, He was a man made a little lower than the angels, yet He had power and authority over all that was created because it was by His Words, spoken as Adonai, that they were created. "*What is man that You are mindful of him, and the son of man that You visit him? For You have made him a little lower than the angels, and You have crowned him with glory and honor. You have made him to have domino over the works of Your hands; You have put all things under his feet*" (**PSALM 8:4-6**). By doing this, many sons of men have been brought to glory in order to share in this sanctification with Yeshua, thereby making mere men His brethren. "*I will declare Your name to My brethren; in the midst of the kahal I will praise You.*".…"*And I will wait on YAHveh, who hides His face from the House of Yaacov; and I will hope in Him. Here am I and the children whom YAHveh has given me! We are for signs and wonders in YisraEL from YAHveh of hosts, who dwell in Mount Zeeon*" (**PSALM 22:22** and **ISA 8:17-18**). All of this was done because of His promise to Avraham and not for the sake of the angels. He became flesh and blood so that He could die in our stead and destroy death, along with the one who had the power over it, hasatan. Originally only the high priest had the authority to make atonement for the sins of the children of YisraEL, so YAH had to become flesh and blood, becoming our High Priest, so that He could be the one who would atone for our sins. He had to be tempted so that He could overcome temptation for our sakes. He was faithful in all that was given to Him, just as Mosheh was faithful to YAH's house when they were given to him. Yeshua was not only faithful to, but was also the builder of that house—that house being YisraEL. To be partakers of His salvation, we need only to hold fast to the confidence and hope of our confession to the very end. "*For He is our*

ELohim, and we are the people of His pasture, and the sheep of His hand. Today, if you will hear His voice: "Do not harden your hearts, as in the rebellion, and as in the day of trail in the wilderness, when your fathers tested Me; they proved Me, though they saw My work. For forty years I was grieved with that generation, and said, 'It is a people who go astray in their hearts, and they do not know My ways.' So I swore in My wrath, 'They shall not enter My rest'"* (**PSALM 95:7-11**). No man can enter into His rest with unbelief. What is His rest? It is the seventh millennium. Just as He rested for a millennium after creation, so will all of those who are called by His Name, YisraEL, rest in His second millennium. *"And on the seventh day ELohim ended His work which He had done, and sanctified it, because in it He rested from all His work which ELohim had created and made"* (**GEN 2:2**). Since His people did not enter His rest after they exited the wilderness, then there is still a rest that lies ahead for them to enter into—they will enter into His Kingdom of Paradise. Disobedience to His Torah is what caused that generation not to have the privilege of entering into His rest—His word still stands. All who have come to believe in His Son, the Living Torah, must also believe in His written Torah by observing its simple ordinances of righteousness/right-living. Our desire to follow His instructions in His Torah is like a two-edged sword—it divides our desire of serving self from our desire of serving Him. His instructions will disclose the thoughts and intents of our hearts through our actions. We must give an account to Him regarding our actions after we discover what is expected of us—His Torah reveals what is expected of us.

Yeshua is able to understand our weaknesses because He was also tempted by hasatan, but He was able to overcome him through true obedience to the Torah. Now He is able to make both intercession and atonement on our behalf because He has become both our High Priest and our sacrifice that was brought to the altar by the High Priest. Before, the high priests were selected from mere men. They may have understood our weaknesses, but they had to offer both sacrifices and blood atonement for us and for themselves. But Yeshua, who was without sin, entered the order of Melchizedek instead of the order of Aaron (Aharon) and became both a Priest and a King forever, offering Himself up as both our sacrifice and our atonement. Therefore, we are redeemed and sanctified and will remain that way forever, unless we deny Him through our disobedience. *"YAHveh has sworn and will not relent, "You are a priest forever according to the order of Melchizedek"* (**PSALM 110:4**). Yeshua knew both the pain and the fear of death and cried out to His Abba to deliver Him; yet He knew what He was sent to do and obeyed the commands of His Abba, up to and including His own death. Because of His obedience, He became the author of eternal salvation for those who obey Him.

The writer continues to admonish his fellow YAHudi brethren because they have stubbornly continued to try to earn their own salvation through the works of the Torah. He said that by now they should be experienced teachers of the Torah both in spirit and in truth, but instead, they still had not yet learned the elementary principles that were taught by the Messiah, Yeshua—they were still in the milk and not ready for the meat of His words. There is only one way to reach maturity and partake of the meat and that is through the exercise and use of the Torah. He said that it was time for them to lay aside the basic milk teachings and to begin exercising the deeper principles of the Torah in their lives. What is the milk of the Word? There are six foundational elementary principles. They are: (1) Repentance from dead works (repentance from your own interpretation of good works). (2) Faith toward ELuah (faith or trust in all of YAHveh's instructions in His TaNaKh). (3) The doctrine of mikvahim/baptisms (teachings regarding dying to self and self-ambitions). (4) The laying on of hands (working in and passing on the authority of YAH). (5) Resurrection of the dead (the promises regarding the events on the last "Great Day"). (6) Eternal judgment (the consequences of disobedience to YAH's Torah). He warns those who have been born-again about the danger of ignoring these kingdom principles and returning to the participation in worldly pleasures—they are in danger of backsliding into permanent rejection. If they have tasted heavenly things and then turn away, heavenly things may never satisfy their spiritual palate again, and they could fall back under the curse of the Torah. At the same time, he knows that those who have truly tasted heavenly things will not really desire to return to their former ways. YAH has established all of these principles, both positive and negative, and this was the reason that He made an oath with Avraham. Avraham knew that YAH could not lie, so his faith was elevated when He said, *"By Myself I have sworn, says YAHveh, because you have done this thing, and have not withheld your son, your only son, "in blessing I will bless you, and in multiplying I will multiply your descendants as the stars of the heaven and as the sand which is on the seashore; and your descendants shall possess the gate of their enemies. "In your seed all the nations of the earth shall be blessed, because you have obeyed My voice"* (GEN 22:16-18). This promise is the anchor that gives us the confidence that we too may enter through the veil into the most Kedosh Place, having been preceded by our High Priest, Yeshua HaMashiach.

The writer explains to his readers the importance of Yeshua's position as High Priest of the order of Melchizedek. Melchizedek was not only a priest of YAH, but he was also the King of Salem (Aramaic for Shalom), the city that later became Yebus of the Yebusi and then, finally, YAHrushalayim (the city of YAH's shalom.). Avraham recognized and acknowledged him as such and gave him a tenth of all of his goods as an offering. In doing so, Melchizedek blessed Avraham and then shared a type of Passover Feast (Seder) with him by bringing out bread and wine. His words were similar to YAH's. *"Blessed be Avram of ELohim Most High, Possessor of heaven and earth; and blessed be ELohim*

WHAT WE WEREN'T TAUGHT ABOUT THE BIBLE AND ITS HISTORY

Most High, who has delivered your enemies into your hands" (**GEN 14:19&20**). (This blessing is similar to the one that most Messianic Believers recite over the wine before the Sabbath meal. *"Baruch Atah, YAHveh ELohenu melech ha-olam, borey p'ree ha-gahfen. Omein."* "Blessed are You, YAHveh our ELohim, King of the Universe, Creator of the fruit of the vine. Amen." An additional blessing is said over the bread. *"Barukh Atah, YAHveh ELohenu melech ha-olam, ha-matzee lechem meen ha-aretz, lechem chaim b'Yeshua. Omein."* "Blessed are You, YAHveh our ELohim, King of the universe, who brings forth the bread from the Earth, the Bread of Life in Yeshua. Amen.") The priestly order that YAH had appointed to minister to Him from within the Mishkahn and then later in His House was to be made up of the descendants of Aharon (the first high priest), who was from the tribe of Levee and a descendant of Avraham. Because Avraham was the father of this priestly order, when they received tithes from YAH's people, they were actually receiving a tribute on behalf of Melchizedek, a higher priest than they. So, it was by decree that all of these priests were to be descendants of Aharon in order to qualify to become priests. But Yeshua was not of the order of Aharon or from the tribe of Levee—He was a descendent of the YAHudi, who were not qualified to be priests. But because Yeshua existed before YAHuda, or Levee, or Avraham, or even before Melchizedek and was also without beginning or end, like Melchizedek, and being the King of all kings, superseding Melchizedek's kingship, He qualified to become the Highest Priest of the order of Melchizedek.

In Chapter One, we mentioned that the importance of the order of Melchizedek would be explained later in this chapter, so here is that explanation. Some believe that Melchizedek was actually Shem, the firstborn of Noah, who lived well beyond the time of Avraham's journey into the land of Canaan. No record was ever scribed by any Hebrew that has shown Melchizedek's birth or death—it was never found in the breathed word of YAH, the Torah. Because there wasn't any record of it, it has been said that he didn't have a mother or a father or any genealogy (meaning that he had no beginning or end of days, which put him on the same spiritual level as YAH—"Eternal"). This was a metaphor of the Messiah being YAH in the flesh, without a beginning or an end and being as perfect as YAH. Perfection could not come through the Levee priesthood, from whom the children of YisraEL received the Torah, but it could through the perfect Melchizedek priesthood. Whenever the priesthood is changed, the principles of the Torah also have to undergo a change. The Torah of the Levee priesthood contained blessings and curses, but the Torah of the Melchizedek priesthood contains only blessings, which were purchased by the cleansing blood of the Messiah. In addition, the office of High Priest of the order of Melchizedek was sealed by the oath that is found in **PSALM 110:4**. Thus, a new covenant, or a covenant (Brit) renewed (ChaDassah), has been made between YAH and the House of YisraEL. This renewed covenant (Brit Chadashah) has a new High Priest, a new Torah, and a new Mishkahn. This High Priest sits at the right hand of YAHveh, our Abba, and has made one final and eternal sacrifice—His own life for our sins—and is our Mediator to that renewed covenant, a Torah with no curse assigned to it. There is now a true Mishkahn, one not made with hands as was the one that was given to Mosheh in the wilderness, which was patterned after Paradise. *"And see to it that you make them according to the pattern which was shown to you on the mountain"* (**EXOD 25:40**). We are now His true Mishkahn with His Ruach dwelling within us. All of this had to be accomplished because the first covenant was lacking, so a second was needed. *"Behold, the days are coming, says YAHveh, when I will make a new* (renewed) *covenant with the House of YisraEL and with the House of YAHuda—"not according to the covenant that I made with their fathers in the day that I took them by the hand to bring them out of the land of Mitsrahyim, My covenant which they broke, though I was a husband to them, says YAHveh; "But this is the covenant that I will make with the House of YisraEL after those days, says YAHveh: I will put My Torah in their minds, and write it on their hearts; and I will be their ELohim, and they will by My people. "No more shall every man teach his neighbor, and every man his brother, saying, 'Know YAHveh,' for they all shall know Me, from the least of them to the greatest of them, says YAHveh. For I will forgive their iniquity, and their sin I will remember no more"* (**JER 31:31-34**). The renewed covenant will supersede the old. This renewed covenant will contain a renewed Torah with no curse because there is no longer a debt to be paid for sin. The old covenant was based on a Torah that relied upon total obedience in order to receive salvation. That total obedience has been achieved by the Messiah, who has offered His own blood as the payment for our sins, thereby canceling the debt.

At this point, the writer begins to explain the articles of worship, their location within the Mishkahn, and their significance in approaching YAH's presence. You will find the explanation of these articles in Chapter Two of this book. Only Levitical priests were allowed to approach its entrance and were required to bring certain articles as sacrifices. Our High Priest, Yeshua, now makes our way clear with a better sacrifice. All of these things were written down as a testament of promise for us as heirs. But we cannot become heirs until the death of the testator. The Messiah Yeshua came down as YAHveh in the flesh in order to explain the testament more clearly to us and then, being the testator, to die in order for us to inherit the promise. The first covenant was sealed with the shed blood of certain innocent animals, symbolizing that a sacrificial life had to be offered as the propitiation for unintentional sins—the only offering for blatant sin was the death of the perpetrator himself. *"So Mosheh came and told the people all the words of YAHveh and all the judgments. And all the people answered with one voice and said, "All the words of which YAHveh has said we will do." And Mosheh wrote all the words of YAHveh. And he rose early in the morning, and built an altar at the foot of the mountain, and twelve pillars according to the twelve tribes of YisraEL. Then he sent young men of the children of YisraEL, who offered burnt offerings and sacrificed shalom offerings of oxen to YAHveh. And Mosheh took half the blood and put it in basins, and half the blood he sprinkled on the altar. Then he took the Scroll of the Covenant and read it in the hearing of the people. And they said, "All that YAHveh has said we will do, and be obedient* (this was an oath of betrothal)." *And Mosheh took the blood, sprinkled it on the people, and said, "Behold, the blood of the covenant which YAHveh has made with you according to all these words"* (**EXOD 24:3-8**). A sacrifice was needed to pay the price for the people's former sins, and only something or someone innocent (without sin) could pay it. Our Messiah became this once-and-for-all sacrifice for those who believe in Him and await His return to collect His inheritance and ours. The things that were sacrificed previously were just a shadow of the heavenly things promised and could never cleanse us or pay for our sins, but our belief in His Messiah can wash us clean and will sanctify us for the better things promised. These other things were done year after year only to remind us of the Promise of the One to come. But the Messiah said through the words of King Dahveed, *"Sacrifice and offering You did not desire; My ears You have opened; burnt offering and sin offering You did not require; Then I said, "Behold, I come; in the scroll of the Book it is written of Me. I will delight to do Your will, O My ELohim, and Your Torah is within My heart"* (**PSALM 40:6-8**). With this promise being made by the Messiah Himself, He is commissioning the system of the new Torah. He prophesies that He will become the offering, according to His Abba's will. We can now enter the presence of our Abba, being sprinkled in our hearts with His blood and washed in the pure water of the words of His Ruach.

The writer goes on to exhort his readers to continue in this truth and to keep reminding each other of this promise. They should not fail to pray for or to minister to one another. They are to continue to assemble as one Kahal of YisraEL—especially as the "Great Day" approaches.

He speaks briefly of his own imprisonment. This statement is why some believe that it was Rav Shaul who wrote this letter. However, this can't be a certainty because Kefa, as well as many others, had suffered the same demise and were in chains for their boldness in proclaiming the "Good News". He speaks of both the judgment and the punishment of those who reject the writings of Mosheh, as well as those who count the blood and death of the Messiah as a small thing. He refers to those who willfully sin and points to their destiny. A willful sin is one deliberately committed and never repented of. This type of sin carries with it both consequences and judgment—unlike sins that are repented of, which carry only consequences. YAHveh said regarding this, *"Vengeance is Mine, and recompense; their foot shall slip in due time: for the day of their calamity is at hand, and the things to come hasten upon them.' "For YAHveh will judge His people and have compassion on His servants, when He sees that their power is gone, and there is no one remaining, bond or free"* (**DEUT 32:35&36**). True repentance consists of both recompense and restitution because all sin has either been committed against ELuah or against a neighbor.

He warns his readers not to turn from the revelation that they have received from the Ruach, but to continue in this revelation. *"For the vision is yet for an appointed time; but at the end it will speak and it will not lie; Though it tarries, wait for it; because it will surely come, it will not tarry. "Behold the proud, his soul is not upright in him; but the just shall live by his faith"* (**HAB 2:3&4**).

At this point, he begins to speak about the nature of true faith and what it consists of. He explains that true and consistent faith will produce whatever you are hoping for when it is a part of the plan and purpose of YAH's work in your life. You may not see the end result of your faith immediately, but if you are patient, it will materialize. He continues by explaining how YAH created all things by faith. Before the beginning of time, there was nothing except the invisible Word of YAH, but when He spoke, time and all the elements that made up the universe came into being in an instant. He speaks of the faith of Ahbel and how his sacrifice was more righteous than Kaeen's because it was the life of an innocent lamb and not something from his own labors. He points to Enoch's rapture as the result of his faith because he chose to walk as close to YAH as a man could. *"Enoch lived sixty-five years, and begot Methuselah. After he begot Methuselah, Enoch walked with ELohim three hundred years, and begot sons and daughters. So all the days of Enoch were three hundred and sixty-five years. And Enoch walked with ELohim; and he was not, for ELohim took him"* (**GEN 5:21-24**). The writer points to the fact that this is the type of faith that pleases ELuah—but first you have to believe that He exists, that He is good, and that He loves to reward those who spend their lives seeking to please Him. He goes on to use Noah as another example who, in spite of ridicule and opposition, continued to follow YAHveh's instructions and build a large wooden container to house his family, as well as many different species of animals. Then he continues with the abba of our faith, Avraham, who embarked on a journey to an unknown destination, the land of promise. He continued this journey of faith for many years, followed by both his son, Yitzyak, and his grandson, Yaacov. Avraham's wife, Sarah, also demonstrated this kind of faith when she believed YAH's promise of having a son past her child-bearing years. This miracle nearly parallels that of the future virgin birth of the Messiah. From the seed of this miracle son, Yitzyak, came two nations, YAHuda and Yosef, who would one day become the forefathers of all Believers. Their faith purchased them a place in the Kingdom. They did not see the Messiah and His salvation firsthand, but their descendants, those who put their trust in YAH's words, would.

Some say that the YAHudi who do not believe that Yeshua is the Messiah will not be allowed to enter the Kingdom. I personally believe that if a person who follows the teachings of the Torah both believes and trusts in YAH's promise of a coming Messiah, he will see the Kingdom and the City of YAH. If a person is given all of the facts about Yeshua being the Messiah and still refuses to believe, then he will be subject to YAH's judgment. But if he wasn't given all of the facts, who then would be at fault?

Avraham also displayed his faith in YAH when he offered up his only son as a sacrifice to Him. He remembered and trusted the promise that YAH had given him when he protested YishmaEL's expulsion. *"But ELohim said to Avraham, "Do not let it be displeasing in your sight because of the lad or because of your bondwoman. Whatever Sarah has said to you, listen to her voice; for in Yitzyak your seed shall be called"* (**GEN 21:12**). Then, by faith, Yitzyak blessed both of his sons, Yaacov and Esau, by prophesying what their futures would be. By faith, Yaacov turned the family name over to Yosef and his two sons, Efraeem and Mahnahseh, and by faith, Yosef left instructions that his bones be taken to the Promised Land when they returned. The writer continues his examples of faith by pointing to Mosheh's parents, who hid him from certain death because they knew that he had a place in the history of the Hebrews. Mosheh also knew that he had a destiny greater than being an heir to Pharaoh's kingdom—his eyes were on the Kingdom of the Promised Messiah of YisraEL. Because of this Promise, he offered up the first Passover celebration and then led the children of YisraEL through the Red Sea, bringing about the destruction of the armies of Mitsrahyim. The writer continues his montage of the works of faith by the fathers with Yoshua, Rahab, Gideon, Barak, Samson, Yephthah, Dahveed, SamuEL, and many other Ne'vim and includes all of the miracles in the lives of those of the Promise. They too did not see the Promise come to pass in their time, but they held true and received their reward. But today many of us have seen Him manifested in our hearts, and now we can share these things with others so that they too may participate in this same Promise.

The writer encourages his readers not to lose heart or faith when they are tested. He tells them that the Promised One, HaMashiach, has already endured to the end for their sins and is both the author and the finisher of their faith. They are told to hold fast to the words of YAH regarding their being the sons of the Most High. *"My son, do not despise the chastening of YAHveh, nor detest His corrections; for whom YAHveh loves He corrects, just as an abba the son in whom he delights"* (**PROV 3:11&12**). Our earthly abba disciplines us because he loves us, and we still love and respect him because we know that he does it for our own good. Our Heavenly Abba does the same through circumstances that may at times seem too harsh in order to train us up for the task that we are called to do. Knowing this, we should endure, endure, and endure until the end because the reward is worth it. We should not be like Esau who gave his birthright away to please his belly because he did not consider his inheritance important at the time. When he repented, it was obvious that he was not sincere because he continued to be motivated by his selfishness.

Yeshua HaMashiach has now led us to a new mountain, Mount Zeeon, a mountain of shalom, to receive our new instructions. Mosheh had led the people to Mount Seenahee, where the Voice of YAH caused the people to tremble with fear. *"You shall set bounds for the people all around, saying, 'Take heed to yourselves that you do not go up to the mountain or touch its base. Whoever touches the mountain shall surely be put to death. 'Not a hand shall touch him, but he shall surely be stoned or shot with an arrow; whether man or beast, he shall not live.' When the trumpet sounds long, they shall come near the mountain"* (EXOD 19:12&13). Mosheh said later, *"For I was afraid of the anger and hot displeasure with which YAHveh was angry with you, to destroy you. But YAHveh listened to me at that time also"* (DEUT 9:19). He warns them that if they who heard His voice from the mountain on the Earth and then felt it shake when He spoke were punished for their rebellion, how much more should we who now hear His Voice from the mountain in Heaven expect? *"For thus says YAHveh of hosts: 'Once more (it is a little while) I will shake heaven and earth, the sea and dry land"* (HAG 2:6).

He now closes his letter with a final series of exhortations. He begins by telling them to walk in YAH's kind of love. Be kind to all people because you never know if you are entertaining an angelic being. Do not forget those who have been imprisoned because of their faith. Stay as true to your spouse as Yeshua has been true to you. Be content with who you are and where you are in Him. *"And YAHveh, He is the one who goes before you; He will be with you. He will not leave you nor forsake you; do not fear nor be dismayed"* (GEN 31:8). And remember, *"YAHveh is my light and my salvation; whom shall I fear? YAHveh is the strength of my life; of whom shall I be afraid"* (PSALM 27:1)? He exhorts them to remember the basics of their faith so that they are not led astray by any teaching other than the Torah and to honor those who have been their instructors and overseers. Men change, cultures change, and nations change, but Yeshua's words never change. He is the living epitome of the Torah and is the same yesterday, today, tomorrow, and eternally. He is the final and our only sacrifice. He fulfilled (or filled up) the TaNaKh and everything that was prophesied about Him. Those who believe in His doctrine are now kosher and nothing they can do, outside of denying Him, will change that. But, because we belong to Him, we need to follow all of His instructions in the Torah that remain to be fulfilled (mainly the Kedosh days, Shabbats, and the Feasts) in order to prepare the way for His final restoration at His second coming. He says to offer up the sacrifice of praise, along with your works of faith, and to continue to glorify His name (HaShem) with your life.

Then he reminds them once more about his imprisonment and the fact that he is in Rome. He also mentions the imprisonment of Timothy. These are more reasons why some believe that this letter was written by Rav Shaul.

Conclusion

As I said at the beginning of this chapter, this letter is one of correction and instruction to the Kahal of the Messianic YAHudi. He wants to be assured that they understand that the Torah has been renewed regarding what has been fulfilled with the coming of the Messiah and what remains unfulfilled. He instructs them that works alone will not cut it in their heavenly Abba's eyes. There is no place for animal sacrifices any longer or any difference between kosher and non-kosher—Yeshua has made all things clean. There is no longer a need for the shedding of blood—it has been taken care of once and for all. These ordinances are now just symbolic. They were only in force until the Messiah came—now they are but shadows. The Feasts are now to be celebrated as memorials or as rehearsals to prepare us for His second coming and are to be practiced as a form of worship to YAHveh.

CHAPTER 26

...about John's Three Letters to the Kahal and the Revelation Given to Him by Yeshua

Four of Yeshua's shelichim saw Him from four different perspectives and wrote the Gospels accordingly. Matthew (MattatiYAH) saw Yeshua as King of kings, the King of YisraEL, and the Lion of YAHuda. Mark (Yochanan Markus) saw Him as the Suffering Servant. Luke (Lucas) saw Him as the Son of Man, who was as much a man as He was Eluah. But Yochanan, the talmid Yeshua loved the most, saw Him mostly as the Son of ELuah—Eluah in the flesh. It is from that perspective that he wrote his "Good News" account of Him. Now he writes four different letters to the Kahal of YisraEL in the capacity of being an original shelichim.

I Yochanan

He began his Gospel account by writing *"In the beginning was the Torah, and the Torah was with ELohim, and the Torah was ELohim. He was in the beginning with ELohim"* (JOHN 1:1&2). Therefore, it is no surprise that he also begins his first letter to the Kahal of YisraEL in this same manner. He not only describes Yeshua as being the Creator of all things, He also compares Him to light. To be able to walk in that light, a person must be without sin—anyone claiming that they have no sin is a liar. But Yeshua has provided a way to be cleansed of sin. He has also provided a way to have fellowship with Him, walking in that light.

Yochanan begins to address his readers as his little children. He does this because he is speaking as the voice of Yeshua, our Advocate and the Savior for the whole world. Yochanan emphasizes that the one and only sign that they are truly walking in His light and having fellowship with Him is if they know and keep His Torah. He says this is nothing new—it was taught to them from the beginning. It was the only training manual that was used by their Rabboni, Yeshua and Mosheh. The only thing new is that the curse from the original Torah has been eliminated. Now they are empowered by the Ruach of ELohim to love both YAHveh and their brother with YAH's kind of love. If any man says he hates his brother, he is still in darkness and is still blind. Those who hate their brothers still love the world and its lusts. The world will pass away and so will everyone who still loves it. He says that whoever walks in the light of Yeshua hates the world and all that it stands for. He addresses his readers as young men or fathers, but more often as children because this is how their heavenly Abba sees them. He reminds them that their sins have been forgiven. He tells them that they have truly come to know Him, who was from the beginning, and that they have overcome the wicked one.

Yochanan warns them that the time is short because the Antimessiah is coming soon. He says that they already know and recognize the attributes of those who are antimessiahs (teachers of the Torah who reject Yeshua as HaMashiach) because they have already come and gone. He says that they are the ones who have come and then, after finding out that they must give up their love for the world and its lusts, turn away. But those who believe that He is the promised Messiah have their eyes opened, through the anointing of the Ruach HaKedosh, to the truth of the Torah and to all of its blessings that were purchased for them by Him. It is this Torah truth that they must abide in no matter what because it is what will give them eternal life, as long as they never turn away from it. This truth will also reveal to them *all* the rest of the mysteries that lie within the TaNaKh.

This truth separates us from the world and its temptations of lust and will abide in us until His coming if we abide in it. This abiding will comfort us until His coming and will assure us that we are born-again and are the children of YAH. How wonderful a thing to know that YAH has loved us so much that He gave His Son that we might be called His children. This truth purifies us and makes us like Him, and when He returns, we will become exactly like Him in every way.

Once we begin to abide in Him, we become completely sinless because He cleanses us from all sin. If we should stumble, He will forgive us if we ask Him, and He will count it as though we were without sin. Those who sin are those who either do not know or do not understand the Torah—since we both know and understand the Torah, we have no sin. Those who sin remain sons of the evil one, hasatan, but we are the sons of the Living ELohim, who is also the Living Torah. The Living Torah, Yeshua, came and destroyed the works of hasatan, which made it possible for us to become born of ELohim and made sinless. Some Believers may have been ignorant of the proper ordinances of the Torah, but if they have been following the teachings of Yeshua, they are abiding in the principles of the Torah because Yeshua taught from the Torah. But once they have become enlightened, they are expected to heed those principles.

To be loved as a son by ELohim is to be hated by the world. The world is under the power of hasatan, who hates us and desires to destroy us. But since we are loved by YAH and are under His power, hasatan has no power over us. As it was said in the beginning of the first book of the Torah, Kaeen hated his brother Ahbel and murdered him because he had no love for his brother. If you are one of YAH's children, you will love your brother. YAHuda should love Yosef, and Yosef should love YAHuda—there should be no division between them. When we love our brother, we should be willing to lay our life down for him. When we love our brother, we should be willing to sell all of our material possessions and come to his aid whenever he is in need. But remember, **our brother** is of the household of YAH and not of hasatan or the world. *"But Yeshua said to him, "Follow Me, and let the dead bury the dead"* (**MATT 8:22**). If our words sound loving but our deeds prove otherwise, the love of YAH does not abide in us.

No one can condemn us, not even ourselves. If we doubt ourselves, be assured that YAH has not forgotten us—that is, if we love His words and live by them. When we abide in Him, He abides in us. He gives us the gift of His Ruach, who dwells in us and empowers us to walk in Him. How can we know if His Ruach is dwelling within us? We can by putting it to the test. If we can confess Yeshua as truly being HaMashiach and that He is YAHveh in the flesh, then we know that His Ruach is within us. By the way, every ne'vee who comes in His Name must be able to pass this same test or he is not to be believed. All who deny His Name are of the spirit of the antimessiah. When His Ruach dwells within you, you are over-comers because His Ruach is greater than the spirit of the antimessiah, who dwells within those who are still under the sinful influence of the world system. Those who are under that influence will not receive the testimony of the "Good News", but those who are known by ELuah will do so gladly. We can use this test to discern those who are being drawn to Him.

A second way to discern those who have a heart for ELuah is if they have compassion and tenderness for YAH and His children. If there was only one word that could describe YAHveh, it would be *"Love"*—He is *"Love"*. Those who abide in His *"Love"* abide in Him, and His *"Love"* is expressed in their love for their brethren. His kind of *"Love"* has power over fear. When we have His kind of *"Love"*, we can endure to the end, knowing that we have the hope of eternal bliss; those who are not of Him or His *"Love"* have only the promise of eternal torment. If we do not have love for the brethren who are daily before us, we cannot have love for Him who is invisible. We are given the opportunity to express our love for Him by knowing, understanding, and obeying His commandments. But first we must know what His expectations are through practicing His commandments and by celebrating His Sabbaths, New Moons, and Feasts. His commandments are not limited to the ten that He gave from Mt. Seenahee—they are only the beginnings of His instructions. Remember, there are a total of six hundred and thirteen. Our lives should express these commandments in one form or another. Knowing and practicing these commandments will determine the extent of our reward in eternity. Those who neglect the greater reward will find themselves agonizing at what they could have had if they had just sought the Kingdom of ELohim more thoroughly. There will be weeping and gnashing of teeth.

When these commandments are kept, we become witnesses to the fact that Yeshua is the one whom the TaNaKh prophesied about. He had to come by water and by blood (natural birth) and also by the Ruach (supernatural birth). By these, the water and the blood, the Ruach bears witness to His Messiahship in the "visible" realm. There are three in the "invisible" realm who bear the same witness: our heavenly Abba—His Son, the Living Torah—His Ruach HaKedosh. They make up what has been referred to as the Kedosh Trinity. They become our heavenly witness, which is far above the witness of mere men. It becomes very simple because he who has the Ruach dwelling inside of him has both the Abba and His Son there also. These three bear witness that he is a new creature born of YAHveh and not just of man. They also bear witness that he has eternal life.

Yochanan closes his first letter by affirming that when you know Him, Yeshua HaMashiach, and His words from the beginning to the end of the TaNaKh, you will know His Abba as your own. You will also have the Ruach within you to teach and guide you on how to live your life in the spiritual realm. You will learn the voice of your Abba, and when you ask anything in His Son's Name, you will not be asking amiss. Instead, you will be asking from your spirit, and it will be granted to you so that you may complete the task for which you were created.

When brethren fall into sin because of the weakness of their flesh, those who are mature in spirit should lead them back into salvation. At the same time, he reminds them that if a brother willfully walks away from YAH's instructions and returns to living in the flesh, he may have no further hope. He must be left in the hands of the Abba because only He knows whether or not future events in his life will re-open his eyes to the truth. It is a personal responsibility for those who have been born-again of the Ruach to keep from sinning. If they stumble, they must return through repentance. If they repent, they will be forgiven as though the sin had never taken place. Therefore, if you remain born of YAH, you have no sin because sin will no longer have a hold on you. The best way to avoid sinning is not to mingle with the world or its temptations because it is ruled for now by the evil one, hasatan.

II Yochanan

Yochanan's second letter is a shorter version of his first and followed soon after. It was apparently directed to the House of the YisraELi Goyim/Yosefs. He begins his greeting by referring to them as the Elect Lady (or betrothed of the Messiah) and Her children (those who are maturing in their faith). He reminds Her to exhort the children to remain in the Torah continually so that they may be built up in their faith. He tells Her to hold on to the key of the Torah, which is to love ELohim with all their heart, strength, and mind and to love their neighbor as themselves. He warns them to be aware of the antimessiahs who lurk about. He also warns them of the possibility of losing their first love, the Torah. If they do, they may find themselves neglecting its teachings and forgetting about their Messiah. If they forget what their Messiah has done for them, they will stand in danger of falling back under the curse of the Torah. If they fellowship with any of those who deny Yeshua's Messiahship, they are also in danger of participating in their evil deeds.

He closes by telling them that he hopes to be able to fellowship with them soon. He also sends greetings from Her Elect Sister (the YAHudi Messianics).

III Yochanan

Yochanan addresses his third letter to a fellow YAHudi by the name of Gaius. He begins by blessing him to be prosperous and to enjoy good health, according to the strength of his faith. This is a blessing that we should all bestow upon one another.

He commends him for treating both his brethren and strangers with equality of love. This is an excellent example of Yeshua's love for all mankind. By setting such an example, he has enabled the brethren to minister to others completely out of their own substance and without any assistance from the Goyim who are around them.

He speaks of a fellow believer, Diotrephes, who had fallen away because of greed and a covetous heart and who speaks evil of all those who are trying to follow Yeshua's teachings. Yochanan promises to confront this individual the first chance he gets in order to turn him back to Yeshua if possible. This kind of evil does not come from anyone who knows YAH. He exhorts them to follow Demetrius' example instead because he is true and obedient to Yeshua's instructions.

He then closes this letter in the same way that he did his second by saying that he hopes to see them soon in person and reminding them to be sure to greet one another with love.

Revelation (Also Known as the "Apocalypse of Yochanan")

Yochanan, like most of the other shelichim, was concerned over the possibility that the Kahal of the Goyim/Yosefs might fall back under the curse of the Torah and annul the atonement that Yeshua had provided for their sins. His concern may have been deeper than the other shelichim because he felt a greater responsibility toward his Messiah. He had been with Yeshua at every major event of His ministry. Then too, maybe it was because Yeshua had shared a special closeness with Yochanan—one that He never had with His own brothers and sisters. He even seemed to trust Yochanan's sense of responsibility because He had given him His own mother to care for. Whatever the reason, he was the one Yeshua chose to reveal the events that would lead up to the final chapter for both the people of the world and the Earth itself.

Yeshua came to Yochanan in seven visions to reveal His final revelation to him for the entire Kahal, which Yochanan referred to as the seven kahal of Asia. Why Asia? It was because Asia represented the kahal of the Goyim where the descendants of the ten tribes of YisraEL were hidden (the lost sheep of YisraEL). The kahal of YAHuda already understood the teachings of the Torah and the TaNaKh—it was the kahal of Yosef/Efraeem/YisraEL who remained ignorant. Yeshua's commendations and admonishments weren't confined to just these seven kahal—they were meant to include all of His Kahal—even up to our present day.

The First Vision

Yochanan begins by sending greetings to the seven kahal in Asia from YAHveh, Yeshua HaMashiach, YAH's Son and firstborn from the dead and ruler over the kings of the Earth, and also from the seven Ruach who are before the throne of YAH. He announces that Yeshua will be returning by the way He left—within clouds (clouds of Believers). This will be a witness to all the inhabitants of the Earth, including those who refused to believe Him and those who were responsible for His being pierced. When He returns, Yeshua's first words will be: *"I AM the Aleph and the Tav* (Hebrew for the *Alpha and the Omega*), *the Beginning*, or Beginnings ("Genesis" in the Greek or "Barasheet" in the Hebrew), *and the End, who is and who was and who is to come, the Almighty* (YAHveh)".

Yochanan explains that he was a prisoner for his faith on an island called Patmos when he received this revelation. He says that he was in the Ruach on the Sabbath, which more than likely means that he was in the process of praying and worshiping YAHveh. Suddenly, he heard the Voice of YAH sounding like a shofar blast—similar to what the children of YisraEL must have heard at Mt. Seenahee. He heard within that sound the same words that Yeshua will probably use when He makes His announcement at His second coming. The Voice then told Yochanan to write letters to the seven kahal of Asia, and He named them: Ephesus, Smyrna, Pergamos, Thyatira, Sardis, Philadelphia, and Laodicea.

Yochanan turned around to face the direction from which the sound was coming and saw a figure standing in the midst of what appeared to be a giant menorah with its standard seven branches. The image that Yochanan saw was probably like the menorah that stood within the House of YAHveh and like the one that Mosheh was given instructions to design for the Mishkahn. The figure that he saw was a man glowing and shimmering and dressed in fine linen and gold. He looked like both a priest and a king who resembled Yeshua, similar to how he remembered Him when he saw Him transfigured on the mount nearly fifty years ago. His hair was white and He had piercing eyes. He spoke with a very authoritative and compelling voice. In His right hand of power, there were seven glowing objects that appeared to be stars. An image of a two-edged sword came out of His mouth when He spoke. The imagery was so overwhelming that Yochanan lost His physical strength and fell down at the feet of this figure. The Voice coming from the figure identified Himself as being both YAHveh and Yeshua (the Echad). He was instructed to write down what he was seeing, including all of the visions that he would be receiving in the future. Then the Voice explained the symbolism of the images that he had just witnessed. The seven branches on the Menorah represented the Kahal of YisraEL, and the seven star-like objects represented the guardian angels who watch over the Kahal.

Notice that He begins each letter to the seven kahal by introducing Himself in terms that identify Him as being the Triune Echad of ELohim. He then closes each by exhorting the reader to listen closely to what is being said. If they do, they will understand that this is part of the process that has been used by YAHveh down through the ages—it's called *progressive revelation*. YAHveh used this method to speak through all of His Ne'vim and Shelichim. Those who have rebelled have had their eyes and ears stopped up to spiritual revelation and understanding since the Beginnings. Now He is ready to reveal these mysteries, when the appropriate time comes, to those who seek His Kingdom in spirit, truth, and humility.

His first letter was to the kahal at Ephesus, where Rav Shaul had spent a great deal of time trying to keep the Goyim Believers from returning to pagan practices and the YAHudi Believers from placing themselves back under the curse of the Torah. Yeshua commends them in their struggle to keep out the false teachers, the Nicolaitans, who taught that Yeshua wasn't really YAHveh in the flesh. They also taught that promiscuousness and indulgence would not be counted against them because they were free from the curse. But He admonishes them for falling away from properly practicing the ordinances of the Torah by substituting their spiritual principles with those of ordinary men. He tells them to return to their first love, the Torah, and warns them that if they don't, He will no longer consider them to be a part of His Kahal. These admonishments not only applied to them but also to anyone in the future who might follow their example.

His second letter was to the kahal at Smyrna. He commends them for their perseverance in not submitting to the trials and testing that has come their way. He commends them for resisting the YAHudi who have tried to put them back under the curse of the Torah with their teachings. He refers to those who have tried to do this as being non-YAHudi and members of the synagogue of hasatan instead. He encourages them not to give in to these lies. If they resist, they will receive the crown of life for their faithfulness.

His third letter was to the kahal at Pergamos. He admonishes them for compromising with the false teachings of both the Nicolaitans and the false ne'vee, Balaam, who have raised their ugly heads in their midst. Their doctrines taught that they could pick and choose the teachings of Mosheh and the Torah and that they could socially mix with those outside of their beliefs, which have led some into succumbing to sexual immorality (See Chapter Three). Those who do nothing but look the other way when these perversions arise are just as guilty as those who commit these same evils. Then He tells those who have held fast to His Name, even when strong persecution came their way, that they will have His mysteries revealed to them. He promises them that all who have stayed faithful to His teachings throughout their lives will one day be presented with a white stone (we are all a part of the living stones that make up His House). On each stone will be a special name for that person. I believe that these stones will be like the stones that were worn on the breastplate of the high priest and the stones that the judge, Yoshua, piled up in the middle of the Yarden River—there will be inscribed on them one of the names of the twelve tribes to which that person has been assigned as a descendant.

His fourth letter was to the kahal at Thyatira. He condemns them for the corruption that they have allowed to come within their kahal. The rebellious and adulterous spirit of Yezebel, who preaches sanctification but practices immorality, He condemns to destruction. All who continue in these practices will suffer the same judgment unless they repent. Those who have been faithful to Yeshua's teachings will not be included under that curse. Instead, they will be given power over the nations to judge those who have rebelled, just as it was given to Him. *"Ask of Me, and I will give You the nations for Your inheritance, and the ends of the earth for Your possession. You shall break them with a rod of iron; You shall dash them in pieces like a potter's vessel'"* (**PSALM 2:8&9**).

His fifth letter was to the kahal at Sardis. He tells them that they think they are alive in the Ruach, but in all actuality, they are dead. They have looked away from the original teachings and instructions and are wandering aimlessly toward destruction. He tells them to watch for Him and warns them not to remain in a spiritual state of slumber, or when He comes, they will be overtaken by surprise, just as a thief overtakes his victim in the middle of the night. To watch for Him is to know and understand the TaNaKh. To forget its teachings will cause them to become numb to sin and complacent to wickedness. Those who fall asleep to its truths will not know what hour it is, and they will be left behind when the Great Shepherd gathers His sheep. Only those among them who are faithful will be counted as worthy and will not have their name blotted out from the Scroll of Life.

His sixth letter was to the kahal at Philadelphia. Yochanan was told to write and tell them that Yeshua is quite aware of their faithfulness. He confirms to them that He possesses the key of Dahveed (true kingship) and has opened the door that will lead them to true fellowship with Him. No man will be able to shut it because it is open and held open by the power of His Ruach. He promises that one day even those of the synagogue of hasatan, who thought that they were true YAHudi but were not, will come to learn the true identity of the Messiah from them. It will be those who have kept both the faith and the truth undefiled who will be kept safe during the tribulation period and will not suffer loss. He also promises them that they who hold fast to His teachings of the TaNaKh and overcome the temptations of the prince of this world are guaranteed to hold a place like a pillar in the heavenly House of YAH and will have written on their foreheads His Name, His Abba's Name, and the name of the New YAHrushalayim.

His seventh and final letter was to the kahal at Laodicea. He admonishes them for being on the fence about their commitment to His instructions. He says that they are neither cold like Sardis nor hot like Philadelphia—they are only lukewarm. Hot springs are good for bathing and cold springs are good for quenching thirst, but a spring that is lukewarm is only good for spitting out. The kahal of Laodicea are like the majority of those in the Church today who say, "If I'm warm, fed, and comfortable, that's all I need—I would rather not rock the boat". But Yeshua says that anyone who has that attitude is really quite miserable and poor and isn't even aware of it. He then offers a simple solution—*repent*. He says that He stands at the door and knocks. If they open it, He will come in, break bread, and have fellowship with them, but it depends upon their taking the initiative. Then and only then will they find true joy. Then they will be able to take part in His Kingdom and become overcomers of the enemy of their souls. They will also be able to come and sit down at His throne, along side of Him and His Abba.

The Second Vision

In Yochanan's second vision, he sees an open door leading into the third heaven, where there is no time and space—the heavenly *"NOW"*. Just as he has been told to do, he writes down what he sees. Those who read his words will have to discern and distinguish between the past, the present, and the future for themselves.

Yochanan is invited to come up and enter through the open door by the Voice of YAH that once again thunders like the blast of a shofar. The Voice declares that in this vision he will be seeing things that are yet to come. Yochanan describes the place he has entered as being YAH's throne room and sees One sitting on the throne closely resembling Ezekiel's (YechezkEL's) vision of YAH. But Yochanan also saw twenty-four elders, not angels, wearing crowns and also sitting on thrones. (Elders are men of wisdom, teachers, and shepherds of His flock.) At the same time, there were present the same four living creatures that YechezkEL had described in his vision—a lion, a calf, a man, and an eagle. (These are the same characteristics that are used in the Gospels to describe the Messiah, as well as the description of the four main ministries to the Kahal— see Chapter Fifteen.) The main purpose of these elders and creatures was to exalt, praise, and give glory and honor to His Majesty.

The Person on the throne had a scroll that was sealed with seven seals, reserved for the only one who had the authority to open it. Yochanan grieved over the fact that no one there seemed to have that authority. Then one of the elders spoke up and drew Yochanan's attention to a Lamb who had been slain. It appeared to have all authority because of its seven horns (which stands for kedosh authority) and seven eyes (which stands for both omnipotence and omnipresence). The Lamb came and took the scroll and began to break the seals. The elders and the four living creatures immediately fell down before Him with harps and golden bowls of incense that represented the prayers of Believers, and they began singing a new song. Joining in with them were angels and Believers too numerous to count. Then all of creation joined in to worship the Lamb.

When the Lamb broke the first seal, the first living creature (the lion) directed Yochanan's attention to the appearance of a rider on a white horse going out into all of the Earth to conquer it in order to bring about salvation and redemption. The second seal was broken and the second living creature (the calf) directed his attention to another rider on a red horse going out to spread sin and wickedness. The third seal was broken and the third living creature (the man) directed his attention to a rider on a black horse going out to spread famine and plagues. The fourth seal was broken and the fourth living creature (the eagle) directed his attention to a rider on a pale horse bringing final judgment upon the wicked. One fourth of all the Earth will be affected by this rider in the final days. So, one fourth of the Earth is to experience the wrath of YAH because of their rebellion. Where do we see these things beginning to happen in one fourth of the Earth today? The Middle East and Asia make up about one fourth of the Earth. Isn't this where we are seeing these events beginning to unfold? This vision represented what would take place over the history of time, but in the last days, its focus will be on one fourth of the Earth.

When the fifth seal was broken, he heard the voices of the Believers who had been martyred crying out for justice for their suffering. They were told to wait awhile longer until the number of all who were to be martyred for their testimony was completed.

When the sixth seal was broken, Earth, along with the cosmos, began to be shaken and catastrophic events commenced, escalating beyond anything like it in its history and causing mankind to tremble. The sun was covered with darkness, and the moon looked red in the night sky. Hail, fire, and plagues, like those that took place in Mitsrahyim, began to happen throughout the Earth. Men began to fear the outcome, with some even calling upon the Name of YAH for His help—judgment had begun upon the Earth.

The Third Vision

In the third vision, Yochanan sees four angels who represent the four corners of the Earth (east, west, north, and south), standing at the ready to bring judgment upon it. They were told by another angel to refrain from their assignments until after the Whole House of YisraEL had received their mark from YAHveh upon their heads (this is a metaphor meaning that they have had all the mysteries of YAH regarding the full understanding of His Torah revealed to them). The number of those who were to be sealed was 144,000, which is 12,000 from each of the twelve tribes of YisraEL (this may not be an exact number, but it means all of those Believers who have received the white stone that identifies their assigned heritage). This 144,000 will be His inner circle, just as His twelve talmidim were before His crucifixion.

The Fourth Vision

In the fourth vision, Yochanan saw another multitude. They too were dressed in white, carried palm branches, and stood before the Lamb, confessing salvation in YAHveh and His Son, Yeshua. He was told by one of the elders that these were the ones who had been delivered out of the great tribulation (persecution of Believers). Now the Great Shepherd, Yeshua, would relieve them from all of the pain that they had endured by comforting them with a clear understanding of all Scripture. Now they would come face to face, and now they would know what He knows because He would completely lift the veil from their ignorance.

Then he saw the seventh seal broken and seven angels standing before the throne of ELuah. They were given seven shofars (this was the official trumpet of YAH, like the ones heard at Mt. Seenahee) to announce YAH's wrath upon the Earth. During this vision, Yochanan recalled what he had seen in his second vision, when the Earth and the cosmos were shaken and hail and fire rained down upon the Earth. Now he was witnessing what triggered that firestorm. He saw an angel with a golden censer that was filled with incense representing the prayers of all Believers. Because of these prayers, the angel took some fire (YAH's wrath), filled the censer, and threw it to the Earth.

At the same time, the first angel sounded its shofar, and the fire came down and burned up one third of the Earth. Scientifically speaking, this could be caused by the Earth entering either a comet's tail or a giant band of asteroids. The one-third area could include the two continents of Europe and Asia, along with the Middle East, because this is where hasatan has warred with YAHveh ever since his rebellion in the beginning.

The second angel sounded its shofar, and what appeared to be a giant meteor, asteroid, or comet struck the Earth's ocean. Now one third of the fish die, and one third of commerce in the shipping industry of the world is disrupted—perhaps the oil coming from the Middle East.

The third angel blew its shofar, and Yochanan saw a star fall from heaven, burning with fire. This star seemed to have demonic forces accompanying it since it had the name of Wormwood. It may have accompanied the cosmic bombardment, bringing with it pollutants and poisons that contaminated one third of the rivers and springs of the Earth, causing death to many.

The fourth angel sounded its shofar, and the light from the sun, moon, and stars are apparently darkened, affecting one third of the Earth for one full day. This could be the aftereffect of the remnants of the particles that were left in the air from the fires and the meteorite strikes. Then another angel made a proclamation that the entire Earth was about to be affected when the remaining shofars are sounded.

When the fifth angel blew its shofar, another star fell. This star is apparently strictly a demonic prince since it is referred to as "him" by Yochanan. This demon, or prince of demons, is able to open the Pit and release what Yochanan describes as locusts that have the power of scorpions. This could be symbolic of some type of deadly plague since it only affects men and not vegetation. It seems to have the authority to affect only non-believers and to last just five months. This plague could be the result of toxic fumes or poisons caused by a series of volcanic eruptions and earthquakes that are further polluting the atmosphere and blotting out the sun and the moon. Then too, because of their overall description, others have offered the theory that these are military gunships, or helicopters, from a world power that are being commanded by the Antimessiah, who has been endowed with the spirit of hasatan.

At the sound of the shofar of the sixth angel, YAHveh speaks and commands the four angels who have been waiting at the Euphrates River to begin killing one third of mankind. Here again, this seems to take place in the area of the Middle East, Asia, and Europe. The description of two-hundred-million warriors could lead to the belief that this was the onset of the battle of Megiddo. In spite of all of these calamities, mankind still had not repented of their wickedness or their worship of things made with their own hands. In other words, they did not recognize that these events were taking place at ELuah's command—they were still depending upon their own technology to deliver them from these catastrophic events.

Then Yochanan saw another angel who, from his description, could have been Yeshua or Michael, the Archangel of YAH, placing His right foot upon the waters and His left foot upon the land. He was holding a small scroll in his right hand and spoke with a Voice of seven thunders. All of these voices originated from the same source, YAHveh. Yochanan was forbidden to write down what he witnessed at that point—they were to be revealed when the seventh shofar had been blown and all of the other events had been completed. Then Yochanan was told by the Voice to go and take the small scroll from the hand of the mighty angel and eat it. He obeyed, and it tasted sweet but made his stomach upset as though he had been poisoned. This seems to suggest that the small scroll contained the events that Yochanan was told not to disclose at that time.

Then he was given a reed to measure the House of YAH. This would indicate that a House for YAH would once more be standing in the city of YAHrushalayim. The surrounding area outside of His House would be governed by the Goyim and not the YAHudi for a period of three and one-half years, or forty-two new-moon phases (Hebrew months). During this time, two men who will represent both houses of YisraEL will appear in YAHrushalayim as YAH's witnesses. These two witnesses were referred to as the two olive trees and the two menorahs (both represent the House of YAHuda and the House of Yosef). These will probably be Mosheh, who represents the Torah and the House of YAHuda, and ELeeYAHoo, who represents the Messiah and the House of Yosef—together they represent the Whole House of YisraEL. Remember, these were also the ones who appeared with Yeshua on the Mount of Transfiguration. They will be given power over nature and power to call down plagues. When their witnessing is completed, the Antimessiah will call upon his demonic powers to have them killed. As a warning to others, their bodies will be left in the streets of YAHrushalayim, which will no longer be considered YAH's city because it will be under the authority of the Antimessiah and his armies. For three and one-half days, the world will rejoice at their death because they brought conviction and shame to its inhabitants. At the end of this time, they will be resurrected and taken up into heaven. The whole world will see, bringing great fear to them. Since there isn't any evidence that either Mosheh or ELeeYAHoo had ever tasted physical death, it makes the probability of their being the two witnesses more likely. At the moment of their resurrection, a great earthquake will split the city into thirds, and one tenth of the city will be destroyed. The Messiah and His court will appear in the heavens, and the judgments of the Earth's inhabitants will begin.

Finally, the seventh angel sounds its shofar, and the entire heavenly host announces His return and the beginning of His reign. The House of YAH in heaven is opened, and the Ark of the Covenant is revealed. The judgments now begin to manifest themselves upon all of those who inhabit the Earth. This is the last trump—the one Rav Shaul referred to when he said the dead in Messiah will rise first, followed by those who have remained and are caught up to meet Adonai in the clouds.

Suddenly, Yochanan has a vision within the vision that appears as a panorama of all of the events that have taken place upon the Earth from its beginning until its end. He sees it in two separate scenarios. In the first, he sees a woman clothed with the sun, the moon under her feet, and a garland of twelve stars on her head. This apparently represents all of the prominent women who were responsible for providing the world with the House of YisraEL and its Messiah—Cheva (Eve), Sarah, Rebekah, Leah, Rahkal (Rachel), and Miriam (Mary). He then sees the image of a red dragon, having seven heads with ten horns and wearing seven crowns, symbolizing the prince of this world (hasatan) and his power within its governments. With his tail, the dragon swept away one third of the stars of heaven (the fallen angels), sending them to the Earth. There, they are kept in chains in the Pit until the time for their judgment (JUDE: 6). Then he, hasatan, sets his sights on the woman to destroy her before she can give birth to her children—YisraEL and the Messiah. But instead, all of his plans are thwarted by YAHveh, and he is forced to try to destroy them at another time. Later, the enemy believes that he has succeeded when he sees the Messiah die on the cross, but he realizes his failure when Yeshua overcomes the power of death and is caught up to the throne of YAH. In his efforts to destroy the woman (who has now become the Kahal of YAH), he wars with her for two-thousand more years. When he again thinks that he is succeeding in destroying her with a plan of persecution and destruction, he sees her being taken away to a wilderness place (a place of protection similar to Goshen), where she stays under YAH's protection until he is finally brought to judgment and imprisonment.

In the second scenario, Yochanan witnesses the very battle that caused hasatan and the rebelling angels to be cast out of heaven in the first place. He saw MichaEL, the Archangel of YAH, overcome the great dragon (hasatan), throwing him down to Earth and away from the presence of YAH. Then Yochanan heard the voices of those who believed on the Messiah as their Savior, singing and praising Him because He had overcome their accuser. They were in Paradise and, like Yochanan, were in a place of perpetual time, where the beginning and the end are the same and they can witness both at the same time. They had been given the power to defeat their enemy and that of their brethren, through their testimony and the power that is found in the blood of their Messiah. They also had been given the responsibility to use their testimony to warn those who did not yet believe in Yeshua about the enemy of ELuah's Creation. The enemy knew that when Messiah's Bride became unified (echad), his time for judgment would soon follow. It was at this time that Yochanan saw the Bride of the Messiah (the Kahal) given wings to take her to the place of protection for a time and times and a half time. Some interpret this as a three-and-one-half-year period of time during which the Bride of Yeshua is taken up (the rapture) to the mansion that He has been preparing for Her since He left two-thousand years earlier. Personally, I see this in millenniums, not in years, and as being the time that YAH has protected the House of YisraEL over the last 3,500 years since Her betrothal to Him at Mount Seenahee.

Yochanan now sees the serpent from the Garden making his first attempt to destroy all of Ahdom's descendants, including Noah and his family (Noah being the one who was carrying the seed of the Messiah from Cheva), with a flood (Remember that it was YAH's flood and YAH's devil.). Instead, they escaped this attempt through faith in YAH's instructions to build an Ark. The serpent (or dragon) thought that he had been successful in bringing about the annihilation of mankind very quickly with this flood. But instead, YAH caused the Earth to swallow up the waters, making new continents, which allowed mankind to survive. The dragon played right into the hands of ELohim, who used this event to establish a new Earth. After that, hasatan's only recourse was to relentlessly war against this woman (the Hebrews) until he achieved his ultimate goal of destroying her. His war against her included his devouring all of her offspring, which meant that he would try to persecute and destroy all believers of the ELohim of YisraEL and His Son until the end.

The visions continued, and Yochanan found himself standing on a beach and seeing a beast (or empire) coming up out of the waters. It had seven heads that contained a blasphemous name and ten horns that had crowns. He compared its appearance to that of a leopard with feet like a bear and a mouth like a lion—three beasts in one. This description is similar to the four beasts that DahneeEL saw in his vision. The beast in Yochanan's vision could be interpreted as being three strong nations or possibly three great religions with a variety of leaders who are held together by a special alliance or treaty. One of these leaders has a near-death experience that seems to help persuade people into pledging him some type of allegiance. He has natural charisma that has its roots in the power of darkness, hasatan. His reign will be accompanied by many signs and wonders that were authorized by his master, hasatan, and will last for three-and-one-half years. Within that period of time, he will have had the ability to sway people's minds into giving him praise and glory over Adonai. His followers will worship him and will persuade others into seeing and treating him as though he were a god (eluah) on Earth. His objective will be to declare war against anyone who opposes him.

Then Yochanan sees another beast (empire) coming up out of the earth. It has two horns, and he describes it as being like a lamb with a voice of a dragon. It has influence over the peoples of the Earth and uses that influence to get the people to give special honor and allegiance to the governmental power of this new-world leader. This more than likely represents a dominant world religion. There are only three predominant religions known on this Earth—Islam, YAHudaism, and Christianity. There is a fourth, but it is a neo-religion that is known as secular humanism. This is the belief that each individual is responsible for their own destiny and that their faith is only in themselves—they are their own god. It has been around for centuries but in many different forms. In modern times, it has taken some theology from the main three, mixed it with eastern theology, and called itself the "New-Age" movement. The likelihood of one or even all four of these spiritual influences playing some part in this end-time religion is highly probable. Great signs will accompany this religion and its leaders. These signs will have their origin within the powers of darkness. Their manifestations will be for the purpose of influencing those who are ignorant of the words of YAHveh and His Torah.

It seems that another predominate leader will immerge—a spiritual leader who is a false ne'vee. Allegiance to these two leaders will become so demanding that anyone not subscribing to it will be considered as lawbreakers. However, those who obey the laws and ordinances that are legislated by these leaders will be given some type of an identity mark, which will numerically equate to the name of the Antimessiah—666. Many have speculated as to the meaning of this *"number of his name"* and have developed theories accordingly. Let me interject mine. Throughout His Scriptures, YAH has used the number six to designate man and the number three to identify His Holy *"Echad"*—thus, three sixes. Therefore, the most obvious conclusion would be that the Antimessiah's number would represent the epitome of secular humanism—man believing that he is his own god. So this Antimessiah will consider himself to be a god and a ruler over mankind's destiny. Now, whether this mark is observable or not is subject to speculation. According to Scripture, the phrase "marks on the hand or the forehead" usually symbolizes a dedication and allegiance to a certain set of instructions and ordinances that result in a covenant relationship between oneself and a higher authority.

Yochanan's attention is suddenly drawn to Mt. Zeeon, where he sees the Lamb of YAH. Accompanying Him are the 144,000 from all of the tribes of YisraEL who have the "number of the Name of YAH" written on their foreheads—777. They are in the presence of the twenty-four elders and the four living creatures, who are singing a special song that expresses praise and adoration to the heavenly Abba. They are referred to as being virgin and not being defiled with women. Describing them as being virgin identifies them as being the Virgin Bride of the Messiah. Not being defiled with women describes their faithfulness for not prostituting themselves to or being prostituted by other religions, as did the House of YAHuda and the House of YisraEL while they were under the curse of the first seven covenants.

Then three angels appear who represent the *"Echad'* of ELohim. The first, representing the declaration of the "Good News", commands all who are present to acknowledge YAHveh as the Creator of all things, including time and space. Then the second angel declares judgment upon the false ne'vee, who he calls *"Babylon"*. Babylon is the name of the spirit of Nimrod that has lived in the hearts and minds of all of those who have rebelled against YAH since the flood. The third angel declares to all who are present that swift judgment will fall upon those who have pledged their allegiance to these two perverse leaders instead of to YAHveh. They also will receive the same punishment as the two leaders, which will be eternal banishment from YAHveh (being tormented by fire and brimstone means to be separated from YAH). At this point, a Voice coming out of heaven declares that all who hear these prophecies and believe them while holding fast with patience will be made happy because of their knowledge of their redemption and the promise of their inheritance in eternity.

Then Yochanan saw Yeshua sitting on a cloud, wearing His crown and carrying a sickle in preparedness for the harvesting and ingathering of the redeemed souls for the restoration of YisraEL. He was waiting for both His Abba's timing and His command when an angel arrived to tell Him to begin the process. Then two more angels appear—one with a sickle and the other with the power and authority to gather in those who were left after the first harvest. These were gathered for the judgment of YAHveh's wrath that would take place outside of the great city of YAHrushalayim.

Yet another sign appears to Yochanan—seven different angels carrying the last seven plagues that represent the wrath of YAHveh. He also sees and hears the 144,000 singing the "Song of Mosheh" while standing on a sea that looked like glass mingled with fire. This sign represents the Judgment Seat of the Messiah.

The Fifth Vision

In Yochanan's fifth vision, he watches as the Heavenly House of YAH is opened and the seven angels with the plagues emerge. As one of the four living creatures gives seven vials to the angels, smoke fills the House of YAH and a Voice comes out of heaven, giving the command to begin pouring out His wrath upon the Earth. The seven vials being poured out upon the Earth seem to parallel the seven shofar blasts that occurred after the seventh seal was broken—the seven shofars usher in the events, while the seven vials usher in YAH's wrath. Both of these are in response to the evil one as he wages his final battle against ELohim, and they seem to occur simultaneously.

The first vial brings sores on everyone who has the mark that identifies their allegiance to the Antimessiah. This seems to indicate something happening in the Earth's atmosphere (the firmament above the waters) that causes a plague to affect only those residing on the one third of the Earth that had experienced the fire and hail when the first shofar blast sounded. Perhaps the meteorite showers that contained the previously mentioned bacteria or radiation triggered the plague (remember that YAH is omnipotent and that He works His miracles and gives His commands within His parameters of physics, both known and unknown).

When the second vial is poured out, it pollutes the sea and causes the death of its creatures. This plague affects the waters (the firmament under the heavens) and parallels the second shofar blast, when one third of life within it died because of what is described as a mountain falling into it.

The third angel causes polluting effects in the rivers and streams when it pours out its vial. Here again, this parallels the blast of the third shofar.

When the vial is poured out by the fourth angel, it affects the bodies of the second heaven, just as the blowing of the fourth shofar affected the sun, moon, and stars. The description of what happens seems to indicate again that the Earth's atmosphere has changed, and now the sun's rays cause physical harm to at least one third of mankind.

The vial of the fifth angel affects only the throne of the Antimessiah and his government. This is the wrath of YAHveh coming down upon this presumptuous and arrogant dictator who dares to touch His kedosh ones. He is the one responsible for the opening up of the Bottomless Pit and releasing all the locusts (demons) of Hell upon the Earth, as described in the blowing of the fifth shofar. Again, this is YAH's wrath coming upon him and his government in response to his rebellion.

When the sixth vial is poured out, the Euphrates River is dried up enough to allow vast armies to come forth and wage war against YAHveh and His armies. The demons from the Bottomless Pit speak words of enticement, which cause the leaders of the world to muster their armies to attack at Megiddo. In the account of the sixth shofar, one third of mankind meets their death here.

Then the seventh vial is poured out, and a loud Voice comes from the House of YAH, declaring that *"it is finished"*. Just as Yeshua had declared the end of His first advent with these very words, He now begins His second. Suddenly, a great earthquake divides YAHrushalayim into three parts, and the mountains and the islands are moved out of place. A rain of hailstones (or meteors) falls upon the Earth, and the great Babylon (or the false religions of the world) meets her judgment.

At this point, one of the angels responsible for the pouring out of the vials (probably the seventh) shows Yochanan a woman sitting upon a red beast that has seven heads and ten horns. She is dressed in red and purple, which means she represents royalty—except she obtained it at the price of the blood of many of the faithful to YAH. She has a name on her forehead identifying her as the "Mother of Harlots". She is found on many waters, symbolizing her influence over all the nations and their leaders through her spiritual guidance. She is the mother of all false religions.

The angel continues to further reveal her identity to Yochanan, who seemed to be overwhelmed at seeing her. The red beast is hasatan who had once manifested himself in Nimrod of Babel, who was the first to falsely claim that he was ELuah on Earth—hence, "he was, but is no more". This was the beginning of the false elohim and ne'veem of the world. Now, in this last hour, hasatan will again manifest himself as Nimrod, only a new one, the Antimessiah—hence, "he was, but is no more, yet is". The seven mountains are where many have built high places for themselves in order to pay tribute to their false elohim. There were seven kings who ruled over these high places—five have fallen, one is, and one is yet to come. The five who have fallen are Assyria, Babylon, Persia, Greece, and Rome. The world power that "is" was ordained by the rest of the world system at the time of the beginning of the shofars and vials. The one "yet to come" will be the one who will also make the claim that he is the Messiah, the ELuah on Earth. He will be the seventh as well as the eighth and final leader of mankind. While he is the seventh leader, he will make an alliance with ten other leaders, just long enough to gain their trust in order for them to transfer their wealth and authority over to him. He will then become the eighth and sole ruler. He will persuade them into helping him overcome all of the spiritual leaders of the false religions in order to set the stage for his claim to be the ELuah of Earth. After all of this, he will become even more bold and arrogant—enough to prepare to make war with the Messiah and His armies at Megiddo.

The Sixth Vision

In this vision, Yochanan sees an angel descending from heaven and proclaiming the fall of Babylon. He also hears the Voice from heaven crying out to those who have yet to renounce her hold on them. They are given one last chance to repent and come out of her system of lies and confess Yeshua as

HaMashiach and Adonai. He reveals to them how she had beguiled them into believing that she was the real thing and how she mixed the principles found in His Torah with the philosophies and theologies of men. But now it is time to renounce her and her false teachings and cling to His truth. She believes her own teachings and claims that nothing will happen to her because she has taught the full truth, but they are lies from the imaginations of men. When she is destroyed by the Antimessiah in just one day, the world will be stunned and devastated. Her wealth will fall with her in one hour, and the repercussions will shake the financial security of the whole world—so much so that the stock markets throughout the entire world will crash as a result. But heaven will rejoice and celebrate because Babylon, the "Great Harlot", has finally fallen, releasing YAH's people from the bondage of her lies.

The Seventh Vision

The seventh and final vision is given to Yochanan as he witnesses the beginning of the marriage supper of the Lamb with all heaven rejoicing. The seven shofars have been sounded, and the seven vials of YAH's wrath have been poured out, which began on the first day, Yom Teruah (Day of Trumpets), of the seventh month, Tishri. The Messiah has made His return to claim His Bride, YisraEL, on the tenth day, Yom Kippur. And for the next five days, Yeshua has taken His position as King of kings to judge the nations at the Judgment Seat of the Messiah (explained in Chapter Nineteen). Now will come Chag Sukkot (Feast of Tabernacles), when Yeshua will consummate His marriage by giving His Bride their resurrected bodies, and they will become One (Echad) with Him. Then He will sit down with Her and begin their eight-day wedding feast.

Then Yeshua appears to him again, looking quite similar as He did in Yochanan's first vision, but this time on a white horse. He also has an army (His Bride), who are mounted on white horses, following Him. They, along with Yochanan, recognize Him as being *"The Word of ELohim"*. On His robe and on a garment (a tallit?) across His thigh were written the words *"King of kings and Adonai of masters"*. He calls for all the birds of prey to come and begin to prepare themselves for a feast on those who will be slain on this coming Day of Judgment. Then the armies of the Antimessiah appear with the leaders who have chosen to follow him. They are then all slain by the sword of His words. Both the Antimessiah and his false ne'vee are captured and thrown into the lake of fire to be tormented for eternity, while the birds of prey feast on the corpses of those who have fallen that day.

Immediately after this, Yochanan sees another angel with a second set of keys in his hands that will again open the Bottomless Pit. He binds hasatan and throws him into the Pit, where he is to be imprisoned during the same period of time that Yeshua is bringing shalom and rest to all the Earth—the seventh millennium. Then he saw all of those who were included in the rapture and in the first resurrection (the five virgins who were ready), along with those who had resisted the persecution and pressures of the Antimessiah to compromise their faith in YAHveh, Adonai (the five virgins who weren't). They were all receiving their just rewards. They are to serve and reign with Yeshua during this entire millennium. According to Scriptures found in the books of the Ne'vim, marriage and family-building will continue by those who resisted the plan of hasatan. But many, because they are still born of the flesh and still have the nature of the natural man, will continue to rebel against the plan of YAHveh Elohenu (the LORD our God). *"I will rejoice in YAHrushalayim, and joy in My people; the voice weeping shall no longer be heard in her, nor the voice of crying; "No more shall an infant from there live but a few days, nor an old man who has not fulfilled his days; for the child shall die one hundred years old, but the sinner being one hundred years old shall be accursed. They shall build houses and inhabit them; they shall plant vineyards and eat their fruit. They shall not build and another inhabit; they shall not plant and another eat; for as the days of a tree, so shall be the days of My people, and My elect shall long enjoy the work of their hands. They shall not labor in vain, nor bring forth children for trouble; for they shall be the descendants of the blessed of YAHveh, and their offspring with them. "It shall come to pass that before they call, I will answer; and while they are still speaking, I will hear. The wolf and the lamb shall feed together, the lion shall eat straw like the ox, and dust shall be the serpent's food. They shall not hurt nor destroy in all My mountains," says YAHveh"* (**ISA 65:19-25**).

At the end of this millennium of shalom, hasatan will be released from his imprisonment, along with his armies, and he will strike the hearts of men to war against Yeshua's authority as King of kings. Rebellious leaders from among the Goyim will gather north of YAHrushalayim to attack it. YAHveh will send down fire from heaven that will destroy all who have come out to make war. At this time, the second resurrection will occur, and all the wicked who have died, along with those of the elect who became redeemed after the tribulation period and during the millennium of the Shalom, will stand before the **"Great White Throne"** for the final judgment. Two scrolls will be opened by YAH, and those whose names are not found in the **"Scroll of Life"**, along with the powers (or angels) of Death, Hell, and hasatan himself, are cast into the lake of fire.

With the seventh millennium coming to a close, Yochanan sees a new heaven and a new Earth being transformed from the old and a "New YAHrushalayim" descending down out of heaven. The final promise is fulfilled, and YAH will now dwell among His people forever. There is no more sorrow or death. Then the seventh angel comes again to Yochanan and takes him to see where the Bride (the Kahal of YisraEL) will dwell. There, he sees the mansion that Her Bridegroom, Yeshua, has built for Her. It is illuminated with the glory of YAH like a precious gem. It has high walls with pearl gates that have the names of the twelve tribes of YisraEL written on them. Only those who were given a white stone with the name of one of the twelve tribes inscribed on it were allowed to enter. Its foundation was laid with twelve of the same kind of gems that were found on the breastplate of the high priest who served in the original Mishkahn. Its inhabitants will be only those whose names were written in the *"Lamb's Scroll of Life"*.

Then Yochanan describes the throne of YAH that stood in the middle of the city of the "New YAHrushalayim". The Gihon River will flow out from under His throne. Alongside of it will be a street, and down its middle and on each side of the river will be growing the "Trees of Life". Each one will produce a new fruit every month of the year. Its leaves will contain healing properties that will sustain this new life. There will be no bodies of water on the Earth, only underground fresh springs. There will no longer be a sun; instead, the Shchinah glory of YAH will light the universe, just as it was in the beginning.

Finally, Yeshua gives His blessings to all who have believed His words and have kept them, reassuring them that He is the Promised One. *"Behold, I AM coming quickly! Blessed is he who keeps the words of the prophecy of this scroll"....."And behold, I AM coming quickly, and My reward is with Me, to give to everyone according to his work. "I AM the Aleph and the Tav, the Beginning and the End, the First and the Last."..."I, Yeshua, have sent My angel to testify to you these things in the Kahal. I AM the Root and Offspring of Dahveed, the Bright and Morning Star."..."Surely I AM coming quickly." Omien.* (**REV** 22:7, 12&13, 16, and 20)

Yochanan has a few last things to share regarding what he has seen, heard, and written. He warns his readers that only those who do YAH's commandments shall share in the right to the tree of life and enter the gates of His city. Anyone attempting to alter or dismiss the prophecies that he has written will be subject to the plagues of the tribulation. They will suffer the loss of their reward and not be allowed to live within the gates of the "New YAHrushalayim". They will also have their name removed from the *"Scroll of Life"*.

Conclusion

Soon after the reign of the Roman Emperor Nero, Emperor Vespasian came into power. He was determined to get things back in order as quickly as he could after the YAHudi uprisings and the suspicious fire in Rome. He immediately began rounding up the prominent leaders of the different YAHudi sects, including the Nazarene sect call the "Way". Yochanan was one of these leaders. He was imprisoned at the island of Patmos until the reign of Emperor Nerva, who freed many who had been imprisoned for what he deemed were minor offenses. Yochanan spent his remaining days at the Kahal of Ephesus, where he brought them the letter that Yeshua had dictated to him. We can only hope that they repented and returned to their first love, the Torah, by honoring and practicing its ordinances and principles again.

During his imprisonment at Patmos, Yochanan received seven visions that revealed the events of the apocalypse that would bring about Adonai's return on the "last day". YAH reemphasized the importance of His pattern of seven throughout Yochanan's writings. In addition to receiving the seven visions, there were the seven letters written to the seven kahal. (Each of the kahal received admonishment that revealed the sins of the Kahal of YisraEL down through the ages and right up to our present day. Their sins consisted of: the loss of their love for the Torah—compromising with the world—corruption—deadness—apathy—promiscuity. He also exhorted them and promised special blessings to those who stayed faithful to Him and to His Word in spite of the persecutions.) There were seven lamps (a menorah) and seven stars (angels). There were the seven "Ruach of YAHveh". And there were the seven seals that revealed the events leading up to the seven shofars and the seven vials. All of these patterns were used to reemphasize the importance of the seventh day of rest, the Sabbath, symbolizing the seventh millennium for our rest in Him.

He also used the number twelve, showing the relevance it had to the restoration of the Whole House of YisraEL. There were twenty-four elders—twelve representing the shelichim and twelve representing the tribes of YisraEL. There were twelve-thousand believers assigned to the twelve tribes, totaling 144,000—they made up the Bride. There were twelve gates to the city of the New YAHrushalayim. There were twelve fruits from the trees of life to feed the inhabitants of the city, one for each of the twelve New Moons (or months) per year.

One final observation—nowhere in Scripture can you find anything indicating that any of the celebrations that YAH had assigned to His people have ceased. Instead, plenty of warnings are given not to change or omit any of His commandments. So why have we? We need to return to the Roots of our Hebrew culture, language, and heritage—besides, all of the rest is just Greek to me!

CHAPTER 27
...about the History of the Church and Christianity Over the Past 2000 Years, Up To and Including the Present

Forty years have passed since Yeshua was crucified, died, and was raised to glory. Yochanan, along with the Messiah's other Shelichim, have been giving their testimony about YAH's promise regarding the coming of the Messiah as already having been fulfilled in Yeshua. During this time, all of those who have heard the "Good News" have been expecting Yeshua's imminent return in order to restore the Whole House of YisraEL to His Kingdom. Yochanan is now the last of the twelve, and he too has been arrested for claiming that Yeshua is the King of the YAHudi. In about 70 CE, the Roman general, Titus, ransacked YAHrushalayim and burned down the Temple that Herod had rebuilt for the YAHudi and their Elohim. Everything was so utterly destroyed that the army was assigned the task of tearing up the very foundation in order to retrieve the gold that had melted and run down to its footers. This fulfilled what Yeshua had said, *"not one stone would be left on top of another"*. Titus saw to it that there wasn't even a trace left for anyone to identify whether or not it had ever existed in order to demoralize the very spirit of the YAHudi. That is why no one can say with any certainty where YAH's House had stood originally. Most of the so-called evidence of its location is purely speculative and not supportive. Eventually, Titus became emperor and was followed by Domitian. Both ruled with an iron rod and brought very heavy persecution to all of the YAHudi, including the Nazarenes. It wasn't until Nerva had become emperor around 100 CE that the majority of the persecution had subsided, and Yochanan was released from prison. He was quite advanced in age by then and spent his final days in Ephesus.

The YAHudi were greatly weakened in their faith after the destruction of the House of YAH and had turned to using local synagogues as its substitute. There could be no atonement for their sins without a House of YAH to bring their sacrifices to, so they attempted to substitute the sacrificial ordinances with prayer and good works. Later, they replicated the Holy of Holies by putting a Torah scroll inside of a cabinet called an *ark* and placing one in each synagogue. This practice continues even to this present day. The priesthood was replaced with the local rabbi, who followed the doctrine of the Pharisees but had no political clout. The Sadducees had lost much of their prestige, the Zealot's and the Herodian's revolt against Rome had subsided due to the persecution, and the Nazarenes had been mostly excommunicated. Rome was surgically and successfully dividing the House of YAHuda.

Since the original shelichim were gone, more Messianics wanted to return to orthodoxy, which even led some to the denial of Yeshua as being the Messiah. The Goyim, because of the persecution of their YAHudi brethren, began to back away from the teachings of the Torah in order to avoid being persecuted themselves. The letters, or epistles, were gathered together and became known as the New Testament, and the TaNaKh became known as the Old. Other writings were kept and were called the extra books, or Apocrypha. There were some who declared that the YAHudi were responsible for Yeshua's crucifixion and claimed that YAHveh had rejected the YAHudi as His children and had substituted them with the *"Church"*. They began to twist the teachings of the shelichim and claimed that the Torah no longer applied because of a New Covenant that had been established by Yeshua. This in turn caused the Messianic YAHudi to separate themselves from the Goyim. The Goyim Believers took on the Greek term "Christian" and vowed to follow only the teachings of Jesus and His apostles and nothing Jewish. Some even stopped following the Hebrew calendar and adopted the Roman's instead. These compromises were the beginning of the reestablishment of pagan practices. (As was said once before, the Roman calendar reflects a pagan-belief system with its months and days named after foreign gods or Roman emperors. For instance, August was named after Augustus, and the month of July after Julius Caesar.) Meanwhile, the YAHudi, in order to protect the TaNaKh further, began to write down all of the oral laws and called it the Talmud. Under all of this persecution and division, the promise of the Messiah restoring the Whole House of YisraEL (YAHuda and Yosef) when He returns became all but dead and forgotten. The hope of this promise would not resurface again for another 1,800 years, when it became the modern day "Jewish" and the "Two-House/YisraELi" Messianic Movement.

The Christians found that the compromising of their teachings did not provide them with any immunity from the persecution because the Romans continued to demand that all citizens of the Roman Empire bow down to the gods of Rome—even Caesar was considered to be a god. Of course, Believers refused this compromise, and their persecution continued even more vigorously. The persecution also continued for the YAHudi, but even more so, and, eventually, they were forbidden to even enter their city, YAHrushalayim. The Hebrew language was outlawed. The Torah scrolls were gathered and burned, and the people were banished from the land and were forced to assimilate into the other nations. The prophecy that all of YisraEL would be scattered throughout the world, including YAHuda, was continually being fulfilled. But to their credit, no matter where they were driven, they never abandoned their commission to keep the Torah alive.

Soon after their dispersion, the role of the visible YisraEL shifted from YAHuda to Yosef. The problem was that Yosef didn't recognize who he was himself because his eyes had been blinded too. He had officially taken on a new name—"The Church". As the teachings of the Torah became less important and as more pagans converted to Christianity, the Church began to acclimate to the traditions of men and further compromise their faith. This was the same path that the YAHudi took during their captivity in Babylon. Still, up until the time of the Emperor Constantine, they continued to keep the appointed feasts—at least Passover. But Constantine's supposed conversion to Christianity changed all of that.

The many emperors who reigned between Nerva and Constantine varied in their attitude toward Christians. The idea that Christian persecution was widespread is incorrect. It depended not only upon who it was that was on the throne, but also who the local magistrates were at the time. Some of the governors and procurators were very tolerant and did not see them as a threat but only an annoyance, while others did. The martyrdom of the Christians varied as well. It became more of a sport than a response to a revolt for them to be thrown to the lions or to become the victims of the gladiators. They were considered to be ghetto trash. They were known as atheists because they refused to worship the Roman gods. Christians were accused of cannibalism and incest because they claimed to partake of the blood and the flesh of their Christ and because they married only those they referred to as "brethren". Because of this, they weren't even considered a part of the human race. Emperors Decius, Valerian, and Diocletian were three of the harshest toward them, while others, such as Gallus, were much more tolerant.

In spite of this, the love that they had for one another could not help but be noticed as the movement of the Ruach continued to change people's lives. The change was so strong that many embraced death rather than denounce their Savior. Christianity began to grow to the point that it dominated the vast of people's spiritual thinking, while the gods of the pagans began to diminish. But history always repeats itself, and false ne'veem and charlatans crept in among the sheep. The idea of the power of the Ruach HaKedosh seemed less and less real to them, while sanctification and redemption were taught to be attainable only through good works instead. It seemed as if all of the redemptive work that Yeshua came to accomplish was put on the back burner, and Christians were beginning to try to earn their salvation by following rules and laws, just like their YAHudi brethren had done.

Two-hundred years had transpired, and the time was ripe for YAHveh's first "Reform" of His people since the resurrection of His Son. YAH's judgment to scatter His people among the nations because of their rejection of both His written and His Living Torah was complete. He was now going to use the Roman Empire to spread the "Good News" of His redemption to all people in all of the nations on the Earth. This would make it possible for anyone who would just believe on His Son's Name and begin to learn to walk by faith and not by sight to receive the gift of eternal life.

Constantine and the First Reform

History records that a man named Constantine became a Roman emperor sometime near 312 CE. His mother, Helena, was a believer in Jesus as the Christ. Constantine's spiritual life, however, consisted first of being a worshiper of Mars, the god of war, then Apollos, and finally Zeus, the sun god, along with Jupiter, his son. Helena had repeatedly tried to convince her son of the reality of the God of the Jews and His Son, Jesus. One day, as the story goes, he found himself in a power struggle with his brother-in-law, Maxentius, over who was to be the next emperor of Rome. A battle between the two was inevitable. When faced with his adversary at the bridge at Milan, Italy, he made a pledge that if he emerged the winner, he would embrace his mother's religion. The night before the battle, he had a dream, and in it, he saw Jesus, who told him that the battle was his. The next morning he had the sign of the Christian's Cross painted on the shields of his soldiers, and they proceeded into battle carrying this as their banner. Now, did Constantine really have this vision, or did he fabricate it? And the painting of signs, or making images, doesn't that smack of pagan superstition? And if the vision itself was real, did it really come from the ELohim of YisraEL?

He did win the battle, and afterward he commanded all persecution of Christians to cease. He also began to close down the pagan temples, and, eventually, he outlawed their rituals and celebrations. But at the same time, he declared the birth of Jesus to be celebrated on December 25th, the day Jupiter (the son of Zeus) was suppose to have been born. He then declared Sunday to be observed as the "Lord's Day", which was also the day of the sun god, Zeus (sun day). Another celebration that he introduced and later was ordained by the bishops of the Church was Easter. Easter was celebrated on the first Sunday after the first full moon that followed the spring equinox. Easter is the English name for Estrus, or Ishtar, the fertility goddess from the Babylonian worship of pagan gods. Passover and the Feast of Firstfruits (the true "Lord's Day") were abolished. Nothing Jewish was allowed to exist. All images of the saints were to have the *sun* displayed behind them as an aurora, or halo, to enhance their personage. All of these changes were to appease the Church leadership in their desire to completely eliminate anything Jewish and, at the same time, to quiet down those who had come out of paganism and still desired their traditional celebrations (another compromise).

WHAT WE WEREN'T TAUGHT ABOUT THE BIBLE AND ITS HISTORY

Constantine transferred some of his political powers to the bishops (overseers) and to the cardinals (the same title that had been given to the priests of their former pagan religions—more compromise). He established a head of the Church called the pontifex maximus, pontiff, papal (Latin for father), or pope. He met with the Church leaders at Nicea and formed the Council of Nicene. They wrote the official creed of the Church known as the Nicene Creed, which was later revised and given a second name, the Apostle's Creed. Five years later, Constantine decided to move the capitol from Rome to Byzantium, which later became Constantinople. This officially made the Roman Empire both an Eastern and a Western Empire with two capitals (the two iron legs of Nebuchadnezzar's edifice). Then he renamed the land of YisraEL and called it Palestine. Other new terms emerged, such as clergy and laity. It was established that the clergy were the only ones who were qualified to interpret the Scriptures—but only those trained in Hebrew, Greek, and Latin could qualify to be clergy. All others had to trust that what they were being taught by the clergy was accurate and true. So, the instructions regarding things such as purgatory, penance, and infant baptism were accepted without question. All of these practices came from, or were related to, or had their origin and roots in pagan doctrine. So, the founder of the Christian Church as we know it today was really Constantine, a Roman Emperor—not Peter or Jesus.

As the Church began to gain more and more political strength, the Roman Empire began to decay from within because of corruption and immorality. In 380 CE, Christianity, after having mingled with so much paganism, became the official state religion of the Roman Empire. In 410 CE, the king of Visigoth, Alaric, invaded Rome and ransacked the city for three days. For the first time in 800 years, the city of Rome fell into the hands of a foreign power. Then, in 476 CE, the Roman Empire ended. The Empire may have fallen, but the idea of its form of democracy (democracy of the Greeks mixed with the republic of the Romans) continued in one way or another throughout history.

I would like at this time to reflect back to the dream that King Nebuchadnezzar had, which was interpreted by the Ne'vee DahneeEL in Chapter Fourteen of this book. In his dream, Nebuchadnezzar saw a colossal statue made up of five different elements. We should now be able to better understand its symbolism and better identify each of the kingdoms that they represented. The head made of gold symbolized Nebuchadnezzar as YAHveh's choice to be the world leader at that time. YAH used him to chastise His people through their temporary captivity. Even though the people of Babylon chose either demons or men to worship, Nebuchadnezzar, their king, came to know YAHveh as his Master. The people of Babylon were the descendants of Nimrod, who led his followers into worshiping demons and men as though they were elohim (gods). YAH used the Babylonian religion as an example of the fact that men had chosen a man as their master over the Creator of the Universe. The Persians and the Medes overthrew the Babylonians and became the second empire, which was represented by the upper torso of the statue. It was made of silver, and its two arms symbolized their divided kingdom. YAH used King Cyrus to release the remaining portion of His people, YAHuda, from their captivity in Babylon. There is a similarity between these two empires that needs to be revisited. They were both represented by precious metals that were used by all religions to represent spirituality because of their extreme value. Both of these empires were made up of people who worshiped either demons or men—or both—as their elohim. Both of their kings had a direct effect on the future of YAH's people, and both came to believe in Him as the One True ELohim of the Earth. The third empire that was chosen by YAH was the Greek with its mix of religion and philosophies, establishing a new democratic type of monarchy. This was what the lower "bronze" torso represented—bronze is a man-made metal consisting of copper mixed with tin. The lower torso also contains the reproductive organs, so you could say that democracy was birthed into history by the Greeks. The leader YAH chose to introduce democracy to the civilized world was Alexander the Great. Our modern government has evolved from this basic form of democracy. Then, of course, the final empire was Rome, initiated by Augustus Caesar and represented by the two iron legs—it ruled with an iron rod. Iron is another metal, like bronze, that man has to refine with his own hands before it can be used. Even though it was represented by iron, the Roman Empire was weakened because of its constant struggle between its two capitols, Rome and Constantinople, trying to establish their authority. Finally, the fifth and last empire is one that is also divided and is represented by the two feet that are made of iron and clay. This also represents the Roman Empire who, in its final days, will attempt to mix religion and spirituality (The City of God) with government and secular humanism (The City of Man)—hence, iron and clay. There was even a bishop within the Roman Catholic Church by the name of Augustine, who, after sensing the beginnings of a second Reform being stirred up by the Ruach of YAH, was inspired to write a thesis that he called "The City of God". This is our condition today. Today's form of world government, whether it is the U.N., the E.U., the U.S., or a mixture of all three, represents the final Roman Empire.

Mohammad

A time period in history that was known as the Middle, or Dark, Ages began about 500 CE, and it was about this same time that the Church became more Roman than Christian. Around 570 CE, a new religious leader by the name of Mohammad was born. His heritage was that of Babylonian descent, and his religion was paganism. At an early age, he found himself in a dilemma

WHAT WE WEREN'T TAUGHT ABOUT THE BIBLE AND ITS HISTORY

as to who out of all of the gods was the one true god. He believed that the god of the Christians and the Jews was Zeus, the god of the sun, who also went by other names, such as YAHveh, EL Shaddia, ELohim, Adonai, or Yeshua. He believed that Zeus was their god because they used the sun to govern not only their four seasons, but also their year with its twelve months and its 360 days. He finally decided that the one true god was the one that the descendants of YishmaEL called Allah (Aramaic for "the god") of the moon because it governed all of the months of their year by the appearance of its crescent. He claimed that in 610 CE, he received what he believed to be his religious calling and started focusing his devotions only toward Allah. He claimed that he was given a revelation, which he wrote down, and this writing later became known as the Qur'an (Koran). The religion that he founded was Islam. It eventually became the predominant religion of all of the Arabs, one of the three largest religions in the world and a declared enemy of both the Christians and the Jews (The Whole House of YisraEL). He was declared as being the prophet of Allah by his followers and put on the same level as Mosheh and Yeshua. He died in 632 CE—but not the religion that he founded. After his death, the believers in Islam took the words of Mohammad from the Koran and set out to fulfill them. It taught that all men outside of the Islamic belief were infidels and were worthy of death, unless they converted to Islam.

Christianity spread like wildfire throughout Asia, Europe, and into the British Isles. It had a tremendous influence on the heads of state of many countries, causing changes within their own politics because of it. The Anglican Church was the first to recant from the beliefs of the Roman Catholic Church. It became known as the Church of England, with its headquarters located in Kent, later called Canterbury. France, England, and Germany became the predominant leading countries in Europe. Meanwhile, the Muslims (Islam) began mounting up attacks against the Christians and the Jews in the Middle East, conquering the lands they inhabited and driving them out. The territories that fell under their siege were Palestine, Syria, Egypt, North Africa, and Spain. In 590 CE, Pope Gregory I became the first papal with any real political influence or power within the European nations. The Muslims built the "Dome of the Rock" upon the site of the Byzantium Church in Jerusalem in 688 CE. It was also thought to be the original site of Herod's Temple of the Jews—thus the decision for its location. The canonization of the saints began to be introduced to the Roman Catholic Church at the turn of the millennium of 1000 CE. Some began to craft their images into statues and to place them within the cathedrals. There, they began to be used as objects of prayer. The main difference in evangelism between the god of Islam and the God of YisraEL was that Allah's method of spreading belief in him was by the sword, whereas YAHveh's was through love. Unfortunately, Rome also turned to the sword as its method for a period of time.

ROGER W. FEARING

The Crusades and the Beginning of the Sixth Millennium

At the beginning of the sixth millennium (1096-1099 CE), the Christians in Eastern Europe requested military aid from the west because of the Muslim invasions and the annihilation of the brethren. The heads of state ignored the request, but not Pope Urban II. He called upon the knights of the surrounding kingdoms to rally. They were mostly made up of wealthy noblemen who had Christian ideals. Their response was overwhelming. They gathered men from the commonwealth of their provinces within the different kingdoms, armed them, and then underwrote their living and traveling expenses in order to defend the faith. The horror stories of the plundering of the weak and the murdering of the Jews were only committed by a few renegade Crusaders, but, as always, they received the most historical attention. Their quest was to rescue the Christians in the east and to liberate Jerusalem, which had been captured by the Muslims. When they accomplished both missions, they began to rebuild Jerusalem into a Christian community.

The second Crusade (1147-1149 CE) didn't fair as well. The Muslims began another attack against the Christians in the east in 1144 CE. The kings of France and Germany sent troops to repel the offensive, but met with defeat. In their attempt to defend Jerusalem, they attacked the Muslims in Damascus, which also was inhabited by some Christians. The result was horrific in that it caused the Muslims to begin slaughtering their Christian neighbors. When the Crusaders finally arrived in Jerusalem, they were battle weary and had little strength to defend the Holy City. So, when the Muslims launched their attack, Jerusalem fell, and the Turks and the Kurds became the primary inhabitants once again. The Muslims, not the Jews, were the targets in the Crusades of the Christians. Anti-Semitism existed within the Church, but not to the extent that some might believe. One example is a monk by the name of Bernard who personally went to Germany to challenge a fellow monk who was using the Muslim uprising as an excuse to lead a personal crusade against the Rhineland Jews. The result was that Bernard took this rebel back to his own convent for disciplinary action.

The third Crusade (1189-1192 CE) came about in response to the failure of the second. The thought was that Jerusalem must be liberated from the Muslims. Three kings from France, Germany, and England (an unholy three) set out on this quest to rescue Jerusalem once more. It was only King Richard I (the Lionhearted) of England that was able to endure the hardships and mainly because of his military experience. But even this was not enough to regain Jerusalem.

The focus of the Fourth Crusade (1201-1204 CE) was diverted from Jerusalem to Constantinople. The Christian leaders there, along with their political friends, made elaborate promises to aid the Crusaders in their efforts to liberate Jerusalem if they would first come and help them to oust the corrupt leadership who were presently occupying the seat of government. Afterwards, the promise of aid was reneged, so the Crusaders turned on the welshers and ransacked the entire city of Constantinople. Pope Innocent III denounced their aggressive action and excommunicated the entire army of the Crusaders. This in turn brought about a split within the Church, and those in the east became known as the Greek Orthodox, while the west remained the Roman Catholic. It was also during this time that Pope Innocent III saw the papacy as being the vicar of the Church. He believed that Peter (Kefa) was given the keys to Yeshua's Kingdom and, therefore, had obtained the authority of the Kingdom—second only to the Messiah. Because of this, he declared Peter (Kefa) as the first pope and that all of those who followed would possess this same seat of authority.

There were two more minor Crusades that once more proved unfruitful—one in 1208 CE and the other in 1212 CE, both led by the Pope from southern France. The Fifth major Crusade (1217-1221 CE), led by King Louie IX of France, took place in Egypt, but it too bore no fruit. The Sixth (1228-1229 CE) and the Seventh (1248-1254 CE), which was a second and a third endeavor that was led by King Louie IX, also failed. The Eighth and last Crusade (1270 CE) proved again to be unsuccessful in regaining control of the Holy City. Instead, the Muslims continued to conquer land throughout the Middle East and even into Europe. As a result, Germany, Italy, and France felt that they too were beginning to be threatened. If the seeds of capitalism, which became known as the Renaissance, had not been planted at this time, Christendom might have been completely wiped out. Education, science, and the first forms of technology became the most effective new weapons against the spread of Islam.

The Renaissance, the Reformation, and the Beginning of the Spanish Inquisition

Continued efforts to uproot the Islamic Revolution in Europe did not come through the use of military force, but through the power of the individual instead. A unique respect for commerce, entrepreneurialism, the Scientific Revolution, and the Age of Exploration led to a time known as the Renaissance, or the age of enlightenment, which was empowered by the religion of secular humanism.

At the same time, the Ruach of YAHveh made a coinciding move to stir the hearts and minds of men who had a hunger for the truth. Considering the events that took place in the ensuing years, YAH's Ruach was taking men back to searching the Scriptures for themselves. Men like John Wycliffe felt the need to bring forth the Holy Scriptures from Latin into an English translation in spite of the opposition from the Church. Wycliffe pioneered an English translation that had to be written by hand for duplication and distribution. Then, with the invention of the printing press in Germany by Johann Gutenberg, the Holy Scriptures could be manufactured and distributed to any man or woman that desired one. Then, a personal crusade by a French woman, known as Joan of Arc, led France to victory against England, who had been oppressing them. Two years later, she was burned as a witch because of her radical-religious beliefs, opposing many of the teachings of the Roman Catholic Church. King Ferdinand and Queen Isabella chose Catholicism to unite Spain in 1478 and began the Spanish Inquisition to drive out the Protestants and the Jews from Spain. Many non-Catholics, including Muslims and Jews, died by the sword in the ensuing years as the king and queen tried to cleanse the land of those whom they had concluded were heretics. In 1490, a young adventurer by the name of Christopher Columbus, who was of Jewish descent, but Catholic turned Protestant, approached the king and queen with the idea of establishing a new trade route to India by traveling west—because he believed that the Earth was round. After several unsuccessful attempts to acquire the financing needed, they finally gave him the money and the authority to set out on his quest in 1492. Some have claimed that Columbus was really a Messianic Jew who had a desire to find a place where all men could worship as they pleased without fear of reprisal. Therefore, after he heard that a New World existed to the west, he devised a plan that would allow him to make his voyage.

The Second Reform

In 1521 CE, a Roman Catholic monk by the name of Martin Luther was excommunicated for challenging the Church for their doctrine of indulgence, setting into motion the second Reform of the Ruach. Luther also questioned the spiritual authority of a political hierarchy being under the authority of one bishop known as the pope. Some of his arguments challenged the unscriptural idea of purgatory. Later, others within this second reform objected to such pagan practices as praying while using rosary beads that are similar to those used by the Muslims and Buddhists and chanting mantras, or prayers, as though they had some mystical power to grab God's attention. The practice of revering Jesus' mother on nearly the same deity level as the Christ and using the "images" of saints and/or of Jesus to pray to (revering these images as being advocates for getting their prayers answered) were also later denounced. These things are in direct disregard of the second commandment, *"You shall not make for yourself any carved image, or any likeness of anything that is in heaven above, or that is in the earth beneath, or that is in the water under the earth; you shall not bow down to them nor serve them;"*..."*For I, YAHveh your ELohim, AM a jealous ELohim, visiting the iniquity of the fathers on the children to the third and fourth generation of those who hate* (have no fear of or regard for) *Me, but showing mercy to thousands, to those who love Me and keep My commandments"* (**EXOD 20:4-6** and **DEUT 5:8-10**).

WHAT WE WEREN'T TAUGHT ABOUT THE BIBLE AND ITS HISTORY

Martin Luther found that corruption had set in deeply within the organized church leadership. He wanted to see all men have a personal relationship with God—one that came through His grace and not by any special works that they could muster up. He recognized that all believers were to be the Lord's priests, but, at the same time, he still believed in a two-tier level between clergy and laity. He was also an advocate for the Scriptures being made available to all men from every nation and in all languages. About this same time, in 1516, Desiderius Erasmus translated and printed the first all-Greek translation of the Scriptures.

The second Reformation of the Ruach had begun, and nothing on Earth was going to stop it—except perhaps the hardness and rebellion of an individual's heart. Catholicism had become so polluted with the ideas of men that those who felt the tug on their heartstrings from YAH repented and began to follow His lead. Not even the Emperor of Rome, Charles V, had any power to challenge this movement. He was unsuccessful when he personally tried to stop it by force and even encountered protest from some of the princes of Germany. Because of this, the movement became known as the Protestant (Protest) Reformation Movement.

A French Catholic by the name of John Calvin was also moved by the Ruach after being introduced to Luther's teaching that salvation comes by grace only. Both he and Luther fully grasped the spiritual understanding regarding what the Ne'vee Habakkuk and the Shelich Shaul taught—"a man must walk by faith and not by sight." Later in life, John Calvin established the first theological seminary that taught Protestantism.

A Catholic Archbishop named Thomas Cranmer helped establish the Protestant Reform in England. He had become a student of Luther's theology and wrote many books regarding the Reformation. His influence even spread to the throne of King Henry VIII. The king denounced Luther's teachings but, at the same time, because of a personal dispute with the pope, ended the pope's power over the affairs of England and declared himself to be the head of the Church of England.

Then another movement began within Protestantism—the Anabaptists. These reformers denounced many things that were still remaining from Catholicism, such as infant baptism. They preached separation of church and state (that civil government had no jurisdiction over the affairs of the Church), that Church authority should remain within the local congregation, and that baptisms should be for those who had repented for their sins and had experienced conversion. Discipleship was the main theme of their doctrine. The "Brethren Church" and the "Mennonites" were off-springs of the Anabaptists. Both the Protestants and the Catholics agreed that the Anabaptists were to be considered heretics. This led to the beginning of YAH's third Reform.

ROGER W. FEARING

The Third Reform

The age of enlightenment, or the Renaissance, was an opposing force against the Reformation. Its focus was on a new form of philosophy with its roots in both Greek philosophy and theology. Another movement within the Reformation was a group known as the Pietists. They developed the idea of personal redemption and sanctification through the new birth (born-again). This new theology was quickly accepted by some Lutherans. These later formed the Puritans, the Quakers, and the Lutheran Pietists.

By this time, all forms of Christianity, whether expressed through Catholicism, Protestantism, or Judaism, had spread to the continents of North and South America. In 1607, Anglican Protestantism came to the commonwealth of Virginia. An Anglican preacher named John Smyth introduced the first Baptist denomination. The first edition of the "King James Version" of the Bible was printed in 1611. In 1620, the Pilgrims signed the Mayflower Compact and set sail for the new world, arriving in what they called the "New England". In 1639, Roger Williams founded the very first "Baptist Church of America" in Rhode Island. In 1679, a Presbyterian Synod was established in Boston, Massachusetts. The "Great Awakening" (the greatest revival ever recorded in the history of America or Europe) began in 1734, which helped prepare the way for the fourth Reform of YAHveh. Oftentimes when YAH has brought about a new revelation to the Body of Messiah in order to mature it, the result has been the birthing of a new denomination. Two brothers by the names of John and Charles Wesley founded the Methodist Church in England in about 1739. The Methodists eventually discovered what became known as "the second touch of grace", or the baptism in the Holy Spirit. YAHveh began to restore the Whole House of YisraEL in Europe with His first three Reforms, but the remaining four will take place in the New World. He seems to be gathering both the believing Jews from the tribe of YAHuda and the Joes (Goyim) from the tribes of Joseph into a type of *land of Goshen* (America). In 1776, the birth pangs of the United States of America began to emerge with the signing of the Declaration of Independence. In 1789, George Washington was elected as the first U.S. President. In 1795, the Methodists separated themselves from the Church of England, and the freedom to worship as each individual pleases continued to grow and be strengthened within America.

In the 1800's, the powers of darkness began to move effectively against YAH's plan to restore His House of YisraEL. Shortly after the beginning of a new denomination known as the "Disciples of Christ", two men from this denomination, Charles Finney and Dwight L. Moody, were able to launch two effective evangelistic ministries. At the same time, however, another man, Joseph Smith, founded a counterfeit ministry know as Mormonism. In

WHAT WE WEREN'T TAUGHT ABOUT THE BIBLE AND ITS HISTORY

1854, Pope Pius IX introduced the idea of the Immaculate Conception of the Virgin Mary, which nearly put her on the same plane of deity as Jesus. In 1865, President Lincoln was assassinated, and in 1866, the Ku Klux Klan was founded. Also, Charles Taze Russell began his counterfeit ministry known as the Jehovah's Witnesses. Then, in 1869, Pope Pius IX declared the infallibility of a papal decision. In 1875, a woman, Mary Baker Eddy, founded another counterfeit ministry, known as Christian Science. But YAH's Ruach was not idle during that time. He began to stir the hearts of the Jews and the Christians alike to birth the Zionist movement for the purpose of helping the Jews return to their homeland, Palestine (YisraEL).

The Fourth Reform

The last century of the sixth millennium is about to begin, and one of the prophecies of the final days of the Earth is about to be fulfilled. *"Behold, the days are coming," says YAHveh, "when the plowman shall overtake the reaper, and the treader of grapes him who sows seed; the mountains shall drip with sweet wine, and all the hills shall flow with it. I will bring back the captives of My people YisraEL; they shall build the waste cities and inhabit them; they shall plant vineyards and drink wine from them; they shall also make gardens and eat fruit from them; I will plant them in their land, and no longer shall they be pulled up from the land I have given them." Says YAHveh your ELohim"* (**AMOS 9:13-15**).

In 1906, in Los Angeles, California, a spin-off group from the Methodist Church, the Holiness Church, was attending a gathering on Azusa Street. There, a phenomenal manifestation of the Ruach took place that was similar to the miracle on the day of Pentecost, nineteen-hundred years earlier. Many began to speak in languages both known and unknown—what has since been labeled as the "Baptism in the Holy Spirit". Later, attempts to explain this phenomenon away by the Organized Church failed because too many Believers from all over the world experienced this same manifestation. This manifestation has been tagged with the term glossolalia or gibberish because at times it has no apparent linguistic origin. From this Azusa Street experience, the Pentecostal Movement began, and the gifts of the Ruach were re-introduced to Believers. Just as the revelation of the redemptive work of the Ruach was re-introduced by the Pietists' doctrine of the new birth, this was the re-introduction of the revelation of the sanctification work of the Ruach. The enemy has tried to counterfeit and discredit this particular work of the Ruach by the raising up of cults that abuse His gifts. But, like the other works of YAH's restoration, this too cannot be stopped by hasatan or by any man who submits to him. YAH has laid the groundwork for His fifth Reform.

Shortly thereafter, in 1917, the enemy threw the world into a World War in an attempt to establish imperialism. But the Ruach causes another event to take place that would counter his plans. Great Britain, who had jurisdiction over the Holy Land at that time, signed the Belfour Declaration that established Palestine as the official national homeland for the Jews as a result of the ongoing work of the Zionist Movement. The final steps for the restoration of the Whole House of YisraEL had begun. Once again, hasatan tried to thwart YAH's plan by incarnating himself in a man by the name of Adolph Hitler, who formed the Nazi Party in 1920 because of his personal ambition to conquer the whole world.

Two different kinds of walls took front-stage in 1929. The Jews and the Arabs clashed over the Wailing Wall, resulting in the Jews being forbidden access to it. Then Wall Street crashed in the United States and brought about a worldwide depression. In 1939, Hitler invaded Poland, and World War II began. He, being an instrument of hasatan, tried to annihilate all of the Jews in Europe. In 1941, the Japanese bombed Pear Harbor and the United States entered World War II. In 1945, the war ended and the world came back into order.

In 1947, a phenomenon began to take place in the heavens—unidentified flying objects started to make their appearance all over the world (signs in the heavens). Coinciding with this, the Dead Sea Scrolls were discovered, and reaffirmation of the authenticity of the Scriptures was established.

The Fifth Reform

The pace of events continued to escalate when YisraEL declared itself an independent state in 1948. Two other significant events took place in the same year in the United States. Two different Catholic Universities, Notre Dame and Duquesne, experienced a move of the Ruach on two separate occasions. In 1948, students at these two universities gathered for prayer with fasting in order to seriously seek the purpose and will of YAHveh. The result was that they were baptized in the Ruach with the manifestation of speaking in tongues and accompanied by many other miracles. This was the beginning of the Charismatic Renewal that quickly spread to all mainline denominations throughout the world in the 50's and 60's. With the Charismatic Renewal bringing the realization of the scriptural truth to the fundamental teachings of redemption and sanctification to the mainline denominations, the stage was set for the next two Reforms.

The Sixth and Seventh Reform

In 1967, at the climax of a six-day war, the military troops of the State of YisraEL recaptured the city of YAHrushalayim, and for the first time in 2,500 years, the Holy City belonged to the Hebrew people once again. There was a coinciding event that took place here in the U.S.—a national convention of Messianic Jews was held in Pittsburgh, Pennsylvania. Since that time, the "Messianic-Jewish Movement" has grown, and numerous local synagogues are being established in most of the major cities inside and outside of our country. This was the sixth-Reform move by the Ruach. At the same time, another Reform began to develop within this movement. More and more non-Jewish believers were given a desire by the Ruach to learn more about their own Hebrew heritage. As they began to search, they discovered the teachings regarding the division between the two southern tribes of BenYAHmeen and YAHuda and the ten northern tribes of Yosef, along with the promise of their restoration in the end times. A seventh Reform called the "Messianic-YisraELi Movement", or the "Two-House Movement", was born. At about the same time, a coinciding event took place within the State of YisraEL. Prior to his becoming the prime minister of YisraEL in 2001, Ariel Sharon, went up to the Temple Mount to pray on Yom Kippur in the year 2000. During the procession, Palestinian-youth rebels began throwing rocks in order to stop them from entering the Mount area. While on the Mount, Sharon began to read from the book of the Ne'vee Ezekiel (**EZEK 37:15-28**). This is where YAHveh explains to Ezekiel His plan to bring the two houses of YisraEL back together in the land of promise in the last days.

Soon after this event, the suicide and homicide attacks began against the innocent people of YisraEL. Many of the rabbim of the State of YisraEL declared these ongoing events as the beginning of "Yaacov's Troubles" that were prophesied by the Ne'vee YirmehYAH. *"The word that came to YirmehYAH from YAHveh, saying, "Thus speaks YAHveh ELohim of YisraEL, saying; 'Write in a scroll for yourself all the words that I have spoken to you. 'For behold, the days are coming,' says YAHveh, that I will bring back from captivity My people YisraEL and YAHuda,' says YAHveh. And I will cause them to return to the land that I gave to their fathers, and they shall possess it.'" Now these are the words that YAHveh spoke concerning YisraEL and YAHuda; "For thus says YAHveh: 'We have heard a voice trembling, of fear, and not of shalom. Ask now, and see, whether a man is ever in labor with child? So why do I see every man with his hands on his loins like a woman in labor, and all faces turned pale? Alas' for that day is great, so that none is like it; and it is the time of Yaacov's trouble, but he shall be saved out of it. 'For it shall come to pass in that day,' says YAHveh of hosts, that I will break his yoke from your neck, and will burst your bonds; foreigners shall no more enslave them. But they shall serve YAHveh their ELohim, and Dahveed their king, whom I will raise up for them. 'Therefore do not fear My servant, O My servant Yaacov,' says YAHveh, nor be dismayed, O YisraEL; for behold I will save you from afar, and your seed from the land of their captivity. Yaacov shall return, have rest and be quiet, and no one shall make him afraid. For I AM with you,' says YAHveh, 'to save you; though I make a full end of all nations where*

I have scattered you, yet I will not make a complete end of you. But I will correct you in justice, and will not let you go altogether unpunished" (**JER 30:1-11**).

Conclusion

Remember, earlier in this book I said that before Yaacov was given the name of YisraEL, his name meant supplanter, replacer, or manipulator and could also mean one who could overcome. This name could describe a politician, a lawyer, a wheeler-dealer, or even a merchandiser—in other words, a worldly or secular person. Before he was known as YisraEL, he was a man who struggled within himself, with men, and even with YAHveh. But because he persevered in his struggle with YAH, he became an overcomer, a conqueror, and a hero. When he came to know YAHveh, he was changed—he became born-again. All Believers were like Yaacov at one time, but after their struggle with YAH and with themselves, they too became heroes of YAH's—His YisraEL.

Also remember that the House of Yaacov, or YisraEL, was made up of twelve sons, or tribes—not just the one called YAHuda. Let me repeat the scenario that I described in Chapter Fifteen. First, trouble came to the two southern tribes (YAHuda and BenYAHmeen) in the fall of the year 2000. They were attacked by the descendants of both YishmaEL (the old enemy of the Hebrews) and Esau (the old enemy of Yaacov) in the land that had been given to YisraEL by YAHveh. Then, one year later, in the fall of 2001, these same two enemies (terrorists) crossed over the waters to the new "Land of Goshen" (America) to attack the descendants of both YAHuda and Yosef there. If these are truly the times of Yaacov's Trouble, then the descendants of all twelve tribes have to experience this testing. And if these are truly the times of Yaacov's Trouble, it will last seven years, according to YAH's pattern of events. That will bring us up to the years 2007 & 2008. This could be the time that Ezekiel (YechezkEL) said that the curse on Efraeem (son of Yosef) would be lifted. At the end of this seven-year period, will there be two more seven-year periods? If I read YAH's pattern correctly, then both Yaacov and Yosef are our examples of the end times. Everything must be established by *two* witnesses. Remember, Yaacov had to struggle seven years before he was able to obtain his beloved bride, Rahkal. First, he was deceived by his Uncle Laban, who gave him his older daughter, Leah, instead. Then, he had to labor for another seven years before he could actually acquire his one true love. After this, he had to labor for a third seven years in order to gather his wages in cattle and servants. Now, in the case of Yosef, he was not recognized by his brothers, just as YAHuda has not recognized the Goy as his brother. In his situation, there was a seven-year period of plenty, followed by a seven-year period of famine. So, is there going to be a seven-year revival throughout the world after the time of Yaacov's Trouble that will lead others into becoming Messianics within both the House of YAHuda and the House of Yosef? Will that be followed by seven years of a famine of persecution and tribulation? And in the middle of those seven years, will YAHuda and Yosef finally recognize one another as brothers? Will Yeshua then return to take those who have been given to Him back to the land of YisraEL so that they might finally dwell in the promised "Shalom" for His Millennium Rest? Right now, within the Messianic Movement, there is strife between the Messianic Jews and the Messianic Joes (those in the Two-House Movement). Right now, the "Church" still thinks that she was ordained by Jesus to replace YisraEL. Right now, the "Church" believes that she only has to follow the teachings of the Shelichim and the Brit Chadashah—not the TaNaKh. They believe that they are not under the "Law" and are not required to follow its ordinances. These things must change before Yeshua will return, and He will see to it that they do change—remember, He did say that five virgins were ready and five were not.

When we look at history from the resurrection of Yeshua until the present, we can see the progressive revelation that YAH, our Abba, has set before us. In His first Reform, He distributed His "Good News" throughout the Roman Empire and the world. In His second and third, He reestablished the understanding of Redemption. In His fourth and fifth, Sanctification was reestablished. Now, in His sixth and seventh, He is bringing about His final promise—the Restoration of all things. Of course, in His eighth and final reform, He will set up His Kingdom here on Earth. And, at its climax, He will establish a new heaven and a new Earth.

Before I close, let me reemphasize one more thing about following the teachings of the Torah and the TaNaKh. Before Yeshua arrived on the Earth to reveal the image of our Abba to us, salvation could only be obtained by keeping all 613 commandments in the Torah, along with having faith in the *promise* of the coming of a Ne'vee like Mosheh—the Messiah. Until the coming of the Messiah, the only payment for sin was the shedding of the blood of an innocent, clean animal for unintentional sins or a person's own blood for intentional sin. This was the "curse" of the Torah—death. But Messiah did come. Yeshua became our example for keeping the Torah, and He shed His own innocent blood as the required atonement for all of our sins. Now all that we have to do in order to be delivered from this curse is to receive this revelation by faith. And all we need to do in order to receive its blessings is to know and be doers of His Torah. Now the keeping of the Torah is a form of worship and a blessing for our lives. It becomes the means that leads us, His Bride, into an intimate relationship with our Groom—Yeshua, the Son of Elohim. When we were commanded to worship Him in spirit and in truth, this is what was meant. When we were told to return to our first love, this is what was meant. To follow Torah is the truest form of worship. Making it legalistic and trying to follow it to the letter is impossible and a burden, or yoke, that no man can endure. Keeping Torah should be enjoyable and not a burden or a task. To demand certain dress codes, being circumcised, the eating or not eating of certain foods, or even baptism was not taught as a condition for salvation. Doing any of these things may be a form of worship, but it is not a requirement. These things within themselves are good, but are never conditional. Always remember that we are not under the curse of the Torah—only under its blessings.

I hope the sharing of my thoughts has inspired you to seek your heavenly Abba in a new way—the Hebrew way, the way in which they were given to us. Shalom ahlekehim (Peace be unto you).

GLOSSARY OF HEBREW WORDS

A

Abba: Father, or Daddy

AbeeYAH (Abijah): Eighth priest of the eighth clan of Aaron of the tribe of Levi

Ahbeemelech (Abimelech)

Adonai: Lord, or Master

Adonai YAHveh: Lord GOD

Afikoman: Hidden loaf

Aharon (Aaron): Moses' brother—First high priest

AhazeeYAH (Ahaziah): Son of King Ahab—Husband to Queen Jezebel—A king over the tribes of Joseph

Ahbeeahthar (Abiathar): The son of the high priest, Ahimelech, who later betrayed David

Ahbeegaheel (Abigail): King David's second wife

Ahbeeshag (Abishag): A concubine of King David

Ahbel (Abel): Adam and Eve's second son

Ahdom (Adam): Mankind—Name of first man

AhdoneeYAH (Adonijah): A second son of David, who tried to usurp the throne of his brother Solomon

Ahee (Ai): A city outside of Jericho

Aheemelekh (Ahimelech): A high priest of God who helped David escape King Saul's attempt to kill him

Aheenohahm (Ahinoam): King David's third wife

AheeYAH (Ahijah): A prophet of God—The name of the second king of the tribe of Judah

AhmahzeeYAH (Amaziah): A king of Judah, son of Joash

Ahmos (Amos): A Minor Prophet of God

Ahsher (Asher): How happy am I—Eighth son of Jacob/Israel

AhzahreeYAH (Azariah): Also known as Abed-Nego—A prophet and one of Daniel's companions

Ahlekehim: Be unto you

Amaleki (Amalekites): One of many warring tribes in the Canaan region bent on the annihilation of Israel

Amee: People

Ammoni (Ammonites)

Amori (Amorites): Descendants of Ammon—Incest son of Lot

Avraham (Abraham): Father of many nations

Avram (Abram): Exalted father

Avshalom (Absalom): Father of peace—One of King David's sons, the one who betrayed him

B

Bahahsha (Baasha): Third king over the tribes of Joseph

Bar: Son

Baruch: Blessed—The name of a scribe for the prophet Jeremiah

WHAT WE WEREN'T TAUGHT ABOUT THE BIBLE AND ITS HISTORY

Bashani (Bashanite): One of the twelve tribes of Ishmael and enemies of Israel

Bat: Daughter

Bathshe`bah (Bathsheba): King David's fourth wife and mother of Solomon

BehnaheeYAH (Benaiah): One of David's mighty men of valor

Beheet (Beit or Beth): House

Beitlechem (Bethlehem): House of bread

Ben: Son of

BenYAHmeen (Benjamin): Son of my right hand—Twelfth son of Jacob/Israel

BietEL (Bethel): House of EL

Brit Chadashah: Renewed Covenant—Eighth covenant made by God with Israel through His Son Jesus—New Testament

C

Canaani (Canaanites): The people living in the land of Canaan, which later became the land of Israel

Chabahkook (Habakkuk): A Minor Prophet of God

Chag Sukkoth: Feast of Tabernacles

Cheva (Eve): Came from man

D

Dahn (Dan): Judge—Fifth son of Jacob/Israel

DahneeEL (Daniel): A Major Prophet of God, also known as Belteshazzar

Dahveed (David): Beloved—Second king of Israel

Deenah (Dinah): Judgment—The feminine equivalent to Dan—Jacob/Israel's only daughter

E

Echad: Oneness, or unity

Edomi (Edomites): Descendants of Esau

ELee (Eli): A priest for God—The one who raised Samuel, the last Judge of Israel

ELeeahkeem (Eliakim): An appointed king of the tribe of Judah—Brother of King Jehoahaz/King Jehoiakim

ELeeshaw (Elisha): Protégé of the prophet Elijah

ELeeYAHoo (Elijah): A prophet of God

ELisheva (Elizabeth): The mother of John the Baptist

Elohenu: Our ELohim, or God

ELohim/elohim: God/gods—Mighty One/mighty ones

ELuah: God in the singular

EmmanuEL (Immanuel): God is with you

Efraeem (Ephraim): Twice fruitful—Joseph's youngest son

Ester (Esther)

Ezrah (Ezra): Prophet, priest, and teacher of God's word

G

GahbreeEL (Gabriel): An angel of proclamation for YAH

Gahd (Gad): A troop—Babylonian word for god, or eluah—Seventh son of Jacob/Israel

Geedehon (Gideon): A judge of the House of YisraEL

WHAT WE WEREN'T TAUGHT ABOUT THE BIBLE AND ITS HISTORY

Gohyeem (Goyim/Gentile): Nations

H

Haggadah: Seder order

Hagahee (Haggai): A Minor Prophet of God

Hahm (Ham): Noah's second son

HahnahneeYAH (Hananiah): Also known as Shadrach, a prophet and one of Daniel's companions

Hahmi (Hahmites): Descendant of Ham and an enemy of Israel

HaMashiach (The Messiah): Christ, or Christo in Greek—The Anointed one

hasatan (satan): The destroyer and the accuser

HaShem: The Name—What most Jews use instead of YAHveh

HeelkeeYAH (Hilkiah): A priest during the reign of King Josiah of Judah

Heerahm (Hiram): A king of Syria

HezehckeeYAH (Hezekiah): A king of the tribe of Judah

Hittitim (Hittites): Descendants of Ishmael, a common enemy of Israel

Hoshea (Hosea): A Minor Prophet of God

HuldYAH (Huldah): A prophetess during the reign of King Josiah of Judah

I

Irvi or Erbee (Hebrew): One who crosses over

K

Kaeen (Cain): Adam and Eve's firstborn

Kahal: Congregation—Assembly—Household—Family—Nation—Ecclesia (Greek for Congregation)—Kirche (Slang for Church)

Kedosh/Kadesh: Holy

Kefa: Peter—Jesus' most impetuous disciple of all

Kethuvim: Writings other than Ne'vim or Torah—Third volume of Hebrew Scriptures

Kosher: Separated—Comes from kedosh/holy

L

Lehvee (Levi): To be attached—Third son of Jacob/Israel

Lukas (Luke): The writer of the third gospel and the book of Acts

M

Mahlakhee (Malachi): A Minor Prophet of God

Mahnahseh (Manasseh): To help forget—Joseph's oldest son

Markus (Mark): A later disciple of Jesus

MattahneeYAH (Mattaniah): A king of the tribe of Judah

MattatiYAH (Matthew): A disciple and apostle of Jesus

Meecah (Micah): A Minor Prophet of God

MeekaheeYAH (Micaiah): Another prophet of God

Meeryahm (Miriam): Mary—Name of Moses' sister—Name of Jesus' mother

Mefeebohsheth (Mephibosheth): One of King Saul's grandsons

Messianic: Follower of the Messiah—Christian

Midiani (Midianite): Descendants of Abraham through his second wife, Keturah

Meekvah (Mikvah): Baptism—Self-washing—Cleansing

MishahEL (Mishael): Also known as Meshach, a prophet and one of Daniel's companions

Mishkahn: Tabernacle—Portable tent or dwelling place for YAH—Used for His meetings and worship services

Mishpochah: Family

Mitsrahyim: Egypt

Mitzvoth: Commandments

Moabi (Moabites): Descendants of Moab—Incest son of Lot

Moedim: Appointed times

Mosheh (Moses): One from the waters (Egyptian meaning)

Mt. Moreeah (Mt. Moriah): The Mountain that YAH's House was built on

Mt. Zeeon (Mt Zion): The Mountain that Jerusalem sets on

N

Nahaman (Naaman): One of the army commanders of the tribes of Joseph

Nahbel (Nabel): King David's second wife's (Abigail) first husband.

Nahohmee (Naomi): Great-great-grandmother of King David

NehchemYAH (Nehemiah)

Nev'eeYAH: Prophetess

Ne'vim: Prophets—Book of Prophets, second volume of Hebrew Scriptures

O

OhbedeeYAH (Obadiah): A Minor Prophet of God

OozzeeYAH (Uzziah): One of the kings of the tribe of Judah—A common name used among all YisraELi

P

Passover/Pesach: Death of the firstborn/feast of the lamb

PekaheeYAH (Pekahiah): Son of King Menahem—A king over the tribes of Joseph

PeneeEL (Peniel): I saw ELohim and lived

Philisti (Philistine): Descendants of both Nimrod and Ishmael—Inhabitants of modern Palestine's Gaza strip

R

Rahkal (Rachel): Second wife of Jacob/Israel

Rosh HaShanah: Head of the year

Ruach: Breath of YAH

Ruach HaKedosh/Kadesh: Breath of the Holy One

S

Sabbath: Day of rest and worship—Seventh day of the week

Sahrah (Sarah): Princess

Saraee (Sarai): One with potential

Seemehon (Simeon): I've been heard—Second son of Jacob/Israel

Seenahee (Sinai): Mountain where Moses received the Torah

Shalom: Peace

Shalomo (Solomon): Peaceable—David's youngest son—Third king of Israel

Shaul (Saul): Name of first king of Israel—Name of thirteenth apostle (Apostle Paul/Rav Shaul), apostle to the Gentiles

Shavuot: The Feast of Pentecost—Feast of Weeks

Shchinah: Glorious aurora of God

WHAT WE WEREN'T TAUGHT ABOUT THE BIBLE AND ITS HISTORY

Sheeloh (Shiloh): A city within the borders of Israel—A description given for the Messiah

Sheemehee (Shimei): A relative of King Shaul, enemy of David

Shehkhem (Shechem): A city in the land of Israel

Shelichim: Apostles

Shimei (Semites): Descendants of Shem and cousins to the Hebrews—Ancestors of both the Ishmaelites and the Edomites from the descendants of Esau, Jacobs's twin brother

Sheh-mah' (Sh'ma): To hear, or to listen

Succoth: Booths—Feast of Tabernacles—Feast of Ingathering, or Harvest

T

Tallit: Prayer shawl, or garment—Worn over the shoulders to represent the Mishkahn/Tabernacle—Worn to display submission to God

Talmidim: Disciples

TaNaKh: Old Testament—Septuagint (Greek version of Old Testament)—Comes from the name of the first three volumes of Hebrew Scriptures (Torah—Ne'vim—Kethuvim)

Torah: Instructions—Law of Moses—Pentateuch (Greek for first five books of Genesis)—First volume of Hebrew Scriptures

TzahkarYAH (Zechariah): A Minor Prophet of God—Name of a son of the chief priest of Judah, Jehoiada

Tzitzits: Tassels—Contains eight strands, one being blue—Worn on the corners of a tallit—Also referred to as wings of a garment

U

UreeYAH (Uriah): Bathsheba's first husband—Name of a prophet of God

Y

Yaacov (Jacob/James): Supplanter, manipulator, overcomer, or hero—Isaac's youngest twin son

Yafeth (Japheth): Noah's youngest son

Yafethi (Japhethites): Descendants of Japheth—An ally of Israel

YAH: Shortened version of YAHveh

YAHdee-deeYAH (Jedidiah): Loved of YAH—Solomon's second given name

YAHoash (Jehoash): A king over the tribes of Joseph

YAHoeeada (Jehoiada): A chief priest of the tribe of Judah

YAHohahaz (Jehoahaz): Son of King Josiah—A king of the tribe of Judah

YAHoheeahkeem (Jehoiakim): A second name given to King Eliakim

YAHoshaphat (Jehoshaphat): Son of King Ahab of the tribe of Judah—A king over the tribes of Joseph

YAHoram (Jehoram): A king of the tribe of Judah

YAHroboam (Jeroboam): Son of Nebat—One of David's mighty men of valor hired to oversee the building of YAH's House—Became the first king over the tribes of Joseph

YAHroboam II (Jeroboam II): Son of King Jehoash—A later king over the tribes of Joseph

YAHrushalayim (Jerusalem): City of YAHveh's peace (shalom)

YAHu (Jehu): A prophet sent to warn King Baasha—A king over the tribes of Joseph

YAHuda (Judah): Praise—Fourth son of Jacob/Israel

YAHudaim: Jewish

YAHuda Yiscariot (Judas Iscariot)

YAHudi: Jew—Jews

WHAT WE WEREN'T TAUGHT ABOUT THE BIBLE AND ITS HISTORY

YAHveh (Jehovah): LORD—The name God called Himself—YHVH (I AM what/who I AM)

YAHveh ELohim: LORD God

Yarden River (Jordan River)

Yaricho (Jericho)

Yebusi (Yebusites/Jebusites): Descendants of Nimrod—First inhabitants of Jerusalem

YekezkEL (Ezekiel): A Major Prophet of God

Yeshua (Hebrew name for Jesus or Iesous, His Greek name): Salvation of God

Yesseh (Jesse): Great-grandson of Nahohmee (Naomi)—Father of David

Yethro (Jethro): Moses' father-in-law

Yezebel (Jezebel): Queen of Beelzebub—Wife of King Ahab, one of the kings over the tribes of Joseph

YirmehYAH (Jeremiah): A Major Prophet of God

Yishbosheth (Ishbosheth): One of King Saul's sons

YishmaEL (Ishmael): God hears—Abraham's firstborn of Hagar, Sarah's concubine

Yishmali/YishmaELi (Ishmaelites)

YishshaYAH (Isaiah): A Major Prophet of God

YisraEL (Israel) One who has wrestled with God and overcome—The name given to Jacob

Yitzhak (Isaac): Laughter—Abraham's son of promise

Yitzsakar (Issachar): I'm for hire/this is a reward—Ninth son of Jacob/Israel

Yoab (Joab): King David's troop commander

YoEL (Joel): A Minor Prophet of God

Yohash (Joash): A child king of the tribe of Judah

Yom Kippur: Day of Atonement

Yom Teruah: Day of Trumpets

Yonah (Jonah): A Minor Prophet of God who was swallowed by a great fish

Yoppa (Joppa): A city in Mesopotamia

Yoram (Joram): A king over the tribes of Joseph

YosseeYAH (Josiah); A king of the tribe of Judah—Possible cousin of the prophet Zephaniah

Yosef (Joseph): Will add more/one of compassion—Eleventh son of Jacob/Israel—Guardian father of Yeshua

Yoshua (Joshua): Derivative of Yeshua, or Jesus—First judge of Israel

Yotham (Jotham): Son of King Uzziah—A king of the tribe of Judah

Yov (Job): Writer of the book of Job

Z

ZedkehYAH (Zedekiah): The last king of the tribe of Judah

Zeebah (Ziba): A servant of Mephibosheth

ZefenYAH (Zephaniah): A Minor Prophet of God

Made in the USA